# australian criminal justice

### Authors' Note

We share responsibility for this book as a whole and each chapter is a collaborative effort of all three authors. However, initial responsibility for preparing the first drafts of the Introduction and chapters 3, 4 and 7 was taken by Mark Findlay, chapters 2, 5, 6 and the first half of chapter 9 by Stephen Odgers, and chapters 1, 8 and 10 and the second half of chapter 9 by Stanley Yeo.

# australian
# criminal
# justice

## Third edition

Mark Findlay
Stephen Odgers
Stanley Yeo

OXFORD
UNIVERSITY PRESS

# OXFORD

UNIVERSITY PRESS

253 Normanby Road, South Melbourne, Victoria 3205, Australia

Oxford University Press is a department of the University of Oxford.
It furthers the University's objective of excellence in research, scholarship,
and education by publishing worldwide in

Oxford  New York

Auckland  Cape Town  Dar es Salaam  Hong Kong  Karachi
Kuala Lumpur  Madrid  Melbourne  Mexico City  Nairobi
New Delhi  Shanghai  Taipei  Toronto

With offices in

Argentina  Austria  Brazil  Chile  Czech Republic  France  Greece
Guatemala  Hungary  Italy  Japan  Poland  Portugal  Singapore
South Korea  Switzerland  Thailand  Turkey  Ukraine  Vietnam

OXFORD is a trade mark of Oxford University Press in the UK
and in certain other countries

National Library of Australia
Cataloguing-in-Publication data:

Findlay, Mark.
  Australian criminal justice.

  3rd ed.
  Bibliography.
  Includes index.
  ISBN  0 19 551738 5.

  1. Criminal justice, Administration of—Australia.
  2. Criminal law—Australia. I. Odgers, Stephen.
  II. Yeo, Stanley Meng Heong. III. Title.

345.94

Typeset by OUPANZS
Printed through Sheck Wah Tong Printing Press Ltd., Hong Kong

# Foreword

## by The Hon. Justice Michael Kirby AC CMG

I was taught criminal law in the first year of my legal studies at the University of Sydney Law School. The year was 1958. The lecturer was the Honourable Vernon Treatt QC, a barrister-turned-politician who squeezed the duties into his other activities. The venue was the fading elegance of the St James Hall in Phillip Street, Sydney, where overflow law lectures were given. The text was *An Introduction to Criminal Law* by Cross and Jones, with only occasional glances at the local *Crimes Act* and Australian case law.

The world has changed. Mr Treatt is no more. The St James Hall has long since been demolished. The Sydney Law School is soon to quit forever its home in Phillip Street. No one in Australia today would think of teaching criminal law from an English textbook. Looked at from a very great height, the basics of the criminal justice system might appear the same. But, as this book illustrates, once one comes closer to the subject, radical changes can be seen that challenge even the fundamentals of criminal law and practice in Australia.

By the end of a year of study, I felt that I understood the fundamentals of the principles of criminal law as the common law had laid them down and as, substantially, we practised the discipline in New South Wales at that time. Today, with the proliferation of local legislation, it is much harder for the Australian law student, practitioner or judge to feel so sure in their knowledge of the fundamental concepts of crime and punishment. Things that had lasted for centuries, and that were described in the old English cases collected by Cross and Jones, have now either been abolished or superseded by statute or radically changed by new practices, institutions and attitudes.

To understand Australian criminal law and practice today, it is essential to identify the applicable jurisdiction and then to plunge deep into the codes or statute laws that govern the content and the exercise of that jurisdiction. In the mass of detail, it is easy for the lawyer to become disoriented, bewildered, confused. So this is the primary value of this book, and especially of this third edition. In a world in which detail is dominant, this book seeks to convey the basic concepts. Once we get those basic concepts into our mind, and see the structure of any particular branch of the law (including criminal law), it becomes easier to understand and remember the detail that governs particular cases.

Lawyers of the civil law tradition are usually astonished by, even critical of, the failure of the common law to elucidate concepts and to see matters of detail in their correct context. It is, all too frequently, a just criticism. It is one that I learned in discharging functions in the Australian Law Reform Commission thirty years ago. It is one that I have sought to remedy in my work as an appellate judge. This book is a tool for conceptual thinking about criminal law in Australia. It will not solve every problem. But it will give the essential overview, a structure, reference points and a thoroughly contemporary understanding of criminal law and practice: the core of every civilised legal system.

Reading this third edition, I was struck by how different the content and practice of criminal law is today from what I learned in 1958. Woven through everything in those days was the 'golden thread' described in *Woolmington v Director of Public Prosecutions* [1935] AC 462 at 481–2: 'The principle that the prosecution must prove the guilt of the prisoner is part of the common law … and no attempt to whittle it down can be entertained'. That thread is still there, in most cases. It was emphasised by the High Court of Australia in *RPS v The Queen* (2000) 199 CLR 620 at 630 [22]. The authors of this book describe and reaffirm the principle. In every chapter, there are references to the basic principles stated in the *Universal Declaration of Human Rights* and in the *International Covenant on Civil and Political Rights*. Neither of these instruments was mentioned by Mr Treatt or cited in Cross and Jones. Indeed, neither was referred to by any of my law lecturers unless Julius Stone mentioned the *Universal Declaration* in passing in his course on international law.

The introduction of the basic principle of universal human rights in this book, as in all other relevant areas of Australian law, is a development that is as inevitable as it is useful: *Mabo v Queensland [No 2]* (1992) 175 CLR 1 at 42. Yet not everyone agrees that this is so: *Al-Kateb v Godwin* (2004) 78 ALJR 1099 at 1111 [51]. In my opinion, the repeated reminder of basic and fundamental rules to which Australia has subscribed is extremely useful. This text shows why that is so. The international instruments cannot override clear and valid local law. But they can help in the elucidation of uncertainties and in guiding us away from temporary over-reactions that sometimes threaten the proper balance between individual rights and community protection which the criminal law is always striving to attain.

So many other issues dealt with in this book demonstrate differences from the criminal law of Australia in my student days. True, the basic principles of criminal responsibility appear to be substantially unchanged. However, even here, the attempt to codify them in the *Model Criminal Code* and to secure uniformity in respect of them throughout the Commonwealth will be an ongoing issue in the years and decades ahead.

The authors illustrate the significant changes that have come about in crime investigation processes. The enhancement of the powers of official interrogation and the growth of new state and federal investigating agencies present significant challenges to the accusatorial system of criminal justice that we have hitherto observed. Powers of governmental search and seizure have been greatly enhanced. Telephonic interception and diminution of the 'right to silence' have, in many cases, shifted the fulcrum that previously existed between the individual and the state. The increasing use of DNA evidence and obligations to supply body samples have likewise changed the equation. The old problem of 'police verbals' has, in large part, been overcome by the electronic recording of confessions to police, adopted under the stimulus of High Court decisions. Yet, as recent cases show, problems in this area remain: *Kelly v The Queen* (2004) 78 ALJR 538.

Pre-trial procedures in Australia today are different in many respects from those of fifty years ago. The increasing number of statutes in Australia obliging disclosure by the defence of its case combine to modify the accusatorial system further. That system is sometimes difficult to explain to lay people and seemingly impossible for tabloid editorialists to understand. Yet casting the obligation on the state to prove beyond reasonable doubt crimes alleged against the individual has been one of the mainstays controlling the exercise of public power in countries like Australia. Indeed, it has helped to define the very character of government as we have known it. The authors illustrate the ways in which this fundamental rule is now being diminished. They voice concern at what they see as the merger in Australia (as elsewhere) of criminal and civil process, despite their very different social functions.

The authors also describe the changes that have come over the conduct of the criminal trial and the law of evidence. One issue that deserves much attention is the blow-out in the length of many criminal trials, which has large consequences for the community of increased costs and enhanced risks of error.

The section on punishment and sentencing records the substantial leap in rates of imprisonment in some Australian jurisdictions over the past forty years. In part, this is attributed to legislation enacted out of 'punitive passions, responding to community fears and political vote bidding. For those who want to see the outcomes to which such developments can lead, there are now the recent High Court decisions in *Baker v The Queen* (2004) 78 ALJR 1483 and *Fardon v Attorney-General (Q)* (2004) 78 ALJR 1519. Apart from these extreme instances, the introduction of mandatory sentences and the provision of 'guideline judgments' has changed the law of sentencing from that which long upheld the right and duty of the sentencer to adjust the punishment to the requirements of the particular offence and individual offender. Now, very often, the law is in a frankly punitive mood.

The section on appeals shows the growing part that appellate courts in Australia have played in reviewing unsafe convictions and also sentences claimed to be excessive or inadequate. It is probably true that, in recent years, the High

Court has become more involved in these subjects than was earlier the case. However, the imperfections of its process, where the would-be appellant is a prisoner without counsel, are illustrated in *Milat v The Queen* (2004) 78 ALJR 672 and *Muir v The Queen* (2004) 78 ALJR 780. In the view of some, such cases demonstrate that 'equal justice under law' is not a principle that the Australian criminal justice system has yet fully attained.

The closing section of this book, concerning vulnerable groups and new terrorism legislation, tends to bear out the authors' proposition that the challenges to the fundamentals of criminal law and practice in Australia continue to arise in large numbers. The outcomes will be reflected in later editions of this book. Whether those editions sustain the authors' gloomy prognostication that, in terms of criminal justice, 'Australia is a civilised nation in steep decline', remains for the future. In the meantime, the authors have accomplished their goal of describing and illustrating the present system 'warts and all'.

Australia's criminal justice system still has great strengths for the avoidance of serious injustice. However, it faces important challenges, which this book identifies. This is a legal textbook, not a polemic. But the law of crime and punishment is not an ordinary branch of the law. It lies at the very heart of the way we define our freedoms. That is why it is essential to understand the fundamental concepts and to look with vigilance upon attempts to change those concepts in ways inimical to the traditions of the past. In writing this legal text, the authors have performed a public service in seeking to engage the reader in the many contemporary debates that they describe. When we fail, as citizens, to understand and enter upon these debates, we must accept responsibility for the erosions of liberty that may ensue.

*Michael Kirby*
*High Court of Australia*
*Canberra*
*1 December 2004*

# Contents

# Preface to the Third Edition

In the six years since the second edition of this work was published, a primary theme played out in the realm of Australian criminal justice has been the purported need for further inroads into individual civil liberties and increased punishment for the sake of community welfare and protection. This theme and its implementation has been driven almost singly by politicians, with the courts fighting a frequently losing battle to protect whatever remaining legal protections individuals have against arbitrary or unjust infringements upon their rights and liberties. A closely related theme is the rapid growth of governmental and legislative measures that encroach upon the traditional functions and powers of the courts.

Thus, we find that in relation to investigation (Chapter 2), there has been a proliferation of legislation empowering law enforcement personnel to conduct invasive body searches. The powers and functions given to newly created specialist investigative bodies (Chapter 3) to combat people-smuggling and terrorism are further examples of this trend. While some judicial safeguards against arbitrary use of these extensive investigative powers remain in place, others have been removed by legislation. The same theme of diminution of individual rights and whittling of judicial powers are present in respect of the pre-trial right to bail (Chapter 4). Similarly, in respect of trials (Chapter 5), legislation has been introduced to override the High Court's recognition in *Dietrich v The Queen* of an accused's right to legal representation in cases involving a serious offence. In the same vein is the continuing rise in the use of imprisonment in most Australian States and Territories (Chapter 7), and the growth of grid sentencing and fixed penalty schemes to restrict the role of the courts in effecting individualised criminal justice (Chapter 8). The dramatic increase in the number of sentencing appeals brought by the prosecution (Chapter 9) is further indication of this worrying trend.

As against this, there have been a few welcome developments. One such development is the rise in the number of jurisdictions legislatively mandating electronic recording of police interrogations to overcome police verbals (Chapter 2). Another is the increase in diversionary programs to promote individualised justice for certain particularly vulnerable groups, with some States creating drug courts that enable drug abusers to be dealt with outside the traditional sentencing exercise (Chapter 8). And most jurisdictions now have conferencing schemes for juvenile offenders (Chapter 10). Mention should also be made of the High Court's continuing role as a guardian of individual civil liberties. For instance, in the recent case of *RPS v The Queen*, the court held that only in 'rare and exceptional cases' was a trial judge permitted to adversely comment on an accused's failure to testify (Chapter 6). More recently, in *Dyers v The Queen*, the court extended the principle to the failure of the defence to call witnesses.

However, the onslaught against civil liberties by politicians in power is the order of the day. The current and ongoing fear of globalised terrorism can only result in still further erosions of individual civil liberties in this country. Indeed, this has already begun in a major way (Chapter 10). If there is any truth in the remark that the condition of a nation's criminal justice system is a barometer of a nation's civilisation, Australia as a civilised nation is in steep decline. Already, many of the hard-won individual freedoms that Australia had forged in its two centuries of nation-building have been diminished or lost, with the spectre of a totalitarian state fast becoming a reality.

Is this the inevitable price for freedom from crime and terror? We have our doubts, and we believe that a properly informed public would too. In this regard, the closing statement of the preface to the second edition of this work remains true. It was that just treatment and outcomes for all participants in the criminal justice system will not be achieved by kneejerk responses to populist cries. Rather, those highly desirable goals can only be secured by an informed understanding of the present system and reforms based on empirical research. We remain hopeful that this new edition will assist that process.

*M. Findlay*
*S. Odgers*
*S. Yeo*
*November 2004*

# An Introduction to Criminal Justice

This book is an introduction to the administration of criminal justice in Australia. It looks at what police do, what judges say, and how people are punished. On another level it points to incidents where decisions are made about crime and justice that require understanding, explanation, criticism or change.

For some people in Australian communities the issues covered in this book will hold little more than vicarious interest. Others will have experienced the impact of criminal justice, or realised its absence, first hand. This book recognises that criminal justice means different things to different people. It is also likely to touch different groups in Australian society in very different ways. We hope to address the differential dimensions of justice in what follows.

From the outset our readers do not require a particular knowledge of any aspect of this book. We have written with the intention of supplementing and directing common-sense impressions about the criminal law, police investigations, trials, sentencing and punishment. To do this we have explored the social context of criminal justice in terms of the rights of the individual, community responsibilities, and international guarantees. But this is an introductory discussion of a complex picture of symbols, systems and situations. If the reader is left asking more questions, or seeking further detail then the intended level of discussion has been achieved.

The structure of the book may incorrectly imply some logical progression of justice from statements and principles of law, through the intervention of agencies, the determination of criminal responsibility and the imposition of penalty. In the administration of criminal justice we are not dealing with an entirely predictable, consistent or certain system. We do not focus only on the workings of formal state institutions. The discussion of criminal justice should rather be viewed as a sequence of decision situations where people apply, distort or ignore rules, and where other people have their lives and futures directly affected by such decisions. If there is a system, it is in the interaction between professional and lay participants in an effort to achieve contested notions of justice.

The discretion exercised by principal players in the criminal justice process is what sets this 'system' apart from other occasions of social control. This discretion starts out with the possibility of changing or developing the law, which through the mechanism of precedent may influence discretion exercised further into the process. Legal doctrines can be affirmed, altered or overturned through the discretion of judges and legislators, and these doctrines have the potential to affect police investigations, the presentation of evidence and the progress of a trial, as well as the verdict and the sentence. In addition, discretion is a significant feature of all those 'justice' resolutions going on outside the formal system comprising the police, courts and prisons.

The exercise of discretion, however, exceeds the demands of substantive justice, regulated as it is by laws and rules. Discretion is delegated to those who administer the various stages of criminal justice, in order to make sense of the process. Both authorised and unauthorised discretion is manifested in the individualised and personal decisions of particular officials. These decisions may be motivated by anything from a desire to confirm individual power to a recognition of the need to cope with limited resources.

An example of the individual dimensions of criminal justice discretion is the operation of police investigations. Police personally see their primary tasks as involving the apprehension of criminals and the maintenance of public order. They work within an organisational structure that strongly rewards and encourages efficiency. Therefore, discretion is employed to satisfy these individual and organisational goals. In some instances, police may exercise discretion in pursuit of these goals and at the expense of an individual's rights. Unauthorised discretion may also be used to avoid what police determine as unjust or an immoral result that might follow the strict application of legal rules and procedures. This obviously challenges aspirations for justice that depend on the law or rely on procedural guarantees. In reality, such laws and procedures may be of limited protection in the face of contrary pressures on discretion. However, formal guarantees do create a framework against which the use of abuse of discretion might be measured, and out of which citizens should be informed of their rights and protections and their limitations. More recently in Australia, much of the political debate about criminal justice reform has centred around the regulation particularly of judicial discretion.

Discretion—as we describe its operation through the various stages of criminal justice—is a mix of both individual and organisational decision-making in legal and political spheres. Administration via the 'rule of law' provides for and endeavours to regulate discretion, as it does the wider activities of the state. Yet an introduction to criminal justice that is simply concerned with what laws and rules say will be done will not record reality.

The political and social environment of justice is replete with policy opportunities and choices that essentially shape discretionary decision-making. Recently such policy dimensions have had particular influence at the dispositional (sentencing and punishment) stage of the process. Because of the ways in which criminal justice policy ranges across a broad field of government, the separation of powers between the legislature undertaking law-making and the judiciary interpreting and applying laws is suspect. Likewise, independent police law enforcement may be illusory and an unhelpful way of understanding the operation of police discretion.

In practice, the criminal justice process in Australia has developed through the growth of legal regulation and bureaucratic administration. Such administration is constrained to a greater or lesser extent by both practical and value-based features. The nature of the task being performed is itself complex and involves relationships of power and dominance throughout heterogeneous communities. The social context where justice is attempted leads to an often imperfect fit between rules, the conduct sought to be regulated and the methods and mechanisms imposed to achieve justice.

Likewise the authority structure of criminal justice, the extent to which it is hierarchical, the degree of autonomy officials have to act as they think best and opportunities for imposing individual interpretations of what is just, sets this process apart within Australian society. Criminal justice is not a simple process of reflecting community morality, as if that could ever be simple. The social background and personal predispositions of criminal justice officials are also significant when it comes to interpreting their responsibilities and shaping their methods of enforcement. For example, the way in which a judge considers the communuty harm posed by a particular offence and the seriousness of the prior criminal record of the offender will affect her or his application of different sentencing principles. This individual approach to balancing public policy against personal interpretation is allowed for when the sentencing process is expected to consider both the requirements of consistency and parity, along with an individualised welfare approach. Added to all of this is the ever increasing need to sieve judicial decisions through some filter of community morality and public opinion.

It is not only the ambiguity in the community regarding crime and justice that makes this administration and its decisions rather problematic, and the criminal justice process seem arbitrary. It cannot simply be put down to the presence of discretion. It is not only a question of rules versus individuals. Criminal justice involves the processing of people in such a way as to protect the community, control crime, endorse the law and recognise the victim, while ensuring the rights of the accused. And it is supposed to produce a just result. The issue of what is justice, and its subjectivity, further complicates the decisions that substantiate this process.

Whether or not, as Pascal suggests, justice and truth are qualities too fine to be measured by our clumsy human instruments, the criminal justice process relies on such individual decision-making for its interpretation and activation. It is the avoidance of injustice through the exercise of individual discretion that is the necessary focus of much of this book. Those closest to the administration of criminal justice may agree that the love of justice is simply in the majority of people the fear of suffering injustice. Yet such a recognition does not bring us closer to the meaning of justice.

For this book, justice is not some abstract concept or unconnected critical comment. We agree with D'Amato's assertion that:

> Justice in any situation depends upon a full and fair accounting of the facts of that situation. If instead of facts, fictions are introduced that are contrary to the facts, then any claimed 'just solution' based on such fictions cannot achieve justice in the real world.[1]

We seek to introduce the problems and potentials for justice in a real world. This does not mean that useful discussions of justice are entirely relative, or only dependent on the facts of a particular situation. We know that emotional demonstrations can sway juries as much or more than hard physical evidence. Despite this, there must exist some essential elements and features of justice that can qualify the facts and the consequences of decisions applied to them. Certainly within the current development of international criminal justice there is a search for universals that transcend jurisdiction, culture and institutional representation.

Before briefly examining some of these elements and features of justice, we should reiterate an important distinction that remains implicit throughout this book. There is *procedural justice*, which appears in the form of written rules and recognised protections. But more significant for people within the process is *substantive justice*, where officials are required to apply standards beyond personal opinion and to reach results sometimes unsupported by popular 'common sense'.

Justice consists of principles. As the machinery of justice examined in this book demonstrates, these principles are not unitary, and may in particular situations contradict one another. But still these principles exist and continually appear in the language of criminal justice officials.

One central principle is *equity*, although between who or what, and at what level is not so easy to agree upon. Yet equality of treatment by police, parity in sentencing and consistency in punishment are expectations for justice in practice. Associated with equity is *uniformity* and resultant *certainty*. Laws should be enforced without 'fear or favour', and the consequences of crime should be known and certain. However, where substantive justice is attempted through the exercise of discretion, justice might only be achieved by the modification and selective application of laws and rules to specific individuals in particular circumstances. Already we have some tension in our definition.

In keeping with our interest in substantive justice, we recognise its 'process' dimension. Justice is found in ways of doing things. The apparatus of criminal justice must translate ideals and principles into decisions and action. The form that this apparatus might take will obviously advance or retard justice. The relationships that exist within and between the apparatus are fundamental to expectations for a just result. Juries, for example, are more than symbols of justice. They are supposed to examine facts within an atmosphere of community sensitivity and shared wisdom. They are intended to produce a fair and just result tempered with common sense.

Justice also takes the form of results. These results must be 'fair' or 'reasonable'. They exist in the resolution of disputes, the solving of conflict, seeing that desert is guaranteed and that injury is retaliated. In this respect, substantive justice is not only achieved through processes, but also in outcomes. Hence the community concern that the punishment 'fits' the crime.

With the acceptance of the position that substantive justice comprises principles, processes and outcomes, we do not lessen the significance of standards and their application. Indeed the recourse throughout the book to comparisons with international instruments that should impact on the administration of justice confirms our belief that standards of justice should, and can, mould the daily practice of justice officials and the operation of justice institutions. Having said this, the reader should be aware that:

> Standards of substantive justice are open-ended and can only imperfectly be embodied in textually fixed rules. Like folk poetry or jazz music they are subtly betrayed if forced into rigid systems. Quite naturally, those provisions which purport to codify precepts of substantive justice employ vague terms such as 'reasonable' or 'fair', terms which allude to old, unwritten and amorphous community standards. However, imperfect expression in terms of rules does not mean that the hall of coordinate judicial apparatus is always dimly lit: decisions need not always be unpredictable, nor incapable of justification in terms of rational discourse.[2]

In chapters 1 and 6, dealing with the criminal law and evidence respectively, we have confronted the scope and confines of rules that determine criminal responsibility and the process for its determination. We have endeavoured to relate these rules to wider principles, such as individual autonomy, protection, community welfare and reliability. These chapters recognise the need for a basic understanding of the normative dimensions of justice, before one approaches issues of procedure and administration. In addition, they represent what some might see as a foolhardy attempt at introduction through the selective summary of vast fields of knowledge. While the content might appear traditional, the particular focus of both chapters ensures an economical and comprehensible coverage of complex issues, without dangerous oversimplification.

The material contained in these chapters essentially informs the discussion of criminal investigation and pre-trial procedures appearing in chapters 2 and 4. These chapters go beyond the boundaries of practice to examine any recognition and impact of justice standards past mere administrative assurance. Discretion is explored, and the participation of the principal players is analysed. Issues of power and authority essentially underpin this aspect of the work.

Crime control agendas are dynamic. Therefore, any analysis of criminal justice in Australia today must recognise the significance of novel institutional and procedural interventions. As regards the investigation of terrorism, corruption, commercial malpractice and organised crime (among other contemporary crime concerns), chapter 3 selects particular institutional inventions and looks at their impact from the point of view of accountability, integration and effectiveness.

The criminal trial as the centrepiece of procedural justice in our justice system is the focus of chapters 5, 8 and 9. Chapter 5 puts traditional imagery to the test, through an examination of the central participants and principal stages of the trial. The important distinctions between what goes on in higher and lower courts are drawn. Chapter 8 discusses sentencing principles and their reality in a variety of sentencing applications. Judicial and legislative measures towards the achievement of just sentences are posed and criticised. The hierarchical protections and review of judicial discretion and trial accuracy offered through the appeal process follow. In chapter 9 both conviction and sentence appeals are addressed.

The chapters that stand apart more as polemic encounters with important conflicts and consequences of criminal justice are 'Penalty and Punishment' (chapter 7) and 'Justice for All?' (chapter 10). Their style, while less self-explanatory than the remainder of the text, is designed to stimulate debate as much as to inform. Here the reader will not so much encounter operational detail as propositions and problems. Chapter 7 is intended to contextualise the sentencing process by challenging the connection between crime and punishment, and discussing the link between criminalisation and penalty in Australian society. Our concluding chapter identifies vulnerable groups when it comes to the determination of criminal responsibility and the operation of criminal justice, and deconstructs their position in terms of distortion, reality and remedies. The issues raised by this analysis are finally considered in terms of victimisation and against international 'rights' instruments.

The collective endeavour of this book has been interpretive rather than definitive. Justice forms the common theme. Opinions are shared where style differs. Our expectations are holistic while we accept that readers will be selective. What follows is an introduction in the literal sense. Critics no doubt would have us alter our emphasis or remain a little longer on certain issues. Some might say we pay too little attention to community justice alternatives and restorative interventions. No doubt these will assume greater significance in future editions as they challenge the monopoly of state institutions and processes. But when it comes to the selection of what to introduce, we have had to sacrifice some detail to be comprehensive, and on other occasions vice versa. We have struggled with the motto 'keep it simple', while not avoiding matters of greater conceptual complexity. We recognise that the diversity of the subject matter and the issues provoked by it make attempts at a harmonious product rather artificial. Our readings range from Law Reform Commission reports to Foucault, and we have strenuously avoided tokenism even down to the book's format.

In a liberal spirit of introduction, we have endeavoured to make available to a wide readership an accurate and well-rounded discussion of Australian criminal justice, warts and all.

# Notes

1    A. D'Amato, 'The Ultimate Injustice: When a Court Misstates the Facts', *Cardozo Law Review*, 11, 1989, pp. 1313–47.

2    M. R. Damaska, *The Faces of Justice and State Authority*, Yale University Press, New Haven, CT, 1986, p. 28.

# Criminal Responsibility

## Introduction

The criminal law identifies certain wrongful behaviour that society regards as deserving of punishment. People breaching the criminal law are labelled as criminals and are penalised by the state. Given these severe consequences, the criminal law is normally reserved for limited kinds of wrongdoing.

This chapter will analyse the major considerations affecting the decision whether certain wrongful behaviour should be regarded as a crime.[1] One of these is the principle of *individual autonomy* whereby people may conduct their lives as they choose with as few restrictions as possible. This principle promotes minimal criminalisation. There is also the related notion of 'individualism', which regards people as capable of choosing their own courses of action. According to this notion, people who lack the capacity to choose should not be made criminally responsible for their actions. A competing consideration is the *community welfare* principle according to which the collective interests of society must be protected. This principle views individuals as belonging to a wider community, which can only be sustained if certain duties are imposed on its members. The criminal law is relied on as one mechanism to ensure that these duties are adequately discharged. These duties serve to protect the rights of other members of the community and, more broadly, the values and interests of the community, which are seen as essential to its successful functioning. Hence, the community welfare principle asserts that individual autonomy may have to be overridden by the collective interests of the community. The criminal law is very much the product of the interplay between these two competing principles of individual autonomy and community welfare.

The first part of this chapter spells out the aims and functions of the criminal law. In the second part, certain specific policies and principles influencing the perimeters of the criminal law are explored. Also included is a brief consideration of the sources of the criminal law and how the law is or should be laid down. The third part covers the essential ingredients of a crime, namely, harm-inducing conduct, a mental or fault element, and the absence of any lawful justification or excuse (that is, defences). The fourth part considers certain concepts that the criminal law has devised to extend the scope of criminal responsibility. The struggle between individual autonomy and community welfare will often appear. It will be observed how justice or fairness is achieved for both individuals and the community to which they belong through a carefully reasoned balancing of these competing considerations. This need to balance individual autonomy with community welfare is so vital that it appears as an Article in the *Universal Declaration of Human Rights*:

(1) Everyone has duties to the community in which alone the free and full development of his personality is possible.

(2) In the exercise of his rights and freedoms, everyone shall be subject only to such limitations as are determined by law solely for the purpose of securing due recognition and respect for the rights and freedoms of others and of meeting the just requirements of morality, public order and the general welfare in a democratic society.[2]

# Aims and functions of the criminal law

The overall aim of the criminal law is the prevention of certain kinds of behaviour that society regards as either harmful or potentially harmful. The criminal law is applied by society as a defence against harms that injure the interests and values that are considered fundamental to its proper functioning. These interests and values cover a wide area. They include the bodily integrity of people, the security of property, protection of the environment and moral values.

It may be easy enough to state this general justifying aim of the criminal law. But the problem comes when we have to locate the key to deciding whether an interest or value is so fundamental as to warrant the protection of the criminal law. This problem is compounded by several factors. First, there are other fundamental interests or values, also crucial to the proper functioning of society, that are incompatible with the threat of criminal sanction. Second, there are methods of social control or prevention besides the criminal law. Third, the primary aim is blurred by its increased use of the criminal law to regulate conduct for reasons of economy and expediency. There is a growing sphere of legislative activity that uses the criminal sanction to endorse policies that stand apart from harm prevention. We shall elaborate upon these factors in the course of our discussion.

## Moral wrongness approach

One suggested key to deciding whether behaviour should be criminalised is 'moral wrongness'. Lord Devlin, an English judge, was a keen proponent of this stance.[3] He regarded morality as underpinning the social fabric of society, and immoral behaviour as eroding that fabric and consequently destabilising society. He therefore had no hesitation in advocating the use of the criminal law to deter 'immoral' behaviour. Lord Devlin applied the strength of feelings of ordinary people to define moral wrongness. If conduct arouses feelings of indignation or revulsion in these people, it is a good indication that the conduct strikes at the common morality and is a proper object of the criminal law. But herein lies a major weakness of Lord Devlin's approach. His definition of moral wrongness is far too imprecise as it leaves the matter to be decided by mere feelings of disgust. Such feelings may well stem from irrational prejudices rather than reasoned moral indignation.

## Individual autonomy approach

Another suggested key to deciding whether the criminal law should be used is the 'harms to others' approach. This may be described as individualistic liberalism.[4] This approach places individual autonomy at a premium and contends that this and its attendant individual freedoms are vital to the proper functioning of society. The approach calls for individuals to be accorded as much freedom as possible, subject only to the minimum restrictions required to provide other individuals sharing the community with those same freedoms. The criminal law should therefore be used only against behaviour that injures the rights and interests of these other people, in other words, behaviour that harms others. Thus, under this approach, homosexual behaviour between consenting adults should not be criminalised since they have mutually agreed to engage in this behaviour. Accordingly, these people should not be subject to the criminal law however reprehensible or immoral their behaviour might appear in the eyes of some.[5]

It should be noted that this 'harms to others' approach relates to individuals who have reached a sufficient degree of mental maturity to competently decide what is best for themselves. Proponents would permit the use of the criminal law to protect individuals who lack such maturity, for example children and intellectually disabled people. This may be described as legal paternalism as it conveys an image of the law acting as a protective parent or guardian to especially vulnerable or dependent individuals. For example, the criminal law may be applied to prohibit children below a certain age from engaging in activities such as homosexual or heterosexual intercourse, drinking alcohol in pubs, or driving a motor vehicle on a public road. The reason why these activities are criminally proscribed is not because they are harmful in themselves, but because they have potentially harmful consequences that immature people may not sufficiently appreciate.

A criticism against this approach is that it fails to explain adequately the use of the criminal law in certain areas. For instance, few would today disagree that the deterrent effect of the criminal law should be applied to ensure that safety belts are worn by drivers, or that motorcyclists should wear helmets. Paternalism is an inappropriate explanation here since we are concerned with individuals who should possess a sufficient degree of maturity to make their own decisions about the risks of such activities. It could be contended that these activities might cause harm because the participants may injure themselves and become a financial burden or source of hardship to their families or the state, which has to care for them. However, these harms are, at best, indirect and their recognition will considerably reduce the limiting principle that makes the approach so attractive.

## Community welfare approach

Perhaps a better explanation for the criminal proscription of such behaviour lies in what we have termed the community welfare principle.[6] This principle justifies the use of the criminal law to protect the continued physical well-being of members of a community. The principle would also take into account the financial cost to the community of permitting activities such as not wearing seat-belts and helmets to continue unrestricted.

It is worthwhile observing here the material difference between the 'harms to others' approach and the community welfare principle. We have already noted that the former emphasises individual autonomy and confines the role of the criminal law to proscribing activities that impinge on the freedoms of other individuals within the same community. In contrast, the community welfare principle places a premium on community interests and would be prepared to override individual autonomy for the greater good of the community. Thus, the principle may impose criminal liability on drug users or on people driving without securing their seat-belts out of concern for the welfare of the community. This would be done at the cost of infringing upon their individual freedom to choose their own course of action. It should be added that the community welfare principle is not confined to explaining those activities that cannot be adequately explained by the 'harms to others' approach. The community welfare principle can and does serve as a key to deciding which behaviour should or should not be criminalised in respect of a full range of 'anti-social' behaviour.

To summarise our discussion thus far, the overall aim of the criminal law may be stated as the prevention of harm. But the criminal law would be drastically over-used if it were to proscribe each and every activity that causes harm or has the potential to do so. The problem for lawmakers is to determine which kinds of harmful activity should fall within the ambit of the criminal law and which should fall outside it. Two competing influences have been located that have a significant bearing on this determination—the principles of individual autonomy and community welfare. Neither can claim to have taken predominance over the other, so that in achieving the overall aim of preventing harm, the criminal law has been moulded in ways that account for both of these principles.

## Major functions

We now turn to examine certain major functions of the criminal law. These involve the processes, operations or activities that the criminal law normally discharges. One of these functions is to distinguish civil wrongs from criminal wrongs. A person who is harmed by a tort[7] or by a breach of contract may sue for damages or obtain some other remedy in a civil court. He or she has been 'wronged' but the harmful conduct may not be regarded as sufficiently serious to constitute a crime. Not all social mischiefs will have aggrieved victims wanting remedies from a civil court. There are some mischiefs that harm the public rather than individual victims. In these cases, the criminal law may be justified in stepping in to ensure that such harmful activities are controlled, even though the mischief may constitute only minor incursions on basic social functioning. These have been described as 'victimless' crimes and include activities such as drug use, prostitution, distribution of obscene literature, and some forms of gambling. Whether the criminal law is the best measure to control this behaviour is open to debate.

Distinguishing civil from criminal cases is only a preliminary function of the criminal law. Its primary task is to stipulate the *degree of seriousness* of criminal conduct. We need to determine not simply whether a social mischief is sufficiently serious to be made a crime but, if a crime, how serious it is when compared with other crimes. Knowing the degree of seriousness of criminal conduct is vital to selecting the proper label of offence and the appropriate penalty. It has also wider practical consequences for matters such as the legality of arrest without a warrant and of searches, the decision to caution or to prosecute, to grant bail, whether to have the case tried before a magistrate or a judge, to try a case with or without a jury, the sentencing options available, and the decision whether to release on parole.

What considerations are material in assessing the relative seriousness of criminal conduct? One factor is the impact of the conduct on victims of the particular kind of crime. Not only the physical injuries, but the psychological trauma of victims of violent crimes may be taken into account. The monetary value of property crimes also affects the degree of offence seriousness. Another factor is the extent of culpability of the offender. This may be gauged according to the offender's mental state in relation to the offence. Thus, intentional wrongdoing would normally be assessed as more culpable than recklessness, which in turn would be more blameworthy than negligent behaviour.[8] A third factor is the degree of likelihood of harm. A case involving conduct that was virtually certain to cause harm would obviously be more serious than one where the risk of harm was remote. Similarly, a case where the harm actually occurred would normally be regarded as more serious than one where the harm did not materialise.

This very brief consideration of how offence seriousness is assessed should be sufficient to indicate its complexity. Numerous value judgments are involved as well as a multiplicity of variables relevant to the assessment exercise. Difficult as the task is in ranking offences, justice to both offenders and their victims requires every effort to be made. To reduce arbitrariness and inconsistency in ranking offence seriousness, it may be necessary to adopt a framework upon which law-makers can pin their deliberations.[9]

So far, we have only discussed crimes that harm the fundamental values and interests necessary for proper social functioning. However, there is an ever-growing proliferation of offences that do not fit this description. These are minor offences that use the threat of punishment to achieve the smooth running of day-to-day social intercourse and activities such as road traffic flow, business regulation, urban planning, licensing procedures and so forth. Accordingly, they have been described as 'regulatory offences'. These offences are often made strictly liable by the legislature so that mere proof of the commission of the proscribed conduct is sufficient to establish the charge against the accused without additionally having to prove that the accused intended, knew of or was reckless of the wrongdoing.[10] But is the use of the criminal law justified in these areas? While the smooth running of these activities may be necessary to realise social and individual goals, it is certainly not as central to social functioning as the protection of physical integrity or the security of property. These regulatory offences seem to have emerged on the basis of economy and expediency. The criminal law and criminal justice system lend themselves to providing cheap, effective and politically convenient means of controlling such comparatively minor infringements. Whether the criminal law should function in these spheres is highly debatable. Such an extension of its operation does not sit well with the overall aim of the criminal law of protecting values and interests considered fundamental to proper social functioning. Furthermore, the stigma and consequences of criminal conviction may be too drastic for these kinds of infringements. It is our view that the better course would be for these infringements to be regulated by some other form of enforcement—for example, insurance, taxation and licensing.[11]

# Sources, prescriptions and influences on the criminal law

In this part, we shall deal firstly with the sources of Australian criminal law—where it is to be found. Next, the form in which the law is presented will be examined. There then follows a brief description of the major categories of crimes. The final section will consider certain policies and principles that narrow or expand the contours of criminal responsibility.

## Sources of criminal law

There is no single body of criminal law governing the whole of Australia. Each State and Territory has its own set of criminal laws. Added to these is Commonwealth criminal law regulating matters within the domain of the constitutional powers of the Commonwealth, such as international and interstate trade, federal taxation, and environmental control.

The criminal laws of these various Australian jurisdictions may be divided into two forms: statutory law, which is enacted by the legislature; and 'common law', which is formulated by judges. Queensland, Western Australia, Tasmania, the Northern Territory and the Australian Capital Territory have criminal codes. These are statutes that comprehensively lay down the criminal law. New South Wales, South Australia, and Victoria have much of their criminal laws formulated and developed by judges. However, in recent years, these common law jurisdictions have witnessed a noticeable increase in criminal legislation. The effect of this is to have the common law gradually replaced by statute.

This variety of criminal laws in Australia is unsatisfactory. While there are some core criminal legal principles commonly shared by all the States and Territories, there remain material differences in much of the substantive criminal laws of these jurisdictions. These differences concern such fundamental matters as the definitions of offences, their range of seriousness, the definitions of defences, and the prescribed punishment. The result is inconsistency and incoherence in outcomes when dealing with like cases in different jurisdictions. Thus, a person performing some criminal conduct in, say, Queensland, may be convicted of a different offence and receive a different punishment from a person who had performed the same conduct in Victoria. Justice dictates that persons engaged in criminal behaviour should be treated in the same way throughout this country.[12] Such a sentiment led the Attorneys-General of all the Australian States and Territories to initiate a uniform criminal code for Australia.[13] Regrettably, after more than a decade, there is little evidence that the State and Territorial governments are prepared to replace their existing criminal laws with the one proposed by the Model Criminal Code Officers Committee.[14] Hopefully, the lead taken by the legislatures of the Commonwealth and the Australian Capital Territory in adopting most of the draft criminal code will eventually persuade the other governments to follow suit.[15]

## Prescription of criminal law

A national criminal code would bring consistency to the criminal law of Australia. This development would have another welcome effect on those jurisdictions whose criminal law is presently founded on a common law base. It would mean that the criminal law would be prescribed and developed primarily by the legislature rather than by judges. This is more in accord with constitutional precepts— since the criminal law is society's most powerful measure in regulating social mischiefs, it should be the legislature who decides what that law should be as opposed to a small number of unelected judges. The legislature, comprising elected representatives of the community, are best equipped to express the views of society on such questions as: Is a particular interest or value fundamental to proper social functioning? If so, are there other competing interests or values that should prevail? Is the criminal law the best medium to protect these interests and values?

Another reason for preferring the criminal law to be cast in statutory form is the greater certainty this achieves when compared with the common law. With the law laid down in statute, members of society are given fair warning of their social responsibilities under the criminal law and can readily find these out. This adheres to the principle of individual autonomy with its notion of sufficient choice. Choices are real if the law clearly spells out in advance the consequences of taking certain proscribed actions.

In contrast, the history of the common law has been to create new offences whenever judges regarded conduct, not previously the object of the criminal law, to be deserving of punishments.[16] The common law has also tended to be much more vague in its pronouncements of the criminal law. This might have been consciously done by the judges to provide room for further creativity should some future occasion so require. The stance of the common law can be supported on the ground of social defence. The judicial power to create new offences and the vagueness of existing criminal law are needed to deal with new variations of social mischief without having to await the lumbering response of legislature. The main criticism against this approach is that it denies individual autonomy (and consequently fairness to individuals) by retroactively penalising previously non-criminal conduct. Indeed, such retroactivity breaches an Article in the *Universal Declaration of Human Rights*, which says that:

> No one shall be held guilty of any penal offence on account of any act or omission which did not constitute a penal offence, under national or international law, at the time when it was committed.[17]

As for the point about the lumbering response of legislature, the pace of legislative enactment has been noticeably much quicker in recent years.[18]

With the move towards greater statutory prescription of the criminal law, what role is left for the courts? This brings us into the realm of statutory interpretation. Judges, with their legal training and expertise, are still the best people to attend to this task. Where the statutory formulation is clear, the court cannot deviate from it. Where the formulation is open to debate, which is often the case, the judges can select from a range of interpretative principles. The judges exercise considerable discretion in both the selection and appreciation of these principles.

The statutory prescription of the criminal law makes it readily accessible to the public. It also provides the impetus to pronouncing the law in simple language so as to be easily comprehensible to ordinary people. Furthermore, the process of encasing the criminal law within the structure and terms of a statute in turn encourages the exercise of ranking offences according to their seriousness.[19] As we have noted earlier, justice requires that a determined effort should be made to perform this task.

## Categories of crime

It is not possible here to mention all the multifarious forms of harms that the criminal law proscribes. The main categories of crimes (not necessarily in order of offence seriousness) may be summarised as follows:

- *Crimes involving death.* Homicide, which is causing death to a human being, is arguably the most serious harm. The crime of murder with its special label and the severity of punishment it attracts places this offence above all other offences involving homicide. A little lower down the scale is attempted murder. This is followed by manslaughter, infanticide and causing death by reckless driving.
- *Crimes involving bodily injury.* Besides offences causing death, there is a whole range of other offences designed to protect bodily integrity. Psychic assault (threats to apply unlawful force) sits at the least serious end of the range. At the other end are physical assaults resulting in very serious bodily injury that brings the victim close to death. In between are numerous varieties of assault, depending on such factors as the degree of force applied, the injury suffered, and the mental state of the offender. Sometimes, the status of the victim is also significant—for example, the relatively serious offence of assaulting a police officer while in the execution of her or his duty. Sexual offences also vary widely and range from minor sexual contact to sexual assault involving serious physical violence.
- *Road traffic offences.* Many of these offences are minor in nature and perform a regulatory function promoting the smooth flow of traffic. However, included in this category are much more serious offences that pose a danger to the lives and safety of other road users. For instance, there is reckless driving and its less culpable counterparts, negligent driving and drunk driving. Besides seeking to prevent bodily injury, road traffic offences seek to provide protection against damage to property.
- *Occupational health and public safety offences.* These are offences designed to prevent physical injury in the workplace, from the consumption of goods, the use of public transportation, and so on. In the past, these offences tended to be

regarded as minor and regulatory in nature when compared with the traditional offences involving bodily injury. However, with greater enlightenment on the extent of injury suffered by victims of these offences, they are beginning to be accorded a much higher rank on the scale of offence-seriousness.

- *Offences against public order.* These offences range from such serious offences as rioting and violent disorder to minor ones such as offensive behaviour or the use of offensive language. They are designed to enable members of society to move about freely without fear of violence, and be spared abuse or nuisance. For offences at the lower end of the range, there is a danger of their being misused by the police to serve or protect their own interests.[20]

- *Offences against the state.* Treason, sedition, and providing assistance to the enemy in time of war are examples of this group of offences. They seek to protect the foundations of the state and maintain the stability of the government, which is considered vital to maintaining peace and good order. Closely related to these offences are those that have recently been enacted to combat the threat of terrorism.[21] As might be expected, these offences are placed very high on the scale of offence-seriousness since they seek to protect national security.

- *Property offences.* The most serious of these offences is robbery (theft accompanied by the use or threat of physical violence). Lower down the range is theft, which is the deprivation of another's property without consent and with the intention of doing so permanently. Then there are the offences of damaging or destroying another's property, that, as with theft, are geared at protecting property interests. Next, are those offences that have an element of fraud—for example, where property has been obtained by deception or by falsifying accounts. The offence of receiving stolen property punishes those who encourage the commission of other property offences by making it economically worthwhile.

- *Environmental offences.* These seek to prevent the pollution of water, air and the earth and to generally maintain a healthy environment. In recent years, there has been an increased awareness of the long-lasting ill-effects of pollution on food, health and the environment. This has resulted in raising many environmental offences up the scale of offence-seriousness. Industries that produce hazardous wastes are being more closely monitored and made to implement anti-pollution procedures under threat of heavy penalties.

- *Paternalistic offences.*[22] Some of these have already been discussed such as the wearing of seatbelts and helmets. Gambling, prostitution, the distribution of obscene literature and drug use may be added to this list. These offences are sought to be justified on the ground that they protect vulnerable people from harming themselves. These are usually the very young, but adults are also included on the basis that the general welfare and well-being of the community is promoted by discouraging such potentially harmful activities.

- *Drug offences.* While the criminalisation of drug use may be motivated by paternalism (as used in a wide sense), there are several other offences connected with drugs, which are seen to exhibit aggravating features. These are drug trafficking, importation, cultivation and manufacture. These offences are placed high on the scale of offence-seriousness because they are designed to eradicate the supply of drugs. The whole issue of drug offences, particularly in relation to so-called 'soft drugs', is a matter of continuing public debate.

## Influences on the perimeters of criminal responsibility

In this section we shall consider certain policies and principles contained in the criminal law that influence the ambit of criminal responsibility. Some of these will have the effect of narrowing the limits of the criminal law while others will have the opposite effect.

The policy of *minimal criminalisation* advocates that the criminal law should be used sparingly due to its coercive and liberty-depriving consequences. Individual autonomy is placed at a premium with the individual given as much freedom of choice as possible. The criminal law should therefore be confined only to censuring those activities that definitely harm the values and interests fundamental to proper social functioning.

As opposed to minimal criminalisation is the policy of *social defence*. This sees individuals as members of a wider community whose social arrangements may need to be protected by the criminal law. The criminal law is permitted to infringe upon individual autonomy should this be required to protect the community from threats to peace and order. We have previously noted this same tension between the two policies when discussing the principles of individual autonomy and community welfare.

The principle of *liability for acts but not omissions* also narrows the ambit of the criminal law. According to this principle, criminal responsibility should be confined to positive conduct. Conversely, the criminal law should not penalise people for failing to take action to protect the bodily integrity or property interests of others. It can be seen that individual autonomy is once again maintained since the principle asserts that people should be free to decide whether or not to act in these circumstances. Proponents of this principle would be prepared to recognise certain exceptions. Positive duties to act may justifiably be imposed by the criminal law where, for example, a parent–child relationship exists, or where the accused had voluntarily assumed the care of the victim.[23] However, these exceptions are still consistent with individual autonomy since the positive duty is imposed only on people who had voluntarily chosen through their previous actions to protect the victim. Accordingly, a failure by these people to protect their charges may deserve punishment.

In contrast, the principle of *social responsibility* asserts that the act-omission distinction should give way to the imposition of duties that help to promote a value

or protect an interest beneficial to society. In partial deference to individual autonomy, there is the proviso that the discharge of the duty is easy and involves no risk
to the actor.[24]

The principles of justification and excuse also operate to narrow the ambit of
criminal responsibility.[25] Under the principle of justification, society approves of
the accused's conduct and seeks to encourage its performance. The accused should
therefore be acquitted of the crime charged. Examples of justification include acting in self-defence or applying force to apprehend a suspected offender. Under the
principle of excuse, society regards the accused's conduct as wrong and to be discouraged. However, the accused is rendered not blameworthy (and therefore
acquitted of the offence) due to certain extenuating circumstances operating at
the time the wrongful conduct was performed. Examples include committing an
offence in order to avoid serious injury or some natural danger. While society
maintains that the accused's conduct was wrong, it acknowledges the pressures
under which the accused operated. As the accused's choices of action were constrained, there was an absence of the individual autonomy required to render her
or him criminally responsible for the resulting harm.

The principles of justification and excuse are subject to the limitations that the
accused's conduct was reasonable and necessary. Reasonableness may be measured
by the concept of proportionate response—the accused's conduct is reasonable
provided the harm it inflicted on the victim was no greater than the harm that
that conduct prevented. Necessity looks at whether there were other less harmful
ways of avoiding the threat or danger to the accused. The concepts of reasonableness and necessity are deliberately kept vague to provide the flexibility needed for
judges to respond properly to a whole variety of situations.

This brief discussion of policies and principles influencing the perimeters of
criminal responsibility highlight two important matters. The first is that there are
no simple explanations as to why the criminal law has taken one direction and not
another over a particular subject. In each case, the explanation will stem from one
or more policies or principles that are selected, and this selection process is value
laden. As Alan Norrie has observed:

> There are principles of rationality and justice in operation within the law but they
> must be seen as elements in tension with other contradictory elements. In exam-
> ining criminal law, we must recognise the limits of rationality and justice: limits
> which are a central and necessary part of the enterprise and not the result of chance
> or contingency. Criminal law is relatively unpredictable in its development and this
> stems from the fundamental ambiguity of its central organising principles.[26]

Second, underlying the whole discussion is the concern that the criminal law
should not be significantly out of touch with society's expectations. These expectations range from individual freedom to conduct one's own affairs with minimal
restrictions, to ideas about shared responsibilities as a member of a community.

Difficult as the task may be, the criminal law should be under continuous scrutiny to ensure that it maintains the respect of society. This is not only an important aspect of democracy, it also has a practical foundation since the law relies on public consensus for its effective functioning.[27]

# Elements of a crime

The elements that must exist before a person can be convicted of an offence vary from one crime to another. All crimes comprise some form of prohibited conduct, which may be an act or (in rare cases) an omission. This conduct element denotes the external or physical component of a crime.[28] Another element found in many (but not all) crimes is the mental state of the person at the time when the prohibited conduct was performed.[29] This may take several forms such as intention, recklessness or knowledge in relation to the prohibited conduct. Most of the traditional crimes developed through the common law require personal awareness of what was being done. However, there are many crimes, known as offences of strict liability and of absolute liability, that do not require any such awareness at all. Even when both the conduct and mental elements are satisfied, a person may still avoid conviction by relying on a defence. These defences constitute justifications or excuses to the prohibited behaviour.

## Conduct elements

A cardinal requirement for all crimes is that the prohibited conduct must have been performed voluntarily. Voluntariness involves the ability to exercise control over one's bodily movements. Examples of states of involuntariness are sleepwalking, a concussion, an epileptic fit, being attacked by a swarm of bees, and being physically overpowered by another person.

The draft Australian Model Criminal Code describes voluntariness in terms of a 'willed act'[30] in line with the High Court ruling that, for conduct to be voluntary, it must be the product of the will.[31] This requirement stems from the principle of individual autonomy, which declares that people may be made criminally responsible for their actions provided they had sufficient choice or control over them. A person who lacks choice or control cannot fairly be described as having *acted* out the conduct in the strict sense of that term. It would be more appropriate to describe the conduct as the result of something *happening* to the person.[32] With the principle of individual autonomy embedded in the requirement of voluntariness, it is easy to incorporate ideas of blame and desert into the discussion. This is consistent with the way a substantial proportion of society views criminal responsibility— a person should be convicted and punished only if he or she was blameworthy in the sense of having freely chosen to perform the proscribed behaviour.

There is a countervailing view to this. It is that human behaviour is determined by causes, some known but others unknown. In this view about the deterministic nature of human conduct, voluntariness, blame and desert play no part in the consideration of criminal responsibility. It calls for a utilitarian approach to be taken when identifying criminal responsibility.

Whether a person will be held criminally responsible will turn on what approach would be most effective in preventing or reducing harmful conduct. How might this view about determinism affect the requirement of voluntariness? It can be safely asserted that there is no real evidence for the truth of determinism in the sense that *all* our behaviour is fully determined. Nevertheless, we should be prepared to accept that there may be instances where a person's behaviour was strongly determined so that he or she should not be held criminally responsible for the proscribed conduct. This proposition has been described as 'compatibilism'.[33] It assumes the notion that individuals are sufficiently free to choose and control their actions so as to be blamed for them, and yet accepts that there may be occasions when circumstances so affect an individual's choice or control as to warrant the negation of blame.

Once conduct has been determined to be voluntary, the enquiry shifts to whether an accused had caused the resulting harm. Take the case of D who stabs V in the arm, leading V to seek medical attention. Unfortunately, the medical treatment is grossly inadequate. Should V die, can D still be said to have caused his death? The test of 'substantial cause' has been devised to resolve this problem.[34] Otherwise, it would be possible to impose liability on conduct of the accused that had some causal effect, however remote or indirect it might be. For example, D invites V to dinner. On the way to D's house, V is killed by a bus. It would be unduly harsh to regard D as having caused V's death, even though it may be true that, but for D's invitation, V would not have used the road that night.

There may be cases involving intervening causes—that is, where another human agent's conduct has come in between the accused's conduct and the eventual harm. Take the case of A who stabs V. As V lies dying, B shoots and kills V instantaneously. The law will conclude that B and not A had caused V's death, even though A might be charged with attempted murder. But what if B's conduct lacked autonomy due, for instance, to A having compelled him by death threats to shoot V? In such a case, A may be regarded as having caused V's death using, as it were, B as his instrument to cause the death. This is further buttressed by the fact that A was the creator of the circumstances that led to V's death. The same reasoning may apply to cases when the intervening cause was by V herself or himself as opposed to a third party. In *Royall v The Queen*, the leading Australian case on causation, R had violently attacked V.[35] On one view of the evidence, V jumped to her death from a high building in an effort to escape the attack. R was regarded to have caused V's death because he impaired her autonomy in respect of her conduct and created the emergency she faced.

There is another way of reaching the same result in these cases of intervening causes. It is to ask whether a reasonable person in the accused's position could have foreseen that her or his conduct might lead to the intervening causal occurrence.[36] If so, then the accused remains causally responsible for the eventual harm occasioned by the intervening cause. To return to the case of shooting, A would have reasonably foreseen both B's act of shooting and V's death from the gun wound since it was he who had coerced B into shooting V. Similarly, with regard to the facts in *Royall*, R could have reasonably foreseen that V might seek to escape from his violent attack by jumping from the building.

## Mental elements

We have just noted the significant impact that the principle of individual autonomy has in moulding the conduct elements of crime. This principle also plays a significant role in linking criminal responsibility to personal awareness about the consequences of one's conduct.[37] Individual autonomy requires people to be judged by their free choice of actions. This choice is present only if individuals knew of the consequences of their conduct or knew the actual circumstances under which they were operating. This may be described as the *subjective approach* in that it places emphasis on the personal viewpoint of the particular defendant.

However, the community welfare principle supports an *objective approach*. According to this principle, individuals should be convicted irrespective of whether they possessed free choice of action, if future crime is prevented or reduced.[38] Additionally, the principle focuses on the actual consequences of an accused's conduct or the actual circumstances under which the conduct occurred rather than on the accused's mental state during the performance of the conduct. An objective approach to criminal responsibility is thereby advocated in that it places emphasis on the *actual* state of affairs resulting from or surrounding the commission of the crime.

Current 'common law' favours the subjective approach to criminal responsibility. The general rule is that the prosecution bears the burden of proving that the accused intended or knowingly risked the consequences of her or his conduct. In contrast, the criminal codes of Queensland, Western Australia and Tasmania lean towards the objective approach.[39] Apart from certain crimes such as murder and many property offences, the prosecution in these jurisdictions does not need to prove a particular mental state of the accused. Instead, the prosecution would only need to disprove that the conduct was done accidentally or under an honest and reasonable mistaken belief, if those issues are raised by the defence. It is worthwhile noting that the committee presently developing a uniform criminal code for Australia has preferred the subjective approach.[40] While acknowledging the good service that the criminal codes had given to Queensland, Western Australia and Tasmania, the committee believed that those codes were out of line with modern thinking about criminal responsibility. The trend is towards presuming a subjective mental state as part of the definition of all offences, accompanied by the prosecution bearing the burden of proving such a mental state.

In the ensuing discussion, the framework incorporating a subjective approach to criminal responsibility will be adopted. First, the salient forms of subjective mental states contained in the criminal law are presented. This will be followed by certain objective principles that have retained a stronghold in the criminal law. It will be observed how the law generally upholds the subjective approach but does occasionally give way to arguments based on community welfare on grounds of 'public interest'.

## Subjective mental states

The mental state of a crime may comprise a variety of mental elements usually classified as intention, recklessness and knowledge. This mental state varies from one crime to another, with some crimes focusing on the consequences of the accused's conduct and others concentrating on the circumstances in which the conduct occurred.

### Intention

The core meaning of this notion is purpose. A person intends a consequence if it is her or his purpose to achieve that result. Seen in these terms, intention in the criminal law is not concerned with desire (for example, one may act out of feelings of duty rather than desire). Furthermore, it shows that the criminal law is only concerned with a particular type of intention, ignoring other intentions that the accused person might have had. For example, in taking a blanket without the owner's consent, D might have intended to permanently deprive the owner of it. She might also have intended to take the blanket to give to a homeless person, or to please a friend who coveted it. For D to be charged with theft, only the first form of intention, which appears in the definition of theft, will need to be proven.

The criminal law has, however, given a wider meaning than purpose to intention. A person may be said to intend a consequence that he or she foresaw was certain to follow the conduct in question.[41] Take the case of D, the owner of a plane, who arranged for it to be blown up while in mid-flight realising that the explosion would certainly kill everyone on board. Let us assume that his purpose was to claim insurance on the plane and not to kill the aircrew and passengers. Since it was not D's purpose to kill, that aspect of the definition of intention is not fulfilled. The issue then is whether D should be classified as a purposeful killer or a merely reckless killer. The criminal law prefers the former as it sees little social or moral difference between the mental state of D (he knew as a matter of virtual certainty that those on board the plane would die, but nonetheless proceeded with the plan) and a person who deliberately set out to kill the people in the plane. Both the core and wider definition of intention have been included in the draft Model Criminal Code:

A person has intention with respect to a result when he or she means to bring it about or is aware that it will occur in the ordinary course of events.[42]

## Recklessness

Given that intention includes foresight of the virtual certainty of a consequence occurring, recklessness must involve a less culpable mental state. Recklessness may be defined as foresight of a risk that a consequence might occur, or that a circumstance exists, and proceeding to act in a way that brings about that risk.[43] Any significant degree of risk (other than virtual certainty, which is covered by intention) will normally suffice for recklessness. A proviso to criminal responsibility based on recklessness is that the accused must be unjustified in taking the risk, which he or she believes to be present. This rarely poses a problem as the bulk of reckless criminal incidents involve socially unjustifiable risk-taking. However, this requirement does explain why a surgeon performing a difficult but necessary operation may not be made criminally responsible for a consequent death even though there was a substantial risk of failure. The proposed draft Model Criminal Code encapsulates these various aspects of recklessness into the following definition:

> A person is reckless with respect to a circumstance when he or she is aware of a substantial risk that it exists or will exist and it is, having regard to the circumstances as known to him or her, unjustifiable to take the risk. A person is reckless with respect to a result when he or she is aware of a substantial risk that it will occur and it is, having regard to the circumstances as known to him or her, unjustifiable to take the risk.[44]

## Knowledge

Knowledge constitutes awareness that a specified circumstance exists or that a consequence will ensue. It is distinguishable from recklessness, which, as we have seen, concerns foresight of a risk of something that may or may not result or be present. In contrast, a person cannot 'know' something unless he or she believes it exists or will exist. The proposed Model Criminal Code subscribes to this distinction by defining knowledge in the following terms:

> A person has knowledge of a circumstance or a result when he or she is aware that it exists or will exist in the ordinary course of events.[45]

Occasionally, a defendant might seek to rebut knowledge on the ground of mistaken belief. For example, an element of the crime of rape is knowledge that the victim did not consent to sexual intercourse. D may have believed, but believed mistakenly, that V had so consented.[46] In such a case, the subjective approach of the criminal law will cause D to be acquitted because his honest mistaken belief rendered absent the knowledge requirement of the offence. Acquittal will lie even if there were no reasonable grounds for such a mistaken belief.[47] This position stems from the principle of individual autonomy, which requires criminal responsibility to be based on what defendants believed they were doing, not on the basis of actual facts that were unknown to them at the time. It should be mentioned that a contrary view exists that sees the need for an element of reasonableness to be added to the mistaken belief. This view takes an objective approach to criminal responsibility. It imposes what is considered to be an easily dischargeable duty on the defendant to ask the victim whether she consents before proceeding to engage in sexual intercourse with her. The criminal codes of Queensland, Western Australia and Tasmania support this approach by insisting on the defendant's mistake of fact to be both honest and reasonable.[48]

## Contemporaneity

Thus far, we have covered both conduct elements and mental elements of a crime. But proof of these elements alone is insufficient to establish criminal responsibility. There is a further requirement that the conduct element must coincide with the mental element of the crime. This has been described as the principle of contemporaneity.[49] It asserts that criminal responsibility should be confined in point of time to when the proscribed conduct was performed together with the requisite mental state. Hence, a person who took a bag believing it to be hers would not be guilty of theft, even though she may have decided to keep the bag for herself upon subsequently discovering the mistake.

Occasionally, the criminal law places a premium on the accused's mental state and downplays the principle of contemporaneity. Take the case of D who strikes V's head with the intention of killing him and then, thinking V to be dead, throws his body into a river. V dies by drowning. D will be found guilty of murder in these circumstances even though, strictly speaking, the prescribed conduct of killing did not coincide in point of time with the requisite mental state for murder.[50]

## Objective principles

The community welfare principle sees individual autonomy as giving way to the greater good of society. In line with this principle, objective criteria such as the seriousness of consequences and the deterrent effect of conviction and punishment should be afforded greater weight than the culpable mental state of individual actors. Some manifestations of this kind of objective approach to criminal responsibility will now be presented.

### Constructive liability

There are instances in the criminal law where people are convicted of serious crimes when they lacked the mental state normally required for those crimes. An example is the 'constructive-murder' rule found in New South Wales.[51] Under this rule, a person may be guilty of murder if, while in the course of committing an offence punishable by imprisonment for 25 years (such as armed robbery with wounding), he accidentally killed someone. The constructive-murder rule may be justified on the ground of social defence. Society needs to deter people from engaging in dangerous behaviour that might cause death. To achieve this, the law takes the mental element of a comparatively minor offence, couples it with the harm caused (which is death), and in this way constructs liability for a more serious offence.

A different example of constructive liability is the doctrine of prior fault. Basically, this doctrine denies a person a defence should the circumstances requiring the need for the defence have arisen out of her or his own fault.[52] For instance, the defences of provocation and self-defence are denied to people who had purposely, through taunts, sought to induce the victim to attack them. In all these cases, the previous acts of the accused are relied upon to prevent them from successfully invoking the defences. The law thereby constructs criminal responsibility by withdrawing the defences on account of the accused's fault occurring, not at the time of the proscribed event, but at an earlier time. Once again, the justification for this form of constructive liability is social defence—society needs to be protected from people who engage in potentially harmful behaviour. It may also be supported on grounds of social responsibility—members of society have an obligation to avoid behaviour that has the risk of causing harm to others.

## Negligence

There are some crimes that base liability on negligence—for example negligent manslaughter and careless driving. The concept of negligence incorporates an objective approach by assessing an individual's behaviour according to what a reasonable person in the same situation ought to have known or done. The personal or subjective awareness of the individual is therefore irrelevant. This approach runs counter to the principle of individual autonomy since it convicts and punishes individuals who, being unaware of the consequences of their actions or the risks involved, lacked the choice necessary for blame.

However, crimes based on negligence can be supported by the competing community welfare principle. This principle argues that the shared obligations that come with belonging to a community require individuals to exercise care in their actions. The more serious the harm that those actions can cause to other members, the greater the care that individuals will be expected to take to avoid them. With regard to the lack of choice, the reply would be that individuals who negligently caused harm have the capacity to behave otherwise. This is because there were sufficient signals to alert a reasonable person to take care. As for the purpose that is served by punishing negligent behaviour, it exerts a general deterrent effect by warning people of the need to take care in certain situations.

The proposed Model Criminal Code defines criminal negligence as:

A person is negligent with respect to a physical element when his or her conduct involves such a great falling short of the standard of care which a reasonable person would have exercised in the circumstances and such a risk that the element exists or will exist that the conduct merits criminal punishment for the offence in issue.[53]

## Strict and absolute liability

Strict liability offences are those offences for which a person may be convicted without proof of intention, recklessness or knowledge. For example, a statute may enable D to be convicted on evidence that he sold adulterated meat without needing to prove further that he knew of the adulteration. However, defendants may escape criminal responsibility by raising the defence of honest and reasonable mistake of fact, which is essentially a claim that they were not negligent when performing the proscribed conduct. Using the above example, D could claim that he honestly and reasonably believed that the meat sold was fit for human consumption because it had been supplied only a few hours earlier by the local abattoir. In contrast, absolute liability offences are more draconian in that they do not permit a claim of honest and reasonable mistake of fact.

The justification for offences of strict and absolute liability appear to be based on economics and expediency. There are numerous trivial social mischiefs that hamper the smooth daily running of society. The threat of criminal sanction is a ready tool to deter them. Whether this is a proper function of the criminal law has already been raised earlier. The point about the triviality of the social mischiefs is significant for two reasons. One is the economic argument that these minor offences are not worth the public expense of requiring the prosecution to prove a subjective mental state. The other reason concerns individual fairness—while fairness may arguably be overridden by economic considerations in cases of minor offences, it cannot be so overridden where the offence is grave.[54]

The severe position created by absolute liability offences and their denial of claims of honest and reasonable mistake of fact is supported by an argument based on social defence. It is that the fundamental values and interests sought to be protected by the criminal law should not be abandoned when their infringements were due to a mistake or accident, however reasonable, on the defendant's part.[55] The criticism that immediately springs to mind is that absolute liability offences are (or should be) confined to trivial harms. The criminal law should not be used to control such minor social mischiefs. Other preventative measures such as education and civil regulation should be relied upon to reduce the minor harms that are currently the subject of absolute liability offences. Of course, this same criticism can be directed against strict liability offences. But at least individual fairness is afforded to people charged with these offences in the form of a claim of honest and reasonable mistake of fact.

# Criminal defences

Accused people may rely on defences to criminal charges against them.[56] Some defences, such as mistake of fact,[57] accident and, to some extent, insanity and intoxication, have the effect of negating the mental element of the crime. Other defences, such as automatism and, again to some extent, insanity and intoxication, negate a conduct element of the crime. Still others, such as duress, necessity and self-defence, serve as excuses or justifications for the criminal behaviour. For this last group of defences, both the conduct and mental elements have been established. However, in respect of excusatory defences, the accused is deemed to be blameless because there were certain extenuating circumstances operating at the time of the offence. With regard to justificatory defences, there were circumstances that made the conduct rightful.

Only some of these defences will be presented here. As with the preceding parts of this chapter, the primary focus of the discussion will be on the tension between the principles of individual autonomy and community welfare.

## Insanity

The insanity defence proceeds in two stages.[58] First, the accused must have been deprived of reasoning power due to a disease of the mind when the offence occurred. Then it must be established that such deprivation of reasoning power caused the accused not to realise what he or she was doing, or at least not realise that it was wrong. The result of successfully pleading this defence is a special verdict of not guilty by reason of insanity. Under this verdict, the accused is not convicted of the crime charged, but is committed indefinitely to an institution for psychiatric treatment.

The principle of individual autonomy explains the defence in several ways. A person who, by virtue of disease of the mind, did not realise what he or she was doing, may be regarded as having acted involuntarily. For example, a person may be so psychotic that her or his conduct could properly be described as that of an automaton (or robot), devoid of the will to act required for voluntary conduct. The lack of realisation of what he or she was doing would also normally result in rendering absent subjective mental states such as intention, recklessness or knowledge. Even if the conduct had been voluntary and the relevant mental state was present, the disease of the mind might operate to render the accused blameless (or excused) for the harm caused. This is because the disease of the mind could have caused her or him to fail to appreciate that the conduct was morally wrong (usually meaning that the accused believed, by some distorted reasoning process, that the conduct was justifiable).

Given the absence of either the conduct or mental element for the crime, the principle of individual autonomy insists on the complete acquittal of the accused. The competing community welfare principle requires that the special verdict be given on grounds of social defence. The reasoning is that, since the accused's involuntary conduct or peculiar mental state arose from insanity, he or she will continue to pose a danger to society. Indefinite medical intervention is therefore warranted. However, of late, the assumption that all criminally insane people are so dangerous as to require indefinite detention has been challenged. There are no clear answers to questions such as what constitutes evidence of future dangerousness, and how accurate are predictions of dangerousness. Accordingly, it would be fairer on criminally insane people for the courts to be given a range of disposition options and to abolish the indeterminate commitment. This proposal has the support of various law reform bodies including the committee responsible for drafting a national model criminal code.[59]

## Intoxication

The defence of intoxication operates to negate the mental state required for an offence. An individual may have been so intoxicated as to lack free and rational choice in her or his actions. Consequently, such a person should be acquitted, following the principle of individual autonomy with its insistence on sufficient choice or control over one's actions before criminal responsibility could lie.

On the other hand, the community welfare principle sees individuals as having certain social duties as part of their membership of a community. One duty is to keep one's behaviour under control at all times. Proponents of this principle criticise the defence of intoxication for promoting the idea of 'more alcohol, less culpability'. They would prefer to confine the defence to offences where an intention to cause a specific result is an element. Under this approach, the defence is unavailable to crimes such as physical assault, rape and manslaughter, which do not require such specific intention. This is the approach taken in New South Wales, Queensland, Western Australia and Tasmania.[60] However, the wider version of the defence, with its emphasis on individual autonomy, has been recognised in other jurisdictions such as South Australia and Victoria.[61] These jurisdictions have not experienced any untoward social effects caused by recognising such a defence. The explanation for this might be the rarity of the defence succeeding in practice. The draft model criminal code for Australia has also recommended the adoption of the defence:

> If a fault element [such as intention, recklessness and knowledge] other than negligence is an element of an offence, evidence of intoxication may be taken into consideration in order to determine whether that fault element existed.[62]

## Duress and necessity

These two defences involve situations where a person claims to have been compelled by a threat to commit the offence charged.[63] In respect of duress the source of the threat is a human agent, while for necessity it may be a human agent or a natural event such as a fire, flood, earthquake or a storm. The defences of duress and necessity do not negate the mental element of the crime since the defendants would have clearly known the nature and consequences of their conduct. Neither could these defences be said to have rendered the proscribed conduct involuntary. Defendants pleading duress or necessity would typically have been conscious and exercised control over their bodily movements. The underlying rationale for acquittal is that the threats, which lie at the core of these defences, have considerably reduced the individual's capacity to exercise free and rational choice of action. Since their freedom of choice had been severely undermined by threats that were not of their own making, it would be unfair to impose criminal responsibility upon them. From this brief discussion it may be seen how the defences of duress and necessity are premised on the principle of individual autonomy.

As against this approach are the arguments based on the community welfare principle. These focus on the protection of the innocent victims injured by the offences claimed to have been committed under duress or necessity. The result is that certain objective considerations have found their way into these defences.[64] One consideration is the reasonableness of the accused's belief that the threat existed and would occur. Hence, an objective evaluation is added to ensure that the perception of the threat was not fanciful. Another is the consideration that a person of ordinary firmness could likewise have succumbed to the threat and done what the accused did. By this consideration, the notion of individual freedom of choice is compromised since the enquiry shifts away from the impact of the threat on the particular accused to its effect on a reasonably steadfast person. Third, the threats recognised for the purposes of the defences are confined to those of death or serious bodily harm so as to restrict the defences to cases of extreme pressure. A fourth consideration is based on the doctrine of prior fault. The defences are denied to people who had created the circumstances giving rise to the threats. For example, the defence of duress is unavailable to a person who was threatened by members of a criminal organisation into committing a crime if he or she had voluntarily joined the organisation in the first place. Similarly, people cannot successfully plead necessity to justify or excuse harm-causing conduct if they had produced the situation of emergency (such as a fire). The criminal law has sought to strike a balance between the principles of individual autonomy and community welfare by reflecting certain aspects of both principles in the elements required for the defences of duress and necessity.

## Self-defence

Through this defence, the criminal law empowers individuals to exercise force against their aggressor for the purpose of protecting themselves or others.[65] The defence is premised on the principle of individual autonomy. Individuals should have a basic right to repel an unlawful attack in situations where society cannot provide the protection. Unlike the other defences previously discussed, which are excusatory in nature,[66] self-defence is a justification. Society regards an accused's act of self-defence as rightful conduct.

Another view of self-defence sees the need to consider the rights of the aggressor. After all, an act of self-defence causes bodily harm and consequently also impinges on the bodily integrity of another. It might be argued that people who initiate unlawful attacks forfeit all their rights to protection of the law.[67] But surely, this goes too far as it places no value whatsoever on the right of aggressors to life and physical safety. This goes against a society that regards life as 'the most basic value and places physical violence high on the range of harms. While society should accord the right of self-defence in cases of sudden attacks, there should be restrictions placed on the application of such a right. These restrictions are needed to prevent the defence from becoming a disguise for revenge or retaliation.

The criminal law does, indeed, impose certain restrictions on self-defensive action in order to accord some recognition of the rights of aggressors.[68] One is that the defendant must have honestly as well as reasonably believed in the existence and nature of the perceived attack.[69] Thus, the defence would be denied to a person whose belief as to the threatened danger was honest but fanciful or unreasonable. Another restriction is that the defensive response must have been reasonable. This requirement of reasonableness is usually seen in terms of the defensive action being reasonably proportionate to the threatened danger posed by the attack. Hence, a defendant should be permitted to use fatal force only in cases of life-threatening attacks or against certain extremely serious offences.[70] A third restriction is that the defensive response must have been necessary. Necessity is measured by several factors, including the imminence of the attack, the availability of alternative means of avoiding the harm posed by the attack, and the value or interest to be protected by the defensive action.

Where a justification (such as self-defence and certain forms of necessity) is involved, the claim is that the harm-causing conduct of the accused was rightful. Accordingly, it is without question that justificatory pleas are integrally connected with the issue of criminal responsibility—that is, whether to convict or acquit a defendant. Where excuses such as insanity, intoxication, duress and some types of necessity are involved, a difficulty arises whether these pleas should be relevant to criminal responsibility rather than to sentencing. It would be possible to regard these excuses only as mitigating factors in the sentencing exercise following a conviction. But, as Andrew Ashworth has succinctly argued:

The objection to this is that a criminal conviction is rightly regarded as condemnatory, an indication of fair labelling which, in turn, should rule out liability altogether in cases where [an accused person's] absence of fault is so high on the 'scale of excuse' that there should be no formal blame.[71]

It is certainly true that the task is a difficult one of delineating between when excuses do and do not reach such a high level as to warrant a complete acquittal. But the task is important to ensure a just and proper apportionment of blame and cannot be abandoned simply on the ground that it involves difficult judgments of degree.

# Extensions of criminal responsibility

Most crimes concern people who have caused one or more of several varieties of harm. But there may be people who, while not causing the proscribed harm, may nevertheless be held criminally responsible. We shall consider two ways in which the criminal law has extended its scope of criminal responsibility. The first is by developing the doctrine of criminal complicity and the second is by recognising 'inchoate' offences.

The doctrine of complicity is designed to convict and punish people who have not actually committed a particular offence but have played a significant role in promoting its commission by others. Hence, criminal responsibility can be imposed on a person who 'aided, abetted, counseled or procured' the commission of a crime by another. Inchoate offences are the preliminary crimes of attempt, conspiracy and incitement. The word 'inchoate' means 'undeveloped' and aptly describes the kinds of offences under consideration—an attempt indicates failure to complete a substantive offence, the objective of a conspiracy may not be achieved, and words of incitement may be ignored. While no harm may have occurred in these situations, the criminal law nevertheless finds it necessary, for various policy reasons, to impose criminal responsibility.

## Complicity

The doctrine of complicity regards people who assist or encourage others to commit a crime as deserving of criminal condemnation in certain circumstances. People who so assist or encourage are called accomplices and those who commit the crime promoted by them are described as principal offenders. Take the case of A who engages a professional assassin to kill her or his enemy, or of B who stands watch while another commits the offence of housebreaking. A and B, in urging or providing support, may arguably be no less culpable than the principal offender.

The conduct element of complicity may be satisfied merely on evidence of some encouragement or assistance. In respect of the mental element, a conflict arises between the principles of individual autonomy and community welfare. The first principle would confine the mental element of complicity to intention in the limited sense of a conscious purpose to promote or facilitate the commission of the principal offence. Criminal liability should be so narrowly construed since, otherwise, the criminal law would spread its net too widely to punish people who, unknown to them, had performed acts that encouraged or assisted the commission of the principal offence. The principle of individual autonomy also advocates a policy of minimal criminalisation. In the context of the law of complicity, such a policy would insist on the most culpable form of mental state (namely, purposeful intention) to be proven given that what is involved is an extension of criminal responsibility beyond its traditional limits. On the other hand, the community welfare principle would extend the net to cover people who may have been reckless as to whether their actions might promote the commission of a crime. This is done on the basis of social responsibility, which regards people as having a social obligation to desist from engaging in conduct that they know has a risk of causing harm. Which principle should prevail is problematic. The current common law has endorsed confining the mental element for complicity to intention[72] and so has the draft Model Criminal Code.[73] However, the High Court has endorsed the principle that, where A agrees with B to participate in a criminal enterprise, he or she should be liable for any offence committed by B so long as A foresaw that B might commit it (even if A did not want it to happen).[74]

## Attempt

The criminal sanction may, in certain cases, be justly imposed on people who tried to commit a crime but were unsuccessful. Take the case of A who snatches at a handbag but it is just out of reach; or B who throws a punch at a person but misses; or C who discharges industrial waste into a blocked pipe leading out to a river. A, B and C all possessed the culpable mental state required respectively for theft, assault and pollution of clean waters. On this basis, the criminal sanction is deserved. It might also be justified on account of the deterrent effect that punishing such people will have on others who may wish to commit similar offences.

Since the culpable mental state forms the primary justification for sanctioning criminal attempts, it would seem that the conduct element is not so important. On this view, any overt act performed by the defendant will be sufficient. The objection to this is that the police may be tempted to arrest and press charges upon the slightest conduct suggesting an intention to commit a crime. This would be too great an infringement of individual liberties and would come dangerously close to creating a society controlled by thought crimes and thought police. To safeguard individual liberties, the law should require conduct that unambiguously indicates the defendant's intention to commit the offence. The extreme manifestation of this latter view is to require proof that the accused performed the last act they were capable of doing in order to carry out the offence. But this may be objected to, on grounds of social defence, for not leaving sufficient time for police intervention, and for enabling the accused to gain an acquittal by casting doubt on what comprised the very last act. We are of the view that concerns over individual liberties and social defence are best served by taking a pragmatic approach to what constitutes the conduct element of criminal attempts. This is achieved by requiring conduct to be performed that was 'more than merely preparatory to the commission of the offence attempted'.[75] This is the proposal of the committee charged with drafting a national model criminal code. While the committee concedes that the distinction between preparation and perpetration may be difficult in some instances, this could safely be left to the jury to decide.[76]

The mental element for criminal attempts requires purposiveness (or intention)—recklessness will not suffice.[77] Further support for this narrowing of the mental element is found in reminding ourselves that, in criminalising attempts, the criminal law is stretched to its outer limits. Since no harm was actually inflicted, cases deserving of punishment should be restricted to those where the accused possessed the most culpable mental state. This argument was also raised earlier when discussing the mental element for criminal complicity.

Occasionally, the law may encounter cases where an individual had done everything possible (with the requisite intention) to complete the offence, but nevertheless failed due to physical impossibility. Take the case of X, who possessed a harmless vegetable matter, which he believed to be cannabis; or Y, who shot at a theatrical dummy thinking it was her enemy; or Z, who poured pure water into a stream assuming it was a potent poison. After some initial uncertainty, the law is now clear that X, Y and Z deserve to be punished.[78] This stance complies with the principle of individual autonomy as these defendants had believed that they were committing an offence and had freely chosen to do so. Their mental state would consequently be as blameworthy if the facts had actually been as they had believed. The law also thereby supports the community welfare principle by promoting social defence against acquitting people who, by pure chance, were thwarted from achieving their objective of causing harm to others.

## Conspiracy

The crime of conspiracy prohibits, on grounds of social defence, two or more people from agreeing to commit some specific offence. The law justifies imposing criminal responsibility for mere agreements on grounds of social defence. Group behaviour results in individuals finding it difficult to withdraw and in participants spurring one another on. Hence the harm intended by the agreement is more likely to materialise than in the case of a sole individual's thoughts about causing harm. There is also the social defence perception that group criminal activity causes greater fear in victims and more public alarm. Such activity should therefore be eradicated, whenever possible, at the earliest opportunity—this is usually at the stage of agreement.

The conduct element of conspiracy is, of course, the agreement. The agreement may be a simple case of a meeting of minds around a table to more complex 'chain' and 'wheel' conspiracies.[79] There is a view that the criminal law of conspiracy goes too far to accommodate social defence at the expense of individual liberties. The concern is that the offence encourages the police to use intrusive tactics of law enforcement (such as bugging phones and premises), and inhibits the exchange and development of controversial ideas. However, we believe that there is a place for conspiracy in the criminal law. In reply to objectionable police intrusions, the remedy lies in internal police disciplinary measures and control, not the abolition of the crime of conspiracy. As for stifling freedom of speech, the remedy would be to confine the subject-matter of conspiracies to crimes alone as opposed to other kinds of unlawful acts such as a tort, corrupting public morals, and outraging public decency.[80]

With regard to the mental element, the law of conspiracy has confined this to intention alone. This may be supported on the ground that any lesser culpable mental state, such as recklessness, will be foreign to an offence based wholly on agreement. It is also justified on the basis that conspiracy, as with complicity and attempt, is an extension of the criminal law. As has already been noted for these other forms of criminal responsibility, the further away proscribed conduct is from the actual infliction of harm, the more culpable should be the mental state.

# Conclusion

This chapter has been necessarily selective in its coverage of substantive criminal law. The discussions on the aim and functions of the criminal law, the major elements of crime, and extensions of criminal responsibility, have all been cast in a particular framework. This framework reveals how the principle of individual autonomy competes with the community welfare principle in moulding the criminal law. Justice to the individual and to the society in which he or she belongs is best served by a careful and reasoned balancing of these competing principles. As the discussion has shown, the criminal law is governed primarily by the principle of individual autonomy. However, there will be many occasions when the community welfare principle is allowed to override the claims of individual autonomy. When this occurs, justice to the individual may still be served so long as lawmakers are keenly aware of their choice of principle. They should, in addition, make every effort to have in place safeguards to ensure that the scope of criminal responsibility is not so widened as to create conditions more in keeping with a police state.

# Notes

1    Much of this chapter is derived from Andrew Ashworth, *Principles of Criminal Law*, 4th edn, Oxford University Press, Oxford, 2003.

2    Article 29. The Declaration was adopted by the United Nations General Assembly in 1948.

3    See P. Devlin, *The Enforcement of Morals*, Oxford University Press, London, 1965.

4    Its proponents include Professor Hart, who engaged in a celebrated debate with Lord Devlin over the role of morality in the criminal law. See H. L. A. Hart, *Law, Liberty and Morality*, Oxford University Press, London, 1963.

5    This was the view of Lord Mustill (dissenting) in the House of Lords decision in *R v Brown* [1993] 2 WLR 556 at 599–600, a case involving a group of sado-masochists who willingly and enthusiastically participated in inflicting violence against one another for sexual pleasure.

6    See N. Lacey, *State Punishment: Political Principles and Community Values*, Routledge, London, 1988, chs 2 and 7.

7    Torts are civil wrongs that attract compensation by way of damages. Some common torts are negligence, trespass, nuisance and defamation.

8    The concepts of intention, recklessness, knowledge and negligence are dealt with later in this chapter.

9    For some examples of suggested frameworks, see J. Feinberg, *Harm to Others*, Oxford University Press, New York, 1984; A. Von Hirsch and N. Jareborg, 'Gauging Criminal Harm: a Living Standard Analysis', *Oxford Journal of Legal Studies*, 11, 1991, pp. 1–38.

10   See further below, under the heading 'Objective principles'.

11   See generally, J. Rowan-Robinson and P. Watchman, *Crime and Regulation*, Butterworths Tolley, Edinburgh, 1990.

12   See M. Goode, 'Codification of the Australian Criminal Law', *Criminal Law Journal*, 16, 1992, p. 5.

13   This occurred in 1991 with the establishment of the Model Criminal Code Officers Committee. For the background to this Australian initiative, see G. Scott, 'A Model Criminal Code', *Criminal Law Journal*, 16, 1992, p. 350.

14   Over the years, the Model Criminal Code Officers Committee has produced several chapters of the Code, commencing with *General Principles of Criminal Responsibility* in 1992.

15   See M. Goode, 'Codification of the Criminal Law', *Criminal Law Journal*, 26, 2004, p. 226.

16   Fortunately, the modern tendency of the courts is to express the need for a new offence and leave its creation to Parliament.

17   Article 11(2).

18   For example, see the proliferation of sexual assault legislation in New South Wales, South Australia and Victoria in recent years. Many of the new offences were enacted within a few months of public debate.

19   Offence seriousness is normally measured by the type of penalty prescribed for the offence. See chapter 7.

20   This is exemplified in chapter 10 when discussing the relationship between the police and Aboriginal people.

21   See further chapter 10, p. 369.

22    Paternalism is here used in a wider sense than as used earlier where capacity and state protection are linked. The offences currently discussed are described as victimless crimes.

23    For a good discussion of the various categories of duties under common law, see *Taktak* (1988) 34 A Crim R 334. The codes expressly impose duties to act: see, for example, ss. 285–90 of the Queensland code; ss. 262–7 of the Western Australian code; and ss. 144–52 of the Tasmanian code.

24    Thus under French criminal law, there is a 'duty of easy rescue': see A. Ashworth and E. Steiner, 'Criminal Omissions and Public Duties: The French Experience', *Legal Studies*, 10, 1990, p. 153.

25    See S. Yeo, *Compulsion in the Criminal Law*, Law Book Co., North Ryde, 1990, ch. 1.

26    A. Norrie, *Crime, Reason and History: A Critical Introduction to Criminal Law*, 2nd edn, Butterworths, London, 2001, p. 13.

27    P. Robinson and J. Darley, *Justice, Liability and Blame*, Westview Press, Boulder, CO, 1995.

28    It has conventionally been described by the Latin term '*actus reus*'.

29    The Latin term *mens rea*, meaning 'guilty mind', is often used to describe these subjective mental states.

30    Section 202.2.1 of the Model Criminal Code prepared by the Criminal Law Officers Committee of the Standing Committee of Attorneys-General (1992). Hereinafter called the 'draft Model Criminal Code'.

31    See *Ryan* (1967) 121 CLR 205; *Falconer* (1990) 171 CLR 30.

32    Ashworth, 2003, p. 99.

33    For a detailed discussion, see M. Moore, *Act and Crime: The Theory of Action and its Implications for Criminal Law*, Oxford, 1993.

34    For primary Australian cases on causation, see *Hallett* [1969] SASR 141; *Moffa* (2000) 112 A Crim R 201; *Royall* (1991) 171 CLR 378; *Arulthilakan* (2004) 178 ALJR 257.

35    *Royall* (1991) 171 CLR 378.

36    See E. Colvin, 'Causation in Criminal Law', *Bond Law Review*, 1, 1989, p. 253; K. Arenson, 'Causation in the Criminal Law: A Search for Doctrinal Consistency', *Criminal Law Journal*, 20, 1996, p. 189.

37    See H. L. A. Hart, *Punishment and Responsibility. Essays in the Philosophy of Law*, Oxford, 1968, chs 2 and 5.

38    The community welfare principle is therefore associated with utilitarian theories that promote general deterrence: see K. Greenawalt, 'Punishment' in S. Kadish (ed.), *Encyclopaedia of Crime and Justice*, Vol. 4, Free Press, New York, 1987, p. 1336.

39    See, for example, ss. 23 and 24 of the Queensland and Western Australian codes, and ss. 13 and 14 of the Tasmanian code. For a further discussion, see R. Kenny, *An Introduction to the Criminal Law of Queensland and Western Australia*, 6th edn, Butterworths, Sydney, 2004, paras 8.13–8.17.

40    Model Criminal Code Officers Committee, *General Principles of Criminal Responsibility*, Commonwealth Attorney-General's Department, Canberra, 1992, p. 25.

41    *Woollin* [1998] J 4 All ER 103. Also refer to B. Fisse, *Howard's Criminal Law*, 5th edn, Law Book Co., Sydney, 1990, pp. 479–81.

42    Section 203.1, draft Model Criminal Code.

43    Fisse, 1990, pp. 62–3.

44    Section 203.3, draft Model Criminal Code.

45  Section 203.2, draft Model Criminal Code.

46  D would not have been reckless since, as far as he was concerned, he knew for certain that V consented. D would be reckless only if he was unsure whether V consented and proceeded nevertheless to have sexual intercourse with her.

47  *McEwan* [1979] 2 NSWLR 926.

48  Queensland and Western Australian codes, s. 24; Tasmanian code, s. 14.

49  See Ashworth, 2003, pp. 161–3; Fisse, 1990, pp. 133–4.

50  *Meyers* (1997) 71 ALJR 1488; *McConnell* [1977] 1 NSWLR 714; *Thabo Meli* [1957] 1 WLR 234.

51  See s. 18 of the *Crimes Act* 1900 (NSW). See also s. 3A of the *Crimes Act* 1958 (Vic).

52  Yeo, 1990, ch. 5.

53  Section 203.4 of the draft Model Criminal Code. This definition is based closely on the one under common law: see *Nydam* [1977] VR 430; *Wilson* (1992) 174 CLR 313.

54  See *He Kaw Teh* (1985) 157 CLR 523.

55  Ashworth, 2003, pp. 165–6.

56  For a full discussion of the available defences, see P. Fairall and S. Yeo, *Criminal Defences in Australia*, 4th edn, Butterworths, Sydney, 2005.

57  This is distinguishable from the defence of honest and reasonable mistake of fact noted in our discussion of strict and absolute liability offences. Here, D need only plead that her or his belief was honest and it would not matter (other than going to the question of honesty) that the belief was unreasonable. For example, D could be acquitted of rape if he honestly believed V to have consented to sexual intercourse.

58  What follows is essentially the *McNaghten* formulation of the defence at common law. For a leading Australian case, see *Porter* (1933) 55 CLR 182. There are some variations under the criminal codes: see, for example, s. 27 of the Queensland and Western Australian codes.

59  Model Criminal Code Officers Committee, 1992, p. 35.

60  See s. 428A–G of the *Crimes Act* 1900 (NSW); s. 28 of the Queensland and Western Australian codes, and s. 17 of the Tasmanian code. See also *Kusu* [1981] Qd R 136; *Cameron* [1992] WAR 1.

61  The leading case is *O'Connor* (1980) 146 CLR 64.

62  Section 303. Where crimes based on negligence are concerned, s. 304 of the draft code specifies that, in determining whether negligence existed, regard must be had to the standard of a reasonable sober person.

63  The defences are recognised by the common law and the criminal codes, although there are certain differences: see R. O'Regan, *Essays on the Australian Criminal Code*, Law Book Co., Sydney, 1979, ch. 7; S. Yeo, 'Necessity under the Griffith Code and the Common Law', *Criminal Law Journal*, 15, 1991, p. 17.

64  At common law, see the leading cases of *Abusafiah* (1991) 24 NSWLR 531 (for duress) and *Rogers* (1996) 86 A Crim R 542 (for necessity). Under the codes, see, for example, s. 31 (for duress) and s. 25 (for necessity) of the Queensland and Western Australian codes.

65  The leading case on self-defence at common law is *Zecevic v DPP* (1987) 162 CLR 645. The codes contain specific provisions covering the defence: see, for example, ss. 271 and 272 of the Queensland code, and ss. 248 and 249 of the Western Australian code.

66  Except certain cases of necessity where the harm caused by the defendant was less than the harm avoided.

67    Such a notion of forfeiture of rights might be supported on the ground that it serves to deter potential attackers and thereby promotes peace: see S. Kadish, *Blame and Punishment: Essays in the Criminal Law*, Macmillan, New York, 1987, p. 117. However, this assertion requires empirical support.

68    For a further discussion of these objective requirements under common law, see S. Yeo, 'Self-defence: From *Viro* to *Zecevic*', *Australian Bar Review*, 4, 1988, pp. 251–67. For the codes, see Kenny, 2004, paras 13.80–13.86.

69    *Zecevic v DPP (Vic)* (1987) 162 CLR 645. Some judges have suggested that an honest belief will suffice: see, for example, *Kurtic* (1996) 85 A Crim R 57. This is the position in New South Wales and South Australia by virtue of the *Crimes Act* 1900 (NSW), s. 418; and the *Criminal Law Consolidation Act* 1936 (SA), ss. 15 and 15A.

70    In New South Wales and South Australia, legislation provides for a defender whose use of fatal force was unreasonable to be convicted of manslaughter instead of murder.

71    Ashworth, 1995, p. 242.

72    See *Giorgianni* (1985) 156 CLR 473.

73    Section 402.1.

74    *McAuliffe* (1995) 183 CLR 108.

75    Section 401.1, draft Model Criminal Code.

76    Model Criminal Code Officers Committee, 1992, p. 75.

77    This is the position under the code jurisdictions and also under the common law: see *Knight* (1992) 63 A Crim R 166. The committee on a national criminal code was of the same view: see s. 401.1 of its draft Model Criminal Code.

78    See, for example, *Britten v Alpogut* [1987] VR 929; *Tran* (1993) 61 A Crim R 140. The uncertainty lay with the common law. The code jurisdictions have always disregarded physical impossibility: see, for example, s. 4 of the Queensland and Western Australian codes.

79    See P. Gillies, *The Law of Criminal Conspiracy*, 2nd edn, Law Book Co., Annandale, 1990, pp. 16–18.

80    These other unlawful acts are recognisable conspirational objects in certain Australian jurisdictions: see Fisse, 1990, pp. 356–63; Kenny, 2004, para. 11.30.

# 2

# Investigation

## Introduction

In the vast majority of cases, what happens before trial determines the ultimate outcome. Part of that process involves the procedural steps from charge to hearing, whether it be a contested trial or a sentence hearing. But perhaps most important is the investigation preceding the charge. The police bear the principal responsibility for the process of criminal law enforcement in its early stages. A major aspect of this responsibility is the investigation of criminal activity, the apprehension of people suspected of breaking the criminal law, and the facilitation of their subsequent prosecution in the courts. As we shall see in chapter 3, new bodies have been created to supplement the role of the police, usually with greater investigative powers than those accorded to the police. Nevertheless, the great bulk of criminal investigation remains in the hands of the police—the central focus of this chapter.

However, we will not examine policing in general. The sociological profile of the police force, the practicalities of police investigation, the structural, organisational and cultural determinants of general policing practices, or the impact of those practices on different sections of society are not our central concern.[1] Our focus is much narrower. This chapter is concerned with the powers of the police to investigate crime and with the rights of people suspected of committing crime. It will focus on major modes of criminal investigation where the law has attempted to regulate both police power and safeguards for the citizen—search and seizure, arrest and detention, interrogation, identification, and the use of informants.

Inevitably, in examining these matters, we shall touch on wider aspects of policing. The legal framework of criminal investigation is only one part of the overall reality of policing in Australia. Indeed, it must always be remembered that what the police actually do does not necessarily reflect what the law says they may do. Nevertheless, legal regulation provides a framework upon which a range of administrative and customary controls should function. It is an indispensable starting point for any discussion of criminal investigation.[2]

In analysing the present legal position with respect to police powers of investigation and the rights of suspects, it is necessary to begin with a consideration of principle. Fundamental issues are at stake, involving basic liberties of the citizen. Powers of arrest and detention, for example, directly impinge on personal liberty. The significance of this cannot be understated. Two members of the High Court of Australia have observed that a power 'to imprison arbitrarily' would 'soon be an end of all other rights and immunities'.[3] Powers of search and seizure qualify legitimate expectations of personal privacy and civil liberties. Occasionally, as we shall see, they also endanger life. Some methods of investigation, notably interrogation, may involve elements of unconscionable pressure or even abuse of people suspected of criminal offences. Other methods of investigation, such as certain modes of eyewitness identification, may create an undue risk of wrongful conviction.

Certainly there is a manifest public interest in effective law enforcement. This, in turn, requires powers of investigation, which will inevitably impinge on individual rights and liberties. But it must always be remembered that the police are investigating only *suspected* offenders. One of the fundamental principles upon which our system of criminal justice is based is the presumption of innocence—people suspected or accused of a criminal offence are presumed innocent until convicted in a fair trial according to law. Executive interference with any citizen's liberties must be justified.

## Balancing public interests

It is helpful to see criminal investigation as an exercise in balancing. On one side of the balance is the degree to which the exercise of a particular power is likely to advance the public interest in law enforcement. This will vary according to such factors as:

- the need for the power (which, in turn, relates to matters such as the incidence and seriousness of the crimes to which the power might be directed and the availability of other powers that serve the same purpose)
- the resources required to exercise the power (given that those resources might be utilised in some other area of law enforcement)
- the reliability of any evidence likely to be obtained by exercise of the power.

On the other side of the balance is the degree to which the exercise of the power is likely to interfere with the public interest in protecting the liberty and legitimate interests of citizens. In making this judgment, it is necessary to consider any safeguards that might ameliorate the impact of the exercise of power. As the

United States Supreme Court has said, 'the history of liberty has largely been the history of observance of procedural safeguards'.[4]

To take one example, interrogation of suspects in police custody involves substantial interference with their liberty. Also, it may, in some circumstances, involve physical or psychological abuse and produce unreliable evidence of guilt. With the full resources of the state behind them, the police are usually in a position of enormous physical, psychological, emotional and legal superiority over the suspect. While they should, in our view, have power to engage in limited questioning of a suspect in custody, the law has created certain safeguards in an attempt to alleviate the imbalance and thereby reduce the risk of abuse or unreliable evidence. Whether they achieve this goal is a matter for debate. One of these safeguards is the recognition of certain 'rights' possessed by the suspect, such as a 'right to a lawyer' and a 'right to silence'. One issue we address is the extent to which these rights comply with those mandated by the *International Covenant on Civil and Political Rights* (ICCPR).[5] Another is whether 'rights' have any meaning other than symbolic if they are simply options that in most cases, for a variety of reasons, are not taken up.

In summary, it is necessary to address the needs of the police for adequate power to conduct criminal investigations while offering proper and practical safeguards for suspects. This balancing task is not assisted by simplistic assertions from protagonists of increased police powers that crime rates will be reduced or that suspects' rights must be sacrificed in a 'war on crime'. Equally, it is not advanced by the assertion that some rights should not be infringed at all. For example, opposition to an extension of police power on the basis that it will intrude on the right against self-incrimination ignores the fact that the community has already accepted compelled self-incrimination in areas such as breathalyser testing and permissible medical examination.

Nor is the task assisted by seeing criminal investigation in terms of an adversarial model adopted at trial. Despite the fact that the criminal trial is only a small part of the criminal justice system, one method of analysing criminal investigation is to draw an analogy with the procedure of a criminal trial. As we shall discuss in subsequent chapters, pre-trial and trial procedure in this country are adversarial. The 'dispute' between the state and the accused person is resolved by an independent third party, according to certain rules giving each side an adequate opportunity to present its side of the case and roughly equalising their positions. In fact, the procedure is more accurately described as accusatorial since a number of procedural advantages are given to the accused in order to minimise the risk of conviction of an innocent person. These procedural advantages are designed to assist the defence and, inevitably, make the task of the prosecution in proving guilt more difficult. However, criminal investigation should not be seen as an adversarial contest in the sense that an attempt is made to equalise the positions of the police and the suspect. Even less should it be seen as a system balanced in favour of the suspect. Rather, it works from the premise that once a person is reasonably suspected of the commission of a crime, the police should be empowered to interfere to some extent with the suspect's normal rights and liberties in order to conduct a proper investigation.

## Other issues

Over and above the balancing exercise, other issues must be considered. The 1981 *Report of the Royal Commission on Criminal Procedure in Great Britain* argued that a prerequisite of effective policing is cooperation between the public and the police. This required public confidence in the integrity of the police. In its report, the Royal Commission sought to create a legal structure that would enable the police to carry out effective criminal investigation and at the same time be sufficiently open to public scrutiny and accountability to gain public confidence.[6] It used three criteria to assess the validity of this structure—whether it was fair, open and workable.

One theme that clearly emerges from a discussion on criminal investigation is the need for clear and comprehensive statutory formulation of the law in this area. At least until recent times, most of the existing Australian law relating to criminal investigation has comprised an amalgam of common law decisions, scattered statutory provisions,[7] administrative directions of varying authority issued by Police Commissioners and, perhaps most important, de facto police practice. It is inexcusable that an area of law of such critical importance to personal liberty has been left in such a state for so long. In this chapter, we will discuss recent Australian legislation enacted in an attempt to remedy this problem.

Finally, it is a striking fact in this area, as in many areas of criminal justice, that relevant empirical data is generally unavailable.[8] There is, for example, very little publicly available information about arrest and detention. This means that an understanding of the reality of criminal investigation is hampered. It also affects the quality of any debate on police powers and practices. Proper record-keeping must become the norm if we are to understand what really happens in criminal investigation. This would foster rational debate and much-needed reform.

## Search and seizure

Under the common law (law developed by the courts) the police do not have any general power to stop people and search them for evidence relevant to the commission of a crime, or to enter and search a person's premises.[9] However, they may search private premises without the consent of the occupier if a number of strict conditions are satisfied.[10] Further, they may enter any premises to arrest a person reasonably believed to be present.[11] Reasonable force may be used but, except in very limited circumstances, there must be a proper announcement before entry so that the occupier has an opportunity to permit entry.[12] If the police have arrested a person, they may, within fairly vague and undefined limits,[13] search the person and his or her premises for items relevant to the crime for which the person was arrested, and items that are potentially harmful or might be used in an escape. If, in the course of this search, they discover goods that reasonably show that person to be implicated in some other crime, these may also be seized.

Apart from the common law, there are in all jurisdictions numerous statutory provisions that confer powers of search and seizure in certain situations. For example, legislation in some jurisdictions permits police to stop, search and detain any person or vehicle reasonably suspected of having or conveying anything unlawfully obtained[14] or used or intended to be used in the commission of certain offences.[15] Legislation in most jurisdictions confers powers to carry out searches of arrested persons, including medical examinations,[16] although sometimes the latter require a court order.[17] Other legislation permits the tapping of telephones, the interception of telegrams and the use of listening devices, but usually only with a warrant obtained in compliance with strict procedural requirements.[18] Some jurisdictions have entirely replaced the common law on search and seizure with a statutory framework, as in the Criminal Code States of Queensland, Western Australia and the Northern Territory.

In Queensland, for example, the Criminal Justice Commission catalogued a vast array of statutory provisions conferring powers to search people, land, premises, vehicles, vessels and aircraft,[19] and in 1997 comprehensive legislation was enacted to deal with police powers in general.[20] This comprehensive Queensland legislation now includes Chapter 8A, dealing with forensic procedures, which permits the police to apply to a magistrate for a 'forensic procedure order' authorising a qualified person to perform an 'intimate or non-intimate forensic procedure' on a named person, if the magistrate is:

> satisfied on the balance of probabilities there are reasonable grounds for believing performing the forensic procedure concerned on the person may provide evidence of the commission of an indictable offence the person is suspected of having committed and carrying out the forensic procedure is justified in the circumstances.[21]

Such forensic procedures extend to physical examination of genitals, internal examination of body cavities and the taking of hair and other samples for analysis. Recognising the conflicting public and private interests operating in this area, section 288 expressly requires a magistrate to engage in an explicit balancing exercise:

(2) In deciding whether performing the forensic procedure on the person is justified in the circumstances, the magistrate must balance the rights and liberties of the person and the public interest.

(3) In balancing those interests the magistrate may have regard to any of the following matters—

(a) the seriousness of the circumstances surrounding the commission of the suspected offence and the gravity of that offence;

(b) the degree of the person's alleged participation in the commission of the suspected offence;

(c) the age and physical and mental health of the person, to the extent they are known to the magistrate or can be reasonably discovered by the magistrate (by asking the person or otherwise);

(d) if the person is a child or a person with impaired capacity—the welfare of the person;

(e) whether there is a less intrusive but reasonably practicable way of obtaining evidence tending to confirm or disprove that the person committed the suspected offence;

(f) if the person has been asked for and refused to give a forensic procedure consent in relation to the suspected offence—the reasons for the refusal to the extent they are known to the magistrate or can be reasonably discovered by the magistrate (by asking the person or otherwise);

(g) if the person is in custody for the suspected offence—

    (i) the period for which the person has already been detained; and

    (ii) the reason for any delay in applying for the forensic procedure order;

(h) any other matter the magistrate considers relevant to balancing those interests.

Other provisions permit senior police officers to authorise the taking of DNA samples by means of a mouth swab or hair sample. Similar, but certainly not identical, legislation now exists in most Australian jurisdictions.[22]

At the Commonwealth level, while the common law continues to operate, search and seizure powers have been regulated by a major 1994 amendment to the *Crimes Act* 1914 (Cth), incorporating Part 1AA into the Act. It includes provisions dealing with powers to conduct searches of arrested persons, searches without warrant in emergency situations and retention of things seized. To illustrate the comprehensiveness of the legislation, methods of search following an arrest that are specifically provided for include 'frisk', 'ordinary', and 'strip' searches. An additional type of search, an internal search, is permitted in certain circumstances by the *Customs Act* 1901 (Cth). Given that such invasive searches are sometimes justifiable (for example, if there are reasonable grounds to believe that a person who has flown into Australia is carrying drugs), it is essential that they are conducted in a manner that protects, as far as possible, the privacy and dignity of the person being searched. Thus, for example, section 3ZI of the Commonwealth *Crimes Act* provides that a 'strip search' must be conducted in a private area by an officer of the same sex without the presence of anyone unnecessary for the purposes of the search. Similar provisions should be generally adopted in other Australian jurisdictions.

Except in those jurisdictions that have abolished the common law, a search may be conducted under a common law search warrant. However, these are limited to searches for stolen goods, and legislation in all jurisdictions has expanded the objects for which a search warrant may be issued. Some permit 'general' warrants; others require more specificity. An example of the former is section 67 of the South Australian *Summary Offences Act* 1953, which permits the Commissioner of Police to issue a 'general search warrant' empowering a police officer, 'at any time of the day or night', to:

> enter into, break open and search any … premises or place where he or she has reasonable cause to suspect that—
>
> (i) an offence has recently been committed, or is about to be committed;
>
> (ii) there are stolen goods; or
>
> (iii) there is anything that may afford evidence as to the commission of an offence; or
>
> (iv) there is anything that may be intended to be used for the purpose of committing an offence.

However, most Australian jurisdictions do not permit search warrants to be issued by a Police Commissioner—they require the authority of at least a quasi-judicial officer such as a magistrate. Further, they have rejected general search warrants, which do not specifically stipulate the premises to be searched, the offence involved or the articles sought, as being an unjustifiable interference with citizens' liberty and privacy. While their use has been justified in terms of the remoteness and isolation problems of law enforcement in many parts of Australia, it is certainly arguable that the possibility of obtaining warrants by telephone negates this problem.

Specific warrants must identify the offence or offences in relation to which they are issued and must, with reasonable particularity and certainty, define the premises to be searched and delimit the thing or class of things for which it is permitted to search. Unlike a general warrant, the need for the power of search and seizure must be capable of justification on every occasion on which it is used. Thus, for example, the New South Wales *Search Warrants Act* 1985 provides that an 'authorised justice'[23] may issue a search warrant to a member of the police force if satisfied that 'the member of the police force has reasonable grounds for believing that there is in or on any premises' a thing that is 'unlawfully obtained' or 'connected with'[24] a wide range of offences. A 'general warrant', allowing the search of unspecified premises or for unspecified things, is not permitted.[25] Except in the case of telephone warrants, the application for a search warrant must be made in writing, setting out the grounds on which it is sought and verified by oath or affidavit. The things to be searched for and the particular offence with which they are connected must be stated in the application for the search warrant and in the warrant itself. On the other hand, in conducting a lawful search of premises under a search warrant, the police officer may seize any property which he or she has reasonable grounds for believing is connected with any offence.[26]

The courts are generally scrupulous in requiring strict observance of the rules governing search warrants,[27] at least when there has been a court challenge to the legality of a warrant. The High Court has stated:

the enactment of conditions which must be fulfilled before a search warrant can be lawfully issued and executed is to be seen as a reflection of the legislature's concerns to give a measure of protection to [property and privacy interests]. To insist on strict compliance with the statutory conditions governing the issue of search warrants is simply to give effect to the purpose of the legislation.[28]

However, as we discuss in chapter 6, evidence obtained by means of a faulty warrant is not necessarily excluded from a trial. Further, it must be said that the courts have only a limited ability to ensure that powers of search and seizure granted to law enforcement authorities are not abused. Examples of such abuse are not uncommon. Perhaps one of the most egregious in recent history involved a police raid on a home in Sydney in 1989.

# A case study

Shortly before 6.00 a.m. on 27 April 1989, David Gundy, a 29-year-old Aboriginal man, was shot by a police shotgun discharged in his bedroom during a raid by SWOS (the Special Weapons and Operations Section of the New South Wales police) on his home in Marrickville, a suburb of Sydney. He died soon after as a result of his wounds. An inquiry into his death was conducted in 1990 by Commissioner J. H. Wootten as part of the Royal Commission into Aboriginal Deaths in Custody.[29]

David Gundy's home had been one of six premises simultaneously raided by SWOS personnel, a quasi-military body designed to carry out dangerous operations using highly specialised techniques. They were searching for a man named John Porter, who was believed responsible for the shooting of two police three days earlier. The police had undoubted power to arrest Porter without warrant as a person they reasonably suspected of having committed a felony. This power extended to arresting him on private premises, but their right to enter premises for the purpose of arresting him depended on the existence of a belief based on reasonable grounds that Porter was on the premises. In fact the police did not have sufficient information to found reasonable grounds for believing that he was in any of the six premises selected as places where he might be.[30]

Curiously, the police decided to obtain search warrants to search for certain 'things' (Porter's gun and clothes) in each of the six premises, even though they had no more reason to believe these things were in any of the premises than they had to believe that Porter himself was there. The obtaining of the search warrants was a subterfuge that the police hoped, wrongly, would improve their legal right to raid the six premises.

The Commissioner found that the rules governing the issue and execution of search warrants 'were treated with contemptuous disregard' by the police.[31] The sworn grounds provided to the justice were highly misleading, lumping together information applying to the six different premises, failing 'to establish any reasonable grounds at all for believing that the things which were the subject of the application were at any particular one of the premises nominated, much less that they were at all of them'.[32] Not knowing where he was, they 'simply spread a wide net in the hope that he would be caught in it'.[33] The Commissioner concluded that:

> clearly what the police were trying to do was to get a 'general warrant' in the sense that goods could be searched for over a lot of premises without their having to supply reasonable grounds for believing that the goods were in any particular one of them.[34]

As the grounds were inadequate, the warrants were invalid.

According to the High Court, a justice approached by the police for a search warrant is required by the law to:

> stand between the police and the citizen to give real attention to the question whether the information proffered by the police does justify the intrusion they desire to make into the privacy of the citizen and the inviolate security of his personal and business affairs.[35]

However, the Commissioner found that the authorised justice approached by the police in this case, a clerk in the Local Courts Administration:

> allowed himself to be prevailed upon to issue the eight warrants without proper grounds for any of them, and he must have been in a much greater state of confusion and less clearly analytical of the situation than he now believes.[36]

Under the New South Wales *Search Warrants Act* 1985, the members of SWOS involved in the raid could enter before 6.00 a.m. if the warrant was so endorsed; were authorised to use such force 'as is reasonably necessary' to enter; and could seize a thing mentioned in the warrant and anything else that they had reasonable grounds for believing was connected with any offence. However, the Commissioner found that '[e]ven if the search warrant had been legally obtained, the actions of the police would have deprived them of protection, because they disregarded the requirements associated with it'.

The police ignored the statutory restrictions on the hours during which the warrant could be executed (since the warrant was not endorsed, the entry shortly before 6.00 a.m. was unlawful); they failed to announce their presence and seek admission before smashing down the front door (the normal SWOS method of entry); they assaulted and falsely imprisoned the occupants by pointing shotguns at them with no legal justification; and they seized things for which there was not the slightest justification. These included a photograph of Gundy and a story book and air rifle belonging to his nine-year-old son, Bradley. No real attempt was made to explain anything to Bradley or to obtain professional assistance for him. It took several hours for Gundy's wife, who was not present at the house, to be informed of her husband's death. A written notice required to be given to the occupier of the premises under the *Search Warrants Act* was never served. The required report on the search to the justice was not made until seven weeks after the raid, instead of the prescribed ten days.

David Gundy had been in his bedroom when SWOS entered the house. One of the SWOS team entered the bedroom and pointed his loaded and cocked shotgun at Gundy, who angrily approached the intruder. The Commissioner noted that:

> although the police officer had been highly trained to enter premises and confront dangerous criminals, he had not been trained to cope with an unarmed, near naked man who reacted angrily when woken from his sleep by armed men bursting into his house.[37]

Occupants were expected to be terrified and freeze. That did not happen on this occasion. During a struggle, the police officer pulled the shotgun back—it accidentally discharged and fatally wounded Gundy.

All police involved in the operation were permeated with an attitude that 'the law will look after police acting to catch a serious criminal, and inconvenient legal rules can be safely ignored'.[38] The result was the death of David Gundy, 'a law-abiding hard-working family man who had had no criminal association with Porter and no contact of any kind with him after his shooting of police'.[39]

## Some conclusions

Many conclusions are suggested by this tragedy. Perhaps the most important is that the law relating to search of premises in order to arrest must be comprehensively regulated. In retrospect, it is clear that the police in this case did not have power to enter any of the premises in order to arrest Porter since they had insufficient basis for believing him present in any of them. The entries were a serious intrusion on the security and privacy of the inhabitants, with the risk of physical or psychological damage to innocent people. They should never have occurred. But, in most Australian jurisdictions the present law is not comprehensively stated, either under the common law or statute, and is certainly not easily accessible. Indeed, it is clear that the entire law relating to search and seizure requires comprehensive regulation. Part 1A of the Commonwealth *Crimes Act*, enacted in 1994, provides one model, notwithstanding criticism that can be made of aspects of it.

Other points may be made. It is unacceptable that the police are able to choose which justice to approach for a warrant in any given case. Such 'forum shopping' is generally discouraged in other areas of criminal justice. Procedures must be implemented that obviate such a practice in this area. The police in this case should have been required to justify armed entry to somebody who had the capacity and experience to balance the conflicting interests involved unaffected by police pressure. It is not a sufficient safeguard in a case of armed entry that the search warrant should be obtained from a court clerk. As the Commissioner recommended, this function should be given to a judge. Indeed, in our view, even run-of-the-mill search warrants, which do not authorise armed entry, should at least require the authorisation of a magistrate.

There was considerable dispute in this case between the police officers applying for the search warrants and the justice who granted them, as to precisely what information was provided by the police. It is critical that procedures be introduced that ensure that there is a complete record of all aspects of an application for a warrant and that the justice is fully informed of all relevant aspects of the matter. This would extend to telephone applications and to the terms of the warrant. The principle must be that the process for obtaining a warrant is subject to the effective supervision of the courts.

This case study also raises questions about the consequences to the police if a search is unlawful. Police complaints mechanisms of various types are available in most jurisdictions, but they are of varying effectiveness, particularly as most involve police reviewing police. A civil action for trespass is theoretically available,[40] at least where the police officer does not act in good faith, but a plaintiff will face delay before the matter is litigated, considerable expense, difficulties of proof, and quantifying damages. There is the (often remote) possibility of exclusion at trial of evidence unlawfully obtained, which we discuss in chapter 6. Whether these are sufficient deterrents to police unlawfulness of this sort is a moot question.

Finally, in Australia there is no constitutional protection against unreasonable search and seizure. Such a constitutional provision exists in Canada, New Zealand and the United States. It places limits on the circumstances in which powers of search and seizure can be validly conferred, and also on the uses that may be made of those powers on particular occasions. We believe that serious consideration should be given to introducing such a provision into the Australian Constitution in order to facilitate compliance with our obligations under the *International Covenant on Civil and Political Rights*, Article 17, which provides that:

> No one shall be subjected to arbitrary or unlawful interference with his privacy, family, home or correspondence …

# Arrest and detention

As we have seen, the law permits the search of an arrested person. Arrest also allows other forms of investigation, including questioning of the arrested person and certain methods of identification. Nevertheless, the common law has always been concerned to limit the powers of the state to detain a person for the purposes of investigation. It has generally prohibited detention without arrest and it has attempted to prevent arrest being used as a mode of investigation.

An arrest involves the deprivation of a person's liberty.[41] The common law confers on the police a power to arrest without warrant[42] on 'reasonable suspicion' of the commission of certain offences. Not only must the police officer have this suspicion, but the circumstances at the time of the arrest known to the police officer must be such that they would create in the mind of a reasonable person such a suspicion.[43] However, the suspicion may be based on material that would not be admissible in evidence at a trial, including the arrested person's criminal record, and hearsay information provided by others.

Legislation has altered this common law position in various respects. The South Australian *Summary Offences Act* 1953 provides, for example:

> A member of the police force, without any warrant other than this Act, at any hour of the day or night, may apprehend any person whom the member finds committing, or has reasonable cause to suspect of having committed, or being about to commit, an offence.[44]

Similar provisions are found in all jurisdictions, with variations. Some require reasonable belief rather than reasonable suspicion in relation to past offences.[45] Several do not cover any offence but are limited to any 'indictable'[46] offence. Victoria has abolished the common law of arrest without warrant and placed the law entirely on a statutory footing. Similarly, the Code State provisions replace, rather than simply supplement, the common law powers. Apart from these general powers to arrest, various Acts in all jurisdictions expressly grant power to arrest without warrant to citizens, police or officers enforcing the specific legislation.[47]

Nevertheless, in all Australian jurisdictions, the law relating to arrest without warrant is not dissimilar and the general common law prohibition against detention without arrest is only exceptionally modified. Thus, for example, the police in some jurisdictions are granted powers to stop a person for a particular purpose and to search that person or his or her vehicle for certain property.[48] Legislation relating to the use of motor vehicles may empower the police to demand certain information from a driver and detain the driver under random breath-testing procedures. These powers are exceptional and the degree of intrusion and detention is limited.

An arrest involves the apprehension of a person for the suspected commission of a criminal offence. Traditionally, the power of arrest has been regarded as a part of the process of prosecution rather than as an investigative power. This has had a number of important consequences. Since one purpose of arrest is to ensure the subsequent attendance of the arrested person before a court should a prosecution be commenced, the power under common law to keep an arrested person in custody is limited in terms of that purpose. Further, the power of arrest cannot be lawfully used for some investigative purpose, for example, in order to detain and interrogate a suspect.[49] However, as we shall see, legislative changes in most Australian jurisdictions have significantly modified the common law position.

# Alternatives to arrest

Arrest is not the only procedure available to commence a criminal prosecution. It can also be initiated by the use of a summons. If a police officer (or any person) knows or suspects that a person has committed an offence, he or she may lay an 'information' before a justice of the peace, who may then issue a summons for the appearance in court of the alleged offender. If the alleged offender fails to appear as required after being served with the summons, an arrest warrant may be issued. A similar procedure is an 'attendance notice' issued by a senior police officer to compel attendance at court. Lastly, infringement notice schemes exist in most jurisdictions in relation to minor offences.[50] Under these schemes, the notice gives the option of paying a fine within a specified time as an alternative to prosecution in court for the offence.

It is critically important that options other than arrest be available in relation to minor offences. Arrest and detention is the direct use of state power on an individual. 'Reasonable force' may be used in effecting the arrest. It is also a dehumanising process. Loss of liberty and personal dignity, embarrassment, isolation from friends and family, and subjection to police procedures are the normal concomitants of arrest. As the dramatic increase in deaths in police custody tragically emphasises, even a brief period of arrest may have drastic consequences. The suspect who is arrested and detained is more likely to be refused bail than is a person summonsed for the same offence, and thus more likely to suffer the prejudicial effects of being held in custody before trial. It follows that arrest should normally be a last resort. Indeed, in respect of many minor offences, arrest should not be an option except in extreme circumstances.

Reforms to simply grant police a discretion to proceed by means of cautions, on the spot fines, infringement notices or court appearance notices, do not address the problem of excessive use of the arrest power as an instrument of control. The Royal Commission into Aboriginal Deaths in Custody found a reluctance within all police organisations throughout Australia to use options other than arrest.[51] While such discretionary power may be appropriate in respect of certain offences—such as assaults and property damage where there is a real possibility of further offences—for many minor offences there is simply no justification for arrest. While the police may argue that it is the only suitable way of accurately identifying a suspect, in matters of minor crime, even this purpose may pose an excessive intrusion into the liberty of the individual. People charged with nothing more than using offensive language, for example, should not be arrested in an exercise of police power and control.

The Commonwealth *Crimes Act* 1914 provides that a statutory power to arrest is only granted if the police officer

> believes on reasonable grounds that … proceedings by summons against the person would not achieve one or more of the following purposes:

(i) ensuring the appearance of the person before a court in respect of the offence;

(ii) preventing a repetition or continuation of the offence or the commission of another offence;

(iii) preventing the concealment, loss or destruction of evidence relating to the offence;

(iv) preventing harassment of, or interference with, a person who may be required to give evidence in proceedings in respect of the offence;

(v) preventing the fabrication of evidence in respect of the offence;

(vi) preserving the safety or welfare of the person.[52]

In jurisdictions where the power to arrest is not so restrained, the courts have sometimes expressed the 'hope' that the police will employ other procedures whenever possible,[53] but it has to be said that such legally unenforceable propositions are little more than wishful thinking. Again, legal regulation is necessary. Article 9(1) of the *International Covenant on Civil and Political Rights* provides that 'no one shall be subjected to arbitrary arrest or detention'. Laws that fail to lay down any clear and objective criteria as to when people may be arrested are defective.[54] An example of a step in the right direction is the 1997 Tasmanian *Youth Justice Act*, which places restrictions on the power of arrest and encourages the use of complaint and summons options, as well as providing a statutory basis for formal and informal cautioning.

## Arrest and criminal investigation

Despite the traditional view that arrest is part of the process of prosecution, it is unrealistic not to see it also as part of criminal investigation. This area of the law cannot be properly understood without some consideration of legal history. Although constables in England were bound to bring an arrested person before a justice as soon as practicable, and were not permitted to detain for interrogation, sixteenth-century statutes required justices of the peace to examine these people before committing them for trial. Their interrogation was regarded as very important in obtaining evidence of guilt.[55]

However, in the nineteenth century, the task of investigating crime and questioning suspects passed from justices to the newly established police force. The role of the justice became one of charging the suspect, if there was sufficient evidence to justify a charge,[56] and determining the question of bail. Unfortunately, there was no real attempt made to resolve consequent uncertainties with respect to the powers of the police. They regularly arrested suspects for questioning before handing them over to a justice, without legal justification. This anomalous situation was inherited in Australia through the colonial reception of English law and has continued into the twentieth century.

Taking New South Wales as an example, section 352 of the *Crimes Act* 1900 requires an arresting constable to take the person arrested 'before an authorised

Justice to be dealt with according to law'. This means a magistrate, or a justice of the peace exercising judicial powers granted under legislation to deal with arrested people.[57] Of course, the arrested person need not be taken before an 'authorised justice' if he or she is to be released. It is now the norm for the police themselves to 'charge' an arrested person and then to grant bail.[58] Only where the police refuse bail is there a need to approach an 'authorised justice'. The real issue, however, is whether the police may delay charging in order to question a suspect and carry out other investigative procedures.

## Period of detention

In *Clarke v Bailey*[59] the New South Wales Supreme Court held that the statutory power under section 352 of the *Crimes Act* 1900, like the common law, requires the arresting police officer to take the person arrested before a justice without unreasonable delay and by the most reasonably direct route. As Chief Justice Jordan observed in *Bales v Parmeter*,[60] any 'detention which is reasonably necessary until a magistrate can be obtained is, of course, lawful, but detention which extends beyond this cannot be justified under the common law or statutory power'. This has at least two consequences in the context of police investigation, including questioning of suspects. An arrest is unlawful if it is carried out for the purpose of investigations.[61] Detention after a lawful arrest will become unlawful if, for the purpose of investigation, the police fail to take the arrested person before a magistrate. However, the police can take advantage of any legitimate delay to engage in investigations.[62]

In these circumstances, the issue becomes whether the arrested person was taken before a magistrate 'without unreasonable delay'. The meaning of this concept was considered by the High Court in *Williams v The Queen*.[63] Williams was arrested by Tasmanian police and it was accepted by the High Court that the relevant legislation required 'the person making the arrest to bring the arrested person before a justice in as short a time as is reasonably practicable'. The members of the court agreed that the rule at common law is the same. Although the actual terminology may vary, from 'in as short a time as is reasonably practicable' to 'as soon as practicable' to 'as soon as is reasonably possible', the High Court took the view that these terms mean precisely the same thing.

In deciding what the concept required, Justices Mason and Brennan stated that it is:

> unlawful for a police officer having custody of an arrested person to delay taking him before a justice in order to provide an opportunity to investigate that person's complicity in a criminal offence, whether the offence under investigation is the offence for which the person has been arrested or another offence.[64]

More eloquently, they concluded, '[p]racticability is not assessed by reference to the exigencies of criminal investigation; the right to personal liberty is not what is left over after the police investigation is finished'.[65] Justices Wilson and Dawson took the same approach, although they had noted that 'obviously there must be reasonable time to formulate and lay appropriate charges for the purpose of bringing a person before a justice'.[66] While all four Justices recognised that this limitation on detention places a considerable curb upon otherwise quite proper investigation by police, they agreed that any modification of the law required legislation.[67] However, the impact of the *Williams* decision was limited by subsequent decisions. For example, in *Attorney-General for NSW v Dean*[68] it was accepted that it will be very difficult for a person who was arrested outside of normal court hours to demonstrate that it was reasonably practicable for the police to take him or her before a justice. As a result, the police could deliberately make an arrest outside court hours in order to gain substantially more time for investigation. Alternatively, when making an arrest during court hours they might, particularly in serious cases, simply ignore the law in order to conduct what they regarded as appropriate investigation. The risks from this are small. As the New South Wales Law Reform Commission has explained, an unlawfully detained person may:

> be able to bring actions for assault, false imprisonment or malicious prosecution. For a plaintiff, however, there are grave problems of delay, costs, proof, and quantifying damages … More commonly, persons who believe that they have been unlawfully detained by police will complain to the Ombudsman or to the Police Board … but basically the investigation of complaints against the police is under police control … In practice, the most likely forum for testing the lawfulness of police treatment of an arrested person is at the subsequent trial of that person …[69]

This is a completely unsatisfactory situation. The *International Covenant on Civil and Political Rights* provides that 'anyone who has been the victim of unlawful arrest or detention shall have an enforceable right to compensation'.[70] Reliance on testing of the legality of the arrest or detention at a subsequent trial is inadequate since the vast majority of prosecutions result in a plea of guilty,[71] so that the issue is never addressed. Moreover, even when there is a contested trial, judges are often reluctant to exclude what may be cogent evidence of guilt because of police impropriety.[72]

In practice, the police have been able to evade the operation of the law relating to arrest and related procedural requirements by defining a person as voluntarily cooperating. If the police merely ask people to 'come to the police station to assist with enquiries' and do not 'plainly convey' the impression that they are not free to refuse, then there may be no arrest, even if the police would have 'arrested' them if they had refused to come and the people believe that they are under compulsion.[73]

In our view, the police should have a realistic opportunity for proper investigation after arrest, subject to a number of important safeguards, which we discuss below. One solution is to give the police a 'reasonable time' after arrest to pursue their investigations, as is the law now in Victoria, Tasmania and the Northern Territory as the result of legislative change. Such a flexible approach permits account to be taken of a wide range of factors in determining the appropriate time for investigation. However, we agree with the New South Wales Law Reform Commission that:

> the 'reasonable time' formula without any fixed limits or presumptions is much too uncertain to regulate an area which touches on the fundamental liberty of the individual. A person in custody would have no idea when he or she is likely to be released, or whether the detention is even lawful.[74]

Equally important is that such an approach offers little in the way of accountability or review mechanisms.

It is far preferable to incorporate some fixed time limits,[75] subject to 'time-out' exclusions when the investigation is legitimately suspended or delayed, and capable of extension after application to a judicial officer. A fixed time period ensures a greater level of certainty on both sides and more effective regulation and review. This view has been accepted in some Australian jurisdictions. Thus, for example, South Australia permits the police to detain a person arrested without warrant in relation to a 'serious offence' for four hours 'or such longer period (not exceeding eight hours) as may be authorised by a magistrate'.[76] A similar provision was enacted in New South Wales, when the *Crimes Amendment (Detention after Arrest) Act* 1997 introduced a new Part 10 into the *Crimes Act*. Queensland legislation introduced in 2000 permits detention for no more than eight hours, subject to extension by a magistrate.[77] During this period of time the police are permitted to carry out legitimate investigative procedures, including questioning and identification parades, which we discuss further below. Legislation in most jurisdictions now confers power to take fingerprints and photographs, conduct medical examinations and take bodily samples, subject to certain conditions.[78]

The uncertainties of the old law and its unreasonable constraint on investigation discouraged many judges from vigorously enforcing the law. Once the police are formally empowered to engage in a limited period of post-arrest investigation, strict enforcement of the limits of that power must follow. Techniques designed to evade such limits—such as 'voluntary co-operation', use of 'holding charges',[79] and immediate re-arrest after termination of a period of detention—must be effectively discouraged. The rules should apply to effective custody, where the suspect is under the control of the police, regardless of whether he or she has been formally arrested.[80] Finally, a number of safeguards must be applied, and rigorously enforced.

## Safeguards over detention

### General

Clearly, all people in police custody must be treated with humanity. Article 10 of the *International Covenant on Civil and Political Rights* provides that:

[a]ll persons deprived of their liberty shall be treated with humanity and with respect for the inherent dignity of the human person.

The Commonwealth *Crimes Act* has been amended to provide that:

a person who is under arrest must be treated with humanity and with respect for human dignity, and must not be subjected to cruel, degrading or inhuman punishment.[81]

However, most jurisdictions do not have any general provision applicable to police detention.

## Allocating responsibility

As the Royal Commission of Inquiry into Aboriginal Deaths in Custody concluded,[82] the police must be made expressly responsible for the safety and well-being of all people in their custody. Division 10 in the New South Wales *Crimes Act*, enacted in 1997, introduced a 'custody manager' system similar to that operating in England.[83] The custody manager is required, orally and in writing, to caution the arrested person regarding his or her rights and to ensure the proper treatment of the suspect while in custody. In this way, responsibility for a person in custody is clearly imposed on one police officer, rather than diffused among several. Indeed, we would support the extension of the custody manager's responsibilities to reviewing the lawfulness and propriety of the arrest and determining whether custodial investigation is necessary.

## Comprehensive records

One way of encouraging a humane and properly regulated system of police detention is to require the maintenance of comprehensive records. As the New South Wales Law Reform Commission has pointed out, this serves several critical functions, including an overview of the period of custody and helping to ensure that procedural safeguards are applied.[84] Under Division 10 in the New South Wales *Crimes Act*, the custody manager must record the following particulars in a custody record:

(a) the date and time:
  (i) the person arrived at the police station or other place where the custody manager is located, and
  (ii) the person came into the custody manager's custody,
(b) the name and rank of the arresting officer and any accompanying officers,
(c) the grounds for the person's detention,
(d) details of any property taken from the person,
(e) if the person participates in any investigative procedure, the time the investigative procedure started and ended,

(f) details of any period of time that is not to be taken into account under section 356F (certain times to be disregarded in calculating investigation period),

(g) if the person is denied any rights under this Part, the reason for the denial of those rights and the time when the person was denied those rights,

(h) the date and time of, and reason for, the transfer of the person to the custody of another police officer,

(i) details of any application for a detention warrant and the result of any such application,

(j) if a detention warrant is issued in respect of the person, the date and time a copy of the warrant was given to the person and the person was informed of the nature of the warrant and its effect,

(k) the date and time the person is released from detention,

(l) any other particulars prescribed by the regulations.[85]

There is considerable variation around Australia with respect to the extent to which, if at all, these safeguards exist. More surprising is the fact that no empirical information exists on police custodial populations beyond that which was provided to the Royal Commission into Aboriginal Deaths in Custody. General adoption of the custody record scheme would be a major step in providing that information.

## Notification of rights

The Australian Law Reform Commission said in 1975:

> It should not be necessary to argue that if a person has rights he should be made aware of them. Whether, once informed, he has the will, the wit or the wisdom to take advantage of them is probably something no criminal justice system can completely ensure. Perhaps it should not try. But no criminal justice system deserves respect if its wheels are turned by ignorance. Any system which pays lip-service to the existence of rights yet does nothing to ensure that they are known and understood—and indeed which may depend on their not being understood—is a system that discriminates against the weak, the unintelligent and the uncomprehending in favour of the strong-willed, the smart and the linguistically competent.[86]

Traditionally, administrative directions have been the only source of an obligation on the police to inform a suspect of his or her rights. These have required the usual caution, informing the suspect that he or she does not have to say anything but that whatever they do say may be used in evidence. There is some uncertainty as to when this caution must be given. On one approach, the police need only caution where they have formally arrested a suspect or they have decided to charge. An alternative position is that they must caution where a suspect is in 'custody' in the sense that it is apparent that he or she is not free to leave. In our view, this position is quite unsatisfactory. Administrative directions are little more than guidelines and should be replaced, as some jurisdictions have already done, with statutory requirements. The police should be required to inform a suspect of his or her rights when in effective custody, where the suspect is under the control of the police. A number of jurisdictions, such as New South Wales, South Australia and Victoria, have now introduced such requirements. However, they are deficient in not requiring the tape recording of the communication of such rights. Part 1C of the Commonwealth *Crimes Act* contains the following provision:

**23U**

(1) If a person is under arrest for a Commonwealth offence, an investigating official who is required by this Part to give the person under arrest certain information (including a caution) must tape record, if practicable, the giving of that information and the person's responses (if any).

(2) In any proceedings, the burden lies on the prosecution to prove whether it was practicable to tape record the giving of that information and the person's responses (if any).

Comparable provisions should be introduced in other jurisdictions to ensure that there can be no dispute that the detained person was informed of his or her rights.

## Interpreter

At common law a suspect with communication difficulties has no right to an interpreter, although a trial judge would have the discretion to exclude evidence obtained if an interpreter were not provided. Most State police forces have standing orders providing for the use of interpreters in the criminal investigation process, but it would be preferable if legislation were generally adopted (as, for example, in Victoria and New South Wales) to ensure that the needs of suspects are properly satisfied.[87]

## Access to relatives and friends

There is no enforceable common law right for people to communicate with a friend or relative during the period between when they are taken into custody and brought before a magistrate. However, most jurisdictions now, formally or informally, allow a friend or relative of a person in police custody to be notified of the circumstances and whereabouts of the person, provided that this does not endanger the investigation. Some jurisdictions also require, subject to limited exceptions, that custodial investigation be delayed until the arrival of a friend or relative if requested by the person in custody.[88] South Australia goes further, permitting a relative or friend to be present during any interrogation[89] and requiring the police to give notice of this right to the arrested person.[90] In the case of questioning of children, New South Wales actually requires the presence of an appropriate person to assist the child.[91]

## Legal assistance

In respect of legal assistance for a suspect, any common law right is limited in practical terms to the proposition that the police should not unreasonably deny a suspect access to his or her lawyer. Given that few suspects have a private lawyer and there is no enforceable common law or 'constitutional' right to free legal assistance at the police station,[92] the 'right' lacks meaning in practice. Again, some jurisdictions have introduced statutory changes. The Commonwealth *Crimes Act* 1914, for example, provides[93] that an arrested person must, subject to very limited exceptions, be allowed to communicate with a legal practitioner before any police questioning. The arrested person must be informed of this right. Further, the legal practitioner must be permitted to be present during questioning 'but only while the legal practitioner does not unreasonably interfere with the questioning'. However, Australian jurisdictions do not in general accord a right to free legal assistance at the police station. This stands in contrast to the position in the United Kingdom and the United States.

There can be no doubt that a lawyer advising a suspect in police custody can provide considerable assistance. The presence of the lawyer will be an important guarantee of proper treatment for the suspect. The lawyer can advise his or her client on the legality of the detention and take appropriate steps in consequence. The lawyer can advise as to options in relation to such investigative procedures as interrogation, identification parades, fingerprints, photographs, medical examinations and the like. There is no doubt that custodial investigation involves elements of negotiation between the police and the suspect over such matters as treatment in custody, the police attitude to bail, the precise formulation of charges, and possible pleas of guilty. A lawyer, acting in the interests of his or her client, could facilitate that process of negotiation. All jurisdictions, therefore, should enact legislation entrenching a full right to publicly funded legal assistance during custodial investigation. It goes without saying that the legal assistance provided must be competent.[94]

# Interrogation

It is a well-known fact that most convictions are virtually ensured by custodial interrogation in the police station. In one small-scale study of New South Wales District Court cases in the early 1980s the following conclusions were reached:

> The vast majority of defendants (96%) made confessions or damaging statements when interviewed by the police. The frequency of such confessional evidence is much higher than has been reported by any overseas study … Although the written confessions were less common than verbal confessions, in nearly 80% of the

cases there was evidence of 'written' or 'oral and written' confessions ... In relation to the question 'who confesses?' the most significant factor appeared to be the nature of the offence. It is somewhat surprising that those charged with more serious offences more frequently supplied incriminating statements ... The defendants generally confessed within a relatively short period of initial police contact ... The giving of a caution, at least as presently worded and administered, seemed to be of little or no significance in regulating the relationship between the suspect and the police during interrogation. Many defendants volunteered or 'blurted out' damaging admissions and most defendants apparently waived their right to silence even after being cautioned ... Few defendants obtained legal advice prior to or during the police interrogation. Furthermore in seven of the ten cases in which the defendant did obtain legal advice it was alleged that the defendant had made damaging admissions at some time prior to the obtaining of legal assistance.[95]

## Verbals

Sometimes the confessions that have emerged from custodial investigation have been fabricated by the police. Such alleged confessions are commonly described as police 'verbals' because the only evidence that the confession was made is the oral testimony of the police. Justice Cave stated at the end of the nineteenth century:

> I always suspect these confessions, which are supposed to be the offspring of penitence and remorse, and which nevertheless are repudiated by the prisoner at the trial. It is remarkable that it is of very rare occurrence for evidence of a confession to be given when the proof of the prisoner's guilt is otherwise clear and satisfactory, but when it is not clear and satisfactory the prisoner is not unfrequently alleged to have been seized with the desire born of penitence and remorse to supplement it with a confession; a desire which vanishes as soon as he appears in a court of justice.[96]

In the Queensland Fitzgerald Royal Commission in 1989, former Inspector Jack Herbert, when asked by Counsel Assisting the Commission about the frequency of 'the practice of verballing' said:

> Very, very frequent—on most occasions, actually ... it was just accepted ... I grew up with it ... I think it is a worldwide practice, actually ... It was a widely accepted practice.[97]

In 1991, a former New South Wales Detective Sergeant admitted that:

> Verbals are part of police culture ... Police would think you're weak if you didn't do it. And prisoners think a policeman who doesn't give him a few words of verbal isn't worth his salt ... The hardest part for police was thinking up excuses to explain why people didn't sign up.[98]

It is true that 'verbals' have become less frequently used in recent years. One reason is that juries have become more sceptical of relying upon the word of police when it is unsupported by evidence from independent witnesses or evidence of a physical sort. Equally important, most jurisdictions have moved towards a legal requirement that most interrogations be recorded on tape. The arguments for some kind of audio- or video-recording of the police custodial interrogation are irrefutable. Recordings offer the possibility of an accurate record of the entire period of questioning, permitting a judge and jury to determine exactly what happened and thus best decide questions of evidentiary admissibility and weight. While the process is not complete, considerable advances have been made.

There is still a way to go. In some jurisdictions the legislation mandating electronic recording has been found to be flawed. In Victoria, for example, the Minister's Second Reading speech relating to sections 464G and 464H of the *Crimes Act* 1958 referred to the 'firm view' that 'universal tape-recording of interviews with suspects by law enforcement officials would have substantial benefits ... for the administration of justice'.[99] However, in *Pollard v The Queen*,[100] the High Court has, by majority, interpreted these provisions as permitting a confession recorded at one place to be admitted—even if an earlier unrecorded questioning had occurred at another place. Members of the majority conceded that this interpretation of the legislation could 'give rise to the very sort of problem against which the relevant provisions provide some safeguards',[101] although one judge suggested that it would still be possible for a court to 'ensure that investigating officials do not try to avoid the operation of [the provisions] by fragmenting their questioning, as to both time and place'.[102] Justice Toohey pointed out other problems with the legislation:

> What if, for instance, a person suspected of having committed an offence is questioned and denies any complicity in the offence, the questioning is tape-recorded and later the person returns to the police station where he or she makes a frank admission of guilt unaccompanied by any questioning? Is that admission excluded by s. 464H(1) unless it is tape-recorded? Again, what if an admission of guilt is made in a written statement provided by the person? Is evidence given of such a statement 'evidence of a confession or admission made to an investigating official'? And if the person is not suspected or ought not reasonably to have been suspected of having committed an offence, that person's admission or confession is not within the terms of s. 464H. These examples demonstrate that the framers of s. 464H may not have achieved all they set out to do.[103]

In 1995, Tasmania enacted legislation that provided that 'on the trial of an accused person for a serious offence',[104] evidence of any confession or admission made by the accused person 'in the course of official questioning' is not admissible unless:

(a) there is available to the court a videotape an interview with the accused person in the course of which the confession or admission was made; or

(b) if the prosecution proves on the balance of probabilities that there was a reasonable explanation as to why a videotape referred to in paragraph (a) could not be made, there is available to the court a videotape of an interview with the accused person about the making and terms of the confession or admission or the substance of the confession or admission in the course of which the accused person states that he or she made a confession or an admission in those terms or confirms the substance of the admission or confession; or

(c) the prosecution proves on the balance of probabilities that there was a reasonable explanation as to why the videotape referred to in paragraphs (a) and (b) could not be made; or

(d) the court is satisfied that there are exceptional circumstances which, in the interests of justice, justify the admission of the evidence.[105]

The term 'reasonable explanation' was defined to include the following circumstances:

(a) the confession or admission was made when it was not practicable to videotape it;

(b) equipment to videotape the interview could not be obtained while it was reasonable to detain the accused person;

(c) the accused person did not consent to the interview being videotaped;

(d) the equipment used to videotape the interview malfunctioned.

In 2004, the High Court held[106] that the phrase 'in the course of official questioning' should be interpreted narrowly. It held that the use of the word 'questioning' means that 'an event cannot be said to have taken place "in the course of official questioning" if the police officer nominates a future time when that course of questioning will commence, and the event happens before that time'. Similarly, it was held that, if an official says after some questioning 'no further questions will be asked', any subsequent statement made by the suspect will not be made 'in the course of official questioning' if 'no further question was asked which triggered the impugned statement'.[107] Applying this analysis, Gleeson CJ, Hayne and Heydon JJ held that 'the course of official questioning' ended when a police officer ceased to ask questions of the appellant in a formal police interview and said '[W]e'll conclude the interview', so that an alleged admission made some time later when the appellant was getting into a police car to be taken to a hospital for the purpose of obtaining samples of blood and hair was not made during 'official questioning'. In dissent, both Justices McHugh and Kirby made the point that such an interpretation renders the provision's operation hostage to the evidence of police officers as to when the questioning commenced and ended.

As it happens, this Tasmanian provision was re-enacted in 2001 in substantially the same terms as the 1995 provision but with the words 'during official questioning' rather than 'in the course of official questioning'.[108] It is unlikely that this change will preclude application of the High Court's narrow approach in *Kelly v The Queen*. Plainly enough, some amendment of the legislation (and similar legislation in other jurisdictions) is necessary to overcome this interpretation and ensure that the legislation provides greater protection against police verbals.

Of course, legislation is not enough by itself. There is a heavy onus on the police themselves to reduce the occurrence of fabrication of confessions. In the past, police representatives have never publicly acknowledged their occurrence or have put them down to a few 'rotten apples'. For whatever reason, it does seem that the use of verbals has declined significantly over the last few years, although it has certainly not disappeared. Nevertheless, loopholes in legislation can be exploited by corrupt police. Different types of fabricated admissions appear. The criminal justice system must remain constantly vigilant against police who are prepared to 'cut corners' to achieve a conviction.

## Compulsion

Apart from the issue of fabrication, the central issue with custodial questioning is the safeguards that operate in respect of it. Article 14(3)(g) of the *International Covenant on Civil and Political Rights* provides that everyone has a right 'not to be compelled to ... confess guilt'. A person being questioned by the police should be protected from physical or psychological abuse. The present legal solution requires that the prosecution prove that any admission or confession was voluntary. Indeed that is how the law also attempts to achieve another legitimate goal—maximising the reliability of any admission or confession. This connection is not surprising. If a confession is obtained after a suspect has been physically or mentally abused, it may well be involuntary and one may seriously question its reliability. Section 149 of the Victorian *Evidence Act* 1958 makes the connection between voluntariness and reliability explicit.

However, there are great difficulties with the concept of 'voluntariness', which we discuss in chapter 6. There would be considerable merit in separating issues of abuse from issues of reliability, as the *Evidence Act* 1995 (Commonwealth and NSW) now does. Further, while the 'voluntariness' test deals adequately with the more obvious kinds of compulsion and abuse, it is inadequate with respect to more subtle forms of pressure. In the High Court case of *Williams*, Justices Mason and Brennan said:

> If the legislature thinks it right to enhance the armoury of law enforcement, at least the legislature is able—as the courts are not—to prescribe some safeguards which might ameliorate the risk of unconscionable pressure being applied to persons under interrogation while they are being kept in custody.[109]

## Legal assistance

As we noted above in relation to detention generally, a number of jurisdictions have legislated a right to legal assistance. Victorian legislation, for example, has impliedly enacted a right to communicate with a legal practitioner.[110] It has also provided for free legal assistance. There is no doubt that this is an important move towards ameliorating 'the risk of unconscionable pressure being applied' to people under custodial interrogation. A lawyer should be present to ensure that the suspect is not coerced, even unintentionally, into confessing, and to ensure that any confession is likely to be reliable. It is likely that the significance of pressures on a suspect to answer questions, and to confess to his or her alleged crimes, would be substantially reduced. Experiments have demonstrated that the effectiveness of external pressures can be significantly reduced by the presence of a third party who is perceived by the suspect as an ally.[111] Further, the lawyer could clarify questions and answers when there was a possibility of ambiguity, which may produce a misleading impression.

The Victorian provisions have been considered by the High Court in the context of custodial interrogation. McHugh J described section 464C of the *Crimes Act* 1958 as follows:

> In pursuance of its objective, the section seeks to neutralize the psychological disadvantage which could otherwise be suffered by a person who is questioned while detained in police custody and isolated from contact with the outside world. It also seeks to ensure that that person will have the opportunity of obtaining legal advice before answering questions, making statements or assisting the police in their investigations.[112]

The High Court accepted, virtually unanimously, that the Victorian provisions apply to the entire process of police questioning, even if it occurs at separate times and places. More important, the members of the court emphasised that these provisions must not be given an unduly narrow interpretation so as to allow the recitation of rights to be little more than a ritualised incantation unlikely to be acted upon by the person being questioned. The police must inform the suspect of his or her rights before any questioning commences. Full information must be provided, conveying the full effect of the rights that the provision confers. In particular, it must be made clear that the person has a right to communicate with a lawyer before the questioning commences. After providing the information, questioning must be deferred for a reasonable time to allow the person the opportunity to have a lawyer present.

However, it has to be said that there is considerable evidence from overseas that most people in custody, even when informed of the right to legal assistance and even when that assistance is freely available, do not take advantage of it.[113] Getting out of the police station as quickly as possible is likely to be a much higher priority for the suspect than obtaining independent advice. One radical option for future reform in those jurisdictions that now accord a right to legal assistance might be to replace the present model of legal assistance as an option with one whereby all suspects received legal advice before being subjected to custodial questioning. In fact, virtually no English-based legal system actually requires the presence of a lawyer during police questioning. Certainly, it is unlikely that the police would support such a scheme, partly because of a belief that legal advisers will usually advise the suspect to exercise the right to silence and so say absolutely nothing at all.[114]

## The 'right to silence'

The 'right to silence' is a legal concept that incorporates a rather disparate group of immunities (including the privilege against self-incrimination), but in this context it primarily refers to the proposition that, except in a limited number of situations,[115] the police cannot legally compel answers to their questions. As the High Court has stated, 'a person who believes on reasonable grounds that he or she is suspected of having been a party to an offence is entitled to remain silent when questioned or asked to supply information by any person in authority …'[116] The traditional caution given to suspects reflects that position. The right not to be compelled to answer questions or confess guilt derives from the principle that the state must prove the guilt of an accused person.[117] More pragmatically, the right to silence in the police station is premised on the idea that those accused of crime tend to be 'inarticulate, poorly educated, suspicious, frightened and suggestible', often incapable of doing themselves justice in their dealings with police.[118] Moreover, there are a number of reasons for silence consistent with innocence:

> The suspect may wish not to disclose conduct on his or another's part which, though non-criminal, is highly embarrassing. He may wish to remain silent to protect other people. He may believe that the police will distort whatever he says, so that the best policy is to say nothing … [119]

However, the right is usually waived by the vast majority of suspects, either explicitly or implicitly by acquiescence to police requests.[120] This is partly because of the pressures to speak and confess noted above and partly because the police will tend to minimise the impact of the caution, perhaps by accompanying it with some kind of 'hedging' to imply that actual invocation would be unwise.[121] Questions will usually begin with minor details such as name and address, making silence very difficult. Having agreed to cooperate by interacting verbally with the interrogator the suspect is committed to an essentially cooperative role. Suspects often seem compelled to try to talk their way out of a difficult situation, inventing false alibis that are easily exposed by the interrogators.[122] Such false exculpatory statements can be more valuable at trial than admissions. Yet false exculpatory statements may be less indicative of guilt than of the pressure of circumstances and a desire to preserve one's dignity by constructing a story for the benefit of interrogators who refuse to believe a simple blanket denial of guilt.

One troubling question in all of this is whether access to legal advice would result in a substantial reduction in the number of suspects willing to talk to the police. The first issue is the kind of advice that is likely to be provided. The advice that a lawyer gives to a suspect will partly depend on the legal consequences of silence. The law in this area is complex and still developing. Nevertheless, it appears clear that where a person who, having been cautioned by the police, chooses to exercise the right, legally any failure to answer questions thereafter cannot constitute any kind of admission.[123] The High Court has again emphasised this: 'an incident of that right to silence is that no adverse inference can be drawn against an accused person by reason of his or her failure to answer such questions or to provide such information.'[124]

If no adverse inference can be drawn from silence then, assuming it is not otherwise relevant, evidence of it should not be admitted at all. The majority judgment stated that 'the Crown should not lead evidence that, when charged, the accused made no reply'.[125] It should also be the case that a refusal to answer any questions asked by police during custodial interrogation before charge should result in similar exclusion, although there is some authority to the contrary.[126]

However, where a suspect does choose to answer some questions, although not others, the entire interrogation will be admitted into evidence and certain negative inferences may be open. The High Court has held that a suspect's 'words, actions, conduct or demeanour' may have evidential value because they manifest a 'consciousness of guilt of the crime charged'.[127] While the various members of the court emphasised that no adverse inference can be drawn from a refusal to answer, there are suggestions in a number of the judgments that such silence or refusal to answer can form part of the accused's relevant conduct.[128] Although the better view of the law is that no inference is permissible from silence where it involves a conscious assertion of the right to silence, inferences may be permissible where the accused answers some questions and omits from his or her answers information that should reasonably have been included. While it now seems established that no adverse inferences should be drawn from selective answering of questions, by itself, such evidence will still get before a jury if only to show that an opportunity to answer questions was given. Given the dangers associated with answering any questions (holding the right to silence in reserve, so to speak), it appears reasonable to assume that many legal advisers will advise their clients in appropriate circumstances to say nothing at all.[129]

Interestingly, a survey of police officers in the north of England after the *Police and Criminal Evidence Act* 1984 (known as the *PACE Act*) was introduced found that 72% believed that the presence of a legal adviser affects the interview 'not at all' or 'not much'.[130] Similarly, 78% of police reported that the presence of a legal adviser did not affect the suspect's exercise of the right to silence.[131] It appears that few advisers recommended silence.[132] This was partly because, as noted above, custodial investigation involves elements of negotiation between the police and the suspect. Where it is apparent that a subsequent prosecution is likely to be successful with or without the suspect's cooperation, vigorous insistence on the right to silence may well not be in the best interests of the suspect, other than as a negotiating tactic. On the other hand, if the prosecution case seems weak or its strength cannot be properly assessed, it is likely that a competent lawyer would give serious consideration to advising silence. The English figures may be partly explained by the fact that the 'legal advisers' are often ex-police clerks, retained because of their contacts and experience, who 'are largely passive and non-interventionist in police interrogations'.[133] Whether this meets the requirements of legal assistance is doubtful. It is also significant that the police in England, unlike in most Australian jurisdictions, may continue to interrogate even though a suspect initially refuses to answer questions. They are also permitted to interrogate for a considerably longer time.

Assuming, for the purposes of discussion, that introduction of a full right to legal assistance did result in a significant increase in assertions of the right to silence, this hardly seems in the public interest. It is in the public interest that a suspect answer police questions, provide any explanations and, where guilty, confess. Just because some suspects choose to say nothing does not mean we should establish a system that encourages every suspect to do the same. There can be little doubt that the right to silence, in its various manifestations, has served important functions in civilising questioning of individuals by the state. But if there are other ways to achieve these goals without incurring the disadvantages, we should consider modification of the right.

One option would be to require prior notice of any defence proposed to be advanced at trial. Already, most jurisdictions require advance notice of a defence of alibi with the possibility of adverse inferences being drawn from failure to provide notice. Extension of this principle to all defences would prevent the prosecution from being ambushed at trial and, in the event that notice is not given, permit the prosecution to explain why there is no evidence to rebut it and also permit the drawing of an inference against the defence.[134]

Another option might be to modify the right to silence so that, if there were reasonable grounds for the questioning and a lawyer was present, the court at any subsequent trial will be told of any refusal to speak and may draw reasonable inferences from that failure.[135] The suspect would be under no compulsion, legal or psychological, to speak—but obviously the possibility of negative inferences would be a strong inducement. If video-recording of interviews became the norm, this would enable to some extent an independent assessment of the circumstances of the interview and any explanation as to why the accused refused to answer questions.

The English Court of Appeal decided,[136] before the introduction of *PACE*, that it is possible to draw a negative inference from silence where the accused and the person asking the questions were 'on even terms'. In that case, the accused had his solicitor present and the court concluded that he was on even terms with the police and that inferences could be drawn against the accused. The status of this authority in Australia is quite unclear. An additional complication is that the suspect in the English case had not been cautioned and this was obviously a significant factor in the decision. It would be quite unfair to draw inferences from silence after the suspect has been informed, at least impliedly, that no adverse consequences will follow from exercise of the right.

This raises the question of whether the present law draws any distinction between post-caution silence and pre-caution silence. Again, the law is unclear on this point.[137] Although the caution contains 'no express assurance that silence will carry no penalty, such assurance is implicit to any person who receives the [caution]', to use the words of the United States Supreme Court.[138] It is therefore possible to argue that the general prohibition on inferences from silence applies only after a caution has been given. It would not be unfair to draw any reasonable inferences from silence if the caution has not been given[139] or if it is reframed by saying that 'silence may be used against you at trial'.

In 1994 the *Criminal Justice and Public Order Act* was enacted in the United Kingdom. It allows a court to draw such inferences as appear proper from the silence of the accused in a number of situations, including police interrogation, and modified the traditional caution to make this clear. In 1996, in the case of *Murray* v *United Kingdom*,[140] the European Court of Human Rights considered the application of similar provisions that had been in force in Northern Ireland for some time. It was argued that the drawing of adverse inferences from the fact that the accused did not answer police questions and did not give evidence at his trial was in violation of the right to a fair trial (recognised in Article 6 of the *International Covenant on Civil and Political Rights*). The court held, by 14 votes to 5, that there was no violation. Provided there was no compulsion, a statute permitting the drawing of adverse inferences amounted to no more than a 'formalised system which aims at allowing commonsense implications to play an open role in the assessment of evidence'. However, in the 2001 judgment of *Condron* v *United Kingdom*,[141] the European Court of Human Rights emphasised the importance of a trial judge's direction to the jury 'striking the right balance' between the right to silence and the circumstances in which an adverse inference may properly be drawn from silence.

This has been a lengthy discussion of the problems that potentially arise from the conjunction between an effective right to a lawyer and a full right to silence. If, in fact, experience shows that there is no significant increase in the rate at which suspects assert the right to silence after receiving legal advice, then any modification of the right to silence should be rejected. We began this chapter with a discussion of the paucity of empirical data in the area of criminal investigation. For the present, there is no clear evidence that the right to silence has any significant effect on prosecution and conviction rates.[142] Clearly, these issues are unlikely to go away, but they should only be resolved on the firm basis of actual evidence.

# Eyewitness identification

Under existing law in all jurisdictions, the police may adopt a variety of procedures in an attempt to identify the perpetrator of a criminal offence and to obtain eyewitness identification evidence in relation to a suspect. Before a suspect is found, and the police are still engaged in the 'detection process', use of photographs to assist detection and identification is often adopted, and not open to criticism. On the other hand, where a suspect has been found and is in police custody, an identification parade or 'line-up' may be used. However, although little statistical data is available, anecdotal evidence in some jurisdictions suggests that the police rarely use identification parades.

The advantages of such a procedure, properly conducted, over photographic identification are considerable. Photographs in police files are generally in black and white, show only head and shoulders and may be several years old. The suspect is not present at the identification to observe the procedure adopted. There is a substantial risk of 'displacement' whereby the memory of the face on the photograph is more clearly retained than the memory of the original sighting of the offender. The mere fact that the police had a photograph of the accused may suggest to a jury that the accused had a criminal record. These problems either do not exist or are much reduced when an identification parade is used.

Accordingly, the courts should actively discourage reliance on photographic identification. In the High Court decision of *Alexander*, some Justices expressed the view that a trial judge should usually exclude evidence of photographic identification obtained after the detection process had ended and a suspect was in custody.[143] However, the majority of the court, while acknowledging the desirability of conducting a parade, preferred to leave the issue entirely up to trial judges. In the result, it is rare for such evidence of photographic identification to be excluded. Reliance is placed instead on warnings to the jury.[144]

This is an unsatisfactory situation. Psychological research and past miscarriages of justice point to eyewitness identification evidence as a potentially serious cause of wrongful convictions.[145] Warnings can only ameliorate the problem. The Australian Law Reform Commission proposed that identification evidence should not be admitted if it was reasonable in the circumstances for an identification parade to be held, and the police preferred to adopt some other procedure.[146] Legislation to implement this proposal has been enacted in the Commonwealth and New South Wales *Evidence Acts* 1995, discussed in chapter 6. Of course, the suspect should not be compelled to take part and, if he or she chose not to, it would clearly be reasonable for the police to use some other method. Where the suspect wished a lawyer to be present at the parade, it should be delayed for a reasonable time to allow this to occur.

Clear procedures should be laid down for the conduct of parades to minimise the risk of mistaken identification.[147] For example, a record should be made of the witness's description of the offender, before the parade occurs. The people in the parade should all be generally consistent with that description and should be dressed alike, with any form of suggestion that a particular person is a suspect avoided. The parade should be photographed. Complete records of all identification parades should be maintained. Legislation to ensure this has been introduced in the Commonwealth *Crimes Act*[148] but other Australian jurisdictions are yet to follow. Other improvements could be made. For example, it would be an improvement on current procedures to do away with line-ups and permit witnesses to see only one purported suspect at a time, so that the witness can make an absolute judgment about each one. When witnesses see a number of people at once, they tend to make relative judgments, comparing them and picking whoever looks most like the offender, rather than evaluating each individually. This is a danger even if the witness is told that the group may not include the offender. Another procedural reform could be to ensure that the police officer running the identification procedure does not know who the real suspect is, and so cannot make leading comments (such as 'would you like to look at number five again?'), for the same reason that good clinical research is double-blind.

# Informers

During the 1980s and 1990s, considerable controversy arose over the use of prison informers giving evidence that another prisoner had confessed some crime to him or her. In New South Wales there developed a belief, particularly in the ranks of prisoners and criminal defence lawyers, that the use of this evidence was in substitution of the discredited verbal. Some referred to this practice as the 'privatised verbal'.

This type of evidence is liable to be unreliable for a number of reasons. It is easily concocted and difficult to disprove. It is likely that the informer is of bad character and may be motivated to fabricate the evidence either by a perception of likely benefit on sentence 'or by reason of any of a variety of pressures of a type which may easily arise in a prison environment and which may not be apparent to a jury'.[149] Further, as one High Court judge has noted:

> evidence given by prison informers is notoriously difficult to break down. The prison-informer is often a skilful liar, with a shrewd knowledge of the criminal courts and their procedures, a quick intelligence well suited to the giving of evidence and withstanding cross-examination and a good demeanour and friendly personality ... At the conclusion of the cross-examination, the jury is likely to be left with the impression of a personable witness whose evidence-in-chief was intrinsically credible and remained unshaken after a 'searching' cross-examination. The danger from prison-informer evidence, therefore lies in the plausibility as well as the character of those who usually give it.[150]

As we will discuss in chapter 6, the High Court now requires that, save in exceptional cases, trial judges must warn juries of the danger of convicting on the potentially unreliable evidence of a prison informer unless it is corroborated by other evidence.

Many doubted whether this was a sufficient response to the problem. The New South Wales Independent Commission against Corruption (ICAC) has considered this issue. One option would be to provide that prisoners can never be relied upon as prosecution witnesses. ICAC rejected this proposition since prisoners will sometimes be the only available witnesses, particularly in the case of gaol murders.[151] It also accepted that benefits (such as reduced sentences) can properly be conferred upon those involved in criminality who help the authorities. However, it concluded that the traditional approach, which relies upon informers to provide information but not to become witnesses, is generally preferable. It also recommended a number of safeguards:

> The first requirement, if prisoners (or indeed criminals) are to be used as witnesses, is that the authorities who deal with them adopt a sceptical attitude. Those dealing with such people as potential witnesses must do their homework, must search and question, and must recognise that lies are likely to be told to them.
>
> The next requirement is to ensure that the fullest possible knowledge is possessed in relation to potential criminal witnesses. No matter how satisfactory rules and systems are, there can be no guarantee that full information will be thrown up about these people. Public officials dealing with them must make themselves fully informed, and convey the information which they obtain to those who need to have it.
>
> The third necessary safeguard is that prisoners and other criminals should only be used where there is substantial external support for what they say.[152]

In relation to the second proposed safeguard, the ICAC accepted that full disclosure should be made to the defence, an issue that we consider more generally in chapter 5. It also proposed that registers of informers be kept by police, prison and prosecution authorities, ensuring that full information about them is recorded and made readily available. This is now generally the practice around Australia.

## Conclusion

The process of legal reform in the area of criminal investigation is slow. As the then Chairman of the Australian Law Reform Commission, Justice Michael Kirby, observed in 1979:

> What is surprising is that we have struggled on for more than a century with a complex body of law made up of a little legislation, much case law (in most jurisdictions), the Judges' Rules and administrative directions of varying authority issued

by Police Chiefs. The argument for collecting, rationalising, simplifying and clarifying the rules seems incontestable.[153]

Citizens would benefit from better understanding of their rights and obligations when subjected to criminal investigation. The police would also gain from
clarification of their powers. It is undesirable that the police, uncertain whether
their investigatory activities are strictly legal, resort to bluff or uninformed and
questionable 'consent' to achieve a desired result.

In the last few years, most Australian jurisdictions have met the challenge, at
least in part. Recent legislation has made substantial changes in the right direction, although more needs to be done. The New South Wales Law Reform
Commission found in 1990 that:

> there is a pressing need for the development of a comprehensive set of rules gov-
> erning the conduct of criminal investigations, with a basic legislative framework
> supplemented by detailed Codes of Practice. The rules must be of practical utility,
> recognising the operational context in which they are to be used. This means that
> the rules must be expressed in language and concepts which enable both ease of
> understanding and certainty in their application. These rules would make it pos-
> sible for the first time for ordinary citizens to have a clear idea of their position
> when they become involved in a police investigation, and for the police to have
> clear guidelines on the treatment of suspects in custody.[154]

As we have noted, New South Wales has enacted legislation in an attempt to
deal with these issues, and most Australian jurisdictions are doing the same.
Nevertheless, we remain unconvinced that there should be any substantial increase
in general investigatory powers. Recent expansion of police stop and search
powers in some jurisdictions, for example, appears to be an overreaction to isolated
incidents. On the other hand, advances in forensic science can justify non-intrusive
searches in limited circumstances, and intrusive searches in even more limited circumstances. As some criminal activities become more complex and inter-jurisdictional, additional powers in specific areas such as telephonic interception must be
provided, subject to careful safeguards. That is the key. Most reports in this area have
recommended a limited increase in certain police powers combined with clarification of the law and stiffening of the rights and protections available to suspects.

Of course, legal constraints on investigation must not be the only focus. The
criminal justice system must be ever vigilant in respect of police who are prepared
to engage in corrupt practices to achieve convictions. As one hole in the system
of criminal justice is plugged, others emerge. We have seen how the incidence of
'verbals' and use of prison informers has declined. But there is reason to suspect a
greater incidence of 'loading up', which involves falsely alleging the finding of
incriminating evidence in the possession of suspects. The greater use of DNA evidence, for example, carries with it the risk that such evidence may be fabricated
or tampered with in order to connect a suspect to a crime scene.

We accept that attempts to influence police behaviour and modes of investigation require more than an examination of the divergences between policing practice and legal ideology. There must be systematic study of the structural, organisational and cultural determinants of that practice. Most police work is carried out in environments largely free from public scrutiny, within which officers have considerable discretion, both legally and practically. It is this idea of discretion that we examine more carefully in following chapters. Nevertheless, the legal ideology relating to criminal investigation provides at least a touchstone against which to measure what the police actually do. We must make every attempt to get that touchstone right.

## Notes

1   For works in this area, see R. Hogg and D. Brown, *Rethinking Law and Order*, Pluto Press, Sydney, 1998; D. Chappell and P. Wilson, *Australian Policing: Contemporary Issues*, Butterworths, Sydney, 1989; I. Freckelton and H. Selby (eds), *Police in our Society*, Butterworths, Sydney, 1988; P. Moir and H. Eijkman (eds), *Policing Australia: Old Issues, New Perspectives*, Macmillan, Sydney, 1992.

2   For a comprehensive discussion of the legal position in the area of criminal investigation, see A. Leaver, 1997, *Investigating Crime: A Guide to the Powers of Agencies Involved in the Investigation of Crime*, Law Book Co., Sydney, 1997.

3   Mason and Brennan JJ in *Williams* (1986) 161 CLR 278 at 279.

4   *McNabb v US*, 318 US 332 at 347 (1943).

5   Enacted in 1966, this Convention was ratified by Australia in 1980.

6   *Report*, chaired by Sir Cyril Phillips, HMSO Cmnd 8092, London, 1981, para. 2.20.

7   In Queensland in 1993, for example, there were more than 90 pieces of legislation that conferred various powers on police: Queensland Criminal Justice Commission, *Report on a Review of Police Powers in Queensland*, Brisbane, 1993, Vol. 1, p. 92. These have now been significantly rationalised in the *Police Powers and Responsibilities Act* 2000 (Qld).

8   A striking exception is in relation to interceptions made under the *Telecommunications (Interception) Act* 1979 (Cth). The Act requires comprehensive information to be compiled and annual reports prepared.

9   Of course, they may search a person or enter premises if consent is given. Such consent may be implied: *Halliday v Neville* (1984) 155 CLR 1.

10  Briefly, the police must reasonably believe that a serious offence has been committed, that the article in question relates to the crime, and that the person in possession is implicated in the crime. See *Ghani v Jones* [1970] 1 QB 693; *GH Photography Pty Ltd v McGarrigle* [1974] 2 NSWLR 635.

11  *Kennedy v Pagura* [1977] 2 NSWLR 810. Compare the Victorian position: s. 459A *Crimes Act* 1958.

12  See *Lippl v Haines* (1989) 18 NSWLR 620.

13  See, for example, D. Meagher, 'Black and white is always grey: the power of the police to conduct a strip search in Victoria', *Criminal Law Journal*, 26, 2002, p. 43.

14  See, for example, s. 68 *Summary Offences Act* 1953 (SA).

15  See, for example, s. 357E *Crimes Act* 1900 (NSW).

16  See, for example, s. 353A *Crimes Act* 1900 (NSW).

17   See ss. 464R–464W *Crimes Act* 1958 (Vic); s. 349ZX *Crimes Act* 1900 (ACT).

18   See, for example, *Telecommunications (Interception) Act* 1979 (Cth); *Listening Devices Act* 1969 (NSW); *Listening Devices Act* 1969 (Vic).

19   Queensland Criminal Justice Commission, Vol. 1, 1992, Appendix 3, Tables 1–6.

20   *Police Powers and Responsibilities Act* 1997 (Qld) (see now the *Police Powers and Responsibilities Act* 2000 (Qld)).

21   *Police Powers and Responsibilities Act* 2000 (Qld), ss. 285–7.

22   See, for example, *Crimes Act* 1958 (Vic), ss. 464R–464ZL; *Criminal Law (Forensic Procedures) Act* 1998 (SA); *Criminal Investigation (Identifying People) Act* 2002 (WA).

23   An authorised justice can be a magistrate or a justice of the peace employed in Local Courts Administration in the Attorney-General's Department (s. 3).

24   A thing is 'connected with' a particular offence if it is a thing with respect to which the offence has been committed, will afford evidence of the offence, or was used in committing the offence (s. 4).

25   *Arno v Forsyth* (1986) 9 FCR 576.

26   Section 7(1)(b)(ii) *Search Warrants Act* 1985 (NSW).

27   See, for example, *Arno* v *Forsyth* (1986) 9 FCR 576.

28   *George v Rockett* (1990) 93 ALR 483 at 487.

29   Inquiry into the Death of David John Gundy (Commissioner J. H. Wootton), Report, Canberra, AGPS, 1991 (referred to hereafter as the Gundy Report).

30   As it happened, Porter had left Sydney 36 hours before the raids.

31   Gundy Report, p. 46.

32   Gundy Report, p. 53.

33   Gundy Report, p. 11.

34   Gundy Report, p. 11.

35   *George* v *Rockett* (1990) 93 ALR 483 (quoting with approval Burchett J in *Parker v Churchill* (1985) 9 FCR 316 at 322).

36   Gundy Report, p. 61.

37   Gundy Report, p. 4.

38   Gundy Report, p. 17.

39   Gundy Report, pp. 4–5.

40   *Feather v Rogers* (1909) 9 SR (NSW) 192.

41   It may involve the physical seizure of the arrested person but may also be constituted by merely touching the arrested person or advising him or her of the fact of arrest. It must be made clear to the arrested person that he or she is no longer a free person. Thus, unless it is not reasonably practicable, the arrested person must be informed that he or she is under compulsion and the reasons for the arrest (see *Christie v Leachinsky* [1947] AC 573). Technically, for an arrest by mere words to be legally valid, the person sought to be arrested must submit to the arrest.

42   An arrest may be made under warrant, both under common law and statutory provisions in all jurisdictions. Similar requirements apply as for search warrants. However, given the extensive powers of arrest without warrant, it is relatively uncommon for the police to seek an arrest warrant.

43   See *George v Rockett* (1990) 93 ALR 483 at 490–1.

44   Section 75 *Summary Offences Act* 1953 (SA).

45 See, for example, s. 3W *Crimes Act* 1914 (Cth).

46 See, for example, s. 459 *Crimes Act* 1958 (Vic). Tasmania grants this power in respect of certain listed indictable offences (s. 27 *Criminal Code* 1924).

47 For example, s. 463A *Crimes Act* 1958 (Vic) allows those people in command of aircraft to arrest, without warrant, people reasonably suspected of offences in relation to an aircraft.

48 See, for example, s. 357E *Crimes Act* 1900 (NSW).

49 *Williams* (1986) 161 CLR 278.

50 For example, minor traffic offences, parking and littering offences and, in South Australia, possession or cultivation for private use of small amounts of cannabis: s. 45a *Controlled Substances Act* 1984 (SA).

51 See D. McDonald, Research Paper No. 13, *National Police Custody Survey, August 1988: National Report*, Canberra, 1989.

52 Section 3W *Crimes Act* 1914 (Cth).

53 *Lake v Dobson*, NSWCCA, unreported, 19.12.1980 per Samuels JA.

54 See ALRC, *Criminal Investigation*, para. 40.

55 See, for example, *Wright v Court* (1825) 4 B&C 596 at 598: 107 ER 1182.

56 The evidence must be sufficient to establish a belief that there is 'reasonable and probable cause' that the person committed the offence. See *Williams* (1986) 161 CLR 278 at 300.

57 See *Ainsworth* (1991) 57 A Crim R 174 at 181.

58 See discussion of bail in chapter 4.

59 (1933) 33 SR (NSW) 303.

60 (1935) 35 SR (NSW) 182 at 189.

61 *Beckwith v Philby* (1827) 6 B&C 635, 108 ER 585; *Nolan v Clifford* (1904) 1 CLR 429; *Christie v Leachinsky* [1947] AC 573.

62 See *Williams* (1986) 161 CLR 278.

63 (1986) 161 CLR 278.

64 (1986) 161 CLR 278 at 295.

65 At 299.

66 At 312.

67 The other member of the High Court, Gibbs CJ, took a rather different view of the law, considering the police are allowed some scope to investigate before bringing the arrested person before a justice.

68 (1990) 20 NSWLR 650.

69 New South Wales Law Reform Commission, Report No. 66, *Police Powers of Detention and Investigation after Arrest*, December 1990, paras 1.54–1.55 (hereafter NSWLRC).

70 Article 9(5).

71 See chapter 5.

72 See chapter 6.

73 See *Miller* (1980) 25 SASR 170 at 184; *Conley* (1982) 30 SASR 226 at 239; *O'Donoghue* (1988) 34 A Crim R 397 (NSWCCA). But cf. *Van der Meer* (1988) 35 A Crim R 232, 239–40 per Mason CJ.

74 NSWLRC, para. 4. 10.

75 They would constitute maximum periods of custodial investigation. Of course, it may well be appropriate to limit this investigation even further by some additional flexible test (as recommended by the NSWLRC and ultimately adopted in NSW: s. 356D *Crimes Act*).

76    Section 78(6) *Summary Offences Act* 1953 (SA). See also ss. 23C, 23D *Crimes Act* 1914 (Cth).

77    *Police Powers and Responsibilities Act* 2000 (Qld), s. 234.

78    See, for example, s. 81(2) *Summary Offences Act* 1953 (SA); s. 464L *Crimes Act* 1958 (Vic).

79    Arrest of a person for one (usually minor) offence when the real intention is to investigate another offence.

80    It is doubtful, for example, whether the recent Commonwealth legislation has achieved this goal. All the provisions apply to a person 'under arrest', defined in s. 23B(2). The definition is arguably too narrow and subjective. In contrast, the Victorian legislation provides a more satisfactory objective test of whether a suspect is in custody (s. 464(1)(c) *Crimes Act* 1958). Similarly, the NSW legislation in this regard appears satisfactory: s. 355 *Crimes Act* 1900.

81    Section 23Q *Crimes Act* 1914 (Cth).

82    Royal Commission into Aboriginal Deaths in Custody (Commissioner Muirhead), *Interim Report*, Canberra, AGPS, 1988, para. 6.4.

83    As recommended by the NSWLRC, para. 4.28.

84    NSWLRC, para. 3.58.

85    Section 356V *Crimes Act* 1900 (NSW).

86    ALRC, *Criminal Investigation*, para. 99.

87    See ALRC, Report No. 57, *Multiculturalism and the Law*, AGPS, 1992, ch. 10.

88    See, for example, ss. 23G, 23L *Crimes Act* 1914 (Cth).

89    Unless the police have 'reasonable cause to suspect that communication between the person in custody and that particular person would result in an accomplice taking steps to avoid apprehension or would prompt the destruction of fabrication of evidence': s. 79a(2) *Summary Offences Act* 1953.

90    Section 79a(3) *Summary Offences Act* 1953 (SA).

91    See s. 13 *Children (Criminal Proceedings) Act* 1987 (NSW), and chapter 10.

92    Contrast the position in a trial: see chapter 5.

93    Section 23G.

94    It would not be satisfactory to follow the English model where it seems that the 'legal advisers' are often ex-police clerks, legally unqualified, retained by legal firms because of their contacts, experience and relative inexpensiveness. D. Dixon, K. Bottomley, C. Coleman, M. Gill and D. Wall, 'Safeguarding the Rights of Suspects in Police Custody', *Policing and Society*, 1, 1990, p. 124; D. Dixon, 'Politics, Research and Symbolism in Criminal Justice: The Right of Silence and the Police and Criminal Evidence Act', *Anglo-American Law Review*, 1991, p. 43; D. Dixon, *Law in Policing: Legal Regulation of Police Practices*, Oxford University Press, London, 1997.

95    N. Stevenson, 'Criminal cases in the NSW District Court: a pilot study' in J. Basten et al. (eds), *The Criminal Injustice System*, Legal Services Bulletin, Sydney, 1982, pp. 140–1.

96    *Thompson* [1893] 2 QB 12 at 18.

97    Q. Dempster, *Honest Cops*, ABC Books, Sydney, 1992, pp. 116–20.

98    Roger Rogerson, in 'Police Story', *Four Corners*, ABC television program, September 1991.

99    Legislative Council Parliamentary Debates, *Hansard*, 3 May 1988, p. 1010.

100   (1992) 176 CLR 177.

101   Per Mason CJ at 183.

102   Per Toohey J at 219.

103   Per Toohey J at 216–17.

104 'Serious offence' is defined to mean 'an indictable offence of such a nature that, if a person of or over the age of 17 years is charged with it, the indictable offence cannot be dealt with summarily without the consent of the accused person and, in the case of a person under the age of 17 years, includes any indictable offence for which the person has been detained'.

105 Section 8 *Criminal Law (Detention and Interrogation) Act* 1995 (Tas). In the same year, similar legislation was enacted in New South Wales: s. 424A *Crimes Act* 1900 and South Australia: ss. 74C–G *Summary Offences Act* 1953.

106 *Kelly v The Queen* [2004] HCA 12.

107 Gleeson CJ, Hayne and Heydon JJ at [49], [53].

108 Section 85A *Evidence Act* 2001 (Tas).

109 (1986) 161 CLR 278 at 296.

110 *Pollard* (1992) 176 CLR 177 per McHugh J at 230.

111 S. J. Odgers, 'Police Interrogation and the Right to Silence' *Australian Law Journal*, 59, 1985, p. 78 at 89. To be effective, the ally should be trusted and well-informed. Moreover, this ally should be present at a fairly early stage—the introduction of an ally once a commitment has been made to a given course of action has a very limited effect.

112 *Pollard* (1992) 176 CLR 177 per McHugh J at 235.

113 For American studies see S. Wald et al., 'Project, Interrogations in New Haven: The Impact of Miranda', *Yale Law Journal*, 76, 1967, p. 1573. All of the English studies of the assertion of rights by suspects after the *PACE Act* reforms in the 1980s indicate that only a small proportion of people in custody actually ask to see a lawyer, even when informed that there is a free-of-charge duty solicitor available.

114 See, for example, J. K. Bowen, 'Suspect's Rights and Police Duties', *Law Institute Journal*, 1986, pp. 1344, 1347.

115 See, for example, s. 45, ss. 59–61 *Road Safety Act* 1986 (Vic); s. 195 *Customs Act* 1901 (Cth); s. 42 *Migration Act* 1958 (Cth).

116 *Petty and Maiden* (1991) 65 ALJR 625.

117 *Sorby v The Commonwealth* (1983) 57 ALJR 248 at 253 per Gibbs CJ.

118 ALRC, *Criminal Investigation*, para. 150.

119 As above.

120 In the small New South Wales study noted above it was found that confessional evidence was tendered by police in over 96% of cases: Stevenson, 1982, pp. 107–8, 140–1. In a survey carried out by the British Royal Commission on Criminal Procedure in 1981 a similar figure was obtained: Royal Commission on Criminal Procedure, p. 84. In the United States, studies have demonstrated that the vast majority of suspects will not take advantage of the right: Ayling, pp. 1195–7. Most of those who did refuse to speak were people with prior criminal convictions or members of the middle class advised by lawyers: see Wald et al., 1967, pp. 1577, 1644, and T. Griffiths and A. Ayres, 'A Postscript to the Miranda Project: Interrogation of Draft Protesters', *Yale Law Journal*, 77, 1967, pp. 300, 312, 318.

121 One American study noted that detectives commonly defused the caution by implying that the suspect had better not exercise his or her right, or by delivering the caution in a formalised, bureaucratic tone to indicate that it was simply a routine, meaningless legalism (Ayling, p. 1552).

122 Ayling, p. 1172.

123 *Ireland* (1970) 126 CLR 321 at 331.

124 *Petty and Maiden* (1991) 65 ALJR 625. This view has been given legislative endorsement in s. 89 *Evidence Act* 1995 (Cth and NSW).

125 *Petty v The Queen* (1991) 173 CLR 95 at 99.

126 See *Reeves* (1992) 29 NSWLR 109, where it was held that police evidence that they had 'put the prosecution's version of the facts to the accused and gave him this opportunity to answer them and to give his own account of the events in question' is admissible 'in order to meet (at least in part) ... anticipated criticism' that the police failed to do this.

127 *Woon* (1964) 109 CLR 529 at 537.

128 *Woon* (1964) 109 CLR 529 per Kitto J at 537, Taylor J at 539.

129 Justice Jackson of the US Supreme Court made the point in 1949: 'any lawyer worth his salt will tell the suspect in no uncertain terms to make no statement to police under any circumstances': *Watts v Indiana* 338 US 49, 59.

130 D. Dixon, 'Common Sense, Legal Advice and the Right of Silence', *Public Law*, 1991, p. 240.

131 D. Dixon, 'Politics, Research and Symbolism in Criminal Justice: The Right of Silence and the Police and Criminal Evidence Act', *Anglo-American Law Review*, 1991, p. 38.

132 See D. Brown, *PACE Ten Years On: A Review of the Research*, Home Office, London, 1997, pp. 171–84.

133 D. Dixon, K. Bottomley, C. Coleman, M. Gill and D. Wall, 'Safeguarding the Rights of Suspects in Police Custody', *Policing and Society*, 1, 1990, p. 124.

134 See *Crimes (Criminal Trials) Act* 1993 (Vic).

135 Odgers, p. 93.

136 *Chandler* [1976] 1 WLR 585. See also *Parkes* [1976] 1 WLR 1251 (PC); *Horne* [1990] Crim LR 188 (CA).

137 *Woon* (1964) 109 CLR 529; *Bruce* (1986) 23 A Crim R 123 at 135–6; *Petty* (1987) 61 ALJR 603 at 604.

138 *Doyle v Ohio* 426 US 610 at 618 (1976).

139 *Jenkins v Anderson* 447 US 230 (1980).

140 (1996) 22 EHRR 29.

141 (2001) 31 EHRR 1.

142 See M. Chaaya, 'The Right to Silence Reignited: Vulnerable Suspects, Police Questioning and Law and Order in New South Wales', *Criminal Law Journal*, 22, 1998 p. 82 at 89.

143 (1981) 145 CLR 395 at 410, 436.

144 See further discussion in chapter 6.

145 See, for example, L. Re, 'Eyewitness Identification: Why so many Mistakes?', *Australian Law Journal*, 58, 1984, p. 509.

146 ALRC, *Evidence*, para. 185.

147 See ALRC, *Criminal Investigation*, paras 121–4.

148 See ss. 3ZM–3ZQ *Crimes Act* 1914 (Cth).

149 *Pollitt* (1992) 174 CLR 558 per Deane J at 586.

150 Per McHugh J at 615.

151 ICAC, *Report on Investigation into the Use of Informers*, Vol. 1, January, 1993, p. 55.

152 ICAC, pp. 59–60.

153 M. D. Kirby, 'Controls over Investigation of Offences and Pre-Trial Treatment of Suspects', *Australian Law Journal*, 53, 1979, p. 632.

154 NSWLRC, para. 1.66.

# The New
# Investigators

*3*

## Introduction

Whether it be the spectre of organised crime,[1] the threat of tax evasion and avoidance,[2] the drug menace,[3] the epidemic of corruption,[4] or the dangers of international terrorism, crime problems of recent decades in Australia have often been portrayed as beyond the competence of conventional criminal justice investigative agencies. Police investigation techniques are criticised for not keeping pace with the sophistication of criminal enterprise. Intelligence gathering, in particular, is accused of failing to support successful prosecutions. And the traditional methods of prosecution have faced accusations of ineptitude and parsimony.

Current crime-control agendas in Australia have been heavily influenced by an official discourse that emphasises the uniqueness of the crime threat and the failure of traditional criminal justice responses to it. For example, reams of reports from state and federal Royal Commissions[5] have portrayed practices of illicit drug commerce and abuse in such common and unequivocal terms that policing priorities would remain tied to the 'war on drugs' for years to come. Along with their apparent failure until very recently[6] to stem the tide of drug trafficking (despite a significant increase in resources for the task), police forces in all jurisdictions have been implicated in the problem.[7] Even their reluctant flirtations with joint task forces have done little more than expose the limitations of jurisdictional rivalry. These tensions, particularly within policing, are not new. They have existed at many levels within all individual Australian police organisations. Jurisdictional barriers have tended to exaggerate the problems of a free information flow between police services. And with the pressure for results against those offences (such as drug trafficking), which do not stop at state borders, traditional policing has not been able to bury the suspicions of the past in favour of a less parochial policing perspective. The advent of DNA/forensic police investigative technologies and the effort to operate a national database is a good example of this problem. In addition, the lack of cooperation and responsiveness between the police and some of the new investigative agencies we discuss later in this chapter have provided the impetus for transforming these agencies and their governance.

Faced with what independent inquiries identified as 'Mr Bigs' and the baffling complexity of criminal enterprise in all its more organised forms, governments conceded the failure of the criminal justice system to go beyond dealing with street crime, and joined in the rush for new institutions. The political answer to public sensitivity over 'new crime threats' has centred around bureaucracy and technology. Along with 'novel' institutional responses to crime such as the Independent Commission Against Corruption (ICAC in New South Wales), the Crime and Misconduct Commission (CJC in Queensland),[8] the Australian Crime Commission (ACC) (formerly the National Crime Authority (NCA)), the Corruption and Crime Commission (CCC in Western Australia) and the Australian Securities and Investments Commission (ASIC), Australia has witnessed new methods of investigation, which Hogg refers to as 'pro-active policing and the "information economy" '.[9] This drive for better crime intelligence is declared as an essential element in the 'home security' response to international terrorism. It was a crucial justification for the recent consolidation of several investigative and intelligence agencies at a federal level, to form the ACC.

This emphasis on specialist responses to meet particular crime threats works from the assumption that traditional investigatory and prosecutorial methods have failed. Any responsibility for this failure seems of little significance in the light of new initiatives and statements of renewed crime-control intentions. Cohen[10] refers to this trend as a *failure model* of criminal justice; where administrators and policy makers accept failure and pursue its consequences; where a new bureaucratic alternative is justified not so much in terms of its own potential but rather as a necessary response to past failure. More recently, this failure model has been applied to the new investigative agencies themselves. The NCA was transformed, and the ASIC has faced sharp criticism in its role as a corporate watchdog, forcing changes in its priorities and practices.[11]

Federal and State governments of different political persuasions have agreed to suspend significant individual liberties and hand over constitutional responsibilities in creating these novel crime-fighting bodies.[12] However, many of these attempts to address particular crime threats have been as conspicuous in their failure as the institutions that they were to augment or, in part, replace.[13] The botched prosecutions of significant public figures have brought calls for not only a reconsideration of agencies' powers, but their very existence.

This chapter recalls an instance of how the new crime investigation and prosecution agenda was set and certain responses orchestrated. Then, through an examination of selected new investigation and prosecution agencies developed to address this and similarly significant crime concerns, the influence over traditional features of the criminal justice process is explored. In particular, issues such as information gathering, investigation and interrogation powers, quasi-judicial functions, accountability, and integration are discussed.

In addition, the analysis of these agencies will highlight their regulatory function. While perhaps not being directly connected with criminal justice, regulation is an interesting framework within which criminal sanctions and civil remedies may be integrated.[14] Further, the imperative for regulation over prosecution reveals the limitations of criminal justice processes and sanctions in certain situations that are the concern of these agencies. Alternative enforcement strategies are apparent in the armoury of the new investigators, in recognition of the novelty of the challenges facing them, the wider expectations of the community, and the need to augment the criminal sanction with concepts such as compliance and best practice.

We focus on the ACC (formerly the NCA) and the ASIC because of their joint federal and State responsibilities, and their integration of conventional investigation/prosecution methods with more modern regulatory strategies. The ICAC has also been selected because it is bureaucratically the largest, and perhaps most intrusive State response to recent concerns about public corruption. We have not focused on other State and Territory agencies, either because they are experiencing a significant period of restructuring and their eventual mandate and operations are uncertain, or they do not present more unique issues, which our selected examples throw up. Also, some other new State institutional responses to corruption, organised crime and fraud regulation are integrated within conventional policing structures or have more limited and determined mandates.

With the ICAC, we have concentrated on its extraordinary powers of public disclosure, and their place within the organisation's investigation strategy. Concerns for accountability are associated with this issue. Regarding the ACC, we have explored measures of effectiveness, and compared these with traditional policing aspirations. In addition, the transition from the NCA to the ACC plots the manner in which concerns over the interface between the new and the conventional investigative institutions can produce pressures for changes in governance structures and priority settings. The ASIC is examined in the light of its necessary 'fit' with the more general prosecutorial authorities and its interaction with these. Obviously conflicts arise where two organisations share similar responsibilities but adopt differing priorities. Further, the interconnection between civil and criminal regulation is novel in the desire for efficient corporate regulation. Each of the agencies chosen has now been operating long enough to merit critical review against the original impetus provided by the failure model.

The following discussion is not intended as a complete summary of these 'new investigators'. Nor is it a full socio-political analysis of the difficulties that have plagued the early years of these new agencies. In keeping with the introductory intentions of this book, some issues are extracted to show the impact that new crime-control strategies can have on the wider operation of the criminal justice process in Australia.

# New methods, new agenda

In the early 1980s a fundamental problem facing the Royal Commission[15] into the Activities of the Federated Ship Painters and Dockers Union in its investigation of criminal enterprises connected with the Victorian branch of the Union was:

> the complete silence of those involved and affected. Apart from using its royal commission powers the Commission turned its attention to making optimal use of a diverse range of other records that were publicly available and might aid communication ... the really important feature of the Commission's approach to its task however rested on the exploitation of the potential of computer technology to store, collate and analyse masses of data collected from these diverse sources.[16]

By the use of an 'open-ended' approach to the investigation process, as well as the computer-based linkage analysis of criminal associations, profiling and matching, made possible through computer technology, the Costigan Commission was able to extend its focus from the misconduct of a few trade union officials, to complex schemes of tax avoidance and evasion, money laundering, corruption, and drug trafficking of significant proportions. The consequent picture of organised crime in Australia that Costigan was able to portray was used to justify calls for a more proactive style of crime investigation and policing.[17] Costigan was critical of traditional policing methods, which had a limited preventative dimension, and as such were too reliant on passive and non-interventionist information gathering and analysis. Costigan argued that an appropriately empowered crime commission should target matters and people involved in those concealed and consensual crimes, rather than await the complaints of individual victims such as those that initiate more conventional justice intervention. Because of the nature and spread of the crimes concerned, the role of the victim informant would be far less evident or effective, and therefore reactive police investigations may not even get off the ground. Why should the police await the next crime if patterns of criminality could be identified, followed and hopefully intercepted?

It is interesting to observe how a new approach to crime investigation, such as that adopted by the Costigan Commission, produced new representations of the crime threat. These in turn fuelled the push towards new investigation agencies and procedures, with wider mandates and more intrusive powers than those granted to traditional policing and prosecution agencies. Organised crime, corruption, and drug trafficking were now placed on a higher level of the crime agenda. Such crime problems were regarded as requiring investigation technologies, prosecution expertise, and special court presumptions and penalties, which were unavailable or thought unnecessary for the more commonplace reactive policing styles.

Frank Costigan emphasised processes as much as personalities when he identified what he saw as the appropriate policing focus against organised crime:

> The first thing to remember about organised crime is that the organisation of crime is directed towards the accumulation of money, and with it power … Two conclusions flow from this fact. The first is that the most successful method of identifying and ultimately convicting major organised criminals is to follow the money trail. The second is that once you have identified and convicted them, you take away their money …[18]

In following the money trail, crime investigators seek to identify the material products of criminal enterprise. This is beyond the traditional interests of police, who accumulate just enough evidence to confirm the individual criminal liability of suspects. More important to Costigan, however, was the potential to identify the overlap between legitimate finance and criminal enterprise. For this purpose, crime investigation may go well beyond the evidentiary needs of a successful courtroom prosecution, and information otherwise accumulated for separate legal and commercial purposes might be obtained. Only this information may not be constrained by the rules of evidence because as much as it may be used as crime intelligence and a tool for investigation, it rarely appears as a legal proof. By avoiding the connotation of justifiable evidence, both its source and use may not be required to be revealed in the courtroom.

To some extent the 'new' institutional and procedural responses to contemporary crime problems became part of a self-fulfilling prophecy for crime control. The crime threat, said to be behind these new agencies, was the motivation for a re-ordering of crime-control priorities. The new crime-control agenda that emerged adopted the language and perspective on crime and control promoted by these new agencies. Their common development seemed mutually supportive to a point where one was soon seen as a justification for the other. Organised crime had to be addressed by a crime commission, and this meant a redirection of control resources. The crime commission becomes the essential feature of the new control agenda, and that agenda demands the development of the commission.

# Divestment of criminal justice

One of the most significant recent developments in Australian criminal justice is the way in which traditional agencies of policing, prosecution, and punishment are retreating from, or are having removed from them, traditional functions in the modern crime-control agenda.[19] The explosion of private security services now largely dominates the protection of corporate private property. Insurance is now seen as the appropriate way of dealing with a wide range of harm to property. Diversion, mediation and compensation have become important alternatives to punishment. However, it would be wrong to assume that this diversification of criminal justice means either a greater involvement of community interests, or a devolution of state power. In fact, with the advent of new investigative agencies, the law enforcement and control dimensions of government have taken on more intrusive powers than traditional criminal justice conventions would allow.

Certain new investigation and prosecution agencies, with enhanced powers and unfettered by protections of due process, operate in ways that do not recognise the traditional sequences of criminal justice. Investigations may produce evidence that is for purposes other than to support an eventual prosecution. Hearings may proceed as little more than fact-finding processes. Penalty may take the form of public disclosure, adverse media comment and community approbation without judicial determination or decisions on guilt. How these new agencies have developed the function and form of criminal justice merits particular examination.

Traditionally, criminal justice in Australia has been conceived as a responsibility of each State or Territory.[20] Except where the Commonwealth has assumed the task of policing those crimes 'imported' into Australia, States and Territories operate their own criminal jurisdiction, and cross-border crime is addressed through mutual assistance or extradition. The wisdom of this has been challenged by those crime threats whose structure does not respect the artificial barriers of jurisdictions. Drug trafficking, money laundering, corporate fraud, and tax evasion have demonstrated the need for policing in particular to be cooperative between jurisdictions. However, these developments have not been without their casualties. Federal lawmakers have grabbed power for drug law enforcement through their customs powers. Joint police task forces have been constructed with strict operational limits, determined through compromise between competing policing styles, and economic expedience. And bodies such as the NCA faced direct challenges over mandates and jurisdiction from State-based investigative initiatives such as the New South Wales Crimes Commission (previously the State Drug Crime Commission).[21] Even so, the single jurisdictional approach to law enforcement in Australia is shifting along with the new crime-control agenda. Commonwealth agencies, whether they be conventional policing institutions such as the AFP or the new investigative agencies such as the ACC, are claiming pre-eminence over criminal justice as a crucial tool for national security. Centralised intelligence gathering is a key to this, as is the language and operational imperative that ties together the new powers given to secret services such as ASIO, and the criminal justice intelligence agencies such as the ACC.[22]

With these preliminary thoughts in mind, we turn to the first of three investigatory agencies.

# Australian Crime Commission (ACC) (formerly National Crime Authority (NCA))[23]

The NCA was established to take a unique position in Australian law enforcement. Given special investigative powers and multi-jurisdictional focus, its investigatory concern was with organised crime as identified in the *National Crime Authority Act* 1982 (Cth). The functions of the NCA were limited to matters relating to 'relevant criminal activity'. Section 4 of the Act established that this may be a relationship of implication or allegation. A 'relevant offence' must be fairly serious, involve two or more offenders and substantial planning and organisation, utilise sophisticated methods, and comprise or be associated with other offences of a serious kind. These other offences were the traditional concerns of organised crime, such as theft, fraud, tax evasion, drug dealing, vice, extortion, corruption, forgery, company offences and bankruptcy.

The reactive nature of conventional policing, the transjurisdictional operations of organised crime, the need for specialist information technology and expertise, and the requirement for more compulsory investigatory powers, were identified as the motivators for a NCA-type response to community and political concern about organised crime.[24] Having its origins in the Costigan Commission, and taking over responsibility for much of its data base, the NCA had a significant crime intelligence function. Initially, the NCA adopted the Costigan approach to investigation, which involved a heavy reliance on information technology and the production of intelligence data. Prior to its demise, the NCA was criticised for its investigation methods and its inability to translate the product of its investigations into successful prosecutions.[25]

Its governing legislation envisaged that the NCA would work in cooperation with State and federal police forces and other crime intelligence agencies such as the Australian Bureau of Crime Intelligence (ABCI).[26] This cooperative intention was not always realised, and the NCA was criticised in other law enforcement circles for a somewhat elitist and dismissive approach to the involvement of other police in the investigation of organised crime.[27]

## Functions and powers

It is important to examine in some detail the powers of the NCA even following its demise. This is because its successor agency, the Australian Crime Commission (ACC), claims all the coercive powers previously exercised by the NCA.[28]

Section 11 of the *National Crime Authority Act* 1982 drew a distinction between 'special' and 'general' functions for the NCA. Special functions included investigating matters referred to it by Commonwealth or State Ministers regarding particular crime occurrences. General functions included:

- collecting, analysing and disseminating relevant crime intelligence
- investigating appropriate criminal activities
- arranging for task forces for the purposes of investigation
- coordinating investigations by task forces.[29]

One commentator summarised the primary functions of the NCA as 'investigating relevant criminal activity and obtaining and disseminating relevant criminal intelligence'.[30] This sounds like the concerns of a conventional police agency. The difference lay in the more direct line of influence between the NCA and governments. Also, the *National Crime Authority Act*, while nominating a wide range of crime concerns, was particularly interested in 'relevant offences', which involve 'substantial planning and organisation' and 'the use of sophisticated methods and techniques'.[31]

The investigatory powers of the NCA were considerable.[32] While being largely based on conventional police powers such as search, seizure and interception, the NCA's investigation powers were exercised in a cross-jurisdictional environment, and beyond the normal protections against self-incrimination. In addition, its 'quasi-judicial' powers to hold hearings were well beyond the powers available to the State, Territory and federal police in Australia.

The NCA was empowered by the Act to conduct the following activities:

- carrying out hearings at which parties may be compelled to appear, to produce evidence, and to answer questions
- assembling of other admissible evidence, and its transfer to other prosecution agencies (section 12(1))
- execution of search warrants and telephone warrants, and seizure of evidence
- conduct of telecommunications interception and utilisation of listening devices
- monitoring of financial institutions' accounts
- accessing otherwise confidential government information such as taxation files
- initiation of proceedings for the confiscation of assets
- issuing indemnities and the protection of witnesses
- charging persons for breaches of its secrecy provisions.

Given the NCA's nature and function, the accountability framework that governed the exercise of its powers was considerably more complex and enunciated than that which affects conventional police services. This has been transferred to and developed for the ACC, with even greater responsibility for that agency vested in the oversight of its board. The NCA was responsible to the Commonwealth Attorney-General, and to an Inter-Governmental Committee whereby relevant State and Territory Ministers had input into the supervision and monitoring of the Authority. In matters of broad policy, the Authority was accountable to the Parliamentary Joint Committee (PJC), which is constituted by members of the Senate and the House of Representatives in the Commonwealth

Parliament. The degree to which the NCA in fact accepted any responsibility to report on operational matters to the Parliamentary Committee caused considerable tension between the Committee and past Commissioners of the NCA.[33] However, as a result of an inquiry into the NCA's investigation and prosecution of John Elliott,[34] the PJC refuted Elliott's attacks on the NCA and endorsed its practices and continued relevance.

In a legislative sense the workings of the NCA could have been reviewed under the *National Crime Authority Act* 1982 (Cth), as well as the *Administrative Decisions (Judicial Review) Act* 1977 (Cth). These review mechanisms did not prohibit a person with standing seeking the conventional common law remedies through judicial review.

As with the other agencies discussed in this chapter, the NCA relied in much of its work on low public visibility and high levels of individual discretion. This made the task of requiring public accountability a difficult one. Further, the claim for operational integrity and investigative anonymity bred a reluctance to share much information relating to the progress of investigations. The 'trust us' approach when it came to the investigation area, and the specialist knowledge it was said to produce, was both prevalent and unhelpful when it came to the public governance of these bodies.

## Effectiveness of the NCA

If one were to assess, as the PJC did, the effectiveness of the NCA simply in terms of its statutory functions against organised crime, several significant obstacles arise. First, there is the issue of measurement itself. As the PJC has observed:

> The success of the Authority cannot merely be measured by successful prosecutions resulting from its investigations. There was also an expectation that the establishment of the Authority would have a deterrent effect: that by its success in its investigations and, possibly, by its very existence, it would increase the fear of detection and apprehension in the minds of those who might be tempted to enter the field of organised criminal activity.[35]

Realistic as these observations are, they are somewhat at odds with the attempts by the NCA, in its evidence to a routine PJC inquiry in 1989, to quantify its successes solely in terms of people charged, individuals prosecuted, convictions obtained, and taxation and proceeds of crime recovered.

Second, comparisons of the efficiency of the NCA in relation to other investigation or prosecution agencies were also problematic. Police forces, for example, are responsible for a plethora of law enforcement duties, and to measure them against NCA operations would require some degree of isolating 'organised crime' functions in respect of other policing agencies. Attempts at such isolation have not met with success. Also, if the joint investigations between the police and the NCA were 'joint' in any true sense, then success in law enforcement of organised crime would be a joint product.

One of the most common criticisms of the NCA, from other law enforcement bodies and those who otherwise supported tough action against organised crime, was its inability to target high-level criminals—the 'Mr Bigs' of organised crime. The NCA eventually chose to de-emphasise successful prosecutions as the primary measure of its success. In its Annual Report for 1996–1997, the NCA identified in its strategic plan the following as 'critical success factors':

*   *resource management:* its people and its physical assets
*   *organisational effectiveness:* its management and contribution to law enforcement
*   *stakeholders and partners:* its direction setters, colleagues and monitors
*   *information management:* its data communication, storage and security.

More particularly, the recovery of the proceeds of crime had been highlighted as another indicator of success. In 1996–97, the NCA boasted a cumulative recovery figure of around $87 million. This should be qualified by the realisation that the vast majority of this figure was property restrained rather than forfeited or confiscated under the relevant legislation.

Whatever were the criticisms laid against the NCA, the debate about its effectiveness and how effectiveness should be measured was a healthy development, particularly if the considerations extended into a more comprehensive trend for the analysis of law enforcement priorities and operations throughout Australian criminal justice.

## End of the NCA[36]

During 2002, public and political dissatisfaction with the operation of the National Crime Authority intensified. This dissatisfaction focused on:

*   several notorious prosecutions of public figures such as John Elliott, which were either mismanaged and criticised at trial, or were represented as vendettas by the NCA against individuals unjustly
*   the lack of sufficient accountability by the NCA to the federal government in particular, and the Parliamentary Joint Committee (PJC)
*   the failure of the NCA to reflect federal and international crime concerns particularly in the context of new terrorist threats
*   the dissatisfaction of federal and State policing authorities with the provision of criminal intelligence through the Australian Bureau of Crime Intelligence (ABCI), and the NCA's autocratic approach to the investigation of crime at a national level.

The Howard Government campaigned politically for the dissolution of the NCA and the creation of a new body to control serious national organised crime threats and the emerging international terrorism. The argument for change was based both on the perceived failure of the NCA to address its mandate effectively (especially in the successful prosecution of major crime), and the assertion that a new body was required to address new crime priorities. The government was supported in its moves for change by federal and State policing agencies dissatisfied with their ability to influence and cooperate with the NCA. Dissatisfaction from other agencies at a federal level responsible for providing criminal intelligence and strategic crime information assisted in the campaign for a realignment of federal crime-control initiatives. In this respect too, federal and State prosecution agencies and other crime-related investigative bodies such as the Australian Securities and Investments Commission (ASIC) were looking for involvement in a federal crime agency different to that of the NCA.

During the 2001 federal election campaign, Prime Minister John Howard announced his intention to convene a summit of State and Territory leaders to consider enhanced national frameworks to deal with trans-national crime and terrorism, including the possible reformation of the NCA. Following the election the Prime Minister commissioned a review of the NCA. The review was conducted by a former commissioner of the Australian Federal Police and a former secretary of the Commonwealth Attorney-General's Department. The findings of the review were reflected in a paper entitled 'Transformation of the NCA', which was prepared by the Commonwealth Attorney-General's Department and circulated to States and Territories.

In April 2002 the Prime Minister convened a leaders summit of Premiers and Chief Ministers in Canberra where it was agreed that a new national framework was needed to meet the challenges of combating terrorism and multi-jurisdictional crime. The leaders agreed to strengthen the fight against organised crime by replacing the NCA with the Australian Crime Commission (ACC). The new ACC was to build on the important features of the NCA for effective national law-enforcement operations in partnership with State and Territory police forces. The leaders also made a number of agreements in relation to the operation of the ACC and noted that any other details would be settled by mutual agreement with the new body to come into operation by 31 December 2002.

An implementation team was formed in May 2002 to oversee the transition of the NCA to the ACC. A Commonwealth/State steering committee was established to coordinate the implementation project and ensure that States and Territories were consulted as the project developed.[37]

The Inter-Governmental Committee (IGC) of the NCA met in July 2002 to discuss the ACC's roles and functions. Subsequently, in August 2002, a special meeting of the federal, State and Territory police Ministers agreed on a number of principles to give effect to the outcomes from the earlier leaders summit in relation to the establishment of the ACC. The Ministers agreed that the ACC would be established to provide an enhanced national law enforcement capacity through:

- improved criminal intelligence collection and analysis
- setting clear national criminal intelligence priorities
- conducting intelligence-led investigations of criminal activity of national significance including the conduct and coordination of investigative and intelligence taskforces as approved by the Board.

The Ministers agreed that the ACC would have in-house and task-force access to all coercive and investigatory powers that were held by the NCA, which included coercive hearings and telephone interception powers and a capability for States and Territories to access these powers where appropriate. The NCA model had relied on ministerial approval but it was now agreed that the coercive powers for the ACC would be authorised by the ACC Board but only exercised through independent statutory officers.

The ACC Establishment Bill was introduced in Federal Parliament in September 2002. The Bill was referred to the Parliamentary Joint Committee of the NCA (PJC) for examination and report and that Committee called for submissions from the public. In addition, it held public hearings and tabled its report in November 2002. The PJC noted in its report that it was aware of the fact that the proposed model for the ACC was the result of negotiation and agreement between the Commonwealth, States and Territories and that its consideration of the Bill took place in the context of that agreement. Nevertheless, the PJC made specific recommendations for changes to the Bill. Its main recommendations related to clarifying and strengthening the role of the Chief Executive Officer of the proposed ACC, ensuring that only the full ACC Board could approve the use of coercive powers, and providing that independent examiners must satisfy themselves that the use of coercive powers was appropriate and reasonable to each case. The majority of these recommendations were accepted by the Government prior to the submission of the Bill to Parliament. Another major amendment to the Bill returned some responsibility to Ministers over the ACC Board in the use of its coercive powers.

All States and Territories agreed to pass complementary legislation to underpin the work of the ACC in each jurisdiction. This was said to reflect the co-operative nature of the ACC and reinforce the multi-jurisdictional mandate for its operations.[38]

In 2002, the Howard Government argued for and enacted the *Australian Crime Commission Act*. From 1 January 2003, the new entity, the Australian Crime Commission, replaced the NCA and took over much of the responsibilities of the ABCI and the Office of Strategic Crime Assessments (OSCA).[39] The ACC was to operate under a structure of governance more closely connected to federal and State governments, and their policing agencies. The Board was to be given more direct power for the management of the Commission's investigation and intelligence capacities, the activation of its powers,[40] and the establishment of its priorities to reflect the federal government's performance commitments on law enforcement and security. In fact the organisation of the ACC and the discharge of its responsibilities[41] clearly reflects a *whole-of-government* approach.[42]

## Role, powers and operations of the ACC

The principal proposed features of the ACC included:

- a focus on criminal intelligence collection and the establishment of national intelligence priorities
- access to task force investigative capabilities to give effect to its intelligence functions and to support its overall operations
- the ACC Board to include representatives from all States and Territories; Ministerial oversight retained by having the Board report to an inter-governmental committee of Commonwealth, States and Territories Ministers
- the process for obtaining investigation references to be streamlined
- the ACC to retain the capability to use coercive powers to investigate criminal activity of national significance.

The principal roles of the ACC are to collect, correlate, analyse and disseminate criminal information and intelligence and to maintain a national data base of that information and intelligence. Associated with this are its investigative and intelligence operations responsibilities in the area of federally relevant criminal activity. The ACC will provide strategic criminal intelligence assessments for federal and State governments and criminal justice agencies. The functions of the ACC are determined by its Board based on national criminal intelligence priorities determined for the ACC.

The special coercive powers of the ACC include the power to summons a person to give evidence under oath, the power to demand the production of documents and the power to demand information from Commonwealth government departments and agencies. The coercive powers can only be used in an intelligence operation or investigation that the ACC Board has specifically determined to be a 'special operation' or a 'special investigation' and only the independent examiners for the ACC can apply those powers. The examiners must be satisfied that it is reasonable in the circumstances to use the coercive powers.

An important function of the ACC is the provision of intelligence services through the maintenance and development of a national criminal database. The Australian Criminal Intelligence Database (ACID) continues to be a major tool in sharing law-enforcement intelligence and it remains the principal intelligence database for many Australian police services. ACID now directly provides intelligence systems support to six police services and plays an important information-dissemination role for the remaining three police agencies and crime commissions. The Australian Law Enforcement Intelligence Net (ALEIN) is a secure national web-based system that facilitates intelligence sharing and dissemination between Australian law enforcement agencies, encouraging the effective use of national intelligence data.

## Governance of the ACC

The ACC operates within an 'outcome and outputs framework'. The federal government's commitment to enhanced Australian law-enforcement capacity has been translated through the ACC into three main fields of operation: criminal intelligence services, criminal intelligence operations, and investigations into federally relevant criminal activity. The performance-management evaluation of the ACC is seen in terms of the output of these fields of operation.

More generally, the corporate governance of the ACC rests with external governance bodies such as the ACC Board, the Inter-Governmental Committee on the ACC, and the Parliamentary Joint Committee of the ACC. These arrangements are in addition to the checks and balances provided by the legal system in general for the investigation and prosecution of criminal offences. Further, the Commonwealth Ombudsman and the Australian National Audit Office have jurisdiction to examine the workings of the ACC.

The internal governance of the ACC is provided by the Chief Executive Officer, who is responsible for the management and administration of the ACC. There are also ACC examiners, who act as independent statutory officers appointed to approve the use of the ACC's coercive powers, to conduct examinations and to issue notices to produce evidence. These examiners are currently barristers who have had some familiarity with the operations of the original federal crime authority.

# Independent Commission Against Corruption (ICAC)[43]

In the years preceding the 1988 return of the Liberal-National Government in New South Wales, the Fitzgerald Royal Commission had rocked Queensland with almost daily revelations of corruption and malpractice at the highest levels of law enforcement and government. Yet this corruption was not presumed to be confined to the northern State. For decades, rumours of widespread corruption in the government and police administrations of New South Wales had gained the status of folk history.[44] Opposition politicians were quick to exploit the new community concern about corruption, which had been sensitised by Costigan and Fitzgerald.

In New South Wales, public respect for the principal officers of government, as well as criminal justice, had been eroded by the jailing of a Chief Magistrate, the alleged corruption of a District Court judge, the conviction of an Assistant Police Commissioner on charges of bribery, the court appearance of a Premier, the imprisonment of the Corrective Services Minister and the conviction of a High Court justice (later overturned on appeal). The traditional ambivalence about corruption in high places had turned, by the end of the 1980s, to a political expectation for change.

The Liberal-National Government won office in March 1988, largely on a platform to clean up corruption in the public sector. The creation of the Independent Commission Against Corruption (ICAC) one year later fulfilled an election promise, and was achieved without comprehensive criticism by any sector of State politics. Ironically, the first major public investigation held by the Commission examined the dealings of the Deputy Premier,[45] and some three years later it would be another ICAC investigation that would lead to the resignation of the then Premier.[46]

## Organisation

The Commission was created as a statutory corporation under the New South Wales *Independent Commission Against Corruption Act* 1988, and the actions of the Commissioner are deemed to be those of the Commission. The Commissioner is appointed by the Governor and can only be removed from office on the address of both Houses of State Parliament. At this level at least, the Commission is assured independence from the government of the day. The Commission is not subject to the direction of any Minister, and reports on investigations and other matters directly to Parliament.

The Commission exists to 'minimise corruption in the public sector of New South Wales'.[47] Its principal areas of function are reflected in the administrative structure of the Commission. These are investigations, corruption prevention and public education.

### Investigations

The Commission carries out investigations in order to ascertain the facts about alleged corrupt conduct, make findings and report. The most prominent element of its investigation function is the public hearing. Through this the Commission exercises some of its most intrusive powers, such as the ability to require witnesses to make self-incriminating statements. The public investigation has caused concern over its potential to endanger the reputation of people appearing before the Commission who are not eventually deemed to be corrupt.[48] This concern is fuelled by the fact that evidence produced in these hearings has been of limited value for criminal prosecutions.

Hearings have, until recently, been one of the principal investigation strategies of the ICAC. It is the public nature of these hearings[49] that has led to politicians from both sides of State Parliament calling for the end of the Commission. The inquisitorial environment of these hearings and the public damage to reputation that they involve have been a cause for concern. Such criticisms no doubt have had an impact on the Commission and its Commissioners. The current Commissioner seems reluctant to invoke a public investigation unless such an investigation is essential, and as a consequence the public profile of the Commission has receded.[50] In 2002, the Parliamentary Joint Committee (PJC) on the ICAC reviewed the conduct of the Commission's hearings and recommended that the ICAC continue to retain its discretion as to whether hearings should be public or private. It said, however, that the Commission should give consideration to only conducting public hearings where the evidence was capable of sustaining findings of corruption. This accords with section 31 of the *Independence against Corruption Act* (NSW), which states that the criterion for determining if a hearing should be private or public is whether the public interest will be served by the particular forum.

## Corruption prevention

The *Independent Commission Against Corruption Act* 1988 (NSW) requires the Commission to examine public authorities with a view to creating strategies that prevent corruption. Besides its general audit function, the Commission cooperates with public sector administrators to reduce organisational opportunities for corruption. Work systems have been developed that identify and encourage operational integrity. For example, the ICAC assisted the Department of Local Government in the creation of a uniform code of conduct for local government officers. In 2002, the Commission established a Strategic Risk Assessment Unit (with intelligence-gathering and surveillance powers) to take responsibility for the strategic identification of corruption in the public sector. Additionally, the Commission initiated a Local Government Research Strategy[51] with the aim of providing relevant and targeted advice and assistance on corruption to local councils. This is consistent with the ICAC's current philosophy of strategic partnership and liaison with other agencies. Allied with this theme of cooperation and consultation, the Commission now provides Corruption Resistance Reviews to agencies and organisations as a tool to help agencies identify areas in which they can improve corruption resistance. The review covers risk management, conduct guidance, internal reporting, human resource management, and complaints and grievance mechanisms. A feature of this 'partnership' model of operations has been the development of specialist legislation for the control of corruption in various government agencies.[52]

## Public education

If corruption is to be effectively reduced, the community must develop an anti-corruption consciousness that is more than a disillusionment with, and distrust of, public officials and government. The Commission has endeavoured to influence the attitudes of school students in particular towards an appreciation of the problem of corruption and its alleviation. In this respect, it exploits the sympathy of the media. However, in the early years of the ICAC, the media has shown a disproportionate interest in the investigations of the ICAC, rather than its other areas of operations. In addition to public education and awareness raising, the Commission has a research capacity, which carries out a limited evaluation, public information and dissemination function.

The Commission relies for its references on the direction of Parliament, and the complaints of the public. It also has power to initiate investigations as an independent authority, and its operational structure is ultimately responsible for determining whether and in what form a reference will be investigated.

The New South Wales Police Integrity Commission (PIC), established in 1997, assumed responsibility for investigating allegations of police corruption. The ICAC retains the responsibility to advise and assist the police service on corruption prevention and education.

## Corrupt conduct

'Corrupt conduct' is defined under the Act both in terms of designated forms of behaviour, and its possible consequences.[53] In its investigative function, the Commission is concerned with corrupt conduct. Section 13(1) of the Act designates among the principal functions of the ICAC, the investigation of allegations or complaints of corrupt conduct. The Commission views this as covering corrupt conduct or conduct connected with it, or liable to allow, encourage or cause its occurrence. Sections 8 and 9 define corrupt conduct in terms of a variety of inclusive behaviours, and the consequences that might flow from these (for example, where the conduct may constitute a criminal offence, a disciplinary offence, or grounds for dismissal).

In a crucial reassessment of the Commission's interpretation of corruption, the New South Wales Court of Appeal criticised the nature, application and effect of this definition of 'corrupt conduct'. In the *Greiner Case* the court had been asked to review a finding by the Commissioner that the then Premier of New South Wales and a Minister, who, while not acting dishonestly or criminally, had committed 'corrupt conduct'. Of the definition, the then Chief Justice Gleeson observed:

> One of the most striking aspects of the legislative scheme is that a conclusion that a person has engaged in corrupt conduct, which is unconditional in form, is necessarily based upon a premise which is conditional in substance ... Thus for example, where an alleged criminal offence is involved, a determination that a person *has* engaged in corrupt conduct is necessarily based upon a finding that the conduct of a person *could*[54] constitute a criminal offence. In the public perception the conditional nature of the premise upon which it is based could easily be obscured by the unconditional form of such a conclusion.[55]

Corrupt conduct may cover a dishonest or partial exercise of official functions, a breach of public trust, or impropriety. Again, in the *Greiner Case*, the judges of the Court of Appeal interpreted the scope of the definition of corrupt conduct employed by the ICAC in the Metherell Report[56] as going beyond meanings given in common usage. Priestly JA in that case preferred to view corrupt conduct as 'corrupt in any ordinary sense of the word', and Mahoney JA designated it as 'corrupt as ordinary people understand it'. Gleeson CJ had:

> the gravest difficulty in understanding how conduct that has not been found unlawful, that was believed to be in all respects lawful, and that would not be seen by a notional jury as being contrary to known and recognised standards of honesty and integrity, could reasonably be regarded [as satisfying the composite definition of corrupt conduct as laid down in sections 8 and 9 of the *ICAC Act*].

Whether section 9 achieves its objective of defining, within 'acceptable' limits, the meaning of corrupt conduct is no longer simply an issue of statutory interpretation. As a consequence of this case the Commission's operating notion of corruption was exposed to wide public discussion.

Following on from the Metherell Report, the New South Wales Parliamentary Committee on the ICAC foreshadowed a recommendation that the definition of corrupt conduct be simplified through the repeal of the section 9 conditions, and the retention of section 8, which sets out the ICAC's jurisdiction. This recognises the problem of a definition dependent on consequences of nominated action to establish the 'corrupt' component of the conduct in question:

> The (then) current definition of corrupt conduct is overly complex and fraught with difficulties. The definition is conditional in nature and as found by the Court of Appeal, 'apt to cause injustice' ... Section 9 should be repealed. Section 8 should remain largely in its present form to describe the ICAC's jurisdiction to enquire.[57]

Not only had the method for determining 'corrupt conduct' become the source of criticism of the ICAC legislation, but concern was also expressed about the process provided for in the 1990 amendment to the Act, which allows the Commissioner to make specific findings of corrupt conduct.[58] In the High Court decision of *Balog & Strait v ICAC*,[59] which was the catalyst for this amendment, the court cautioned that:

> the Commission is primarily an investigative body whose investigations are intended to facilitate the actions of others in combating corrupt conduct. It is not a law enforcement agency and it exercises no judicial or quasi-judicial function. Its investigative powers carry with them no implication, having regard to the manner in which it is required to carry out its functions, that it should be able to make findings against individuals of corrupt or criminal behaviour.

The High Court felt that if the government wished the Commission to make express findings of corrupt conduct, this should be specified in the Act. This was because of the Commission's broad communication and reporting function, and the fact that the evidence that it assembled and from which it drew its conclusions was not necessarily bound by the rules and considerations that govern judicial proceedings. Without such a power, then Commissioner Temby was quoted as saying that:

> it would seem a terrible shame and waste if most of the work done in hearings to date went for naught … If Parliament wanted the Commission to produce useful reports, then the ICAC Act would have to be amended.[60]

The government complied, and amended the legislation so as to endorse the ICAC's custom of making specific findings. Since that time the Commission has been challenged in court and regularly attacked in Parliament for doing just that.

Former Assistant Commissioner Adrian Roden QC has stridently argued against the specific findings power:

> What I believe the Commission should not do is make legal or quasi-legal decisions about individuals … The Commission is looking for facts, seeking the truth, trying to determine what in fact happened, who did it, and in what circumstances it was able to occur. The performance of this task is not aided by complex or technical definitions. What the task requires is the exercise of special powers which have been conferred on the Commission for that very purpose. The Commission and the courts have their respective functions to perform … If the Commission does not make findings that named individuals engaged in corrupt conduct, the main reason for having the definition in the first place disappears. If any need for the definition remains it can only be to indicate the area of the Commission's jurisdiction—that is to say, to identify the type of circumstance it is empowered to investigate.[61]

Clearly, if the Commissioner is to retain the power to find that certain conduct is corrupt, the substance of and process through which such conduct is defined bears much significance. In particular this requires that parties appearing before the Commission and the community at large are confident that the Commissioner is not biased in his or her deliberations. In 1998 the ICAC was involved in a highly publicised public investigation into benefits given to a State politician, Paul Gibson. Both Gibson and his lawyers alleged that the Commissioner was biased against them, and the Supreme Court upheld their contention that an appearance of bias arose from the Commissioners' conduct of the public hearings. This determination not only jeopardised the investigation in question but brought the Commission into disrepute.

It is also difficult to argue, given the present arrangements, that the Commission's hearings do not possess a quasi-judicial appearance. It would be incorrect, however, to simply view the role of the Commissioner as equivalent to a judge in a criminal jurisdiction. The ICAC Commissioner is more similar to an investigating magistrate in the civil law system, whereby he or she is actively involved in the interrogation of those brought before him or her and in eliciting evidence. An ICAC hearing is more inquisitorial than accusatorial; hence the Commissioner is more likely to face conflict and criticism than a judge might be.

# Powers of the ICAC

The Commission has been given powers, which the High Court has described as 'far reaching', to perform its investigative functions. These powers are based upon the commencement of an investigation, which in turn relies on a specific reference.

## Powers to require information

Under section 21, the Commission may, by notice in writing served on a public official or public authority, require them to produce a statement of information. In terms of similar notification, the Commission may require attendance before the Commissioner to produce specific documents.

## Entry, search and seizure

Powers of entry and inspection of premises, as well as the examination and removal of documents found there, are given to the Commission by section 23. Section 40 empowers the Commissioner, on application by an officer of the Commission, to issue a search warrant if satisfied that there exist reasonable grounds for doing so. These grounds are a reasonable belief that the premises in question contain something connected with a Commission investigation. Section 19 of the Act permits the Commission to apply for the issue of a warrant for the use of a listening device under the New South Wales *Listening Devices Act* 1984. The power is rarely utilised.

The powers in sections 21 and 22 were amended in 1990 to allow for the production of statements and documents to officers of the Commission, and not only to the Commissioners. The exercise of powers in sections 21, 22 and 23 may be resisted on the grounds of legal or professional privilege, but no public immunity privilege based on the occupancy of public office, or any conflicting duty of secrecy, can be raised successfully. Nor does privilege against self-incrimination prevent compliance with this order, although the substance of these disclosures may not be used against the person producing them if it is done under objection.

## Contempt of the Commission, and other offences

The Commission also has powers to deal with contempt, principally in the conduct of its hearings. The Commission can inquire into and certify a contempt to the Supreme Court, but cannot impose punishment.[62]

Part 9 of the *ICAC Act* creates a number of offences to punish and deter conduct that interferes with the Commission's pursuit of its investigative function. These include (without lawful excuse) obstructing the Commission; refusing to comply with a lawful requirement of a Commission officer; making a false statement or misleading the Commission; and disrupting a Commission hearing.

## Hearings

Section 30 enables the Commission to hold both public and private hearings. Following ongoing debate over the adverse effects on witness reputation flowing from some ICAC hearings, and a Parliamentary Committee report on the matter, private hearings will now be available where the Commissioner determines that a party otherwise accused of an indictable offence requires that her or his right to a fair trial not be prejudiced. The Commissioner has the discretion to decide how to conduct hearings, and whether to publish reports where associated criminal proceedings might be affected.[63]

The Commission may authorise a person who is substantially or directly interested in any subject matter of a hearing to appear and may authorise that person or a witness to be legally represented.

In 2004, the NSW Government constituted another inquiry into the ICAC's operations, which, among other broad ranging concerns, is to report on the appropriatenesss of public and private hearings.

## Referral power

The Commission has power to refer matters for investigation or other action to an appropriate body or person, before or during any ICAC investigation (Part 5). These bodies include the Road Traffic Authority, the Director of Public Prosecutions (DPP), and the Commissioner of Police. The Commission can ensure that the prescribed action is taken following such a referral.

A number of amendments that concerned the Commission's powers were made to the *ICAC Act* in 1996. Notably, its powers to provide protection for witnesses were enhanced.

# Accountability of the ICAC

While the Commission is independent of direct political influence, it is made accountable through several mechanisms. These are the Operations Review Committee (ORC), the Parliamentary Joint Committee (PJC), the annual report to Parliament, and the scrutiny of the media. Despite these various levels of accountability, Bersten rather prophetically observed:

> The independence of the ICAC puts it in an invidious position. If it is perceived to have failed or gone wrong, the government may feel entitled to shift the blame onto Mr Temby [then Commissioner] on the basis that the government should not be responsible for an agency which it created but could not and did not control. Yet when the independence of the ICAC is likely to count most, in an investigation affecting the political survival of the government of the day, the ICAC might then experience the most strenuous attempts to interfere with its independence.[64]

This is readily borne out in the history of the ICAC. For example, the Commission's early investigations into land dealing[65] on the New South Wales north coast brought a swift and bitter attack from the leader of the National Party. Later, when the Premier resigned as a result of the Metherell report,[66] his supporters both inside and outside of the Parliament preferred to 'shoot the messenger'.

The Operations Review Committee (ORC) is charged with advising the Commissioner whether the Commission should investigate a complaint made under the Act, or discontinue an investigation. It also has a general advisory function covering matters that the Commissioner refers to it. The Committee receives statutory reports relating to the handling of complaints by the Commission but does not have an individual or detailed oversight of the Commission's complaints capacity.

The ORC consists of the Commissioner of the ICAC, an Assistant Commissioner, the Commissioner of Police, a person nominated by the Attorney-General, and four people appointed by the Governor, on the recommendation of the Minister, who each reflect or represent 'community views'. The Committee meets on average once a month to consider reports and recommendations prepared by Commission officers. In most cases the recommendations of officers are concurred with, or the Commissioner is advised to seek further information. The Commissioner follows the advice of the ORC.

For the ORC to render the ICAC more accountable, it should focus on the exercise of the Commissioner's discretion to investigate. A major problem encountered by the ORC has been the way information is 'packaged' by the Commission for the ORC's consideration. Packaged presentation may prevent the ORC from dealing in any real or challenging fashion with the central subjects of its oversight.

The Parliamentary Joint Committee has been much more effective in making the ICAC accountable for the exercise of its functions. Since it began, it has required explanations of the Commissioner regarding matters of operational detail that may have been considered beyond its mandate to monitor and review. The PJC has a more powerful tool to require accountability of the Commission than any available to the ORC—namely, the opportunity to report to both Houses of Parliament on any matter pertaining to the Commission and its functions. In addition, the PJC can hold its own public inquiries into the Commission, and it has done this frequently with considerable public impact. The Committee requires the Commissioner to appear before it to answer questions on any nominated matter of concern. This it arranges on a regular basis.

The Commission's Annual Report (1991), which is itself subject to the review and reporting function of the PJC, emphasised that the Committee 'cannot involve itself in individual matters (such as decisions to investigate, and the reconsideration of findings), but can obtain information from the Commission, and others, to assist it in performing its functions'.[67]

The PJC has carried out a major inquiry into the Commission's hearing procedures and the rights of witnesses. Following the Metherell report, the PJC instituted a general review of the *ICAC Act*, which included consideration of the definition of corrupt conduct, the Commission's powers to make findings, and the Commission's response to recommendations by the PJC. At a more particular level, the PJC has required the Commission to clear up certain public complaints, and to clarify nominated investigation procedures.

The ICAC's actions are reviewable by the New South Wales Supreme Court to ensure the proper exercise of its functions and proper use of powers. The public reports of the ICAC, and the practice of providing information and explanation to complainants, are also means by which the ICAC is held to account by the community regarding its daily operations.

Internally the ICAC has in place a number of systems to ensure accountability and transparency. During 2002–03, the Commission reviewed its internal committee structure, reporting requirements and performance-measurement systems.[68]

Because of the atmosphere that surrounded its inception, and the high media profile of the ICAC in its early public hearings, community expectations of the Commission need to be considered when identifying appropriate measures of its effectiveness, efficiency and accountability.[69] It has been argued that even at this level, and despite its independent position, the ICAC can be evaluated in a quantifiable fashion in terms of its impact on corruption in New South Wales public life, its impact on the conditions that create corrupt practice, its influence towards creating an 'anti-corruption' consciousness, and the way it has used or abused its powers. The Commission's own version of its worth can be evaluated in a limited way through its annual report to Parliament. Media treatment of the ICAC and the manner in which it feeds public debate about the Commission's operations has moved beyond issues of newsworthiness. The fundamental reasons for the existence of the ICAC in any new crime agenda are now being questioned as much as whether it can actually carry out its objectives. Certainly in significant areas such as police corruption, the ICAC has had its mandate reduced. Perhaps the recent trend towards strategic partnerships and liaison with other agencies reveals a less confrontational and more collaborative dimension to the Commission's anti-corruption strategy. Even so, this should not diminish the significance of its compulsory powers (such as phone tapping, and document production), which it continues to use with vigour.[70]

# Australian Securities and Investments Commission (ASIC)[71]

In January 1991 the National Securities Scheme came into force. The *Commonwealth Corporations (Amendment) Act* 1990 established a system of cross-vesting of jurisdiction for corporation law matters between federal, State and Territory courts. The corporations laws of each jurisdiction are now identical in substance. Offences created by these laws may now be treated as if they were offences against Commonwealth law, so that the Commonwealth provisions (and not those of the States) dealing with investigation and arrest, prosecution, trial, and conviction, appeal, sentencing, fines, and proceeds of crime all apply to breaches of the corporations law.

In 1991, the Australian Securities Commission (ASC) replaced the National Companies and Securities Commission (NCSC) as the agency responsible for the administration and enforcement of the Commonwealth corporations law. Broadly, the charter of the agency was to restore and maintain community confidence in companies and the market, which had been undermined by the corporate excesses of the 1980s. To achieve this, the ASC was invested with wide investigative powers to uncover corporate misconduct, as well as routine regulation responsibilities to govern the legal life of companies. Unlike the NCSC, the ASC was offered a role in the prosecution of corporate deviance.

In 2001, the Howard Government put the *Australian Securities and Investments Bill* before Parliament. The Bill did not substantially alter the regime set down in the 1989 Act but it did rename the Commission. It also gave the ASIC a mandate under federal laws to operate nationally rather than only under an aggregate of State and Territory laws. In performing its functions and exercising its powers, the ASIC must now strive to achieve uniformity throughout Australia over the way the Commission and its delegates do business.

The Australian Securities and Investments Commission (ASIC) is the sole administering authority for the National Securities Scheme and, together with the Commonwealth Director of Public Prosecutions (DPP), has responsibility for prosecuting offences under the corporations legislation. Information gathering from surveillance investigations and public hearings provides an important source of evidence for potential prosecutions. Assistance in its investigation and prosecution function is provided to the ASIC by the Federal Police. The ASIC itself prosecutes all minor statutory offences under its charge and automatically issues penalty notices to company secretaries for breaches such as the failure to lodge returns required by the Act. The administration of the public register of information on corporations is kept separate from the ASIC's other regulatory and enforcement functions. This is obviously so that its function as the repository of information on legitimate corporate practice is not confused with its accumulation of crime intelligence information.

## Enforcement policy

As the national regulator of corporations law, the ASIC has developed an enforcement policy that employs a number of strategies. Its statutory scheme of enforcement includes:

- prosecutions by the ASIC
- civil actions by the ASIC

- intervention in third party civil actions
- provision of information to third parties
- final reports of investigations.

The focus is on preservation of assets, recovery of wealth, and prosecution remedies. In relation to prosecution remedies, the Commonwealth Director of Public Prosecutions and the Chairperson of the ASC disagreed early about the extent to which the ASC was willing to pursue the corporate excesses of the 1980s through the use of the criminal sanction, by attending to individual liability as well as civil recovery. While continuing to recognise its role as an investigation and prosecution agency the ASIC holds that, along with taking action against offenders, it has responsibilities to protect and help investors, provide information about companies and deliver high-value services.

The ASIC's predecessor, the National Companies and Securities Commission (NCSC), was not prosecution oriented. While it had legislative power to bring prosecutions, it was required (by Ministerial direction) to delegate that power to State Corporate Affairs Offices to bring forward prosecutions in the NCSC's name. However, the NCSC could not direct the Corporate Affairs Office to prosecute. This discretion lay with the State offices or, in some cases, the State DPP. This factor, combined with a lack of funds, led the NCSC to adopt a practice of commercial settlement and the threat of adverse publicity to require compliance or to force the company to the negotiating table.

The Australian Securities and Investments Commission has the power to commence and conduct criminal proceedings in relation to the *Australian Securities and Investments Commission Act* 2001 (Cth) and the *Corporations Act* 2001 (Cth). Since its creation, the ASIC has initiated prosecutions, and has continued criminal court actions inherited from the previous cooperative scheme (the NCSC). Where serious breaches are detected, the conduct of the prosecution is referred to the Commonwealth DPP in accordance with written guidelines developed and agreed between the DPP and the ASIC. These guidelines state:

> Ideally in the first instance, civil recovery actions to preserve property will be taken
> and disposed of as quickly as possible for the benefit of the members and creditors
> of a particular company. Thereafter, the wider public interest should be satisfied and
> appropriate criminal prosecutions brought.

It has become clear from the manner in which the ASC originally concluded many of the investigations inherited from the Corporate Affairs Commission and the NCSC that it was more interested in committing resources to civil sanctions rather than criminal investigations and prosecutions. Despite this appearance, in its 2003–04 annual report the ASIC boasted that as a result of its work, it '[a]chieved record enforcement outcomes including 29 criminals gaoled for fraud, criminal· breach of duties and insider trading'.[72]

Against this, in 2002–03, the ASIC undertook 67 civil proceedings, resulting in orders against 151 people or companies, $121 million in recoveries and compensation orders and $2 million frozen. The Commission had 16 people fined or banned from directing companies and 39 people from offering financial services. Eight company auditors and liquidators were disciplined for misconduct. In addition, the report relied on $506 million in funds protected, compensation orders or assets frozen for the public creditors.[73]

The investigation and prosecution strategy of the 336 ASIC staff involved in these activities relies on the following indicators:

- the number of corporate criminals gaoled
- the high profile cases concluded
- banning and disciplinary proceedings
- the dollars recovered for investors in civil cases
- the identification and reduction of insider trading.

In this respect it is the status of the offender and the proceeds of crime, along with conviction and sentence, that are priorities. These are seen against the anticipated impact on corporate behaviour and morality.

However, in recent years, and perhaps due to criticism of its enforcement role, the Commission has emphasised its regulatory functions, which have been enhanced through the additional powers given it under the *Financial Services Reform Act* 2002 (Cth).[74] In addition, the ASIC indicates that increases in public reporting of misconduct and greater information delivery through website and search facilities are indications of its relevance.

What is sometimes forgotten in all this talk of enforcement, is ASIC's financial regulation functions, which are not enforcement oriented. While not being distinctly 'criminal justice' in orientation, these functions can be used in tandem with the enforcement powers and are designed to ensure commercial probity compatible with crime-prevention aspirations.

## Financial regulation

The ASIC regulates companies and financial services and promotes investor, creditor and consumer protection under a variety of regulatory, insurance, superannuation and retirement legislation. It conducts this function in association with other bodies such as the Australian Prudential Regulation Authority, State and Territory fair trading or consumer affairs agencies, and the Reserve Bank of Australia.

It was in relation to this function that the ASIC has received its most vocal criticisms in recent times with the collapse of some major Australian companies through alleged fraud and corporate malpractice. In particular, the demise of the giant HIH insurance group and the resulting severe economic fallout has been put down in no small measure to incapable regulators, the ASIC included.

# Relationship with the DPP: criminal v civil remedies

In a response to early criticisms of the ASC's priorities, the then Chairperson has declared:

> The public thirst for blood sees this process as all too slow and not resulting in quick convictions. I can take no responsibility for the timetables of the Australian courts once major criminal proceedings are commenced in them. Like the majority of the Australian population I do not understand why they take so long. What I do understand is that the time taken between the 'first' finalisation of an investigation by the ASC and the consideration of the results by the DPP … is a slow, frustrating process which has been taking as long as the initial investigation—sometimes longer. The only way I know to speed up that process is to integrate the officers of the DPP more closely with the officers of the ASC from the start of a serious investigation.[75]

The Commonwealth DPP, on the other hand, explained the delay in terms of the need to get the lead-up to a prosecution right, and ensure that complex criminal proofs are established. Despite the frustrating time-frames governing the prosecution of criminal fraud, the DPP argued that these should not be used to support assertions that the criminal sanction is an inappropriate mechanism for corporate regulation:

> There is a need to resist the public pressure for quick convictions or 'runs on the board'. That expression is unfortunate but marginally better than 'scalps on the wall'. That there is a public expectation that corporate entrepreneurs face the court and be dealt with is understandable. Nevertheless, we must be careful to ensure that the prosecution response is a proper and appropriate one.[76]

The ASIC, with its responsibilities as a corporate and cooperative administrator, as well as a regulation agency, may be reluctant to see scarce investigation resources devoted to what it sees as purely offences under State and Territory legislation, such as fraud or misappropriation by entrepreneurs. State police forces or the ACC might be deemed to be more appropriate for these investigations. Yet, if these matters fall outside the mandate of the ACC, or the expertise and resourcing of State police, then the ASIC, either independently or as a joint initiative with the police, becomes the responsible investigatory institution.

As a corollary to its responsibility for administering and enforcing corporations law, the ASIC has a policy (now indeed a duty) to develop mutually beneficial relationships with other government, law-enforcement, and regulatory agencies both in Australia and overseas. Where, however, the ASIC's intention to see civil recovery is advanced in preference to criminal prosecution, this may lead to tension with other agencies of criminal investigation and prosecution.[77]

Because of its concerns to run parallel modes of civil and criminal regulation, and to spread what its Chairperson refers to as a 'deterrent net', the structure of accountability for the ASIC is not without problems. The ASIC says that the traditional 'head counting' by the media in terms of successful ASIC prosecutions is neither a fair nor an effective means towards public accountability for a corporate regulator. Qualitative factors, such as the complexity of investigations and their resource-consuming nature, require consideration. The ASIC also argues that as their 'deterrent net' programs have no real precedent in the language and ideology of conventional law enforcement, quantifiable objectives are even less relevant for their operations.

Despite this more balanced approach to the evaluation of success, the ASIC has in recent times returned to the head counting of successful prosecutions and grounded much of its impact on the profile of the corporate offenders it has helped send to prison. Given that the ASIC and other new investigatory agencies are aided by vast mixes of information beyond the usual temper of the rules of evidence, they must be made accountable for the proper exercise of these powers, at least to the extent we expect of the police. In this regard, successful conclusions in the conventional criminal process are expected. With the ASIC and its reliance on the DPP, the inextricable connection between the new investigation agencies and the traditional institutions of criminal justice is exposed.

# Australian Secret Intelligence Organisation (ASIO)

In the present atmosphere of incorporating criminal justice as a crucial component of the Australian response to terrorism, it is worth briefly mentioning the new investigative powers to be given to the Australian Secret Intelligence Organisation (ASIO).[78] We do this bearing in mind that agencies such as ASIO have a close historical association with police intelligence operations, and are now very much concerned with the civil dimensions of homeland security.

In 1999, the *ASIO Act* (Cth) was amended to enable ASIO to:

- under a warrant approved by the Commonwealth Attorney-General, use tracking devices, to access data in computers and to open mail carried by private mail contractors
- enter premises after a warrant has expired, to remove a listening or tracking device
- collect foreign intelligence by using non-technical means (for example, using agents)—until this change ASIO could only collect foreign intelligence by technical means (under warrant)[79]
- pass information received from overseas liaison partners onto Australian law-enforcement agencies

- charge non-Commonwealth agencies for protective services and security-assessment advice
- give security assessments for the 2000 Olympic Games in Sydney, directly to State and Territory authorities.

Other changes to the *ASIO Act* now mean that:

- search warrants issued to ASIO can be valid for 28 days rather than the previous seven and may come into force on the date of issue or when a specified event occurs
- the Minister may appoint a person to act as Director-General when it was previously the province of the Governor-General to make any such appointment
- the Director-General of ASIO will be able to issue any type of warrant in an emergency, except a warrant to collect foreign intelligence.

The *Financial Transaction Reports Act* 1988 (Cth) and the *Taxation Administration Act* 1953 (Cth) have been amended to enable ASIO, for security purposes, to access information held by the Australian Transaction Reports and Analysis Centre (AUSTRAC); and for the Taxation Commissioner to disclose tax information to ASIO. This provides a telling example of where the integrity and privacy of sensitive personal information gathered for a specific purpose is open to access from unrelated criminal justice and security agencies. The use of AUSTRAC information by ASIO is audited by the Inspector General of Intelligence.

Amendments to the *Telecommunications (Interception) Act* (Cth) enhance ASIO's ability to advise governments on threats to security and to collect foreign intelligence, by obtaining telecommunications interceptions warrants, and targeting named persons if such warrants prove ineffective.

In 2003, the Howard Government, after much debate and considerable public discussion, passed a package of anti-terrorism legislation.[80] The extension of security powers was justified as a necessary response to the threat of international terrorism in Australia in the wake of the Bali bombings, and September 11. The major features of this initiative are:

- an expansion of the warrant and search powers to cover groups as well as individuals, and to retain material
- detention of persons up to 168 hours continuously
- expanded powers to require the production of information including computer data
- use of force in detaining a suspect and taking them into custody
- restriction on access by a suspect to a lawyer of his or her choice, during interrogation
- surrender of passports and restriction of movement
- strip searching
- secrecy provisions covering warrants and questioning.

Some of these powers and their extent were, up until this time, unknown in the history of law enforcement and security practices in Australia.

# Ramifications for individual rights

As we have noted in other parts of this work, a significant recent trend in Australian criminal justice is the federal government's growing interest and involvement in criminal jurisdiction. Federal agencies not only have wider functions and reach into the activities of citizens in Australia and abroad, but these agencies also benefit from a steady increase in their powers and coordinated capacities. This trend has meant, purportedly in the name of national security, that the rights of individuals and communities are potentially exposed to the impact of unjustifiable criminal justice interventions.

The *Australian Securities and Investments Commission Act* 2001 (Cth) states that examinees must assist the ASIC with their inquiries unless they have a reasonable excuse not to do so. The Act indicates that self-incrimination is in this situation not deemed to be a reasonable excuse. If, however, the examinee claims immunity in relation to any compulsory disclosure, such immunity is available from using the disclosure in a criminal proceeding or any proceeding resulting in penalty. The immunity depends on a judicial determination that the disclosure might tend to incriminate the examinee (or accused person).[81]

There can be little argument that the powers vested in these new agencies present a potential challenge to the rights of suspects, and those under investigation. In particular, the abrogation of protections against self-incrimination, and the rights of witnesses to such investigations and inquiries in general require critical evaluation. This is particularly so when in ASIO investigations now the onus may be on the suspect to explain the details of an accusation about which he or she might know nothing.

The ACC, the ICAC and the ASIC all have the power to require witnesses to answer questions or produce documents, which might tend to incriminate them. For example, the right to silence in these situations has been removed (see chapter 5). The rationale is that these authorities must be able to investigate where the known facts concerning the individual or company give rise to a suspicion that they are involved in illegitimate, corrupt or fraudulent activity, or are being mismanaged.[82] As these institutions are involved in investigations that are often beyond the particular purpose of criminal prosecutions, the normal protections available to a suspect in a criminal investigation are seen as not so essential.

The protection against the abuse of these powers, and the interference with a fundamental civil right, is supposed to be contained in various use immunities referred to in the Commission's enabling legislation.[83] These immunities exist because successful investigations in these contexts do not always need to rely on an eventual criminal prosecution.

The lure of successful prosecutions might not be so great for the ICAC, but the NCA saw such results as a measure of its success, and, along with the ASIC, has been criticised for not providing sufficient evidence to support convictions in criminal trials. In 1991, the Commonwealth Parliament Joint Statutory Committee on Corporations and Securities (JSCCS) examined the 'use immunity provisions' contained in the ASC law, and concluded that the 'effective regulation of the corporate sector may include legislative provisions which vary the established common law rights available to the ordinary citizen'.[84] The Committee recommended that section 579(12) of the Corporations Law and section 68(3) of the ASC law be amended to remove the derivative use immunity provisions and that section 68(3) also be amended to remove the use immunity with regard to the fact that a person has produced a document. In addition, they recommended that the use immunities should not be available to corporations. The *Corporations Legislation (Evidence) Amendment Act* 1992 (Cth) endorsed these recommendations so that the protection afforded by the privilege in relation to further inquiries that may yield incriminating evidence is no longer available.

Legal professional privilege also cannot generally be asserted as a reasonable excuse not to disclose. A legal practitioner may claim this privilege; however, this is heavily qualified by the legislation. Where the client is required to disclose, a use immunity (against criminal prosecution) may apply.

Despite the concerns expressed by the Commonwealth DPP and the ASIC that they are reluctant to bring a prosecution where the evidence may not support its success, we are not convinced that this reluctance is well founded without more empirical or judicial testing. In addition, the threat to successful convictions in the criminal courts might not simply be overcome by the removal of use immunities. Further, the failure of prosecutions while immunities remain may be testimony to the appropriateness of civil remedies above criminal proceedings in these situations. We agree with the submission of the Queensland Premier to the Committee on this matter:

> Any decision to abrogate use immunity or derivative use immunity clearly involves a choice between an encroachment on the right to privacy of the individual, on the one hand, and the need to ensure that the Australian Securities Commission is not prejudiced in the pursuit of its regulatory responsibilities, on the other …[85]

We also echo the reservations of the Committee's dissenting report:

> We note with unease the growth in powers given to investigators over the last decade. Their ability to legally tap telephones has been markedly increased. Financial transactions have been opened up to their scrutiny … The state must look to order and good government but must not intrude unduly on people's rights in so doing. Were

a trend to develop of allowing it whatever powers it declared were necessary for the detection of crime, the sort of community we now enjoy would be devalued.[86]

# Conclusion

The emergence of these new investigatory bodies is evidence of the strain under which the traditional criminal justice process has been placed through recent shifts in the crime-control agenda. The perception, both in criminal justice circles and throughout the commercial community, that conventional law enforcement is unable to address fundamental challenges to good governance, legitimate financial practice, and honest business enterprise, has fuelled the development of these new agencies and processes.

In the case of the three investigative agencies featured in this chapter, their existence and operations have presented a challenge for traditional criminal justice institutions to better integrate their service delivery in order to reclaim community confidence in the more complex and sophisticated crime-control enterprise. The new agencies and the repositioned traditional institutions all now enjoy more extensive and intrusive investigation powers justified by more generic and less jurisdictionally confined crime threats. As we suggest, this is significantly eroding the conventional criminal justice protections available to suspects and accused, particularly when criminal justice investigations are merged with national intelligence, security and defence concerns.

The creation of specialised investigation agencies with powers beyond those accorded to normal police and prosecution institutions has brought with it a range of new opportunities for the intrusion of crime control into public life and commercial relationships. These concerns have been heightened by the intentions of these new agencies to share resources, and to access other realms of public information, in ways that ignore the integrity of the original data collection. The pervasive justification of criminal intelligence collection and dissemination exacerbates the data-protection controversy. This is due to the slippery concept 'intelligence', and the problems facing the subject of data collection in challenging the integrity of the data–collection process.

The shift towards specialisation in investigation has had the contradictory effect of breaching jurisdictional barriers across Australia, while at the same time further polarising the traditional institutions of policing and prosecution. This in turn has added to the pressure prevailing on criminal justice as a coordinated and systematic administration.

The tenuous balance that is criminal justice comes into stark reality when the special powers possessed by these new omnibus investigative and prosecution agencies are unveiled. Not only is the conventional separation of criminal justice functions between investigation and prosecution compromised; as a result, the traditional protections (such as public accountability and institutional scrutiny) are exposed as largely dependent on the operational morality of these institutions despite complex and apparent frameworks of responsibility and review.

However, it would be unfair to represent the appearance of these new agencies in a singularly suspicious light. Their existence and operation have confirmed a re-emphasis of control commitment away from traditional images of crime and criminals, towards those with the far greater potential to undermine economic stability and democratic freedoms.

## Notes

1    A. R. Moffitt, *Quarter to Midnight: The Crisis for Australia*, Angus and Robertson, Sydney, 1985.

2    F. Costigan, Royal Commission on the Activities of the Federated Ship Painters and Dockers Union, *Final Report*, Canberra, 1984.

3    I. Dobinson and P. Ward, *Drugs and Crime*, NSW Bureau of Crime Statistics and Research, Sydney, 1985.

4    I. Temby, 'ICAC: Working in the Public Interest', *Current Issues in Criminal Justice*, 2, 1991, pp. 11–16. Also see, Justice J. Wood, Royal Commission into the NSW Police Service, *Final Report*, Sydney, 1996.

5    Justice E. Williams, Australian Royal Commission of Inquiry into Drugs, *Report*, Canberra, 1980; Justice P. Woodward, New South Wales Royal Commission into Drug Trafficking, *Report*, Sydney, 1979.

6    In NSW, in particular, the police have in the past few years claimed success in stemming the tide of heroin on Sydney streets. The Australian Federal Police and the Customs service also contend that their initiatives have had an influence, resulting in a cutback on the availability of cocaine throughout Australia.

7    B. Bottom, *Without Fear or Favour*, Sun Books, Melbourne, 1984.

8    For a useful discussion of the workings of the CJC, see A. Leaver, *Investigating Crime*, Law Book Co., Sydney, 1997, ch. 8.

9    R. Hogg, 'Criminal Justice and Social Control: Contemporary Developments in Australia', *Journal of Studies in Justice*, 2, 1988, pp. 89–122.

10    S. Cohen, *Visions of Social Control*, Polity Press, Oxford, 1987.

11    The collapse of the national insurance giant HIH, in particular, called into question the capacity of governments, professional bodies and investigative agencies to act to prevent such threats to Australian business and commercial life and stability.

12    See *Report on National Crime Authority Bill*, Senate Standing Committee on Constitutional and Legal Affairs, Canberra, 1983. See also, M. Findlay, 'International Rights and Australian Adaptations: Recent Developments in Criminal Investigation', *Sydney Law Review*, 17(2), 1995, pp. 278–97.

13    C. Corns, 'Evaluating the National Crime Authority', *Law Institute Journal*, 1991, pp. 829–30.

14    The importance of the regulatory function at national and international levels was recognised by the Australian Securities Commission (ASC) in particular. The ASC Chairperson commented: 'We regulate investments in the worldwide market, yet we have only national regulatory remedies. Increasingly we will depend on the cooperation of overseas regulators. Without that help we cannot regulate effectively' (ASC, *Annual Report 1996–1997*, 9).

15   Chaired by Frank Costigan QC.

16   R. Hogg, 1988, p. 99.

17   F. Costigan, 'Control of Organised Crime with Reflections on Sydney', *Proceedings of the Institute of Criminology*, 1986, pp. 10–16.

18   Costigan, 1986, p. 12.

19   Recent explorations of systemic police corruption and malpractice in NSW, Queensland, Western Australia and Victoria have tended to endorse the view that conventional policing may be enmeshed with organised crime and drug trafficking to such an extent as to debar them from effectively investigating and regulating key features of the new crime-control agenda.

20   This is not to ignore the very significant work done by the Gibbs Committee in codifying the criminal law of the Commonwealth.

21   Details regarding the establishment, powers and operations of the Commission may be found in Leader, 1997, ch. 8.

22   See J. Hocking, *Terror Laws: ASIO, Counter-terrorism and the Threat to Democracy*, University of NSW Press, Sydney, 2004.

23   The NCA is discussed in detail in Leader, 1997, ch. 9. This reference is particularly useful for information on functions, powers and the accountability of the authority.

24   Parliamentary Joint Committee on the National Crime Authority, *The National Crime Authority: An Initial Evaluation, Report*, Canberra, 1988.

25   A topical case in point is the recent extensive investigation of Melbourne businessman John Elliott for alleged share transaction frauds. On acquitting Elliott, Justice Vincent was highly critical of the methods employed by the NCA during its investigation and for the construction of the case against Elliott.

26   *National Crime Authority Act* 1982, s. 17.

27   E. Strong, 'The Proliferation of Investigative Agencies: Demarcation and Intelligence Tensions', *Current Issues in Criminal Justice*, 1990, pp. 9–18; C. Corns, 'Inter-agency Relations: Some Hidden Obstacles to Combating Organised Crime', *Australian and New Zealand Journal of Criminology*, 25, 1992, pp. 169–87.

28   Australian Crime Commission, 2003, *Annual Report 2002–2003*, Sydney, p. 12.

29   When considering the task force dimension of the NCA's work, this should not be simply conceived of as cooperation with State and federal policing agencies. Other Commonwealth bodies, such as AUSTRAC, the Australian Taxation Office and the Australian Customs Service, also feature. Recently, the NCA has also engaged in task forces on a regional and international level.

30   Corns, 1991, p. 829.

31   *National Crime Authority Act* 1982, s. 4.

32   L. Robberds, 'The National Crime Authority: A National Perspective on the Investigation of Organised Crime', *Current Issues in Criminal Justice*, Vol. 1, No. 2, 1990, pp. 25–34.

33   The PJC objected to the literal interpretation, by Justice Stewart, of the secrecy provisions, as restricting the NCA from disclosing any operational information to anyone outside the NCA, even to the PJC itself. This led to a prolonged period of strain between the then Chairman of the NCA and the PJC.

34   See *R v Elliott and Ors* (Victorian Supreme Court, 22 August 1996).

35   PJC Report, 1988, p. xii.

36    In this section (and throughout the book) we use 'federal' and 'Commonwealth' to refer to the same national government. The term 'federal' seems to be used more commonly now, by and with reference to, national law enforcement agencies.

37    The steering committee comprised the Police Commissioners of South Australia, NSW, Tasmania and the ACT, senior officials from NSW Ministry of Police, the Victorian Department of Justice, the Chairperson of the ASIC, the Secretary of the Commonwealth Attorney-General's Department and an observer from the Victorian Department of Premier and Cabinet.

38    The *Australian Crime Commission (State Provisions) Act* 2003 (Vic) received assent on 16 June 2003. The *Australian Crime Commission (NSW) Act* received assent on 30 June 2003. Similar legislation was moved in other jurisdictions.

39    The *Australian Crime Commission Act 2002* brought into being the ACC, specifically incorporating the roles of the former NCA, the ABCI and OSCA. The three organisations played an important role in Australian law enforcement and merging them was intended to better integrate their strengths in strategic intelligence, operational intelligence, and investigative capabilities.

40    The ACC has special coercive powers to assist in intelligence operations and investigations. The ACC Board is responsible for priority setting in the intelligence responsibilities of the ACC.

41    The ACC now operates under a performance-management structure incorporating specific outcome and outputs frameworks agreed for the ACC in May 2003 Budget Papers presented to Federal Parliament.

42    This is where the important functions and responsibilities of government are addressed in an integrated fashion across ministerial portfolios and departmental administrations.

43    The workings of the ICAC are discussed in Leader, 1997, ch. 8.

44    D. Hickie, *The Prince and The Premier*, Angus and Robertson, Sydney, 1985.

45    ICAC, *Report on Investigation into North Coast Land Development*, Sydney, 1990.

46    ICAC, *Report on the Metherell Resignation and Appointment*, Sydney, 1992.

47    ICAC, *Annual Report to 30 June 1990*, Sydney, 1990.

48    Parliament of New South Wales, Committee on the ICAC, Inquiry into Commission Procedures and the Rights of Witnesses, *First Report*, Sydney, 1990.

49    The reliance on public hearings is a feature that significantly distinguishes the NSW ICAC from its namesake in Hong Kong.

50    In 2002–03, the Commission held 18 days of public hearings in respect of four investigations when compared with 54 summons for private hearings in relation to 14 investigations.

51    Recognising that 36% of its public complaints were against the local government sector (2002–03).

52    For example, *Local Government Amendment (Anti-Corruption) Act* 2002 (NSW); *Environmental Planning and Assessment Amendment (Anti-Corruption) Act* 2002 (NSW).

53    *Independent Commission Against Corruption Act* 1988 (Cth), ss. 8 and 9.

54    This was removed in the 1990 amendment to s. 8.

55    *Greiner & Moore v ICAC* (Court of Appeal) CA 40346–7/92, 21 August 1992. Judge's emphasis.

56    ICAC, 1992.

57    Parliament of New South Wales, Committee on the ICAC, *Review of the ICAC Act*, Sydney, 1993, p. 25.

58    *Independent Commission Against Corruption Act* 1988 (Cth), s. 13(3a).

59    (1990) 64 ALJR 400.

60    *Sydney Morning Herald*, 26 June 1990, p. 1.

61    A. Roden, 'Submission to the Parliament of New South Wales Committee on the ICAC on its Discussion paper of September 1992', Submission, Sydney, 1992.

62    *Independent Commission Against Corruption Act* 1988 (Cth), ss. 98, 99, 100.

63    *Independent Commission Against Corruption Act* 1988 (Cth), s. 18(2).

64    M. Bersten, 'Making the ICAC Work: Effectiveness, Efficiency and Accountability', *Current Issues in Criminal Justice*, 1, 1990, p. 110.

65    ICAC, *Report on Investigation into North Coast Land Development*, 1990.

66    ICAC, 1992.

67    ICAC, *Annual Report to 30 June 1991*, pp. 109–10.

68    For details of this see ICAC, 2003, *Annual Report 2002–2003*, Sydney, p. 69.

69    See Bersten, 1990.

70    For details on trends in use over recent years see ICAC, 2003, p. 34.

71    The Australian Securities Commission is discussed in Leader, 1997. Chapter 10 covers in particular the investigations power, the production of documentary evidence, privilege, and procedural fairness. Note that the ASC changed its name to the Australian Securities and Investments Commission (ASIC) in mid 1998.

72    ASIC, 2003, *Fighting Fraud and Misconduct: Annual Report 2002–2003*, Sydney, p. 25.

73    ASIC, 2003, p. 27.

74    These powers have been criticised by trade organisations such as the Financial Planning Association and the Investment and Financial Services Association.

75    A. G. Hartnell, 'Regulatory Enforcement by the ASC: An Inter-relationship of Strategies', conference paper, Sydney, 1992, pp. 11–12.

76    M. Rozenes, 'Prosecuting Regulatory Offences', conference paper, Sydney, 1993, p. 6.

77    Rozenes, 1993, p. 10.

78    In concentrating on ASIO, it would be wrong to ignore the other important military and civil intelligence agencies in this strategy. For a discussion of these see McCulloch, 2004.

79    As for the gathering of intelligence within Australia, ASIO has always relied on its operatives or the intelligence gathered by State and Federal Police officers.

80    The *ASIO Legislation Amendment (Terrorism) Act* 2003 (Cth); *ASIO Legislation Amendment Act* 2003 (Cth).

81    See *ASC v Kippe* (1996) 137 ALR 423, where the Federal Court narrowly interprets the concept of 'penalty' and limits the scope of the use immunity. Section 128 of the *Evidence Act* 1995 (Cth) indicates that the privilege may still be claimed by a company director as a personal right. The privilege may not be claimed by a corporation—*Evidence Act* 1995 (Cth), s.187.

82    See (Eggleston Committee) Standing Committee of State and Commonwealth Attorneys-General, 1990, 'Company Law Advisory Committee', Government Printer, Melbourne.

83    Use immunity cited in the Corporations and ASC laws relates to indemnification against the consequences of giving evidence by making the oral evidence and, in the case of s. 68(3) of the ASC law, the signing of the record and the production of a document, inadmissible in

any criminal proceedings. The legislation goes further and indemnifies the person against the use of evidence gained indirectly from 'leads' provided by the answers to questions or documents produced to investigators. This is the derivative use immunity.

84    Parliament of the Commonwealth of Australia, Joint Statutory Committee on Corporations and Securities (JSCCS), *Use Immunity Provisions in the Corporations Law and Australian Securities Commission Law*, Canberra, 1991, p. 26.
85    JSCCS, 1991, p. 25.
86    JSCCS, 1991, p. 35.

# 4

# Pre-trial

## Introduction

Most decisions taken in criminal justice occur long before a matter ever gets to trial. In fact, criminal justice is administered as a process comprising stages at which significant (and essential) opportunities arise for diversion from the necessity of progression further through the process. Diversion is not only a feature of our criminal justice administration for reasons of efficiency. A process that depends for its operation on the regular exercise of discretion by its principal players will invariably focus on those points at which the flow-through can be regulated.

The police have been described as 'gatekeepers' of the criminal justice process. This analogy is not simply confined to their role as the initial detectors of crime, since this function largely relies on the cooperation of the community in reporting crime. Instead, it is the control that police exercise over the initiation of individuals into the early stages of the process that confirms their gatekeeper 'filtering' capacity.

The police have an obvious and major filtering role in the selection of those people who will eventually appear in the criminal courts. In addition, they have a powerful influence upon subsequent stages of the criminal justice process in ways that are less obvious than their responsibilities over arrest, charging and bail. For example, the deployment of particular police resources in certain localities, and operating with specific target strategies may have ramifications for the 'crime rate' and its impact on sentencing principles.

Having recognised the significance of the police at the pre-trial stage, the question arises as to what extent the police are the sole or principal gatekeepers of the process. What is the form and extent of interaction between the police and other criminal justice agencies, both in terms of their aims and objectives, and in relation to the operational strain that exists within and between different players at each major stage?[1]

Before proceeding further, it is worthwhile reminding ourselves of one of the central paradoxes in our criminal justice system. While there is an assumed unity of purpose within the system, the administration of the process of justice is characterised by its piecemeal treatment of decision stages, often in isolation from one another. In practice, this challenges the tenability of any binding and shared objective. To appreciate the tensions that underlie criminal justice, it is not only necessary to examine the role and function of the major agencies at particular stages, but also an understanding is required of the interaction between agencies as they exercise discretion throughout the principal stages of the process.

As with so many contradictions existing within the criminal justice process, the reconciliation of sometimes competing individual and occupational aims and interests of the parties involved in the pre-trial stage depends on discretion. Our detailed discussion of pre-trial procedures of the police, defence attorneys, the DPP, and the magistracy, will be enhanced by some preliminary thoughts on the operation of discretion.

# Discretion

Discretion, as it operates within criminal justice, is the principal focus of decision-making, the style employed to make decisions, and the designation of where the responsibility for decision-making resides:

> Discretion is a tool indispensable for the individualisation of justice—governments of laws and men (*sic*)—rules alone cannot cope with the complexities of modern government ... Where law ends, discretion begins and the exercise of discretion may mean either beneficence or tyranny, justice or injustice, reasonableness or arbitrariness.[2]

As the grist for criminal justice, discretion exists and operates in a variety of forms, such as:

- decisions by individual criminal justice agencies
- organisational and procedural frameworks within which decision-making is structured
- ideological imperatives that impact on decision-making (for example, independence and impartiality)
- opportunities and situations where criminal justice and law enforcement responses rely on discretionary decision-making (for example, decisions by police to arrest, or to grant or oppose bail).

All decision-making in the criminal justice process relies on discretion. Despite policy initiatives to formalise, regulate, and make accountable instances of discretion within criminal justice, discretion remains inbuilt within the formal and informal structures of policing, sentencing and punishment. The position of discretion within the criminal justice process is complicated by its exercise beyond the bounds of formal legality. These situations are not limited to where a lawful power or authority is exercised illegally. They may also include instances where a lawful result is achieved by means that are arguably outside the limits of the law. As discussed in chapter 2, police employ methods of investigation in order to produce what they view as the just outcome of a criminal trial, but their methods have violated due process or legal restrictions on the accumulation of evidence.

The significance and meaning of particular discretionary decisions within the criminal justice process will be determined by the status of the parties involved, and the points at which the decisions are taken. The characteristics and situations of individual 'clients' are taken into account in criminal justice decision-making. In so doing, the exercise of discretion is very likely to be influenced by the individual characteristics and values of the decision-makers themselves.[3] It would not be surprising that the discretion not to arrest or charge might be exercised in the suspect's favour if a police officer viewed a suspect as respectful.

In addition, the fact that parties in criminal proceedings operate within an adversarial setting means that their discretion is directed towards opposing objectives. The very nature of the adversarial process—with the presentation of opposing versions of the evidence, and opposing arguments—provides some legitimate basis for competing exercises of discretion. Even at its earliest stages, the criminal justice system proceeds in an atmosphere of contest where win, lose or compromise are motivations for discretion beyond any objective distillation or shared vision of justice. Very often it is the adversary against which a discretionary decision is directed.

Discretion originates in the notion of independence, which is essential to our conceptualisation of the police, the courts, sentencing and punishment. However, it operates within a framework of laws, rules and definitions. Issues such as the elements of the offence, the demeanour of the offender, the visibility of discretion's exercise and regulation, public expectations, and accountability may determine the outcomes of any discretionary decision-making.[4] At an operational level, discretion may be regulated by:

- perceptions of how justice agencies will function, and whether these come from within the system, or are presented from community and media interests
- internal bureaucratic constraints such as the structures of disciplined services (for example, the police)
- interpretations of the law where its substance and application depend on the decisions of individuals
- professional standards and job satisfaction
- pressure from other agencies, whether direct such as the DPP on the police, or indirect where the operation of one component of the system impacts on

the potentials of another (for example, sentencing practice and prison over-crowding)

• occupational solidarity, which is an isolating and consolidating feature of all criminal justice agencies.

Discretion allows for compromise and expediency to act as considerations in the criminal justice process. For example, some observers of policing[5] suggest that con-flict between the law governing police powers and police operations in practice is resolved through the individual and collective exercise of discretion. In settling any such conflict, police may even usurp the roles performed by other agencies of the determiners of guilt or the executors of penalty (see chapters 3 and 7).

The major stages of the criminal justice process where discretion is exercised are:

• police pre-trial decision-making (for example, apprehension, caution, arrest, diversion, charge, bail, evidence gathering)

• prosecution pre-trial decision-making (for example, *nolli prosequi*, alternative charges, plea bargaining, witness selection)

• defence pre-trial decision-making (for example, plea bargaining, bail review, plea, witness selection)

• magisterial pre-trial decision-making (for example, issue of warrants, 'case to answer' determinations, committal for trial)

• judicial discretion at trial (for example, acceptance of plea, admission of evidence, jury instruction and direction, sentencing)

• decisions on appeal (for example, granting leave, new evidence, conviction and sentence)

• discretion during punishment (for example, classification, variation, conditions, parole, executive release).

This chapter will deal with some of the matters raised in the first four stages. The remaining stages will be taken up in later chapters.

# Pre-trial police decision-making

In their role as official gatekeepers of the criminal justice process, the police receive and interpret information in order that other stages of the process can be invoked or avoided. In most crime situations, victims or other members of the public inform the police of the commission of an offence, of certain circumstances surrounding its commission, or of the parties involved in the offence. The police may then take charge of the crime investigation and the preparation of the prosecution case on behalf of the state. Rather than require any further initiative from the victim beyond presenting evidence, the police assume the role of the informant.[6]

## Diversion and cautions

Diversion is the process where criminal justice officials take decisions to remove suspects and offenders out of the criminal justice process or to redirect them to other social control agencies. Diversion therefore constitutes those resolutions at the pre-trial stage which avoid eventual recourse to trial. The police realise that an efficient administration of an already overtaxed criminal justice system depends on diversion. They are also more able to transact these informal resolutions than might be possible for other criminal justice agencies at later stages of the process because almost all crime-related matters must come first to police attention. Usually, also, the quicker the diversion, the less publicly visible will be its consequences. In addition, the exercise of their discretion is more individualistic and anonymous and therefore often less accountable than at the later stages of the criminal justice system. The informal 'justice without trial' approach is possible in a functional sense because of the general low visibility of conventional 'street' policing. Further, the practice of stereotyping, so essential to police investigation practice, means that many police decisions opting for diversion can be taken quickly on the basis of ready-made pre-judgments.

More recently, police have been invested with expansive opportunities for pre-trial diversion. Cautioning and restorative justice conferencing have greatly enhanced the formal diversionary alternatives at pre-trial.

Provided the offence is not so serious as to require prosecution above all other interests, the police may decide not to proceed against a suspect despite their confidence that there would be a case to answer. Often it is the nature of the suspect and considerations of public interest that militate against the application of further steps in the criminal justice process. This discretion to refrain from charging an offender has been formalised in some States and Territories through processes such as the administration of juvenile cautions. Cautioning is a system (either formal or informal in its structure) in which the police admonish and discharge juveniles they have apprehended for criminal offences. These cautions are usually accompanied by a warning about the consequences of reoffending.[7]

## Decisions on arrest or summons

Once a suspect has been identified and a 'reasonable suspicion' exists in the mind of a police officer connecting the suspect with a particular offence, the police have a choice of ways in which they may initiate trial proceedings. They can either physically arrest the accused (or have a warrant issued for that purpose), or they may draft and serve a summons. The summons spares the accused from being physically restrained but requires the accused to satisfy certain conditions, including appearing at court on the nominated date.

For offences of a minor nature, and those where the security of appearance or the protection of witnesses is not required through bail procedures, the summons may be a preferred way to proceed. In some jurisdictions such as the Australian Capital Territory, police are required to determine that the summons 'route' will be 'ineffective' before opting to arrest. The economic and resource incentives to summons have led to a new function for the police—that of punisher, as well as investigator and prosecutor. Particularly with traffic offences, the police administer the infringement notice process right up to the collection of the penalty. Recently, similar infringement notice strategies have been used for minor drug and street offences. Some concerns have been expressed over the use of infringement notices. They include:

- the real risk that the strategy is driven by fiscal rather than correctional objectives
- the risk that persons believing themselves to be innocent pay up because of the pressure of convenience and threat of costs
- the undesirability of permitting the police to impose penalties without independent judicial scrutiny of the alleged facts.[8]

Normally, where police officers reasonably suspect that an arrestable offence has been committed, they may arrest anyone reasonably suspected of that offence without first obtaining a warrant of arrest. To proceed 'reasonably' appears to be the overriding determinant in the law of arrest but, as the determination of what is reasonable is in the mind of the arresting officer, its measurement is not objective. For example, the degree of force used in an arrest must be reasonable. However, much of the case-law in point views the discretionary decision exercised by the police in the use of force as unfettered, or at least only dependent on the satisfaction of conditions that precede the decision. The decision to arrest is viewed as arising from a balancing of the need, on the one hand, to protect public safety and order and, on the other, the recognition of rights to individual liberty.

In principle at least, the police are not able to detain without arrest simply for the purposes of gathering information. Nor are they empowered to arrest as part of the investigation process, without the intention of eventually laying charges. As we have noted in chapter 3, the law governing detention for questioning provides for some discretion on duration, the provision of reasons, bringing before a justice, and the consequences of unlawful detention.

The determination over whether or not to charge a suspect for an offence may not only be an issue of the strength of that suspicion. Factors such as the age of the suspect, the minor nature of the offence, the reaction of others in the vicinity, whether the person is intoxicated, and other features of the offence situation and its consequences might persuade the police not to proceed. Tolerance of criminality is not an infrequent feature of police discretion; it could be for the public good or simply the administrative convenience of the police.

## Charges and 'bargaining'[9]

The police not only decide whether to initiate the criminal justice process but they also pre-determine to a large degree the future progress of the accused through the criminal justice system: they are the investigators of an offence, the accumulators of evidence, and the initial interpreters and appliers of the law.

If charging a suspect is contemplated, then the initial collection of information sufficient to support a charge is regulated in various ways. These include the Instructions issued to police by their Commissioners and the adverse consequences of the rules of evidence and associated case-law relating to admissibility of evidence (see chapter 7). From as early as 1975 the Australian Law Reform Commission has been recommending some uniformity in the legislation that governs police practice at the investigation and charge stage (see chapter 3). One reason for resistance to this proposed change is the belief among police that they should retain extensive discretion over the initiation of consequent criminal justice responses. Legislation in most States and Territories has recognised this discretion within the notion of reasonable police behaviour or police-adjudicated exceptions to statutory limitations over the exercise of their investigation powers.

Once the decision to arrest and charge has been made, naturally a presumption of guilt pervades the investigation process in respect of the suspect in question. This presumption is essential for all police involved at future stages of the prosecution of the offence, for its absence would undermine the justification in their own minds to initially arrest and charge. Such a presumption of guilt might be alleged right up until the commencement of the trial and the reading of the indictment. Charges can be amended, added to, or dropped throughout the pre-trial stage. This presumption explains the police culture to see their part of the prosecution process as a contest that they should, wherever possible, win. It has also provided an explanation for police malpractice in the investigation and prosecution process where they deem a conviction at all costs to be for the greater good, and where the police may not trust lawyers and magistrates to produce the just result.

After arrest and charge, the task for the police is governed by general crime-control concerns, considerations of organisational efficiency, and individual notions of 'proper' police work. Crime control is achieved from the police point of view by opposing bail and gaining convictions. The police have a vested interest in these convictions—they are a measure of their success. In addition, a conviction is viewed as a re-affirmation by other agencies that the police were right and that their efforts should be rewarded. Acquittals, on the other hand, can tend to fuel police suspicion concerning the competence and motives of other players and agencies in the criminal justice process. Therein also lies motivations to divert or to plea bargain and avoid the perceived dangers of a committal hearing.

Charge bargaining in some State systems has recently been recognised by police, lawyers and magistrates as a legitimate means for expediting justice in an atmosphere of limited resources. This is especially for the purpose of producing guilty pleas from the accused and thereby complying with the 'myth' about contrition, which may be rewarded with a modified sentence.[10] Once admitted, however, the questions of how such bargaining is to be regulated and by whom become pressing. In those jurisdictions that employ an independent prosecution service, it might be deemed appropriate that the bargain process be theirs to monitor. Yet, it is rare that Directorates of Public Prosecutions have sole or complete responsibility for prosecutorial discretion at all levels, and therefore the police will also need to be involved in the oversight of the bargaining process. The courts will find it increasingly difficult to maintain a 'hands-off' policy to the practice of plea bargaining if it becomes more institutionalised within the prosecution process.

## Police and bail

Next to arrest and charge, the bail determination is one of the main ways in which police discretion affects the process of criminal justice. Bail is a decision on the liberty or otherwise of an accused, between the time of arrest and the verdict. Where bail is considered by police following arrest, it is described as police bail. Court bail is determined by a justice at the initial court presentation, or a judge on appeal.

Due to legislative restrictions on bail such as the reversal of the presumption in favour of bail for certain offences, bail has become more difficult to obtain throughout Australia. Remand rates and periods of remand are on the increase. In these circumstances, the routine opposition to bail from police is likely to have direct and increasing penal consequences.

Legislation governing bail throughout Australia provides both the police and the court with powers to determine bail entitlements, depending on the time and situation at which the determination is to be made. The higher courts have inherent jurisdiction to review bail decisions.[11]

Police bail is a legislative creation in all Australian jurisdictions and usually confers on certain police officers the power to release arrested people on bail on their undertaking that they will appear in court. Following the laying of charges, the accused must be informed in writing as soon as possible of their entitlement to bail, and a determination must be made by the police in writing. Whether it is police or court bail under consideration, the same criteria apply. These include the likelihood of court appearance, the seriousness of the offence, the severity of possible sentence, the probability of conviction, prior criminal history, potential interference with prosecution witnesses, court delay, the requirements for preparing a defence, and the view of the police/prosecution. The significance of this final condition should not be underestimated. There is no doubt that police opposition to the granting of bail is influential over a determination by a judge to refuse bail, and their opposition leading to refusal will affect impressions of the accused at trial, and the eventual determination of the sentencer. Even something as simple as the accused being in custody during the trial may impact on attitudes toward the accused. It also has an effect on the practical running of the defence case, in terms of the ability of the accused to conveniently instruct her or his lawyers.

If the police oppose court bail or resist a Supreme Court application for review, bail is less likely to result. As discussed later, the higher courts have jurisdiction to review decisions to refuse bail and these review hearings will usually receive police or prosecutor's views about the suitability or otherwise of the applicant for bail.

Legislative presumptions either in favour or against bail will vary depending on the offence charged. Rights to bail are very much dependent on the status of the accused and the nature of the alleged offence. For example, those charged with possession of certain amounts of narcotics, which are then deemed trafficable quantities (for the purposes of sale), may face a reverse onus when applying for bail. This obstacle may otherwise have nothing to do with the accused's satisfaction of any or all of the criteria for determining bail. Recently, bail has become a potent political issue in the law and order debate throughout Australia. The trend is to restrict access to bail and water down traditional bail rights (originating as they have done from the fundamental presumption of innocence) as evidence of a government's commitment to crime control. As a consequence remand populations in prison have soared but offending while on bail has decreased.[12]

The decision as to whether or not bail should be granted depends to a large extent on offence seriousness and the assumption that it will have an adverse influence on an accused's reliability to appear at court.[13] Broadly speaking:

- if the crime charged is not punishable by a gaol term, then the person generally should have a right to bail
- for most other offences the person should be entitled to bail unless:
  - refusal of bail is justified in accordance with conditions set out in the Act that designates the offence in question, or
  - the person is convicted, or is serving another term of imprisonment for another offence that would not expire before the completion of the bail period
- for certain serious offences there is no entitlement to bail.[14]

Bail considerations arise in the following situations or stages of the criminal justice process:

- on preliminary remand
- on any bail review by the Supreme Court
- on any other bail re-hearing before a superior court
- on committal
- at trial
- awaiting sentence
- pending appeal.

Bail is either granted unconditionally, or with the requirement that money be lodged as surety or that the applicant comply with reporting or surrender requirements. A police decision to refuse bail often relates to an accused's inability to appreciate bail conditions. It is not uncommon for intoxicated prisoners to be held in police custody, for instance, until they demonstrate a level of sobriety that enables them to understand the terms of their bail.

There have recently been developed in Australian jurisdictions long-term presentence conditions that take on the appearance of sentencing dispositions but might also be seen as conditions for the extension of bail. In Western Australia, for instance, the *Sentencing Legislation (Amendment and Repeal) Act* 2003 creates the Pre-Sentence Order (PSO), which allows the court to adjourn sentence for a period of up to two years provided the offender addresses his or her criminal behaviour. The *Crimes Legislation Amendment (Criminal Justice Interventions) Act* 2002 (NSW) provides for an 'intervention program order' available to a court after arrest but prior to trial, or after a finding of guilt or conviction. These orders invite the offender to enter into rehabilitation, treatment or restorative justice programs in order to prevent reoffending while at liberty. Such an order can be used as a condition of bail or as a deferred sentence or as a condition of a good behaviour bond. The distinction between conditional bail and sentencing disposition is in this way becoming blurred.[15]

## Police and court delay

Police usually prefer to avoid their day in court. At a local court level, significant policing resources are invested in the prosecution of criminal cases. Police may act as informants and witnesses, prosecutors, and even court orderlies. Trials are extremely disruptive of normal policing duties through the paperwork that they generate, and the uncertainty of their scheduling and duration. In addition, police are a class of witness that faces attacks on their character in the witness box—this can be seen as undermining respect for police authority.

With the spectre of delay[16] hanging over much of the exercise of pre-trial and trial discretion, the motivation for efficiency is as important for pre-trial decisions as will be concerns for justice. Police realise that a pre-trial agreement with an accused party to plead guilty has advantages that directly impact on court delay. In addition, efforts to establish agreed facts and to rationalise the calling of witnesses will work towards a speedier trial.

If pre-trial delay is the result of unreasonable police or prosecutorial action (or inaction), it has been held[17] that this could be justification for a stay of proceedings.[18] However, this decision would rest on establishing that the delay was 'improper'. The court would determine whether the delay caused the defendant to be left without a fair opportunity to defend him- or herself.

# Pre-trial obligations of the prosecution and defence— pre-trial hearings

In the next few sections we will explore the obligations that rest on both prosecution and defence at the pre-trial stage. Many such obligations arise from common law or conventions of practice. Certain statutory obligations exist, but in Australia they are neither comprehensive nor codified. These obligations have led to a formalised process of pre-trial hearings in particular, to facilitate the mechanics of disclosure. Pre-trial hearings may even provide the opportunity for the evidence from a witness to be taken where the availability of that witness is in question, or where a statement from the witness was not included in the hand-up brief conveyed to the defence.[19]

Such obligations are to the court as well as to the accused. In this regard they may be seen as constraining the exercise of discretion by prosecutors and defence counsel. Both the nature and form of any such constraint should be reflected upon when determining the impact of such obligations. For instance, an obligation created through prosecution guidelines might be important for best practice but may not be appellable through the creation and violation of a legal right.

## Prosecutor's obligations

The common law obligations on a prosecutor at the pre-trial stage fall into two general categories: to specify with particularity the charge(s) the accused person must answer at trial, and to advise the defence of the relevant evidence for the prosecution case. In relation to the latter, the prosecution has a duty to indicate all the evidence they will lead at the trial, and to adduce all material evidence at the committal. The prosecution should give notice to the accused of any evidence additional to that presented at the committal upon which it proposes to rely at the trial. This only refers to such evidence as will help the defence and relates to any matter or issue that could arise in the trial.

In Victoria, for instance, section 6 of the *Crimes (Criminal Trials) Act* 1999 requires the prosecution to prepare, file in court and serve on the defendant, in not less than 28 days before the trial commences:

• a summary of the prosecution opening statement
• a notice of pre-trial admissions.

The summary of the prosecution opening must outline:

• the manner in which the prosecution will put the case against the accused
• the acts, facts, matters and circumstances being relied upon to support a finding of guilt.

The notice of pre-trial admissions must contain a copy of the statements of witnesses whose evidence, in the opinion of the prosecutor, ought to be admitted without further proof, including evidence that is directed solely toward matters involving:

- continuity, or
- a person's age, or
- proving the accuracy of a plan, or that photographs were taken in a certain manner or at a certain time.

Section 8 of the Act determines what matters must comprise the openings for the prosecutor and the defence and, obviously, this has a bearing on the nature and content of the disclosure. Provision is made for notice to be given by either party that they intend to depart substantially from a matter nominated in this disclosure.

In other jurisdictions the magistrate or judge may expect at least the preparation and submission by the prosecution of a summary of agreed facts.

As discussed later, most prosecution agencies throughout Australia have created their own guidelines, which establish a range of obligations of practice and disclosure. For instance, the recently revised DPP's guidelines in New South Wales[20] provide 'guidelines (not prescriptions) for the conduct of all prosecutions and appeals by the DPP in NSW'. They include detailed provisions for disclosure. These guidelines may, from time to time, also restrict discretion not to prosecute certain classes of offences, reflecting strong public concerns about justice and community protection.

In addition to these obligations to disclose, the prosecution retains a general duty to bring the case against the accused to trial as expeditiously as is practicable. More generally, the prosecutor has an overarching requirement, as an officer of the court, to always act in the public interest.

## Defence's obligations

In most jurisdictions legislation requires the defendant wishing to rely on an alibi to give notice of such a defence, and particulars of the alibi, to the prosecution.

The *Crimes (Criminal Trials) Act* 1999 (Vic) imposes limited obligations of disclosure on the accused. The purpose of this is to identify, prior to trial (at a directions hearing called for the purpose), the real issues in dispute between the prosecution and the defence. This might mean an indication from the accused of any elements of the charge(s) that he or she admits, and the facts and issues that the defence will challenge. Section 7 is drafted as a defence response to the summary of the prosecution's opening and as a notice of pre-trial admissions. The defence must respond within 14 days of trial by identifying 'acts, facts, matters and circumstances (in the prosecution summary) with which they take issue and on what basis issue is taken'. Specifically, the defence response to prosecution admissions must indicate what evidence set out by the prosecution is agreed to be admitted without further proof and what evidence is in issue, and the basis on which issue is taken. The defence is not required to identify their witnesses unless they are experts, nor whether the accused will give evidence.

In addition, at an initial pre-trial directions hearing the court can require parties, including the defence, to:

- provide an estimate of the time required for the trial
- advise on the estimated number of witnesses to be called and their availability
- require the accused to indicate whether he or she is legally represented and has funding for the continued legal representation up to and including the trial
- indicate the need for any special requirements such as interpreter facilities.

At a subsequent directions hearing, the court may require advice (or specify a time for its provision) on any questions needing determination before trial, indicating any question of law or procedure anticipated to arise at trial, determine any question of fact (or fact and law) for the judge alone, or order the filing of any material required under the Act.

Difficulties with requiring defence disclosure, as evidenced through recent problems with the Victorian scheme, relate to incentives for compliance (or sanctions against non-compliance). In practice, the accused would prefer not to disclose and give the prosecution the time to investigate and prepare an answer to the defence. Even, such as in Victoria, where a judge has the right to comment on failure to disclose, the defence may risk this in preference to forewarning.[21]

# Prosecutor's pre-trial decision-making

In jurisdictions where police still act as prosecutors in the local courts, much of the previous discussion on the exercise of police discretion is relevant. In some local courts, and in the superior courts, the role of prosecution may be discharged by various players besides the police. These include solicitors employed by the Director of Public Prosecutions (DPP),[22] counsel retained by the Crown as prosecutors or briefed by the DPP, or special prosecutors. The trend is now away from using the police to prosecute criminal matters in the lower jurisdiction.

Lawyers employed by the DPP or directly by an Attorney-General in a prosecutorial capacity retain a large degree of discretion to set the direction of a criminal trial.[23] This discretion operates in the following areas.

## Bail

In the case of court bail, prosecutors may oppose bail on behalf of the police or the Crown, or seek to have conditions imposed. They can intervene in this manner at each stage of bail consideration, except on preliminary remand, which is unlikely to take the form of police custody.

## Charge bargaining and plea bargaining

The prosecutor has wide discretion in framing charges against the accused. Since alleged criminal activity can usually be analysed in different ways, the prosecutor will often be able to frame a number of different charges against the accused. This paves the way for plea bargaining. A prosecutor may accept a plea of guilty to a count not charged in the indictment in full satisfaction of the charge or charges in the indictment. Where the prosecutor accepts a guilty plea to a lesser offence, the trial judge must accept such a plea even though there may be evidence before the judge supporting a more serious charge.[24]

Plea bargaining comprises a range of matters, which are the subject of negotiation between the prosecution and defence in respect of the charge or charges to be proceeded with. Charge bargaining is the most frequent form of plea bargaining in Australia. Such bargaining may result in the accused pleading guilty to only some of the charges he or she is facing, with the remaining charges either not proceeded with or taken into account. Other forms of plea bargaining involve a reduction in the charge to a lesser offence, a withdrawal of other charges or a promise not to proceed on other possible charges, and a recommendation as to the type or severity of sentence that can be expected.

Charge bargaining usually occurs (if at all) following the initial charge or charges by the police. Once prosecutors have become involved in the matter, they are in a position to re-negotiate the charges on behalf of the Crown. The advantage of charge bargaining to the prosecutor is that the need for a contested trial is avoided. So too may be the risk of a total acquittal from a charge that a jury believes not to reflect the actual nature and seriousness of the facts. Charge bargains may also be struck in situations where the accused agrees to assist the Crown case in this or other matters.

A later occasion for bargaining may arise where the judge at trial sees the parties in chambers and gives an indication of the view he or she is taking and the penalty being considered. If a lenient sentence is talked of, then charge bargaining may occur between the accused and the prosecution. The accused may at that stage plead guilty in order to expedite the matter.

It is the secrecy surrounding plea bargaining that gives rise to criticisms that it is nothing more than an invitation to sloppy practice or a temptation to trade innocence for leniency. The recent endeavours by some DPPs to tighten up the practice through the construction of guidelines addresses some of these concerns. For example, the Commonwealth Director of Public Prosecutions has provided guidelines for the framing of charges. The charge or charges should bear a reasonable relationship to the nature of the accused's criminal conduct, they should provide an adequate basis for an appropriate sentence in all the circumstances of the case, and they should be supported by evidence.[25]

Prosecutorial discretion also affects the charge process when, following committals, the prosecutor is required to decide on the type of charge to be heard at the trial. Charges (that is, indictments) can be altered right up until the morning of the trial.

## Prosecutors in committal hearings

The impact of prosecutorial discretion at the committal stage will be dealt with more fully later in this chapter.[26] Suffice it to say now that the prosecutor is really the 'master of ceremonies' for the committal hearing. After all, it is the prosecution case that is at stake at this point. Even so, the magistrate retains the right to reject pleas accepted by the prosecution and thereby to activate the trial committal and trial process.[27]

The prosecutor determines what evidence is to be written, and what witnesses are to be called for oral evidence at a committal hearing. However, in jurisdictions such as New South Wales the prosecution evidence at committal is required to be submitted in writing.[28] The magistrate relies, for the matters that he or she is eventually to determine, on the presentation of the prosecutor.

The prosecution case may be assisted at committals by seeing how their witnesses perform under the pressure of cross-examination. Without the presence of a jury, cross-examination technique has a potential to be more harsh than that which witnesses might confront at trial.

In several States, recent law reform initiatives have been concerned with committals. The tenor of these reforms has been to limit the significance of the committal as a hearing and to restrict the discretion of the prosecutor and the magistrate. One such proposal has been to transfer responsibility for the decision to send the case for trial from the magistrate to the prosecution authority (DPP).[29] By so doing the DPP would have independent responsibility for deciding if a matter should continue after arrest and, if so, what should be the appropriate charge. The DPP would also decide whether a matter should be dealt with summarily (by a magistrate or judge without a jury) or on indictment (trial by jury) where this is possible (see chapter 5). The prosecution evidence would then be disclosed to the defence and the names of the prosecution witnesses would also be revealed. The only role for the magistrate here would be to see that the rules of evidence were complied with. Following the hearing, the DPP would decide if the matter would proceed to trial, and a bill would be found (see next section). In fact, through the 'bill' process the prosecutor confirms or denies the committal process as presently operating. Of course, the suggestion that the role of the magistrate in the committal process should be diminished has not found favour with some defence lawyers.[30] There are also interesting parallels here with the criminal process as it operates in civil law jurisdictions, with its heavy reliance on the discretion of the prosecutor to confirm (or divert from) future stages of the trial.

## Finding a bill, and deciding 'no bill'

In the event that the magistrate presiding over the committal hearing decides that there is sufficient evidence for the accused to stand trial, and that there is a reasonable prospect that a jury would convict the accused, the prosecuting authority (usually the DPP) will then decide whether to continue with the proceedings for the offence charged. If the prosecutor thinks that the case should go to trial, he or she will determine the exact nature of the indictment. This process is known as 'finding a bill'. If the prosecutor considers that the case against the defendant is not sufficient, he or she recommends to the DPP that 'no bill' be found, and further proceedings on these charges will not be taken against the defendant. In some jurisdictions the 'no bill' determination is made by the Attorney-General on the advice of the prosecutor. A 'no bill' may be found at any time up until the trial. In this respect the impact of prosecutorial discretion over the progress to trial is pre-eminent.

In *Barton v The Queen*[31] it was held by the High Court that a decision by an Attorney-General to bring a matter to trial via an 'ex officio information'[32] is not reviewable by the courts. Through such an information, a prosecuting authority has the power to commence criminal proceedings either without committal, or where otherwise a bill may not have been found.

There are several reasons why the DPP may 'no bill' beyond the belief that a magistrate has wrongly committed an accused for trial. Predominant among these is the decision that there is 'no reasonable prospect of conviction'. In such cases, it is possible that the committal hearing revealed an important weakness in the Crown case, which makes the expense and time involved in a trial unwarranted. The request of the victim not to proceed with a charge or the loss of a prime witness may also influence 'no bill' decisions. Where application is made to the prosecutor for a 'no bill', the prosecutor is normally required to support her or his decision with written reasons. There is no formal appeal process from a finding of a bill.

## Indictment

After a committal for trial, the prosecutor is responsible for drafting the indictment, which will be read out at the commencement of the trial by jury and to which the accused must direct her or his plea. Indictments are the documents that formally put a charge before an accused and the judge or jury. The indictment is not required to rigidly adhere to all the findings of the committal hearing, although new indictable offences that were not considered at the committal, must not find their way into the indictment. If this were to happen the judge may stay the proceedings, require the preparation of new or additional indictments, and order a new committal. The trial judge may make comment on the adequacy and appropriateness of the indictment; prosecution cases have sometimes failed simply because the indictment was not prepared with due care.

## Suspension of prosecution

It is possible for the prosecution to suspend prosecution prior to trial for a variety of reasons that may not constitute an acceptance of the innocence of the accused, or a fatal flaw in the prosecution's case. In these situations, it is conceivable that the prosecution might be reactivated at some future date. We would argue that in order to prevent the prevailing uncertainty for any accused that such a situation presents, there is a need for the formalisation of suspensions of prosecution, which exists in Japan and various civil law jurisdictions worldwide.[33]

# Defence pre-trial decision-making

The nature of legal representation for an accused will depend on their financial resources, the legal support services available in the jurisdiction concerned, the stage that the defence has reached, and the type of offence with which the accused is charged. For more serious offences, some jurisdictions provide the service of a public defender's office.[34] It should be remembered that while the absence of an opportunity for legal representation may, for some accused, impact on the fairness of the trial, there is no right to a defence lawyer in Australian jurisdictions.[35] Because of the court's power to stay proceedings until an indigent person can arrange legal representation, these conditions are sometimes construed as the circumstances for a legal right.

The success of the defence case is in significant measure dependent on the accused having legal representation.[36] However, the issue is not simply one of representation *per se*, but the quality of that representation, and the stage or stages of the pre-trial and trial process during which it was available.

## Legal aid[37]

In 1992 the High Court rejected the submission that in Australia the accused has a universal common law right to legal representation at the public's expense.[38] However, a judge should, in the absence of exceptional circumstances, adjourn, postpone or stay a trial where an indigent person charged with a serious offence is, through no fault of her or his own, unable to obtain legal representation.

State, Territory, and federal jurisdictions have legal assistance bureaucracies, which either provide lawyers at public expense to an accused without means (and whose case fits within certain merit or seriousness criteria), or will fund the engagement of private lawyers. Particularly in the lower courts, the very high case loads managed by legal aid solicitors mean that the time available for lawyer–client consultation and the attention that the lawyer can pay to any single case are very restricted. If legal aid is granted, the involvement of a lawyer of choice or one nominated by the aid authority will commence. This can happen at any pre-trial stage. The briefing of counsel to represent the accused at trial will obviously depend on the nature of the legal aid grant. In some jurisdictions, State-financed legal aid is not available for committals.

Special provision for legal assistance for Aboriginal and Torres Strait Islander peoples is provided through the Aboriginal Legal Service (ALS). The ALS is a recognition of the special problems faced by Aboriginal people in gaining appropriate legal representation and also the over-representation of Aboriginal people in the criminal justice process.[39] The national prosecution services and many judges recognise the unique service provided by the ALS not only in relation to the particular needs of their clients, but also to the courts and the effective and fair administration of criminal justice. Even so, the Howard Government has recently endeavoured to throw open the service to competitive tender.

Legal assistance is also provided by community legal centres, clerks of local courts or chamber magistrates, and certain motor vehicle associations. There is also emerging an important pro bono movement among major law firms, the various Bars and professional associations, and even Australian law schools have become involved through trial support services.

In recent years Australian governments have generally retreated from legal aid funding: 'The prospects for achieving adequate public legal services in Australia are bleak'[40] As Mark Richardson, the ex-director of the New South Wales Legal Aid Commission has observed:

> it is probable that (legal aid commissions) will need to review the way in which legal aid services have been delivered. Rather than making cuts to numerous programmes, the [commissions] may achieve more significant savings by altering the manner in which legal aid services are provided to the community ...[41]

However, the problems do not simply lie with strains on funding as a result of economic rationalist policy. The National Principles on Legal Aid of the now defunct National Legal Aid Advisory Committee (NLAAC) assert that governments 'in Australia have a duty to ensure that sufficient funds are provided for ... the fair and effective application of the law, and the efficient administration of the Federal, State and Territory legal systems'.[42]

Despite the *de facto* right to legal aid for the poor, where assistance is forthcoming it has been so reduced as to be only available in some situations, while being excluded arbitrarily from others. For instance, beyond the realm of administrative convenience or budgetary constraint, there seems no justification for providing legal aid for bail application hearings and not for committals. Recent law and order debates in Australia have gone so far as to suggest that legal aid for appeals should be denied if the offence is one where community safety is particularly vulnerable or the appellant has a bad criminal history.

There is a strong case for a more uniform and rational system of legal aid provision for criminal cases across jurisdictions. In addition, it would be unfortunate if the coverage of legal aid services was to be determined in such a way as to diminish the practical significance of equality before the law, or undermine the preferential position of the accused in a criminal trial. In May 1994, the Commonwealth Attorney-General's Access to Justice Advisory Committee (AJAC) delivered its report, which advocated a national strategy of access to justice. The federal government's response to the report, which came a year later, included initiatives in legal aid funding and services, although these were primarily in the fields of civil and family law. Another governmental response was to replace the NLAAC with a new Australian Legal Assistance Board 'to actively pursue a national approach to the delivery of legal aid to increase access, equity and efficiency'.[43] Given the grossly disproportionate levels of expertise and resources between the prosecution and an indigent accused and the highly damaging consequences of criminal conviction and punishment, it is lamentable that the federal government did not see fit to extend the same initiatives and degree of funding to the criminal law field.

In a similar vein, several States of Australia have moved to cut their legal aid budgets, reducing the scale of fees paid and the nature of services covered by legal aid, and restricting the scope of the jurisdictions and tribunals for which legal aid would be available. In some jurisdictions legal aid funding was denied for retrials, for appeals by convicted drug traffickers, and for trials that ran too long. Entire legal aid initiatives, such as the Aboriginal Legal Service, have had their funding cut and their administration wound down either as a result of a shift in government policy or an overall reduction in budget allocation. These cutback measures have significant ramifications for the right to legal advice and representation. If fair access to legal services is to depend upon the largesse of the legal profession or the financial resources of the accused, then all the nominal protections of a right to legal advice become little more than well-meant intentions.

## Right to defence counsel on arrest[44]

Defendants should usually be given the opportunity to contact and instruct a lawyer from the commencement of their detention in police custody. In fact, with certain classes of defendant, such as juveniles, it is necessary for the police to establish that the presence and counsel of a lawyer was offered, and accepted or refused, so that the results of any interrogation might later be admissible in evidence.

The presence of a lawyer during the police interview process is important to ensure that the relevant police guidelines or Commissioner's Instructions regarding proper investigation practice are complied with, and that no form of threat or inducement prevails over the record of interview. The lawyer is able to advise her or his client against answering those questions which might tend towards self-incrimination, where it is not intended. In addition, the lawyer can confirm the veracity of the record of interview and this may avoid time-consuming *voir dires* (trial within trial) at the trial.

With such protections in place, and being supported by the audio or audio-visual recording of police interviews, it has been argued that the rules of evidence regarding admissions and confessions, or the assumptions that can be drawn from the refusal of an accused to answer police questions, should be relieved.[45] The nature of the assistance that may be provided by legal counsel in such situations is an important consideration for the balance between the presumption of innocence and the effective investigation of crime. Having a lawyer present during police questioning may improve the quality of the interrogation, the admissibility of its results, and the sense of equity between the police and the suspect, which may be in question where such representation is not available.

## Advice on construction of defence

Defence lawyers have a responsibility to advise their clients in the construction of their defence. As may be imagined, the comprehension of the law and rules of evidence and procedure, and the strategy of mounting a good defence are obtained through long years of study and experience, which most defendants would not have. The availability of legal advice is particularly crucial where an accused person is on remand and therefore limited in the avenues open to him or her for the development of a defence case. As remand populations in Australian prisons grow, the pressure on prisoner legal services increases. Not only the presence but also the accessibility and quality of legal services available to prisoners is under threat.

With the advent of legal aid for criminal trials throughout Australia, the role of the defence lawyer within the criminal justice process, particularly in the lower courts, has assumed greater significance. However, because of cutbacks in government funding, there is a growing proportion of unrepresented defendants still appearing in courts throughout Australia. Unfortunately, those most in need of legal representation often will be least able to claim its benefit. Judicial officers are becoming called on more often to support the unrepresented accused.[46]

## Defence at committal hearings

Beyond the opportunity to test the Crown's case, the committal hearing will produce recorded evidence against which the defence can compare evidence and answers given by witnesses at the trial. This is particularly so now in those jurisdictions where the prosecution is compelled to reduce the evidence of their witnesses into writing.

Dishonest or unreliable witnesses can be exposed more effectively before a jury if contradictions with the committal transcripts are put to these witnesses.

With the recent trend to restrict the availability of committal hearings, the accused may find that they are increasingly reliant on the product of 'paper' committals. No doubt this will reduce the discretion available to the accused in the committal environment, and its ultimate utility.

A defendant committed for trial is entitled to apply for 'no bill' to be found by the prosecuting authorities (or where appropriate, the Attorney-General) prior to trial, as may any witness or member of the community. Having discussed the significance of discretion from the perspective of principal players in the pre-trial process, it is necessary now to examine important arenas within which such discretion is in contest.

# Committal hearing

The committal hearing as a preliminary to trial of a serious criminal charge has long been regarded as an indispensable part of the criminal justice system. However, calls for its reform or abolition have been increasing in recent years. The jurisdiction of committal hearings is now very much reduced on the basis of offence type and the nature of the trial venue.

## Procedure

When a person is charged with an indictable offence, the accused is usually tried before a judge and jury unless there is provision for her or him to elect to be tried by a judge alone. The level of court that will try the case will depend on the seriousness of the offence charged. Before an indictable offence is sent to trial, a preliminary investigation is carried out by a magistrate. This takes the form of a committal hearing but, more recently, many prosecution cases have been determined on the basis of documentary evidence alone. This is referred to as a 'paper committal'.

Traditionally, the purpose of a committal hearing has been to test the prosecution case and determine whether it provides sufficient evidence to justify moving on to trial. Traditionally, the committal process should include giving the defence the fullest opportunity to investigate all aspects of the prosecution brief. The trend to cut back on committals and the reduced significance of the committal hearing may to some extent be compensated for by other methods of pretrial disclosure discussed earlier in this chapter.

The committal allows the defence to see and test the Crown case without any reciprocal obligation to declare their own position. This means that the defence is not required to place any evidence on its behalf before the committal hearing. Thus the committal provides an open check on the exercise of the discretion to prosecute.

The committal hearing involves the prosecutor, the defence lawyer where the accused is represented (legal aid is often not available for committals), the magistrate, and the defendant. In most States and Territories, and federally, the prosecutor represents the Director of Public Prosecutions (DPP), who has responsibility for the carriage of all indictable offences prosecuted on behalf of the Crown.

Prior to the committal hearing, the prosecution collects evidence from its witnesses in the form of written statements. The defendant (and her or his lawyer) may be given copies of these statements. Decisions are then made as to the witnesses who will be required to attend the hearing and give oral evidence.

At the commencement of the hearing, the charge is read and the accused is required to enter a plea. Assuming that the case is to be defended, or at this point the prosecution does not withdraw the charges, the hearing will proceed. If the accused decides to plead guilty at this point, the prosecution usually submits to the magistrate their written statements of evidence (the 'hand-up brief'). If upon reading the evidence the magistrate accepts the plea, he or she will commit the prisoner to a superior court for sentence.

A defended committal hearing normally revolves around the presentation of evidence by prosecution witnesses, and where witnesses are available beyond their written statements, their cross-examination by the defence. In certain situations, the magistrate may restrict the cross-examination of victims of violent crime or child witnesses. If the prosecution evidence consists in part or whole of written statements tendered to the magistrate, and the defence declines to present any witnesses, the written documents may nevertheless be objected to by the defence or rejected by the magistrate.

Following the presentation of the Crown case, the defence makes their submissions to have the defendant discharged. The magistrate then determines whether there is evidence from the prosecution 'capable of satisfying a jury beyond reasonable doubt that the defendant has committed an indictable offence'. This should not be equated with a finding of guilt, but it does require a forecast of the likely outcome of the trial.[47] In New South Wales, for example, section 64 of the *Criminal Procedure Act* 1986 obliges the magistrate to determine whether there is a reasonable prospect, on the evidence presented, that a jury would convict. If the magistrate determines that the prosecution evidence would not be likely to persuade a reasonable jury to convict, the defendant is discharged.

Where the prosecution case is deemed sufficient, the accused will be committed to stand trial in a superior court. The defendant may be committed for trial on *any* indictable offence supported by the evidence and not only for the offence charged.

In certain circumstances, post-committal conferences are available to the parties as soon as possible after the committal. In Victoria, the purposes of such a hearing are:

- for the prosecution to disclose the major evidence relied upon to support a finding of guilt
- to identify matters that a party believes will require resolution prior to trial

- to identify witnesses that the DPP, with the agreement of the defence, will not be required to call at trial
- to disclose whether any of the evidence of these witnesses is admitted by the accused
- to identify evidence that is disputed by the defendant and the nature of that dispute.[48]

# Purposes of committal

Committal hearings serve several purposes.

## Eliminating weak cases

A survey in 1992 by the New South Wales Bureau of Crime Statistics and Research[49] of Local Court committal hearings in that State found that the outcome of the majority of these hearings (88.8%) was committal for trial. This indicates that magistrates are not unreasonably disposed to commit to trial. The 1991 annual report of the New South Wales Director of Public Prosecutions proffers the opinion that magistrates wrongly commit in only 3% of cases.

For a small proportion of cases the charges were withdrawn by the prosecutor (3.6%) at the committal stage. The discharge rate for committal hearings is particularly low when compared with the proportion of matters 'no billed' by the prosecutor after they have been committed for trial in a superior court.

## Disclosure of the prosecution case

Guidelines issued by the DPP in New South Wales at a committal hearing indicate that the prosecution should fully disclose their case and all other evidence relevant to the guilt or innocence of the accused. Only when 'there is a real need to protect the integrity of the administration of justice, including the need to prevent danger to life or personal safety may disclosure be withheld'.[50] In practice, the extent to which the prosecution case can be tested depends on whether the defendant can achieve effective cross-examination. This rarely occurs without legal representation.

Prosecution disclosure relies on the discretion of the prosecutor. Critics of this position say that the defence will not be in a position to confirm that all that should be disclosed has been disclosed. In addition, this discretion is difficult if not impossible to challenge, particularly in court.

## Identification of guilty pleas early in the prosecution process

If accused persons refrain from initially entering a guilty plea, they may do so on hearing the strength of the prosecution case. In New South Wales in 2002, well over half the cases committed to the higher courts eventually were committed to sentence, whereas a decade earlier, over one-third of the cases committed to higher courts were cases where the accused had pleaded guilty.[51] Not only does this early opportunity to plead save court time and expense, it minimises the stress on victims and witnesses and means that sentence can be imposed closer to the date on which the offence was committed. In addition, the matter will be resolved far more quickly than if it went to trial.

### Clarifying the issues of the case

At the committal hearing, both the prosecution and the defence have another opportunity to clarify and narrow the matters at issue in the case. Alternative charges can be disposed of and conflicting testimony discarded. If the magistrate is willing to confront matters of prevailing confusion, their settlement will inevitably lead to a shorter trial.

### Public venue for the testing of the prosecution case

Committal hearings, as with most court hearings, are open to public scrutiny. Although some criticisms have been raised concerning the potential of committal hearings to prejudice a fair trial through the public nature of these pre-trial disclosures,[52] the general maxim of criminal procedure that justice must be seen to be done in order to protect the presumption of innocence, should prevail.[53]

# Reform

In a misguided reform, several States have enacted legislation that substantially negates the central purposes of the committal. This not only creates procedural unfairness for the accused but has serious consequences in terms of court delays and costs.

By way of example, section 106(3) of the South Australian *Summary Procedure Act* 1921 provides that a prosecutor need not call a witness for oral examination in a committal hearing unless 'the Court grants leave'. The magistrate cannot grant leave unless 'satisfied that there are special reasons for doing so'. In determining whether there are 'special reasons', the magistrate must have regard to various factors including the 'interests of justice'. If, however, the witness is the victim of an alleged sexual offence or a child under the age of 12 years, the court must not grant leave unless satisfied that the interests of justice cannot be adequately served except by doing so.

In New South Wales, section 93 of the *Criminal Procedure Act* 1986 provides that, in any committal proceedings where a defendant has been charged with an 'offence involving violence', a magistrate shall not require the attendance of the victim (who has provided a written statement) to give evidence 'unless … satisfied that there are special reasons why the alleged victim should, in the interest of justice' so attend. An 'offence involving violence' is defined to include most sexual offences and the more serious forms of assault.

The term 'special reasons' has received some judicial consideration in South Australia. There the courts have suggested that the magistrate should take into account whether or not the alleged victim may be embarrassed by cross-examination; whether the defendant has given an undertaking to give evidence at the committal hearing; whether any tactical advantage will be lost if the alleged victim is not called; and whether cross-examination was desirable to establish important facts concerning the foundation of a defence. Since the burden of satisfying the magistrate of special reasons is on the defence, it will have to be clearly demonstrated that the defendant will suffer a disadvantage over and above the loss of the opportunity to cross-examine.

There can be no doubt of the good intentions behind these legislative enactments to restrict the formality of committal hearings. Such hearings often involve extensive, sometimes unnecessary, cross-examination of all the witnesses whom the prosecution proposes to call at the subsequent trial. Further, it can be very stressful for an alleged victim to be subjected to two cross-examinations, once at the committal and once again at the trial. When proposals were advanced in New South Wales in 1990 for sweeping changes to committal procedures, the Bar Council defended the committal but suggested that the *Justices Act* (now largely incorporated into the *Criminal Procedure Act* 1986) should be amended to produce a category of witnesses who should not be called without good reason. However, the Council had in mind scientific and non-contentious witnesses, not the alleged victim. The reason is the central concern of the criminal justice system with ensuring fairness to a person accused of criminal offence. In *Barton v The Queen*[54] the High Court considered that the 'preliminary examination' of committal proceedings is usually required as a matter of fairness to the accused in proceeding to trial:

> [the cases] show that the principal purpose of that examination is to ensure that the accused will not be brought to trial unless a prima facie case is shown … it is one thing to supplement the evidence given before the magistrate by furnishing a copy of a [witness's] proof; it is another thing to deprive the accused of the benefit of any committal proceedings at all. In such a case the accused is denied (1) knowledge of what the Crown witnesses say on oath; (2) the opportunity of cross-examining them; (3) the opportunity of calling evidence in rebuttal; and (4) the possibility that the magistrate will hold that there is no prima facie case or that the evidence is insufficient to put him on trial … The deprivation of these advantages is … a serious departure from the ordinary course of criminal justice.

If the alleged victim is not called as a witness in the committal hearing, the determination of whether a prima facie case exists, and whether there is sufficient evidence for the case to go to trial, must become a mere technicality. The magistrate will have no choice but to rely on the written statements presented by the prosecution, including the statement of the alleged victim, and nothing the defence says about them is likely to affect the result. While the defence will have the opportunity to call evidence in rebuttal, this is unlikely to be of much use since the quality of the prosecution case has not been subjected to proper scrutiny.

When the case does go to trial, the defence will have been denied knowledge of what the central prosecution witnesses say on oath. In addition, the accused is denied the opportunity to test that account under cross-examination before the trial, despite the view of the High Court that it is a necessary protection for the accused. Equally, the prosecution will not know what their central witnesses say on oath or under cross-examination. Formulation and revision of the appropriate charges will be disadvantaged and there will be less chance that the true issues between the parties will be identified.

Equally unsatisfactory is the expectation that delays and procedural problems will be simply pushed up the line to already congested and over-worked trial courts. Indeed, delays will be increased by attempts to obtain judicial review of magistrates' decisions declining to order the attendance of alleged victims. Pleas of guilty will probably reduce in number because the defence will not have had an opportunity to properly assess the strength of the prosecution case. Magistrates who have to decide whether a matter should be determined summarily or by trial in a higher court will have little option but to send the matter to the higher court. These enactments are fundamentally flawed and should be reconsidered.

# Pre-trial discovery and disclosure

There has been much discussion in Australian law reform circles about the attractions and appropriateness of pre-trial discovery and disclosure. This has been further fuelled by calls for the simplification of the trial process. An important way of achieving this is by providing mechanisms for finding common ground on evidentiary issues prior to trial, such as the 'freeing up' of access to the prosecution brief at the committal stage.

Requirements for discovery and disclosure prior to hearing have long been a part of civil pleadings. Not only is it expected that such disclosure would lead to a clarification of the matters at issue, but parties will also be given a less formal opportunity (compared to the trial) to resolve disputes, and the hearing itself will be expedited. However, confusion arises out of simple comparisons with civil proceedings. The presumption of innocence and differential burdens of proof mean that there is no level playing field, nor is there intended to be any, in the criminal trial. Therefore, calls for more balance in the status of parties before the criminal courts may be misplaced.

At present, much of the dissemination of information between the police, the prosecutor and the defence occurs at an informal level. In other common law jurisdictions, such as Canada and England, this has been augmented by pre-trial conferences held between prosecution and defence in the presence of a judicial officer. As mentioned in the preceding section, such conferences are now a more common feature in Australian jurisdictions, particularly where the trial proposed may involve the use of complex forensic evidence or other matters where expert evidence needs clarification and, where possible, agreement.

The difficulty in applying civil law case management procedures to the criminal trial rests in the special status and rights of the accused. Despite the fact that many of these rights are currently under challenge (see chapter 3) the presumption of innocence prevails.

As stated earlier, the prosecution has a general duty to disclose all evidence on which it relies, as well as evidence that may not be used by it but could be of benefit to the accused in the preparation of her or his defence. Such disclosure, while discretionary, is compatible with the prosecutor's obligations to the court as well as to the defence to see that the accused is able to answer the particularities of the charge.

In addition, the prosecutor may claim immunity from disclosure on the basis that to do so would be against the public interest. Here it must be alleged that the public interest in preserving otherwise material evidence from disclosure outweighs the prejudice to the accused through non-disclosure.

In certain trials it is not only the concealment of evidence but the fact that it is in contest that may tend to confuse the issues before the court, or complicate the presentation of either case. Trials may be complex because of the nature and form of evidence presented in a hearing.[55] Obviously, complexity is not only dependent on evidentiary concerns, but as recent controversial trials in which expert evidence was crucial have revealed,[56] much confusion in the minds of judge and jury may have been averted if the parties had agreed to issues of expert opinion prior to coming to trial. An example of this is where the science of DNA profiling may be accepted by both sides as not in contest while the interpretation of the profile and its evidentiary significance is challenged. In such a case, the evidence of the DNA analyst regarding this science could be put before the judge and jury in a simplified and schematic form, and the credibility of the expert would not be at issue here.[57] Where it is, on the other hand, at the minimum, the conflict over the credibility of expert opinion might be better settled outside the courtroom, and thus avoid the risk of confusion for the fact finder arising out of which expert is to be believed.

Of particular concern is the absence of discovery at magistrates' courts level. If the maximum amount of uncontested information could be produced at the earliest stages of the court process, this would have positive ramifications for the later issues of complexity and court delay.

There are significant dangers involved in the suggestion that, as an incentive for cooperation with pre-trial discovery, cooperation by the defendant could be recognised in her or his favour when it comes to sentencing. In addition, we would oppose the Victorian position that a convicted person who unreasonably refuses to admit facts that were not in dispute, or to adequately identify the issues in the case, should pay the resultant prosecution costs. In New South Wales, these defence penalties are more specific and wide reaching. Section 148 of the *Criminal Procedure Act* 1986 (NSW) identifies sanctions for non-compliance with pre-trial disclosure requirements. These include:

- a court failing to admit evidence from a party not complying with a pre-trial disclosure requirement
- dispensing with formal proof requirements in respect of evidence about which no earlier indication of dispute was disclosed
- adjournments where a party who has failed to disclose evidence, seeks to adduce it at trial and as a result the other party is prejudiced
- comment by the judge (or with leave, any other party) to the jury concerning a failure to disclose evidence, which should not go so far as to suggest that the non-disclosure is an indication of the accused's guilt
- adverse comment or a restriction on evidence as a result of the accused's non-disclosure, which cannot be allowed unless the prosecutor has fully complied with his or her disclosure obligations.

In the Victorian scheme, judges are allowed to comment in the trial on any departure from a pre-trial disclosure or a failure to comply with a pre-trial order. As mentioned earlier, judges appear reluctant to do this in case they appear to be punishing an accused person for failing to condemn themselves out of their own mouths.[58]

The Australian Law Reform Commission's (ALRC) reports on *Evidence* (1987) and *Customs and Excise* (1992) have things to say about pre-trial discovery and disclosure. The work of the ALRC, however, promotes the fundamental policy bases of the criminal trial that should not be ignored or undermined by any particular law reform endeavours. These include:

- *Fact finding.* While the criminal trial is not a search for truth, its fact-finding task must remain pre-eminent.
- *Accusatorial system.* The criminal trial is not about resolving disputes between parties, but rather the prosecution of guilt, and the accused is not obliged to assist in this process.
- *Concern to protect the innocent.* The objectives of the criminal trial are different to those of a civil trial, and the presumptions influencing the status of participants in the former are unique. In that respect, the acquittal of the guilty is less in the interest of the community than the conviction of the innocent.
- *Time and cost.* So far as reform proposals are consistent with the above considerations, the time and cost of court proceedings should be minimised.[59]

In both the United Kingdom and Australia there is a currently developing interest in the potential to merge aspects of civil and criminal procedure from civil law jurisdictions, wherever appropriate, into common law procedure. A significant motivation behind this is the efficiencies that would flow from a simpler and less contested trial process. The pre-trial procedures in civil law jurisdictions have been suggested as offering this result. For instance, the Royal Commission on Criminal Justice in England and Wales (1991–93) explored ways in which the criminal trial might be made less complex through the promotion of agreed evidence, settling expert opinion outside the trial, and the reliance on documentary evidence. Difficulties were identified in stimulating greater levels of disclosure during the investigation stage in a system that recognises a presumption of innocence. The Australian Law Reform Commission examined similar issues as part of its wider reference on the synthesis of civil and common law systems.

# Abuse of process in pre-trial

To conclude our discussion of pre-trial procedure, it is necessary to explore some critical abuse of power issues at the pre-trial stage. Many of the protections discussed in our chapter on evidence (chapter 6) have their origins in concerns for such abuse. The reality of a fair trial is largely dependent on the way in which power is exercised against the accused by investigation and prosecution agencies at the pre-trial stage.

In the protocol that precedes the United Nations *Code of Conduct for Law Enforcement Officials*,[60] there is the recognition of 'the potential for abuse which the exercise of [their] duties entails'. As any close examination of evidentiary disputes at trial or grounds of appeal will reveal, the abuse of process at the pre-trial stage is a major concern in the proper operation of the criminal justice process. Abuse of process almost always involves the irresponsible, improper or unlawful exercise of discretion. And as the penalties for such abuse are far from universal or certain, it becomes difficult to deter such practices.

The English Royal Commission on Criminal Justice evaluated the consequences for criminal justice of a series of impugned trials, which shook public confidence in policing and the judiciary to such an extent that the 'reality' of justice was questioned.[61] As a result, the government could not simply isolate individuals or agencies as being responsible for injustice, while leaving the rest of the criminal justice process untouched. The ramifications for the perception of justice following on from revelations concerning the fabrication of evidence in these trials were so far-reaching as to implicate prosecutors, judges and the prison service, in addition to the practices encouraged or condoned throughout all levels of policing. The Commission took the view that where abuses of power had become so institutionalised as to compromise all stages of the investigation, trial, appeal and punishment process, remedies must be sought in terms of the justice system as a whole. Unfortunately some commentators were disappointed in the Commission's recommendations for failing to do this or 'change the shape of the system significantly'.[62]

For criminal justice to prevail or at least retain the support of the community, the ideologies on which it rests must be respected throughout the process. One of these is the presumption of innocence, which is said to be at the heart of our notion of justice. If this presumption is to be acknowledged right up until the pronouncement of verdict, then the suspect or accused should also be in a more secure position than the police or the prosecution. Evidence of this being so would be an acceptably high acquittal rate. There is no point in police, prosecutors or judges bemoaning such an acquittal rate if the presumption of innocence is given its due operation. Whether it is through clandestine police manipulation of evidence, heavy-handed prosecutorial plea bargaining or preferential judicial interpretation of the prosecution case, justice is not the winner through any attempts to 'redress the balance' by having more convictions. Further, the recent push for a 'level playing field' in the investigation and prosecution of criminal offences fails to recognise the preferred position of the accused and the profound protections that conventionally ensure this position. Attacks on the right to silence, and demands for the accused to disclose, are fundamental challenges to features of common law criminal justice that set it apart from civil law systems.

The criminal justice process as it presently operates in Australia reflects the tensions created by criminal justice ideology and allows for their resolution through the regulated exercise of discretion. Thus the procedures for the investigations of crime and the accumulation of evidence are only selectively restricted through legislative enactment.

All too often, however, it is through the abuse of power that the preferred position of the accused is denied. One of the justifications for the presumption of innocence is the recognition that an individual defendant will be relatively powerless against the state's criminal justice 'machine'. Therefore, the possibility of a fair trial might only be realised where the power of the prosecution is checked. Discretion allows for abuse of power as much as it flexibly interprets criminal justice. Such abuse at the pre-trial stage is most serious due to the influence it may have over all other stages of the process. Furthermore, because the exercise of discretion before trial is rarely a public event, the potential for abuse of power is at its greatest. In particular, the powers exercised by the police must be clear and consistent in order to reduce the risk that they will be abused to punish someone who has not been convicted or to convict someone who is innocent. What follows is a presentation of areas that especially lend themselves to abuse of process.

For a detailed discussion of abuse of power in respect of police powers of arrest, detention, the questioning of suspects, search and seizure, information interception, and the fabrication of evidence, the reader should consult chapter 2 on investigation.

## Use of criminal informants

As Russell Hogg observes:

> The cultivation and use of criminal informants has been a critical if shadowy part
> of criminal investigation practice in Australian police forces for at least 100 years …
> The constitution of such practices under certain conditions as misconduct or 'cor-
> ruption' conceals the routine part they play in criminal investigation and their cus-
> tomary acceptance by the police as necessary and effective detective work.[63]

Both at an organisational and an individual level, the use of criminal informants as part of acceptable police practice is motivated by the expectation that the
quotient of police success is 'clear-up' figures and prosecution victories:

> The organisational and operational inducements are for a detective to use every
> means at his disposal to gather information which might lead to further convic-
> tions. So strong is the supposed public expectation, and the organisational pressure
> towards crime solving that it is not surprising that certain fundamental dichotomies
> arise within the framework of detective policing as it is traditionally practised in
> NSW. Chief amongst these is the contradictory invitation on the one hand for
> detectives to closely associate with criminals in order to gather information, while
> at the same time police are said to be governed by strict laws and regulations
> designed to prohibit consorting with known criminals.[64]

In its 1993 Report, *Investigation into the Use of Informers*, the New South Wales
Independent Commission Against Corruption (ICAC) identified a variety of
situations where criminals and prisoners were induced to fabricate evidence. In
chapter 8 of the report ('Fair Trials: The Legal Theory') the Commission identified 'information flows' that essentially influence the outcomes of certain trials. It
recommended that the DPP should issue guidelines to the Commissioner of
Police, which would ensure that the prosecutors were fully informed of the source
and nature of informer evidence on which the police brief relies. These have since
become an important feature of the prosecutor's guidelines in New South Wales.
In addition, the Commission recommended that a register of informers, combined
with certificates of disclosure, be employed by the DPP, the police, and the
Department of Corrective Services. Such registers are now a feature of justice
practice in that State.

Having said this, the ICAC recognised that the use of informers depends on
the individual integrity of the law officers involved:

> What all this comes down to is that the wrongful means must not be used to
> achieve noble ends. There is no point trying to enshrine that proposition in a rule
> or regulation. It is simply a question of integrity, and that depends on organisations
> being imbued with an ethical sense, and the ultimate moral responsibility of indi-
> vidual officers.[65]

To what extent this integrity is present in the police force and what measures can be invoked to raise the level of integrity are matters of grave concern. The recent Royal Commission into the New South Wales Police Service identified all too many occasions where the investigator–informant relationship led to abuses of power, police misconduct, miscarriages of justice, and corruption.[66]

## Bail conditions and remand

As mentioned earlier in this chapter, the deprivation of a suspect's liberty prior to trial is governed by clear legal principles and legislative safeguards. Consistent with these legal principles and safeguards, nowhere in the schemes of bail and remand operating within Australia is there formal provision for a refusal of bail (by the police or the courts) in order to facilitate the preparation of the prosecution case.

It is not unknown for police to use the threat of remand or their power over initial bail applications to 'encourage' suspects to provide information. Such 'overbearing' may range from the imposition of onerous bail conditions, to the promise that when a reapplication for bail is heard, the police or the prosecutor will no longer oppose it. These are instances of the use of police and prosecutorial power well beyond the spirit of any bail legislation.

## Unfair inducements to plead

Associated with the above-mentioned abuses of power is the practice by police, prosecutors or sentencers to encourage an accused party to plead guilty. Some critics of 'plea bargaining' argue that any inducement to plead is stretching justice beyond the bounds of fairness. Clearly, this view is not held by the appellate courts, which have condoned sentence discounting on the basis of the assumed contrition of the offender who pleads guilty.[67] Recent sentencing legislation in Australian jurisdictions has enacted the discount approach and thereby legitimated the potential disadvantage for an unsuccessful accused in electing their right to put the prosecution to proof. With the trend towards increasing maximum sentences, and through judicial guidelines and the like, limiting the sentencer's discretion to recognise the individual circumstances that may have encouraged a not guilty plea, accused persons who have a case may still be reluctant to gamble on an increased prison term for exercising their rights.

Of much greater concern is the practice whereby police or prosecutors are willing to drop certain charges if an offender agrees to pleading guilty to other charges. This cannot operate without bringing into question the veracity of the original charge process. In some instances, as the investigation of offences and the preparation of the prosecution brief proceeds, some original charges may appear unsustainable. However, if this is the case, then a bargain could not be struck. The real issue is whether there was any real intention by the prosecuting authorities to call evidence on all charges and, if not, what does this say about the charge process itself?

Another method of inducement by the Crown is to suggest that only one matter will be proceeded against, and if the accused agrees to plead guilty to a number of similar but unrelated matters, they will simply be heard by the court together with the original charge. This is attractive to police in particular because it enables them to 'close the files' on a number of matters, using the one trial and single offender, and in so doing, increase the police 'clear up' rate. This hidden agenda can subvert the principle of justice itself: 'The essence of any plea bargaining arrangement is a short-circuiting of the normal process. As such, there are fundamental interests and issues at stake and developments in this area should be monitored and assessed with considerable care'.[68]

## Denial of a prisoner's rights[69]

Generally, a prisoner's rights at the pre-trial stage are a more complex and vulnerable issue than the rights of sentenced prisoners. Whether the situation is police custody or imprisonment on remand, the need to prepare the best defence case influences all other general issues on rights.

Access to legal advice while in custody is a right that should prevail unchallenged from the first instance of police detention, up until the prisoner awaits sentence, and on until any appeal mechanisms are exhausted. Unfortunately, the very nature of the custodial environment restricts the freedom of such access. Criminal justice is served only if the custodial authorities are proactive in assisting the prisoner's access to such advice.

Many prisoners in police cells or on remand are held under worse physical and psychological conditions than those that apply to sentenced prisoners. Placed against the prevailing presumption of innocence, this should not be so.

This is compounded by prisoner safety, which is now a significant concern for police and correctional administrators in Australia. Sexual assault in gaol, particularly for young inmates is a likely occurrence. Suicides and self-injuries in custody have reached alarming proportions. In addition, the infiltration of the HIV/AIDS virus into prison communities makes even the briefest stay in gaol dangerous.

# Conclusion

The pre-trial stage is one of the most volatile and dynamic sites within the criminal justice process. All one needs do to confirm this is to examine the developments (and debates) surrounding police powers. Throughout Australia, legislation has been introduced to allow police to engage in 'body sampling' for the purposes of DNA testing. The prevalence of DNA evidence in police investigation practice has generated criticism that the rights of the suspect vary from jurisdiction to jurisdiction depending on the idiosyncrasies of forensic evidence legislation across Australia.[70] It is indeed regrettable that the uniform approach to forensic investigation and evidence practice proposed in the Commonwealth Model Forensic Procedures Bill has not been achieved. Queensland consolidated and extensively revised its police powers legislation in 1997, creating a range of new and intrusive powers, such as the power to allow police to stop citizens and require information of them. In New South Wales the government has passed legislation allowing police to detain suspects prior to arrest for a reasonable period, and to reduce the impact of the 'dock statement' (see chapter 2). New South Wales has also consolidated police powers,[71] creating a range of new opportunities for police in the management of crime scenes and the accumulation of evidence. In addition, and in response to the increase in youth violence, the New South Wales police have been given new powers to stop and search people suspected of carrying weapons, to confiscate offending property and to seek personal information, all without reasonable suspicion of the commission of an offence. These expansions of police pre-trial powers are occurring piecemeal in a 'law and order' political environment, and despite law reform bodies recommending some consistency and accountability in the rules of evidence that relate to the production of police evidence.

The pre-trial stage is crucial for realising criminal justice. Not only does it present the earliest occasions in which the individual citizen and the agencies and institutions of criminal justice interact but it also provides a vital opportunity for the diversion of whole classes of suspects and offenders. This will avoid the negative consequences of trial and penalty, as well as increase the efficient and just use of valuable and limited trial resources. The pre-trial stage provides the chance for creative innovations in criminal justice, which might otherwise be constrained by the formal procedures of trial and punishment.[72]

Having said this, the pre-trial stage is also one where strenuous criticisms have been raised about the justice and fairness of police and prosecution practice in the production of evidence. Even a cursory examination of what led to the deliberations of the Royal Commission on Criminal Justice in the United Kingdom and the Royal Commission into the New South Wales Police Service demonstrates the potential compromises and dangers to justice that abound at the pre-trial stage. Given the adversarial nature of our criminal justice system, justice demands that the significant powers and resources of the police and prosecution should be effectively and constantly counterbalanced by the provision of legal representation for indigent defendants. Courts must also be vigilant in their oversight of the exercise of discretion by police, prosecutors, defence lawyers and other justice agents in situations outside the courtroom where the exercise of such discretion is less visible, and therefore more open to abuse.

A major attack against our conventions of criminal justice has recently been launched around pre-trial process. Whether this has taken the form of requirements for defence disclosure, attempts to nullify the right to silence, limitations on committal hearings, and the under-resourcing of legal aid, the overall impact is to endanger the legitimate status of the accused. These attacks cannot be traded off against reforms in police investigation practice or the rules of evidence. The level playing field is not a place where pre-trial justice can be played out.

## Notes

1　For a detailed discussion of this and other aspects of police powers see M. Findlay, *Introducing Australian Policing*, Oxford University Press, Melbourne, 2003.

2　K. C. Davis, *Police Discretion*, West Publishing, Saint Paul, MN, 1975.

3　See G. Travis, 'Police Discretion in Law Enforcement: A Study of Section 5 of the NSW *Offences in Public Places Act* 1979' in M. Findlay et al. (eds), *Issues in Criminal Justice Administration*, Allen & Unwin, Sydney, 1983.

4　See Travis, 1983.

5　J. Skolnick, *Justice Without Trial: Law Enforcement in Democratic Society*, Wiley & Sons, New York, 1966.

6　Since the state has generally assumed the responsibility for prosecuting criminal offences, and prosecutions by private individuals have become rare, the police rather than the victim take on the role of putting the initial information about the alleged offence before the court.

7　For example, see C. Cunneen, 'An Evaluation of the Juvenile Cautioning System in NSW', *Proceedings of the Institute of Criminology*, 75, 1988, pp. 21–8.

8　R. Fox, 'Infringement Notices: Time for Reform?', Australian Institute of Criminology, *Trends and Issues*, No. 50, 1995.

9　In the literature on criminal justice, particularly in the United States, discussions of 'bargaining', which is designed to encourage a plea of guilty, often involves bargains about the charges to be presented by the prosecution, as well as the plea to be offered by the accused. The charge and the plea form the opposite sides of a potential bargain.

10　In some Australian jurisdictions, sentencing legislation further disadvantages an accused who fails in his or her not guilty plea because this is seen as a denial of contrition.

11　For a fuller discussion of the court's role in bail determinations see M. Aronson and J. Hunter, *Litigation: Evidence and Procedure*, Sydney, 1995, paras 8.98–8.126.

12　NSW Bureau of Crime Statistics and Research, 'Evaluation of the *Bail Amendment (Repeat Offenders) Act* 2002', *Crime and Justice Bulletin*, 83, 2004, p. 1.

13　In addition, there has developed in public debate the often erroneous assumption that the more serious the offence, the more likely it is that the accused will reoffend if out on bail. For the facts about who absconds while on bail see NSW Bureau of Crime Statistics and Research, 'Absconding on Bail', *Crime and Justice Bulletin*, No. 68, 2002, Sydney.

14　NSW Bureau of Crime Statistics and Research, 'Bail in NSW', *Crime and Justice Bulletin*, 2, 1987, pp. 1–4.

15　See A. Freiberg & N. Morgan, 'Between Bail and Sentence: The Conflation of Disposition Options', *Current Issues in Criminal Justice*, 15, 2004, p. 220.

16　NSW Bureau of Crime Statistics and Research, 'Grappling with Court Delay', *Crime and Justice Bulletin*, 19, 1993, pp. 1–8. See also NSW Bureau of Crime Statistics and Research,

'Managing Trial Court Delay: An Analysis of Trial Case Processing in the NSW District Criminal Court', *General Report*, 47, 2000.

17 See *Jago v District Court of NSW* (1989) 168 CLR 23 at 33–4.

18 See A. L-T. Choo, 'Abuse of Process and Pre-Trial Delay: A Structural Approach', *Criminal Law Journal*, 13, 1989, pp. 178–87.

19 See, for example, *Crimes (Criminal Trials) Act* 1999 (Vic), s. 11.

20 See the NSW DPP's website, <http://www.odpp.nsw.gov.au/>, Prosecution Guidelines (1998), guideline 18.

21 It would appear that some judges in Victoria are also treating defence compliance, even to orders to disclose, as voluntary. In this respect they are refraining from adverse comment for fear that it might jeopardise the fairness of the trial.

22 The Director of Public Prosecutions is a statutory office in most Australian jurisdictions, responsible for the carriage of criminal prosecutions at various levels of the court. It should be distinguished from the Attorney-General, who is a politically appointed principal law officer, and from the Solicitor-General, who provides a wider range of legal advice and assistance to governments.

23 For a discussion of the nature and significance of prosecutorial discretion, and of the move away from police prosecutors, see Office of the DPP, NSW, *Future Directions: Conference Papers*, NSW DPP, Sydney, 1997.

24 *Maxwell v R* (1996) 70 ALJR 328.

25 Commonwealth Director of Public Prosecutions, *Prosecution Policy of the Commonwealth*, <http://www.cdpp.gov.au/Prosecutions/Policy/ProsecutionPolicy.pdf>, para. 2.18.

26 It should be remembered that because of the expansion of the summary jurisdiction and the greatly diminished significance of the committal hearing as a process for commencing the trial, this exercise of discretion is relatively rare. Having said this, its significance for the trial of serious offences should not be overlooked.

27 See *Maxwell* (1995) 184 CLR 501.

28 See *Criminal Procedure Act* 1986, s. 74.

29 See J. Dowd, 'Committal Reform: Radical or Evolutionary Change?', *Current Issues in Criminal Justice*, 2, 1990, pp. 10–18.

30 See G. James, 'The Future of Committals', *Criminal Law Journal*, 14, 1990, pp. 145–56.

31 (1980) 147 CLR 75.

32 Where out of the office of the DPP, rather than through a police informant, a criminal information is laid.

33 See M. Findlay, 'Prosecutorial Discretion and the Conditional Waiver: Lessons from the Japanese Experience', *Current Issues in Criminal Justice*, 4, 1993, p. 175.

34 A description of the NSW office is found at: <http://www.lawlink.nsw.gov.au/lawlink/pdo/ll_pdo.nsf/pages/pdo_index>.

35 See *Dietrich* (1993) 67 ALJR 1.

36 See P. Cashman, 'Representation in Criminal Cases' in J. Basten et al., *The Criminal Injustice System*, Legal Services Bulletin, Sydney, 1982. See ch. 5, p. 232.

37 For a useful description of the operation of legal aid and the issue of 'unmet need', see J. Disney et al., *Lawyers*, Law Book Co., Sydney, 1986, ch. 14.

38 *Dietrich* (1993) 67 ALJR 1.

39 See chapter 10, pp. 305–10.

40    D. Kemp, 'Legal Aid in the Early 1900s: A Broad View of a Black Picture', *Alternative Law Journal*, 17, 1992, pp. 124–6.

41    M. Richardson, 'A Background to the Current Legal Aid Funding Issues', *Current Issues in Criminal Justice*, 9(2), 1997, pp. 162–3.

42    National Legal Aid Advisory Committee, *Legal Aid for the Australian Community*, Canberra, 1991, p. 56.

43    Commonwealth Attorney-General's Department, *The Justice Statement*, May 1995, p. 102.

44    See chapter 2.

45    See S. Odgers, 'Regulating Police Interrogation: Back to First Principles' in I. Freckelton and H. Selby, *Police and Society*, Butterworths, Sydney, 1988.

46    Also noteworthy are legislative provisions that allow for a hearing to proceed in the absence of the accused; for instance, see *Criminal Procedure Act* 1986 (NSW), s. 196.

47    Section 64 of the *Criminal Procedure Act* 1986 (NSW) required that if the magistrate determined that there is a reasonable prospect that a reasonable jury, properly instructed, would be likely to convict of an indictable offence, on the evidence presented, then the accused should be committed. The standard to be employed in the predictive process would be whether the outcome was 'likely'.

48    *Magistrate's Court Act* 1989 (Vic), Schedule 5, s. 24(6).

49    NSW Bureau of Crime Statistics and Research, 'Understanding Committal Hearings', *Crime and Justice Bulletin*, 18, 1992, pp. 1–4.

50    NSW DPP's website, <http://www.odpp.nsw.gov.au/>, Prosecution Guidelines (1998), guideline 18.

51    This seems to suggest a significant impact as a result of more apparent sentencing-discount regimes.

52    NSW Law Reform Commission, *Procedures from Charge to Trial: Specific Problems and Proposals*, Vol. 1, Sydney, 1987.

53    For a recent discussion of these and other reform themes in NSW, see Australian Institute of Criminology, *Crisis in Bail and Remand: Seminar papers*, 2002, Sydney.

54    (1981) 147 CLR 75 at 99–100.

55    M. Findlay, 'Jury Comprehension and Complexity: Strategies to Enhance Understanding', *British Journal of Criminology*, 41, 2001, p. 56.

56    See R. Harding, 'Jury Performance in Complex Commercial Cases' in M. Findlay and P. Duff, *The Jury Under Attack*, Butterworths, London, 1988.

57    See M. Findlay & J. Grix, 'Challenging Forensic Evidence? Observations on the Use of DNA in Certain Criminal Trials', *Current Issues in Criminal Justice*, 14, 2003, p. 269.

58    See J. Henry, 'Serious Fraud, Long Trials and Criminal Justice', *Denning Law Journal*, 75, 1992, p. 82.

59    See S. Mason, 'Background Paper: Evidence and Procedure Reforms', unpublished conference paper, Melbourne, 1992.

60    General Assembly Resolution, 34/169, 17 December 1979.

61    The Commission delivered its report in 1993 (Cmnd 2263).

62    A. Sanders, 'From Suspect to Trial' in M. Maguire, R. Morgan and R. Reiner (eds), *The Oxford Handbook of Criminology*, Oxford University Press, Oxford, 1997, pp. 1051–93 at 1060.

63    R. Hogg, 'The Politics of Criminal Investigation' in G. Wickham (ed.), *Social Theory and Legal Politics*, Local Consumption Publications, Sydney, 1987, pp. 120–40, 130.

64    M. Findlay, 'Acting on Information Received: Mythmaking and Police Corruption', *Journal of Studies in Justice*, 1, 1987, pp. 19–32, 23.

65    Independent Commission Against Corruption, *Report of Investigation into the Use of Informers*, January 1993, p. 118.

66    D. Dixon (ed.), *A Culture of Corruption: Changing an Australian Police Service*, 1999, Hawkins Press, Sydney.

67    See chapter 8, pp. 249–52.

68    P. Sallmann and J. Willis, *Criminal Justice in Australia*, 1984, p. 99.

69    A general discussion of prisoners' rights in Australia is to be found in D. Brown & M. Willke (eds), *Prisoners as Citizens: Human Rights in Australian Prisons*, 2002, Federation Press, Sydney.

70    See J. Gans, 'Something to Hide: DNA, Surveillance and Self Incrimination', *Current Issues in Criminal Justice*, 13, 2001, p. 168.

71    *Law Enforcement (Powers and Responsibilities) Act* 2002.

72    Compare the initiatives such as sentence indication schemes, community aid panels, family conferencing and juvenile cautioning.

# 5

# Trial

## Introduction

The criminal trial. These words tend to conjure up certain images. A robed and bewigged judge (invariably male) presiding from the 'bench'; similarly dressed lawyers—the Crown prosecutor and defence counsel—engaged in a verbal and tactical battle of wits and aggressively cross-examining each other's witnesses; the defendant sitting in the 'dock'; arcane ceremonies and procedures; complex rules of evidence; a jury of twelve silently observing proceedings and listening to arguments until required to hand down a verdict of guilty or not guilty. These images reflect the importance of the trial as the central and most public part of the criminal justice system. It is the showcase where the community can observe the law in action and assess whether justice is being done. The ritual and formality are designed to demonstrate the importance of the proceedings and the power of the law. The procedures and rules are, for the most part, designed to ensure fairness to both sides and hopefully ensure that only the guilty are convicted. The presence of the jury ensures community involvement in the determination of guilt.

These images, while still a part of the criminal justice system in Australia, are rather misleading. In the first place, a large majority of persons accused of serious crimes, which would be heard in the higher courts, do not go to trial. They enter a plea of guilty. More than 70% of cases in the higher courts are sentencing hearings on pleas of guilty.[1] This is just as well. A contested trial in the higher courts is generally time-consuming and costly. As we have noted in chapter 4, this is one reason for the delays that have become increasingly common in the criminal justice system. One practice whose effect, if not intention, is to facilitate the processing of cases through the courts, is to encourage pleas of guilty. We will return to this topic in chapter 8.

An even more important reason why the traditional image of the criminal trial is misleading is that the vast majority of criminal trials in this country (certainly more than 95%)[2] take place not in the higher courts with a judge and jury, but in the lower courts before a magistrate (often referred to as 'summary' proceedings). Further, the proportion of guilty pleas in the lower courts is even larger than in the higher courts.[3] As we shall see, there are important differences between these two modes of trial. For example, in a criminal trial in the lower courts the prosecutor is likely to be a member of the police force, the defendant may lack legal representation, there will be less emphasis on ritual and formality and, most obviously, there will be a magistrate rather than a judge and jury. Such differences have led some to argue that the traditional image of a criminal trial in the higher courts is little more than a deliberate facade. Thus, Doreen McBarnet has asserted:

> Legal policy has established two tiers of justice. One, the higher courts, is for public consumption, the arena where the ideology of justice is put on display. The other, the lower courts, deliberately structured in defiance of the ideology of justice, is concerned less with subtle ideological messages than with direct control. The latter is closeted from the public eye by the ideology of triviality, so the higher courts alone feed into the public image of what the law does and how it operates.[4]

There are two aspects of this critique. The first is that the operation of the higher courts is designed to be the showcase of the criminal justice system. Justice being seen to be done is as important as justice actually being done. In such circumstances, those parts of the system hidden from public gaze tend not to receive the critical examination they deserve. The other aspect of the critique is that there are fundamental differences in the way the system operates in the higher and lower criminal courts.

We shall consider these arguments in what follows. However, some preliminary qualifications should be noted. It may be that what we have discussed in the preceding chapters—the modes of investigation and pre-trial procedure—are more significant in terms of substantive and procedural justice than whether the mode of trial is that of the higher or lower courts. Further, it should be borne in mind that the rules of evidence, which we discuss in the following chapter, do not, at least in theory, distinguish between the two different modes of trial. Finally, while it is true that public discussion of criminal trials tends to involve those in the higher courts, the fact remains that any person's first-hand experience of the criminal justice system is likely to be in the lower courts. What happens to them is likely to shape their view of the courts and, ultimately, to have a bearing on public perceptions of the system as a whole.

# The higher courts

Each Australian State and Territory has a superior court, referred to as the Supreme Court, and some have an intermediate higher court called the County

Court or District Court. These higher courts hear more serious offences, in the sense that they carry long potential maximum sentences, usually referred to as indictable offences because of the procedure (tendering an indictment or 'presentment') adopted to initiate the prosecution and the fact that trial is by judge and jury. As we shall see, other offences are dealt with in the lower courts, by 'summary' procedure, without a jury.[5]

The mode of trial in the higher courts is based on an adversarial model. As we noted in the previous chapter, the parties, not the court, determine the issues that they will fight. The parties, not the court, obtain the evidence in support of their case. This model is carried over to the criminal trial. The parties conduct the case and judicial intervention is, as a general rule, comparatively minor. The law provides the rules according to which the contest is to take place and the judge acts as referee. But within this framework the parties are accorded a considerable degree of choice and flexibility. Justice Dawson of the High Court of Australia has explained this system:

> A trial does not involve the pursuit of truth by any means. The adversary system is the means adopted and the judge's role in that system is to hold the balance between the contending parties without himself [*sic*] taking part in their disputations. It is not an inquisitorial role in which he seeks himself to remedy the deficiencies in the case on either side. When a party's case is deficient, the ordinary consequence is that it does not succeed. If a prosecution does succeed at trial when it ought not to and there is a miscarriage of justice as a result, that is a matter to be corrected on appeal. It is no part of the function of the trial judge to prevent it by donning the mantle of prosecution or defence counsel.[6]

As we noted in chapter 2, the adversarial model is modified in the criminal justice context by altering the balance to accord the accused certain procedural safeguards. The prosecution, accusing the citizen, must prove guilt. The accused is granted a right to silence. Such procedural benefits given to the defence are a response, at least in part, to the reality that the accused is pitted against the power, resources and professionalism of the state prosecution service. An adversarial model has fundamental drawbacks if the adversaries are completely mismatched. Despite these modifications, however, adversarial elements predominate. That is why the courts have attempted to ameliorate the potential problems with such a system of trial procedure by emphasising the general requirement that every accused must receive a 'fair trial according to law'. As Chief Justice Mason and Justice McHugh explained in the High Court case of *Dietrich v The Queen*:

> The right of an accused to receive a fair trial according to law is a fundamental element of our criminal justice system. As Deane J correctly pointed out in *Jago v District Court of New South Wales*, the accused's right to a fair trial is more accurately expressed in negative terms as a right not to be tried unfairly or as an immunity

against conviction otherwise than after a fair trial, for no person can enforce a right to be tried by the State; however, it is convenient, and not unduly misleading, to refer to an accused's positive right to a fair trial. The right is manifested in rules of law and of practice designed to regulate the course of the trial.[7]

The majority of the High Court has clearly determined that the courts have the inherent jurisdiction to stop criminal proceedings that will result in an unfair trial. There is no requirement that the circumstances causing that situation constitute an 'abuse of process' by the prosecution—the simple fact that the trial would be unfair requires (in the absence of any other effective remedy) that it be 'stayed'. Indeed, as was apparent in this case itself, such a trial must be stayed even if there is no 'abuse', the trial would be one taking place 'according to law', and the court had no capacity to remove the source of the unfairness. On the other hand, it has been held that this principle does not extend to a situation where the unfairness arises from the operation of a legislative provision.[8]

However, despite the significance of the decision in *Dietrich*, some aspects of it require careful thought. The majority of the court emphasised that appellate intervention on the basis of 'fairness' will depend on a conclusion that the appellant lost a real chance of acquittal. Chief Justice Mason and Justice McHugh explained:

[A]ppellate courts in this country do not interfere with convictions entered at trial purely on the basis that there was unfairness to the accused in the conduct of the trial. The appellate jurisdiction in criminal matters depends upon a conclusion that there was a 'miscarriage of justice' such that the applicant 'has thereby lost a chance which was fairly open to him of being acquitted' … or 'a real chance of acquittal', to repeat the expression used by Brennan, Dawson and Toohey JJ in *Wilde v R*.[9]

This approach raises the question whether appellate review is a sufficient safeguard to ensure fair trials in general, an issue we return to in chapter 9. Perhaps more important, the High Court was unwilling to directly apply international norms in determining the content of a fair trial. It emphasised the traditional view that 'rights' jurisprudence in other countries has limited application to Australia. Even the international covenants to which Australia is a party will have little effect on domestic law except where that law is uncertain or ambiguous. Indeed, the courts are reluctant to attempt to list exhaustively the attributes of a fair trial. One can anticipate that there will be increasing pressure to give more precision to the concept of fairness in particular contexts, so as to give greater guidance to judges and lawyers in practical situations, recognising that 'the practical content of the requirement that a criminal trial be fair may vary with changing social standards and circumstances'.[10] In considering the mode of criminal trial in the higher courts, therefore, a central issue is whether it reflects contemporary standards of fairness.

The ensuing discussion will focus on the major participants in the trial—the prosecution, the defence, the judge and the jury. This is not to suggest that there are not other important participants. The witnesses, called by the prosecution or the defence, are obviously a central part of a trial. We will discuss some of the rules relating to the testimony of witnesses in the next chapter. It may well be that the alleged victim of the offence charged will be called as a witness, and this raises important and controversial issues. Indeed, since the victim is not directly represented under the adversarial model, his or her interests may not be fully protected. This is an issue to which we return in chapter 10. The court staff, the judge's associate, the police, the press, the public—all may play a role in the trial—and we will refer to some of them in our discussion.

## The prosecution

The charge against the accused is brought by the executive branch of government, traditionally referred to as the 'Crown'. The prosecution represents the community, rather than any individual victim; in some cases, so called 'victimless crimes', there is no victim to represent. In this context, the system attempts to balance two conflicting principles: prosecutorial independence and ensuring fairness to the accused.

The former principle, premised on the adversary model, means that the courts are reluctant to interfere in the conduct of a prosecution except in extreme situations. It has also seen the development of prosecutorial independence from the executive. Traditionally, prosecutions have been brought by the Crown through the Attorney-General. Crown prosecutors have been under the control of the Attorney-General. However, the trend has been to create an independent office of public prosecutions. Thus, for example, the federal government established the Office of Commonwealth Director of Public Prosecutions in 1983 and, in 1986, the New South Wales government created the Office of the Director of Public Prosecutions to undertake all indictable prosecutions and to decide no-bill applications. The latter principle results in prosecutors being subject to a number of ethical, common law and statutory duties in conducting a trial. It also means, as we have seen, that the courts should, in theory, act to ensure that any conduct by the prosecutor is not allowed to make the trial 'unfair'.

Beginning with the determination of charges brought against an accused person, the prosecutor determines them without judicial interference. But, as we have seen, certain rules apply to ensure fairness to the accused and certainty as to what the trial is to determine. The indictment/presentment must inform the accused of the precise nature of the charge and identify the essential factual ingredients of the actual offence.[11] Sufficient 'particulars' must be provided to isolate precisely what alleged actions of the accused will be under scrutiny at the trial.

Several charges ('counts') may be contained in the one indictment, as long as each count contains a single charge only.[12] The usual rule is that the charges in the indictment should be 'founded on the same facts or are, or form part of, a series of offences of the same or similar character or a series of offences committed in the prosecution of a single purpose'.[13] From the perspective of efficiency, a single trial of several charges will require less time and resources than separate trials of each charge. On the other hand, the primary goal must be ensuring fairness to the accused. Allowing multiple counts sometimes tempts the prosecutor to 'overload' the indictment. The more charges there are, the greater the scope there is for utilising prosecutorial discretion to drop some charges in return for a plea of guilty on the remainder.

More important in the context of a fair trial, while the evidence adduced on each charge is theoretically only to be used in determining that charge, there is an obvious danger that prejudicial material admitted in respect of one charge will be used in respect of another. Further, multiple counts may improperly enhance the apparent criminality of the accused, cause jury confusion, and encourage a compromise verdict (acquittal on some counts, conviction on others). For these reasons, the courts bear a heavy responsibility in ensuring that 'where there is a real risk of impermissible prejudice to the accused, the sound exercise of the [judicial] discretion generally (if not universally) requires a direction for separate trials'.[14] Similar principles should apply where several accused are joined in an indictment for a single trial. However, in practice, trials are not separated where the offences substantially arise out of the same or closely related facts, regardless of the risks of prejudice.[15]

In conducting the trial, and presenting evidence, the prosecutor again has considerable independence from judicial interference. By way of example, the High Court has held, as a 'general proposition', that the 'Crown Prosecutor alone bears the responsibility of deciding whether a person will be called as a witness for the Crown'.[16] The trial judge may question the prosecutor to discover the reasons for a decision not to call a particular witness, may suggest that the prosecutor reconsider the decision, and may comment to the jury on the decision. But the trial judge 'cannot direct the prosecutor to call a particular witness' and, 'save in the most exceptional circumstances, the trial judge should not himself [sic] call a person to give evidence'.[17]

It is true that the ethical responsibilities imposed on a prosecutor are considerable, although they vary from jurisdiction to jurisdiction. The New South Wales Bar Association Rules, for example, provide in part:

62. A prosecutor must fairly assist the court to arrive at the truth, must seek impartially to have the whole of the relevant evidence placed intelligibly before the court, and must seek to assist the court with adequate submissions of law to enable the law properly to be applied to the facts.

63. A prosecutor must not press the prosecution's case for a conviction beyond a full and firm presentation of that case.

64. A prosecutor must not, by language or other conduct, seek to inflame or bias the court against the accused.

65. A prosecutor must not argue any proposition of fact or law which the prosecutor does not believe on reasonable grounds to be capable of contributing to a finding of guilt and also carry weight.

66. A prosecutor must disclose to the opponent as soon as practicable all material (including the names of and means of finding prospective witnesses in connexion with such material) available to the prosecutor or of which the prosecutor becomes aware which could constitute evidence relevant to the guilt or innocence of the accused, unless

    (a) such disclosure, or full disclosure, would seriously threaten the integrity of the administration of justice in those proceedings or the safety of any person; and

    (b) the prosecutor believes on reasonable grounds that such a threat could not be avoided by confining such disclosure, or full disclosure, to the opponent being a legal practitioner, on appropriate conditions which may include an undertaking by the opponent not to disclose certain material to the opponent's client or any other person.

...

67. A prosecutor who has reasonable grounds to believe that certain material available to the prosecution may have been unlawfully obtained must promptly:

    (a) inform the opponent if the prosecutor intends to use the material; and

    (b) make available to the opponent a copy of the material if it is in documentary form.

68. A prosecutor must not confer with or interview any of the accused except in the presence of the accused's representative.

69. A prosecutor must not inform the court or the opponent that the prosecution has evidence supporting an aspect of its case unless the prosecutor believes that such evidence will be available from material already available to the prosecutor.

70. A prosecutor who has informed the court of matters within Rule 69, and who has later learnt that such evidence will not be available, must immediately inform the opponent of that fact and must inform the court of it when next the case is before the court.

Some prosecution guidelines produced by Directors of Public Prosecutions (DPPs) require prosecutors to inform the defence of 'all facts and circumstances and the identity of all witnesses reasonably to be regarded as relevant to any issue likely to arise at trial'.[18] This duty of disclosure extends to 'any statement by a witness that may be inconsistent with the witness's intended evidence, including any statement made in conference'.[19] It is obviously necessary that similar guidelines be adopted throughout Australia. However, the real issue is whether reliance on ethical guidelines is sufficient. The New South Wales Independent Commission Against Corruption (ICAC) has commented:

> At the moment much depends upon the sense of fairness, and the demanding nature or otherwise, of the individual prosecutor. They can call for information from the police, but not all will do so. The requirement is to be aware of the cards which the State holds, and ensure they are laid on the table. This can be galling

where the defence has, and frequently exercises, the right to perpetrate ambushes upon the prosecution. However the obligation upon those involved on the prosecution side to be fully fair at all times is one that all espouse. Just a few pay only lip service to it.[20]

There is another problem, which may be more serious. A totally ethical prosecutor remains dependent on the police who conduct the investigation and obtain the evidence to be produced in court. Even if that evidence has been obtained improperly or fabricated, the prosecutor may be completely unaware of this. The prosecutor may not know that a witness has prior criminal convictions or has made earlier statements inconsistent with the testimony they propose to give. Indeed, the prosecutor has little incentive to investigate such matters. The police have little incentive and, traditionally, no obligation to disclose such matters to the prosecutor. The system has worked on the premise that it is for the defence, rather than the prosecutor or the judge, to bring such matters to light. Unfortunately, the defence may not be in a position to do this. In some jurisdictions, the police are now required by DPP guidelines to certify that all 'documentation, material and other information [that] might be of relevance to either the prosecution or the defence' has been disclosed to the DPP, but it may be doubted whether such certification is a sufficient safeguard against police misconduct.

Reliance on appellate review is not entirely satisfactory. An appeal may never even be brought because the defence may not have become aware of withheld information. Even if the information is discovered, the problem remains that the courts are reluctant to actively enforce these guidelines. While they accept that, for example, a prosecutor should not be an advocate fighting for conviction, it is rare for an appeal to be allowed on the basis that such conduct has deprived an accused of a fair trial and caused a miscarriage of justice.[21] This is true in other contexts. A decision of a prosecutor not to call a particular person as a witness will only result in a successful appeal if it gave rise to a 'miscarriage of justice', when 'viewed against the conduct of the trial taken as a whole'.[22] To give another example, an appeal would rarely succeed on the basis that a prosecutor in his or her final address had misrepresented the evidence or the law, or resorted to emotional arguments rather than reason. As long as the trial judge in the summing up to the jury had corrected these matters, the appeal court is likely to conclude that there is no risk of a miscarriage of justice. In one Queensland case, for example, the Crown Prosecutor addressed the jury in a way that the Court of Criminal Appeal described as 'clearly reprehensible' and involved language that was 'inflammatory' and 'emotive'.[23] However, the appeal was dismissed because the trial judge directed the jury to ignore the remarks and because the Crown case was a 'strong one'.

It is our view that the present system is unsatisfactory. Reliance on a prosecutor's ethical duties is little compensation to an accused person unlucky enough to be prosecuted by someone who fails, for whatever reason, to comply with appropriate standards. Appellate intervention on fairness principles has two major disadvantages—it is limited in available remedies, and usually emphasises that there must be a risk of miscarriage of justice. In a report of the Australian Institute of Judicial Administration it was observed that:

> Quite apart from tactical considerations, the time is long overdue for placing an obligation upon the prosecution, an obligation, moreover, which is continuous … Time and again, calls for such an obligation are resisted on the ground that all Directors of Public Prosecutions have office guidelines requiring disclosure upon request. It is reasonable to require a request, but it is not reasonable to require that the requester identify the exculpatory material which may be in the government's possession. Besides, if disclosure already occurs (upon request) on a voluntary basis, the passage from voluntary compliance to statutory obligation should not prove too onerous.[24]

The ICAC has recommended that prosecution internal guidelines be strengthened and made as objective as possible.[25] It has also recommended that guidelines be issued requiring the police to provide to prosecutors all material and information held by any police officer 'concerning any proposed Crown witness with material or information that might be of assistance or interest to either the prosecution or the defence'.[26] As we have seen, this has been done in some States. It is up to the appeal courts to actively enforce such guidelines and ensure that prosecutorial zealousness does not endanger a fair trial for the accused.

## The defence

In the higher courts, the accused is usually seated in a special dock separated from the rest of the court and he or she is normally referred to as 'the accused' rather than by name. These customs add to the theatre of the trial, but tend to subtly undermine the presumption of innocence. In some trials, there is also a practical consideration—isolating the accused in this way is very suggestive when a witness is asked to carry out an in-court identification. It would be preferable if such symbolism were avoided. In the United States, the accused sits with his or her counsel, reflecting the constitutionally protected right to a fair trial and due process.[27] Some Australian jurisdictions give a judge the power to order that the accused may 'remain on the floor of the court'[28] but it would be preferable if the use of the dock were simply abolished. Security concerns may be met in other ways. Any procedure that undermines the presumption of innocence and trial fairness should be discontinued. Thus, the Unites States Supreme Court has held that an accused person held on remand must be permitted to wear civilian clothing in court to avoid the fact-finding process of the jury being tainted by extraneous considerations that may render the trial unfair.[29]

An issue of more general importance, however, is the question of legal representation. An accused person may choose to conduct his or her own defence, but in the vast majority of criminal trials the representation of a barrister or solicitor is sought for very good reasons. There can be no doubt that a criminal accused who lacks legal representation in our adversarial system of criminal justice is usually at a substantial disadvantage. Various studies have shown that represented accused have a statistically far better chance of acquittal.[30] The effective conduct of a criminal defence calls for knowledge not only of the criminal law but also of the rules of procedure and evidence. Both examination-in-chief and cross-examination of witnesses require skill and experience, and some degree of objectivity, as do many tactical decisions to be made during a criminal trial.

One of the apparent merits of the adversarial model is that, in theory, if not always in practice, it facilitates and encourages the resolute examination and testing of all propositions of fact advanced in a court.[31] Given the continuation of the present model of criminal justice, the availability of legal assistance is critical to prevent the forms and formalities of legal procedures constituting little more than a sham of justice. More eloquently: 'In such a case, the adversarial process is unbalanced and inappropriate and the likelihood is that, regardless of the efforts of the trial judge, the forms and formalities of legal procedures will conceal the substance of oppression.'[32] For these reasons, the *International Covenant on Civil and Political Rights* expressly provides that, in the determination of any criminal charge, everyone shall be entitled:

> to defend himself in person or through legal assistance of his own choosing ... and to have legal assistance assigned to him, in any case where the interests of justice so require, and without payment by him in any such case if he does not have sufficient means to pay for it.[33]

But while the proposition that legal representation is advantageous has long been recognised in this country, it is only recently that the further proposition that it is nearly always essential for a fair trial has achieved a measure of general acceptance. The reason, of course, was the financial implications of such a proposition in respect of those accused people unable to pay for legal representation. Legal aid schemes, funded in large measure by both federal and State government money, expanded rapidly during the 1970s. The increase in demand for legal aid generated by its increased availability resulted in further need for expansion, as government policy and then economic recession limited available funds. As a result, the various legal aid bodies have faced the difficult, if not impossible task, of reconciling demand for legal aid with tight and inadequate budgets. Indeed, the federal government has significantly reduced legal aid funding over the last few years. Inevitably, this will have an impact on the availability of legal representation in criminal cases (see also the discussion of legal aid in chapter 4).

Until recent years, the High Court had been unwilling to endorse the proposition that a fair trial usually required access to legal representation. However, it changed its position in *Dietrich v The Queen*. On a strict analysis, the High Court decided that a person charged with a criminal offence has no enforceable 'right' to legal representation. But the position of the majority, as articulated by Mason CJ and McHugh J in their joint judgment, is that where a trial judge:

> is faced with an application for an adjournment or a stay by an indigent accused charged with a serious offence who, through no fault on his or her part, is unable to obtain legal representation … [then] in the absence of exceptional circumstances, the trial in such a case should be adjourned, postponed or stayed until legal representation is available.

Further, where the trial in fact proceeds to conviction in such circumstances, the majority held that if:

> by reason of the lack of representation of the accused, the resulting trial is not a fair one, any conviction of the accused must be quashed by an appellate court for the reason that there has been a miscarriage of justice in that the accused has been convicted without a fair trial.

The majority of the High Court has in fact recognised a right to legal representation in substance, at least where the charge involves a 'serious offence'. This conclusion follows from the proposition that an accused person has a right to a 'fair trial', or at least a right not to be subjected to an unfair trial. The majority considered that inability to obtain legal representation for a trial of a serious offence would, 'in the absence of exceptional circumstances', render such a trial inevitably unfair. It should thus be stayed, at least until representation is available. Failure to stay it will usually result in a successful appeal against conviction.[34]

Two members of the High Court dissented, considering that the responsibility of the courts is to ensure that an accused person receives the fairest possible trial in all the circumstances. Those circumstances may include the absence of publicly funded legal representation. On this approach the trial must go ahead even though, in an ideal world, the accused would be legally represented. In respect of this argument, it may be accepted that the legislature and the executive bear the responsibility of obtaining and allocating public funds. It is also true that, in a real world, difficult choices have to be made as to how the pie of available funds is to be divided. More legal aid dollars may well mean fewer hospital beds.

As a general proposition, it is not the role of the courts to second-guess such decisions in a parliamentary democracy. On the other hand, if the state chooses to bring to bear the weight of the criminal law on an individual citizen, and to utilise the resources at its disposal to advance the prosecution, the citizen is entitled to something in return. Whether this is because every citizen in a democracy must be accorded certain rights when dealing with the state, or because there is some 'social contract' according to which the grant of power to the state is subject to certain conditions, is a matter more of language than of substance. This decision of the High Court does not mean that the courts are interfering in the process of allocation of public monies. What it does mean is that the courts will not allow the state to take a person to trial without certain basic prerequisites to a fair trial.

It is likely that the boundaries of this decision will come under pressure. The High Court has had to make it clear that the reference to 'through no fault on his or her part' was '*not* intended to indicate that' any form of improvidence or mis-behaviour on the part of a defendant 'which had contributed to his or her lack of representation must automatically preclude entitlement to a stay'.[35] The nature of 'exceptional circumstances' was not explained by the majority of the court, although Justice Toohey provided some guidance (not necessarily endorsed by the rest of the majority) when he said:

> It is not possible to say that the trial judge must adjourn the trial [when it is likely that the accused will be prejudiced by lack of representation] for there are other considerations to be taken into account … The situation of witnesses, particularly the victim, may need to be considered as well as the consequences of an adjourn-ment for the presentation of the prosecution case and for the court's programme generally. But ordinarily the requirement of a fair trial will be the prevailing con-sideration.

Given the fundamental importance of ensuring a fair trial for an accused per-son, it has to be said that such considerations as the court's program carry little weight. It is to be hoped that 'exceptional circumstances' are truly exceptional. More problematic is the requirement that the offence charged be 'serious'. Since virtually all offences charged in the higher courts would be classified as serious on any cal-culus, we will defer comment on this issue until the discussion on lower courts.

Some jurisdictions have sought to override the decision of the High Court in *Dietrich*. In South Australia, for example, the *Criminal Law (Legal Representation) Act* 2001 provides in section 11 that:

> [t]he fairness of a trial (or a prospective trial) cannot be challenged (and a trial or prospective trial cannot be stayed) on the ground of lack of legal representation unless [the Legal Services Commission has] contrary to this Act, refused or failed to provide legal assistance for the defendant.[36]

The rest of the Act regulates the basis upon which legal assistance is to be pro-vided to defendants in criminal proceedings. The object of the legislation, as specifically stated in section 3, is:

> to ensure that legal representation is available to persons charged with serious offences; … as a consequence of the provision made for legal representation—to limit the application of the rule under which the trial of a person charged with a serious offence may be stayed on the ground that the trial would be unfair for want of legal representation; and … to ensure, as far as practicable, that trials are not dis-rupted by adjournments arising because the defendant lacks legal representation.

Another problem is the situation that may arise where the accused has financial assets that are sufficient to engage private legal representation but she or he is reluctant to bear such a heavy burden. Justice Deane recognised this issue when he said in *Dietrich*:

> In the context of the current level of legal fees, it is arguable that no accused should be required to devote a substantial part of his possessions to obtaining legal representation in resisting a prosecution for an alleged offence of which the law presumes him to be innocent.[37]

At present, recovery of costs in criminal cases is rigidly circumscribed by legislation in most jurisdictions.[38] One solution to this dilemma would be to liberalise the recovery of costs, with the qualification that payments to lawyers be according to the legal aid scales. In this way, a measure of equality would be achieved. Given some proposals to introduce costs awards in certain criminal trials as a mechanism for ensuring compliance with court orders and to encourage admission of facts not in dispute,[39] there is merit in a more sweeping application of the principle that a successful defendant should be able to recover at least some of the costs of the defence.

Just as legal representation is a prerequisite to a fair trial and an indigent accused should receive legal aid, the cost of providing interpreter services (where needed) should be borne by the state. This right should extend to all non-English speakers and the deaf.[40] Indeed, the Constitutional Commission recommended that a right to an interpreter should be constitutionally recognised, extending not merely to translation of oral evidence but also translation of documentary evidence.[41] Justice Deane has put the position clearly:

> If, for example, available interpreter facilities, which were essential to enable the fair trial of an unrepresented person who could neither speak nor understand English, were withheld by the government, a trial judge would be entitled and obliged to postpone or stay the trial and an appellate court would, in the absence of extraordinary circumstances, be entitled and obliged to quash any conviction entered after such an inherently unfair trial.[42]

Of course, a trial judge must retain a discretion to prevent any abuse of a right to an interpreter.[43] A multilingual defendant should not be able to insist on an interpreter as a device to ensure greater time to consider questions put in cross-examination. However, the principle remains that all defendants must, without discrimination, be able to understand what is occurring in the trial.

## The judge

Judges are appointed by government from the ranks of successful barristers and, to a much lesser extent, solicitors and legal academics. They are tenured positions, only subject to dismissal by Parliament in the most extreme circumstances. Their task in a criminal trial is, traditionally, to supervise proceedings, to act as umpire, to determine questions of law, and direct the jury in their task of determining the factual issues.

The judge determines all questions of law that arise during the trial. Most importantly, these include application of the law of evidence, which we discuss in the following chapter. As we shall see, many evidentiary rulings involve difficult questions of degree and 'discretion', which means that the trial judge has enormous power over what evidence is admitted and over the ultimate result. While this is to some extent unavoidable, it is essential that judges be put in the best position to resolve these issues. Greater use of pre-trial hearings on evidentiary questions would encourage careful reflection, as would a greater willingness in appeal courts to interfere with such determinations—a theme we return to in chapter 9.

It goes without saying that a judge must not only *be* impartial but must also *appear* impartial. As a general principle, the judge should be circumspect about 'descending into the arena'. Thus judges may seek clarification of points from witnesses to clear up doubts or confusion or to allow a better understanding of the evidence, but not so as to interfere in the parties' own examinations of the witness or to engage in some form of investigative interrogation.

On the other hand, as we have seen, the law requires that a trial judge ensure that an accused person receives a 'fair' trial. Where the accused is legally represented, the judge will be unlikely to intervene unless the representation is grossly inadequate. But if the accused is unrepresented—a relatively rare event in the higher courts—the trial judge is under an obligation to provide a degree of assistance during the trial. While it is not the judge's role to assist the accused in making tactical decisions, the High Court in *MacPherson v The Queen* explained what is required:

> [T]here is, of course, a distinction between telling the players how to play and telling them the rules of the game. If the distinction is not observed, and an unrepresented accused is kept in ignorance of the rules, the procedural rules which are designed to protect an accused and to ensure a fair trial become a trap, for an unwitting failure to make objection would avoid the judicial duty to control the admission of evidence ... Whether any and what advice should be given to an accused depends upon the circumstances of the particular case and of the particular accused. What can be said is that if it is necessary to give any advice, the necessity arises from the judge's duty to ensure that the trial is fair. That duty does not require, indeed it is inconsistent with, advising an accused how to conduct his case; but it may require advice to an accused as to his rights in order that he may determine how to conduct his case.[44]

It has to be said that this 'solution' to the problem of the unrepresented accused is unsatisfactory. In most cases, it would be quite unrealistic to expect an accused person to be able to make effective use of such information provided by the trial judge. To tell an unrepresented accused that she can cross-examine a police witness will not give her the skill or the experience to do so with any degree of effectiveness. On the other hand, the adversary model makes it inappropriate for the judge to actively coach or assist the accused. Either legal representation must be provided, as we have discussed earlier, or some greater modification of the adversary model must be tolerated in those cases where it cannot properly function because the parties are hopelessly mismatched.

It is our view that the adversary model should not be regarded as sacrosanct. It is already qualified by various procedural advantages accorded to an accused. Ensuring a fair trial for the accused may require its qualification in other contexts. There is a strong argument for the proposition that a judge should be permitted greater leeway to call witnesses, for example, at least in some circumstances. Given that a party who calls a witness is not permitted to engage in the questioning techniques of cross-examination, there may well be cases where it would be unfair to force the defence to call a witness who is likely to prove unfavourable without the defence having the option of testing such evidence. The judge should be allowed to call the witness, giving both sides the opportunity to ask leading questions.[45]

Another area where the calling of witnesses by the judge should be considered is in relation to matters of expertise. One of the problems with the adversary model is that it encourages the parties to litigation to call expert witnesses who will tend to be biased in favour of that party. As Justice Deane of the High Court has said, 'there is much to be said in favour of the introduction of a system of "court witnesses" or expert "assessors" to advise or guide a jury in such areas'.[46] The opinions of such neutral court-appointed experts could be circulated to both sides before trial and full cross-examination allowed.

A further aspect of the limited role of a trial judge is that the judge cannot direct a jury to acquit if he or she feels that the evidence is so weak that it would be 'unsafe' to convict. The High Court has affirmed that while a jury may be directed to acquit if 'there is a defect in the evidence such that, taken at its highest, it will not sustain a verdict of guilt',[47] the case must be left to the jury where the evidence is capable of supporting a conviction. It rejected the argument that the trial judge should be permitted to stop the trial if the prosecution evidence was tenuous or lacking in credibility, since:

> the purpose and genius of the jury system is that it allows for the ordinary experiences of ordinary people to be brought to bear in the determination of factual matters. It is fundamental to that purpose that the jury be allowed to determine, by inference from its collective experience of ordinary affairs, whether and, in the case of conflict, what evidence is truthful.[48]

On the other hand, as one judge has pointed out,[49] appeal courts have the power to overturn a conviction on the basis that it is 'unsafe'. If this is appropriate as a safeguard against wrongful conviction, it is not entirely clear why the trial judge, with all the advantages that derive from presence at the trial, should not also be permitted to intervene in a weak case. The existence of such an additional safe-guard to minimise the risk of convicting an innocent person is no more a dero-gation of the role of the jury than the comparable power of an appeal court or the power of the prosecution to withdraw a charge because the evidence is weak.

The judge directs the jury as to the relevant law, including alternative verdicts and the legal requirements of any defences that may be available on the evidence, even if the accused has not relied on the defence for tactical reasons. In many cases, such directions will be complex and trial judges should try to maximise juror comprehension of the applicable principles. Such techniques as providing written summaries of the relevant law, expressed in clear and simple language, would be a step in the right direction.

Another option is to alter the substance of the applicable legal doctrine in order to make it more comprehensible to a jury. This was what happened in the case of *Zecevic v DPP*[50] when the High Court simplified the law of self-defence by abolishing the doctrine of excessive self-defence, which reduced murder to manslaughter. It is our view, however, that a limited defence of excessive self-defence is justified in principle and should not be removed simply because of doubts about the abilities of juries to understand it.[51] While much more should be done to assist juror comprehension of difficult legal concepts, principle must not be sacrificed to expedience in the criminal law.

The same point may be made in respect of judicial comments on the evidence. The New South Wales Court of Criminal Appeal has set out the obligations of the trial judge in directing the jury in these terms:

(1) In summing up a trial judge will normally direct his attention to matters of law and then to any relevant matters of fact, and assist the jury by such discussion as is necessary to enable the jury to relate the relevant principles of law to the matters of fact falling for their determination.

(2) A trial judge does not bear the responsibility of analysing all of the conflicts and inconsistencies in the evidence adduced during the course of the trial.

(3) A trial judge is under no obligation to put the entirety of the evidence before the jury; all that is required is that he put a fair summary.

(4) A summing up must present a balanced account of the conflicting cases, but when one case is strong and the other is weak it does not follow that a bal-anced summing up will be achieved by under-weighting the strong case and over-weighting the weak case. If one case is strong and the other is weak, then a balanced account inevitably will reflect the strength of the one and the weak-ness of the other.[52]

A trial judge is permitted to indicate his or her personal opinion about the merits of the case, provided that it is also made clear to the jury that they are the judges of the facts and are free to accept or reject such comments as they see fit. It has to be said that recitation of such incantations, while protecting the judge on appeal, is unlikely to prevent such opinions influencing the jury. If the system is to retain the adversary model in which the judge is supposed to play the role of neutral umpire, where the emphasis is on minimising the risk of convicting an innocent person, it would be far better if trial judges avoided such expressions of opinion. Indeed, there is a strong argument that trial judges should avoid any discussion of the evidence or the facts at all. The practice is based on the assumption that the jury is assisted by such a discussion, but it shows little faith in their ability. In the United States, judges give only directions on the law and there is no reason to think that juries in that country are consequently less able to understand the evidence or determine the facts.

Judges in this country sometimes have difficulty in avoiding impermissible comment. In a trial in South Australia in 1992 involving allegations of marital rape, the trial judge directed the jury in terms suggesting that it was permissible for a husband to use 'a measure of rougher than usual handling' in order to 'persuade' his wife to engage in sexual intercourse. Not surprisingly, these directions generated a storm of negative publicity around the country since they appeared to approve the use of force to obtain sex in marriage. Of course, the accused was charged with rape and not assault. It was incumbent on the trial judge to make clear to the jury that an assault before intercourse does not necessarily constitute rape. But the way he chose to do this clearly went too far, as a majority of the South Australian Court of Criminal Appeal subsequently concluded. Although one juror later told the press that the trial judge's summing-up did not play a part in the verdict of acquittal, he could not know for certain what factors operated on the minds of his fellow jurors.

This does not in any way derogate from the principle that the independence and autonomy of the judiciary must be maintained. Once appointed, judges should be protected from dismissal at the whim of the government or any other form of governmental control. But care should be taken in judicial appointments to ensure participation by all sections of the community while retaining qualifications based on merit. Further, more must be done to minimise the expression of sexist or racist attitudes by the judiciary.[53] This country has been slow to recognise the value of judicial education. Yet, judicial education is consistent with judicial independence and autonomy. While institutions such as the Australian Institute of Judicial Administration have been established with that goal in mind, more can be done to keep judges abreast of developments in both the law and society.[54] This is required even though most questions of fact arising in a criminal trial in the higher courts are answered not by the trial judge but by the jury.

## The jury

In the higher criminal courts, it is the jury that determines the ultimate factual question—whether the prosecution has proved the accused guilty of the offence or offences with which he or she is charged. In determining this issue, the jury will have to consider a whole range of factual matters, the evidence adduced in the trial by the prosecution and the defence, and the directions on the law given by the trial judge.

As a general principle, a jury is drawn randomly from all adult members of the community. However, there are several important qualifications to this principle. Certain people, such as those sentenced to imprisonment within a prescribed period, are disqualified while others, such as practising lawyers, police, and people unable to understand English are ineligible. Some people, such as doctors, dentists and pregnant women may claim exemption.

In most jurisdictions, both the prosecution and the defence may 'peremptorily challenge' for any reason a number of potential jurors (the number varying from jurisdiction to jurisdiction). Both the prosecution and the defence may success-fully challenge any juror 'for cause', which apart from categories of disqualifica-tion or ineligibility, involves juror bias. Few such challenges are made because little or no information is available regarding potential jurors—unlike in the United States, where extensive questioning of prospective jurors is permitted. This absence of information also means that peremptory challenges are usually based on appearance and stereotyping. In a 1990 Queensland trial, the accused used all of his eight peremptory challenges to challenge potential women jurors and then told the trial judge that 'as a Christian man, it was against his religious beliefs to be judged by women'. The judge treated this as a proper challenge for cause but, on appeal, the Court of Criminal Appeal rejected the notion that an accused per-son can object, on religious or any other grounds (other than demonstrated par-tiality), to people entitled by law to sit as jurors.[55]

Criticisms of the jury come from a number of quarters. There is clearly force in the argument that a jury of ordinary men and women drawn at random from the community is likely to lack the knowledge and experience necessary to responsibly determine some complex scientific issues that may arise in the course of a criminal trial or some of the detailed technical questions that may be involved in the trial of white-collar corporate and computer crime. Yet the vast body of opinion and research indicates that the jury is a reliable and competent fact-finding body, provided the evidence and issues are put to it sensibly and practi-cally.[56] This is not to suggest in any way that juries do not make mistakes or that, in some circumstances, reliance on a jury is inappropriate. Some of the arguments in support of the jury system are unverifiable and rather doubtful, such as the claimed ability to best judge demeanour and witness credibility. Overall, however, it has to be said that the arguments in favour of retention of the jury system, appropriately reformed, outweigh the arguments for abolition.

The fact that a jury comes from the general community, on a transient basis, means that it is likely to be some guarantee against the arbitrary exercise of power by the state. The United States Supreme Court referred to the knowledge gained 'from history and experience that it was necessary to protect against unfounded criminal charges brought to eliminate enemies and against judges too responsive to the voice of higher authority'.[57] An independent judiciary is one protection against arbitrary government action; juries are another: providing 'an accused with the right to be tried by a jury of his peers [gives] him an inestimable safeguard against the corrupt or overzealous prosecutor and against the compliant, biased, or eccentric judge'.[58]

Further, the jury is significant in terms of popular democratic participation in the criminal justice system. Although, as we have noted, the role of the jury is circumscribed by judicial directions and by procedural limitations, it still is a method of infusing community values into the operation of the criminal law, particularly where the law requires the making of fine moral judgments. For example, in a complex fraud trial in the New South Wales Supreme Court in 1992, the jury was discharged when it failed to reach a verdict after 15 days of consideration. The trial of four people accused of defrauding the Commonwealth, by stripping the assets of companies and making them unable to pay tax, had begun on 4 February and involved 111 sitting days before the jury was sent out to consider its verdict. The jury had been taken through the asset-stripping exercises on 141 companies, given a crash course on relevant parts of the Commonwealth *Companies Act*, *Income Tax Assessment Act* and *Crimes Act*, and read the expert advices by eminent lawyers given to the four accused when devising their schemes 13 years before. It was clear from a relatively early stage of the trial that the task of the jury in achieving unanimity would be difficult. On 22 June, 84 days into the trial, the trial judge received a letter from the foreman indicating that one of the jurors had stuck cotton-wool in her ears during some days of the Crown's closing address, had done the same thing in the jury room, put her head on a cushion and refused to take part in jury discussions about the case. This could make it impossible for the jury to reach a unanimous decision, the foreman wrote, thus making 'a mockery of the jury system'. The trial judge recalled the jury and emphasised the need for all jurors to take part in jury room discussions and listen to the points of view of other jurors. Nevertheless, the jury was never able to agree on a verdict. Some would draw from this example an argument for abolishing jury trials in such cases. But even in complex trials of this type, there are often fundamental issues at stake that should remain the province of a randomly selected cross-section (at least as a fair approximation) of the community. As was written in an article in the *Sydney Morning Herald* commenting on this case:

> Did the outcome of the latest bottom-of-the-harbour tax case represent a failure of the jury system? Far from it. The charges were uniquely suited to trial by jury. The four accused were charged with conspiring to defraud the Commonwealth of tax revenue to which it was, or might be, entitled, by dishonest means, knowing they were dishonest. Justice James ruled that dishonest means dishonest by the standards of

ordinary reasonable people at the time the alleged conspiracy took place—that is, in 1979 and 1980. Who better to decide whether the accused were dishonest by such standards than 12 reasonable people drawn at random from the population at large.[59]

There are other ways in which a jury can introduce community values into the criminal law. In cases of wives killing their husbands after prolonged periods of domestic violence, the law may provide very little in the way of defence. Pleas of provocation and self-defence may be so defined that they are not available in such circumstances. Yet a jury may nonetheless acquit the accused. While it is the view of the High Court that a jury would be acting improperly if it brought in a verdict inconsistent with its findings on particular facts, it is clearly the position that it is within the exclusive province of the jury to decide the verdict.[60] As Justice Murphy said:

> Anyone acquainted with the modern operation of the system of criminal justice will be aware that juries do invoke their traditional power to acquit for reasons which are extraneous to the strict legal issues, for example, where the charge is trivial or stale or there has been serious misconduct by the prosecution.[61]

There are other benefits to be derived from the system of jury trial. It encourages the trial to be conducted in a way comprehensible to the public and seen to be fair. As Justice Deane has explained:

> Trial by jury also brings important practical benefits to the administration of criminal justice. A system of criminal law cannot be attuned to the needs of the people whom it exists to serve unless its administration, proceedings and judgments are comprehensible by both the accused and the general public and have the appearance, as well as the substance, of being impartial and just. In a legal system where the question of criminal guilt is determined by a jury of ordinary citizens, the participating lawyers are constrained to present the evidence and issues in a manner that can be understood by laymen ...
>
> Equally important, the presence and function of a jury in a criminal trial and the well-known tendency of jurors to identify and side with a fellow-citizen who is, in their view, being denied a 'fair go' tend to ensure observance of the consideration and respect to which ordinary notions of fair play entitle an accused or a witness.[62]

In summary, jury trials must be retained in the higher criminal courts. This is not to say that judge-only trials should not be an option, only that they should require the consent of both the defence and prosecution (as is presently the position in New South Wales). Nor is it to deny that there is scope for reform of the jury system. Some issues may be addressed shortly.

With regard to the composition of juries, the principle that they are selected at random from a cross-section of the community should be strongly defended. While it is appropriate that some categories of people should not sit on juries, care is required in circumscribing these categories.[63] Equally important, the principle of randomness demands that no extra information is given to the prosecution about any antecedents or reputation of jury members. In some jurisdictions that has been the practice[64] and it is, as one judge has stated, 'a process of artificial selection derived from the special knowledge available to the prosecution authorities ... contrary to the spirit and principle of jury service'.[65] It must be stopped. In Queensland, both the prosecution and defence are given access before trial to the list of potential jurors who will be summonsed on the day the trial is listed to commence. This has permitted investigation into their background and attempts to use the information gained in choosing the jury (as seen in the trial of the former Premier of Queensland, Joh Bjelke-Petersen). Although legislation was introduced in 1995 imposing some limits on such investigation,[66] the danger remains that any jury chosen in such circumstances will not be truly random. Indeed, there is considerable force in the argument that the right of peremptory challenge, exercised either on the basis of a 'hunch' or extra information, is inconsistent with the principle and should be abandoned. On the other hand, it is possible to introduce procedures designed to reduce the likelihood of partiality while retaining the principle of randomness. Potential jurors might, for example, be required to swear that there is nothing that would make it difficult for them to be impartial.

There is much scope for assisting juries in their task.[67] The practice in some jurisdictions of providing jurors with a document containing basic information about court procedure and their rights and duties should be generally adopted. Use of technology such as video recorders, overhead projectors and, in appropriate cases, computers, should be encouraged. Copies of all documentary exhibits and photographs must be provided to each member of the jury when they are admitted into evidence. While it is increasingly common to allow jurors to take notes during the trial, they are still discouraged from taking an active part in the trial. To take one example, the courts are reluctant to allow juries to ask questions of witnesses. Allowing juries to interact in the trial in this way, subject to the normal controls, would not only emphasise the element of public participation in the justice system, it would also give the other participants a better idea of what issues are of interest to the jury.

In Western Australia, South Australia, Tasmania, Victoria, and the Northern Territory, legislation provides that, in most criminal trials, if a jury has failed to reach a unanimous verdict after a fixed term (at least two hours), an agreed verdict of ten of those jurors will suffice for conviction or acquittal. While the High Court has held that such verdicts are prohibited by the Constitution in respect of Commonwealth offences,[68] supporters of majority verdicts assert that too many juries fail to convict because of one or two obstinate or corrupt jurors who are determined not to convict whatever the evidence, and that the result is the enormous delay and cost incurred in retrials. However, research overseas indicates that where there is a requirement of unanimity, it usually requires a large number of dissenting jurors early in the deliberations to prevent an ultimately unanimous verdict.[69] In a 1997 New South Wales study, it was found that only modest benefits could be expected from introduction of majority verdicts.[70] If all re-trials were avoided in all cases where an 11–1 or 10–2 split occurred, the reduction in total trials would be less than 5%. However, many presently hung trials do not result in a re-trial, so the consequent benefits from the introduction of majority verdicts would be substantially reduced. Further, the requirement of unanimity forces the jury to take seriously the views of a dissenting minority, a minority that may in fact reflect a minority group within the community. While it may be going too far to say that majority verdicts are inconsistent with the principle of proof beyond reasonable doubt, there does not appear to be sufficient evidence to justify introducing them in those States that presently require unanimity.[71]

There are difficult issues concerning the extent to which freedom of public discussion should be restricted in order to protect the impartiality of criminal juries and the confidentiality of their deliberative processes. In respect of the first issue, the present law of contempt prohibits publications before verdict if 'as a matter of practical reality', they have a 'real and definite tendency to prejudice or embarrass' the trial, subject to defences of 'innocent publication', 'fair and accurate reporting in good faith' and 'comment on matters of public interest'. Because a jury's role is to decide the case according to the relevant law and the admissible and admitted evidence, it would cease to be impartial if, for example, it was aware of, and influenced by, allegations or material not admitted during the trial.

It is true that there are remedial measures available such as warning the jury to ignore prejudicial publicity, adjournment, change of venue or, finally, jury discharge. However, it cannot always be assumed that warnings are effective. According to one account of a jury's deliberations published in an Australian newspaper, when the jury was told to ignore press reports their response was to make a special effort to find out what had been said in the press and to discuss its significance among themselves.[72] As the Australian Law Reform Commission has pointed out:

> It cannot, in short, be assumed that members of a jury are wholly obedient and passive in the face of instructions from the judge on a matter such as this. In familiar human style, their attitude to an instruction to behave in a certain way may range from more-or-less complete obedience through qualified obedience to outright disobedience. The last reaction seems most likely to occur when the jury feels that 'something is being hidden from them'.[73]

Research studies support the common-sense view that some kinds of information, such as suggestions that the accused had confessed to the crime charged or had a substantial criminal record, are likely to have a prejudicial impact on any jury.[74] Directions to ignore such information are unlikely to have any effect.[75]

It follows that contempt laws are necessary, although we share the view of the Australian Law Reform Commission that the present rules are both over- and under-inclusive. More guidance is required on what is prohibited so that, for example, statements to the effect that an accused is innocent or guilty, has prior convictions or is of good or bad character, or has confessed to the offence, should be specifically prohibited subject to available defences.[76] On the other hand, a general principle of 'substantial risk of prejudice' should be retained. The defence of 'public interest' should be narrowed so as to prevent it automatically exonerating prejudice to a fair trial. As the Commission has recommended, the 'media should, in effect, be required to show that the discussion is genuinely important, that the material in question forms an integral part of the discussion and that the discussion would suffer significantly if the publication were delayed'.[77]

With regard to the issue of confidentiality of jury deliberations, the situation is equally complex. While the present law is not entirely clear, contempt and evidentiary rules discourage both disclosure and publication of what occurs in the jury room. The most commonly advanced justification for this secrecy is that jury verdicts must be final and conclusive, subject to appeal on specified limited grounds. Such secrecy and finality, so the argument goes, is crucial to maintaining public confidence in the jury system.

While consistent with the system's concern to maintain the appearance of justice, we are not impressed by this argument. If there have been serious irregularities with consequent risk of miscarriage of justice, they should be brought to light. Indeed, there is a public interest in research into the behaviour of juries to permit more intelligent discussion of the issues which we have touched upon. On the other hand, we do not accept the argument that the secrecy of jury deliberations constitutes the best instrument 'for achieving uncertainty, capriciousness, lack of uniformity, disregard of former decisions—utter unpredictability'.[78] Some restrictions are necessary, if only to give jurors the security and privacy that is essential for the proper performance of their task. The extent of the restriction should vary, however, depending on such considerations as whether disclosure or publication is involved, whether the particular trial or the names and addresses of jurors are disclosed, and the timing and purpose of disclosure.[79] Above all, there should be no inhibition on a juror disclosing matters that suggest a miscarriage of justice.

In respect of complex[80] white-collar criminal trials, there are options for reform short of removing the right to trial by jury. The Standing Committee of Attorneys-General has been considering possible reforms and there are moves for procedural changes in some of the States. There is scope for the general reform and simplification of the rules of evidence, which we discuss in chapter 6. In particular, some of the rules of evidence relating to admission of documents, usually a central part of white-collar crime trials, may be modernised and simplified. The use of charts, summaries and other aids might simplify complexity without any risk of injustice. There should be much greater use of formal pre-trial proceedings to ensure disclosure of relevant evidence, determine questions of admissibility, and obtain agreement on non-contentious issues. Indeed, it is possible to develop procedures that encourage early disclosure of an accused's line of defence, thereby simplifying and shortening trials, without impinging on the right to silence. What must be avoided is a knee-jerk reaction to perceived difficulties in prosecution and the removal of existing rights when less radical options are available.

Given the central role of the jury in the criminal justice system, it is worrying that its role is being whittled away. Many offences have been created by statute, which may, or must, be determined summarily. There are no provisions regarding jury trial in the State Constitutions. It is true that section 80 of the Australian Constitution reads, in part:

> The trial on indictment of any offence against any law of the Commonwealth shall be by jury ...

On one interpretation of this section, it provides a right to trial by jury in trials of 'serious' offences under Commonwealth law. However, the majority of the High Court has traditionally taken a very narrow approach to the provision, holding that it has a merely procedural effect: only if the prosecution is by indictment (as distinct from some summary procedure) must the trial be by jury.[81] It is true that the High Court has held that, where a trial of a Commonwealth offence is by jury, majority verdicts are prohibited under section 80 of the Constitution.[82] But there is no constitutional restriction imposed on any government in Australia in creating criminal offences that may be heard and determined summarily.

In 1987, the Rights Advisory Committee of the Constitutional Commission recommended that section 80 of the Australian Constitution be amended to provide that neither the Commonwealth nor a State shall:

> provide for or permit trial without jury for an offence which is punishable by imprisonment for twelve months or more, but may provide for or permit such a trial if a magistrate or a judge so orders upon the application of the accused.[83]

A referendum in 1988 included a proposal in accordance with this recommendation but it was defeated.

# The lower courts

The names of the lower courts vary from jurisdiction to jurisdiction, with titles such as Court of Summary Jurisdiction, Magistrates' Court, Local Court and Court of Petty Sessions. In New South Wales, for example, the lower courts are the Local Court, the Children's Court and the Coroner's Court.

The Local Court in New South Wales has jurisdiction over a wide range of summary offences (for example, traffic offences, offences against public order or safety, public health offences). It has jurisdiction over a large number of indictable[84] offences, which may be dealt with summarily (unless the defendant or the prosecuting authority elects otherwise).[85] It also has jurisdiction over a range of indictable offences, which are dealt with summarily unless the prosecuting authority elects otherwise (that is, the defendant has no say in the matter). These include offences against property where the value of the property does not exceed $5000 and such serious offences as assault occasioning actual bodily harm, indecent assault and assault with intent to commit a felony. In such cases, the maximum penalty of the offence is reduced to, at most, two years' imprisonment.[86] As we have seen in chapter 4, the Local Court also has jurisdiction over committal hearings. The Children's Court has jurisdiction over both summary and most indictable offences in relation to young people under the age of 18. In terms of procedure, the major difference from Local Courts is that most cases are heard in closed courts. Lastly, the Coroner's Court investigates a wide range of deaths and fires. If, at the conclusion of the inquest, the court finds that the evidence establishes a prima facie case against any known person for an indictable offence, the coroner is required to have that person charged with the offence and may commit the person for trial.[87] The coroner may make such further and other findings as to the facts and circumstances as seem appropriate.[88]

One issue that arises from this brief analysis is that there has been a steady increase in the number of indictable offences that can be heard and dealt with summarily in the lower courts. This has been the general tendency in all Australian jurisdictions, and it is designed to reduce the number of trials in the higher courts in front of judge and jury. The lower potential penalties, while still severe, encourage many accused people to proceed summarily. It has been argued by some that this improperly deters accused people from insisting on trial by jury,[89] but this is perhaps an overstatement. Realistically, the system would grind to a halt if a substantial number of those accused who now opt for summary jurisdiction chose to proceed by jury trial. Yet that would most likely be the result if similar sentences were likely, regardless of which option were chosen. It does not seem wrong in these circumstances to offer an accused the option of a different procedural and sentencing regime, as long as the ultimate decision is left with the accused. On the other hand, it is a question of degree. If even more serious offences could be dealt with summarily, perhaps with a corresponding increase in the maximum penalty available in the lower courts, there would be cause to suspect an attack on the institution of trial by jury.

An even more difficult issue concerns the vast number of offences that are triable only summarily. Most new statutory offences are in fact only triable in the lower courts. The question is whether this can cause injustice to the accused or, put differently, whether the lower courts' tier of justice is 'deliberately structured in defiance of the ideology of justice, [and] is concerned less with subtle ideological messages than with direct control', to use the language of Doreen McBarnet quoted at the beginning of this chapter.

The problem is that there are both similarities and differences between the higher and lower courts. On the one hand, many of the procedures are similar to those adopted in the higher courts. In principle, the laws of evidence that apply in the higher courts apply, with some modifications to take into account the absence of a jury, in the lower courts. On the other hand, there are obvious differences. The buildings themselves are often old, badly designed, lacking essential amenities, and generally inadequate to serve the needs of the courts. Proceedings tend to be conducted with less formality and ritual in the lower courts, with the emphasis being to get through the cases and avoid congestion and delay. The common perspective, given the less serious penalties generally imposed, is that most of the cases involve mundane, if not trivial, issues of little interest to the general community. This led Doreen McBarnet to observe, with regard to the similar division in the English system, that:

> it is the relative triviality of the penalties that provides the crucial legitimation in law for the lack of due process in summary justice. Due process of law is required in the ideology of democratic justice before a person's liberty may be interfered with. The reasoning which legitimises reducing due process in the lowest courts is based on this premise, but with a refinement. 'Liberty' ceases to be an absolute and becomes subject to a measuring rod. The limited penalties available to magistrates means that they can interfere less with one's liberty than the higher courts, so defendants in these courts need less due process. The less one's liberty is at risk the less one needs protection. This is perhaps most explicitly stated in the criteria for awarding legal aid.[90]

Assessment of the validity of this critique requires some consideration of the major parties involved in a criminal trial in the lower courts.

# The prosecution

In terms of the formulation of charges, the position is very similar to that in the higher courts. The prosecution determines the charges against the defendant. The information or complaint must inform the accused of the precise nature of the charge, identifying the essential factual ingredients of the actual offence.[91] Sufficient 'particulars' must be provided to isolate precisely what alleged actions of the accused will be under scrutiny at the trial. Most jurisdictions permit several charges in one information. While in some other jurisdictions only one charge may be contained in each information, the prosecutor may bring several charges by laying more than one information. In both situations, the courts have the power to order the matters heard separately where desirable.

However, there is a significant difference between the higher and lower courts with regard to the independence of the prosecution. Traditionally, and with exceptions, prosecutions in the lower courts are conducted by members of the police force. They are sometimes legally trained, but are neither independent lawyers nor members of an independent office of public prosecutions. As a result, they are more likely to identify with the police point of view, to come under pressure to obtain convictions, and to have relatively little concern to ensure a fair trial for the accused. In this context, it should be noted that, apart from this lack of independence, police prosecutors are not necessarily subject to the ethical responsibilities imposed by the Bar Association rules on Crown Prosecutors. It must be concluded that one of the mechanisms adopted in the higher courts in an endeavour to ensure a fair trial for an accused is simply not present in the lower courts. For this reason, we can only support the trend to transfer responsibility over lower court prosecutions to the office of public prosecutions. In New South Wales, for example, this has been done with respect to all committal proceedings. There are proposals to take prosecutions at the Local Court level entirely out of the hands of the police. It should be done forthwith.

It might be argued, on the other hand, that this absence of prosecutorial independence and ethical obligation to ensure a fair trial for the accused is less of a problem in the lower courts given the greater availability of appellate review. It is true that appeals from the lower courts tend to be less constrained than appeals from the higher courts. The reason is that an appeal from a lower court conviction will be a full rehearing in a higher court—effectively a completely new trial. As a result, the conduct of the prosecution in the lower court hearing is, at least in one sense, less significant. Yet this would be little consolation to the convicted accused who cannot afford to bring such an appeal, or to a convicted accused who is refused bail after such a conviction and must wait until the appeal is heard to obtain justice and freedom. It is simply not good enough to excuse flaws in the lower courts by saying that an appeal may be brought in the higher courts.

## The defence

Many accused people in the lower courts are not legally represented. In a 2000 study by the New South Wales Bureau of Crime Statistics and Research it was found that about half of defendants in the New South Wales Local Court were unrepresented.[92] In fact, the proportion of unrepresented defendants had been steadily increasing over the preceding years.[93] This had significant consequences for defendants. The success rate, in terms of having all charges dismissed, of represented defendants entering a plea of not guilty was more than double that of unrepresented defendants. While more represented defendants entered pleas of guilty, this may have merely reflected a realistic assessment of the prosecution case and would have tended to result in a reduced sentence.

Despite the fact that proceedings in the lower courts are not conducted with the same degree of ritual formality that occurs in the higher courts, they are nonetheless highly structured and formal from the point of view of the lay defendant. The procedures, the rules, the architecture of the court, the language of the professional participants, all combine to make the experience a confusing and frightening one for defendants and witnesses. In part, as we have noted, there is a purposive element to this—to demonstrate the importance of the proceedings and the power of the law, and to ensure an orderly flow of cases. In a democracy, however, this is no justification. The operation of the law and its institutions must be comprehensible to all. This is particularly important for the accused, who is entitled to understand what is happening during the trial of the charge against him or her and entitled to participate in its process.

We noted above that there is an obligation on a judge in the higher courts to provide information to an accused who is without legal representation in order to ensure a 'fair trial'. The same obligation is imposed on magistrates in the lower courts. As we concluded there, some modification of the adversary model must be tolerated in those cases where it cannot properly function because the litigants are completely mismatched. But, short of such radical changes, much more can be done to simplify procedures and court discourse. Much greater information should be provided to defendants about their rights and the operation of the court system.

Of course, however, such modifications would not address the central issue here, which is the availability of publicly funded legal assistance. In *Dietrich*, the majority of the High Court held that inability to obtain legal representation for a trial of a 'serious offence' would, in the absence of exceptional circumstances, render such a trial inevitably unfair. The majority did not attempt to define the meaning of 'serious offence' although Justice Deane stated that an example of a non-serious offence would be one 'where there is no real threat of deprivation of personal liberty'.[94] He did not suggest that this example provided the boundary. Interestingly, in an earlier case considering the connected issue of a right to trial by jury, Justice Deane had discussed the same term. He indicated the tentative view that the 'boundary will ordinarily be identified by reference to whether the offence is punishable, when prosecuted in the manner in which it is being prosecuted, by a maximum term of imprisonment of more than one year'.[95] Other boundaries are possible—the possibility of any imprisonment[96] or proceedings where imprisonment is in fact to be imposed.[97] In the United States there is no right to counsel when the accused is not in fact to be sentenced to a term of imprisonment. In a 1996 decision by the New South Wales Court of Appeal it was held that an offence under the *Prevention of Cruelty to Animals Act* (NSW) prosecuted in the Local Court was not a 'serious criminal offence' even though it carried a maximum penalty of $4000 and imprisonment for one year (although the defendant was, in fact, only fined).[98] Whatever test is ultimately adopted, the fact remains that it will exclude a substantial number of defendants in lower courts from the protection of *Dietrich*. This is a matter for concern.

There are likely to be cases that cannot be classified as serious in the sense that there is a risk of a substantial period of imprisonment and yet there appears to be a strong argument for legal representation. In truth, it is difficult to understand what the nature of the potential sentence has to do with the fairness of the trial (although, as Deane J noted, the absence of a jury may reduce some of the potential benefits of legal representation). Offences that may appear relatively minor when compared with many charges heard in the higher courts will often be regarded as very significant by the individual accused. The same is true in respect of the penalties imposed. Any period of imprisonment is traumatic and a fine may be extremely onerous, quite apart from the stigma of conviction. As Doreen McBarnet has argued:

> offences and penalties may seem trivial from the outside but far from trivial from the perspective of the accused—unless they have become so only through the folk memory of the lower-class people who pass through the court, to whom police and law have become enemies, and prosecution for trivial offences a risk of every-day life ... It is these trivial offences [that are] first, most open to the direct intervention of the state in the sense that the police are the only complainants; second, most open to the imposition of a criminal label on 'marginal' behaviour; and third, most open—because their content is so open—to post hoc law-making. In short, it is exactly in the area of minor offences that the operation of the law, in terms of democratic justice, becomes most suspect.[99]

One argument for not ensuring legal aid in all lower court prosecutions might be that summary cases tend to be less complex than trials in the higher courts. There is some truth in this. Many offences dealt with in summary proceedings, for example, do not include any *mens rea*, or 'guilty mind', element. All that the prosecution needs to establish is that the defendant acted, or failed to act, in a certain way and the offence will be proved. Yet, the fact that the definition of the offence so simplifies the facts in issue is a rather curious basis for reducing the entitlements of accused people. As we said in chapter 1, such strict or absolute liability offences are often difficult to justify. Making it easier to impose criminal liability by limiting the definition of an offence is a strange justification for taking away procedural rights, making it even easier to impose liability.

Another aspect of the limited complexity of many summary trials is that they often involve police–accused encounters, rather than resulting from citizen's reports. In such circumstances, the trial is usually limited to the issue of the accused's word against that of the police. Again, however, this is no justification for reducing procedural safeguards. There are many things that a competent counsel can do in cross-examining the police, for example, which may be beyond the skills and experience of the accused. Similarly, it would be wrong to conclude that summary cases are simple cases from the fact that they are, on average, concluded in far less time than trials in the higher cases. That situation is more likely to be the product of the limited resources allocated to such proceedings and the absence of defence counsel, who, if present, would be engaged in aggressive defence of the accused.

Of course, there are policy reasons for placing some limitation on any *de facto* 'right' to legal representation. Greater availability of legal assistance would tend to result in longer hearings, with consequent further delays in the legal system. Equally, the cost of legal aid is very considerable. Over the last few decades, there has been a great increase in the number of people being legally represented at public expense in the lower courts. Duty solicitors employed by legal aid bodies provide the bulk of this assistance. In New South Wales in 1991–92, for example, there were 16 198 appearances before magistrates in the Local Courts on behalf of adults, and 18 551 for juveniles in Children's Courts.[100] But many accused people in the lower courts are not eligible for legal assistance. In New South Wales, guidelines have been introduced restricting legal aid for people appearing on drink-driving charges and as respondents in domestic violence matters.[101] In Victoria, assistance will not normally be provided unless there is a substantial risk of conviction and the imposition of imprisonment or some other significant sanction.[102]

The issue is whether greater delays and costs are a sufficient justification for denying a right to legal assistance or should be seen as an unfortunate consequence of providing a fairer system of criminal justice. In our view, at the very least, legal assistance should be provided when there is a possibility of imprisonment. The High Court will eventually have to set, and justify, a precise dividing line.

Our view is not inconsistent with the proposition that the money spent on legal aid should be used as efficiently as possible. In New South Wales in 1997, for example, 55% of criminal case and duty work was performed by employed duty solicitors, with the rest provided by private lawyers funded by legal aid.[103] There is increasing reliance on solicitor advocates and public defenders. If it proves more efficient in the delivery of legal services, greater use of salaried lawyers must be considered. Further, there are other options for legal assistance short of complete representation. Unrepresented defendants might receive financial assistance for some procedures, such as the issuing of subpoenas. Paralegals could usefully perform some roles, such as guilty pleas in straightforward cases, under the supervision of lawyers. Ultimately what is required is that each defendant receive that degree of legal assistance necessary to ensure that a fair trial is not put at risk.

## The magistrate

As a general proposition, the lower courts are presided over by magistrates. They are appointed under special legislation, will almost invariably have a law degree, and have quasi-judicial tenure. This is a fairly recent development. In many jurisdictions, criminal matters traditionally could be determined by a justice of the peace, without legal training. However, lay justices have been almost entirely excluded from exercising criminal jurisdiction around Australia. Equally, while magistrates have not always been required to have a law degree, since 1985 it has been mandatory for new appointments. Until the last few years, magistrates in some jurisdictions were members of the public service appointed under the terms

of the relevant Public Service Act. Now they are appointed under separate legislation from the public service and are more clearly independent of the executive
government. They usually have, or are close to having, the degree of tenure or
independence that is the norm with judicial rank, although there is considerable
variation around the country.

Removal of justices of the peace from the lower criminal courts is a welcome
development. Equally, there has long been a clear need for all magistrates to be
legally qualified and independent of the government with security of tenure. But
more can be done. Greater emphasis should be placed on professional competence
and experience in appointments. There should be a clear formulation of ethical
standards for the magistracy. As with the judiciary, continuing legal education
should be the norm. Indeed, there is a case for integration of the magistracy
within the judicial hierarchy to emphasise the judicial nature of their function and
the importance of the lower courts.

Yet, whatever improvements are made to the magistracy, the fact remains that
the ultimate factual issues in lower court criminal trials are not decided by a jury.
We have discussed the arguments for and against the jury system in our discussion
of the higher courts and concluded there that the jury should be retained.
Inevitably this raises the question whether the absence of juries in the lower courts
means that accused people there are not receiving 'due process' or a 'fair trial'.
Some commentators argue that this is the case and that:

> in the face of a vastly expanded state, and the near-extinction of jury trials, it is
> more important than ever to argue not merely for the retention, but for a radical
> expansion of popular, democratic participation in the administration of criminal
> justice. This is best done not by mutely treating the jury as sacrosanct but by recov-
> ering the historical and political legacy of the jury, piercing the existing mythology
> that jury cases are the standard method of trial, and holding those who so loudly
> proclaim the importance of the jury to their rhetoric.[104]

In considering this issue, one factor is how well magistrates perform their task.
Perhaps significantly, conviction rates tend to be higher in the lower courts than
the higher courts. While we have noted that juries tend to acquit up to half of
accused people who plead not guilty, the figure in lower courts is more like a
third. Of course, this is no real guide to competence and there is little hard evidence available on this. One by-product of the attitude that lower court criminal
trials are trivial has been that little research has been done into the operation of
these courts, making evaluation effectively impossible. Clearly, there is a need for
comprehensive evaluation of the performance of the lower courts. The lack of
comprehensive information about the operation of the court system encourages
ad hoc adjustment at the expense of informed and principled reform.

In our view, whatever the result of such an evaluation, an ideal system of criminal justice would employ juries at all levels of the system. The arguments in favour

of juries apply just as strongly in the lower courts as in the higher courts. Yet we recognise that there is no practical possibility of juries being introduced in the lower courts. The effects on court delay and the costs of justice would be simply too great and there is no prospect of vastly greater public funds being spent on courts to overcome these problems. As it is, the criminal justice system in the lower courts is stretched to breaking point. One reason is the extremely heavy work load that is commonly imposed on magistrates. It is not uncommon for a magistrate to have to hear more than twenty cases a day, involving a wide range of offences, which require determination of both verdict and sentence. Introduction of juries would see the whole structure collapse.

# Conclusion

Article 14(1) of the *International Covenant on Civil and Political Rights* enunciates the principle that a criminal trial must be 'fair'. It draws no distinction between different types of trial, nor should it. In our view, a strong case can be made for the proposition that the quality of justice offered in the lower courts does not match that provided, notwithstanding any flaws, in the higher courts. Given the fact that the vast majority of criminal trials are dealt with in the lower courts, the critique of Doreen McBarnet at the introduction of this chapter is entirely supportable in Australia.

Yet the argument should not be overstated. We do not share the view that lower court trials are 'deliberately structured in defiance of the ideology of justice'. Rather, they are the product of history and tradition. The problem has been the relatively recent massive expansion of their criminal jurisdiction at the hands of the Australian Parliaments. This requires reform of the lower courts to ensure justice and fairness to accused people. Prosecutions in the lower courts should be taken from the police. Improvements should be made in the professionalism of the magistracy. While we do not believe that it is a practical option to introduce jury trials in the lower courts, we conclude with the observation that a preoccupation with administrative efficiency and cost cutting, while understandable, must not be allowed to endanger the principle that all criminal trials must be fair, open and just.

## Notes

1   In NSW in 2002, for example, more than 75% of persons appearing in the District and Supreme Courts pleaded guilty to all charges against them: NSW Bureau of Crime Statistics and Research, *Criminal Court Statistics:* <http://www.lawlink.nsw.au/bocsar1.nsf/pages/courtstatindex>.

2   In 2002, the number of cases registered in the NSW higher courts was 3771 compared with 130 555 in the Local Court: NSW Bureau of Crime Statistics and Research, *Criminal Court Statistics*, <http://www.lawlink.nsw.au/bocsar1.nsf/pages/courtstatindex>.

There were 683 concluded trials in the NSW higher courts compared with 17 698 in the Local Court.

3  NSW Bureau of Crime Statistics and Research, *Criminal Court Statistics*, <http://www.lawlink.nsw.au/bocsar1.nsf/pages/courtstatindex>. Between 1998 and 2002, more than 85% of defendants in the NSW Local Court entered a plea of guilty.

4  D. McBarnet, *Conviction: Law, the State and the Construction of Justice*, London, 1981, p. 153.

5  There are some exceptions to this proposition. For example, higher courts have extensive powers to punish for contempt of court. This is a summary jurisdiction, triable without a jury. Historically, another mode of distinction of some importance has been between felonies and misdemeanours. However, such distinctions have little analytical importance today.

6  *Whitehorn* (1983) 152 CLR 657 at 682.

7  *Dietrich* (1992) 109 ALR 385 at 387.

8  *PJE v The Queen* (CCA, NSW, unreported, 9 October 1995); special leave to appeal to the High Court refused: *PJE v The Queen; Grills v The Queen* (1996) 70 ALJR 905. Suggestions in some High Court judgments that there is a constitutionally entrenched right to a fair trial have not been adopted by a majority of the court.

9  *Dietrich* (1992) 109 ALR 385 at 396.

10  Deane J at 409.

11  *John L Pty Ltd v Attorney-General (NSW)* (1987) 164 CLR 508.

12  This rule against duplicity is designed to ensure that the ultimate result of the trial is certain, whether it involves conviction or acquittal. In the event of breach of this rule against duplicity, the indictment may be amended.

13  *Queensland Criminal Code*, s. 567(2).

14  *Sutton* (1984) 152 CLR 528 per Brennan J; endorsed in *De Jesus* (1986) 68 ALR 1.

15  *Ditroia* [1981] VR 247; *Guldur* (1986) 8 NSWLR 12.

16  *Apostilides* (1984) 154 CLR 563.

17  *Apostilides* (1984) 154 CLR 563 at 575. See also *Harry; Ex parte Eastway* (1985) 39 SASR 203 and *Damic* [1982] 2 NSWLR 750.

18  See, for example, guideline 7 of the NSW DPP Prosecution Guidelines.

19  As above.

20  Independent Commission Against Corruption (ICAC), *Report on Investigation into the Use of Informers*, Vol. 1, January 1993, p. 71.

21  A rare example of an appeal succeeding on this basis is *Robinson*, unreported, Victorian Court of Criminal Appeal, 19 December 1997.

22  *Apostilides* (1984) 154 CLR 563 at 575.

23  *Pernich and Maxwell* (1991) 55 A Crim R 464 at 466, 472–3.

24  M. Aronson, *Managing Complex Criminal Trials: Reform of the Rules of Evidence and Procedure*, Australian Institute of Judicial Administration, Sydney, 1992, p. 111.

25  ICAC, 1993, p. 80.

26  ICAC, 1993, p. 81.

27  R Edney, 'Use of the prisoners' dock under Australian criminal law: desirable practice or impediment to a fair trial?', *Criminal Law Journal*, 25, 2001, p. 194 at 203–4.

28  *Criminal Procedure Act* 1986 (NSW), s. 34.

29  *Estelle v Williams* 425 US 501 (1976).

30  T. Vinson and R. Homel, 'Legal Representation and Outcome: A progress report on the relation between legal representation and the findings of Courts of Petty Sessions through-

out New South Wales', *Australian Law Journal*, 47, 1973, p. 133. But cf. P. Cashman, 'Representation in Criminal Cases' in Basten et al. (eds), *The Criminal Injustice System*, Legal Services Bulletin, Sydney, 1982, pp. 195–220 and P. Cashman, 'Legal Representation in Lower Courts' in Zdenkowski et al. (eds), *The Criminal Injustice System*, Vol. 2, Pluto Press, Sydney, 1987.

31   It should be noted that while there are professional rules that apply to defence counsel, such as prohibiting misleading conduct, there is a fundamental difference between the role of defence counsel and prosecutor. The former is ethically obliged to use all lawful and legitimate means to obtain an acquittal.

32   *Dietrich* (1992) 109 ALR 385 at 415 per Deane J.

33   Article 14(3)(d).

34   *Dietrich* (1992) 109 ALR 385. Victoria has amended its *Crimes Act* (s. 360A) to prevent the adjournment of jury trials on the ground that the accused is unrepresented, but has recognised the right to legal representation by permitting a court to order the Legal Aid Commission to grant legal aid.

35   *Craig* v *South Australia* (1995) 184 CLR 163 at 184.

36   An alternative basis is that the Legal Services Commission has withdrawn legal assistance for the defendant on the ground that it has been unable to reach agreement with the Attorney-General on a case management plan.

37   *Dietrich* (1992) 109 ALR 385 at 416.

38   For example, NSW has amended s. 81 of the *Justices Act* 1902 to overturn the effect of the High Court decision in *Latoudis v Casey* (1991) 170 CLR 534, which had held that a successful defendant is normally entitled to costs. On the other hand, *Latoudis* still applies in Victoria.

39   Proposal contained in the report of the Standing Committee of Attorneys-General on 'Complex Fraud Trials', 7 August 1992. Legislation implementing this proposal for  all criminal trials was enacted in the *Crimes (Criminal Trials) Act* 1993 (Vic), s. 11. It appears that it has had little practical impact because of the absence of any sanctions for non-compliance or incentives for compliance.

40   See Australian Law Reform Commission, *Multiculturalism and the Law*, ch. 3.

41   *Final Report, Constitutional Commission*, Vol. 1, Sydney, 1988, para. 9.626.

42   *Dietrich* (1992) 109 ALR 385 at 412.

43   See *Gradidge v Grace Bros Pty Ltd* (1988) 93 FLR 414.

44   *MacPherson* (1981) 147 CLR 512 at 546–7 per Brennan J.

45   Another solution, adopted in the new Commonwealth and NSW Evidence Acts, is to make it easier for a party to cross-examine its own witness.

46   *Kingswell* (1985) 159 CLR 264 at 303.

47   *Doney* (1990) 171 CLR 207 at 215.

48   At 214.

49   A. Asche, 'The Trial Judge, the Appeal Court and the Unsafe Verdict', *Criminal Law Journal*, 15, 1991, p. 416.

50   (1987) 162 CLR 645.

51   See S. Yeo, 'The Demise of Excessive Self-defence in Australia', *International and Comparative Law Quarterly*, 37, 1988, p. 348. Both South Australia and NSW have reintroduced a statutory partial defence of excessive self-defence.

52   *Ali* (1981) 6 A Crim R 161.

53   See chapter 10 for some examples.

54   See P. Sallmann, 'A Note on Judicial Education in Australia: An Australian Institute of Judicial Administration Perspective', *Journal of Judicial Administration*, 2, 1992, p. 28.

55   *A Judge of District Courts at Brisbane and Paul Shelley; Ex parte Attorney-General for Queensland* (1990) 48 A Crim R 139.

56   See, for example, J. Baldwin and M. McConville, *Jury Trials*, Oxford University Press, London, 1979, ch. 1; New South Wales Law Reform Commission, *The Jury in a Criminal Trial: Empirical Studies*; New South Wales Law Reform Commission, *The Jury in a Criminal Trial*; M. Findlay and P. Duff (eds), *The Jury under Attack*, Butterworths, Sydney, 1988.

57   *Duncan v Louisiana* (1968) 391 US 145 at 156 per White J (majority opinion).

58   As above.

59   V. Carroll, 'The Trials and Tribulations of the Jury', *Sydney Morning Herald*, 20 August 1992, p. 13.

60   *Gammage* (1969) 44 ALJR 36.

61   *Jackson* (1976) 134 CLR 42 at 55.

62   *Kingswell* (1985) 159 CLR 264 at 301.

63   See W. T. Westling and V. Waye, 'Promoting Fairness and Efficiency in Jury Trials', *Criminal Law Journal*, 20, 1996, p. 127 at 129.

64   A. Freiburg, 'Jury Selection in Trials of Commonwealth Offences' in M. Findlay and P. Duff, 1988, p. 117.

65   Shaw LJ in *Crown Court at Sheffield; Ex parte Brownlow* [1980] 2 All ER 444 at 456; cited by Vincent J in *D* [1988] VR 937 but cf. *Robinson* [1989] VR 289.

66   *Jury Act* 1995 (Qld), s. 31.

67   See W. Young, Y. Tinsley and N. Cameron, 'The effectiveness and efficiency of jury decision-making', *Criminal Law Journal*, 24, 2000, p. 89.

68   *Cheatle* (1993) 116 ALR 1.

69   For example, see H. Kalven and H. Zeisel, *The American Jury*, Little Brown and Co., New York, 1966, pp. 462–3.

70   NSW Bureau of Crime Statistics and Research, 'Hung Juries and Majority Verdicts', *Crime and Justice Bulletin*, No. 36, Sydney, 1997.

71   See also W. Young, Y. Tinsley and N. Cameron, 'The Effectiveness and Efficiency of Jury Decision-making', *Criminal Law Journal*, 24, 2000, p. 89 at 99–100.

72   C. Petre, 'View from the Jury Room', *National Times*, 4–10 May 1984.

73   Australian Law Reform Commission (ALRC), *Contempt*, Report No. 35, Sydney, 1987, p. 163.

74   As above, p. 164.

75   The ALRC noted that 'psychological findings as to whether it is genuinely possible to put information out of one's mind through a conscious act of will-power are equivocal' (at 164). It should be said that this is no argument for replacing juries with judges—there is no evidence to suggest that judges are better able to achieve such compartmentalisation. More important, juries at least offer the possibility of keeping such material from the fact-finder (where appropriate under the rules of evidence).

76   As above, p. 174.

77   As above, p. 195.

78   J. Frank, *Law and the Modern Mind*, Stevens and Sons, London, 1949, p. 172.

79   The ALRC has made recommendations in this area. See *Contempt*, ch. 7.

80　The concept of complexity in criminal trials is itself not a simple measure. Critics of the jury in complex commercial trials have failed to determine satisfactorily the nature and form of complexity to which they refer.

81　See *Kingswell* (1985) 159 CLR 264.

82　*Cheatle* (1993) 116 ALR 1.

83　The Constitutional Commission adopted this proposal but limited the applicable offences to ones punishable by imprisonment for more than two years. However, the failure of the referendum in 1988 meant that further constitutional review was shelved.

84　This term refers to the procedure (tendering an indictment) adopted to initiate the prosecution of more serious criminal offences. Subject to statutory modification, trial of such prosecutions is by judge and jury.

85　*Criminal Procedure Act* 1986 (NSW), Part 9A. Most offences carrying a maximum penalty of up to ten years' imprisonment (if dealt with in the higher courts) may be dealt with summarily on this basis, although the maximum penalty that may be imposed in the Local Court will be, at most, two years.

86　*Criminal Procedure Act* 1986 (NSW), ss. 33K and 33J. Even multiple sentences imposed by a magistrate in such circumstances cannot total more than three years' imprisonment: s. 444(4)(b) *Crimes Act* 1900 (NSW). In Victoria, the maximum total sentence is five years: s. 16(6) *Sentencing Act* 1991 (Vic).

87　Section 19(2), *Coroners Act* 1980 (NSW).

88　Section 22(1A), *Coroners Act* 1980 (NSW).

89　Per Murphy J in *Beckwith* (1976) 135 CLR 569 at 585.

90　D. McBarnet, *Conviction: Law, the State and the Construction of Justice*, Macmillan, London, 1981, p. 145.

91　*John L Pty Ltd v Attorney-General (NSW)* (1987) 164 CLR 508. But cf. s. 30(l)(a) of the Tasmanian *Criminal Code*.

92　NSW Bureau of Crime Statistics and Research, *New South Wales Criminal Courts Statistics*, 2000, Table 1.5.

93　NSW Bureau of Crime Statistics and Research, *Key Trends in Crime and Justice*, NSW, 1999, Figure 2.4.

94　*Dietrich* (1992) 109 ALR 385 at 416, citing *Argersinger v Hamlin* (1972) 407 US 25 at 37–8, 40.

95　*Kingswell* (1985) 159 CLR 264 at 319.

96　*Lowenstein* (1938) 59 CLR 556 at 583 per Dixon and Evart JJ (dissenting). See also *Argersinger v Hamlin* (1972) 407 US 25.

97　The present position of the United States Supreme Court: *Scott v Illinois* (1979) 440 US 367.

98　*Khalifeh* v *District Court Judge Job* (1996) 85 A Crim R 68.

99　D. McBarnet, *Conviction*, pp. 146–7.

100　Legal Aid Commission of NSW, *Annual Report 1992*, p. 24.

101　As above, p. 15.

102　R. G. Fox, *Victorian Criminal Procedure*, Monash Law Book Co-op Ltd, Clayton, 1992, para. 2.8.2.2.

103　Legal Aid Commission of NSW, *Annual Report 1997*, p. 25.

104　D. Brown and D. Neal, 'Show Trials: The Media and the Gang of Twelve' in M. Findlay and P. Duff, *The Jury under Attack*, Butterworths, London, p. 135.

# 6

# Evidence

## Introduction

The laws of evidence applied in Australian courts serve a number of functions: they regulate what material a court may consider in determining factual issues; how that material is to be presented in the court; and how the court actually decides the factual issues on the basis of the evidence. These laws are the product of long historical development by the courts, and statutory modification, reflecting a variety of principles and values. For this reason, in all of these areas the law is complex and technical. Nevertheless, while substantial rationalisation and reform is long overdue, it would be wrong to assume that rules of evidence were unnecessary.

In any trial system, there must be some rules regulating how evidence is produced in the court and how the court is to perform its task of deciding the issues before it. This is particularly true in an adversarial system, where the parties to the litigation take the active role in obtaining and producing evidence, and seek to persuade the court to reach particular factual findings. Rules limiting the evidence that the court may consider are not essential since the court could receive whatever evidence the parties produced and give it the importance (or 'weight') the court thought appropriate. However, there are good reasons why the law of evidence does in fact exclude certain types of evidence. Evidence may be excluded because it is more likely to inhibit than help the fact-finding task. Thus, some evidence may be of doubtful reliability and it may be impossible to test it. An example is hearsay evidence, discussed below. The danger is that the court (particularly, but not exclusively, a jury) may give it too much importance. Some evidence is likely to be more prejudicial than helpful, tending to produce an emotional reaction out of proportion to its real value. Evidence that an accused person has prior criminal convictions is a good example. Then there may be policy reasons justifying the exclusion of evidence—for example, to deter the police from obtaining evidence unlawfully, or to keep trials as short as possible.

In assessing the law of evidence as it operates in criminal trials, it is necessary to bear in mind some important points. While the principles of justice that we have discussed in previous chapters may be used as a touchstone to judge the various rules of evidence, it will rarely be the case that powerful arguments cannot be presented on both sides of any issue. Given the different types of evidence, the differing issues they raise, and the variety of assumptions upon which the law is based, any other conclusion would be surprising. Moreover, different mechanisms are available to deal with evidence. Strict rules offer precision and clear guidance to the people who use the courts. On the other hand, they can produce arbitrary and apparently unjust results despite the creation of (often numerous) exceptions to the strict rules. More flexible rules, or discretions, allow for greater flexibility, but confer greater power on the judge and produce greater uncertainty of result. Inevitably, the law of evidence is a mixture of rules (with exceptions) and discretions.

Perhaps a useful starting point for consideration of evidence law in criminal trials is to consider the differences between civil and criminal proceedings. In respect of all the functions that evidence rules serve, there are important differences between these two kinds of proceedings. For example, in relation to the material that the court may consider in determining factual issues, there is a much greater concern in criminal trials with certain categories of potentially unreliable evidence, such as identification evidence and evidence from accomplices. These concerns sometimes result in the exclusion of evidence. More often, they result in the giving of warnings about placing too much reliance on the evidence.

Another difference between civil and criminal proceedings exists in respect of how the court actually decides the factual issues on the basis of the evidence. Perhaps the most notable distinction between civil and criminal proceedings is the standard of proof. This is the standard that must be met by the party bearing the burden of proof on any issue. Sufficient credible evidence must be admitted that satisfies the court to the requisite standard. In civil trials the plaintiff must prove the elements of the cause of action on the 'balance of probabilities'. However, in a criminal trial the prosecution must prove the guilt of an accused person 'beyond reasonable doubt'. All elements of the offence must be proved to this standard and, indeed, in most cases, the prosecution must rebut any defences raised by the accused to this standard.

These, and other, aspects of the laws of evidence in relation to criminal proceedings will be considered in greater detail in the discussion that follows. Before doing so, however, it is worth considering why it is that there are these differences between civil and criminal trials. One possibility that springs to mind is the much greater use of juries in criminal proceedings. Juries, it can be said, are likely to be less experienced than judicial officers with the dangers associated with certain types of evidence. As a result, such evidence might be excluded or, at least, care would be taken to ensure that the jury is not led astray.

In fact, the presence of juries in the criminal justice system is a relatively poor explanation for these differences in the rules of evidence. For a start, many of the differences, such as with the standard of proof, appear largely unrelated to the nature of the court. Further, the differences continue to exist (at least in principle) even if the factual issues are being decided by a magistrate or a judge sitting without a jury. It is true that there is a tendency in practice for legal practitioners not to assert the rules of evidence as strongly as in jury trials. That is a tactical choice made in the circumstances of the trial, taking into account the reality that a magistrate or judge sitting without a jury will have to look at evidence before ruling on its admissibility. Even if excluded, the evidence may have some impact. Nevertheless, there is no doubt that the rules of evidence apply with only minor modifications in summary trials and they are often rigorously enforced. This is not to deny that the presence of juries has had a bearing on the development of the rules of evidence, only to point out that other considerations are more significant.

Arguably the most important distinction between civil and criminal proceedings is in terms of their respective goals. It is true that any formulation of those goals is inevitably controversial. Nevertheless, it can be said with some confidence that the primary goal of civil proceedings is dispute resolution. This means that the courts attempt to accurately determine facts, but this is not crucial—what matters is resolving the dispute between the litigants. In criminal trials, greater importance is given to accurately determining the facts, to 'getting at the truth'. But this goal is qualified too, and not simply because the trial is based on an adversarial model. There is an important difference from civil proceedings in that the primary aim of criminal trial procedure, it may be said, is to minimise the risk of convicting an innocent person, as is evident in the following observation:

> The Romans had the maxim that it is better for a guilty person to go unpunished than for an innocent one to be condemned ... Sir Edward Seymour ... said [in 1696]: 'I am of the same opinion with the Roman, who, in the case of Catiline, declared, he had rather ten guilty persons should escape, than one innocent should suffer.' Hale took the ratio as five to one; Blackstone reverted to ten to one, and in that form it became established.[1]

Of course, there is a contrary view. No doubt many members of the community believe that there is just as great a public interest in convicting the guilty as in acquitting the innocent.[2] On this basis, there should be no weighting of the system in favour of the accused. Nevertheless, for the time being at least, the balance of the criminal trial is tilted in favour of acquitting the innocent rather than convicting the guilty.

Many of the differences in the rules of evidence between civil and criminal proceedings derive from this difference in goals. Thus, the particular rules in criminal trials relating to certain categories of potentially unreliable evidence usually only apply to evidence led by the prosecution against the accused, not vice versa. The criminal standard of proof only applies to the prosecution; where the accused has the burden of proof on some issue, the civil standard is applied.

Yet there are other considerations. As Peter Sallmann has explained:

> The convictions of 'guilty' persons are not to be pursued and obtained at virtually any cost. The conviction of the guilty is important … but … accused persons are entitled to the benefits of certain rights and protections as a matter of recognition of their personal dignity and integrity, and also, on a far broader scale, as a measure of the overall fairness of the society to the individuals within it.[3]

These are more problematic concepts than the idea of minimising the risk of convicting an innocent accused. And yet we have stressed throughout this book the importance of broad conceptions of justice and fairness, as well as respect for individual rights. The very idea of democracy incorporates recognition of individual rights. However, the difficulty is in determining the content of individual rights in the context of the law of evidence. Everyone can agree that an accused person should be treated with 'dignity' and 'fairness', but what do these terms mean in practical terms in relation to particular types of evidence?

It is significant that the international human rights conventions have almost nothing to say about the rules of evidence in criminal trials. They do provide that accused people have the right to a 'fair and public hearing' and to be presumed innocent until proved guilty.[4] The content of such rights, however, is inevitably ambiguous and the conventions do not provide greater precision. It appears that one reason for this was the inability of the drafters of these conventions to agree on appropriate minimum procedural safeguards. This is hardly surprising given the differences of perspective between European 'civil' lawyers familiar with inquisitorial procedure and lawyers from common law adversarial systems. The *International Covenant on Civil and Political Rights* does recognise that an accused person has a right 'not to be compelled to testify against himself or to confess guilt', but even this concept has, as we shall see, difficulties of interpretation. Nevertheless, the difficulty of the task of giving content to these generalities does not mean that it should be avoided.

There are factors that theoretically relate to both civil and criminal trials but in practice have a greater impact on the latter. The laws of evidence include many rules that are based on policy concerns that are only indirectly connected with the trial system. One illustration is provided by the rules of privilege, under which various classes of people are entitled to refuse to give information at a trial, even though it may be very significant and probative. Thus, communications between a lawyer and her client (who may subsequently become an accused in a criminal trial) cannot be given in evidence unless the client consents. Similar privileges exist for communications with a priest and between spouses. Such rules demonstrate the priorities given to various competing values in the community so that the interest in obtaining all relevant evidence is given less weight than the perceived need to encourage full and frank disclosures between lawyer and client; to respect the religious beliefs and practices of members of the community; and to promote openness and trust between married couples. Yet this priority is not given to communications with doctors, accountants or journalists—although New South Wales has in recent years given courts a discretion to protect the confidentiality of such communications.[5]

Sometimes no clear rule is adopted, but a judge is required to balance the conflicting public interests in the circumstances of the case. One example concerns disclosure of material relating to national security or confidential governmental communications. Another involves the rules designed to deal with unlawful or improper methods of obtaining evidence. The latter example is clearly one that more commonly arises in criminal proceedings. The policies behind such rules must be carefully examined.

The point of this lengthy introduction is that we cannot understand, or criticise, the laws of evidence in criminal proceedings without first considering the assumptions upon which the rules are premised. Arguments over particular rules often reflect more fundamental disagreement over basic values. On the other hand, it can be confidently said that criticisms can be levelled at the rules, which have nothing to do with values. The common law and statute law applying in this area in most Australian jurisdictions is often over-complicated, obscure and irrational. Substantial reform has been long overdue.

To take one example, the hearsay rule prohibits evidence of 'statements made outside the court room, if the purpose of the party seeking to have the evidence admitted is to prove the truth of any assertions contained in the statement'. Thus, a witness in a murder trial would normally not be permitted to testify that she had heard X say: 'I saw Smith [the accused] kill Jones [the victim].' The rule applies to both oral and written statements. One rationale for it is the doubtful reliability of hearsay evidence. Experience and research have shown that information passed from one person to another is often not recorded or remembered accurately. Of course, this might justify treating the evidence with care rather than excluding it completely. A more important reason for the exclusionary rule is that it encourages the calling of X as a witness, so that he or she can be subject to cross-examination in order to test the reliability of the evidence.

Yet, while there is much common-sense behind the rule, it can confuse witnesses and make the task of proving even the most basic and non-controversial matters both difficult and expensive. Calling the person who made the statement may in fact be impossible because he or she is dead or overseas or cannot be found. It may be pointless because the person has no memory of what was said or written. In some circumstances, the hearsay evidence may be more reliable than the testimony of the person who made the out-of-court statement. The courts have created a large number of exceptions to the rule designed to meet some of these problems, but they are technical and often arbitrary in application, often without clear rationale. Legislation has also introduced exceptions, particularly in the area of documentary hearsay, but it has limited operation in criminal proceedings. Despite all the exceptions, evidence is sometimes excluded with worrying consequences. In a famous South Australian murder trial, for example, evidence was not admitted that another person had confessed to the crime for which the accused was ultimately convicted.[6]

In the 1980s there were signs that the courts were prepared to do something about the complex and confusing nature of the law in this area. In 1989 the High Court handed down a judgment that dealt comprehensively with the scope and application of the hearsay rule and suggested a more flexible approach, and a willingness to apply it as a principle rather than a strict rule. Chief Justice Mason was most explicit:

> The hearsay rule should not be applied inflexibly. When the dangers which the rule seeks to prevent are not present or are negligible in the circumstances of a given case there is no basis for a strict application of the rule. Equally, where in the view of the trial judge those dangers are outweighed by other aspects of the case lending reliability and probative value to the impugned evidence, the judge should not then exclude the evidence by a rigid and technical application of the rule against hearsay.[7]

However, a subsequent decision of the High Court very much muted these moves towards a more flexible approach. Thus, one member of the High Court strongly opposed judicial reform of that type:

> It would be possible, no doubt, to redesign the law of evidence with the assistance of psychologists and philosophers versed in epistemology but it cannot be done piecemeal or by extensions which are not linked to an underlying principle. To attempt such alterations, however pragmatically desirable in one case, will throw the next case into confusion. The law of evidence, though adjectival, is the working tool which a trial judge must keep constantly at hand and the principles of the law of evidence are, so to speak, the ground on which the dynamics of a trial, especially a criminal trial, are played out. There is an attraction in the notion that the admissibility of hearsay should be governed by a judicial assessment of its reliability, but there are countervailing arguments ...[8]

The trend in the common law seems to be to retain a strict rule with the possibility of new exceptions being developed as seen to be appropriate. Unfortunately, this does nothing to simplify the law or clarify the principles behind it.

Finally, in 1995, substantial reform of the law of evidence took place in Federal Courts and in New South Wales and the Australian Capital Territory, with enactment of comprehensive uniform evidence legislation (hereafter referred to as the

Uniform Evidence Law).[9] Tasmania adopted the same legislation in 2001. Largely based on the recommendations of the Australian Law Reform Commission, these reforms have done much to simplify the operation of law (although there have been inevitable teething problems with the legislation). Major changes in the law have also been introduced.[10] Thus, in relation to the hearsay rule, it is easier to have admitted first-hand hearsay where the person who made the out-of-court representation is 'unavailable' to testify. Out-of-court representations made when events were 'fresh in the memory' of the person who made the representation are more likely to be admitted into evidence. In general, it is easier for the defence in a criminal trial to have admitted evidence of first-hand hearsay. Substantial changes have also been made in other areas of evidence law. In what follows we shall consider both the common law and the Uniform Evidence Law. The discussion will inevitably be selective since the law of evidence is an enormous field. We focus on the more controversial topics that have a particular significance in the criminal justice system. Most of these concern the exclusion or special treatment of particular categories of evidence. However, we will begin our overview with a brief consideration of the law relating to proof, followed by the presentation of evidence in criminal trials.

# Proof

As was noted in the introduction to this chapter, one of the most significant distinctions between civil and criminal proceedings is the standard of proof. While the plaintiff in civil proceedings must prove the elements of the cause of action on the 'balance of probabilities', the prosecution must prove the guilt of the accused 'beyond reasonable doubt'.

There are two aspects to this proposition. Proving 'guilt' means that the prosecution must prove all the elements of a crime and must also, in general, disprove any defences to the crime raised during the trial.[11] However, at least one common law defence must be proved by the defence[12] and many examples may be found in all jurisdictions of the legislative imposition, expressly or by implication, of the burden of proof of some fact on the defendant.[13] In 1982, the Senate Standing Committee on Constitutional and Legal Affairs found at least 220 provisions in federal legislation that imposed a burden of proof on defendants,[14] and a similar report in Victoria in 1983 found over 600 such provisions in Victorian statutes.[15]

As we saw in chapter 1, crimes may be defined in different ways. They may include an element of 'guilty mind', they may be crimes of negligence, and they may be crimes of 'strict' or 'absolute' liability. But over and above this differentiation, offences vary in terms of the allocation of the burden of proof. A statutory offence might require knowledge of some fact as an element, but place the burden of proof on the defence—requiring it to prove absence of knowledge. An offence of negligence might require the defence to prove absence of negligence. The proliferation of offences that place a burden of proof on the accused is a worrying tendency and conflicts with the principle that an accused person is presumed innocent until proved otherwise by the prosecution. As Lord Sankey said in the famous English case of *Woolmington v The Director of Public Prosecutions*:[16]

> Throughout the web of the English Criminal Law one golden thread is always to be seen, that it is the duty of the prosecution to prove the prisoner's guilt subject to what I have already said as to the defence of insanity and subject also to any statutory exception ... No matter what the charge or where the trial, the principle that the prosecution must prove the guilt of the prisoner is part of the common law of England and no attempt to whittle it down can be entertained.[17]

One reason for this principle, which has been endorsed by the High Court of Australia,[18] is that it serves as a counter-balance to the superior resources of the state. It also seeks to overcome any presumption of guilt from the simple fact that a criminal charge has been laid. While it is reasonable that an accused should bear the burden of leading some evidence supporting a defence before the issue is effectively raised for the consideration of the jury, to impose the ultimate burden of proof on the defence seems rarely justifiable. Indeed, it creates practical problems in the event that the accused is convicted by a jury, since the sentencing judge does not know whether the jury was sure of guilt or simply not sure of innocence. For example, if drug legislation places the burden on the accused to prove that he or she did not know that a substance was an illegal drug, a guilty verdict could mean that the jury was sure the accused knew, or that the jury was not satisfied the accused did not know. The sentencing judge is given little guidance and is left to determine the issue in order to sentence, thus downgrading the role of the jury.

Various reasons are advanced for such reversals—for example, to facilitate enforcement of the law, to deter serious crime, to overcome the difficulties of proving a negative (for example, that the accused did not have some reasonable excuse) and matters peculiarly within the knowledge of an accused. However, we believe that it should be most exceptional to depart from the general principle. Difficulties of proof are often exaggerated. Juries and magistrates are quite capable of drawing inferences from conduct to state of mind. Even where the legal burden is on the prosecution, the tactical reality will often be that the defence will have to explain apparently incriminating circumstances. The principle should not be eroded in order to appease public anxiety regarding particular types of crime. Once an offence is defined to contain a particular element, the presumption of innocence requires proof by the prosecution rather than disproof by the defence. While this will sometimes make the obtaining of a conviction difficult, it is a price worth paying.

The second aspect of the proposition that the prosecution must prove guilt beyond reasonable doubt is the criminal standard of proof. What it means is that if the tribunal deciding the facts in the case (a jury or a judicial officer sitting without a jury) has a doubt that it considers reasonable as to the guilt of the accused, it must find the accused not guilty.[19] This does not mean that guilt must be certain. The criminal justice system does not indulge in the absolutes of philosophy or science. Yet the standard is set at such a high level as to (hopefully) minimise the risk of convicting an innocent person. Even if guilt is likely, reasonable doubt as to guilt requires a finding of not guilty. This means that many guilty people may be acquitted but, again, it is the price the system is willing to pay.

Where the tribunal of fact is a jury, the trial judge must direct them as to this standard of proof. The courts have often emphasised that it is generally unwise to elaborate upon the conventional formula, except by way of contrasting it with the standard of proof in civil proceedings. Such elaborations as 'comfortable satisfaction' and 'more than theoretical or fanciful doubt' should generally be avoided. However, where a case involves circumstantial evidence, rather than direct evidence of guilt, it may be necessary to direct the jury that guilt should not only be a rational inference, it should be the *only* rational inference that can be drawn from the circumstances.[20] Such a direction is no more than an amplification of the requirement that the prosecution must prove its case beyond reasonable doubt.[21] Similarly, where an intermediate conclusion of fact constitutes an 'indispensable link in a chain of reasoning towards an inference of guilt', this fact must itself be proved beyond reasonable doubt.[22]

In order to ensure that a jury does not convict in a case where it would not be reasonably open to find an accused guilty, it is the duty of the trial judge to direct a verdict of not guilty if such a situation exists at the end of the prosecution case.[23] Expressed in traditional terms, there is no case to answer. However, the trial judge must assume the prosecution evidence to be truthful and reliable and evidence favouring the defendant must be disregarded. The trial judge may not direct a verdict of not guilty on the basis that a verdict of guilty would be unreasonable or that the prosecution evidence is 'tenuous or inherently weak or vague'.[24] If there is a case to answer, the defence must proceed and the jury must decide the issue.[25] Under these rules, the role of the jury as the ultimate finder of fact is maintained, notwithstanding that the trial judge determines questions of law (including whether it would be 'open' to convict). We discussed the merits of the law on this topic in chapter 5.

# Presenting evidence

By and large, a criminal trial proceeds in much the same way as a civil trial. Unless there are any preliminary legal questions, the prosecutor opens by summarising the case against the accused and the evidence that will be produced to prove it. Then the prosecution witnesses are called, 'examined' (asked questions) by the prosecutor and cross-examined by the defence, subject to the various exclusionary rules.

Documents and exhibits will be put into evidence, again subject to the exclusionary rules. At the end of the prosecution case, the defence may make a 'no-case submission' (submit that a conviction could not reasonably be based on the prosecution evidence) and, if this submission fails, the defence may[26] proceed with its case in much the same way as the prosecution. Then both sides make a final address. If there is a jury, the trial judge directs them on the law and the evidence, and the case proceeds to verdict.

However, there are some important and controversial differences between civil and criminal trial procedure. The most significant relates to the position of the accused.[27] A criminal defendant, as with a civil defendant, may but need not give sworn evidence.[28] However, there are additional protections for an accused who chooses not to give sworn evidence. At common law, the trial judge should not suggest that the silence of the accused can displace the burden on the prosecution to prove guilt.[29] In addition, in some Australian jurisdictions there are statutory provisions that prohibit 'comment' on the failure of the defendant to give evidence, either by the prosecutor or, in some cases, the trial judge. Prohibited 'comment' is any statement that directly or indirectly suggests that the defendant could have given evidence on oath (which would then be subjected to cross-examination) and did not do so. These rules have been based on the argument that, if an accused cannot be 'compelled' to testify, he or she should not be 'penalised' for choosing not to. However, some jurisdictions have substantially removed the prohibition on comment by the judge.[30] One rationale for this is that a jury is likely to draw negative inferences anyway, and it would be preferable for the trial judge to provide assistance to the jury than ignore the issue entirely. Thus, the jury should be told:

> that the fact that an accused does not give evidence at trial is not of itself evidence against the accused. It is not an admission of guilt by conduct; it cannot fill in any gaps in the prosecution case; it cannot be used as a make-weight in considering whether the prosecution has proved the accusation beyond reasonable doubt.[31]

The more difficult issue is what the jury should be told about permissible adverse inferences that might be drawn from the failure of the defendant to testify. In a 1993 judgment of the High Court, it was held that, in appropriate circumstances, the jury might be directed that 'hypotheses consistent with innocence may cease to be rational or reasonable in the absence of evidence to support them when that evidence, if it exists at all, must be within the knowledge of the accused'.[32] However, subsequent judgments of the High Court, emphasising the principles discussed above, have very much restricted the making of any adverse judicial comment. In *RPS v The Queen*[33] the majority judgment stated:

> What is presently significant is that a criminal trial is an accusatorial process in which the prosecution bears the onus of proving the guilt of the accused beyond reasonable doubt. In a trial of that kind, what significance can be attached to the

fact that the accused does not give evidence? … In a civil trial there will very often be a reasonable expectation that a party would give or call relevant evidence … By contrast, however, it will seldom, if ever, be reasonable to conclude that an accused in a criminal trial would be expected to give evidence. The most that can be said in criminal matters is that there are some cases in which evidence (or an explanation) contradicting an apparently damning inference to be drawn from proven facts could come only from the accused. In the absence of such evidence or explanation, the jury may more readily draw the conclusion which the prosecution seeks.

The High Court subsequently emphasised that only in 'rare and exceptional' cases would it be appropriate for an adverse comment to be made by the judge.[34]

Another difference between civil and criminal procedure is worthy of mention. In civil cases, if the defence chooses not to call any evidence, then it has the right to address the court after the plaintiff, but the right is lost if it calls evidence. In criminal trials, in some jurisdictions the defence is always allowed to go last, allowing it the opportunity to respond to the prosecution submissions. In other jurisdictions, the civil practice is followed—an arbitrary rule inconsistent with the basic principles of criminal justice. Such a rule can lead to anomalies and artificial practices. Thus, the defence may choose not to tender available and relevant evidence in order to preserve a right of reply. The civil model should be abandoned in all jurisdictions, as has occurred in South Australia in 1993.

Indeed, there is also a case for altering the normal rules regarding the opening address. In most cases the accused merely pleads orally 'guilty' or 'not guilty' in response to the reading of the charge in court. There are some other rarely used technical pleas that need not concern us here. While a plea of 'not guilty' requires the prosecution to prove guilt, it is possible for the defence to formally admit certain facts so as to obtain some tactical advantage. Given that the burden of proof rests on the prosecution, it is entirely appropriate that it presents its case and then the defence is given the opportunity to respond. In some complex trials, this can mean a long delay between the prosecution opening and the jury hearing the defence response. There is merit in allowing the defence the option of a response immediately after the prosecution opening, as is now permitted in Victoria and New South Wales. It allows the defence an early opportunity to put a contrary position and to alert the jury to the issues in the trial. It is also a way of reducing the length of the trial if certain matters are not in dispute.

One final difference in practice between the manner of presenting evidence in civil and criminal trials should be noted. Legislation in a number of jurisdictions[35] allows the evidence-in-chief of young complainants in sexual offence and serious assault cases to be given at trial by way of a pre-recorded video and audio tape, but the complainant must be available at court to be cross-examined.[36] It is also becomingly increasingly common for the evidence of certain classes of alleged victims, such as children and sexual assault complainants, to be given by way of audiovisual links. Designed to reduce the trauma associated with giving evidence in open court in the presence of the accused, there is a danger that such procedures convey the assumption that the accused is guilty. However, where the procedure is adopted in a jury trial, the judge would be required to give an appropriate warning. For example, section 42V of the Victorian *Evidence Act* 1958 provides that:

> the judge must warn the jury not to draw any inference adverse to the accused person or give any evidence given by the witness or the accused person any greater or lesser weight because of the making of the direction or the appearance by audio visual link.

So long as the jury understands that the procedure is one adopted in all such cases, there is unlikely to be any adverse prejudice to the accused. As it happens, there is reason to believe that many prosecutors encourage complainants to testify in open court, believing that the impact of such evidence is likely to be greater than seen through an audiovisual link.

# Admission and use of evidence

The bulk of the law of evidence is concerned with those rules that regulate the admission and use of particular categories of evidence in trials. Basic administrative efficiency demands that the evidence admitted be limited to material that is relevant to the issues in the trial. It is the trial judge's task to exclude irrelevant evidence—material that has no rational bearing on any issue. But over and above that requirement, there are a number of significant exclusionary rules and discretions. We have already discussed the hearsay rule in the introduction to this chapter. Other major exclusionary rules include those relating to propensity evidence and opinion evidence. Further, certain categories of evidence, while admitted, may have their use limited by other rules. For example, certain types of evidence require a warning to be given to the jury in a criminal trial regarding their potential unreliability, although they are not seen as so unreliable as to require exclusion. What follows is a selective consideration of some of the more controversial rules.

## Improperly obtained evidence

One of the most heated continuing debates in the American criminal justice system involves what is commonly referred to as the 'exclusionary rule'. In simple terms, the rule provides that evidence obtained in breach of constitutionally protected rights must be excluded from evidence in any ensuing trial. According to the doctrine of the 'fruit of the poisoned tree', if other evidence is indirectly obtained as a result of that breach, then it also is tainted and must be excluded.

Now it is true that there are exceptions to these rules, of varying importance, but they can still have a dramatic effect. Occasionally, critical and damning evidence of an accused person's guilt of a serious crime is excluded because of what may be a relatively technical breach by the police of procedures required by judicial interpretation of a constitutional provision. Not surprisingly, the consequent acquittal of an almost certainly guilty accused in such circumstances, although a rare occurrence, generates heated controversy.

In contrast, the traditional position in the United Kingdom in respect of unlawfully or improperly obtained evidence has been (at least until the enactment in 1984 of the *Police and Criminal Evidence Act*) that the way in which the evidence was obtained is irrelevant at the trial, unless it had an effect on the quality of the evidence. The position of the House of Lords was that responsibility for control over police practices was a matter for the executive, not the judiciary. Not surprisingly, the courts in the United Kingdom seem to be moving away from this strict position in the last few years, partly because the *Police and Criminal Evidence Act* appears to require a more interventionist approach, but also because of recent revelations of police malpractice in such cases as those involving the Guildford Four and the Birmingham Six.

There is no doubt that control over police investigative practices involves broad and largely political judgments about such issues as the powers, organisation, training and discipline of the police and their relationship with government—issues that extend well beyond the conduct of criminal trials. On the other hand, the courts must protect their processes from abuse. More generally, they cannot simply ignore illegality by those seeking to have the law enforced against others. If the Australian legislatures had produced a potent response to illegal or improper police practices, then the courts could concentrate on their primary function. But this has not happened.

Consequently, the High Court has acted to produce a halfway house between the extreme positions considered above. In *Bunning v Cross*, Stephen and Aickin JJ, who delivered the leading judgment, stated that a trial judge has a 'discretion' to exclude evidence that is 'the product of ... unlawful or improper conduct on the part of the authorities'.[37] What this discretion involves:

> is no simple question of ensuring fairness to an accused but instead the weighing against each other of two competing requirements of public policy, thereby seeking to resolve the apparent conflict between the desirable goal of bringing to conviction the wrongdoer and the undesirable effect of curial approval, or even encouragement, being given to the unlawful conduct of those whose task it is to enforce the law.[38]

It is significant that these Justices emphasised that the discretion is not based on 'fairness'. As the courts have tended to interpret that term, the focus is on evidentiary reliability and any dangers that the evidence might be given more significance than it is worth. In many cases, evidence that has been unlawfully or improperly obtained is highly reliable and cogent proof of guilt, and its admission would not be unfair to the accused on this analysis. Yet there may still be sound reasons of policy justifying exclusion. Justices Stephen and Aickin explained the reasoning behind their approach:

> The liberty of the subject is in increasing need of protection as governments, in response to the demand for more active regulatory intervention in the affairs of their citizens, enact a continuing flood of measures affecting day-to-day conduct, much of it hedged about with safeguards for the individual. These safeguards the executive, and, of course, the police forces, should not be free to disregard. Were there to occur wholesale and deliberate disregard of these safeguards its toleration by the courts would result in the effective abrogation of the legislature's safeguards of individual liberties, subordinating it to the executive arm. This would not be excusable however desirable might be the immediate end in view, that of convicting the guilty. In appropriate cases it may be 'a less evil that some criminals should escape than that the Government should play an ignoble part'—per Holmes J in *Olmstead v United States*. Moreover the courts should not be seen to be acquiescent in the face of the unlawful conduct of those whose task it is to enforce the law. On the other hand it may be quite inappropriate to treat isolated and merely accidental non-compliance with statutory safeguards as leading to inadmissibility of the resultant evidence ...[39]

Various criteria were articulated as relevant to this balancing of public policies. Fairness to the accused was one, but equally important were other factors, including whether the actions of the police involved a deliberate or reckless disregard of the law, the cogency of the evidence obtained, and the nature of the offence charged.

A number of points need to be made. Because this approach is discretionary, although guided by criteria, and appellate review is limited, it relies heavily on the judgment of the individual judge. Not only does this sacrifice predictability to flexibility, but it also imposes a sensitive and essentially political task. There have been no empirical studies of how this discretion is actually exercised in Australian courts, but it is the experience of most practitioners that judges rarely exclude illegally obtained evidence. For this reason, the Australian Law Reform Commission recommended that such evidence should be presumptively inadmissible, with the prosecution bearing the burden of convincing the court to admit the evidence,[40] and this approach has been adopted in the Uniform Evidence Law.[41] Whether such a change will have much effect in practice is difficult to predict.

A particularly controversial application of this discretion occurred in *Ridgeway v The Queen*.[42] In that case, the accused was convicted of an offence in relation to the possession of a 'prohibited import', heroin, which was in fact brought into Australia by an undercover officer of the Malaysian Police Force with the assistance of the Australian Federal Police. Although the whole exercise was done with the intention of prosecuting Ridgeway for his involvement in the importation, and the heroin never reached the streets, the fact was that the police were in (technical) breach of the law. A majority of the High Court held that there is 'a discretion to exclude evidence of the accused's guilt either of an alleged crime or of an element of it in circumstances where the actual commission of the crime was procured by such unlawful conduct'. Indeed, they went further, holding that 'where the illegal police conduct is itself the principal offence to which the charged offence is ancillary or creates or itself constitutes an essential ingredient of the charged offence' and the illegal police conduct 'would appear to be condoned by those in higher authority', then 'an extremely formidable case for exclusion will be raised'.[43] Not surprisingly, the legislative response was swift, effectively ensuring that evidence obtained by such undercover operations will not be excluded by the courts in subsequent prosecutions.[44]

Putting this exceptional situation to one side, it is arguable that deliberate or reckless police unlawfulness should always result in exclusion of evidence so obtained—as a majority of the High Court hinted in *Foster v The Queen* when they stated that 'deliberate or reckless disregard of the law by those whose duty it is to enforce it' is the 'real evil' at which the discretion is directed.[45] The arguments of discouraging impropriety and preventing abuse of the criminal justice process are much stronger in such circumstances. Indeed, the United States Supreme Court is apparently moving, albeit slowly, to an approach limiting the strict exclusionary rule to circumstances of 'bad faith'.[46] On the other hand, even in these cases there may be good reasons not to exclude the evidence. If the government were to introduce meaningful alternative remedies for police impropriety, whether criminal, civil or disciplinary, the police involved might be punished without the disadvantageous effects on the trial process associated with evidentiary exclusion. Until that happens the courts must vigilantly 'police the police'. Lastly, in some cases, automatic exclusion of the unlawfully obtained evidence rule is appropriate. For example, the police should not be able to evade the strict requirements imposed by the legislature for telephonic interception. Although the Commonwealth *Telephonic (Interceptions) Act* 1979 originally left the issue of evidentiary exclusion to the common law balancing test, it has now been amended to provide that evidence obtained in breach of its terms is inadmissible. In areas of fundamental liberties where the law is precise and objective in application, an exclusionary rule makes sense.

## Confessions

Perhaps the most contentious area of the criminal trial is the issue of confessional evidence. Police investigations, especially in relation to more serious crimes, often proceed upon information (for example, 'informers', rumours, 'whispers') that will not be allowed as evidence at trial, but that may well convince the police as to the identity of the criminal. Their next task is to obtain evidence that will be admitted at the trial and result in the conviction of the accused. Confessional evidence admirably fulfils these requirements. Admissions of guilt, both oral and written, express or implied, made out of court by an accused person are admissible as evidence against the accused. Such evidence is commonly tendered by the prosecution and very often plays a crucial role in influencing the outcome of the trial.[47]

There are two major problems with confessional evidence. It can be fabricated with considerable ease by unscrupulous police who are prepared to go to any lengths to obtain a conviction. Alternatively, it may be obtained by use of improper methods such as threats, inducements or deceptions.

There is no doubt that an accused person at trial, confronted with police evidence of a confession allegedly made during interrogation will sometimes contend that it is a fabrication (or, to use the vernacular for disputed oral confessions, a 'verbal'). The police, of course, will assert that the confession was made, perhaps with the accused refusing to sign a record of interview because he 'never signs anything'. Sometimes this will be true but, as we noted in chapter 2, there were numerous reports during the 1970s and 1980s concluding that 'verballing' was commonplace among some members of the police.[48]

Because fabrication of confessional evidence is often extremely difficult to detect, trials often descended to slanging matches between police and accused, and there is no doubt that time spent in disputing such evidence occupied a substantial amount of the time of the courts. For a long time it had been apparent that the best solution was to introduce some form of electronic recording of police interviews with suspects. Unfortunately, police forces tended to oppose tape-recording or video-recording on various grounds, including cost, the potential for editing and alteration of tapes, the impracticality of taping in many situations, and a belief that some suspects would be inhibited from confessing. These objections were basically of little substance and one tended to wonder, as did Professor Glanville Williams, 'whether the real objection of the police to tape-recording (though it is never avowed) is their fear of the consequences of public inspection of what happens in the interviewing of suspects'.[49]

Not surprisingly, the courts and particularly the High Court became exasperated with this. Thus, in *Driscoll v The Queen*,[50] the High Court concluded that unsigned records of interview should generally be excluded by a trial judge although the police would still be permitted to give oral testimony of any alleged confession, using the record of interview to refresh memory. Then, in *Carr v The Queen*,[51] the High Court decided that, although there is no rule of law or practice requiring corroboration of evidence of an alleged oral confession, there may be occasions when a warning should be given to the jury of the need to look carefully at such evidence. Finally, in *McKinney v The Queen*[52] a majority of the court concluded that whenever police evidence of a confessional statement allegedly made by an accused while in police custody:

> is disputed and its making is not reliably corroborated the jury should be informed that it is comparatively more difficult for an accused person held in police custody without access to legal advice or other means of corroboration to have evidence available to support a challenge to police evidence of confessional statements than it is for such police evidence to be fabricated, and, accordingly, it is necessary that they be instructed … that they should give careful consideration as to the dangers involved in convicting an accused person in circumstances where the only (or substantially the only) basis for finding that guilt has been established beyond reasonable doubt is a confessional statement allegedly made whilst in police custody, the making of which is not reliably corroborated. Within the context of this warning it will ordinarily be necessary to emphasize the need for careful scrutiny of the evidence and to direct attention to the fact that police witnesses are often practised witnesses and it is not an easy matter to determine whether a practised witness is telling the truth.[53]

This warning was premised on the 'existence and increasing availability of reliable and accurate means of audio-visual recording'. Fortunately, all Australian jurisdictions have now introduced some form of electronic recording. However, it must be stressed that recording of part only of an interrogation is insufficient; the entire process of questioning should, where reasonably practicable, be recorded. Further, such procedures must be mandatory to ensure that there is no fabrication and, indirectly, to discourage improper modes of interrogation. Significantly, a majority of the High Court has stated that, in a case where the arrest and detention of the appellant was unlawful, that:

> to admit evidence of the appellant's alleged [and disputed] confessional statement was to compound the wrong done to him by his unlawful arrest and detention by subjecting him to the risk of conviction upon police evidence of what had occurred while he was unlawfully held in a police environment and deprived of any possibility of independent confirmation of his evidence.[54]

They concluded that, in such circumstances, 'it is plain that the case was one in which a proper exercise of the learned trial judge's discretion required the exclusion of evidence of the confessional statement'.

The issue of improper police methods has been considered in a general sense above. The High Court has held that the public policy balancing test applies to unlawfully or improperly obtained confessions.[55] However, long before the development of that doctrine, the courts had formulated rules relating to the methods used to obtain confessional evidence. These rules continue to operate and the High Court in 1998 clarified the relationship between them.

The primary common law rule is a test of voluntariness: the prosecution must establish that the confession was voluntarily made, in the sense of an 'exercise of a free choice to speak or be silent'.[56] There is no doubt that this doctrine is closely related to an accused person's right to silence, which in turn is related to the privilege against self-incrimination. We discussed the right to silence in chapter 2, but the precise interrelationship between these two doctrines is uncertain. While the requirement of voluntariness may be another way of saying that an accused shall 'not be compelled to testify against himself or to confess guilt', as provided by Article 14 of the *International Covenant on Civil and Political Rights*, the concept remains amorphous. On the one hand, it is clear that a confession will not be involuntary simply because some factor external to the accused was a cause of the confession. Some kinds of pressure are permissible, such as putting a suspect in a bare room, surrounded by strangers, unable to leave, scared that the police have (or think they have) enough evidence to convict. 'Voluntary' does not mean 'volunteered'. On the other hand, a confession will not be voluntary simply because the accused exercised a choice. A person who chooses to confess after being tortured does not make a voluntary confession. Partly in an attempt to overcome these difficulties, various categories of involuntariness have been formulated: confessions obtained by 'oppression' or 'inducements held out by a person in authority' will be inadmissible. These categories provide some assistance to judges, but have themselves developed a complex and artificial jurisprudence.[57] The rule copes fairly well with the obvious forms of abuse but is unsatisfactory in relation to more subtle pressures. Judges usually say that they know an involuntary confession when they see one, but the truth is that they do not often think that they see one.

A considerable degree of pressure is tolerated, particularly the myriad of psychological techniques that the police can use to encourage a suspect to talk, and to confess. The police usually carefully structure the physical conditions of the interrogation environment to maximise the suspect's anxiety and compliance: the interrogator dresses in a way that emphasises the disparity in social status, reduces stimuli available to the suspect, infringes the socially required area of personal space by close physical proximity, and removes the usual props that provide psychological support or relief from tension, such as paper clips and cigarettes. The social science literature generally confirms that such an environment heightens anxiety and promotes compliance.[58] The mere fact of incarceration is inherently coercive, inducing in perfectly normal individuals a depressed and pathological state of mind. Even if the interrogator acts in good faith and does not physically or psychologically abuse the suspect, the suspect is still under enormous pressure to confess, even if innocent. Indeed, subtle coercion is the most effective coercion. For example, the remarkable ease with which human conduct can be manipulated by inducing feelings of guilt has been demonstrated experimentally.[59] The

Chinese during the Korean war were able to use this technique to extract sincerely felt false confessions from entirely normal American prisoners.[60]

The Australian Law Reform Commission proposed replacement of the voluntariness rule with an objective test that requires the prosecution to prove that there was no 'violent, oppressive, inhuman or degrading conduct' involved in the making of the confession. The Commission also proposed that the prosecution be required to prove that the circumstances of interrogation were unlikely to affect adversely the reliability of the confession. The general public policy discretion would continue to apply to unlawfully or improperly obtained confessions and there would also be a general discretion to exclude such evidence on 'fairness' grounds. These proposals have been adopted in the Uniform Evidence Law. Similar developments have occurred in the common law. Initially, the problems with the voluntariness rule led to the development of a broad discretion to exclude confessional evidence if, having regard to the conduct of the police in obtaining it, and all the circumstances of the case, it would be 'unfair' to admit the evidence.[61] Not surprisingly, the courts had great difficulty in defining the idea of fairness in this context, a difficulty exacerbated by the yet additional general discretion to exclude improperly obtained evidence on public policy grounds. In 1998 the High Court reconsidered, and reformulated, the common law rules. The majority judgment in *Swaffield and Pavic*[62] held that admissibility of confessional evidence should be seen, in general terms, as:

> turning first on the question of voluntariness, next on exclusion based on considerations of reliability and finally on an overall discretion which might take account of all the circumstances of the case to determine whether the admission of the evidence or the obtaining of a conviction on the basis of the evidence is bought at a price which is unacceptable, having regard to contemporary community standards.[63]

The 'overall discretion' is intended to invest 'a broad discretion in the court', which may take into account considerations of fairness, public policy and 'protection of the rights and privileges of the accused'. One aspect of the latter is a focus on whether 'the accused's freedom to choose to speak to the police' has been 'impugned'.

Of course, such reforms of the law of evidence cannot provide a complete answer to questionable methods of obtaining confessions. Another solution is to lay down rules enforced by the courts as to what the police can and cannot do during interrogation, relying on audio or video recordings to ensure compliance. Statutory reforms in all Australian jurisdictions, considered in chapter 2, go a significant way in this direction. However, there are considerable difficulties in defining unacceptable police conduct, particularly in the grey area of psychological coercion. A more direct way to ensure absence of coercion and maximising reliability would be to require that a person independent of the police and possessing adequate legal knowledge be present during interrogation, in other words a lawyer acting for the suspect. This was considered in detail in chapter 2.

# Propensity evidence

There is a general common law rule, with exceptions, that evidence disclosing an accused person's bad character or criminal record (and thus a 'propensity' to commit the crime charged) may not be admitted against him or her. Similarly, each jurisdiction has statutory provisions that create a rule, also with exceptions, that an accused who chooses to testify is not required to answer questions seeking such evidence.

The reasons for this general prohibition derive from the principles considered earlier. Given that the primary aim of criminal trial procedure is to minimise the risk of convicting an innocent person, the courts should be careful about admitting prosecution evidence that is likely to be misused or given too much weight by the tribunal of fact. The primary danger with this kind of propensity evidence is that the jury (or, indeed, a judge or magistrate sitting without a jury) may be influenced to convict as punishment for conduct other than that charged. Clearly this is a great danger where the propensity evidence tends to show the commission of other crimes by the accused, particularly where they remain unpunished.

In addition, there is likely to be a tendency to overestimate the significance of such evidence. Once a criminal, always a criminal, some may think. Yet human behaviour is as much dependent on surrounding circumstances as it is on inherent character traits. We tend to think our own behaviour is the result of particular situations, but assume other people's behaviour is the result of character traits. More important, proving that someone accused of stealing has stolen before would normally be of little significance in identifying the perpetrator of a theft, since there are likely to be thousands of such people who might also have had the opportunity to commit the crime, but the tribunal of fact may fail to properly take this into account.

For these reasons, and others, propensity evidence under both the common law and the Uniform Evidence Law is not admissible against an accused unless the value of the evidence clearly outweighs its likely unfairly prejudicial effect.[64] A trial judge has a general power to exclude prosecution evidence that is more prejudicial than probative (tending to prove guilt), but the law in this area is that there is a rule of exclusion of the evidence unless the trial judge is satisfied that probative value outweighs the inevitable prejudice. There are differing formulations as to the degree of probative force required. However, there is High Court authority indicating that such evidence must be so probative that 'it bears no reasonable explanation other than the inculpation of the accused in the offence charged'.[65]

In assessing the real value of this evidence, it is important to consider how it is sought to be used—the reasoning process involved. If 'propensity reasoning' is involved (that is, A has committed a particular type of crime before, therefore he has a propensity to commit that type of crime, therefore he acted in conformity with that propensity to commit the crime charged), the evidence is likely to have little value. But the more specific the propensity, then the more probative it will be in the circumstances of the case. Other factors may enhance the value of the evidence, such as the degree to which the propensity is unusual.

Even if evidence disclosing an accused person's criminal record is not led by the prosecution for the purposes of propensity reasoning, but the prosecution relies on similarities in the offences to conclude that it is probable that the accused committed all of them (including the one being prosecuted), this evidence may still have an unfairly prejudicial effect. For that reason, the same exclusionary rule applies. However, striking similarities between two crimes, one of which was certainly committed by the accused, may be sufficiently probative that the accused committed the other crime to justify admission of the evidence.

Significantly, and consistently with the principles we have discussed, these rules do not apply to propensity evidence led by the defence. In traditional terms, the defence may lead evidence of the accused's 'good character', perhaps by calling witnesses as to his or her good reputation in the community. Such evidence of good character may be used as relevant directly to the issue of guilt and also, if the accused gives evidence, as bearing on his or her credibility as a witness. Of course, the court should not be misled. If the defence raises the issue of the accused's character, by (even inadvertently) advancing evidence of good character or suggesting that the accused is of good character, the prosecution may tender evidence of bad character (which would not otherwise be allowed) in rebuttal.

Perhaps the most troubling area in principle involves propensity evidence led by the defence in relation to an alleged victim. Such evidence is, with exceptions, admissible if relevant to a fact in issue. Thus, a man accused of murdering his wife is allowed to call evidence that she has behaved violently on other occasions to support a defence of self-defence.[66] Where the alleged crime is a sexual offence, however, special statutory rules apply to the adducing of propensity evidence in all jurisdictions.[67] These provisions are complex and vary from State to State, but the overriding theme is a desire to reduce the trauma experienced by complainants in such trials.

There is no doubt that the traditional approach in the area of sexual offences was unacceptable, based on discredited generalisations relating to a woman's 'chastity' and allowing offensive cross-examination into the highly sensitive but often irrelevant area of sexuality. Equally, there is little doubt that this approach discouraged a number of victims of sexual offences from coming forward to give evidence. Nevertheless, it must be said that blanket exclusion of a rape complainant's sexual history may well conflict with the central principles of the criminal justice system. Whatever indignities are suffered by the complainant in a criminal trial are not likely to compare with those a convicted sexual offender must suffer. If the evidence is in fact probative of the innocence of the accused in the particular circumstances of the case, there should be very good reasons advanced before it is excluded. No doubt, the real danger that the evidence might be given too much weight by a jury or prejudice them against the complainant ('she got what she deserved') may justify exclusion of general sexual history, which has minimal probative value. But probative value cannot be assessed in isolation. It will vary depending on what fact it is used to prove, the way it is established, and the mode of reasoning involved.[68]

The present law in New South Wales imposes a strict exclusionary rule, with limited exceptions, but this runs a serious risk that innocent people will be hampered in their defence so that genuine rapists may be more easily convicted. Under section 409B of the *Crimes Act* 1900 (NSW) evidence that discloses that the complainant in a sexual assault prosecution 'has or may have taken part or not taken part in any sexual activity is inadmissible' unless it falls within one of six exceptions spelt out in the rest of the provision. Unlike every other jurisdiction in Australia, there is no discretion granted to a trial judge in New South Wales to let the evidence in if it does not fall within one of the exceptions. As a result there have been several cases in the last few years in which trial judges have accepted that the evidence in question is highly relevant in tending to undermine the credit of the complainant or in tending to establish the innocence of the accused—and yet cannot be admitted as evidence. After criticism of the legislation by several members of the High Court, it was finally referred in 1997 for reconsideration by the New South Wales Law Reform Commission. The Commission advised that the strict exclusionary rule should be replaced by a judicial discretion to admit such evidence in appropriate circumstances. However, the Commission's report has been ignored by the New South Wales Government.

## Confidential communications privilege

In 1997, the New South Wales Parliament enacted the *Evidence Amendment (Confidential Communications) Act* 1997, which amended the *Evidence Act* 1995 by incorporating two new privileges relating to confidential communications.[69] The first, a 'professional confidential relationship' privilege, gives courts in New South Wales the power to protect confidences made (by a 'protected confider') to such persons as psychiatrists, psychologists, therapists, journalists and social workers. A court must direct that such evidence not be adduced in a proceeding in a court if it is satisfied that:

(a) it is likely that harm would or might be caused (whether directly or indirectly) to a protected confider if the evidence is adduced, and

(b) the nature and extent of the harm outweighs the desirability of the evidence being given.[70]

This is an important reform. The discretion allows courts to determine in a particular case whether the interest in confidentiality outweighs the desirability of the evidence being adduced. Of course, in respect of criminal proceedings it could be argued that it is difficult to see any circumstances in which the desirability of evidence being given to support an accused person's case could ever be outweighed by the harm that might be caused to a protected confider, bearing in mind the availability of protections other than evidentiary exclusion (such as closing the court or making suppression orders). In addition, it may be doubted whether the argument advanced to protect confidentiality in therapeutic situations—to encourage full disclosure—can hold good. Those persons who might choose not to seek therapy or counselling where they know their files may be used in evidence will be in no different position. They will have no guarantee that a court will not find that 'the desirability of the evidence being given' outweighs the interests in favour of non-admission of the evidence. Thus, they will continue to avoid counselling (assuming that is presently the case) and no benefit is gained. The only change will be that, on occasion, evidence sought to be adduced by a criminal defendant will be excluded.

Nevertheless, assuming the courts exercise the discretion with care, there is little that can be said against the substance of this provision. That cannot be said, however, in respect of the other privilege created by this legislation: a 'sexual assault communications privilege'. Evidence of a 'protected confidence' (defined to mean a communication made in confidence in the course of a relationship where a counsellor is treating 'for any emotional or psychological condition' a person, 'the protected confider', against whom a sexual assault offence has allegedly been committed) will not be admissible unless:

(a) 'reasonable notice in writing' of the intention to adduce the evidence has been given to 'each other party', 'the protected confider' (if not a party) and 'the counsellor' (if not a party), and

(b) the evidence is of 'substantial probative value', and

(c) 'other evidence of the protected confidence … is not available', and

(d) the public interest in non-disclosure is 'substantially outweighed' by the public interest in admitting the evidence, and

(e) 'the court gives leave for the evidence to be admitted'.[71]

It may be asked what justification there can be for excluding evidence that would fail the test of exclusion under the general 'professional confidential relationship' privilege. As noted above, it is difficult to see any circumstances in which the desirability of evidence being given to support an accused person's case could ever be outweighed by the harm that might be caused to a protected confider, bearing in mind the availability of protections other than evidentiary exclusion. Under the test adopted, even if that balancing test is not satisfied (that is, the court is satisfied that the desirability of the evidence being given outweighs the harm that may be caused if the evidence is adduced), the evidence may still be inadmissible.

In essence, this legislation reflects a distrust of judges. The New South Wales Parliament was not prepared to simply allow a court to balance the conflicting

interests at stake. Rather, it required that the evidence must have 'substantial probative value' and that the public interest in non-disclosure be 'substantially outweighed' by the public interest in admitting the evidence. To impose such a
burden on the accused is not only unfair but it is wrong in principle.

A more specific criticism may be made of the requirement that 'other evidence
of the protected confidence ... is not available'. An earlier draft of this provision
referred to 'other evidence concerning the matters to which the protected confidence or document relates'. This appeared to have the effect that evidence of a
protected confidence given to a counsellor would not be admissible, even if it
were directly inconsistent with the complainant's account at trial, where the
defence called another witness to give evidence and another communication to
the same effect in non-confidential circumstances—no matter how lacking in
credibility that defence witness may be. The new version contained in the Act
overcomes this problem, but it is difficult to understand what effect it will have.
Presumably any 'other evidence of the protected confidence' will be subject to the
same pre-conditions to admissibility as the evidence in question. How could the
'availability' of such evidence ever affect the admissibility of the evidence adduced
to prove the confidential communication?

Finally, in relation to the notice requirement, there is no provision for the
court waiving the requirement in appropriate circumstances (unlike comparable
provisions in the *Evidence Act*).[72] Thus, for example, it may be that an unrepresented accused who has failed to give notice through lack of knowledge of the
requirement cannot be protected, unless 'reasonable' is defined in terms of the
capacities of the party required to give notice rather than the parties required to
be notified.

Nevertheless, despite these legitimate criticisms, the legislation remains in
force. A very similar privilege relating to 'sexual assault communications' has been
introduced in Victoria.[73]

## Expert evidence

The rules relating to opinion evidence in criminal trials can be summarised in a relatively short compass. This evidence is excluded unless it is the opinion of an 'expert'
or, less commonly, it is relevant for some reason other than to establish the truth of
the opinion.[74] The reason for this exclusionary rule is that the drawing of inferences
from facts is a matter for the tribunal of fact, and the expression of what may be
little more than uninformed speculation is unlikely to be helpful and may be positively misleading. However, the opinion of a legitimate expert may well be helpful:
there are many areas of specialised knowledge that are relevant to matters in issue
before the courts and are needed to assist the tribunal to reach a correct conclusion.

At one time, it was thought that special technical rules limited the admission
of expert evidence.[75] The better view, however, is that the rules are very flexible

and this approach has been adopted in the Uniform Evidence Law. If the witness really is an expert in a legitimate area of expertise, able to supply helpful opinion evidence on an issue in the trial, the witness may testify (subject to the general discretion to exclude evidence that is more prejudicial than probative).[76] An example of such a flexible approach has been the admission of evidence relating to 'battered woman syndrome' in several murder trials. Thus, in a 1991 decision,[77] the South Australian Court of Criminal Appeal allowed opinion evidence, from professional psychologists, that women subjected to 'habitual domestic violence are typically affected psychologically to the extent that their reactions and responses differ from those which might be expected by persons who lack the advantage of an acquaintance with the results of those studies'.[78] Such evidence is likely to assist in understanding the actions of a battered woman, notwithstanding the danger that a jury may too readily defer to the views of the experts.

While flexibility is preferable to the arbitrary distinctions of the past, there is no doubt that evidence admitted under the guise of 'expertise' can sometimes result in miscarriages of justice. Justice Dawson of the High Court listed some of the dangers with expert opinion evidence:

> Although the modern attitude towards expert evidence is, perhaps, less exclusionary than in the past, it is nevertheless still important to recognise the dangers of wrongly admitting it. The admission of such evidence carries with it the implication that the jury are not equipped to decide the relevant issue without the aid of expert opinion and thus, if it is wrongly admitted, it is likely to divert them from their proper task which is to decide the matter for themselves using their own common sense. And even though most juries are not prone to pay undue deference to expert opinion, there is at least a danger that the manner of its preparation may, if it is wrongly admitted, give to it an authority which is not warranted. In addition the calling of unnecessary expert evidence tends to prolong a trial, particularly when it provokes the calling of further expert evidence in reply. Moreover there is then a risk that the focus of the trial will shift from the evidence of the facts in dispute to the conflict between the competing theories of the various expert witnesses.[79]

Perhaps the most recent example of serious concerns about the admission of expert evidence was the trial of Lindy and Michael Chamberlain. Their baby daughter, Azaria, disappeared from a tent in the camping area near Uluru (Ayers Rock) on 17 August 1980. Her body was never found. The claim by her parents that she was taken by a dingo came under challenge from a number of experts, who argued that the available evidence established facts that suggested that Mrs Chamberlain had murdered her daughter and that Mr Chamberlain helped in disposing of the body. A trial based almost entirely on the testimony of expert witnesses resulted in the conviction of the Chamberlains in 1982 and subsequent appeals were unsuccessful. But doubts persisted. The evidence of the prosecution experts was challenged and new evidence was obtained. A Royal Commission set up to inquire into the case concluded in 1987 that the evidence fell 'far short of proving that Azaria was not taken by a dingo. Indeed, the evidence affords considerable support for the view that a dingo may have taken her'.[80] The Chamberlains were eventually pardoned.

The Royal Commissioner, Justice Morling, concluded that it was the expert evidence at the trial that caused the miscarriage of justice. It is not possible to deal with all of the expert evidence considered by Justice Morling or, indeed, with all of the problems that he identified. However, perhaps the most significant was the evidence of a forensic biologist, who testified that immuno-chemical tests on material taken from the Chamberlains' car demonstrated the presence of a significant amount of blood from a baby. Justice Morling found that difficulties posed by the age of the red material in the car and the temperatures to which it had been exposed, difficulties of which the forensic biologist was not aware, raised considerable doubts as to the reliability of her results. He also found compelling evidence demonstrating that the alleged blood was in fact sound-deadening compound. He concluded that only a very small quantity of blood was in the car, if any, for which there was an innocent explanation.

Justice Morling made some observations on why some of the most damaging of the trial evidence was 'either wrong or highly suspect':

- Some experts who gave evidence at the trial were over-confident of their ability to form reliable opinions on matters that lay on the outer margins of their fields of expertise.
- Some of their opinions were based on unreliable or inadequate data.
- Other evidence was given at the trial by experts who did not have the experience, facilities or resources necessary to enable them to express reliable opinions on some of the novel and complex scientific issues that arose for consideration.
- The failure of the defence to put in issue some of the scientific opinions at the trial may have been due, in part, to lack of access to the necessary expert witnesses.[81]

It is clear that the courts have to be careful to maintain the basic rule that an expert may testify only with respect to those matters on which he or she is truly expert. It may also be that the courts should do more to test the reliability of data introduced into evidence and used to form the basis for crucial expert opinions.[82] Difficulties with the presentation and understanding of complex expert evidence (for example, in relation to DNA analysis) should be addressed.[83] Appellate review should be strengthened.[84] Finally, some modification of the adversary nature of the system may be appropriate in this area. There is no doubt that some of the problems with expert evidence derive from that adversary structure: the parties may have greatly different resources to obtain expert evidence, they will choose only those experts who will provide favourable evidence, and the expert will tend to identify strongly with that party in giving evidence. An autonomous national forensic science centre, equally available to prosecution and defence, should be established and properly funded, pre-trial disclosure and consultation should be required, and consideration should be given to judges calling independent expert witnesses in appropriate cases.[85] Experts must be encouraged to see that their role is to assist the court, not to advance the interests of the party paying their fee.

Another option would be to remove some factual issues from the lay jury, but this should not be considered until less radical options are tried. In a New South Wales case dealing with complex (and conflicting) scientific expert evidence relating to DNA analysis, the trial judge excluded the evidence on the basis that the jury 'even if properly directed, could fail to appreciate the complexity of the inter-relationship of the various pieces of the forensic evidence or the limits that might be placed on the forensic evidence'. However, the New South Wales Court of Criminal Appeal overturned this ruling. The court stated:

> It is one thing to say that, in such a case as is exemplified by the present particular case, it will be, obviously, difficult to put into simple lay language the concepts which the jury must have firmly in its grasp; and to assist the jury with a similar clarity and simplicity to apply those concepts to the evidence adduced in the trial, both by the prosecution and by the defence. It is, however, an entirely different thing to take it as, more or less, self-evident that the jury, even if given that assistance, will be either unwilling or unable, or both, to carry out in a proper way the jury's critical fact-finding function.[86]

The court concluded that, with careful judicial directions, the jury could be trusted to assess the conflicting expert evidence.

## Eyewitness identification evidence

In many criminal trials the crucial issue is identification: is the accused in fact the person who committed the crime charged? Often the prosecution will call one or more witnesses to identify the accused in the court room (a 'dock' identification). Almost invariably, this identification evidence is accompanied by evidence of an earlier identification, whether from a group of photographs, or in some other way. Often this evidence will be very impressive. The identification witness or witnesses will usually be confident that the accused is the culprit and testify accordingly.

Yet the fact is that eyewitness identification evidence is by far the greatest cause of wrongful convictions. There are numerous publicised cases around the world that illustrate the dangers with this evidence. One of the most famous was the Adolph Beck case, which led to the creation of the English Court of Criminal Appeal in the early part of the twentieth century. Beck was picked out of a line-up by 11 different witnesses (all of whom knew the culprit well), convicted, spent seven years in prison, was released, charged with more offences, and identified by another four witnesses. Only then was the real criminal, who surprisingly did not look much like Beck, caught.

There are many reasons why mistakes are made.[87] The circumstances of observation may not have been conducive to accuracy. The stress of the situation may have impaired perception. Subsequent information may have affected memory, producing unconscious transference whereby a person seen in one situation is confused with a person seen in another situation. The circumstances of first identification may be highly suggestive, such as where the witness is presented with a single suspect or photograph.

At the trial, there may be additional problems. According to the 'rogues' gallery' effect, a jury may be prejudiced by the fact that photographs used for a photographic identification may suggest that the accused has a prior criminal record or at least has been arrested on a prior occasion.[88] They may be unduly impressed by the confidence with which the witness makes the identification. Cross-examination of the witness may not be an effective test of the quality of the evidence since there is no story to dissect, only an (apparently) simple assertion of identity.

Given all these concerns, one may ask whether the present common law approach to eyewitness identification evidence is sufficiently concerned about minimising the risk of convicting innocent people. Visual identification evidence is not subject to any exclusionary rule but may be excluded under the general discretions based on conceptions of 'unfairness', whether relating to unfairly prejudicial evidence, or unfairness in the way the evidence was obtained. Thus, failure to use an identification parade after the 'detection process' has ended is, in the absence of some explanation, usually improper and may result in exclusion.[89] If the first identification is a dock identification, exclusion will often follow if the subject was not previously familiar to the witness and another mode of identification on an earlier occasion was reasonably possible.[90]

Nevertheless, there are no statistics on the rate of discretionary exclusion and it is arguable that the courts have not been sufficiently insistent that the police adopt the safest possible methods. The Australian Law Reform Commission recommended that eye-witness identification should be the subject of rules of admissibility and tighter discretionary controls.[91] Most of its proposals have been adopted in the Uniform Evidence Law. One effect of the new provisions is that, in substance, such evidence is not to be admitted unless an identification parade was held or it was not reasonable to hold one.[92] While this does still incorporate a discretionary element, it provides a welcome encouragement of the preferred mode of identification.

One reason the courts have not taken a strong line on exclusion of doubtful or tainted identification evidence is because of a traditional reliance on jury warnings. A jury must be appropriately warned about the dangers with identification evidence, both generally and in the particular circumstances of the case.[93] This will often include the considerations referred to above, as well as some reference to past miscarriages of justice deriving from identification evidence. One can only hope that these warnings encourage careful assessment of the real value of the identification evidence in the particular case. However, the efficacy of many jury warnings is doubtful.[94] It is our view that the proposals of the Australian Law Reform Commission, largely adopted in the Uniform Evidence Law, offer a more realistic way of maximising the reliability of this extremely dangerous form of evidence.

## Other types of potentially unreliable evidence

Warnings to the jury[95] are the primary way in which the law of evidence deals with most types of potentially unreliable evidence. Perhaps the classic example is the evidence of an alleged accomplice of the accused, called by the prosecution. Under the common law, the jury must be warned by the trial judge that it is dangerous to convict upon such evidence unless it is corroborated. Several reasons have been advanced for this rule, but the primary justification is that the accomplice may have an interest in giving false testimony, which is not necessarily apparent to the jury. Thus, the alleged accomplice might try to exculpate herself or minimise her own part in an offence by fabricating or exaggerating the role of the accused.

The corroboration warning encourages the jury to look for other independent evidence of guilt on which to found a conviction even though it may, after scrutinising the evidence with great care, convict even in the absence of corroboration if satisfied of the truth and accuracy of the evidence. Corroborative evidence 'confirms', 'supports' or 'strengthens' other evidence in the sense that 'it renders [that] other evidence more probable'.[96] However, it is not enough that it simply confirms the other evidence in some respect. It should confirm it in a 'material particular' by 'tending to connect the accused with the crime charged'.[97] On the other hand, it need not, standing alone, establish the guilt of the accused, or any other proposition, beyond reasonable doubt.

Traditionally, several categories of evidence, including the evidence of children and the evidence of complainants in sexual offence proceedings, have required corroboration warnings. Thus, it was thought that the evidence of young children is generally unreliable because immaturity and lack of responsibility may lead them to lie, exaggerate, fantasise or make mistakes. However, modern research has tended to undermine the view that children are inherently unreliable witnesses, although they may be more suggestible than adults. Similarly, the argument that complainants in sex cases are unreliable has been largely discredited: rape is underreported rather than over-reported, there is no evidence of large numbers of false allegations, and there is little evidence that juries are swayed by emotional sympathy for the complainant.

More generally, corroboration rules are unduly arbitrary. They throw a group of witnesses into a category of unreliable witnesses without any discrimination according to the circumstances of the case. Further, they direct a jury to look for corroboration without fully explaining why the evidence is potentially unreliable. Some studies suggest that the jury may focus its attention on the question whether there is corroboration and be more willing to convict as soon as it is satisfied such corroboration exists, ignoring the problems with the evidence that led to the giving of the warning in the first place.

For these reasons, most of the categories of evidence requiring corroboration warnings under the common law have now been abolished by statute. Indeed, the Uniform Evidence Law has abolished them all.[98] But this does not mean that no warnings are ever given by a trial judge. Currently the preferred approach is that, where the evidence of a particular prosecution witness is potentially unreliable, the jury must be made aware, in words appropriate to the particular case, of the need for caution before placing reliance on it.[99] Such a warning will be particularly necessary where the jury may not have fully perceived the dangers, or the jury's attention may have been diverted from them. Examples of witnesses who may be potentially unreliable include a witness who has a mental disability that may affect his or her capacity to give reliable evidence; a witness who is a young child; a witness who is giving evidence of events many years in the past; and a witness of bad character. The direction should be clear and the reasons for it should be appropriately explained to the jury.

In 1992 the High Court added another category to the types of witnesses likely to require a jury warning: prison informers. At that time, there had been several prosecutions based largely on evidence of an alleged confession made by a person in prison to another prisoner who then informs the authorities. We have discussed this development in chapter 2 and considered there the dangers with such evidence. In *Pollitt v The Queen* the High Court agreed that, in all but exceptional cases, it was necessary for a trial judge to warn of the danger of convicting on evidence of that kind unless corroborated by other evidence connecting or tending to connect the accused with the crime charged. However, as a number of the Justices pointed out, in the usual case where the accused asserts that the conversation with the informer did not take place, such a warning will not direct attention to the real issue of the unreliability of such evidence. Indeed, because there is usually some corroborative evidence, this 'may lend some semblance of reliability to what is essentially unreliable evidence'.[100] As a minimum, a very strong judicial warning should be almost invariably given, drawing attention to the unreliability of the evidence, the need for very careful scrutiny of it, and the dangers of basing a conviction upon it. The Uniform Evidence Law imposes similar obligations on a trial judge. In the second edition of this book, we expressed the view that the dangers with this evidence necessitated rather stronger measures. We argued that there 'must be very close scrutiny of the informer and his history, and of the benefits, direct and indirect, promised and hoped for, that may come from his evidence'. We suggested that 'the courts should carefully consider taking the more interventionist approach of excluding the evidence entirely', so as to 'reduce the incidence in criminal trials of what some have referred to as the "privatised verbal" '. However, since that edition, it appears that this type of evidence has become much less common, suggesting that the High Court's intervention has had a real impact.

# Conclusion

It is clear that the rules of evidence applied in the criminal courts cannot be approached in a simplistic manner. They reflect diverse principles and values and perform a number of different functions. The courts continue to develop the rules in response to changing political and social demands, but it is nevertheless apparent that comprehensive legislative reform is essential. We have indicated our support for many of the reforms introduced by the Uniform Evidence Law, now applying in Federal Courts, New South Wales, Tasmania and the Australian Capital Territory. We would support enactment of similar legislation in other Australian jurisdictions, although progress to date does not give many grounds for optimism in that regard. In the first edition of this book, we observed that 'such is the complexity of the law in this area, and the disagreement over values inherent in many of the controversial topics', that legislative implementation of the Australian Law Reform Commission's proposals was far from certain. We noted that 'resistance from legal practitioners, particularly barristers, is almost inevitable, if only because they have invested time and effort to master the present law and derive much of their prestige from such arcane knowledge'. While we have been pleasantly surprised by the enactment of the Uniform Evidence Law, and its recent adoption in Tasmania, it remains to be seen whether it will be extended to other parts of Australia.

One final point must be emphasised. Most of the rules of evidence operate in the context of the adversary system. That system can only function effectively if the parties are roughly evenly matched. In practical terms that means that, as a minimum, the accused should be legally represented. As we saw in chapter 5, that is not the norm in the lower courts. If that were to remain the position, there is a strong argument for radical simplification of the rules of evidence when applied in such circumstances. Of course, as we have noted, while the rules of evidence theoretically apply in full force in summary trials, there is a tendency in practice for legal practitioners not to assert them as strongly as in jury trials. That is a tactical choice made in the circumstances of the trial. If the defendant has no legal representation, however, the complexity of the rules means that such a choice is not even available.

## Notes

1   Glanville Williams, *The Proof of Guilt*, 3rd edn, Stevens and Sons, Oxford, 1963, pp. 186–7.

2   For a strong assertion of this position, see the views of the United Kingdom Criminal Law Revision Committee, 11th Report, *Evidence (General)*, para. 27.

3  P. A. Sallmann, 'The Criminal Trial on Trial: A Response to Some Recent Criticisms', *Australian and New Zealand Journal of Criminology*, 16, 1983, p. 31.

4  *International Covenant on Civil and Political Rights*, Article 14.

5  *Evidence Amendment (Confidential Communications) Act* 1997 (NSW). It is discussed below.

6  *Re Van Beelen* (1974) 9 SASR 163. Admittedly, the confession was of doubtful reliability since the person who made it was receiving psychiatric treatment and was unable to provide any information confirming its truth. It was also almost immediately withdrawn.

7  *Walton* (1989) 166 CLR 283 at 293.

8  *Pollitt* (1992) 174 CLR 558 at 573–4 per Brennan J.

9  *Evidence Act* 1995 (Cth); *Evidence Act* 1995 (NSW).

10  For a detailed summary and discussion of these changes, see S. Odgers, *Uniform Evidence Law*, 6th edn, Law Book Co., Sydney, 2004.

11  *He Kaw Teh* (1985) 157 CLR 523.

12  The defence of insanity, which must be established on the balance of probabilities.

13  For example, s. 30R *Crimes Act* 1914 (Cth); s. 417 *Crimes Act* 1900 (NSW); s. 168 *Magistrates (Summary Proceedings) Act* 1975 (Vic).

14  Senate Standing Committee on Constitutional and Legal Affairs, *Report on the Burden of Proof in Criminal Proceedings*, AGPS, Canberra, 1982, pp. 87–92.

15  Legal and Constitutional Committee of the Legislative Council of the Victorian Parliament, *Report on the Burden of Proof in Criminal Cases*, Melbourne, 1985, pp. 91–6.

16  [1935] AC 462.

17  As above at 481–2.

18  *Mullen* (1938) 59 CLR 124, *He Kaw Teh* (1985) 157 CLR 523.

19  *Thomas* (1960) 102 CLR 584 at 595 per Kitto J; *Green* (1971) 126 CLR 28 at 33. This principle is enacted in the Uniform Evidence Law (s. 141).

20  *Peacock* (1911) 13 CLR 619.

21  *Shepherd* (1990) 170 CLR 573 at 579 per Dawson J (Mason CJ, Toohey and Gaudron JJ agreeing).

22  As above at 579, 581.

23  *May v O'Sullivan* (1955) 92 CLR 654 at 658; *Doney* (1990) 171 CLR 207 at 212.

24  *Doney* (1990) 171 CLR 207 at 214.

25  Although the trial judge may invite the jury to stop a trial on the basis that it does not need to hear all the evidence in order to conclude that it should find a verdict of not guilty: *Prasad* (1979) 23 SASR 161.

26  In some States, the defence obtains a procedural advantage if it does not call any evidence—defence counsel can make a final address (to judge or jury) last (i.e. after the prosecutor). If the defence calls evidence, this advantage is lost. However, most jurisdictions have abandoned this curious and rather unfair rule, always allowing the defence to address last.

27  There are also special rules relating to the spouse and family of an accused person but space does not allow discussion of them here.

28  Curiously, in the nineteenth century an accused person did not have the right to give evidence, on the assumption that his or her evidence would be inherently untrustworthy. Now, an accused may, but cannot be compelled to, testify. Not only is this position consistent with civil parties, it also reflects the human right of an accused person 'not to be compelled to testify against himself' (Article 14, *International Covenant on Civil and Political*

*Rights*). The right of an accused person to make a 'dock statement', an unsworn statement not subject to cross-examination, has been abolished in all Australian jurisdictions.

29 *Bridge* (1964) 118 CLR 600.

30 Uniform Evidence Law, s. 20.

31 *Azzopardi v The Queen* (2001) 205 CLR 50 (High Court).

32 *Weissensteiner v The Queen* (1993) 178 CLR 217 at 229.

33 (2000) 199 CLR 620 at [22] – [27].

34 *Azzopardi* at [68]. For a critique of these High Court judgments, see D. Hamer, 'The Privilege of Silence and the Persistent Risk of Self-incrimination', *Criminal Law Journal*, 28, 2004, p. 160.

35 Victoria, Queensland and Western Australia.

36 See H. Jackson, 'Child Witnesses in the Western Australian Criminal Courts', *Criminal Law Journal*, 27, 2003, p. 199; C. Corns, 'Videotaped Evidence in Victoria: Some Evidentiary Issues and Appellate Court Perspectives', *Criminal Law Journal*, 2004, p. 43.

37 *Bunning v Cross* (1978) 141 CLR 54 at 75.

38 As above at 74.

39 As above at 77–8.

40 Australian Law Reform Commission, Report No. 38, *Evidence,* para. 164(a).

41 Uniform Evidence Law, s. 138.

42 (1995) 184 CLR 19.

43 At 39.

44 *Crimes Amendment (Controlled Operations) Act* 1996 (Cth). The High Court has held this legislation to be constitutional in *Nicholas* v *The Queen* (1998) 151 ALR 312. See also the *Criminal Law (Undercover Operations) Act* 1995 (SA); *Law Enforcement (Controlled Operations) Act* 1997 (NSW); Chapter 5 of the *Police Powers and Responsibilities Act* 2000 (Qld).

45 (1993) 113 ALR 1, at 10.

46 By means of a 'good-faith exception' to the exclusionary rule: see *United States v Leon* 468 US 897 (1984) (search made in good faith on the basis of a subsequently invalidated search warrant).

47 Unfortunately, as elsewhere in this area, there is a paucity of empirical studies. But see N. N. Stevenson, 'Criminal Cases in the NSW District Court: a pilot study' in J. Basten et al. (eds), *The Criminal Injustice System*, Legal Services Bulletin, Sydney, 1982, pp. 106–45.

48 Report of the Committee of Inquiry into the Enforcement of Criminal Law in Queensland (the Lucas Report), Brisbane, 1977, pp. 14–15, 30–1.

49 G. Williams, 'The Authentication of Statements to the Police', *Criminal Law Review*, 1979, p. 14.

50 (1977) 137 CLR 517.

51 (1988) 165 CLR 314.

52 (1991) 171 CLR 468.

53 (1991) 171 CLR 468 at 475–6.

54 *Foster* (1993) 113 ALR 1 per Mason CJ, Deane, Dawson, Toohey and Gaudron JJ at 10.

55 *Cleland* (1982) 151 CLR 1.

56 *Lee* (1950) 82 CLR 133 at 149.

57 Although it should be noted that judgment of McHugh J in the High Court decision of *Foster* (1993) 113 ALR 1 at 18 does offer an attractive rationalisation of the law in this

area, emphasising that where inducements are used by the police the prosecution must show that they had no causal impact at all on the accused.

58  C. Y. Ayling, 'Comment—Corroborating Confessions: An Empirical Analysis of Legal Safeguards against False Confessions', *Wisconsin Law Review*, 1984, pp. 1121, 1162–78.

59  Ayling, p. 1121.

60  Ayling, p. 1161.

61  *Lee* (1950) 82 CLR 133 at 154.

62  (1998) 151 ALR 98.

63  At 121.

64  *Pfennig* (1995) 182 CLR 461; s. 101 Uniform Evidence Law.

65  *Pfennig* at 481.

66  *Re Knowles* [1984] VR 751.

67  NSW: ss. 409B, 409C *Crimes Act* 1900; Qld: ss. 4, 5 *Criminal Law (Sexual Offences) Act* 1978; SA: s. 34i *Evidence Act* 1929; Tas: s. 102A *Evidence Act* 1910; Vic: s. 37A *Evidence Act* 1958; WA: ss. 36A–BC *Evidence Act* 1906; ACT: s. 76G *Evidence Ordinance* 1971.

68  See S. J. Odgers, 'Evidence of Sexual History in Sexual Offence Trials', *Sydney Law Review*, 11, 1986, p. 73. For a different perspective, see E. A. Sheehy, 'Feminist Argumentation before the Supreme Court of Canada in *Seaboyer, Gayme*: The Sound of One Hand Clapping', *Melbourne University Law Review*, 18, 1991, p. 450.

69  It should be noted that this amendment has been neither adopted by the Commonwealth for Federal Court proceedings nor enacted in the ACT. Consequently, the 'Uniform Evidence Law' is, to this extent, somewhat less uniform.

70  Section 126B(3) *Evidence Amendment (Confidential Communications) Act* 1997.

71  See s. 126H *Evidence Amendment (Confidential Communications) Act* 1997.

72  Compare ss. 67 and 100.

73  *Evidence Act* 1958 (Vic), ss. 32B–32G.

74  It is sometimes said that there is another exception for opinion evidence, based on actual perceptions of factual events and necessary to give a complete account of the perceptions. However, such evidence is better seen as evidence of fact even though expressed in the form of an opinion.

75  For example, the 'common knowledge' rule and the 'ultimate issue' rule.

76  The leading decision in this area of the law of evidence is *Murphy* (1989) 63 ALJR 424.

77  *Runjanjic and Kontinnen* (1991) 53 A Crim R 362.

78  King CJ at 366.

79  Dawson J in *Murphy* (1989) 63 ALJR 424.

80  Royal Commission of Inquiry into the Chamberlain Convictions (Commissioner, Justice T. R. Morling), Commonwealth Parliamentary Paper No. 192/1987, p. 338.

81  As above, at pp. 340–1.

82  See J. Bourke, 'Misapplied Science: Unreliability in Scientific Test Evidence', *Australian Bar Review*, 10, 1993, pp. 123, 183.

83  See M. Findlay and J. Grix, 'Challenging Forensic Evidence? Observations on the Use of DNA in Certain Criminal Trials', *Current Issues in Criminal Justice*, 14, 2003, p. 269.

84  See chapter 9.

85  But see M. N. Howard, 'The Neutral Expert: A Plausible Threat to Justice', *Criminal Law Review*, 1991, p. 98.

86 *Lisoff* [1999] NSWCCA 364 at [49].

87 See L. Re, 'Eyewitness Identification: Why so many Mistakes?', *Australian Law Journal*, 58, 1984, p. 509; B. Cutler and S. Penrod, *Mistaken Identification: The Eyewitness, Psychology and the Law*, Oxford University Press, New York, 1995

88 *Alexander* (1981) 145 CLR 395 at 401, 409, 412; *Aziz* [1982] 2 NSWLR 322.

89 In *Alexander* (1981) 145 CLR 395 a minority of the High Court (Stephen and Murphy JJ) considered that photographic identification after the detection process had ended should, in the absence of explanation, almost invariably result in exclusion of the evidence (at 417, 436–7). However, the majority of the court rejected any such general rule (at 402–3, 431, 437).

90 See *Davies and Cody* (1937) 57 CLR 170 at 181–2.

91 Australian Law Reform Commission, Report No. 38, *Evidence*, para. 184.

92 See ss. 114 and 115 Uniform Evidence Law. An identification parade will not be required if the suspect was not in police custody at the time.

93 *Domican* (1992) 173 CLR 555. See also ss. 116 and 165 Uniform Evidence Law.

94 See 'Juries and the Rules of Evidence', [1973] *Criminal Law Review*, p. 208.

95 It should be noted that if a judge is sitting without a jury, she or he should warn her- or himself. *Collett v Bennett* (1986) 21 A Crim R 410 at 415–16. The same applies to magistrates.

96 *Doney* (1990) 171 CLR 207 at 211.

97 As above.

98 Section 164 does, however, retain the requirement for corroboration in respect of perjury charges.

99 *Bromley* (1986) 161 CLR 315, 319 per Gibbs CJ.

100 *Pollitt* (1992) 174 CLR 558 at 601 per Dawson and Gaudron JJ.

7

# Punishment
# and Penalty

## Introduction

In Australia at present, much doubt, confusion and controversy surround the issue of what to do with those who are found guilty of breaking the criminal law. While there is a broad acceptance of some need to punish, divisions arise over how particular penalties are to be justified, and most fairly and effectively imposed. Even for serious offences, there seems little consensus on what punishments fit which crimes, or what the particular relationship between offence, offender and penalty should be.

Punishment is one of the essential elements of our criminal justice process. It gains a legal dimension through the connection between criminal sanctions and penalty. In this regard, the legal sanction to punish involves the consequences of a guilty verdict leading to the sentencing process and the awarding of penalty.

The 'justice' of punishment exacted through criminal sanctions and penalty, however, is open to criticism. The air of arbitrariness surrounding the sentencing situation, the deliberate infliction of suffering, which penalties involve, and the considerable uncertainty about their consequences, mean that the place of punishment within any system of criminal justice cannot be taken for granted.

This chapter examines the significance of punishment and penalty within criminal justice.[1] Penalties are seen as a reflection of the system out of which they emerge, and of community values, which they are supposed to reflect. They represent the 'whole of the penal complex including its sanctions, institutions, discourses and representations'.[2]

Punishment is connected to crime through the criminal justice process, and appears both legitimately and illegitimately at various stages of its operation. Specific forms of penalty depend on the historical and cultural setting within which they are enforced.[3] Penalties are imposed on people by institutions, and therefore the significance of any penalty should first be understood from the perspectives of the actors involved in the sanction. In addition, an appreciation of the place of a particular penalty within the process requires consideration of the procedures and rules governing sentencing discretion.

It is important when looking for causal connections in the criminal justice process that punishment and penalty receive individual consideration. In this way one might concede the appropriateness of punishment in criminal justice and yet still dispute the nature of particular penalties. This chapter situates punishment and penalty within the justice process and speculates on their impact across Australian society. To achieve this we realise how the criminal sanction leads on to specific penalties for individual offenders convicted of particular offences. The criminal law's general requirement to punish once criminal liability is established does not satisfactorily explain the existence and operation of specific penalties, and vice versa. These depend on the expectation of punishment being focused down through a system of justice and on a crime event.

When discussing punishment and penalty, it is useful to recognise that crime and its imposed punishment share similar features. As our later consideration of sentencing indicates (see chapter 9), the legal criteria and the administrative processes for identifying crime also have relevance for punishment, and the determination of penalty.

# Crime and punishment

One of the assumptions that underlies our system of criminal justice is that crime and punishment fundamentally differ. However, in some situations, the behaviour that comprises the offence may be similar to the nature of the penalty, or the harm that flows from these: for example, theft and the fine, or homicide and capital punishment. Therefore something beyond behaviour or actions must distinguish crime and punishment.

In seeking to distinguish crime and punishment one is confronted with whether:

- we are dealing with phenomena universal to all cultures
- there are intrinsic characteristics and attributes of crime and punishment that warrant the assumption that they operate as independent classes of behaviour.

The state's control over the determination of criminal liability (see chapter 1), the sanction process, and the imposition of punishment is a common thread that runs through the administration of criminal justice. Such control is confirmed by the state's assumption of responsibility for criminal prosecutions, and its monopoly over the power to punish or pardon. In this respect, it is state interest and authority that connects a crime to the criminal sanction and to the imposition of penalty.

To simply maintain that crime causes or essentially requires punishment is to ignore the separate significance of the processes of criminalisation and punishment. Such a basic causal approach assumes that the exercise of police or judicial discretion is inevitable after a crime is committed, and therefore sanction and penalty always follow every crime. As we know, this is not the case. While being fundamentally influenced by crime, punishment also relies on wider socio-political considerations, similar to those that designate the nature of crime in the first place.

The concept of an inextricable connection between crime and punishment overlooks many important policy questions, which are regularly side-stepped in the traditional administration of criminal justice. These include:

- In what manner is crime created or abolished through the imposition or removal of penal sanctions, and by selective law enforcement?
- What is the relationship between criminalisation and the wider socio-political imperatives, as distinct from legal requirements, which determine the nature of criminal offences and penalties?
- How does social structure affect (or is affected by) crime, punishment, and criminal justice?[4]

Recently, serious miscarriages of justice have emerged in several Australian jurisdictions, which have raised some fundamental questions about the motivations behind criminalisation. In addition they have demonstrated the inherent distinction between crime and punishment.[5] All too often, punitive political responses to 'law and order' concerns become criminal justice policy, at the expense of justice for the individual.[6] Punishment should not be regarded always as the most appropriate response to the 'crime problem'. This leads to the false proposition that the more punishment the state advocates, the more concerned it is about crime.

## The social reality of punishment

Punishment is a 'complex set of interlinked processes and institutions rather than a uniform object or event'.[7] The nature of these processes and institutions is determined by the historical development of the society out of which they emerge.[8] The connection between punishment and social structure explains much of the early development of penal colonies that grew to form Australia.

Transportation, along with the newly emerging prison system, was viewed in Britain as another option for the banishment of human social problems. So too, the destination of the convict was as much hidden from the 'onlookers' as is the prisoner behind prison walls. Yet it would be an over-simplification to see present Australian society, or even its attitude to punishment, as a direct consequence of the penal colony history. In modern Australia, multicultural communities have not necessarily grown out of the penal colony experience; they may have diverse appreciations of punishment relevant to their own cultural memory. However, on arrival, new citizens become subject to a system of punishment that reflects the complexity of modern Australian society.

As the criminal law developed largely in an atmosphere of punishment in early Australia, so too the criminal sanction became a primary technique for state control. With a community of guards and prisoners, other influences of social control were a long time coming in convict New South Wales.

In the 1800s, penalty developed from a reason for being in Australia, to a consequence of police investigation, court hearing and the determination of the criminal sanction by local judges and magistrates. The impact of punishment came to depend more on the criminal sanction and its formal operation within a system of criminal justice. The expectations for penalty also changed in accordance with the courts of Australia sanctioning the individual, rather than the courts of Great Britain imposing terrible penalties on classes of exiles.

In the colonial period of Australia's development, penal reformer Jeremy Bentham declared of New South Wales that it was 'an outrage to Law, Justice, and Humanity'.[9] The 'outrage' didn't simply stop at the physical dimensions of punishment. The nature of colonial government and the discrimination resulting from its administration created institutions and processes that uniquely determined the status and community obligation of its citizens. On the way to becoming a free society, there were actions of law-makers, judges, police and the military that were neither just nor equitable, and the imposition of penalty[10] was prominent among these.

In respect of the historical development of Australia, the processes and institutions of punishment have been both a driving force behind the construction of our brand of criminal justice, and the background against which our traditions of government initially struggled for identity.[11] Individual and community rights, as well as the duties to protect these under the development of democratic government, were gradually (if sometimes selectively) confirmed through Parliaments and the courts[12] rather than through patronage and influence. With the emergence of an elected government's responsibility for policing, adjudication and punishment, rather than a reliance on the interests of military governors or influential landholders, there was an associated professionalisation of all aspects of criminal justice. The connection between the offender and victim was removed by an expanding bureaucracy of justice administration in which policing, prosecution and penalty became inextricably interwoven.

The development of a criminal justice administration in Australia was a critical factor in the transition from a penal colony.[13] The transition has led to both the new state and its justice agencies being largely concerned with the imposition and oversight of penalty. In a nation where its first generation relied on 'tickets of leave' to confirm emancipation and the road to prosperity, the consequences of crime and punishment took on unique dimensions.[14] For example, with the colony as the prison far away from the traditions of capital crimes and the class-motivated process of pardon, which was a feature of British justice,[15] offenders were able to return to all levels of community life in a way not possible in the mother country. With the development of Australian society through the Victorian era, the agencies of criminal justice grew more able to imitate their English counterparts and this potential for reintegration declined.

The abolition of capital (death) and corporal (physical beating) punishment by all Australian jurisdictions, left imprisonment as the final institution of punishment by which all other sentencing options are confirmed. The prison has dominated the landscape of penalty since the establishment of the penal colonies and their various systems of criminal justice.[16]

The place of punishment within Australian society now is determined through legal requirements and social convention. The wider social reality of punishment cannot be expressed singularly as directions from the judges and prison superintendents, statements by the offender, or the expectations of the victims.[17] The consequences of punishment go beyond the situations in which penalty is imposed.

Punishment viewed as a fact of social life extends responsibility for the administration of sanction and penalty beyond the state or the law alone. A focus on punishment as a community phenomenon helps to explain the essential variations in the form, institutions and processes of punishment. A wider social appreciation of punishment also invites an understanding of the relationship between penalty and other techniques of social control, and a measuring of the significance of penal forms against other methods of social regulation. For example, the principle of insurance, which underpins so many modern social relations, also has an impact on the intervention of criminal sanctions, and even the selection of penalty.[18]

Many other modes of regulation and control contain elements that resemble punishment and its purposes, but operate in contexts of contract, or property, or licensing. As such they may not rely on the force of the criminal sanction. But, as recent developments in the areas of corporate regulation and commercial sanctioning demonstrate,[19] sanctions within the criminal justice system and its penalties may incorporate and overlap traditional civil regulatory processes in order to heighten their impact on modern corporate situations of criminal liability.

The wider social consequences of punishment should also be considered when imposing particular penalties. This is the issue at the heart of recent debates over whether fines should be set relative to an offender's ability to pay. As Hogg argues of the fine, 'it might be regarded not only as a retreat from prison discipline, but also a penalty which positively seeks to minimise disruption whilst still punishing'.[20] Practically speaking, sentencers not only settle on the fine as a penalty because it is appropriate to the offence, but because it is quick and cost-effective, and presents minimal social disruption to the offender and the community. These are the type of 'social' considerations that influence the imposition of penalty.

## Sanction and penalty

As punishment is not simply the province of one agency in the system, so too those involved in overseeing the actual terms of a sentence are not the sole decision-makers on criminal sanctions. For instance, the legislature in New South Wales, through the provisions of the *Sentencing Act* 1989,[21] has fettered both executive and judicial discretion when it comes to setting down and administering sentences, while recognising that the legislature, executive and judiciary still have roles to play. It would be incorrect to suggest that the moves towards 'truth in sentencing', as it was referred to in New South Wales political parlance, were motivated by concerns about the operation of judicial discretion alone.[22] Recognising the other important influences over sanction and penalty, the legislation also was directed against executive intervention in the sentence initially served.[23]

The intentions for influencing the sanction process may vary, and even conflict, depending on the agency of government from which they emanate. For example, one of the reasons behind the expansion of executive involvement in actual sentence length might be to counteract sentencing practice that did not recognise its consequences for prison populations and overcrowding.[24]

The relationship between prison conditions and the existence of imprisonment as the ultimate penalty has increasingly important ramifications for the administration and management of criminal sanctions and the range of sentencing options that flow on from these.[25] If, for example, it was the expressed policy of the legislature that the punishment component of imprisonment must be nothing beyond the deprivation of individual liberty, then the factors responsible for poor prison conditions would be appropriate issues of government concern and intervention. Prison overcrowding, with its direct bearing on gaol conditions and institutional security would be, against different expectations for the prison, a serious concern for justice administrators. The relevance of prison conditions for measures of penalty is also not lost on the international community. For example, the United Nations *Standard Minimum Rules for the Treatment of Prisoners*, when dealing with prison accommodation, hold that:

> All accommodation provided for the use of prisoners, and in particular all sleeping accommodation shall meet all requirements of health, due regard being paid to climatic conditions, and in particular the cubic content of air, minimum floor space, lighting, heating and ventilation (Rule 10).[26]

Any discussion of the relationship between criminal sanctions and penalty can potentially distort the significance of punishment for criminal justice unless one appreciates that most crime within the community goes unpunished. All too often, examinations of the social significance of punishment ignore the balancing issues of tolerance and pardon.

## Tolerance and pardon

As the criminal justice system is unable to investigate all forms of criminal behaviour, and efficiently process every offender, a large proportion of crimes will go unpunished. This 'tolerance' of crime is significant, not only for any measure of the actual social impact of punishment, but also because it influences the realistic expectations for penalty. As Phillip Bean suggests, punishment:

> is *for* something and directed *at* someone … Punishment is one of the ways in which we can show that rules exist and are broken. It is not the only way nor is it necessarily the most reliable way … It will show which category of person is exempt from punishment and which is punished less severely.[27]

Therefore, tolerance needs to be considered in any analysis of the process of penalty. Whether it be due to the partial manner in which criminal sanctions are created and interpreted, limitations in the system for exposing crime, the selective nature of law enforcement, or the discriminate application of penalty, punishment is as much a discretionary event as any other element of criminal justice.

Tolerance, demonstrated through the exercise of discretion at various stages within the criminal justice process, influences the imposition of sanction and penalty, and puts into context the occasions when punishment is a consequence of crime. Notions of justice and injustice are as readily confirmed through a reluctance to punish as they have been through the relentless application of penalty. Tolerance also reflects the forms of penalty a society will accept, and the limitations on punishment its sense of humanity demands.[28]

In certain situations, the severity of potential punishments have had a vital influence over tolerance and pardons. Juries reluctant to bring in guilty verdicts for capital crimes have been known to acquit in the face of the facts so as to protect an accused from this awful consequence. And, in periods of history when capital punishment was the penalty for a wide range of offences, the judiciary more readily entertained, indeed came to expect, pleas for pardon.

Thus we see that formal instances of tolerance such as pardon are an important counterbalance to punishment and penalty, not only in their potential to act as a pressure valve on the process of justice, but by the way they identify sources of discretionary power. The choice to punish or refrain from punishment, even after sanctions are warranted, is as powerful a discretion as that which rests with police, judges and legislators to select or impose a particular penalty.

# Principles of punishment

Much that is said and written about philosophies of punishment is based on idealised, one-dimensional views of punishment as an essential response by the state to the individual who 'rationally chooses' to violate the law. Classical notions of criminal responsibility such as that which common law jurisprudence incorporates, require a punishment response that is entirely explicable in terms of its purposes. Punishment becomes both the means to a necessary end, and the end itself.

A consideration of principles of punishment is important not only for testing the fairness, justice and efficacy of particular penalties, but also because punishment merges principle and practice through a process of contest and compromise. For example, theories about the causes of crime will influence the selection, adoption, and endorsement of principles of punishment. Using these principles, judges structure penalties around institutions and practices in order to influence these causes.

In their simplest form, the principles of punishment include:

- *retribution or 'just deserts':* where the offender's behaviour merits a response that demonstrates community outrage proportional to the nature of the offence
- *rehabilitation or reform:* where the penalty is designed to influence the offender away from future criminal behaviour in favour of law-abiding behaviour
- *individual or general deterrence:* where the penalty will discourage the offender, and others of like disposition in the community, from engaging in further criminal behaviour
- *community protection:* where the penalty is designed to protect the community from the offender, and criminal behaviour
- *reintegration:* more usually considered as a motivation for non retributive determinations, restoration and reintegration have assumed importance particularly in international criminal justice, where punishment is an ancillary concern in respect of restitution.

These each suggest that punishment should serve some social purpose beyond vengeance or terror. They imply that there is some acceptable logic behind sanction and penalty. Each is designed to bring about a desired consequence.

Since the recent official disenchantment with rehabilitation as the overriding principle for punishment,[29] general justifying aims of punishment have focused on retribution.[30] As noted by the Australian Law Reform Commission, 'In general it would appear that the Australian community subscribes to the view that retribution and deterrence should be the major goals of sentencing policy'.[31] Justice Nagle, in his report as Royal Commissioner into New South Wales prisons, observed that the aims of corrections should be 'imprisonment as punishment, retribution, deterrence and the protection of society'.[32] Rehabilitation and just and humane treatment were relegated in his analysis to positions of secondary importance. Other concerns for deterrence, reform, or protection relate to the manner in which they can limit or direct the unqualified pursuit of retribution as the single social aim of punishment.

It would be incorrect to imply, however, that there is some overarching and consistent opinion throughout heterogeneous Australian society on issues of punishment. Perhaps fuelled by the prevailing ignorance and misinformation that surrounds issues of punishment, there is what Sallman and Willis refer to as 'an ebb and flow of penal thinking'.[33] As principles come and go from political or public favour, guiding philosophies for punishment rarely possess the singularity of logic or principle which might guarantee long-term administrative commitment. This ambivalence is evidenced daily in appeal courts throughout the country where principles are endorsed in what appears to be an interchangeable fashion. Consistency is not a characteristic of discussions about sentencing principle.

While retribution is presently popular as a justification for penalty, it does not stand on its own, nor does it deny other intentions for punishment. The return to retribution was promoted by the desire to emphasise and measure 'what works' in the field of penalty. In these terms, it was argued, no other penological objective could be sufficiently supported on empirical or moral grounds. Interestingly, since the resurgence of retribution in Australia, little if any research has been done to 'measure' whether retribution is 'working', and the infiltration into penal policy of a variety of other rationales continues unabated. Justice Nicholson (as he then was) of the Victorian Supreme Court indicated the ambivalence of the judiciary to a singular search for philosophies of punishment:

> For my part I see the doctrine of just deserts as useful in setting an upper limit on sentencing so that no person receives a sentence which is disproportionate to the offence involved … I would like at this point to express what is an unfashionable view as to the rehabilitative aim of sentencing … It seems to me that the process of labelling the aims of punishment has tended to produce a knee-jerk reaction as one or other theory has vogue from time to time.[34]

Justice Nicholson went on to warn that obvious paradoxes will arise if one seeks to assert the predominance of a single principle for punishment. Equally illogical is the practice of many sentencers to assert the influence of principles that might be mutually exclusive (for example, rehabilitation and deterrence, just deserts and community protection).

The formulation of policy for punishment by those responsible for its execution relies on identifying its general aims or aspirations. These may incorporate several principles, but they all feature some hope for the reinstitution of justice for the victim and the community, and the control of crime. Recent aspirations have included principles of just deserts, denunciation, less eligibility, and compromise.[35]

## Just deserts

To view punishment as possible or appropriate only where it is deserved places punishment squarely within a moral dimension. Desert is a more basic *raison d'être* than legal liability, or even guilt. Where activated only as a result of the conscious or moral choice of the offender, punishment becomes a denial of wrong, through an assertion of right. The state can restore the victim and the community to a previous balance if the offender is punished in proportion to what his culpability deserves. The fundamental difficulty with desert-based justifications for punishment rests in its reliance on proportionality.[36]

A 'just deserts' model for punishment is motivated by desires for deterrence, protection, and retribution. Yet, unlike deterrence or protection, retributive punishment is an end in itself rather than a means to an end. It relies on the link between punishment and responsibility, both in moral and logical terms. The justifications for retribution are argued as self-evident, and necessary as a consequence of rule violation. Retribution is not concerned with matters outside the direct connection between crime and punishment.

For a 'just deserts' model of punishment also to lay claim to a deterrent potential, it must present punishment as being grounded, efficacious and profitable. The consequence of deterrent punishment must either be to induce actual or prospective offenders to commit less harmful offences, to refrain from crime, to cause as little harm as possible, or to exact as little social cost as possible.

Where the immediate object of deterrence and protection is control, for retribution it is simply the reaffirmation of just desert. Logic and morality are linked only through considerations of when to punish, and when one ought to punish.

## Denunciation

Denunciation or condemnation is one of the often unstated intentions for punishment. More usually, discussions of retribution in a sentencing situation degenerate into (or never leave the bounds of) debates about tariff and penalty.[37] Limiting debate in this manner ignores vital issues that should precede penalty such as: Who is punishment awarded for? Whose interests should it reaffirm? What influence will it have on the punished and the unpunished?

Punishment as social reprobation has its origins in community condemnation. Primitive forms of punishment focused on the ridicule and degradation of the body of the offender in order to demonstrate condemnation by the immediate community. More recently, the shaming of reputation has been advocated to punish the corporate personality.[38] For such ridicule or shaming to have effect it should go beyond mere social disapproval and yet not be seen as vengeance. It needs to surpass a simple recognition of wrongdoing, registering some effective measure of public condemnation. In order to establish an inevitable link between punishment and condemnation, one must assume that the sanctioning agency has some legitimate mandate to impose penalty.

## Less eligibility

Writing in the early nineteenth century, Jeremy Bentham enunciated the principle of 'less eligibility' for prison management.[39] He argued that if conditions in prison were not harder than those experienced by the lowest of the honest labouring classes, then the deterrent effect of the penalty would be lost. This principle had significant influence over the development of penal strategies in Australia, and we would suggest that it informs the thinking of many justice officials and politicians today.[40] Much of its persuasive power derives from its concordance with 'common sense' perceptions of the relationship between crime, sanction and penalty.

One of the central philosophies underlying the *Report of the Royal Commission into New South Wales Prisons* is revealed in the widely quoted aphorism, 'A person is sent to prison as punishment, not for punishment'.[41] The conditions under which prisoners are constrained are crucial to any assessment of prison as a punishment.[42] For the less eligibility principle to accord with justice, the comparative standards of prison life should not fall below a level where the conditions themselves become the punishment to bear.

Expectations for the experience of imprisonment vary enormously, and have been used to justify the expansion and diversification of the penal sanction. In their most modest representation, however, 'it is hoped that by treating all prisoners humanely in a manner befitting their human dignity … prisoners will at least leave prison no worse than when they entered it'.[43]

It is commonly asserted by those who are opposed to prison reform that gaols resemble motels or holiday camps, and prison life is too easy. According to this view, prisons should be made as harsh and unpleasant as possible so that their occupants will suffer stiffer punishments, and potential criminals in the community will be deterred. Whether there is substance in such a causal assertion, or in the assumptions on which it is based, has been actively challenged.[44] The reality for most prison systems is that, as institutional conditions decline, the pressures on occupancy increase, and vice versa. Thus the relationship is not so much one between the nature of the penalty and the culpability of the prisoner, but rather conditions of punishment are determined by issues well beyond the offence or the offender.

## Compromise

The announcement and application of sometimes mutually exclusive principles of punishment requires compromise. When considering the dimensions of punishment, H. L. A. Hart noted that 'what is needed is the realisation that different principles (each of which in a sense may be called a justification) are relevant at different points in any morally acceptable account of punishment'.[45]

He indicated the importance of distinguishing between justifying punishment as a social institution and justifying individual sentences. Strategies of justification that concentrate on the wrong done should be separated from those that stress the utility of punishing crime in a social sense or to satisfy some community imperative. In this respect, 'blameworthiness' might have both absolute and conditional influences on the consequent imposition of sentence: absolute when put against concerns of social harm, conditional when considered from the particular perspective of each offender. However, with the divergence in expressed purposes for sentencing, the expected effect on both the offender and the community has become somewhat problematic.

It would certainly be a devastating criticism of sentencing throughout Australia, were it demonstrable that both in principle and practice it lacked any coherent intellectual account of aims and intended functioning. However, recent reviews of sentencing in Victoria, New South Wales, South Australia, and at a federal level have striven with varying degrees of success to identify such accounts.

Whether the predominant application of principle to punishment is one of 'honesty', rationality, justice, or certainty, sentencing-reform initiatives throughout Australia have directed the sentencing process towards identifiable principle rather than expedience or compromise (see chapter 9). Yet, despite law reform in the area of sentencing and punishment, the wide public perception in most States that the actions of certain police, prosecutors and judges in a number of celebrated cases have led to unjust and inconsistent punishment, has not been overcome.[46]

Debate about which principle of punishment should be paramount reflects on society's perception of citizenship, as well as the structure and institutions within which it exists. If, for example, rehabilitation and reintegration are put forward then the value of the individual is placed above desires for revenge. On the other hand, the protection of the rest of the community reflects greater concern for deterrence-based punishment. The predominance of each punishment principle has shifted throughout the historical development of criminal justice in Australia. With each shift has evolved new connections between punishment, the processes of criminal justice, and public opinion.[47]

The language of restitution and reform of 1970s Australia was replaced, along with a swing to more conservative politics, by a more pragmatic tone of control and containment. The trust invested in 'treatment models' for penalty, including the professionals who were responsible for them, was gradually replaced with suspicion and a fundamental mistrust of rehabilitation professionals and their programs. The policy compromises that plagued the period of rehabilitation in recent Australian penal history[48] were an inevitable result of confused principles for punishment. Now, with pragmatism and rationalism the order of the day, condemnation the objective, and neutralisation the best result, the official horizons for punishment in Australia are narrow indeed. What remains of a commitment to the restoration or reintegration of the offender seems now directed well before the imposition of penalty or as with restorative justice being the alternative to it. Diversion and community intervention are now considered as legitimate directions for criminal justice. John Braithwaite's call for the reintegration of offenders back into a caring and responsible community[49] is yet to have real influence beyond the early stages of the justice process. This is because of the domination in the trial of a retributive ethic demanding punishment as its determination.

# Penalty

An examination of punishment set out in legislation leads to the consideration of forms and ranges of penalty, as well as sentencing options. This is not surprising when we realise that the actual practice of sentencing is the calculation of tariff against options and ranges set down in statutes (see chapter 8).

However, this is not the level at which a consideration of the nature of punishment should be confined. To do so would be to imagine that punishment is a creature of legal drafting; this is obviously not the case. Also, to concentrate entirely on particular penalties as the focus for punishment is to ignore the wider social dimensions of punishment within criminal justice. It is often convenient for politicians and administrators to consciously ignore these wider dimensions. But in emphasising such singular purposes as crime control above all other consequences of punishment, legislators and criminal justice professionals are not in a position sensitively and subjectively to manage punishment as a potent force for change.

Any over-concentration on penalty also fails to appreciate the broad connections between punishment and discipline. The social and moral components of punishment have an important impact on the institutions of socialisation that tend to discipline citizens and communities (such as religion, education, health care, and industrial labour). To simply view the effects of punishment in criminal justice terms is to be unprepared for many of the socially negative consequences that affect those who are punished, beyond the expected impact of the penalty imposed.

When considering the nature of punishment it is useful to view the type of 'outrage' that generates calls for punishment, and the nature of the response that is anticipated. In this way, the shared emotional reaction of communities and governments finds release and satisfaction through punishment. And, as such, using punishment as penalty assumes great significance for the aggrieved. The media 'drama' that surrounds 'horror crimes' and the calls for tougher penalties might be viewed as the present-day incarnation of the mob that enjoyed public hangings in earlier times. What David Garland refers to as the 'punitive passions'[50] is as much a part of the nature of punishment as are its often criticised representations as various penalty options.

## Distribution of penalty

'A penal system must be conceived of as a mechanism intended to administer illegalities differentially, not to eliminate them all.'[51] Such selectivity is a feature of all stages (both formal and informal) of criminal justice administration. Discretionary decision-making influences the distribution of penalties by judges, as much as it does selective law enforcement by police.

The distribution of penalty is not simply an issue of numbers, or the location of either offenders or institutions of justice. It relates to questions of identifying liability and sanction. Who may be punished is linked to the issue of what value punishment is to promote. Initially, penalty is a consequence restricted to the relationship between the offender and the offence. This relationship, even as set down in the criminal law and procedure, cannot be explained as a natural result of any particular general justifying aim of punishment. Penalties and their distribution depend on actual offence situations, and the criminal justice conditions that influence any particular criminal sanction.

Differences in penalties, and their distribution, should have some connection with offenders and offences. The more serious the offence, the higher should be the penalty. Using this general principle, one might expect that fairly consistent trends in penalty and distribution would prevail across jurisdictions. Similarly, with serious offences one would assume that police would have less discretion in selective enforcement. In addition, with the offences resulting in serious penalty, extraneous characteristics of the offender (such as race) would have less bearing on the exercise of discretion. This is not so, it appears, particularly for the last assumption.

Take, for example, recent developments in imprisonment rates in Australia. For the years 1993–2003 there has been an increase in prisoner populations throughout Australia of 50%.[52] This increase has exceeded the 15% growth in the Australian adult population, resulting in the adult imprisonment rate increasing from 119 to 153 per 100 000 adult population over that period. The female prisoner population has increased over the decade by 110% in comparison with a 45% increase for male prisoners. The rate of increase varied significantly for the States and Territories, ranging from a marginal increase in New South Wales and South Australia[53] to over 80% in Tasmania and the Australian Capital Territory. All other States and Territories experienced increases.[54]

Indigenous prisoners have accounted for an increasing proportion of the total prisoner population (15.2% for the period), particularly with females. The total figure masks more significant shifts on a jurisdictional basis. The over-representation of Aboriginal and Torres Strait Islander people (as a proportion of the total prison population) varies significantly from jurisdiction to jurisdiction. For instance, in 2003 the proportion was 4.6% in Victoria, 35.1% in Western Australia and 78.3% in the Northern Territory.[55] The national average of over-representation was a proportion of 20.5% for that year. Indigenous persons were 16 times more likely than non-Indigenous persons to be in prison and this proportion is on the increase. The highest Indigenous imprisonment rate was recorded in Western Australia, where it was 14% higher than in the preceding year.[56]

# Institutions of punishment

The variety in values and purposes expected of and expressed through criminal justice institutions is well represented in the institutions of punishment themselves, such as the prison. When called upon to give effect to diverse values and purposes for punishment, it is not surprising that criminal justice institutions and programs are occasionally riddled with internal conflict and tension. For example, the prison is supposed to deter while at the same time a term of imprisonment is intended to be reformative, and Community Service Orders (CSOs) are supposed to benefit the victim's community, while recognising that the individual commitments and responsibilities of particular offenders must not be too disrupted.

The institutions of punishment are fundamentally influenced by penal ritual. What we mean by this is that the symbols, routines, and requirements of punishment are either shared by, or linked across, the range of penalty. For instance, the institutions of punishment might represent degrees of custody and incapacitation, or be backed up by these. They all operate within atmospheres of compulsion. They each involve interference with the rights of citizenship. They all intend to inflict pain. Even what might be considered as a lenient penalty, such as a suspended prison sentence, imposes a burden of uncertainty and apprehension that prevails for the duration of that sentence. And the ritual element of most sentences, such as their 'public' nature, becomes important when measuring their impact on both the offender and the community.

The 'pain' component of punishment has been justified through its exercise by the state on behalf of the aggrieved victim and the community. In Australia, until the recent experiments in Queensland, New South Wales, Victoria, and South Australia, the principal institution of punishment, the prison, has always been a state-owned and operated concern. This has not been the case with custodial institutions for juveniles, female offenders, Aboriginal people, and offenders with mental and emotional disabilities. Where religion, welfare, or paternalism has gained a foothold in the criminal justice process, the state has been willing to share the domain of punishment with private interests.[57]

The issue of who controls the institutions of punishment is significant against the trend towards a state monopoly over the earlier stages of the criminal justice process.[58] The state police have largely assumed the informant's role and, in most jurisdictions, control crime investigation and the initial phases of prosecution. The courts are state institutions and the criminal trial is funded from state coffers and governed by state rules. If the system is to be bound by common interests, it is only logical that it should remain predominantly in state hands.

## Development of penalty options

Most discussions of punishment tend to revolve around practical issues only: the sentencing process and its calculation, and the administration of formal penalties. For an understanding of penalty beyond the justifications for imprisonment, one needs to recognise the variety of sanction practices and agencies of punishment in Australia. To get the complete picture requires an examination of the formal legal penalties administered by the courts and the correctional authorities in State and federal jurisdictions as well as those informal modes of sanctioning administered both within and beyond the state-based criminal justice process. The formal sentencing options are set out in legislation and often appear in terms of a range of available sentences. Informal modes of sanctioning can involve situations such as the use of police detention in a punitive fashion, or the way that conditions of imprisonment are selected and applied to an individual.

## Increased use of the penal sanction

An examination of prison statistics published by the Australian Bureau of Statistics[59] reveals that imprisonment rates are on the increase, and have been so for decades, radically outstripping the increase in the Australian population. For instance, in December 1989 the daily average of people held in prison in New South Wales was 4864. In June 2004 the figure was 8764.[60] The imprisonment rate (per 100 000 general population) was 83.4 for December 1989. By 2003 the figure had risen to 169.4. Apart from the Northern Territory, which has an exceptionally high rate of imprisonment, New South Wales, Queensland and Western Australia have the highest rates in the Commonwealth. This has remained constant over the past decade. The rate for Victoria is less than half the rate of these States. As Angela Gorta observes,[61] the average increase in prison numbers for recent years has been higher than the general growth in prison population for New South Wales shown this century.

Ivan Potas lays partial blame for the increase in New South Wales on the sentencing legislation:

> While there may be other factors such as increasing crime and police clearance rates, which may be contributing to the burgeoning prison population, there is little doubt that the *Sentencing Act* (NSW), as translated into practice has meant that 'real time' served for those sentenced to imprisonment has increased.[62]

The consequences of this increase have been differentially felt across the New South Wales community, and certain groups have been affected more than others. In addition, the disparity in time served between prisoners sentenced before and after the legislation was enacted has generated claims of injustice.[63]

When dealing with average prison population measures, one should be aware that they conceal sometimes huge weekly fluctuations. Even so, the relatively recent increases overall in the prison populations of most States are considerable. Again, taking New South Wales for example, from 1988 to mid-1991:

> the daily average prison population ... increased by the equivalent of nine times the design capacity of Parklea prison, in Sydney (210 inmates). To have kept up with this increase at this time we would have had to have been building at the rate of more than one Parklea every 4.7 months.[64]

Instead, the then New South Wales Government settled for overcrowding prisons such as Parklea, in the western suburbs of Sydney, to in excess of 70% above optimum capacity.

The increase in prison population since changes in sentencing legislation is not explained simply by the fact that more people are going to gaol. In New South Wales, for instance, over the decade 1990–2000, penalties imposed by both the higher and the lower courts became more severe. In significant offence areas the percentage of offenders given custodial sentences increased.[65] While prison sentences may not have increased in all offences, the actual period during which prisoners are held in custody is on the rise. For certain offences affected by intense adverse public opinion (such as sexual assault, and drug trafficking), actual sentence length may have doubled in recent years. Mandatory sentencing, and sentencing guidelines, have also contributed to an atmosphere among trial judges that if imprisonment is a sentence available it should be used more often, for more offenders and for longer. And once a sentenced offender is serving his or her time, there is far less opportunity for sentence reduction through remissions for good behaviour, or early parole.

It seems clear that determinate sentencing leads to an increase in prison populations.[66] Despite the contrary assurances[67] that if such increases occur they are merely continuations of pre-existing trends, there is ample evidence in the States of Australia, and in the United States,[68] that when there is a move towards determinate sentencing, accompanied by a rejection of executive intervention for early release, pressures towards prison overcrowding will be exacerbated. The abolition of remissions, of release on licence schemes, and the requirement to serve longer minimum terms of imprisonment prior to consideration for parole, ensures determinacy and consequent population growth in prisons.

Because sentencers prefer to see prison overcrowding as a problem of the prison administrator, there is no guarantee that the provision of non-custodial options, or lower maximum penalties, may bring about a reduction in the use of the prison. In fact, it has been argued that policy initiatives towards decarceration, which do not require a reinterpretation of judicial discretion, are not successful in reducing the use of imprisonment:[69] 'Australian imprisonment rate data from 1961 to 1985, the period during which community based corrections measures were introduced, show some slight decline in some States and substantial fluctuation in others'.[70]

There is evidence that alternatives to imprisonment are frequently used for offenders who would not have been incarcerated in the first place. To this extent, these sentencing options are not true alternatives. Furthermore, if the conditions of these options are breached by the offender, they create another pathway to the prison.

## Controlling the growth of prison populations

Effective strategies to counter the use of the penal sanction beyond already strained custodial resources must countenance some reordering of judicial discretion. Judges consistently pronounce that it is not for them to consider prison crowding when setting an 'appropriate' sentence. However, this removal from the reality of punishment is more difficult to justify when overcrowding vitally affects the physical conditions of a penalty.

How can the inflow of prisoners, and their length of stay, be influenced without judicial discretion? Assessing possibilities would include an examination of pre-sentence negotiations, the sentencing process itself, and post-sentence interventions. Independent variables such as court delay may also play a part.[71] In New South Wales, prior to the *Sentencing Act* (1979), the preferred method for regulating prison population involved executive interference at designated or discretionary occasions following sentence.[72] This is not to say that the pre-sentence stage was not influential. As John Willis[73] has identified, whether it be as a result of prosecutorial discretion, sentence discount for pleading guilty, or the less significant practices of charge or plea bargaining, negotiations before the trial have the potential to constrain judicial discretion (see chapter 2).

Beyond legislative regulation, judicial discretion is controlled in some jurisdictions through sentencing guidelines. However, this device has not been seriously explored in Australia as a uniform means of rationalising the use of imprisonment at the sentencing stage. Some State jurisdictions in the United States have taken a numerical approach to the construction of guidelines where, given constant conviction rates, the aggregate prison population would not exceed the capacity of the State's prisons.[74] To achieve this result, sentencing must be informed by a prison population target either slightly higher or lower than capacity populations, to allow for policy fluctuations. Such a target is the responsibility of the executive and is determined through the consideration of wider administrative issues, which may not have influence over sentencing discretion. Having said this, both sentencers and administrators are mindful of matters that directly influence the nature of imprisonment as a general penalty, and an individual sentence. Therefore, the interaction between sentencing guidelines and the population ceiling provides a mechanism for population regulation that does not rely on prison administrators alone in the face of judges continuing to sentence beyond reasonable capacity. Sentencers are made responsible for the consequences of their decisions through the relative neutrality of externally imposed guidelines.

We are in favour of rational and open methods for ensuring that the sentencing process is mindful of its consequences. Sentencers must take some responsibility for the nature of the penalty imposed, in the same way that they attempt to tailor a sentence to the requirements of an individual's criminal liability. Broad public policy concerns are not foreign to the principles of sentencing that courts apply, and therefore the real conditions under which a sentence will be served should also not be ignored.[75]

## Sentencing options: the construction of a penalty

In looking at sentencing options, it is advisable to avoid discussions of alternatives. Alternative sentences usually imply a disposition that avoids or replaces imprisonment. However, if the term 'alternative' is used to refer to any other sentence outside imprisonment, as is commonly the case, it may be misleading. Indeed, many so-called alternative sentencing options may result in an offender ending up in prison through a sequence of default situations that might otherwise not have eventuated if the initial sentence had not been inextricably bound to the prison.

Where the fear of imprisonment lies behind any alternative, it is not in fact an alternative in any absolute sense. Employing alternative sentencing structures that rely on imprisonment as the consequence of default actually may endorse rather than diminish the ultimate status of imprisonment in the sentencing hierarchy.[76] By not breaking the connection between the prison and other sentencing options, the appearance that the prison is the essential institution of last resort for modern systems of punishment is not challenged:

> When alternatives to imprisonment are discussed, it is suggested that they must be seen as viable; often a euphemistic phrase which implies they must bolster up rather than threaten the continued existence of the prison as the central criminal sanction.[77]

The present range of sentencing options available to Australian courts, limited as they are, demonstrates the general misconception that they operate as alternatives to a prison sentence:

> Some schemes are alternatives to prison only to the extent that they form the latter part of a sentence which involves imprisonment, such as parole, or the use of a halfway house as a pre-release measure. Others, of course, such as probation, community service orders, and pre-trial or pre-sentence diversion are alternatives to the extent that imprisonment will usually only be a threatened possibility in the event of failing to comply with the conditions of community release. Others still, such as education and work release, involve imprisonment during certain hours with release for specific purposes. Community correctional programmes may be institutional, and to the extent that any programme involves institutionalisation, it must be asked whether it is imprisonment by any other name.[78]

It is preferable to discuss sentencing options as choices on a graduated and progressional scale of penalties. If this is done, then the prison will assume its appropriate significance. The principal sentencing options that exist throughout the criminal jurisdictions of Australia include the following:

> *Imprisonment* covers periods of incarceration in a variety of State-run institutions (and in New South Wales, South Australia, Victoria[79] and Queensland, some that are privately operated). These vary in their levels of secure detention (for example, maximum, medium, minimum), in their occupational focus (for example, prison farms), the age limits of their occupants (for example, juvenile detention centres), and their integration into the community (for example, day release centres). The characteristic that makes each of these environments imprisonment is the deprivation of individual liberty.

- *Periodic detention* is a special form of imprisonment that usually requires incarceration for a limited and regular period (for example, weekend detention). The class of offence and status of offender towards which this penalty is directed is limited (for example, drink driving, and offenders who are employed and possess stable family ties).

- *Home detention* is incapacitation in the home or within a designated distance from the home. This form of 'house arrest' has been monitored in some settings with electronic devices attached to the body of the offender.

- *Suspended sentence of imprisonment* is where a sentence of imprisonment is suspended or deferred for a designated period, during which certain conditions may be stipulated. At the expiration of that period, and the satisfaction of these conditions, the imprisonment will lapse. Should the conditions be violated or further crimes committed, imprisonment may be imposed for all or part of the original sentence. This penalty is sometimes imposed in conjunction with a fine.

- *Therapeutic orders* are where usually specialist courts (such as the Drug Court in New South Wales) will suspend a sentence of imprisonment or refrain from ordering a prison term depending on the successful completion of an agreed therapeutic program.[80]

- *Fines* are monetary confiscation. In Australia, fines are generally not related in amount to an offender's ability to pay. Therefore, in the case of some offenders, the fine has been criticised as a *de facto* prison sentence where imprisonment is the penalty for fine default. Fines are by far the most common form of penalty. The confiscation of assets or the seizure of the proceeds of crime should not be viewed as a fine penalty.

  Fines may be issued automatically in situations such as the infringement notice system, which applies to minor traffic violations. In other situations, a fine will be determined by a sentencer in the normal course of the sanction. Other occasions where fines arise are those where a licensing body regulates stipulated conditions or practice.

  Until recently in the English courts, magistrates had the power to award fines in terms of units. The valuation of these units, and therefore the monetary value of the penalty, could be varied depending, among other things, on the accused's ability to repay the fine.

  The unit fine system in Australian jurisdictions is primarily designed to allow the executive to vary the total amount of the fine without legislative amendment.

- *Compensation or restitution.* In conjunction with other penalties, the court may require that compensation for loss or injury be paid by the offender (or in some situations, the state) to the victim. Failure to comply with a compensation order may result in an additional penalty.

- *Confiscation of assets.* Though more in the form of a civil remedy than a criminal penalty, the criminal courts in State and federal jurisdictions can confiscate the assets of an accused person if they are deemed to be the profits of crime.

Usually the onus of proof rests on the accused to establish that these assets were obtained legitimately in order to avoid confiscation.

• *Probation orders* are where the court requires the offender to enter into a bond of supervision with the probation service, during which the offender must comply with certain nominated conditions and be of good behaviour. Recently, probation supervision case-loads throughout Australia have become so burdensome that the enforcement of the conditions of the order is in doubt. Breach of the probation bond usually has imprisonment as a consequence.

• *Community service orders (CSOs)* are a court order that an offender carry out unpaid work or service in a designated form and for a nominated community organisation (or, in some situations, for the victim), over a period of hours. The work may be supervised. Breach of a CSO usually results in imprisonment. Along with the suspended sentence and probation, CSOs are the next most popularly used penalty after the fine.

• *Attendance centre orders* are imposed on juveniles, usually requiring that the offender attend an activity centre either before or after school, or at other 'criminogenic' times, for a nominated number of hours per week.

• *Good behaviour bonds* are similar to suspended sentences or probation orders but without the automatic consequence of imprisonment on breach, or the requirement that the bond be supervised. The conditions of the bond are generally that the offender keep the peace, and be of good behaviour.

• *Admonition and discharge* is where the sentencer, without the imposition of further penalty, publicly remonstrates with the offender for the crime. Usually this is limited to offences of a minor nature, or first offenders. In certain State jurisdictions, such as New South Wales, the sentencer can award a nominal penalty of detention until the rising of the court, where the accused person remains in custody until the court adjourns.

• *Finding of fact but no conviction* is a provision in most jurisdictions for the sentencer to find the facts of a charge proven, but to refrain from proceeding to conviction. This also is reserved for first offenders.

As this list shows, there is not a wide variety or particular creativity in the options available to sentencers. In addition, many of the more popular sentencing options have been in existence since the establishment of European settlement in Australia.

Figures that measure the application of each option reveal how limited a sentencer's choice is in practice. The fine is by far the most popular penalty in Australia, followed by bonds and probation orders. In New South Wales, for example, fines and bonds comprise more than 80% of the total sentences handed down by the local criminal courts (fines are twice as frequent as bonds and both are a hundred times more likely than imprisonment).[81] Detention in custody only accounts for 6% of the local court determinations (compared with 60% in the higher courts). If we were to examine these rates relative to the race, age, or socio-economic background of the offender, the results may skew disproportionately towards (or away from) prison sentences, depending on the characteristics of the offender. For example, Aboriginal prisoners in New South Wales are tending to be imprisoned for individual offences that are on average not that different to those of non-Aboriginal offenders. However, though they are receiving significantly shorter average minimum terms, they are being imprisoned at rates almost 11 times that of non-Aboriginal offenders.[82]

In recent years, the inadequacy of sentencing options has been recognised in the move towards diversion at the pre-trial, the pre-sentence or the pre-release stage. Diversion involves screening out:

- offenders inappropriate to the criminal justice process (for example, the mentally ill)
- low-risk offenders, or those not posing a threat to public safety (for example, the non-violent)
- vulnerable offenders (for example, juveniles)
- special offenders (for example, child sexual assault perpetrators)
- offenders involved in treatment programs (for example, drug abusers)
- offenders with a potential to reform (for example, drink drivers).

Diversion is usually seen as a move away from state intervention, institutions, and experts, or a move away from individual responsibility. The purposes for diversion can range from financial considerations to the recognition of the brutalising influence of institutional regimes. For example, in the case of offenders charged with drug-related crimes, commitment to a therapeutic community may be more advantageous to the offender and to the community at large than a prison sentence where a therapeutic regime is not available. The creation of the Drug Court in New South Wales, and its therapeutic orders, are recognition of this. Even so, imprisonment is the fall back for a candidate's failure to comply with those orders.

Particularly in the processing of juvenile offenders, the police and the courts have been active in initiating routes of diversion from the inevitable consequences of conviction. Police cautions, family conferencing,[83] and community aid panels[84] are three of the major diversionary creations of recent years, each possessing varying degrees of formality, and different distances from the courts and the police. With juveniles, it has been recognised that a wider, more flexible, and potentially individualised range of sentencing options is a way of advancing greater possibilities with justice for the offender. For other marginalised or vulnerable groups when it comes to criminalisation (for example, Aboriginal people, drug abusers, the mentally ill), diversification has not been developed to any large degree.

The problem with the relationship between diversion and punishment (or more accurately the adverse consequences of retributivism) is that in our criminal justice system it is almost entirely confined to the pre-trial stages. There is an argument now, particularly in international criminal justice, that judges should be given the opportunity to divert offenders into restorative processes if and when they see this as more appropriate, particularly in the interests of victims.[85] In certain civil law countries, such as Germany, prosecutors have a limited power in this regard although they too almost always make this determination at the pre-trial stage.

## Punishment without trial

If one defines punishment as a process by which power and authority are communicated and confirmed through the imposition of a penalty (rather than as a specific institution, object, or event), then punishment can be identified in other situations within the criminal justice system, beyond the sanction and sentence. This might seem logical if we accept that punishment also has a place outside the court room and in the wider community. The police, as the initial exponents of power in the justice system,[86] obviously possess the potential to impose punishment without trial. This potential is heightened by the importance of individual and organisational discretion for policing.

Some of the more common representations of police-based punishment include:

- *Summary justice*—the application of physical force by police in order to resolve disputes, enforce authority, claim respect, confirm notions of justice, and avoid the oversight and interference of courts and lawyers
- *Juvenile cautions*—occurring at both formal and informal levels, as a response to an admission of guilt, and used as a threat to proceed to more serious levels of punishment should the offending behaviour not be stopped, and contrition not occur
- *Infringement notices and citations*—the awarding of penalty in an almost automatic administrative process if the facts of the accusation are not formally denied.

For a wider discussion of the punishment potentials existing at other stages of the justice process, examine chapter 2 on investigation and chapter 4 on pre-trial procedure.

# Correctional models of punishment

Both conservatives and reformers have embraced a variety of correctional models for punishment, and justifications for the imposition of penalty. While adopting the guise of a humanitarian response to the offender, a correctional emphasis for sentencing can be supported by any of the following justifications:
- if successful, it is the ultimate form of individual deterrence
- if successful, it provides another guarantee of individual protection and public safety
- if successful, it reaffirms the potential for social and medical science to overcome individual pathology

- if successful, it works against social disorganisation from the individual's perspective
- if successful, it may invest the offender with the social skills necessary for reintegration
- even if it is not successful, it has the consequence of widening the state's involvement in, and potential for, social control.

In most Australian jurisdictions, the correctional component in criminal justice has grown out of more punitive sanctions and intentions. For example, rehabilitation appeared in the 1960s as a major concern of prison management, as well as providing the impetus for the development of semi-institutional 'alternatives'. Periodic detention and work release, while manifesting some commitment to custodial forms of punishment, were also represented as correctional and rehabilitative through time spent in the community.

Correctional expectations for punishment and penalty are fraught with contradictions. The problems inherent in expecting some form of rehabilitation through, or as a consequence of, penalties designed as much for non-corrective purposes pervades much of criminal justice policy in Australia. Further, a commitment to corrections through punishment assumes:

- the pathology of the offender
- the origins of criminality as social disorganisation, maladjustment or abnormal behaviour
- the belief that 'correction' is both possible and appropriate within the institutions and processes of criminal justice.

While a treatment model for corrections may require any or all of these, no such assumptions are necessary to underpin the operations of punishment. Therefore, it is wrong to use 'corrections' as synonymous with punishment or penalty.

Not only are there obstacles in the way of developing correctional dispositions for sentencing policy but, it might be argued, a correctional commitment in penal policy is doomed to failure.[87] One merely has to reflect on the irreconcilable dilemmas that arise when attempting to transfer a treatment regime into a prison, and the connection between punishment and corrections seems tenuous indeed.

# Community corrections

Three major grounds are usually offered in support of community correctional programmes against traditional imprisonment. Firstly, it is argued that prisons have little if any rehabilitative effect and they may contribute to future criminality.[88] It is therefore suggested that community correctional programmes will be more successful in rehabilitating offenders so they do not take them out of the ordinary social environment, suspending constructive relationships and contacts. Secondly, it is argued that community correctional programmes are less costly than prisons. Finally, proponents of community correctional programmes argue that they are more humane than prisons because they avoid the harmful effects of institutionalisation.[89]

With the disillusionment surrounding the rehabilitative influence of the prison, the treatment model has been transposed to what is fashionably termed a 'community setting'. Economic considerations have stimulated this trend.[90] While not denying the relevance of punishment to the proper operation of criminal justice, it has often been viewed as relegated to the perimeter of the prison. Community 'corrections' can therefore promote a reform and reintegration agenda within the framework of sanction and penalty.[91]

It is interesting to note that at the same time that the principal rationale for punishment has contracted to simple notions of control and containment, the culmination of the criminal justice process has fanned out into a wide range of institutional control settings that aim for correction rather than punishment. Whether the community direction for penalty under the guise of reintegration and correction can be deemed legitimate in a classical criminal justice model tied to the determination of guilt and responsibility, is more than a nice problem of jurisprudence.

Community corrections in most States have evolved not so much as a complete alternative to imprisonment, but rather as an appendage to it. The rhetoric of community corrections often conceals and legitimates an extension of the penal sanction into more marginal areas of deviance as well as into the community and the lives of the offender in a broader sense. For example, a person sentenced to a community service order may end up in prison for defaulting on its conditions. In times when these orders were not available to the courts as a sentencing option, the offender may have received a good behaviour bond or a probation order, where the consequences of breach were not so automatic.

With the talk of community corrections, certain problems are disguised. First, what is meant by the term? Does it simply imply correctional programs located within the community, or does it extend further to implicate the community in the correctional process?

> Perhaps the most positive thing that can be said about this generic term is that many offenders can be held in community service, attendance centres, probation hostels, on probation and parole etc., as successfully within the community as in the prison and at a cheaper cost. But is this really community corrections?
>
> I assume by the notion of community corrections that to some extent it is intended that the community will become involved in and responsible for correcting its own. However, this involvement of the community in the exercise of punishment is directly contrary to developments in criminal justice over the past few centuries. The state has taken on the general role as the legitimate exerciser of punishment. The community has willingly divested itself of its role in this regard. The community chooses to remove itself as far as possible from the actuality of punish-

ment. In so doing it can objectify the process of criminal justice and thereby avoid being implicated in its consequences.

How then can the community be convinced that it should take back some meaningful responsibility in the punishment process, even if it is in a correctional sense?[92]

An additional problem with community corrections, and alternative sentences at large, is that all too often they are expected to fulfil the same conflicting and inconsistent philosophies, as is the prison. In addition, the measures of their success, such as reoffending rates, are as flawed and unreasonable as those expected of the prison. If we are to justify a sentence in terms of its rehabilitative value (and we also recognise that rehabilitation depends on wider community reintegration beyond the terms and conditions of the sentence), then it would be unreasonable to blame the sentence alone for any eventual lapse back into other crimes by the offender concerned.

# Punishment and welfare

With the development of 'welfare states' during the last century, welfare has become related to penalty in shaping the environment for punishment. Where welfare fails, penalty is often the consequence. Both in terms of a just deserts philosophy for punishment, and a state paternalism motivation for welfare, the confluence of punishment and welfare seems logical.

During the 1960s and 1970s in Australia, welfare was a prominent factor in penal change. It became an indicia of the social organisation within which forms of penalty existed. Social work policy and language infiltrated courts and corrections. There was a direct co-option of welfare within penalty in forms such as probation and parole. Welfare could be guaranteed through the authority of the state and imposed on a subjugated audience.

The institutions of penalty came to support and extend those of the social realm, especially under the umbrella of community corrections. The benefits of social welfare became conditional on conduct reinforced by penalty. Penalty took over the failures of welfare, processing these through institutions that either intended to reintegrate or remove. The image of state-controlled penalty was softened by its connections with the positive and reformist character of welfare.

The traditional hierarchy of punishment severity has become skewed towards the diverse and differentiated dispositions within a welfare framework. The language of punishment has changed to where guilt is no longer the determinant for state intervention. Individual responsibility is no longer the reason for punishment. In addition, welfare professionals have become part of the necessary landscape of punishment. Some penalties are still imposed conditional on the involvement of welfare professionals.

The problem with this confusion between punishment and professional intervention is that responsibility for the welfare of the offender, and the community at large, in situations of punishment is diffused. In addition, the danger exists that systems of penalty and institutions of punishment may develop for the convenience of the professionals involved. Stan Cohen[93] warns that with the expansion of professional influence particularly on the peripheries of punishment, there is the likelihood of a 'net-widening' effect. This arises where individuals who might otherwise not have become involved in the criminal justice system are sucked into its system of punishment (for example, failure to fulfil the conditions of a community service order, resulting in imprisonment).

# Penal reform

Some have argued that the prison, as the dominant institution in the history of punishment in Australia, has failed to achieve any of the expectations held for it, be they rehabilitation, deterrence or community protection.[94] Whether it be simply based on questions of economics, or on the more extensive realisation that the philosophy on which it rests is internally inconsistent, the prison, up until the late 1980s at least, lost favour with most State governments in Australia. Even so, 'despite the massive weight of evidence built up against imprisonment over the past 200 years, the prison walls stand firm, unmoved and seemingly uninfluenced by such documentation of failure'.[95]

The histories of the States of the Commonwealth are characterised by cycles of penal reform. The circumstances and motivations for this reform went far beyond the specifics of crime and punishment. As Cohen comments more generally: 'the motives and programmes of reform within the penal system were more complicated than a simple revulsion with cruelty, impatience with administrative incompetence, or sudden scientific discovery'.[96] The push for deinstitutionalised sentencing options may rely as much on considerations of economy and expedience, as on desires for reform. So too penal reform movements have gained momentum from tensions in the operation of justice, and the politics of penalty at large.[97]

In his critique of criminal justice reform in general, David Brown points to the fact that too often in Australia, the satisfaction with short-term goals has diverted reformers from broader and more long-lasting aims, and in a sense has corrupted the logic and consistency of their goals.[98] Therefore, the results have been, particularly in the field of punishment, that we are left with a strange mishmash of programs and directions in policy, the objectives for which often clash and are sometimes doomed to failure through having to satisfy conflicting philosophies.

# Conclusion

There can be no conclusion to any discussion on punishment and penalty as it relates to the criminal sanction. As the sentence at the end of a trial is merely the commencement of another phase of criminal justice, so too an overview chapter such as this merely promotes rather than resolves a range of interesting questions for the student of criminal justice to ponder. In addition, the process of reform and development as directed towards punishment and penalty is at worst cyclical, and at best at an early stage of development in terms of sentencing options, and the institutions of criminal justice punishment.

It is encouraging that writings on punishment and penalty have recently demonstrated levels of sophistication and insight that generally stand in stark contrast to social policy initiatives in sentencing and punishment. As sentencing options are often criticised for their lack of imagination, and penalties are accused of a 'blunt edge' approach to the realisation of sentencing principle, the importance of recent critiques on sentencing and punishment outstrip the developments in the topic with which they are concerned. David Garland, John Pratt, Nils Christie and Thomas Mathiesen from an international standpoint, and David Brown, Mark Findlay, David Neal, Janet Chan, Mark Finnane and Don Weatherburn in Australia have turned the reader's attention to the critical social reality of sentencing and punishment. We are fortunate then in that, while the practice of sentencing and punishment may lag behind community expectations, historical and socio-political writings about punishment and penalty provide us with a fresh understanding of the limitations of this phase of criminal justice.

## Notes

1   While punishment is viewed as an essential concluding phase in many criminal justice models, penalty is the consequence of the determination and imposition components of the criminal sanction.

2   D. Garland's notion of penalty, in *Punishment and Welfare*, Gower, Aldershot, 1985, p. x.

3   In this respect penalties, while distinct legal phenomena, cannot be separated neither from considerations of penal institutions and systems nor from punishment as a culturally specific, generic concept.

4   K. Bottomley and C. Coleman, 'Law and Order: Crime Problem, Moral Panic, or Penal Crisis?' in P. Norton (ed.), *Law and Order in British Politics*, Gower, Aldershot, 1984, p. 55, cite the following well-established penological facts when criticising the perceived simple causal relationship between crime, criminal justice, and punishment:

    •   Increased resources to the police are most unlikely to reduce the crime rate, and may quite feasibly produce an increase in what is recorded.

    •   Harsher sentences upon convicted offenders will have no effect in deterring them (or other potential offenders) from future crime, nor indeed will more rehabilitative sentences achieve greater success in changing their behaviour patterns.

- Detaining offenders in prison for long periods on the grounds of incapacitation is a policy that will have only marginal effects on the crime rate, even if the prison population were to be increased three- or four-fold.

5    See K. Carrington et al., *Travesty! Miscarriages of Justice*, Pluto Press, Sydney, 1991.

6    For instance, parental responsibility legislation in NSW makes parents to a certain extent liable for the actions of their delinquent children (*Children (Protection and Parental Responsibility) Act* 1997). For a discussion of other such legislative intervention throughout Australia see R. Hogg and D. Brown, *Rethinking Law and Order*, Pluto Press, Sydney, 1998.

7    D. Garland, *Punishment and Modern Society*, Clarendon Press, Oxford, 1990, p. 16.

8    See M. Finnane, *Punishment in Australian Society*, Oxford University Press, Melbourne, 1997.

9    J. Bentham, *Bentham Papers*, British Library, Add MS 33543, p. 1802.

10   In discussing penalty at this stage we are not so much interested to examine in detail the process of fixing or setting penalty. These matters are examined in chapter 8. The actual impact of penalty (and the real form that it takes) cannot, however, be entirely separated from the sentencing process and its participants.

11   See D. Neal, *The Rule of Law in a Penal Colony: Law and Power in Early NSW*, Cambridge University Press, Melbourne, 1992.

12   For the original Aboriginal inhabitants the guarantees offered by the rule of law have yet to fully articulate their 'citizenship', and in many situations remain illusory. See, C. Cunneen, 'Judicial Racism', unpublished conference paper, 1992.

13   See G. Woods, *A History of Criminal Law in NSW: The Colonial Period 1788–1900*, Institute of Criminology, Sydney, 2002.

14   See H. V. Evatt, *Rum Rebellion*, Angus and Robertson, Sydney, 1938.

15   See D. Hay et al., *Albion's Fatal Tree*, Allen Lane, London, 1975.

16   See R. Hughes, *The Fatal Shore: A History of the Transportation of Convicts to Australia*, Pan, London, 1988.

17   Although recent victims' legislation in most States has given greater emphasis to victims' interests, particularly in prolonging terms of imprisonment.

18   Insurance affects policing in situations where selective non-enforcement might be justified because the 'loss' to the victim is indemnified. As for penalty, the impact on the victim of punishing the offender may be far less significant than the impact of loss indemnification through insurance.

19   See B. Fisse, 'Towards a Framework for the Design of Sanctions Against Corporations: Differential Implementation of the Criminal Law, Elements of Sanction Design, and the Punitive Length of the Chancellor's Foot', unpublished conference paper, 1992.

20   R. Hogg, 'Criminal Justice and Social Control: Contemporary Developments in Australia', *Journal of Studies in Justice*, 2, 1988, pp. 89–122.

21   For a full discussion of the many complex issues surrounding this reform of the law on sentencing, see *Current Issues in Criminal Justice*, 3, 1992.

22   See J. Chan, *Doing Less Time*, Sydney Institute of Criminology, Sydney, 1992.

23   Now the *Crimes (Sentencing Procedure) Act* 1999 (NSW). In most jurisdictions in Australia the relevant Minister, or committees and boards with delegated authority, can reduce the actual sentence of imprisonment to be served by a prisoner. This influence may be directed through parole orders, or executive release determinations.

24    With respect to the calculation of penalty, the factors initially that should influence the mind of a judge are now seen to extend to executive decision-making as it affects the actual nature of any sentence. In New South Wales at least:

- All the considerations that are relevant to the sentencing process, including antecedents, criminality, punishment and deterrence, are relevant both at the stage when a sentencing judge is considering whether it is appropriate that the convicted person be eligible for parole at a future time and at the subsequent stage when the parole authority is considering whether the prisoner should actually be released on parole at or after that time (*Shrestha*, High Court of Australia, 20 June 1991).

- Hence all the factors considered, when sanctions are imposed and penalties set, may have ongoing influence over the course of a prisoner's incarceration even beyond the expiration of the minimum term of the sentence.

25    See R. Mitchell, *South Australian Criminal Law and Penal Methods Reform: Report No. 1: Sentencing and Corrections*, Adelaide, 1973.

26    Such aspirations are honoured more in the breach in almost every penal administration. Of the British prison system a press editor tellingly has observed that 'if the prison system came under the same health regulations governing shops, factories and offices, the Prison Director would have been taken to court years ago on one of the longest indictments our criminal justice system has witnessed' (*Guardian*, 31 October 1978).

27    P. Bean, *Punishment*, Martin Robertson, Oxford, 1981, pp. 191–3.

28    'Our sense of what constitutes a conscionable, tolerable, civilised form of punishment is very much determined by cultural patterns, as is our sense of what is intolerable or, as we say, inhumane' (Garland, 1990, p. 196).

29    For a discussion of this both in custodial and community settings, see M. Findlay, 'The "Demise of Corrections" Fifteen Years On: Any Hope for Progressive Punishment', *Current Issues in Criminal Justice*, 2, 2004, pp. 57–70.

30    A. Von Hirsch and A. Ashworth, 'Not Not Just Deserts: A Response to Braithwaite and Pettit', *Oxford Journal of Legal Studies*, 12, pp. 83–98.

31    This position was endorsed by the NSW Court of Criminal Appeal in *Hayes* [1984] NSWLR 740 in affirming a sentence that approached the statutory maximum, on a conviction for breaking and entering: 'The invasion of people's homes and the plundering of their property is a social evil from which the community looks for protection to law enforcement agencies and the criminal courts … the time has come for a hardening in the policy of the criminal courts when sentencing for this offence. There has developed a tendency not to give inadequate weight to the legislative policy which fixes fourteen years as a statutory maximum for this offence. That tendency needs "correction".' The court was of the view that if the legislature sets maximum penalties, and public concern about the prevalence of the offence is high, then a sentence approaching the maxima is appropriate to reflect the intention of the legislature and public attitude.

32    J. Nagle, *Report of the Royal Commission into NSW Prisons*, Sydney, 1978, p. 380.

33    P. Sallmann and J. Willis, *Criminal Justice in Australia*, Melbourne, 1984.

34    I. Potas (ed.), *Sentencing*, Australian Institute of Criminology, Canberra, 1987, pp. 79–80.

35    An example of this is Schedule 1 *Crimes (Sentencing Procedure) Act* 2002 (NSW), replaced by the new s. 3A of the Act.

36    T. Mathiesen, *Prison on Trial: A Critical Assessment*, Sage, London, 1990.

37    For an explanation of tariff, see C. Emmins, *A Practical Approach to Sentencing*, Blackstone Press, London, 1986, pp. 47–50.

38    See J. Braithwaite, *Crime, Shame and Reintegration*, Cambridge University Press, Cambridge, 1989.

39    In J. Bentham, 'Principles of Penal Law', *Works*, J. Bowring (ed.), Edinburgh, 1962.

40    M. Yabsley, *Prisons: Firm but Fair*, Department of Corrective Services, Sydney, 1990.

41    Nagle, p. 40.

42    See Mathiesen, 1990; M. Fitzgerald and J. Simm, *British Prisons*, Basil Blackwell, London, 1982.

43    Nagle, p. 41.

44    M. Findlay, *The State of the Prison: A Critique of Reform*, Mitchellsearch, Bathurst, 1982; F. Zimring and G. Hawkins, *Deterrence: The Legal Threat in Crime Control*, University of Chicago Press, Chicago, 1973.

45    H. L. A. Hart, *Punishment and Responsibility: Essays in the Philosophy of Law*, Oxford University Press, Oxford, 1968.

46    See Carrington et al.

47    D. Garland, 1990, p. 210, says: 'in discussing terms such as "less eligibility", "equality", "uniformity", "proportionality", or the "principles of surveillance and discipline" and linking them to wider networks of power and economy, theorists … were in fact explicating penal culture and grounding it in the structure of social life. However, in linking penal culture to social structure in this way, these accounts tend to leave out large stretches of the mediating cultural framework within which penalty exists …'

48    R. Tomasic and I. Dobinson, *The Failure of Imprisonment: An Australian Perspective*, George Allen and Unwin, Sydney, 1979.

49    Braithwaite, 1989.

50    In Garland 1990, pp. 61–5.

51    M. Foucault, *Discipline and Punishment*, Penguin, Harmondsworth, 1977, p. 74.

52    From Australian Bureau of Statistics, *Prisoners in Australia*, No. 4517.0, Canberra, 2004. In 2004 there was the first decrease in the rate (1%) for over a decade.

53    Which had both experienced significant increases over the previous decade.

54    Lowest to highest: SA, NSW, Vic, WA, NT, Qld, Tas, ACT.

55    Interestingly for the Northern Territory, at 1626 Indigenous prisoners per 100 000 adult Indigenous population, its rate remains below the national average.

56    This partly reverses the 20% decrease the year before.

57    See R. Harding, 'Prison Privatisation in Australia, A Glimpse of the Future', *Current Issues in Criminal Justice*, 1992, pp. 9–27.

58    Harding, 1992.

59    Australian Bureau of Statistics, *Corrective Services, Australia*, No. 4512.0, Canberra, June 2004.

60    This figure includes sentenced and unsentenced persons at a proportion of about two-sevenths.

61    In 'Impact of the Sentencing Act 1989 on the NSW Prison Population', *Current Issues in Criminal Justice*, 3, 1991, pp. 308–17.

62    I. Potas, 1992, p. 317.

63    See Amnesty International, Sydney, 1993.

64    Gorta, 1991.

65    See NSW Bureau of Crime Statistics and Research, 'Trends in Sentencing in the NSW Criminal Courts: 1900–2000', 2002.

66    See J. Chan, 'The Limits of Sentencing Reform' in G. Zdenkowski et al. (eds), *Criminal Injustice System*, Vol. 2, Pluto Press, Sydney, 1987; Chan, 1992; Gorta, 1991.

67    A. Blumstein et al. (eds), *Research on Sentencing: The Search for Reform*, National Academy Press, Washington, 1983, p. 32.

68    See D. Greenberg and D. Humphries, 'The Cooperation of Fixing Sentencing Reform', *Crime and Delinquency*, 26, 1980.

69    See also A. Scull, *Decarceration: Community Treatment and the Deviant: A Radical View*, Polity Press, Oxford, 1984.

70    Chan, 1987, p. 219.

71    See NSW Bureau of Crime Statistics and Research, 'Court Delay and Prison Overcrowding', *Crime and Justice Bulletin*, 1989.

72    Chan, 1992.

73    J. Willis, 'Pre-trial Decision-making' in G. Zdenkowski et al. (eds), 1987.

74    A. Von Hirsch, 'Guidance by Numbers or Words? Numerical versus Narrative Guidelines for Sentencing' in M. Wasik and K. Pease (eds), *Sentencing Reform: Guidance or Guidelines*, Manchester University Press, Manchester, 1987.

75    N. Christie, *Crime Control as Industry*, Routledge, London, 1993.

76    See T. Mathiesen, *The Politics of Abolition*, Martin Robertson, London, 1974, pp. 84–5.

77    Findlay, 1982, p. 153.

78    Tomasic and Dobinson, 1979, p. 61.

79    In recent years there has been a concerted effort by the Victorian government to take back responsibility for custodial institutions from private contractors.

80    See chapter 8 where the sentencing of drug offenders is discussed.

81    NSW Bureau of Crime Statistics and Research, New South Wales Criminal Court Statistics 2002, Sydney, 2003.

82    S. Eyland, 'Truth in Sentencing: A Koori Perspective', unpublished research paper, 1993.

83    See J. Hudson, A. Morris, G. Maxwell and B. Galaway, *Family Group Conferences: Perspectives on Policy and Practice*, Federation Press, Sydney, 1996.

84    See J. Bargen, 'Going to Court CAP in Hand', *Current Issues in Criminal Justice*, 4, 1992, pp. 118–40.

85    For a presentation of this argument see M. Findlay and R. Henham, *Transforming International Criminal Justice*, Willan, Devon (forthcoming).

86    See K. Baldwin and A. K. Bottomley, *Criminal Justice: Selected Readings*, Part II, Martin Robertson, Oxford, 1978.

87    See M. Findlay, 'The Demise of Corrections' in B. Cullen et al. (eds), *Corrective Services in NSW*, Law Book Co., Sydney, 1988, pp. 326–32.

88    P. Bean, *Rehabilitation and Deviance*, Routledge and Keagan Paul, London, 1976.

89    Tomasic and Dobinson, 1979, p. 61.

90    See Chan, 1992.

91    See M. Findlay, 'The "Demise of Corrections" Fifteen Years On: Any Hope for Progressive Punishment', *Current Issues in Criminal Justice*, 2004, pp. 57–70.

92    M. Findlay, 'The Possibility of a Criminal Justice Corrections Model', *Proceedings of the Institute of Criminology*, 60, 1984, pp. 15–16. Also M. Findlay, 'The "Demise of Corrections" Fifteen Years On: Any Hope for Progressive Punishment', *Current Issues in Criminal Justice*, 2, 2004, pp. 57–70.

93    S. Cohen, *Visions of Social Control*, Polity Press, Oxford, 1985.

94    See Tomasic and Dobinson, 1979.

95    Fitzgerald and Simm, 1979, p. 139.

96    Cohen, 1985, pp. 18–19.

97    See M. Findlay, 'The Politics of Prison Reform' in M. Findlay et al. (eds), *Issues in Criminal Justice Administration*, George Allen & Unwin, Sydney, 1983, pp. 139–56.

98    D. Brown, 'Criminal Justice Reform: A Critique' in D. Chappell and P. Wilson (eds), *The Australian Criminal Justice System*, Butterworths, Sydney, 1977, pp. 471–91.

# 8

# Sentencing

## Introduction

At the hub of the criminal justice system is punishment. All the processes leading to the conviction of the offender such as arrest, interrogation, the laying of charges and the trial hearing would be superfluous if there was no penalty[1] awaiting the offender. Similarly, the correctional institutions and personnel who deal with the offender after conviction are primarily concerned with implementing the penalty imposed by the court.

What then is punishment? The classic statement of the elements of punishment was made by Professor H. L. A. Hart:

> I shall define the central case of 'punishment' in terms of five elements:
> (i)   It must involve pain or other consequences normally considered unpleasant.
> (ii)  It must be for an offence against legal rules.
> (iii) It must be of an actual or supposed offender for his offence.
> (iv)  It must be intentionally administered by human beings other than the offender.
> (v)   It must be imposed and administered by an authority constituted by a legal system against which the offence is committed.[2]

The first element specifies the infliction of something that is assumed to be unwelcome to the recipient. The second and third elements confine its infliction to people who have been determined by the criminal justice process to have breached the criminal law. The fourth element dictates that only those unpleasantries that are administered by people other than the offender constitute punishment. The final element places the responsibility for imposing and administering punishment on an authority of the state. This authority is the courts, and their exercise of imposing and administering punishment is called sentencing.

The courts, when sentencing, discharge a significant function of the criminal justice system. They represent the whole public and invoke the 'common conscience' when pronouncing sentence. Hence, sentencing constitutes a highly symbolic and public declaration of how society regards the offence, the offender, and society's formal reaction to them. It may be that the pronouncement of sentence has in reality a minor impact on crime control and that other agencies of the criminal justice system are better equipped in combating crime.[3] However, the highly public, symbolic and representative nature of sentencing ensures its prominence and importance. This is evidenced by the number of law reform bodies in several Australian jurisdictions that have looked into the sentencing process. The public aspect of the sentencing process cannot be overly emphasised. Indeed, it is entrenched in international instruments to which Australia and a host of other nations are signatories. For instance, Article 14(1) of the *International Covenant on Civil and Political Rights* declares that:

> In the determination of any criminal charge against him ... everyone shall be entitled to a fair and public hearing by a competent, independent and impartial tribunal established by law ... [A]ny judgment rendered in a criminal case ... shall be made public.[4]

The reference to the 'determination of any criminal charge' covers both the adjudicating on guilt or innocence and determining the appropriate sentence.

Given this public nature of sentencing, it should be vital for the sentencing process to be both just and seen to be just. The above Article stipulates as much by requiring the sentencing hearing to be fair. A sentencing hearing, practice or pronouncement that is perceived by the public to be unjust would bring disrepute to the system. Offenders, victims and the general community would feel aggrieved by the failure of the courts to discharge justice, and would regard the sentencing judges as not being in tune with community demands and expectations. The Australian Law Reform Commission (ALRC) has identified two main criteria by which the community will determine whether justice is being achieved:

> First, the criminal justice system must involve imposing on offenders punishment of sufficient severity that it is possible to say that a breach of the law, when detected, is attended by significant consequences. Secondly, the system must be consistent in the apprehension, identification and punishment of offenders. The need for consistency pervades all elements of the system.[5]

The first criterion concerns the quantum of punishment and requires the sentence imposed to be of a severity appropriate to the offence. The penalty must be *appropriate*, meaning that it must strike a balance between the two extremes of being excessively harsh and being too lenient. The second criterion of consistency requires similar offenders who commit similar offences in like circumstances to be punished in a similar way. The High Court had this to say about the matter:

Just as consistency in punishment—a reflection of the notion of equal justice—is a fundamental element in any rational and fair system of criminal justice, so inconsistency in punishment, because it is regarded as a badge of unfairness and unequal treatment under the law, is calculated to lead to an erosion of public confidence in the integrity of the administration of justice.[6]

A sentence pronouncement is preceded by a public hearing during which facts that are relevant to the sentencing decision are presented and debated. These facts would certainly include the evidence already received at the trial hearing but could also comprise facts that are presented for the first time. To achieve justice, it is again crucial for the receipt and consideration of facts relevant to sentencing to be performed in a procedurally fair manner.[7] This includes such measures as the onus of proving facts, the opportunity to challenge disputed facts, and cooperation from both prosecuting and defence counsel to assist the court to reach a just sentence.

This chapter will examine the sentencing process in the light of justice. 'Sentencing aims' will deal with the traditional aims of sentencing and point to the possible injustices served by the eclectic treatment of these justifications by our courts. In 'The sentencing hearing', certain aspects of the sentencing hearing will be discussed with an eye to procedural fairness. 'Facts relevant to sentencing' considers several factors that are regarded as relevant to decision-making in sentencing. The discussion will consider whether these factors should justly be taken into account by the sentencer and, if so, in what way. In 'Sentence disparity', the problems of inappropriate and inconsistent sentences will be canvassed, and the major reasons for these problems aired. 'Remedies for achieving just sentences' will present various possible solutions to these problems. The chapter will continue with a brief discourse about the relationship between sentencing policy and public opinion concerning crime, offenders and punishment. Finally, two recent developments will be evaluated with considerations of justice in mind—the use of mandatory sentences, and the sentencing of drug-dependent offenders.

# Sentencing aims

Having an understanding of what punishment is does not tell us *why* society regards it as necessary to punish the offender. There are several justifications for punishment or, as some might describe them, aims of sentencing.

## Retribution

One justification or aim is *retribution*. Punishment is inflicted on people who break the law so as to cancel out, at least symbolically, the ill-gotten benefits they have received from their breach. Failure to punish these offenders would make it unfair on law-abiding people who have denied themselves those illicit benefits. Retribution is sometimes justified on the basis of the need to prevent the community from taking the law into its own hands. Nowadays, retribution takes the form of 'just deserts', which provides that offenders should receive only such a penalty as they deserve. The principle of proportionality is invoked here, which insists that only grave wrongs merit severe penalties and minor ones deserve lenient penalties.

## Deterrence

Another aim of sentencing is *deterrence*. Two effects are said to occur whenever a sentence is passed. The first effect, which is called 'general deterrence', is the inhibition of people other than the offender being sentenced from committing similar crimes. By punishing this particular offender, potential ones are warned of the unpleasant consequences that await them should they commit crimes, be apprehended, and convicted. The second effect, called 'special deterrence', inhibits the offender being sentenced from committing further crimes. Built into the justification of deterrence are limiting principles, which are different from the principle of proportionality in retribution. One is that punishment is justified provided the unpleasantness it causes to the offender is not greater than the unpleasantness that would result if the offender or others, undeterred, offended in the future. Another restriction requires that, in the event of several possible penalties having a deterrent effect, only that penalty is justified that causes the least unpleasantness.

## Rehabilitation

A further aim of sentencing is *rehabilitation*. Under this rubric, criminal behaviour is seen as a product of antecedent causes that can be scientifically identified. This identification enables remedies to be developed, which can effect changes in the behaviour of offenders, transforming them into law-abiding people. The type of sentence handed down is accordingly regarded as a therapeutic measure tailored to the specific needs of each offender. Any measures are justifiable as long as they are needed to cure the criminal behaviour of the particular individual. It follows then that, unlike retribution and deterrence, there are no limiting principles governing rehabilitation.

It will be evident from even this cursory description of the aims of sentencing that they promote sentencing policies that are in conflict with one another. A sentencing policy based on retribution would be largely retrospective in its approach. It would concentrate on such matters as the seriousness of the offence, the culpability of the offender and the severity of penalties, while relegating issues of future offending to a secondary position. In contrast, both deterrence and rehabilitation take a prospective approach to the sentencing exercise, with the primary goal of future crime reduction. The clash between retribution on the one hand and deterrence and rehabilitation on the other occurs when the former rejects any harsher or lighter penalty, which the latter are attracted to because they have the best chances of reducing future offending. As for the conflict between deterrence and rehabilitation, these go their separate ways when it comes to the measures they would be prepared to support to achieve their shared goal. For instance, a form of treatment might be enthusiastically embraced under rehabilitation, but regarded as infringing one or the other of the limiting principles contained in the deterrence justification.

The preceding discussion makes it obvious that the conflict between sentencing aims can only be resolved by ranking them into some order of priority. The ranking could be done by the legislature or the courts. Regrettably, neither has done so. Instead, an eclectic approach has been taken, with the sentencer having to select from the whole range of sentencing aims the one (or more) that best serves the particular case. An example of legislative eclecticism is contained in section 16A of the Commonwealth *Crimes Act* 1914. The provision, while not indicating an overriding aim of sentence for Federal offenders, requires a court to take into account specific deterrence, the need to ensure adequate punishment and the prospect of rehabilitation.

As for judicial eclecticism, there is the following passage from the High Court in *Veen (No. 2) v The Queen*:

> The purposes of criminal punishment are various: protection of society, deterrence of the offender and of others who might be tempted to offend, retribution and reform. The purposes overlap and none of them can be considered in isolation from the others when determining what is an appropriate sentence in a particular case. They are guideposts to the appropriate sentence but sometimes they point in different directions.[8]

When presented with such an approach, choosing the aims of sentencing becomes a highly subjective exercise to be left to the individual judge. Thus, until such time as a ranking order of sentencing aims is drawn up, we should rightly speak of a particular judge's justification for sentencing and avoid such erroneous expressions as '*the* justification for sentence'.[9]

The lack of a coherent structure of sentencing aims has resulted in the so-called 'intuitive' technique to sentencing. The exercise of sentencing is hailed as an art and not a science and the sentencing decision is declared as 'the sentencing judge's instinctive synthesis of all the various aspects involved in the punitive process'.[10] The same objection to the lack of a hierarchy of sentencing aims may be directed at such a technique, namely, that it leads to disparate and, consequently, unjust sentences. This will be discussed more fully in the later parts of this chapter. For now, we turn to some aspects of the sentencing hearing that have a direct bearing on justice.

# The sentencing hearing

The sentencing hearing takes place immediately after the accused has pleaded guilty or, where a trial has occurred, been found guilty of the offence charged. In order to arrive at the appropriate penalty, the judge must consider the factors that are relevant to sentencing. For factors to be relevant, they must relate to such matters as the culpability of the offender, the nature and seriousness of the offence committed, and the impact of a sentence on the offender and third parties. Some of these factors will be discussed in the section dealing with facts relevant to sentencing. For now, we are concerned with whether the courts evaluate and use the factors in a procedurally fair manner.

In chapters 5 and 6, we noted the detailed rules of procedure and evidence, which regulate the trial hearing. These stand in contrast to the relative scarcity of rules governing the sentencing hearing. However, there has lately been a gradual development of rules in this area. As a starting point, it can be safely asserted that the sentencing judge is dutybound to form a view of all the facts relevant to sentencing and to determine the facts in dispute. This development is the result of the sentencing hearing being more clearly recognised as being as adversarial as the trial proper so as to call for minimum procedural safeguards in respect of all disputed matters. A cogent reason for expediting this development is contained in the following observation:

> There certainly are stark contrasts between the sentencing and trial processes, and for the great majority of defendants—that is, those who plead guilty—the sentencing hearing is the only part of the court process to which they are exposed.[11]

It is vital for the maintenance of respect for the criminal justice system for justice to be seen to be done by this vast group of offenders and other interested parties, such as victims and family members of offenders and victims. The rules governing the sentencing hearing may be presented under several sub-headings: the types of facts permitted to be considered; the opportunity to challenge disputed facts; the standard of proving facts; and the roles of prosecuting and defence counsel in ensuring procedural fairness and justice at the sentencing hearing.

## Types of facts considered

In accordance with the public nature of the sentencing hearing and the concomitant need to secure justice, the sentencing judge is required to come 'to a judgment strictly and exclusively upon the materials regularly placed before him in open court'.[12] This principle disallows the sentencing judge from discussing the sentence with the prosecution or the defendant out of earshot of the other party.

The sentencer is required to take into account all the circumstances surrounding the offence for which the offender was convicted. Justice requires the sentencer to ignore those circumstances that are ingredients of a more serious offence for which the offender has been acquitted or which he or she may not have been charged. In the words of the High Court:

> the general principle that the sentence imposed on an offender should take account of all the circumstances of the offence is subject to a more fundamental and important principle, that no one should be punished for an offence of which he has not been convicted.[13]

In cases where a trial has taken place, the judge has had the opportunity to hear evidence of the facts relating to the offence and the culpability of the offender. No difficulty arises in respect of summary trials as the sentencer is the same person who has decided on guilt. With regard to jury trials, the sentencer must accept the necessary and clear factual implications from a verdict of guilty. Where the implications are ambiguous, the judge is empowered to either question the jury or draw her or his own conclusions without further reference to the jury.

For cases where the offender has pleaded guilty, there has not been an opportunity to test the facts as related by the prosecution. The sentencer can regard the offender who pleads guilty as admitting all the essential facts necessary to constitute the offence charged. Should the statement made by the prosecution be unchallenged and is not inconsistent with the defendant's version of the facts, that statement may properly be acted upon. The court cannot compel an offender to give evidence, even at the sentencing stage.[14] However, it can require the prosecution to clarify and elaborate on aspects of the facts of a case. It is observed that a guilty plea does not admit any of the aggravating circumstances that might be alleged by the prosecution, nor does it negative any mitigating circumstances that might be relied on by the offender. These are matters that should be raised and perhaps challenged at the sentencing hearing.

Another source of facts considered at the sentencing stage appears in the form of pre-sentence reports. These reports are not compulsory but are prepared at the request of the courts. They provide information on the social background of the offender to assist in choosing the most appropriate sentence. The reports always comprise an interview with the offender, and often contain interviews with other people such as a psychologist, psychiatrist or some other expert witness.

While this information usually concerns the rehabilitative needs and prospects of the offender, the sentencer is not restrained from giving more weight to other facts that support the competing aims of retribution or deterrence. Furthermore, the sentencer is not bound to accept as true the information set out in the reports. In practice, unless challenged, the courts tend to admit the contents of the report even though they appear in hearsay form.

Another source of facts is the victim impact statement, which is supplied by the prosecution to the sentencing judge. The statement contains information about the crime victim that may not be contained in the other sources, in particular, the impact of the crime on the victim and the victim's views concerning the sentencing of the offender.

## Fact finding and standard of proof at the sentencing stage

The accuracy of any facts tendered by the prosecution may be challenged by the defence. Likewise, the prosecution is entitled to challenge any claims by the defence of mitigating circumstances, by calling evidence in rebuttal or, if the offender gives evidence, by cross-examination. With regard to pre-sentence reports, the judicial practice is to supply the defence with a copy so as to allow for the opportunity of challenging it. Where certain facts of the report are challenged, the court can decide either to disregard those facts or call evidence to resolve the question. The testing of disputed facts in the pre-sentence report is performed in the same way as other disputed matters at the sentencing hearing.

The sentencing judge may take into account facts that are adverse to the offender only if those facts have been proven by the prosecution beyond a reasonable doubt.[15] However, where the facts to be taken into account are in the offender's favour, those facts have to be proven by the offender on a balance of probabilities. Imposing such a burden of proof on the offender may run counter to the fundamental principle of the criminal law that it is for the prosecution to prove the case against the accused. While accepting that there are differences between the sentencing hearing and a trial, these differences do not relieve the courts of the need to maintain this 'golden thread' of the criminal law.[16]

Where material available to the court on some disputed fact cannot be resolved in a way that goes either to increasing or decreasing the sentence, the judge should not make a finding one way or the other. Overall, the sentencing judge does not undertake an inquisitorial role in the fact finding process of sentencing, relying on the prosecution and defence to initiate and provide material to support or deny a fact that may be relevant in the sentencing determination.

## The roles of prosecution and defence counsel

Obviously, the quality and accuracy of facts placed before the sentencer greatly contribute to the outcome of the sentencing hearing. Just decisions are possible only if they stem from a consideration of relevant, balanced and accurate information. The ensuing discussion builds on what has already been said regarding the prosecution and defence as providers of facts relevant to sentencing.

Traditionally, the prosecution has been regarded as not concerned with sentence; its role has largely been discharged after the summing-up of the prosecution's case at the trial stage. However, the Australian courts have increasingly engaged the prosecution in the task of sentencing. This has primarily been due to the availability in Australia of the prosecution's right to appeal against sentence.[17] With this right comes a need for fairness to the defendant: silence on the prosecution's part at the sentencing hearing denies the defendant the opportunity of challenge there and then. The right also carries with it a duty to prevent the sentencing hearing from committing errors requiring appellate correction.

The prosecution performs several functions at the sentencing hearing. It may be called upon to assist in clarifying or providing facts pertinent to the sentencing decision. These include providing full details of the circumstances surrounding the commission of the offence, the effect of the offence upon the victim, the offender's character such as relevant prior convictions, and the treatment facilities available. Given the vast range of sentencing laws, the courts are having to rely on the prosecution to bring to their attention those laws that affect the case. The prosecution may also be required by the court to express its views on the appropriateness of various types of sentences. This is to be contrasted with recommendations as to the quantum of sentence, which the courts regard as solely within their own domain.[18] In all its submissions on sentence, the prosecution is required to act in a fair and even-handed manner and should not, as an adversary, press for a heavy sentence.[19] However, the adversarial nature of the hearing does entitle the prosecution to challenge any defence claims that mitigating factors exist. The tenor of the prosecutor's role in sentencing is succinctly expressed in the following judicial comment:

> It is very well established that prosecuting counsel are ministers of justice who ought not to struggle for a conviction nor be betrayed by feelings of professional rivalry, and that it is their duty to assist the court in the attainment of the purpose of criminal proceedings, namely, to make certain that justice is done as between the subject and the state.[20]

A failure to allow the defendant or her or his counsel the opportunity to be heard on sentence amounts to a reviewable denial of natural justice.[21] In cases where the defendant is legally represented, the primary aim of counsel is to secure the least severe sentence available for the offence. Counsel does so by presenting the court with mitigating factors supported by evidence and by challenging disputable aggravating circumstances raised by the prosecution. Defence counsel may also, upon a request by the court, suggest an appropriate sentence. The court's acceptance of this suggestion will depend on counsel's familiarity with the range of sentencing options available for the offence. Where the sentencing options have prerequisites to their use, defence counsel should supply the court with evidence and other material to satisfy them.

It is clear from this brief description of the functions of defence counsel in the sentencing hearing that expertise and experience is necessary. Unfortunately, there is no obligation under Australian law requiring a defendant to be legally represented at trial or at the sentencing hearing.[22] The vast majority of defendants are inexperienced and incompetent to properly present their version of the circumstances of the offence and any mitigating factors. One outcome might be that relevant information that may be known only to the defendant is not told to the court. Furthermore, these defendants will not normally have the expertise to suggest an appropriate sentence from a range of possible sentencing options pertinent to their offence. With the courts favouring more involvement from the prosecutors at the sentencing hearing, it has become even more necessary for legal representation to become mandatory so as to achieve procedural fairness.

Overall, there has been a gradual move by the courts towards regarding the sentencing hearing as adversarial in nature. From this move, there has emerged a body of jurisprudence on the conduct of sentencing hearings that was not so evident twenty years ago.[23] Certainly, the sentencing hearing still lags far behind the trial proper insofar as measures ensuring procedural fairness are concerned. But a real start in the right direction has been made.

# Facts relevant to sentencing

At the sentencing hearing, the judge is presented with an array of facts (or factors) by the prosecution and defendant, all of which are claimed to be relevant to the sentencing decision. The judge has the formidable task of sifting through these facts and deciding what weight, if any, should be attached to each of them. In this exercise, the judge must bear in mind the significance of these facts to the justifications or aims of sentencing, namely, retribution, deterrence and rehabilitation. Additionally, account must be taken of sentencing laws and practice as well as the current attitudes of the public towards the offence, the offender and punishment.

The sentencer's task cannot be discharged without a measure of discretion. To serve the ends of justice, the sentence is required to be tailored to the particular facts of each case. This can only be achieved by providing the sentencer with a wide discretion to meet the infinite number of different combinations of facts, varying in form and potency, from case to case. However, this discretion is not an unfettered power since it must be exercised only according to relevant criteria. Furthermore, there should be a body of principles and policies guiding the exercise of the sentencing discretion. These principles and policies must be geared at achieving justice, should be clearly expressed, and should be capable of being put into practice.

The facts relevant to sentencing may be classified into several categories. First, there are those concerning the nature of the offence—such as the gravity of the offence, the mental state of the offender during the commission of the offence, the harm to the victim, and the prevalence of the crime in the community at the time. Next, there are facts concerning the offender—such as being a first offender or having prior convictions, her or his age, and whether the offender showed remorse. Then there are the effects of the offence and the sanction on the offender and on others such as her or his family members. Finally, consideration is given to whether there should be parity with the sentences of co-offenders. Clearly, some facts serve as matters of aggravation and others as mitigating circumstances. The judge is required to balance these facts and at the same time determine which sentencing aim or aims are best served in the particular case. Some of these facts will now be discussed.

## Facts concerning the nature of the offence

The following are some of the main facts relevant to sentencing that relate to the nature of the offence. Generally, these facts will be contained in the prosecution's case or its statement to the court. Where there are gaps in the information, the court may require the prosecution to supply the necessary facts.

## Gravity of the offence

The sentencing judge receives some indication of how the legislature regards an offence by examining the procedural and penalty provisions governing the offence. The legislative view may be gleaned from the classification of the offence as indictable or summary and from the maximum penalty prescribed. The maximum penalty provides the sentencer with a crude yardstick against which to measure all cases falling within the particular offence description. This penalty is reserved for the worst cases. Should legislature increase the maximum ceiling, the courts are required to reflect that increase throughout the whole range of cases involving the particular offence. However, justice dictates that the increase should not be applied retrospectively, in consonance with Article 15(2) of the *International Covenant on Civil and Political Rights*.[24] The justifications for legislature prescribing the particular maximum penalty are often obscure. A heavy maximum penalty could be aimed at retribution or deterrence or both. However, even for such offences, the absence of a mandatory minimum penalty equips the courts with sufficient flexibility to select a sentence on rehabilitative grounds.

Another indication of the gravity of the offence comes from the previous sentencing practice of the courts themselves. Cognisance may be taken of the permissible sentencing range for the offence in question. As the Victorian Full Court has said:

> So, too, a judgment as to what is appropriate by way of sentence must depend upon knowledge of sentences for the same or similar offences which is derived from personal experience or any other source.[25]

Of course, such adherence to a common permissible sentencing range in respect of the same offence facilitates consistency in sentencing. The Australian courts are reluctant to be circumscribed by a sentencing 'tariff' in the sense of a 'going rate' for a sentence, which is the practice in England.[26] While the sentence is restricted to the permissible range, our courts have considerable leeway within that range to choose an appropriate sentence.

## Mental state of the offender

As with substantive criminal law, the offender's state of mind in relation to the consequences of her or his criminal conduct is most relevant. An offender who intended the consequences is more culpable than one who was negligent about them. Likewise, an offender who knew of the risk of engaging in certain conduct but persisted nonetheless is more blameworthy than one who was unaware of the risk but ought reasonably to have known about it. In the same vein, premeditated conduct will be treated more severely than acts done impulsively or in the heat of passion. It may be readily seen that the mental state of offenders has a direct bearing on the aims to be achieved in punishing them. A deliberate or premeditated mental state would attract a stronger retributive response than if the offender were negligent. Deterrence would also be regarded as being more effective in the case of intentionally or deliberately performed criminal conduct. Conversely, an impassioned mental state could suggest that the offence was a 'one off' incident (as when the offender kills her or his provoker) so that deterrence is superfluous. The same may be said of an offender who is affected by some mental disorder when committing the crime. In such a case, the disorder may serve as a mitigating circumstance and call for a sentence based on treatment or rehabilitation.

## Harm to and involvement of the victim

Certain characteristics of the victim will be relevant to sentencing. For example, the victim's vulnerability due to age, or mental or physical disability would be regarded as an aggravating fact. So too would the fact that the offender had been motivated by hatred or prejudice against the victim due to the victim's race, religion or sexual orientation. The impact on the victim is also significant and would call for an increased penalty should there be evidence of severe physical or psychological injury, or substantial damage to the victim's property. To assist the court in receiving information on the impact of the offence on the victim, there is legislation admitting victim impact statements at sentencing hearings. These statements contain particulars not already known to the court of any injury, loss or damage suffered by any person as a result of the offence.[27] Legislature may further enhance the penalty on account of the particular status of the victim, for example, as a member of the clergy or the police force. The primary justification for this legislative measure would be deterrence and, perhaps, to denounce[28] this particularly abhorrent behaviour of assaulting or obstructing these people from discharging their public duties.

On the other hand, the victim's wish that no punishment be imposed on the offender may serve as a mitigating factor in sentencing. So too might the victim's contribution to the crime be viewed as mitigatory. For instance, the victim might have actively cooperated with the offender in committing the crime, or may have provoked the offender. However, the courts will not regard as mitigating the fact that the offender had acted in revenge against the victim for previous unlawful acts or that the victim was an obnoxious person.

## Prevalence of the offence

Current sentencing practice permits the courts to take cognisance of the prevalence of an offence in a particular locality or time period. Such prevalence is treated as justifying an increased penalty for the purposes of general deterrence. Where the offence is rarely committed, the deterrence may be disregarded although this will not be regarded as a mitigating circumstance. A major problem with taking prevalence of the crime into account in sentencing is the lack of rigour in assessing the correctness of that perceived state of affairs. Usually, the sentencer relies on personal observations or media reports as opposed to detailed and methodically sound statistics. It is for this reason that the Australian Law Reform Commission has recommended that prevalence should not be taken into account in determining sentence.[29] The Commission regarded the legislature or the executive as the proper bodies to respond to the prevalence of offences. To date, only the Australian Capital Territory has adopted the Commission's recommendation.[30]

It is observed that some variations in sentencing can occur when dealing with facts pertaining to the nature of the offence. For instance, for the same offence, one offender could receive a harsher sentence than another to reflect her or his more culpable mental state accompanying the commission of the offence. Or a stiffer penalty than, say, a year ago, is considered appropriate for the same offence on account of its increased prevalence.

# Facts concerning the nature of the offender

Further variation in sentencing will result when the sentencer considers the characteristics of each offender. The relevant personal data of the offender may not always be found in the prosecution's case or statement. Other sources of information will be from defence submissions and pre-sentence reports.

## Character of the offender

The offender's criminal character, as evidenced by a prior criminal record, may be an aggravating consideration. Prior convictions can be directly pertinent to the aims of sentencing. As the High Court has stated:

> The antecedent criminal history is relevant ... to show whether the instant offence
> is an uncharacteristic aberration or whether the offender has manifested in his
> commission of the instant offence a continuing attitude of disobedience of the law.
> In the latter case, retribution, deterrence and protection of society may all indicate
> that a more severe penalty is warranted.[31]

However, the High Court was not saying that prior convictions were a justification for imposing a sentence that was disproportionate to the gravity of the instant offence.[32] To do so would run counter to the principle of justice that a person should not be punished twice for the same crime. This principle is expressed in the *International Covenant on Political and Civil Rights* as follows:

> No one shall be liable to be ... punished again for an offence for which he has
> already been convicted ... in accordance with the law and penal procedure of
> each country.[33]

The prior criminal record of an offender can be relevant in ways that do not contravene this principle. It could be relevant in denying the offender any leniency, which might otherwise have been accorded to a first offender or person of good character. Furthermore, the prior record could inform the court that certain sentencing measures had previously failed.

Previous good character of the offender is generally regarded as a mitigating factor. Lack of previous convictions may properly be reflected in the sentence on the ground that the gravity of the offence is tempered by its having been the offender's first criminal act. However, the courts are disinclined to permit evidence of good character to mitigate crimes that were committed for profit with a rational and premeditated state of mind. Also, previous good character might actually be an aggravating factor in criminal breach of trust cases where it was used to manipulate and deceive the victim.

## Age of the offender

Youthfulness is generally regarded as a mitigating consideration. Both the legislatures and courts tend to regard rehabilitation as the primary aim when sentencing young offenders.[34] However, a deterrent sentence might be called for in cases where the particular offence was one that was prevalent among the younger age group in the community. Examples of these are car theft, house burglary, criminal damage and drug offences.[35]

Old age might be a mitigating factor preventing the sentencer from imposing a term of imprisonment for retributive purposes. When old age is combined with illness, imprisonment could have a significant deleterious effect on the offender. Furthermore, imposing a penalty on account of special deterrence would have little effect on an elderly offender.

## Gender

Some courts have justified imposing a lighter sentence on the ground that the offender was a woman. However, there are cases that have refused to adopt this approach and it cannot be said with any certainty that being a woman constitutes a mitigating factor in sentencing.[36]

## Cultural background

There is legislation providing for the cultural background of an offender to be a relevant mitigating factor in sentencing.[37] This endorses the proposal of the Australian Law Reform Commission for legislation to be passed to ensure that the offender's cultural background not be overlooked when it is relevant.[38] Where Aboriginal people are concerned, the courts have taken into account the offender's cultural outlook regarding the proscribed behaviour, the fact that the offender would suffer payback from tribal punishment, and the wishes of the tribal community of which the offender was a member. For some charges, the courts will not impose a sentence aimed at general deterrence where the offender is Aboriginal. For example, offensive behaviour through drunkenness, assaulting police and resisting arrest by Aboriginal offenders may be explained by society's neglect of the welfare of Indigenous Australians.[39] In a recent case, the impact of an Aboriginal offender being separated when young from his parents and the sexual abuse he experienced during foster care were regarded as critical factors relevant to sentencing.[40]

## Disabilities

Physical disabilities such as blindness and deafness may be mitigating factors in sentencing, and so would intellectual disability such as low intelligence. The degree of intellectual disability is, of course, relevant, with below-average intelligence not amounting to intellectual retardation given less weight than intellectual retardation as a mitigating factor in sentencing. As may be expected, the courts will tend to give less relevance to general and specific deterrence when sentencing physically or intellectually disabled offenders.

## Cooperation with authorities

Substantial 'discounting' of sentences may be obtained by an offender giving information to the authorities that leads to the conviction of other criminals.[41] The extent of the discount will depend on the nature of the crime and the quality of the cooperation. Also, voluntarily surrendering to the police and making a full confession are mitigating factors in sentencing. However, the sentence must not be so reduced as to inadequately reflect the seriousness of the offence. Neither are the courts permitted to increase a sentence for an offender's failure to cooperate.

## Remorse and guilty pleas

Evidence of contrition on the offender's part can be used to mitigate a sentence. In the words of the High Court: 'Contrition, repentance and remorse after the offence are mitigating factors, leading in a proper case to some, perhaps considerable reduction of the normal sentence'.[42] The offender will be required to do more than claim to have suffered remorse or declare an intention to reform. Concrete evidence of contrition is required such as restitution to the victim, cooperation with the police and prosecution, and admission of other offences.

A guilty plea may imply contrition but cannot of itself be conclusive of this. The plea might have simply been the response of an offender who was resigned to an inevitable conviction. Also, the courts have observed that it is possible for people who have opted to be tried to have experienced repentance.[43] Where the guilty plea is supported by other concrete evidence of contrition, no problem arises. However, should the courts recognise a guilty plea as a mitigating factor solely on the basis that it has promoted administrative convenience? The Australian Law Reform Commission saw the following arguments for and against such a recognition:

> Allowing a 'discount' would have the advantages of encouraging shorter trials; relieving delays and backlogs by lightening the court's workload; in many cases, saving the expense (often at the cost of legal aid) and inconvenience of a trial; [and] saving trauma to witnesses, especially victims.
>
> But doing so may penalise those who plead not guilty; undermine the principle that the defendant's plea must be made voluntarily; weaken the requirement that the Crown proves its case beyond reasonable doubt; [and] create the risk that innocent persons will plead guilty.[44]

In a recent case the High Court objected to recognising a guilty plea purely on the ground of administrative convenience.[45] The court ruled that a guilty plea could be taken into account independently of any question of remorse only if the offender had displayed a subjective 'willingness to facilitate the course of justice'. On this view, a guilty plea will not be recognised on the sole basis that it saved the community the expense of a trial. The New South Wales legislature has rejected the High Court ruling by introducing a provision that makes it incumbent on a sentencing judge to take a guilty plea into account even where there was no evidence that the offender had intended to facilitate the administration of justice.[46] It is submitted that the High Court's view on the issue is to be preferred for placing the individual offender's subjective mental state and motivation ahead of the objective utilitarian value of the guilty plea.

## The effect of the offence and penalty

The offender might have suffered injury in the course of engaging in the offence. The type of penalty chosen might also have an especially adverse effect on particular offenders due to some particular characteristic of theirs. In addition, the penalty imposed could cause significant hardship to the offender's family members and dependants. These facts could be relied on to reduce the sentence or to justify a community-based penalty.

### Hardship to the offender

The injuries suffered by an offender as a result of the offence may be regarded as a mitigating factor. For instance, the sentence of an offender has been reduced if he shot himself, causing gross disfigurement, after he had shot and killed his victim. Another example is of a person convicted of dangerous driving who had suffered severe injuries in the motor accident.

Some weight may be given to psychiatric evidence of the ill effects of imprisonment on a particular offender. Old age and attendant illness is a related instance of when the courts might be disinclined to impose a custodial sentence. The deprivation of present employment or the loss of reasonable future opportunities for employment may be accepted as mitigating factors. This may be justified for reasons of rehabilitation and retribution. Also, public humiliation and acts of revenge directed at the offender may be mitigating factors in sentencing.

## Hardship to others

Current sentencing practice seems to be against giving any or much weight to the hardship caused to an offender's family or dependants as a result of the penalty imposed. This is clearly borne out in the following comment of the Victorian Court of Criminal Appeal:

> when one appeals for mercy on the grounds of hardship to a wife or family, the accused ought to have had regard to that before embarking on a life of crime, and the Court cannot be blamed because it deals with an accused on the merits having regard to the gravity of the offence, the past circumstances, and so on. The Court is not so inhuman as not to be very sorry for those placed in the position of this wife and child because of the criminal activities of the husband, but our task is not to yield to pleas based on sentiment or emotion.[47]

However, in exceptional circumstances the adverse impact on these other people might persuade the court to forego imposing a sentence of imprisonment. An example would be when imprisonment of a single parent or of both parents would leave young children without any parental care.

The Australian Law Reform Commission has recommended legislation that recognises the hardship of others as a mitigating factor in sentencing. Besides noting the potentially deleterious effects of the penalty on third parties, the Commission thought that these effects 'can itself be a form of punishment of the offender'.[48] Following this recommendation, the Commonwealth *Crimes Act* 1914 includes an offender's family or dependants as a consideration to be taken into account when sentencing a federal offender.[49] There is similar legislation in the Australian Capital Territory and in South Australia.

## Parity with sentences of co-offenders

Where a crime has been committed by more than one offender, justice requires a comparison between the sentences imposed on these various offenders. In the words of the Tasmanian Court of Criminal Appeal:

> The obligation to have regard to the sentence imposed upon a co-offender thus does not rest merely upon the need to avoid imposing a sentence which could engender a feeling of grievance or resentment in the person being sentenced, but is a corollary of the fundamental postulate of the common law that like cases should

be treated alike and its converse and is a factor which must accordingly be given substantial weight in the sentencing process.[50]

Hence, the courts should ensure that the sentences of co-offenders are similar to one another should the facts relevant to sentencing be similar for all the offenders. Conversely, the courts should ensure that disparate sentences are imposed when the antecedents of the offenders are quite different. To ensure parity in sentencing, the sentencing of co-offenders should preferably be done by the same judge. Where this has not been done, the High Court has urged that 'at least the judge imposing the later sentence should inform himself of the sentence already imposed and the circumstances in which it was imposed'.[51]

## Judicial expression of facts relied upon in sentencing

The preceding discussion covers only a selected number of facts (or factors) relevant to sentencing. There is a vast array of other facts, such as the method of committing the offence, the degree of participation, weapons used, whether there was a breach of trust, the significance of profits from the offence, the effect of alcohol or drugs, voluntarily seeking treatment, personal crisis, informing on other offenders, and trial delay.[52] The sentencer has the daunting task of assessing the weight to be given to each of these facts, deciding what aim of sentencing is to be attached to them, and eventually choosing an appropriate sentence. It is small wonder that the judges opt for what has been described as the 'intuitive' technique or approach to sentencing.

But this intuitive approach should not mean that it is impossible for a judge to indicate how he or she made the sentencing decision. The facts that were considered most significant and for what reasons should be stated. Similarly, the judge should explain why certain facts carried little weight. The judges themselves see the value of this, and believe that it can be achieved without overburdening the courts. For example, in the opinion of a judge of the South Australian Supreme Court:

> I think that, as a general rule, [a judge] should state his reasons for sentence. He does not have to make a long speech about it. It will be enough to indicate, briefly but comprehensively, on what view of the facts he is acting and what considerations, including any relevant opinions or judgments have led him to his decision. Then the parties, including the man most affected, will know why he is being dealt with in a particular way and upon what factual basis, and the Supreme Court in the event of an appeal will not be left to proceed by dubious assumptions or conjecture.[53]

Unfortunately, however, the current practice is that, while reasons are desirable, the failure to provide reasons is not a sufficient ground for setting aside a sentence on appeal. The Australian Law Reform Commission has argued for sentencers to provide reasons in all cases where imprisonment is ordered or is a sentencing option.[54] The Commission considered this to be integral to securing justice in the sentencing exercise:

> The giving of reasons is necessary in the interests of consistency and fairness. The provision of detailed reasons is just to the offender and supplies a guide to other courts, enforcement agencies and correctional personnel and to the community. Such a requirement would allow trial and appellate courts to participate actively in developing a more consistent sentencing jurisprudence.[55]

# Sentencing disparity and problems with quantum of punishment

In this section, we return to the main criteria mentioned in our introduction to this chapter by which society determines whether justice is being achieved in the sentencing process. The first criterion is consistency in sentencing, and the second is that the quantum of punishment must be of a severity appropriate to the offence.

Consistency or parity in sentencing is a basic requirement of justice. Consistency here means that courts should prescribe similar sentences on similar offences committed by offenders in similar circumstances. The importance of achieving and maintaining consistency in sentencing was expressed by the High Court in the following terms:

> Just as consistency in punishment—a reflection of the notion of equal justice—is a fundamental element in any rational and fair system of criminal justice, so inconsistency in punishment, because it is regarded as a badge of unfairness and unequal treatment under the law, is calculated to lead to an erosion of public confidence in the integrity of the administration of justice. It is for this reason that the avoidance and elimination of unjustifiable discrepancy in sentencing is a matter of abiding importance to the administration of justice and to the community.[56]

It is observed that the High Court acknowledged a difference between unjustifiable and justifiable disparity (or inconsistency) in sentencing. The concern over justice relates to the former kind of disparity. As for the latter, the objective of sentencing consistency does make allowances for individual differences in both the circumstances of the offence and of the offender. Some of these facts or circumstances were discussed in 'Facts relevant to sentencing' where we noted the ways in which they have a bearing on the aims of sentencing. Hence, disparity in sentencing is permitted provided there are good grounds for differentiating between offences or offenders.[57] Overall, the approach to achieving just sentences may be presented thus—while sentencing consistency should generally be adhered to for similar offences committed by offenders in similar circumstances, judges have the discretion to adjust sentences to take account of the particular facts found in individual cases.

Another aspect of sentencing, which justice requires the courts to have, is a clear and coherent policy relating to the type and quantum of punishment. This is a separate issue from sentencing consistency as it is concerned with matters such as severity or leniency of penalties, proportionality between the offence and the penalty, and generally the appropriateness of a sentence. While consistency has to do with procedural fairness and equality, the quantum of punishment is concerned with just deserts, humanity and effectiveness of the penalty. The Australian Law Reform Commission described this relationship between justice and the quantum of punishment as follows:

> the punishment imposed for a particular offence must be just—that is, of a sever-ity appropriate to the offence. This is not a justification for punishments of any severity. A criminal justice system which delivered punishments that were exces-sively harsh would be as ineffective and unjust as one which delivered punishments that were too lenient. In the latter case, the law is likely to be simply disregarded. In the former, informal means may well be taken to avoid subjecting offenders to the excessively harsh punishments. The level of severity of punishment must strike a balance between these two extremes.[58]

Clearly, the aims of sentencing are closely related to this aspect. A lack of clar-ity in these aims would invariably cause problems in determining the quantum of punishment.

While it is difficult to assess the extent of unjustifiable sentencing disparity and problems with quantum of penalties in Australia, disparity and problems certainly exist. Recent Australian law reform bodies have relied on local research findings of unjustifiable sentencing disparity to recommend ways of reducing disparity.[59] As for the quantum of punishment, the courts themselves have lamented the lack of guidelines or principles in the use of particular penalties, and how they com-pare in severity with other penalties. Possible explanations for unjustifiable dispar-ity in sentencing and the problems of quantum are discussed below.

## Ambiguity of sentencing aims

The preceding discussion has referred to the significance of sentencing aims to both the issues of sentencing consistency and quantum of penalties. Many of the problems surrounding these issues have been created by the uncertainty of these sentencing aims. In particular, neither the legislature nor the courts have attempted to formulate priorities among the competing aims of retribution, deter-rence and rehabilitation. This has led to unjustifiable disparity in sentencing on account of individual judges sentencing according to their own ideas about these aims. Furthermore, relating these aims to the decision as to type and quantum of punishment is often extremely difficult, if not impossible. This is due to the absence of guidelines on the use of these penalties and of a hierarchy of penalties.

The incoherence of sentencing aims is compounded by two matters. There is first the frequent shifts in sentencing reform policy.[60] Thus, in the nineteenth and first part of the twentieth century, the predominant aims of sentencing were retribution and deterrence. These took a back seat to rehabilitation in the 1960s and 1970s. Most recently, retribution has re-emerged in the form of 'just deserts' as the major aim. This 'pendulum of ideas' swinging from one idea to the next clearly discourages any efforts to lay down a fixed priority of sentencing aims. Second, there is the felt need in some political and judicial circles for sentencing aims to reflect community expectations and attitudes on punishment. Studies have revealed that the public are themselves divided over the priority that should be given to the competing justifications for punishment.[61] Not surprisingly, this ambivalence is reflected in the views of sentencers.

## Lack of legislative guidelines

The failure of the legislature to prescribe the priority of sentencing aims has already been noted. The usual legislative guidance on sentencing is the maximum penalty for particular offences. This leaves the courts with extensive discretion to choose the type and quantum of penalty in individual cases. Certainly, this absence of narrower legislative guidelines promotes the instinctive approach to decision-making in sentencing. But critics of this approach, such as the Australian Law Reform Commission, point to its 'largely unregulated' discretion, which is seen as promoting inconsistency in sentencing.[62] Even with respect to what the legislature does do, it has been criticised for being arbitrary in setting down maximum penalties for various offences. As the Victorian Supreme Court judges have scathingly noted:

> there is no logical or rational basis upon which the maximum penalties are set by Parliament. It is only necessary to refer to the maximum of 25 years for armed robbery and to compare it with a maximum of 15 years for manslaughter to make the point. Yet, from the point of view of the Courts, the only way to determine how seriously a particular offence is to be treated is to look at the maximum sentence prescribed for it.[63]

A further problem created by the legislature is its recent proliferation of a whole variety of penalties. Such a proliferation is in itself not a bad thing as the sentencer's choice of the appropriate sentence is widened. However, the legislature has aggravated the problems of sentencing inconsistency and quantum by failing to provide guidance on the conditions of the use of these new penalties. It has also failed to order these penalties in terms of relative severity. Thus, sentencers may be at a loss as to whether a community service order is only to be used in lieu of imprisonment, whether such an order is to be regarded more as a punitive measure or for rehabilitative purposes, and how it is to be compared with, say, a probation order.

This ambiguity also occurs with the enactment of a provision such as the following: that a sentence of imprisonment is not to be imposed unless the court 'having considered all other available sentences, is satisfied that no other sentence is appropriate in all the circumstances of the case'.[64] The Victorian Court of Criminal Appeal criticised this provision for raising certain 'unanswerable' questions:

> The questions are provoked because the legislation is couched in general terms which omit to make Parliament's intention clear and thus greatly increase the work of the courts. If Acts of Parliament are couched in general terms which do not make Parliament's intention clear, much time is taken up in the courts by arguments as to the meaning of the section and how the court should apply it. Costs and delays are increased and injustice may follow.[65]

These remarks apply generally to the virtual absence, apart from maximum penalties, of legislative guidelines on the sentencing decision and the use of a growing range of sentencing options.

## Lack of judicial guidelines

We have already noted the eclectic nature of sentencing decisions. This is largely the result of a judicial refusal to formulate a priority of sentencing aims. Judges laud the instinctive approach to sentencing on the ground that it best enables the sentence to be tailored to the particular case. While no one would deny the need for a wide discretion to be afforded to sentencers, there is deep concern that the instinctive approach is insufficiently regulated, leading to sentencing disparity and problems with the appropriate quantums of punishment. Nigel Walker has described one of the dangers inherent in the present system as 'emotional eclecticism'.[66] Under this notion, sentencers may perform their decision-making in a rational way until they encounter a case that so shocks them that they resort to homilies about desert. It is as if, when an offender's culpability rose above a certain threshold, a different sort of reasoning was applied. Sentencing inconsistency occurs because this threshold is high for some judges and low for others.

Traditionally, the courts have loathed any external attempts to guide their decision-making in sentencing, often invoking the principle of judicial independence. Efforts by law reform bodies to establish sentencing guidelines have often been met with judicial resistance and opposition to change.[67]

This judicial reticence about sentencing guidelines is also evident within the appellate review structure itself. Courts hearing appeals against sentence interfere with the original sentence only when there has been some manifest injustice. The appellate courts have rarely handed down sentencing guidelines that could be applied in future cases, preferring instead to restrict their comments to particular cases. In the following passage, Richard Fox sums up the inadequacies of Australian appellate review of sentences:

In many cases, appeal decisions on sentencing ... do not state any explicit priniple. They merely affirm the correctness of the original sentence, or illustrate the balancing of principles, or give an example of how a certain type of problem can be approached. Their coverage of sentencing law is patchy, with serious crimes and extreme sentences ... predominating. They say nothing, or very little, about sentencing for the average type of offence, especially ones decided in the lowest level courts, because very few of these reach the upper echelons of criminal appeal. The vast majority of sentencing appeals are unreported and major problems of accessibility limit the use of such cases as authorities at first instance.[68]

## A non-integrated criminal justice system

One reason for sentencing disparity in this country is the Federal system. Different States have different approaches to certain offences, producing different sentencing outcomes. This may be an acceptable consequence of federalism, reflecting different circumstances and priorities. More problematic is the issue of sentencing persons convicted of offences under Commonwealth law. In Australia, there are no Federal prisons as such. Convicted Federal offenders are held in State or Territory prisons. It is therefore inevitable that problems of equity of punishment will arise. Out of recognition that they are housed side-by-side with State offenders in State prisons, should their punishment be assimilated, approximately, with that of State prisoners? Or should Federal offenders be treated, in respect of their Federal offences, as equally as possible throughout Australia, wherever their offence occurred? Part 1B of the Commonwealth *Crimes Act* chooses the latter option, attempting to ensure consistency between the sentences served by Federal offenders throughout Australia.

Regrettably, there is a more far-ranging reason for unjustifiable sentencing disparity and problems with the quantum of punishment. The criminal justice system is comprised of separate sub-systems, each with its own ideology and interests.[69] For example, the police and prosecution are dominated by the ideology of law and order and interested in controlling crime through the deterrent effect of punishment. The courts are eclectic in their sentencing ideologies, relying on retribution, deterrence and rehabilitation as they deem fit. Their interests include protecting judicial independence, efficient movement of caseloads and reducing court delays. The corrective services are motivated by public protection and some form of rehabilitation. They are concerned with the professional and efficient management of cases.

It will readily be seen that the competing ideologies and interests of these sub-systems have a direct impact on sentencing. This phenomenon has been described as analogous to a hydraulic system where pressure at one point inevitably produces a corresponding effect at another point.[70] Thus, the prosecutorial decision on the type of charge, the mode of trial, and whether to inform the court of prior convictions and other matters of aggravation, all directly affect the nature and scope of the sentencing decision. Another example is the measures taken by corrective services to reduce the actual time offenders spend in custody. The courts would construe this as a usurpation of their sentencing function. Judges would also be deeply concerned that the public will perceive the courts as failing to discharge their responsibility of ensuring that offenders are adequately punished for their crimes. George Zdenkowski sums up the situation as follows:

> The pursuit by such agencies of different objectives (whether articulated or not) is likely to lead to an incoherent sentencing policy however conscientiously the protagonists in each sector exercise the responsibility vested in them. This in turn contributes to, reinforces and indeed recycles, the confusion about objectives which bedevils discussion of sentencing, whether amongst professionals involved in the field, in the media or in the community at large.[71]

What is urgently needed is an integrated ideology, one that is shared by all the sub-systems comprising the criminal justice system. In the next section, it will be suggested that Parliament must take the lead in constructing this.

# Remedies for achieving just sentencing

The preceding section presented the major causes of injustice in our sentencing system. They are the absence of any clear articulation of sentencing aims; grossly inadequate sentencing guidelines by the legislature; and the judicial resistance to laying down sufficiently detailed sentencing principles for the judges themselves. These combine to produce unjust sentences as measured by the dual tests of sentencing consistency and the sufficient severity (or quantum) of punishments. In this section, we shall consider the main measures that have been suggested to alleviate such injustice. The first of these is to select just deserts as the primary aim of sentencing. Next, there are legislative measures such as the endorsement of just deserts as the primary sentencing aim, grading offences according to seriousness, laying down facts to be taken into account in sentencing, and providing a sanctions hierarchy. Then there are measures that the courts could implement such as guideline judgments, making it a duty to provide reasons for sentences, and relying on the data pertinent to sentencing supplied by specially created information-gathering bodies. Finally, there is the invocation to establish an integrated criminal justice system. The proposal is for each sub-system of the criminal justice system to have clearly established policies and guidelines that, together with those of other sub-systems, work towards achieving shared goals.

# Establishing a hierarchy of sentencing aims

The competing aims of retribution, deterrence and rehabilitation have already been explored. To allay sentencing inconsistency and the disparate use of penalties for like offences and offenders, a hierarchy of sentencing aims is required. We are of the view that heading this hierarchy should be the principle of 'just deserts'.[72] This has been described as the 'just deserts model of sentencing' and it has received much support from law reform bodies and judges. The 'just deserts' principle provides a ceiling on punishment, both an upper and lower limit, beyond which the sentencer cannot traverse. In this respect, just deserts is utilitarian in nature and is therefore a modification of retributivism. For a pure retributivist, the state has a moral duty to inflict punishment on an offender who deserves it and it does not matter whether the punishment has a utilitarian value.[73] Between the upper and lower ceilings set by the just deserts principle, the other aims of deterrence and rehabilitation are allowed to operate. The Victorian Committee on Sentencing advocated just such a model when it said:

> In the Committee's view the just deserts principles ought to set the maximum sentence that can be imposed on an offender in any particular case, however, the effects of the just deserts principles should be modified by giving appropriate weight to … the other aims of sentencing—rehabilitation, deterrence and denunciation. In no circumstances should a sentence be increased beyond that which is justified on just deserts principles in order that one or more of the secondary aims are met.[74]

The courts have generally been resistant to putting the sentencing aims into some order of priority. But in the first case where the High Court granted special leave to appeal against a purely sentencing matter, it appears to have given its support to the just deserts model of sentencing.[75] The High Court had to consider a mentally disordered offender who had been imprisoned for manslaughter and who killed again when he was released. The court had to decide on the weight to be given to societal protection when fixing the sentence. It held that sentences should be:

> proportionate to the gravity of the offence … [and] … that the sentences should not be increased beyond that which is proportionate to the crime in order merely to extend the period of protection of society from the risk of recidivism on the part of the offender.[76]

In a recent case involving the sentencing of a paedophile, the High Court noted that rehabilitation was the primary aim of punishment in the mid-twentieth century but, in more recent years, the retributive aspect of punishment had reasserted itself.[77] A reason for the shift was the persistently punitive attitude of the community towards criminals, which meant that public confidence in the judiciary would be weakened if the judges ignored the retributive aim of punishment. We submit that judges would do well to promote a 'just deserts' model of sentencing that incorporates this retributive aim.

The High Court's reference to proportionality goes to the heart of what is meant by 'just deserts'. For the sentence to be just, the severity of the punishment must be commensurate with the seriousness of the offence. The seriousness of the offence is measured by the magnitude of the harm suffered and the extent of the offender's culpability. Proportionality dictates that the greater the harm inflicted and the higher the degree of culpability, the harsher should be the penalty.[78] However, tempering this concept of proportionality is the principle of 'parsimony'. This principle requires the least restrictive or punitive penalty necessary to achieve defined social purposes to be chosen. In advocating the principle of parsimony, the Victorian Sentencing Committee relied on the following comment: 'The principle is utilitarian and humanitarian; its justification is somewhat obvious since any punitive suffering beyond societal need is, in this context, what defines cruelty.'[79] The principle of parsimony has received statutory endorsement in Victoria and Queensland.

Incorporated into the just deserts model is the stipulation that the sentencer must choose only penalties prescribed for the offence at the time when it was committed. Hence, the sentencer is disallowed from considering an increased maximum penalty that came into being after the offence was committed. This restriction appears in the following terms in Article 15(1) of the *International Covenant on Civil and Political Rights*:

> Nor shall a heavier penalty be imposed than the one that was applicable at the time when the criminal offence was committed.[80]

This provision maintains justice by preventing changes made to the law after criminal conduct had been committed to prejudice the actor.

As to which should be the appropriate body to adopt the just deserts model—the legislature or the judiciary—it is suggested that it should be the legislature. One reason is that it is unlikely that the courts can be persuaded to take this initiative. The High Court aside, we have observed the judicial preference for eclectic sentencing, which refuses to present the sentencing aims into any order of priority. Another reason is that the legislature is most suitably placed to create an integrated criminal justice system. It has plenary power to enact rules and guidelines not only for sentencers, but also for the police, prosecutors, corrective service personnel, and other institutions or personnel who have an input in the process of sentencing. Currently, there is Australian legislation identifying the aims of sentencing but without ranking them. In contrast, the Finnish and Swedish Penal Codes identify just deserts as the primary rationale for sentencing.[81]

Adopting the just deserts model is certainly the first step towards achieving consistently just sentencing practices and results. But it must be complemented by an array of other measures to become operative. This is because concepts such as proportionality and parsimony can only be properly applied when there are in place clear gradations of offence seriousness and a hierarchy of penalties. The legislature is the only body equipped to tackle these tasks.

# Legislative measures

At the outset, it should be declared that legislative guidelines on sentencing need not usurp an integral judicial function. While it is true that these guidelines would regulate judicial decision-making more than if the courts were left to their own devices, the discretionary power of judges remains sacrosanct.[82] Within the limits imposed by the legislature, there will be a wide range of issues and matters upon which the sentencer would be the sole decider. Hence, the proposed legislative measures regulating sentencing are not so restrictive as to deprive the sentencing process of the human element, which comes in the person of the sentencer. In the following comment, Norval Morris succinctly places the need for legislative guidance in the context of judicial discretion in sentencing:

> Judicial discretion is essential to achieve the fine tuning needed in ascertaining punishment. I think it lies beyond society's intellectual competence to create a system in which the judge is not the fine tuner of punishment. Therefore I see the problem of sentencing as one of providing guidance and a frame of reference to the judge, and of shaping and controlling judicial discretion; not of supplanting it.[83]

With this in mind, the major legislative measures aimed at reducing sentencing inconsistency and disparity in the quantum of punishments will now be presented.

## A hierarchy of offences according to seriousness

Since the legislature comprises the elected representatives of the community, it is the best body to decide on the appropriate levels of seriousness for each offence. These decisions should be based on research findings on such matters as judicial and public perception of the gravity of specific offences, and the harm suffered by victims of these offences. This exercise would replace the many illogical or irrational maximum penalties currently found in the statute books with ones that more accurately reflect judicial and community expectations. Another effect may be to cause the legislature to remove the least serious offences from the criminal process altogether. The prosecutorial sub-system has a vital input in working out an integrated strategy here. Based on these research findings, types of offences could be sub-divided according to seriousness, assigning 'starting points' and ceilings of penalties to each sub-division. A court should be bound by these lower and upper limits, unless it states special reasons for departing from them. That the courts themselves would welcome such a legislative measure is evident in the following Victorian Supreme Court submission to the Victorian Sentencing Committee:

> It is, therefore, urgent and vital that all maximum sentences be revised so as to prescribe sentences which reflect modern notions of the seriousness of the various offences or at least Parliament's view of such seriousness.

It is thought that the most important service which the Sentencing Committee could render to Victoria would be to recommend a rational scale of penalties for all offences.[84]

The Supreme Court regarded this legislative initiative as a significant step towards achieving an integral criminal justice system, saying that '[a] new level of sentencing would inevitably follow and some easing of the tension which presently exists between Parliament and the Courts would, it is hoped, ensue'.[85] Following the recommendations of the Sentencing Committee, there is now Victorian legislation detailing the maximum and minimum penalties for a wide range of offences according to their seriousness.[86]

## A hierarchy of penalties according to severity

For the just deserts model of sentencing to operate effectively, there must be a graduated scale of penalties to match the graduated scale of offence seriousness. Again, the legislature is the best body to grade penalties and to conduct this matching exercise. A scale of penalties is also essential to avoid unjustified sentencing disparity, especially given the ever increasing range of types of penalties made available to sentencers by the legislature. Without it, we cannot know whether one sentencer has been more punitive or lenient than another. In working out the scale, the legislature should initiate research on judicial and public perceptions of the types of penalties. With this information, the penalties should be drawn up, as far as possible, according to their perceived severity. Where penalties serve as alternatives, rather than a correctional progression, legislature should make this clear.[87] This is especially so among the middle range of penalties such as fines, probation and suspended sentences.

A legislative method of controlling judicial discretion in sentencing is the enactment of offences that contain an aggravating feature not shared by the generic offence. An example is the offence of home invasion, which attracts a more severe penalty than the generic offence of break and enter. Through this arrangement, the legislature identifies particular features of criminal conduct that it wants judges to punish more severely.

The courts themselves have called for a hierarchy of penalties to be declared by the legislature. An example is found in the following comment by the Victorian Supreme Court:

> The maintenance of the balance between Parliament and the Courts is not easy. But Parliament cannot escape responsibility. The balance should be maintained by Parliament's prescribing maximum sentences for particular offences, indicating (if it wishes to) for what offences imprisonment is generally thought appropriate (without binding the Court to imprisonment in each case), and indicating in general terms what it regards as the descending order of severity of punishment.[88]

It is observed how the Supreme Court was keen to guard against too great an infringement of its sentencing discretion by legislature, while at the same time appreciating the need for some legislative clarification of the severity of penalties.

## Detailing facts relevant to sentencing

The legislators of most jurisdictions have undertaken the process of identifying and tabulating facts relevant to sentencing. The sentencing legislation typically contains a list of matters for which a court should have regard and other matters that cannot be used to increase the severity of sentence. In all models, the lists are not exclusive, permitting other matters to be considered. The legislators have not listed the matters in any order of priority or importance, preferring to leave this task to the courts.

In New South Wales and Western Australia, the legislation has gone further and identified the matters as aggravating or mitigating.[89] The New South Wales legislation has sought to regulate judicial decision-making through a three-pronged strategy comprising a restatement of sentencing aims, a specific declaration of aggravating and mitigating factors, and the setting of non-parole periods for certain serious offences.[90] However, in practice, judicial sentencing discretion appears to be largely retained.[91]

# Judicial measures

While legislative measures are vital to eliminate sentencing inconsistency and problems of quantum of punishment, these measures have to be expressed in general terms. Justice in individual cases can only be served by leaving the courts with sufficient flexibility to consider the particular circumstances of the offence and the offender and the appropriate penalty to be imposed taking into account those circumstances. The judiciary could devise various measures of its own to supplement the legislative efforts at achieving just sentencing.

## Guideline judgments

Guideline judgments are those delivered by appellate courts that go beyond the point raised in the particular case on appeal. In giving these guideline judgments, the appeal court takes the opportunity to lay down principles on the sentencing of types of offence. The advantage of these judgments is that they expand and consolidate the principles which should govern the area concerned, thereby sparing sentencing courts from trying to extract these sentencing principles from a line of cases. The experience of the New South Wales Court of Appeal has been positive in this respect and has thus far delivered guideline judgments on culpable driving,[92] armed robbery, drug offences and break and enter.[93] It should be observed that this innovation is aimed at structuring rather than restricting sentencing discretion.

To date, New South Wales, Victoria and Western Australia have made statutory provision for guideline judgments. The New South Wales legislation[94] grants statutory power to the Court of Criminal Appeal to give a guideline judgment of its own motion or at the request of the Attorney-General. The senior Public Defender, Director of Public Prosecutions or the Attorney-General may appear in guideline proceedings to oppose or support the giving of a guideline judgment or to make submissions with respect to the framing of the guidelines. The legislation also provides for the guideline judgments to be reviewed, varied or revoked by a subsequent guideline judgment. To similar effect, the Victorian and Western Australian legislation empowers the Court of Criminal Appeal to deliver judgments containing guidelines that must be taken into account by sentencing courts.[95]

## Duty to state reasons for sentence

Currently, courts are encouraged but not duty-bound to explain how they arrived at a sentence. Sentencing consistency and sufficient severity of penalties will be better secured by requiring sentencers to provide reasons. This change from discretion to duty in giving reasons can be initiated by the courts themselves, or by the legislature. It is only when adequate reasons are given and recorded that useful comparisons can be made between cases. The provision of reasons will make it clear what facts the sentencer regarded as significant and the weight that was attached to them. The sentencer would also have to explain why he or she regarded the particular sentence imposed to be the most appropriate and the sentencing aims being promoted by such a sentence.

The Australian Law Reform Commission has recommended that more extensive requirements for the giving and recording of reasons for sentencing should be introduced. It saw the need for this measure in terms of promoting justice:

> The provision of adequate reasons is also fundamental to achieving justice within the criminal justice system. The imposition of punishment is of such importance to the state and to individual offenders that reasons for particular sentencing decisions must be given as a matter of fairness. The availability of reasons for decisions will lessen the possibility of those decisions being, or appearing to be, unjustified or arbitrary.[96]

## Indeterminate sentences

Consideration should be given to introducing special sentences for people convicted of serious crimes and liable to lengthy terms of imprisonment. Instead of being sentenced to, say, ten or fifteen years' imprisonment, the offender might be given an 'indeterminate sentence' according to which the determinate sentence would not be imposed for a number of years (perhaps five years) after conviction.[97] No judge can, at the time of conviction, confidently predict how a prisoner will respond to many years of incarceration. It may be that at a resentencing

hearing some years later the prisoner will be able to present evidence of significant rehabilitation, persuading the resentencing judge to impose a relatively short
determinate sentence. Such a scheme would reduce difficulties of prediction at the
time of conviction and provide considerable inducement to prisoners to good
behaviour and rehabilitation in the prison environment.

## Judicial education and training

In recent years, the rapid advancement of computer technology has greatly assisted
the education of sentencing judges. The New South Wales Sentencing
Information System is an excellent example of this development. The system is a
highly comprehensive computerised database of sentencing statistics, legislation
and case law that informs judges of the general pattern of sentences for a particular offence and enables them to specify key factors such as the offender's age,
guilty plea and prior conviction so as to more closely match the statistics they
require to the case before them. Clearly, the use of the system has been highly
effective in tackling the problem of unjustified disparities in sentencing.

Although the use of computerised databases has helped tremendously, sentencing judges remain ill equipped to conduct the research needed to evaluate public
perceptions about crime and punishment and formulate guideline judgments. It is
also unrealistic to expect the parties to criminal proceedings to generate the necessary research or to present their cases in ways that promote the development of
sentencing principles. Noting this deficiency, some States have established a
research and advisory body, with the courts being directed to take account of the
findings and recommendations of such a body. For example, the Victorian legislature has created a Sentencing Advisory Council whose functions include:

- providing to the Court of Appeal its views on the giving or review of a guideline judgment
- providing statistical information on sentencing to the courts and other interested persons
- conducting research and disseminating information on sentencing matters to
the courts and other interested persons
- gauging public opinion on sentencing matters
- consulting, on sentencing matters, with government departments and other
interested persons and bodies as well as the general public
- advising the Attorney-General on sentencing matters.[98]

## Towards an integrated criminal justice system

It is observed that the functions of research and advisory bodies such as a Sentencing
Advisory Council are not confined to the sentencing decisions by judges. The
Australian Law Reform Commission was keenly aware of the 'hydraulic press' effect
where restricting the exercise of discretion in one sub-system of the criminal justice

system would result in greater disparity in the use of discretions in other sub-systems. The Commission therefore advocated that the Sentencing Advisory Council should conduct a wide-ranging review covering all the sub-systems having an input in variations in sentence. From this one body, a coordinated effort at achieving an integrated policy on sentencing could emerge. Obviously, such a Council must receive legislative empowerment to carry out its tasks. And the legislature should, after a period of consultation and public debate, cast the Council's recommendations (or modifications to them) in statutory form. Through this process, legislative guidelines for the various sub-systems—from the police, the prosecution, the courts, to the corrective administrators—will be established by the same body.

The interrelatedness between the legislature, judiciary and executive sub-systems in the sentencing process cannot be overly emphasised. The following comment by George Zdenkowski, the Commissioner in charge of the Australian Law Reform Commission reference on sentencing, provides an excellent summary of how best to achieve justice in sentencing:

> On balance, I would argue for a more detailed and coherent articulation of sentencing principles by statute, so that the court's discretion is exercised by reference to known and publicly available principles. The judiciary should, however, retain the important role of developing a jurisprudence based on those principles. This would have the advantages of providing some guidance, retaining flexibility and giving due prominence to a reasoned determination in a public forum and accountability through the appellate process. Appeal courts could, however, be more actively involved in sentencing policy in that they would have regard to the conformity of the decision of trial courts to the criteria prescribed by statute. The executive functions in the sentencing process (through prosecution and parole board decisions and the like) should operate by reference to guidelines which also relate to the clearly articulated objectives.[99]

The problems of integration in a Federal system will remain. Where Federal offenders are sentenced in State courts and serve their sentences in State prisons, difficult parity issues are inevitable. For example, section 16G of the Commonwealth *Crimes Act* was enacted in 1990 to ensure that a Federal offender sentenced in a State jurisdiction that did not offer remissions on sentence would be treated equally with a Federal offender sentenced in another State jurisdiction that did offer remissions. It was repealed in 2003 because all States have abolished remissions, or soon will. The surprising, and arguably unjust, result seems to be that sentences for Commonwealth offences in jurisdictions such as New South Wales (which abolished remissions in 1989) will increase by 50%.[100]

# Sentencing policy and public opinion

This chapter began with highlighting the highly symbolic and public character of sentencing. When imposing a sentence, the court issues a public declaration that the offender deserves to be punished for engaging in criminal behaviour. Furthermore, the sentence is a warning to both the defendant and potential offenders in the community of the painful consequences that flow from committing such criminal behaviour. The court might also declare the need for the offender to undergo treatment for the purpose of making her or him a law-abiding person. Hence, we observe how the retributive, deterrent and rehabilitative aims of sentencing are very much served by the public declaration of the sentence. However, it is one thing for judges to impose sentences for these purposes; it is quite another matter whether members of the community regard the sentences in the way the judges do. Public disagreement over the sentence having a sufficiently retributive or deterrent effect, or that a penalty aimed at rehabilitation was inappropriate, would work against what the sentencer hoped to achieve.

The notion of justice that is posited as the hallmark of good sentencing practice is also very much connected with public opinion. We have already observed how the Australian Law Reform Commission was concerned to measure justice according to community perceptions. In the context of sentencing, the public would consider that justice was done if the sentence was sufficiently severe and there was consistency in sentencing of offenders committing similar offences in similar circumstances. While judges might regard the sentence as sufficiently severe, to be consistent with sentencing practice for the kind of offence and offender, the public might think otherwise. Again, such disagreement undermines the sentencer's objective of selecting a sentence that is just by community perceptions. Mindful of the significance of public opinion on sentencing, the courts have accepted the need to account for 'informed' public opinion. Such opinion notionally includes an awareness of the facts relating to the offender and the range of penalties imposed in the past in like cases.[101]

Given the tremendous significance that public opinion has on sentencing goals and, more generally, on community support for the criminal justice system, it is surprising that little research has been done in this area. Although the situation has slightly improved since,[102] the following comment by researchers at the Australian Institute of Criminology still holds true:

> Judges, magistrates, politicians and others concerned with crime and punishment often assert that the sentences given by courts or fixed in legislation by government are 'What the public want' ... In Australia it has been rare for public opinion to be systematically elicited on issues relating to how serious certain crimes are seen as being. Generally, it has been judicial or political perceptions of the public mood in relation to crime and punishment that exerted a far greater influence on policy than public opinion itself.[103]

The situation is worsened by the fact that these judicial and legislative perceptions have largely relied on media reports, which are often sensationalised and ill-informed.[104] For justice to be done and seen to be done, there is a pressing need for more detailed and accurate information about public attitudes on sentencing.

Lately, the courts and legislatures have shown a willingness to openly engage the public on sentencing matters. For example, when the New South Wales Court of Criminal Appeal delivered its first guideline judgment, the Chief Justice appeared on television and wrote a newspaper article explaining the importance and impact of the decision.[105] Another example is the legislative creation of Sentencing Advisory Councils in New South Wales and Victoria, whose functions include monitoring sentencing trends and practices and conducting research on public opinion on sentencing. Representatives of the community who sit on these Councils are expected to facilitate broad community input into the deliberations and activities of the Councils.

While sensitivity to public opinion could considerably affect sentencing policy and practice, it should not degenerate into simply pandering to the swings of public sentiment. As a British legislative committee has asserted:

> that would be a negation of responsible leadership and a dangerous and undemo-
> cratic course to follow. It is up to the leaders of public opinion to inform, educate
> and persuade the community.[106]

In this regard, given the significant role of the media in educating the community, emphasis should be given to ensuring that it receives accurate information about sentencing policy and practice. This function could be performed by a body such as the Sentencing Advisory Council or specially created media liaison officers attached to the courts.

Public opinion has certainly not gone unnoticed of late. Indeed, much of recent sentencing reform in Australia has been motivated by the need to account for evolving public opinion on crime and punishment. For instance, there is now in place Victorian legislation materially revising afresh the maximum penalties for a whole range of offences.[107] This initiative seeks to meet public cynicism over the disparity between the statutory maximum penalties prescribed by the legislature and the sentences actually imposed by the courts. Similarly, the abolition of remissions by several jurisdictions[108] was a direct response to public dissatisfaction over prisoners being released well before the terms that were handed down by the judges.

We can usefully conclude our discussion on sentencing practice and public opinion with the following words of caution offered by Sir Anthony Mason, a former Chief Justice of the High Court of Australia:

> The way in which the courts apply the law necessarily takes account of the com-
> munity's standards of behaviour and expectation. But this does not mean that the
> courts automatically give effect to community behaviour or expectations or, for
> that matter, the community's moral values and attitudes …
>
> There are powerful reasons why it is not helpful for the judge to have regard
> to public opinion about the sentence to be imposed in the particular case. For one
> thing, how does one ascertain what that opinion is? For another thing, how could

the judge be satisfied that the opinion was an informed opinion, based on relevant sentencing principles and reflecting knowledge of all relevant circumstances of the case? And thirdly, there is the risk that opinion about the particular case may represent an emotional reaction to one or more aspects of the crime.[109]

# Mandatory sentences

Thus far, the discussion has centred on the legislature setting the maximum limit of sentences and leaving the courts with discretion in the prescription of sentences for individual offenders. However, the legislature is paramount and, if it considers that there are good reasons for doing so, may deprive or further restrict the sentencing discretion of the courts. This occurs whenever the legislature specifies a mandatory fixed sentence for an offence.

A prime example of a mandatory sentence was section 53AE of the *Juvenile Justice Act* 1983 (NT), which, until it was abolished in 2001, provided for mandatory minimum terms of detention for some categories of juvenile repeat offenders. The section required a magistrate or judge to impose a period of at least 28 days' detention on a juvenile (defined as a person between 15 and 17 years of age) who had been convicted of any one of a list of property offences and had at least one prior conviction for a property offence committed after a prescribed date.

Another example is the Western Australian so-called 'three strikes legislation', which was introduced in 1996.[110] It applies to both adult and juvenile offenders and makes it mandatory for a judicial officer to sentence a repeat offender convicted of home burglary to a minimum of 12 months' imprisonment (for adults) or detention (for juveniles). The legislation defines a repeat offender as a person who had committed and was convicted of a relevant offence committed in respect of a place ordinarily used for human habitation and subsequent to that conviction again committed and was convicted of a relevant offence committed in respect of such a place.

A third example of mandatory sentencing legislation is found in the *Migration Act* 1958 (Cth), which forms part of the Howard Government's efforts at 'border control'. Introduced in November 2001, the legislation imposes mandatory minimum penalties for a number of offences involving illegal entry into Australia. For example, a person who 'facilitates' the entry into Australia of five or more unauthorised people will face a minimum of 5 years imprisonment. The same penalties apply to a person who provides misleading information to immigration officials with respect to a group of five or more such arrivals.[111]

The main criticism against mandatory sentences is that they ignore the sentencing principle that offenders must be examined individually and that prescribed penalties should be mitigated in some cases depending on the outcome of the examination. As observed in the bulk of this chapter, it has been traditionally left to the courts to impose individualised sentences to ensure that the punishment not only fits the crime but the offender as well.

Other objections could be raised against the use of mandatory sentences. The efficiency of the criminal justice system would be adversely affected since offenders would be less willing to plead guilty to offences that carry a mandatory sentence. This means increased pressure of time and resources on the courts and legal aid services. The introduction of mandatory minimum sentences also leads to an increased use of detention centres and prisons. The cost to the public purse is immense, as is shown by Northern Territory Department of Corrective Services figures estimating that nearly $12 500 is needed to accommodate each young offender sentenced to the mandatory 28-day period of detention. One must wonder whether the money would not be better spent on schools, job schemes, public housing and health services for young people.

While on the subject of young offenders, imposing mandatory sentences on them is contrary to other State and Territorial sentencing legislation. For instance, the preamble to the *Juvenile Justice Act* 1983 (NT) refers to:

> the intention that juveniles be dealt with in the criminal law system in a manner consistent with their age and level of maturity (including their being dealt with, where appropriate, by means of admonition and counselling) and to extend to juveniles the same rights and protections before the law as apply to adults in similar circumstances...

There is also section 7(h) of the *Young Offenders Act* 1994 (WA), which stipulates that detaining a young person in custody for an offence should only be used as a last resort and, if required, should only be for as short a time as is necessary.

Another adverse effect of mandatory sentences is that they provide prosecutors with too much bargaining power with which to influence defendants into pleading guilty to lesser offences when there is a substantial chance of acquittal of the original charge. Yet another reason against the use of these sentences, especially in respect of young offenders, is that they will, in practice, tend to be directed against already disadvantaged groups. The link between poverty, unemployment and property crime is well documented. Young unemployed people, the homeless and the poor make up a significant number of people who commit property crime. The matter is compounded further when it is realised that Indigenous Australians comprise a substantial proportion of this disadvantaged group. For example, a study conducted in 1994 found that an Aboriginal youth was fourteen times more likely than a non-Aboriginal to be charged with a property crime.[112] Added to this is the fact that the clear-up rate for property crime in Aboriginal communities is generally much higher than the clear-up rate in urban centres because people in Aboriginal communities have nowhere to hide. This state of affairs has led one commentator to express the deep concern that the mandatory sentencing laws under discussion 'have all the hallmarks of the next chapter of the "stolen generation" report' and that 'mandatory sentencing is the "next round" of witnessing the State removing young Aboriginal children from their families'.[113]

A final reason against the use of mandatory minimum sentences in respect of juveniles is that it infringes certain articles of the *United Nations Convention on the Rights of the Child*, which was ratified by Australia in January 1991. In particular, the Northern Territory and Western Australian legislation are very likely to be in breach of Article 37(b) of the Convention, which states that 'the detention or imprisonment of a child ... shall be used only as a measure of last resort and for the shortest appropriate period of time'. Similarly, the legislation under consideration contradicts Article 40(1) of the Convention, which requires parties to:

> recognise the right of every child ... to be treated in a manner consistent with the promotion of the child's sense of dignity and worth, which ... takes into account the child's age and the desirability of promoting the child's reintegration and the child's assuming a constructive role in society.

These infringements heavily influenced the Senate Select Committee on Legal and Constitutional References when delivering its report on the Human Rights (Mandatory Sentencing of Property Offences) Bill 2000 (Cth).[114] That report was highly critical of Western Australia's 'three strikes' laws. The passing of the Bill would have overridden the Western Australian legislation for conflicting with Australia's international obligations. However, the Bill did not proceed because a majority of the committee recommended that the State government should have the opportunity to address the 'deleterious effect of mandatory sentencing on Indigenous youth'.[115] Regrettably, the Western Australian government has, to date, refused to restrict or abolish the offending legislation. We submit that the federal Parliament should act forthwith to abolish the legislation because the concept of mandatory sentences is offensive to the principles of judicial independence and individual justice (especially when it concerns Aboriginal juveniles), which are fundamental to the rule of law.

In the final analysis, the emergence of fixed penalty schemes such as mandatory penalties and grid sentencing should be seen for what they are—efforts by the legislature to restrict or curtail the traditional role of the courts of effecting individualised criminal justice.[116] Unless the legislature has a sound reason for tampering with this time-honoured sentencing practice in these very intrusive ways, it should desist from doing so. One such reason might be that the courts have displayed regular and unacceptably high levels of leniency in sentencing. However, the reality is that, except for a few instances that may have been dramatised by the media, the courts have largely followed long-established sentencing principles that require the punishment to fit the particular crime as well as the offender. A more plausible reason is that the politicians regard the area of sentencing as a rich lode from which to feed their political agenda of winning votes by being 'tough' on crime. In the following comment, Neil Morgan describes the current situation and sets out what should be done:

Sentencing has become the most politicised area of law in Australia and mandatory and [grid] schemes represent the most overt attempts to impose political control over sentencers. Consequently, advocates of fixed penalties cannot simply propose abstract structure: they must first explain how we can develop a regime which is above excessive political pressures. Then, a second issue would arise: once the legislature has control over sentencing levels, how can the grid or other model be protected from future political pressure and tinkering?[117]

# Sentencing drug-dependent offenders

The failure of traditional law enforcement efforts to deal with drug-related crime is well documented.[118] This includes the whole range of sentencing measures that have been tried at one time or another to deal with drug-dependent offenders.[119] The likely explanation for this is that the courts have inclined towards a punitive rather than a rehabilitative solution to the problem. For example, particularly in cases of serious offences where deterrence is considered necessary, the courts are likely to discount the fact that the offender had committed the offence to fund his or her drug addiction.

Recently, several jurisdictions have trialled the use of specialist courts to deal with drug-dependent offenders.[120] The ideology of these drug courts differs from that of the conventional courts in recognising that drug-addiction is not a form of wilful self-indulgence that can be deterred by punishment. Instead, the offender requires treatment and other means of support to help him or her break the drug habit. The drug courts have a mixture of criminal justice and therapeutic aims. Thus, the *Drug Rehabilitation (Court Diversion) Act* 1999 (Qld) provides that its objectives are to reduce:

- the level of drug dependency in the community
- the level of criminal activity associated with drug dependency
- health risks to the community associated with drug dependency
- pressure on resources in the court and prison systems.[121]

The Act goes on to provide that these objectives are to be achieved by establishing a pilot program to:

- identify drug-dependent persons who are suitable to receive intensive drug rehabilitation
- improve their ability to function as law-abiding citizens
- improve their employability
- improve their health.

The structure, administration and powers of drug courts vary with each jurisdiction. The Queensland model provides a good idea of what these courts do. There, drug courts are presided over by a magistrate who has jurisdiction over all drug offence cases. After hearing the relevant pleas and assessment, the court may make an Intensive Drug Rehabilitation Order. Under this order, the court must record a conviction and sentence the offender to a term of imprisonment, which sentence is then suspended. The order will include requiring the offender to undergo drug-abuse education, preventing and managing relapse programs, anger management, and ending offending and social reintegration and life skills programs. The court may also order the offender to pay compensation or perform community service or other tasks that the magistrate considers may assist with rehabilitation. Upon termination of the order, due either to its successful completion or failure, the court must reconsider the initial sentence and impose the 'final' sentence, which may be any sentence that the court is empowered to otherwise impose. When considering the final sentence, the court will consider the extent to which the offender participated in the rehabilitation programs. Should the court decide to impose a term of imprisonment, the term must be no longer than the initial sentence, and it may be suspended.

The following comment by Arie Freiberg sums up the use of drug courts to date, and offers a view concerning their future potential:

> On balance, Australia is right in experimenting with drug courts, providing that they are rigorously and carefully evaluated and carefully targeted at those who are most likely to benefit. Probably, like the children's court a century before, they will find a small, but important niche in the judicial system, after having provided it with a wider range of ideas and innovations which the broader system will have absorbed and which will come to be regarded as part of the 'traditional' justice system ...[122]

# Conclusion

Sentencing is a complex function. The sentencing judge has the unenviable task of sifting through a host of facts in a procedurally fair manner, deciding along the way whether they are relevant to the sentencing decision. Having accomplished that, he or she will then have to categorise the facts into aggravating and mitigating factors and determine the weight to be given to each. But accounting for these facts alone is not enough. In deciding on the appropriate sentence, the judge must reflect on the often competing aims of sentencing, comply with any judicial or legislative guidelines on sentencing, note any relevant sentencing trends and practices, and hope that the proposed sentence is in tune with community standards and expectations. Throughout these deliberations, the judge is required to keep in mind that the proposed penalty should meet the dual requirements of sentencing consistency and sufficiency in the quantum of punishment.

Quite clearly, the judge requires every possible assistance in discharging the sentencing function. Assistance can come from the judiciary itself by way of detailed sentencing guidelines from the higher courts, stating the reasons for sentencing, and conducting judicial training courses on sentencing. However, these are inadequate. There is a need for some legislative regulation of the instinctive approach to sentencing. Legislative measures include a prescribed hierarchy of sentencing aims, a hierarchy of offences according to seriousness, a hierarchy of penalties according to severity, and the drawing up of a list of facts relevant to sentencing. Another important source of assistance would be in providing sentencers with ready access to vital information such as statistics on sentences imposed for the same offence, the prevalence of the offence, and public opinion about it. Only with such measures in place can there be a good chance that justice will properly be meted out in the sentencing exercise.

While legislative measures are needed to improve the quality of justice in sentencing, they must not be allowed to replace the sentencing discretion of the courts. In this respect, the recent emergence of mandatory minimum penalties is disturbing. On the other hand, a strong case can be made for legislative measures requiring certain types of offenders, on account of their special needs, to be dealt with outside of the traditional sentencing exercise. The disposal of juvenile offenders before children's courts is one example, and the newly established drug courts for offenders with drug-abuse problems is another.

## Notes

1   In line with chapter 7 the term 'punishment' denotes, conceptually, the consequence of breaching the criminal law. 'Penalty' is the particular form of sentence that is imposed on an offender.

2   *Punishment and Responsibility: Essays in the Philosophy of Law*, Clarendon Press, Oxford, 1968, pp. 4–5, and endorsed by the Victorian Sentencing Committee in its report, *Sentencing*, Vol. 1, Melbourne, 1988, para. 3.2.

3   A. Ashworth, 'Criminal Justice, Rights and Sentencing: A Review of Sentencing Policy and Problems' in I. Potas (ed.), *Sentencing in Australia: Issues, Policy and Reform*, Proceedings of a seminar on Sentencing: Problems and Prospects, Canberra, 1986, pp. 43–4.

4   Entry into force in 1976 and adopted by Australia in 1980. For a similar provision, see Article 10 of the *Universal Declaration of Human Rights*.

5   Report No. 44, *Sentencing*, Sydney, 1988, para. 26.

6   *Lowe* (1984) 154 CLR 606 at 610–11, per Mason J.

7   See *Pantorno* (1989) 63 ALJR 317 where the High Court displayed a healthy obsession with procedural fairness at the sentencing stage.

8   (1988) 164 CLR 465 at 476; *Scholes* [1999] 1 VR 337 at 346; *Ryan* [2001] HCA 21 at para. [49].

9   N. Walker, *Why Punish?*, Oxford University Press, Oxford, 1991, p. 3.

10   *Williscroft* [1975] VR 292 at 300.

11   P. Sallmann and J. Willis, *Criminal Justice in Australia*, Melbourne, 1984, p. 184. Recent research suggests that about 90% of all criminal charges are dealt with when an offender is convicted on her or his own plea of guilty: Australian Law Reform Commission, Discussion Paper No. 29, *Sentencing: Procedure*, Sydney, 1987, p. 25.

12  See *Warby* (1983) 9 A Crim R 349; *Marshall* [1981] VR 725; *Tait and Bartley* (1979) 24 ALR 473.

13  *De Simoni* (1981) 147 CLR 383 at 389, per Gibbs CJ.

14  *Law v Deed* [1970] SASR 374 at 379; *Nash v Haas*, Tasmanian Supreme Court, unreported, 15 February 1972, per Burbury CJ.

15  *Olbrich* (1999) 166 ALR 330; *Weininger* (2003) 196 ALR 451.

16  S. Odgers, casenote on *Olbrich*, *Criminal Law Journal*, 23, 1999, p. 376 at 380.

17  See chapter 9.

18  *Jamieson* (1988) 50 SASR 130; *Casey and Wells* (1986) 20 A Crim R 191.

19  *Tait and Bartley* (1979) 24 ALR 473 at 477. See also *Travers* (1983) 34 SASR 112 at 116.

20  *Lucas* [1973] VR 693 at 705.

21  *Hunter* (1988) 62 ALJR 432; *Ex parte Kent; re Callighan* [1969] 2 NSWR 184.

22  Of course, the need for legal representation arises earlier in the criminal justice process such as at the investigation stage, and the preparation for the defence.

23  Sallmann and Willis, 1984, pp. 183–8.

24  The Article states in part: 'Nor shall a heavier penalty be imposed than the one that was applicable at the time when the criminal offence was committed'. See also Article 11(2) of the *Universal Declaration of Human Rights*.

25  *Williscroft* [1975] VR 292 at 301, per Adam and Crockett JJ.

26  D. Thomas, *Principles of Sentencing*, 2nd edn, Heinemann, London, 1979, ch. 2.

27  For example, see *Criminal Law (Sentencing) Act* 1988 (SA), s. 7(1); *Sentencing Act* 1991 (Vic), Part 6 Div 1A; *Sentencing Act* 1995 (WA), ss. 13, 24–26. See further chapter 10, pp. 364–5.

28  Denunciation is a justification for punishment often associated with retributivism: see the Victorian Sentencing Committee report, 1988, para. 3.8.

29  ALRC, *Sentencing*, 1988, para. 181.

30  *Crimes Act* 1900 (ACT), s. 429B(e).

31  *Veen (No. 2)* (1988) 164 CLR 465 at 477.

32  This is borne out in the later case of *Baumer* (1988) 166 CLR 51 at 57 where the High Court said: 'It would clearly be wrong if, because of the record, his Honour was intending to increase the sentence beyond what he considered to be an appropriate sentence for the instant offence'.

33  Article 14(7).

34  For example, see *Ainsworth v D (A child)* (1992) 7 WAR 102; *R v T* (1993) 67 A Crim R 272; *Child Welfare Act* 1960 (Tas), s. 4; *Children and Young Persons Act* 1989 (Vic), s. 139(1).

35  The legislatures of some jurisdictions have reacted to repeat offenders of some of these offences by implementing a scheme of mandatory sentences: see below, p. 270.

36  For a further discussion, see chapter 10, pp. 339–41.

37  Obviously, it would be racist for an accused's ethnicity to be regarded as an aggravating factor in sentencing: see chapter 10, pp. 329-30.

38  Australian Law Reform Commission, *Multiculturalism and the Law*, Report 57, Canberra, 1992, paras 813 ff.

39  *Gordan* (1994) 71 A Crim R 459. Principles to be applied in the sentencing of Aboriginal people are discussed in *Fernando* (1994) 76 A Crim R 58 at 62–3.

40  *Fuller-Cust* [2002] VSCA 168 at para. 65 per Eames J. See further, R. Edney, 'Sentencing of Indigenous Offenders in Victoria', *Law Institute Journal*, 32, 2003, p. 32.

41  *R v C* (1994) 75 A Crim R 309; *Gallagher* (1991) 23 NSWLR 220; *Golding* (1980) 24 SASR 161. For examples of legislation, see *Sentencing Act* 1995 (NT), s. 5(2)(h); *Penalties and Sentences Act* 1992 (Qld), s. 9(2)(i).

42  *Neal* (1982) 42 ALR 609 at 617, per Murphy J citing *Harris* [1967] SASR 316.

43  *Gray* [1977] VR 225 at 231.

44  ALRC, *Sentencing*, 1988, para. 173.

45  *Cameron* (2002) 76 ALJR 382.

46  *Crimes (Sentencing Procedure) Act* 1999 (NSW), s. 22 and discussed in the New South Wales Court of Criminal Appeal case of *Sharma* (2002) 130 A Crim R 238.

47  *Polterman*, unreported, 2 August 1974, and discussed in R. Fox and A. Freiberg, *Sentencing: State and Federal Law in Victoria*, Oxford University Press, Melbourne, 1985, pp. 488–9.

48  ALRC, *Sentencing* (1988), para. 172.

49  Section 16A (2)(p).

50  *Riley*, unreported serial no. 73/1986 and quoted in K. Warner, *Sentencing in Tasmania*, Federation Press, Sydney, 1991, p. 289.

51  *Lowe* (1984) 154 CLR 606 at 622, per Dawson J. See now *Postiglione* (1997) 189 CLR 295 where the High Court has held that parity of sentencing of co-offenders should be tempered by the totality principle. This principle requires the court to have regard for the total effect of a series of sentences imposed on an offender and to avoid imposing a sentence that is so 'crushing' as to discourage rehabilitation altogether.

52  These are discussed in detail in Fox and Freiberg, 1985, ch. 11, 'The Laws of Australia', *Criminal Sentencing*, Law Book Co., Sydney, 12, 1996, para. 12.2.

53  *Leech v McCall* (1986) 41 SASR 96 at 99–100, per Cox J.

54  ALRC, *Sentencing*, 1988, para. 164.

55  As above, para. 163.

56  *Lowe* (1984) 54 ALR 193 at 196, per Mason J.

57  ALRC, *Sentencing*, 1988, para. 155.

58  As above, para. 28.

59  For example, the Australian Law Reform Commission, Report No. 15, *Sentencing of Federal Offenders*, Sydney, 1980, paras 162–6; Victorian Sentencing Committee's Discussion Paper, *Sentencing*, Melbourne, 1987, para. 5.6; ALRC report, *Sentencing*, 1988, para. 156.

60  See Sallmann and Willis, 1984, pp. 166–70.

61  D. Weatherburn, 'Sentencing for What?' in M. Findlay, S. Egger and J. Sutton (eds), *Issues in Criminal Justice Administration*, George Allen & Unwin, Sydney, 1983, p. 126.

62  ALRC, *Sentencing*, 1988, para. 156.

63  Extract from submission of Supreme Court judges to the Victorian Sentencing Committee, reproduced in the Committee's Report, 1988, at para. 2.10.13.

64  *Penalties and Sentences Act* 1985 (Vic), s. 11. This Act has since been replaced by the *Sentencing Act* 1991 (Vic), which does not contain such a provision.

65  *O'Connor* [1987] VR 496 at 499.

66  Walker, 1991, pp. 124–5.

67  For example, ALRC, *Sentencing*, 1988; the Victorian Sentencing Committee, 1988; and the Victorian Sentencing Review, 2002.

68  R. Fox, 'Controlling Sentencers', *Australian and New Zealand Journal of Criminology*, 20, 1987, p. 226. See further chapter 9, p. 311.

69   J. Chan, 'The Limits of Sentencing Reform' in G. Zdenkowski, C. Ronalds and M. Richardson (eds), *The Criminal Injustice System*, Vol. 2, Pluto Press, Sydney, 1987, p. 207.

70   G. Zdenkowski, 'Sentencing: Problems and Responsibility' in D. Chappell and P. Wilson (eds), *The Australian Criminal Justice System: The Mid-80s*, Butterworths, Sydney, 1986, p. 213.

71   As above, pp. 213–14.

72   See chapter 7.

73   Walker, 1991, p. 9 and Part III.

74   Victorian Sentencing Committee report, 1988, para. 3.14.11.

75   *Veen (No. 1)* (1979) 143 CLR 458 and its sequel, *Veen (No. 2)* (1988) 164 CLR 465. See R. Fox, 'The Killings of Bobby Veen: The High Court on Proportion in Sentencing', *Criminal Law Journal*, 12, 1988, p. 339.

76   *Veen (No. 2)* (1988) 164 CLR 465 at 472. See also *Hoare* (1989) 167 CLR 348 at 391; and *McGarry* [2001] HCA 62 at para. [60] in relation to legislatively prescribed indefinite sentences.

77   *Ryan* [2001] HCA 21 at para. [46] per McHugh J.

78   See further R. Fox, 'The Meaning of Proportionality in Sentencing', *Melbourne University Law Review*, 19, 1994, p. 489.

79   N. Morris, *The Future of Imprisonment*, University of Chicago Press, Chicago, 1974, pp. 60–1 and cited in the Committee's report at para. 3.12.

80   The Article goes on to provide for the most favourable law to be applied where there has been a reduction in the criminal penalties after the commission of an offence.

81   A. Ashworth, 'Four Techniques for Reducing Sentences' in A. von Hirsch and A. Ashworth (eds), *Principled Sentencing: Readings on Theory and Practice*, Oxford University Press, Oxford, 1998, pp. 229–30.

82   Certain legislative measures, notably grid sentencing systems, do unduly curtail judicial discretion and should be avoided. These systems impose a presumptive sentence for specific offences, deviation from which will create an automatic right of appeal. The Western Australian government proposed such a system in 1998, which was abandoned after it was strongly criticised by the judiciary.

83   N. Morris, 'The Sentencing Disease', *Judges Journal*, 18, 1979, p. 11.

84   Victorian Sentencing Committee report, 1988, para. 2.10.13.

85   As above.

86   *Sentencing Act* 1991 (Vic), and see R. Fox, 'Order Out of Chaos: Victoria's New Maximum Penalty Structure', *Monash University Law Review*, 17, 1991, p. 106. Earlier, a similar but less comprehensive penalty structure was introduced into South Australia by the *Statutes Amendment and Repeal (Sentencing) Act* 1988 (SA).

87   Review of Commonwealth Criminal Law, General Principles of Criminal Responsibility, Fifth Interim Report, 1991, ch. 16.

88   Victorian Sentencing Committee report, 1988, para. 2.10.11.

89   *Crimes (Sentencing Procedure) Act* 1999 (NSW), s. 21A; *Sentencing Act* 1995 (WA), ss. 7 and 8.

90   *Crimes (Sentencing Procedure) Act* 1999 (NSW), ss. 3A, 21A and 54A.

91   *Way* [2004] NSWCCA 131.

92   This issue was the subject of the first guideline judgment of the court: see *Jurisic* (1998) 45 NSWLR 209.

93   K. Warner, 'The Role of Guideline Judgments in the Law and Order Debate in Australia', *Criminal Law Journal*, 27, 2003, p. 8; D. Shroff, 'The Future of Guideline Judgments', *Current Issues in Criminal Justice*, 14, 2003, p. 316.

94  *Crimes (Sentencing Procedure) Act* 1999 (NSW), ss. 36–42A.

95  *Sentencing Act* 1991 (Vic), s. 6AB; *Sentencing Act* 1995 (WA), s. 143.

96  ALRC, *Sentencing*, 1988, para. 161.

97  J. Nicholson, 'Resentencing Serious Offenders: A Commentary on the New South Wales Model', *Criminal Law Journal*, 16, 1992, p. 216.

98  *Sentencing Act* 1991 (Vic), s. 108C. See also the New South Wales Sentencing Council, which was established by the *Crimes (Sentencing Procedure) Act* 1999 (NSW), Part 8B.

99  Zdenkowski, p. 236.

100  *Kevenaar* [2004] NSWCCA 210.

101  *Inkson* (1996) 6 Tas R 1; *Causby* (1984) 17 A Crim R 461.

102  For example, see the study by D. Indermaur, 'Public Perception of Sentencing in Perth, Western Australia', *Australian and New Zealand Journal of Criminology*, 20, 1987, p. 163; A Lovegrove, 'Judicial Sentencing Policy, Criminological Expertise and Public Opinion', *Australian and New Zealand Journal of Criminology*, 31, 1998, p. 287.

103  P. Wilson, J. Walker and S. Mukherjee, 'How the Public Sees Crime: An Australian Survey' in P. Wilson (ed.), *Trends and Issues in Crime and Criminal Justice*, No. 2, 1986, p. 1.

104  N. Cowdery, 'Whose sentences: the judges', the public's or Alan Jones?' *Australian Journal of Forensic Sciences*, 34, 2002, p. 55.

105  D. Spears, 'Sentencing Discretion: Sentencing in the Jurisic Age', *University of New South Wales Law Journal*, 22, 1999, p. 300.

106  Fifteenth Report of the Expenditure Committee, *The Reduction of Pressure on the Prison System*, 1977–1978, Vol. 1, para. 33. For a recent comment on the English position, see S. Shute, 'The Place of Public Opinion in Sentencing Law', *Criminal Law Review*, 1998, p. 465. See also, Cowdery, as above, pp. 54–6.

107  *Sentencing Act* 1992 (Vic). See R. Fox, 1991, p. 106.

108  For example, in New South Wales and Victoria.

109  'The courts and public opinion', *Bar News*, Winter, 2002, pp. 33, 35.

110  By virtue of the *Criminal Code Amendment Act (No. 2)* 1996 (WA). For a review of the Northern Territory and Western Australian laws, see Jonas, *Human Rights and Equal Opportunity Commission, Social Justice Report 2001*, 2002, available at <http://www.human-rights.gov.au/social_justice>.

111  *Border Protection (Validation and Enforcement Powers) Act* 2001 (Cth), Schedule 2, amending the *Migration Act* 1958 (Cth), ss. 232A and 233A.

112  *Katherine Juvenile Justice Crime Workshop Outcome Document*, 1995.

113  R. Funston, 'Mandatory Sentences for Juveniles: Misguided Policy', paper presented at the National Conference of Community Legal Centres, Adelaide University, 9 September 1997, p. 7. See also M. Flynn, 'One Strike and You're Out!', *Alternative Law Journal*, Vol. 22, 1997, p. 72.

114  The Bill was introduced by three senators and provided that Commonwealth, State and Territory laws must not require a court to sentence a person to imprisonment for an offence committed by a person under 18 years of age, and existing laws with such a requirement were to have no force and effect after the Bill's commencement as an Act.

115  Report on the Inquiry into the Human Rights (Mandatory Sentencing of Property Offences) Bill 2000 (Cth), 2002.

116  D. Brown, 'The Politics of Law and Order', *Law Society Journal*, 40, 2002, p. 64.

117  N. Morgan, 'Why We Should Not Have Mandatory Penalties: Theoretical Structures and Political Realities', *Adelaide Law Review*, 23, 2002, p. 141.

118   See the Victorian Premier's Drug Advisory Council, *Drugs and Our Community*, Melbourne, 1996.

119   They include assessment panels, bail schemes, conditional sentences, deferred sentences, suspended sentences, and treatment regimes in and after custody.

120   For a good description and critique of these courts, see A. Freiberg, 'Australian Drug Courts', *Criminal Law Journal*, 24, 2000, p. 213.

121   Section 3.

122   Freiberg, 2000, p. 235.

# 9

# Appeals

## Introduction

Article 14(5) of the *International Covenant on Civil and Political Rights* states:

> Everyone convicted of a crime shall have the right to his conviction and sentence being reviewed by a higher tribunal according to law.

However, it is questionable whether this principle is fully applied in Australia, at least in appeals from the higher courts. As we noted in chapter 5, there are important differences between trials in the lower and higher courts. Similarly, there are significant differences between appeals from decisions made in the lower and higher courts. However, in the case of appeals, their relative position is reversed. Whereas trials in the lower courts lack a number of the procedural safeguards operating in higher court trials, appeals from the lower courts are easier than from the higher courts. These appeals are usually as of right and involve a full rehearing. The higher up the court hierarchy a case proceeds, the more restricted is the possibility of appeal and the more formalistic appeals become.

Thus, convictions in the lower courts tend to be more easily appealed against than convictions in the higher courts. In most jurisdictions, appeals against conviction and sentence in the lower courts tend to be as of right, whereas an appeal against conviction in a higher court will only be available as of right if it involves a question of law, rather than a question of fact, or mixed fact and law. Similarly, as we shall see below, appeals against a sentence imposed in a higher court always require leave to appeal.[1]

Further, the nature of the appeal varies, depending on whether the conviction was imposed in a lower or higher court. Appeals against conviction by a jury usually require the appellant to demonstrate appealable legal error or that the verdict was completely unreasonable. In contrast, in most jurisdictions, an appeal from a summary conviction in the lower courts is by way of a complete rehearing of the original charge, although the appeal court may (with the consent of the parties) rely on the transcript of the first trial. While this system of complete rehearing provides magistrates with little guidance,[2] it offers the convicted defendant an unlimited opportunity to seek acquittal before a new court.

In this chapter we shall focus on appeals from conviction and sentence in the higher courts, since it is these that impose significant procedural and substantive limitations. However, we should also note other types of appeal available within the criminal justice system. Appeals are not limited to appeals against conviction or sentence. It is usually also possible to appeal against court decisions regarding investigative powers, such as search warrants, and aspects of pre-trial procedure, such as committal hearings.

Even during the conduct of a summary trial, issues may arise that permit appellate review. Thus, the Supreme Courts in all jurisdictions possess a general power to supervise lower courts and tribunals to ensure that they are acting lawfully, within the scope of their powers. This supervisory jurisdiction is invoked by application for one of the prerogative writs, or for a declaration, or some statutory remedy of a similar nature.

Further, a 'case stated' procedure is commonly available to refer a dispute regarding a question of law arising during a trial in both the lower and higher courts. Thus, for example, section 446 of the Victorian *Crimes Act* 1958 provides that if, on the hearing of any appeal in a criminal proceeding to the County Court from the Magistrates' Court, a question or difficulty in point of law arises, the judge may reserve the question of law for determination by the Full Supreme Court. The judge who reserves the question of law must state a case, setting out the questions that have been reserved and the relevant facts of the case. The superior court then decides the questions of law on the basis of the facts found by the lower court. Similarly, it is usually possible for the prosecution in a criminal trial to have a question of law reviewed on this basis, without challenging any acquittal.

Finally, the possibility of a second appeal to a higher level of the court hierarchy is rigidly circumscribed. Thus, appeals to the High Court of Australia may only take place by special leave.[3] Broad criteria for the granting of special leave are contained in the *Judiciary Act* 1903 (Cth), which include the general importance of the question of law involved and the need to resolve differences of opinion between different courts and jurisdictions. The High Court normally refuses special leave on issues of fact or cases where it is being asked to take a different view of the evidence than the court below. In respect of sentencing appeals, the High Court has made it clear that it will only grant special leave to appeal in exceptional circumstances. It will never grant special leave simply on the basis that the sentence imposed was excessive.[4] While these restrictive rules are unfortunate, it must be accepted that the High Court can only hear a small number of appeals each year and has no alternative but to be very selective.

# Appeal against conviction

## Conditions of appeal

While in almost all Australian jurisdictions it is not possible for the prosecution to appeal against a verdict of not guilty in a higher court,[5] statutory provisions in all jurisdictions allow a person convicted in such a court to have certain prescribed bases for appeal. In Queensland, for example, a person convicted on indictment may appeal to the Court of Criminal Appeal under section 668D of the *Criminal Code*:

(a) against his conviction on any ground which involves a question of law alone; and

(b) with the leave of the Court, or upon the certificate of the judge of the court of trial that it is a fit case for appeal, against his conviction on any ground of appeal which involves a question of fact alone, or question of mixed law and fact, or on any other ground which appears to the Court to be a sufficient ground of appeal.

Some jurisdictions limit the right to appeal even further by providing that appeals regarding some questions of law will require leave where there had been no objection on the issue by defence counsel at the trial. Thus, rule 4 of the *Criminal Appeal Rules* in New South Wales provides:

No direction, omission to direct, or decision as to the admission or rejection of evidence, given by the Judge presiding at the trial, shall, without the leave of the Court, be allowed as a ground for appeal or an application for leave to appeal unless objection was taken at the trial to the direction, omission, or decision by the party appealing or applying for leave to appeal.

Such provisions do not apply where the defendant is unrepresented. Even if there was legal representation, leave to appeal will be granted if the 'direction, omission to direct, or decision as to the admission or rejection of evidence' is shown to have caused a miscarriage of justice.[6] The purpose of these provisions is to ensure that potential problems are raised at the trial and hopefully corrected— not simply left as a possible basis for appeal. Even those jurisdictions that do not have a formal provision of this type take a similar approach to grounds of appeal regarding alleged errors where no complaint was made at the trial.[7] On the other hand, the failure of defence counsel to complain may have arisen from incompetence. The courts have recognised that in extreme circumstances of 'flagrant incompetence' a miscarriage of justice may well result.[8]

# Basis of review

The basis of appellate review against conviction[9] is contained within statutory provisions in all jurisdictions. For example, section 6 of the New South Wales *Criminal Appeal Act* 1912 provides:

> (1) The court on any appeal under section 5(1) against conviction shall allow the appeal if it is of the opinion that the verdict of the jury should be set aside on the ground that it is unreasonable, or cannot be supported, having regard to the evidence, or that the judgment of the court of trial should be set aside on the ground of the wrong decision of any question of law, or that on any other ground whatsoever there was a miscarriage of justice, and in any other case shall dismiss the appeal; provided that the court may, notwithstanding that it is of the opinion that the point or points raised by the appeal might be decided in favour of the appellant, dismiss the appeal if it considers that no substantial miscarriage of justice has actually occurred.

The proviso to this section is very significant. It means that an appeal court may dismiss an appeal, even if satisfied that there was some error at the trial or risk of miscarriage of justice. The justification for this is that, despite the popular idea that appeals are allowed on 'technicalities', an appeal should not succeed unless the appeal court is satisfied that there is a real risk that an innocent person was wrongly convicted.

In *Dietrich v The Queen*, the majority of the High Court emphasised that appellate intervention will depend on a conclusion that the appellant lost a real chance of acquittal. Chief Justice Mason and Justice McHugh explained:

> [A]ppellate courts in this country do not interfere with convictions entered at trial purely on the basis that there was unfairness to the accused in the conduct of the trial. The appellate jurisdiction in criminal matters depends upon a conclusion that there was a 'miscarriage of justice' such that the applicant 'has thereby lost "a chance which was fairly open to him of being acquitted" … or "a real chance of acquittal" ', to repeat the expression used by Brennan, Dawson and Toohey JJ in *Wilde v R*.[10]

This approach raises the question whether appellate review is a sufficient safeguard to ensure fair trials in general. There is another line of authority within the High Court to the effect that a 'fundamental flaw' in a trial will necessitate a miscarriage of justice without any investigation of the prospects of acquittal. The issue then becomes when a 'flaw' is sufficiently important to be 'fundamental'. In *Wilde v The Queen*, Justices Brennan, Dawson and Toohey stated:

> the proviso has no application where an irregularity has occurred which is such a departure from the essential requirements of the law that it goes to the root of the proceedings. If that has occurred, then it can be said, without considering the effect of the irregularity upon the jury's verdict, that the accused has not had a proper trial and that there has been a substantial miscarriage of justice.[11]

This approach was endorsed by a majority of the High Court in *Glennon v The Queen*.[12] However, as Justice Deane said in *Wilde*, the 'fundamental prescript of the administration of criminal justice in this country is that no person should be convicted of a serious crime except by the verdict of a jury after a fair trial according to law'.[13] If there has not been a fair trial according to law, the conviction is intrinsically flawed and it should not be open to an appeal court to say that, in its view, the appellant 'is so obviously guilty that the requirement of a fair trial according to law can be dispensed with'.[14] Justice Deane explained:

> If it were otherwise, the fundamental prescript of the criminal law could be reduced to a mockery and the injustice of a conviction without a relevantly fair trial according to law could be made the occasion for trial by appellate judges who had seen no witnesses, heard no evidence and had no direct contact with the atmosphere, the tensions, the nuances or the reality of the actual trial.[15]

Justice Deane, along with Justice Gaudron, repeated this view in *Glennon*, but they were in the minority of the court. Yet, in our view, even their approach would not go far enough. The principle should not be limited to ensuring a fair trial. If there has been significant malpractice in the process of investigation[16] or prosecution,[17] that should also result in a successful appeal and, as a minimum, a new trial.

In certain circumstances, an appeal court will admit new evidence at the appeal. For example, section 574 of the Victorian *Crimes Act* 1958 permits the Full Court of the Supreme Court of Victoria to allow the admission of new evidence upon an appeal if it thinks it necessary or expedient in the interests of justice. It does not matter that the evidence is not 'fresh' in the sense that it was not available to the defence and could not have become available by the exercise of reasonable diligence. The appeal will succeed if the new material shows the appellant to be innocent or raises such a doubt about guilt that the verdict should not be allowed to stand.[18] If the evidence is in fact 'fresh', the verdict will not be allowed to stand and a new trial will be ordered if the appeal court considers the evidence was capable of being accepted by a jury and there is a significant possibility that the jury would have acquitted the defendant.[19] This may be the case even where the evidence only goes to the credibility of a prosecution witness.

Where no legal error occurred in the course of the trial and there is no new evidence, appeal courts have traditionally been slow to allow an appeal on the ground that the conviction was 'unreasonable, or cannot be supported, according to the evidence' (to use the statutory language) or 'unsafe and unsatisfactory' (to use the terminology that was, until recently, more fashionable). In *Chamberlain v The Queen*, the High Court stated that the test was:

> whether the jury, acting reasonably, must have entertained a sufficient doubt to have entitled the accused to an acquittal, that is, must have entertained a reasonable doubt as to the guilt of the accused.[20]

We discussed the *Chamberlain* case in chapter 6. In deciding the appeal against conviction by the Chamberlains, a majority of the High Court took the view that it is not open to a jury to be satisfied beyond reasonable doubt that a fact exists where there is a conflict between two groups of expert witnesses on the issue, no real challenge is made to the expertise or impartiality of either group of experts, and the jury is not in a position to resolve the conflict.[21] They concluded that the evidence relating to the finding of foetal blood in the Chamberlains' car was in this position and they excluded it from their consideration of whether the convictions were safe. However, this did not result in the appeal being allowed.

The majority, after considering all the problems with the prosecution evidence, concluded that there was still sufficient evidence in the case to justify the jury's verdict. In contrast, Justice Murphy, dissenting, pointed out that:

> it is not good enough to take the view that this evidence of foetal blood can be set aside, and to look at the rest of the evidence to see if the verdict can be sustained. If that is done the reasoning runs like this. Because of the verdict the jury must have disbelieved not only Mrs Chamberlain and Mr Chamberlain but also [other witnesses present at the scene] and rejected other evidence which might have raised a reasonable doubt. They therefore rejected the dog or dingo hypothesis leaving murder as the only possibility; therefore the verdict can stand. The error in this approach is that the jury's view of the exculpatory evidence may well have been taken in the light of their acceptance of the scientific evidence as reliable, an acceptance contributed to by the trial judge's summing up. Likewise with other adverse conclusions, and the finding of guilt itself. If in accordance with the directions, the jury accepted the evidence that the blood was foetal, it was inevitable that they should then disbelieve Mrs Chamberlain and the other evidence pointing to her innocence ... Once it is accepted that it was unsafe to conclude that there was foetal blood in the car then the conviction of Mrs Chamberlain was unsafe.[22]

One would have to say that this dissenting view was vindicated by the conclusion of the subsequent Royal Commission that the evidence fell 'far short of proving that Azaria was not taken by a dingo'. Cases such as that of the Chamberlains raised serious questions concerning the adequacy of the appeal process and the narrow approach adopted by some appellate judges. In 1994, in *M v The Queen*, the High Court reconsidered the test for concluding that a verdict is 'unsafe and unsatisfactory'. The majority of the court stated that:

> the question which the court must ask itself is whether it thinks that upon the whole of the evidence it was open to the jury to be established beyond reasonable doubt that the accused was guilty. But in answering that question the court must not disregard or discount either the consideration that the jury is the body entrusted with the primary responsibility of determining the guilt or innocence, or the consideration that the jury has had the benefit of having seen and heard the witnesses ... In most cases a doubt experienced by an appellate court will be a

doubt which a jury ought also to have experienced. It is only where a jury's advantage in seeing and hearing the evidence is capable of resolving a doubt experienced by a court of criminal appeal that the court may conclude that no miscarriage of justice has occurred.[23]

Despite this somewhat ambivalent language, it appears that the High Court intended in this case to expand the scope of appellate review of convictions. On this approach, if appeal court judges themselves harbour a reasonable doubt as to the defendant's guilt then, in most cases, they should allow an appeal against conviction. However, many appellate judges continue to show a marked reluctance to overturn jury verdicts.[24] For example, there was a period when a significant number of appeals succeeded on the basis that the apparent inconsistency of a jury in convicting on some counts in an indictment but not on others tended to indicate that they had been 'unreasonable' (perhaps 'compromising' to achieve unanimity), but the High Court has acted to limit such appeals by emphasising that an appeal must fail if there is some plausible explanation for the verdicts consistent with the jury proceeding in accordance with their oath.[25]

## Powers of disposal

In each of the Australian jurisdictions the appeal court may, if it allows the appeal, either direct a judgment and verdict of acquittal to be entered or direct the holding of a new trial. The High Court has explained:

> The power to grant a new trial is a discretionary one and in deciding whether to exercise it the court which has quashed the conviction must decide whether the interests of justice require a new trial to be had. In so deciding, the court should first consider whether the admissible evidence given at the original trial was sufficiently cogent to justify a conviction, for if it was not it would be wrong by making an order for a new trial to give the prosecution an opportunity to supplement a defective case ... Then the court must take into account any circumstances that might render it unjust to the accused to make him stand trial again, remembering however that the public interest in the proper administration of justice must be considered as well as the interests of the individual accused.[26]

Alternatively, the appeal court may substitute a verdict of guilty of some other offence if it was one of which the accused could have been convicted on the indictment, and the appeal court concludes that the jury must have been satisfied of facts that prove that the defendant was guilty of that offence.

## Other review mechanisms

Before we leave the topic of appeals against conviction, we should note another mechanism available to a convicted person for review of the conviction (apart from the possibility of a Royal Commission). Some jurisdictions have statutory provisions which permit the establishment of an inquiry (usually by a higher court judge) into the correctness of a conviction. For example, Part 13A of the New South Wales *Crimes Act* 1900, enacted in 1993, provides that, where 'there is a doubt or question as to the convicted person's guilt, as to any mitigating circumstances in the case or as to any part of the evidence in a case', the Governor or the Supreme Court 'may direct that an inquiry be conducted by a prescribed person into the conviction or sentence' or the case may be referred to the Court of Criminal Appeal to be dealt with as an appeal. Where an inquiry by a prescribed person is held, the person conducting it has the powers and immunities of a Royal Commissioner. A report is prepared and the matter may then be referred to the Court of Criminal Appeal for consideration of whether the conviction should be quashed or the sentence reviewed. The Court of Criminal Appeal is required to consider the report, and the rules governing the admissibility of evidence do not apply to the proceedings.

These procedures offer a convicted person an avenue of review less formalistic than the traditional appellate structure. Most important, they permit full investigation of all relevant evidence and factual circumstances. The experience in New South Wales (in relation to pre-1993 modes of review) has been a general reluctance to take full advantage of the opportunity offered to provide a 'fail safe' diminishing 'the risk of unredressed injustice'[27] but there are signs that the new procedures are being used more frequently.

# Appeal against sentence

Anyone who is aggrieved by a sentence imposed on her or him may seek to have that sentence reconsidered by a higher court. In addition, legislatures have felt the need to permit the prosecution to appeal against 'manifestly inadequate' sentences.

The nature of appellate review of sentences varies from jurisdiction to jurisdiction, and also depends on whether the offence was indictable or summary. It is not intended here to spell out the law governing sentencing appeals in any detail. A general picture of appeals to Courts of Criminal Appeal in most jurisdictions will suffice to raise the broad question of whether the existing appellate criminal procedure is fair and just. Whether appellate courts have been effective in reducing sentencing disparity will also be pursued further in this section.

There are generally three matters for consideration by appellate courts. The first is the validity of the sentence, that is, whether the court at first instance was legally empowered to impose the particular sentence. Next, the appellate court is empowered to review sentences decided on the basis of some error of fact or law, particularly in terms of sentencing principles. A third consideration is the merits of the sentence, that is, whether the sentence is within the permissible range of penalties for the particular offence or offender. When reviewing sentences for these purposes, the appellate courts are supposed 'to lay down principles for the governance and guidance of courts having the duty of sentencing convicted persons'.[28] In the ensuing discussion, it will be seen that such principles are rarely forthcoming. This is in keeping with the appellate courts' general attitude of not interfering, as far as possible, with the sentencing decision of the court of first instance.

We turn now to examine some of the conditions that must be present before an appeal will be heard. This will be followed by the basis for appellate review of the sentence. We shall then consider the relevance of fresh evidence at the appeal stage before turning to the powers of the appellate court to dispose of the case. Finally, a critical appraisal will be made of the prosecution's power to appeal against a supposedly lenient sentence. In all of these matters, a primary consideration will be on whether procedural fairness is maintained and justice achieved.

## Conditions of appeal

The defendant does not have an absolute right to have her or his sentence reviewed by an appellate court. The leave of the appellate court must first be obtained, and this will not be granted unless certain conditions are met. One condition is that appeals are predicated upon the existence of both a conviction and a sentence. As to what constitutes a conviction, the High Court has held that the return of a guilty verdict by the jury or the proffering of a guilty plea is insufficient; these must be accepted by the court before there can be said to be a conviction.[29] Hence, the law insists on a determination of guilt by the court before there can be said to be a conviction.

A sentence has been defined by the High Court as a 'definitive decision by the judge on the punishment or absence of it which is to be the consequence of the conviction'.[30] We note in this statement the connection between the sentence and the conviction, with the former directly flowing from the latter. Before it will consider granting leave, the appellate court will require the sentence to be a final judgment of the sentencing court. Thus, it has been held that an order remanding a defendant for sentence in 12 months provided she or he enter into a good behaviour bond for that period is *not* a sentence.

Usually there are time limits on applications to appeal against sentence. Thus, in Victoria, the defendant must lodge a notice of application for leave to appeal against sentence to the Court of Criminal Appeal within 14 days of conviction and sentence. The court has power to dismiss an appeal without any hearing if the appellant has failed to follow the timetable of filing grounds and written submissions. This restriction serves to secure finality of the original sentence after the time period has lapsed. However, the appellate courts have a discretion to extend the time for lodging an application by the defendant. There must be special and substantial reasons for extending the time, and a reasonably satisfactory explanation of the failure to comply with the time restriction.[31] Possible explanations include intellectual disability and lack of access to legal advice and representation.

The grounds for appealing against a sentence are lodged together with the application for leave to appeal. The grounds of appeal comprise a statement expressing the particular objections to the sentence and reasons of the sentencing judge, and a statement of the argument as to why leave to appeal should be granted. In prosecution appeals, the prosecution must provide a statement of the argument as to why the court should interfere with the sentence imposed, including, if appropriate, details of the range of sentences imposed in similar cases. Early notice should be given to all parties concerned, including the sentencing judge, of any changes to the grounds of appeal. A party to the trial or an appellate judge may request the sentencing judge to furnish her or his notes of the trial and also an opinion on the case. The appellate court will then examine the grounds of appeal and the trial judge's records and opinion. The court must consider the views of the trial judge expressed in the records but those views cannot be taken as conclusive. Indeed, it has been held that the appellate court should, if necessary, be critical of the trial judge's remarks on sentence since sentencers often operate under immense pressure of time when handing down their decisions.[32] The appellate court will grant leave to appeal when the applicant has raised an issue deserving of consideration or presents a sufficiently arguable case. In practice, the High Court rarely grants special leave applications in relation to sentence appeals, preferring instead to resign the field to the Courts of Criminal Appeal of the States and Territories. Expressing a dissenting view, one High Court judge has urged the court to 'break with the "hands-off" sentencing tradition which has so far been followed' and argued that the court should 'develop principles and give guidance to other courts in the same way as it does in other branches of the law'.[33] We submit that there is much merit in this view. Lately, the High Court appears to have shown a greater willingness to consider sentence appeals, at least where issues of general principles arise.[34]

## Basis of review

Upon granting leave to appeal, the appellate courts conduct their review of the sentence appealed against by assuming, in the absence of demonstrated error, that it is appropriate. This assumption is justified by virtue of the special advantage the trial judge has over appellate judges in having personally viewed the offender, the victim, or the witnesses giving evidence concerning the seriousness of the offence. Of course, this presumption is weakened where the defendant has pleaded guilty, obviating the need for a trial hearing.

The appellate courts are granted various powers to assist them in their review of the appeal. They have discretionary power to order the production of documents that an appellant wishes to have before the court. But a sentence may not be increased at appeal on the basis of any evidence that was not given at the trial.

The appellate court may order the attendance of any person to give evidence but may decline to make such an order if insufficient grounds are made out. The appellate court is also empowered to remit a matter to the trial court for determination of any fact or issue and report back to it. This procedure may be necessary since appeal courts have practical difficulties in determining matters of fact.

The appellate courts will interfere with the sentence only if there is an error. It is an insufficient reason to overturn the sentence that the appellate judges would have chosen another sentence had they been sentencing in the first instance. The error may be specific or expressly contained in the sentencing decision, or it may be a non-specific error. As to the first type of error, the High Court in the case of *House v The Queen* has provided some examples:

> If the judge acts upon a wrong principle, if he allows extraneous or irrelevant matters to guide or affect him, if he mistakes the facts, if he does not take into account some material consideration, then his determination should be reviewed and the appellate court may exercise its own discretion in substitution for his if it has materials for doing so.[35]

Regarding non-specific errors, the High Court in the same case described them as follows:

> It may not appear how the primary judge has reached the result embodied in his order, but, if upon the facts it is unreasonably or plainly unjust, the appellate court may infer that in some way there has been a failure properly to exercise the discretion which the law reposes in the court of first instance. In such a case, although the nature of the error may not be discoverable, the exercise of the discretion is reviewed on the ground that a substantial wrong has in fact occurred.[36]

As a ground of appeal against sentence, non-specific errors are usually framed as an assertion by the convicted person that the sentence was manifestly grossly excessive or (if the prosecution was appealing[37]) manifestly inadequate. In order to decide whether the sentence was manifestly excessive or inadequate, the appellate court will examine the range of penalties established in other cases for the particular offence. Should the sentence clearly fall outside that range, the appellate court will quash the sentence if it does not find any circumstances justifying such a diversion. The following comment by the Court of Criminal Appeal of New South Wales sums up the approach:

> What must be looked at is whether the challenged sentence is within the *range* appropriate to the objective gravity of the particular offence and to the subjective circumstances of the particular offender, and not whether it is more severe or more lenient than some other sentence ... which merely forms part of that range.[38]

Occasionally, new evidence is sought to be tendered at the appeal stage. The appellate courts will sparingly admit such evidence for reasons of fairness. Similar principles operate here to fresh evidence adduced in appeals against conviction. The new evidence must have the quality of probably causing the sentencing judge to decide upon a critical issue differently from the way he or she did. Appellate courts have been prepared to admit evidence of relevant material that failed to come before the sentencing judge due to the incompetence of legal counsel or through administrative oversight. Fairness to the appellant also dictates that it is impermissible to increase the sentence on the basis of the new evidence.

The principle of error, which currently forms the basis of appellate review, has been severely criticised. The Victorian Sentencing Committee has proposed that it be replaced by the appellate courts deciding on the right or correct sentence.[39] A 'right' sentence was defined by the Committee as 'that sentence which the court on appeal, after having considered all the relevant facts, considers to be right'.[40] The Committee cited the practice of the English Court of Appeal to impose a different sentence, providing that there was no error and the sentence was within the range of permissible penalties. Ultimately, the Committee saw the present practice based on the principle of error as promoting injustice. The Committee bluntly dismissed the Victorian Supreme Court Judges' submission against its proposal in the following way:

> The substance of the criticism of the Judges is no more or less than a statement that the determination of the correct sentence on an appeal is a difficult task, and they feel that there ought to be a fair leeway for error. It is doubtful whether the public, and in particular the prisoner before the court, will take a similar view.[41]

A more general criticism against appellate review of sentences is the 'stand-off' policy of appellate courts to interfere with sentences. Where they do intervene, the appellate courts tend to regard their function as putting right a sentence that was wrong, without providing guidance to courts of first instance in the discharge of their sentencing duties. Regrettably, the appellate courts thereby forego the opportunity to reduce unjustifiable sentencing disparity and, consequently, injustice.

## Powers of disposal

Should the appellate court find an error in the sentencing decision of the court of first instance, it must quash the sentence and substitute one that it considers should have been imposed. The substituted sentence can be more severe than the original one, and this is so even when the defendant has brought the appeal. The High Court has questioned the continued existence of this power to increase sentences, since legislation now provides for the prosecution to appeal against sentence.[42] Accordingly, the court thought that, where the appeal has been brought by a defendant, the power to increase sentences should be redundant except in special cases. The Victorian Sentencing Committee has gone even further to recommend the abrogation of this power because it was unjust:

> The only justification that has been advanced for that power to the Committee is
> that it is a means by which the Court of Appeal can discourage frivolous appeals.
> The essence of this argument is that the appeal provision which has been provided
> for the purpose of ensuring that justice is done, can be used in an arbitrary and friv-
> olous way to punish an offender for exercising his statutory right to seek leave to
> appeal. The Committee finds that provision abhorrent and believes that the power
> to increase a sentence on appeal by an offender should be repealed.[43]

It is true that, in most jurisdictions where the prosecution may appeal against sentence, it is the general practice not to increase a sentence on an appeal by the defendant without giving the defendant the opportunity to withdraw the appeal against sentence. Invariably, the opportunity will be taken. Nevertheless, we agree with the Victorian Sentencing Committee that reliance on this practice is unsatisfactory.

On appeals against conviction, the appellate court may find that the defendant should not have been convicted of a particular offence but could properly have been convicted of another offence. It may then dismiss the appeal against conviction and substitute a verdict of guilt in respect of the other offence. The appellate court will then resentence the offender for the substituted offence, but the new sentence cannot be more severe than the original. The appellate court is also empowered to alter sentences in cases where the defendant was convicted of several counts and had successfully appealed against conviction in respect of one of them. The appellate court may affirm the sentences in respect of the remaining counts or modify them. For example, the court may increase the remaining sentences on the basis that they would have been more severe but for the sentence imposed for the quashed conviction. These various empowerments to modify sentences in respect of appeals against conviction are not controversial and are consistent with notions of justice.

## Prosecution appeals

Appeals against sentence brought by the prosecution have contributed towards a more balanced pronouncement of sentencing principles by allowing challenges to be made in respect of both the leniency and severity of sentences. However, the High Court has called for the prosecutor's right to appeal to be exercised sparingly. It should be regarded as 'an extraordinary remedy, intended to be invoked only rarely … and then only for reasons of great public importance'.[44] This stems from the judicial concern that such appeals could unjustly expose the offender twice to the trauma of a sentence hearing. In the words of the New South Wales Court of Criminal Appeal:

The prisoner's liberty, pocket and reputation are put in jeopardy both before the sentencing judge and before the appellate court … In addition, the prisoner suffers the anxiety and stress caused by the situation of uncertainty arising from the delay in resolving his or her position.[45]

The result of this judicial concern is that appellate courts are, at least nominally, reluctant to increase the original sentence. There is also the view that prosecution appeals should be disallowed from unduly circumscribing the substantial discretion of sentencing judges over the assessment of the facts and circumstances of individual cases. This judicial assessment includes exercising mercy and allowing for a degree of leniency towards the convicted person.[46]

The general attitude of the appellate courts is to assume, in the absence of anything expressly to the contrary, that the sentencing judge has determined the facts in a way that is most favourable to the defendant. Even when there is an error in the sentencing decision, the appellate courts might decide not to alter the sentence on grounds of fairness to the offender.[47] Hence, lenient sentences have not been disturbed because the offender had already served a considerable portion of the sentence as a result of delay in hearing the appeal. Other factors are whether the inadequate sentence is shown to have had a significant rehabilitative impact on the offender; whether an unappealed sentence by a co-offender might be seen as imposing a ceiling; whether the prosecution's argument on appeal had been raised before the sentencing judge; and whether the appeal would not have arisen but for the prosecution's failure to challenge sentencing facts or principles relied on by the sentencing judge. Where the appellate court allows the prosecution's appeal, it will follow the convention of imposing a substituted sentence that is closer to the lower end of the range of available sentences.[48]

Until recently, the Directors of Public Prosecutions have paid heed to the judicial reservations concerning the lodging of prosecution appeals against sentence. For instance, the New South Wales Director of Public Prosecutions has issued the guideline that prosecution appeals on the question of sentence are exceptional rather than usual and should only be instituted where there is a real prospect of success.[49] In a similar vein, the Victorian Director of Public Prosecutions has declared that public outrage, no matter how widespread, is not a factor to be taken into account when determining whether or not to launch an appeal against sentence.[50] However, a recent study has found that, between 2002 and 2004, prosecution appeals against sentence have increased dramatically, and that a majority of them have been successful.[51] The explanation for this may be because the courts consider these appeals as meritorious on account of their perceived rarity, with the successful outcome in turn encouraging the prosecution to lodge more appeals.[52] If this is correct, the courts should counter this self-fulfilling prophecy by allowing an appeal only where the sentence was outside the range for a particular offence, and not because the prosecution believed that the penalty was inadequate.

# Sentencing disparity

The preceding discussion has revealed the general reluctance of the appellate courts to interfere with sentences. This reluctance extends to the giving of sentencing principles to guide the lower courts. Hence, sentencing disparity is not being tackled, since the appellate judges are doing no more than replacing the original sentencer's discretion with their own. In a study of the practice of the Court of Criminal Appeal of New South Wales in its review of sentencing decisions, Don Weatherburn identifies the reasons for the failure of that court in tackling sentencing disparity:

> For many of those cases where a Court of Criminal Appeal seeks to intervene there will be no formal justification for its intervention at all. The sentencer will not have said anything which conflicts with established sentencing principles. In these cases the Court of Criminal Appeal is thrust into a somewhat awkward position. It cannot justify its intervention on the grounds that the sentence under review is one which it would not have imposed ... It must therefore argue that the sentence in question is so lenient (or excessive) as to disclose an error of sentencing principle. For all its utility this line of attack plainly begs the central question at issue. Even if justice is served by the Court of Criminal Appeal's intervention in these cases, courts lower in the appellate hierarchy will be no wiser after a judgment of this kind than before.[53]

Furthermore, the few rulings that do contain sentencing guidelines are often too selective or else too broadly stated to be of practical application. Richard Fox and Arie Freiberg raise another concern:

> [the appellate courts'] coverage of sentencing law is patchy, with serious crimes and extreme sentences predominating. They say nothing, or very little, about sentencing for the average type of offence, especially ones decided in the lowest level courts, because very few of these reach the upper echelons of criminal appeal.[54]

Besides fostering sentencing disparity, this unfortunate situation promotes injustice of another kind. The scarcity of sentencing guidelines and readily available information about appellate decisions may dissuade people who are convicted from appealing against their sentences even though they may have a good case. This is further promoted by their lack of confidence that the appellate courts will overturn an unjustly severe sentence. There is additionally the concern that their sentences might be increased on appeal.

Measures that the appellate courts could utilise to rectify these injustices have already been discussed above and in chapter 8. They include the use of guideline judgments; the judicial duty to provide clear and detailed reasons for sentencing; the requirement that appellate courts impose the right sentence instead of having to find an error before allowing appeals; and the establishment of a Sentencing

Council to provide the much-needed information on sentencing practices, the effect of sentences on offenders and crime rates, and the like.

# Conclusion

While procedures for appeal from conviction and sentence in the lower courts appear satisfactory, the higher one goes up the judicial hierarchy the more restrictive and formalistic the procedures become. This is incongruous given the seriousness of the crimes charged and the sentences imposed. The rights articulated in Article 14(5) of the *International Covenant on Civil and Political Rights*, while not strictly enforceable, should be given liberal scope in this country—not only to ensure justice for the individual appellant (or, at least, to try to minimise the risk of miscarriage of justice) but also in order to exercise effective review over the entire process of criminal justice.

## Notes

1     That is, judicial permission to hear an appeal.

2     See *Goldfinch* (1987) 30 A Crim R 212 at 219 per McHugh J.

3     Section 35(2) *Judiciary Act* 1903 (Cth). Appeals to the Privy Council in England are no longer available.

4     *Radenkovic* (1991) 170 CLR 623.

5     One exception is Tasmania.

6     *Abusafiah* (1991) 24 NSWLR 531 at 536.

7     For a full discussion, see M. Weinberg, 'The Consequences of Failure to Object to Inadmissible Evidence in Criminal Cases', *Melbourne University Law Review*, 11, 1978, p. 408.

8     *Birks* (1990) 48 A Crim R 385.

9     It is possible to appeal against conviction even after a plea of guilty, but the courts will ordinarily only consider such an appeal if it appears that the appellant did not appreciate the nature of the charge, or did not intend to plead guilty, or on the admitted facts he or she could not, in law, be convicted of the offence charged: *Kardogeros* [1991] 1 VR 269.

10     *Dietrich* (1992) 109 ALR 385 at 396.

11     *Wilde* (1988) 164 CLR 365 at 373.

12     (1993) 179 CLR 1.

13     *Wilde* at 375.

14     As above.

15     As above.

16     For example, unlawful detention of the defendant for the purposes of interrogation.

17     For example, inadequate disclosure of relevant evidence to the defence (see *Maguire* [1992] 1 QB 936 and *Ward* [1993] *Criminal Law Review* 312 for two English examples of this approach, the result of bitter experience).

18     *Ratten* (1974) 131 CLR 510.

19  *Mickelberg* (1989) 167 CLR 259 at 273.

20  (1984) 153 CLR 521 at 534 per Gibbs CJ and Mason J.

21  (1984) 153 CLR 521 at 558–9 per Gibbs CJ and Mason J.

22  (1984) 153 CLR 521 at 576.

23  (1994) 181 CLR 487.

24  This made it necessary for the High Court to reaffirm the principles stated in *M v The Queen* in its recent decision of *Jones v The Queen* (1997) 72 ALJR 78.

25  *MFA* (2002) 77 ALJR 139.

26  *Director of Public Prosecutions (Nauru) v Fowler* (1984) 154 CLR 627 at 630.

27  Kirby P in *Varley v Attorney-General for NSW* (1987) 8 NSWLR 30 at 41.

28  The High Court in *Griffiths* (1977) 137 CLR 293 at 310 per Barwick CJ.

29  *Griffiths* (1977) 137 CLR 293.

30  As above at 307, per Barwick CJ.

31  See *Varney* [1964] VR 143; *O'Keefe* [1979] VR 1.

32  *Mason (Daniel)* [2000] NSW CCA 207, 29 May 2000, per Sully J at para. [4].

33  Murphy J in *Veen* (1979) 23 ALR 281 at 311.

34  *Postiglione* (1997) 189 CLR 295.

35  (1936) 55 CLR 499 at 504. The decision in *House* has been recently approved by the High Court in *AB* (1999) 198 CLR 111; and in *Dinsdale* (2000) 74 ALJR 1538.

36  As above.

37  See below, pp. 290–1.

38  Hunt CJ at CL in *R v Warfield* (1994) 34 NSWLR 200 at 207 (Judge's emphasis) and approved of by the New South Wales Law Reform Commission, Report 79, *Sentencing*, Sydney, 1996, para. 1.14.

39  Report on *Sentencing*, Melbourne, 1988, para. 4.20.16.

40  As above, para. 4.16.11.

41  As above.

42  *Neal* (1982) ALR 609.

43  Report, 1988, para. 4.20.15.

44  *Griffiths* (1977) 137 CLR 293 at 329 per Murphy J. See also *Everett* (1994) 181 CLR 295 at 299–300; *Dinsdale* (2000) 74 ALJR 1538 at para. [62] per Kirby J.

45  *Hayes* (1987) 29 A Crim R 452 at 469. See also *Comptroller-General of Customs v D'Aquino Bros Pty Ltd* (1996) 85 A Crim R 517.

46  *Osenkowski* (1982) 30 SASR 212 at 212–13 per King CJ; *Kalache* (2000) 111 A Crim R 152 at para. [101] per Sully J.

47  *Warfield* (1994) 34 NSWLR 200 at 209. See also F. Rinaldi, 'Dismissal of Crown Appeals Despite Inadequacy of Sentence', *Criminal Law Journal*, 7, 1983, p. 306.

48  *Dinsdale* (2000) 74 ALJR 1538 at para. [62] per Kirby J.

49  N. R. Cowdery, Director of Public Prosecutions, New South Wales, *Prosecution Guidelines*, Sydney, guideline 19.

50  Victoria, *Annual Report of the Office of the Director of Prosecutions for the year ended 30th June 1994*, p. 44. For sentencing policy and public opinion, see pp. 268–70.

51  R. Edney, 'The rise and rise of Crown Appeals in Victoria', *Criminal Law Journal*, 28, 2004, p. 351.

52   As above.

53   D. Weatherburn, 'Sentencing Principles and Sentence Choice' in M. Findlay and R. Hogg (eds), *Understanding Crime and Criminal Justice*, Law Book Co., North Ryde, 1988, p. 269.

54   S. R. Fox and A. Freiberg, *Sentencing—State and Federal Law in Victoria*, 2nd edn, Oxford University Press, Melbourne, 1999, para. 2.

# 10

# And Justice for All?

## Introduction

Throughout the preceding chapters, our discussion of the criminal justice system has presumed the existence of an important consideration without which there would be injustice. It is that the law and the criminal justice process are applied consistently and equally to everyone. Should the law or its application operate in ways that discriminate against particular individuals or groups, injustice results, and the administration of criminal justice will fall into disrepute. This demand for equal treatment by the law and its system stems from the fact that it is a basic human right. The following Article in the *International Covenant on Civil and Political Rights* expresses this right in the following terms:

> All persons are equal before the law and are entitled without any discrimination to the equal protection of the law. In this respect, the law shall prohibit any discrimination and guarantee to all persons equal and effective protection against discrimination on any ground such as race, colour, sex, language, religion, political or other opinion, national or social origin, property, birth or other status.[1]

Lawmakers and criminal justice personnel are meant to jealously guard against discriminatory laws, policies and practices and to guarantee equal and effective protection of the law to everyone.

The sad reality is that discrimination does exist in our criminal justice system. A broad explanation for this may be found in the power imbalance between various groups in our society. Powerful groups protect their own interests by using the law as a tool of control over the other groups. Proponents of this explanation have been described as conflict theorists. They see conflict among various groups in society and postulate that the conflict is resolved only when particular groups achieve control. Hence:

> It is our contention that, far from being primarily a value-neutral framework within which conflict can be peacefully resolved, the power of the State is itself the principal prize in the perpetual conflict that is society. The legal order—the rules which the various law-making institutions in the bureaucracy that is the State lay down for the governance of officials and citizens, the tribunals, official and unofficial, formal and informal, which determine whether the rules have been breached, and the bureaucratic agencies which enforce the law—is in fact a self-serving system to maintain power and privilege. In a society sharply divided into haves and have-nots, poor and rich, blacks and whites, powerful and weak, shot with a myriad of special interest groups, not only is the myth false because of imperfections in the normative system: It is *inevitable* that it be so.[2]

Sometimes, the discriminatory law, policy or practice may be deliberately created or discharged. At other times, the discrimination may stem from ignorance or neglect on the part of those wielding the power. Examples of these will be given in the ensuing discussion.

This chapter deals with specific areas in our criminal law and criminal justice system where discrimination occurs. We shall be examining the unequal treatment afforded to five groups of offenders, namely, juveniles, Aboriginal people, women, the intellectually disabled, and corporations. Juveniles have been selected because they comprise one of the foremost concerns in our crime-control agenda. This concern arises from the large numbers of juvenile offenders and the need for effective crime-prevention strategies to deal with young people going through adolescence. Aboriginal people are a significant group because they have been adversely affected in social, economic and political terms by Australian colonial history. With regard to women, the women's movement has increased community awareness that women's experiences and perspectives are different in material ways to those of men. The intellectually disabled have been chosen because they are among the least visible and least protected of disadvantaged groups in society. Of course, there are other groups who also experience discrimination, such as the unemployed, the working class, ethnic minorities, drug users and homosexuals for example, but unfortunately space does not permit dealing with them. In respect of corporations, we shall see that, unlike these groups, discrimination works in their favour rather than against them.

For each of the five selected groups, particular features of injustice are highlighted, and some major concerns canvassed. The circumstances of each group are presented and followed by remedies that attempt to eradicate or reduce the discriminatory effect of the laws, policies or practices. The discussion then transfers our attention from defendants (or offenders) to those who have been injured by crime—the victims. Recognising the rights of these victims and meeting their needs is a major growth area of criminological thinking and policy-making. The final part of this chapter briefly considers the governmental efforts to combat threats of terrorism in Australia, and the impact these efforts have on traditional principles of criminal justice. Of particular concern is that the newly created counter-terrorist investigative bodies will target especially vulnerable groups in our society.

# Juveniles

Juveniles are children and young people, usually between the ages of 10 and 18, who may be criminally responsible for their actions. Although juveniles comprise 12.5% of our population, they have limited or no power in protecting themselves against injustice. Power lies in the hands of adults to protect or to discriminate against juveniles.

## Exaggerating the problem

The usual picture painted of juvenile crime is aptly drawn in the following comment made to the Australian Law Reform Commission when it was examining the sentencing of young offenders:

> Notions of a 'juvenile crime wave' about to engulf the community have wide popular currency. It seems to be commonly believed that juveniles commit a disproportionately large number of serious personal and property offences, or that new legislation and programs lead to an increase in juvenile crime, or that society is getting soft on its delinquents, and that tougher institutions and harsher penalties would help curb juvenile crime.[3]

The new legislation and programs refer to various initiatives that seek to divert juvenile offenders away from the criminal justice system.

Who paints and presents this picture to the community? The police play a large role by supplying information and crime statistics that have been manipulated so as to show an increase in juvenile crime.[4] The gain to the police is increased allocation of resources and power in combating crime. The police rely heavily on the media to use this information to inform the community. The media in turn see these 'official' pronouncements of crime waves, or depictions of particularly horrendous individual cases, as newsworthy. The gain to the media in publishing these stories is greater readership. It may also be that these stories conform to, and support, the ideology of the company interests who own the media concerned.[5]

With the exaggeration of the juvenile crime problem by the media, politicians have in recent years become actively engaged in this issue as a matter of political survival. There have been many occasions where political parties have used 'law and order' as a platform in their election campaigns. For example, in the New

South Wales State election of 1988, juvenile crime was given much attention, especially in relation to car theft, graffiti and vandalism, the cautioning system and juvenile institutions. The electoral promises of tougher responses against juvenile offenders are usually kept, and these are publicised by the media. The illusion is thereby created that the government is actively tackling the 'problem' and engaged in reform and change.

Another example of the interplay between juvenile crime, the police, media, politicians and the public is the background to Western Australian legislation on the sentencing of serious and repeat offenders. In late 1991, there were several incidents of car thefts by juveniles and the involvement of these vehicles in police car chases where several fatalities occurred. The police expressed their concern over the apparent increase of these cases and sections of the media drummed up a sizeable public demand for tougher penalties against the juvenile offenders. Bowing to this demand, the government implemented legislation that made a custodial sentence mandatory in certain circumstances.[6] This was a remarkable turnabout of government policy at the time, which, at least according to the public record, regarded rehabilitation as the dominant concern in sentencing juvenile offenders.

The major impact of perceptions that juvenile crime is escalating is a greater adherence by lawmakers and criminal justice authorities to the so-called 'justice model' over the 'welfare model'. Simply stated, the justice model regards juveniles as being primarily responsible for their deeds. The sentencing court has therefore the duty of imposing punishment that is proportionate to the juvenile offender's deeds. This model also grants the same legal safeguards and due process rights that the law accords to adults. In contrast, the welfare model regards juvenile offending as the result of complex biological, psychological and sociological factors. The sentencing court has consequently to respond to the juvenile offender's needs, rather than deeds. In line with this perspective, child welfare administrators are provided with wide discretionary powers needed to develop a treatment strategy in the best interests of the juvenile. The justice model is more in keeping with a 'law and order' agenda with its insistence on the punishment being proportionate to the crime committed. This model assumes that an appropriate and proportionate sentence will deter people from offending and reoffending. This requirement of proportionality in sentencing also ensures that juveniles are not unduly punished on the basis of their 'needs' (as the welfare model is prone to do), nor are they treated 'too leniently'.[7]

## A more accurate portrayal

Contrary to police and media reports and the claims of politicians, there is in Australia no juvenile crime wave and no large increase in serious juvenile crime. This was the finding of the Australian Law Reform Commission and the Human Rights and Equal Opportunity Commission in their joint report on children in the legal process:

The levels of children's court appearances and formal diversions from the juvenile justice system have remained stable for the last 15 years. Despite this there is a public perception that youth crime is increasing.[8]

The New South Wales Youth Justice Coalition report entitled *Kids in Justice* has summarised some of the major findings of several Australian studies on juvenile crime. They are:

- the levels of numbers of young people being formally dealt with in the juvenile justice system, by cautions and court appearances, has remained relatively stable …;
- juveniles are disproportionately under-represented in arrest rates for serious offences, both personal and property; and over-represented in arrest rates for offences such as car theft, burglary and 'good order' offences;
- serious assaults are overwhelmingly committed by young adult males, as opposed to juveniles;
- a disproportionate small number of juveniles commit a large proportion of juvenile offences;
- young people are less likely to cause injury and to use a weapon, and cause less damage or injury when committing an offence than adults;
- the cost of juvenile crime is substantial … but is probably significantly less than adult crime, especially drug, corporate, organised, environmental and taxation crime.[9]

Thus, the general picture gleaned from empirical studies is that there has not been any significant increase in juvenile crime rates, and that crimes committed by juveniles are less serious than those committed by adults, especially in relation to the amount of property involved and the extent of injury suffered by victims.

Another significant finding of these studies is that the reoffending rate of juveniles is very low.[10] Juvenile offenders are overwhelmingly 'one-off' offenders. Furthermore, most offenders grow out of crime. As Diagram 1 indicates, the offending pattern based on age is a rapid rise during the mid and late teenage years, and then dropping off significantly after that.

On the other hand, those who do reoffend are responsible for a large proportion of juvenile crime.[11] Also, most people held in adult prisons would have had contact with the juvenile justice system.[12] What these findings tell us is that the criminal justice system needs to proceed with caution and restraint in dealing with the lives of juvenile offenders. The popular 'get tough' solution to juvenile crime is misconceived. It runs the real risk of wrecking young lives and at the same time increasing rather than reducing the incidence of such crime. As the New South Wales Youth Justice Coalition has argued:

> More police, more powers, more courts and more institutions may have some immediate effect; but they ultimately add to the levels of reported crime over the long-term because of the self-generating effects of intervention, and the criminogenic

**Diagram 1** Rates of recorded offences in Queensland per 100 000 population age group (2002–03)

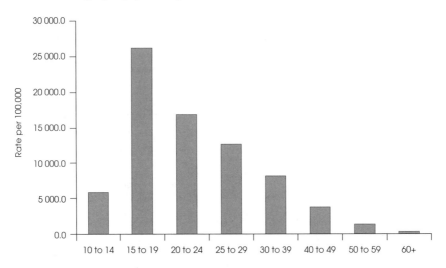

Sources: Queensland Police Service (QPS) 2003, *Statistical review 2002–03*, Brisbane; Australian Bureau of Statistics (ABS) 2004, *Population by age and sex*, cat. no. 3201.0, Australian Bureau of Statistics, Canberra

effect of institutionalisation. Such an approach does not reduce crime, nor does it make the community feel more secure. It is doubtful whether even cost–benefit analyses would support our current and growing investment in control.[13]

Some other matters may usefully be canvassed here. First, relations between the police and juveniles are frequently marred by tension and conflict. The police tend to relate aggressively to youth who are unemployed, homeless, Aboriginal or belonging to certain minority ethnic groups.[14] By approaching their work in this manner, the police create a dynamic of fear, lack of respect and resistance on the part of these young people. Second, governments that have sought to tackle the problem of juvenile crime by greater intervention in the lives of juvenile offenders and tougher penalties are merely applying a knee-jerk response to the problem. In so doing, they fail to come to terms with the deeper underlying social and economic causes of juvenile offending. Reducing welfare benefits, cutting expenditure on education, disbanding family counselling and related support services, and failing to resolve problems such as housing and unemployment are sure ways of encouraging the incidence of juvenile crime. Third, contrary to popular belief, the public is not as vindictive as the media and politicians appear to believe. A study by the Australian Institute of Criminology found that two out of three members of the public interviewed felt that it was more important to rehabilitate juveniles than adult offenders, and the same ratio regarded the main purpose of the juvenile courts was to treat and rehabilitate rather than to punish.[15] Furthermore, 56% preferred spending on counselling and job training programs for juvenile offenders compared with only 9% who felt that money should be spent in building more institutions for juveniles. Given that public opinions about crime and punishment are more sympathetic and sophisticated than the media and politicians would have us believe, a change of direction may well succeed.

## Remedies

Following from the preceding discussion, juvenile justice agencies should make a concerted effort to provide accurate and balanced information about juvenile crime to the media, politicians and the community. Journalists should be educated and persuaded to cover the broader debates and theories underlying the administration of criminal justice, and to move away from purely sensational news reporting. A more informed public would hopefully influence politicians to move away from a law and order strategy against juvenile offending to a strategy with hallmarks of diversion, protection and rehabilitation.

As a broad strategy, juvenile justice agencies should collaborate with a wide range of government departments to prevent or reduce juvenile offending. Presently, some of these departments may not regard crime prevention as a core business of their work. The authors of a recent youth justice research project sponsored by the Australian Institute of Criminology have thus commented:

> Genuine effective crime prevention strategies will need to involve arms of government as diverse as Housing, Education, Health, Police, Families, Treasury, Public Amenities (parks, roads, swimming pools etc.) and Transport. A coordinated whole-of-government approach to crime prevention would yield very substantial benefits over the long term, but would also produce significant benefits in the short term if properly developed and implemented.[16]

More specifically, diversion of a juvenile offender away from the criminal justice system to community support services is the optimal response to the problem of juvenile crime.[17] In this way, they are spared the destructive effects of formal proceedings of the criminal justice system, including the stigma of conviction and the negative effects of punishment. Furthermore, by keeping the juvenile within the setting of her or his family and community, the social controls that these institutions have on the juvenile remain intact. The focus on diversion is evident in the United Nations *Standard Minimum Rules for the Administration of Juvenile Justice*, commonly described as the 'Beijing Rules'.[18] Rule 11, entitled 'Diversion', states in part that:

> 11.1 Consideration shall be given, wherever appropriate, to dealing with juvenile offenders without resorting to formal trial by the competent authority [such as a court, tribunal, board, council etc.].

11.2 The police, the prosecution or other agencies dealing with juvenile cases shall be empowered to dispose of such cases, at their discretion, without recourse to formal hearings, in accordance with the criteria laid down for that purpose in the respective legal system.

The police cautioning scheme, found in many Australian jurisdictions, is a good example of such a diversionary measure.[19] Under this scheme, young offenders who admit guilt may be taken to a police station with her or his parents attending, and warned by the police about the criminal behaviour and the consequences of reoffending. There is no court appearance or court record of the caution. A concern about this scheme is the possibility of 'net-widening', that is, having more people coming into formal contact with the criminal justice system than would otherwise have occurred. However, net-widening need not result as is well illustrated in Victoria. In that jurisdiction, cautioning is used extensively and yet Victoria has low rates of court intervention and boasts one of the country's lowest recorded rates of juvenile crime.[20]

Net-widening may, however, be created by New South Wales legislation, which provides the police with wide discretionary powers to remove young people below 16 years of age from the street and take them home or to a safe house.[21] While the legislative intention may be to protect children, concerns have been expressed that the police are likely to pick up young people who have caused them trouble before and who will resist persons in authority.[22] As the Australian Law Reform Commission and the Human Rights and Equal Opportunity Commission have observed:

The legislation ... allows police to monitor youth behaviour that is not criminal. It sanctions preventive apprehension but provides little or no accountability for police actions or judicial supervision. It allows police to act on stereotypes about young people. Many submissions argued for the repeal of this and similar legislation in other jurisdictions. The Inquiry agrees with them.[23]

Another diversionary measure is mediation, an idea that was trialled by the New Zealand Family Group Conference Scheme established in 1989.[24] Several similar schemes have been established in at least six Australian jurisdictions. A good example is the one found in South Australia.[25] Family group conferences operate as a second level of diversion, dealing with cases that were too serious for a police caution but not serious enough for a formal court hearing. Each conference comprises a youth justice coordinator, the juvenile, her or his family, the victim or representative, and officials from the police and welfare services. The family group conference explores alternative ways to resolving the matter rather than prosecution. Through negotiation, the needs, rights and interests of both the offender and victim are taken into consideration in an effort to reach a mutually satisfactory response to the offence and the harm caused.

Where juveniles cannot avoid going through the criminal justice system, there should be procedural safeguards in place that ensure that they are treated fairly and humanely by the system and its administrators. This prescription appears in the *Convention on the Rights of the Child*, Article 40(1):

> State Parties recognise the right of every child alleged as, accused of, or recognised as having infringed the penal law to be treated in a manner consistent with the promotion of the child's sense of dignity and worth, which reinforces the child's respect for the human rights and fundamental freedoms of others and which takes into account the child's age and the desirability of promoting the child's reintegration and the child's assuming a constructive role in society.[26]

This Article emphasises the reciprocal nature of rights and responsibilities between adults and young people. Adults cannot expect respect and responsibility from juveniles if they do not themselves show respect for and responsibility over the rights of juveniles. Breaches and denial of rights by adults bring the law and those who enforce it into disrepute, and have counter-productive effects on the juveniles' belief in adults and the criminal justice system.[27]

It is not possible here to canvass the full range of areas in the criminal justice system where the rights of juvenile suspects may be jeopardised. A few instances will have to suffice, and are confined to contacts between the police and juveniles.[28] One area where a juvenile's rights may be denied is police questioning. Given the gross power imbalance between police officers and a juvenile suspect being interrogated in a police station, procedural safeguards are required to ensure the protection of the suspect's rights and the gathering of reliable evidence. Safeguards should include a clear explanation of all rights of the suspect before questioning begins; informing the juvenile's parents, guardian or an adult nominated by her or him of the arrest; encouraging these people to be present during the interrogation; and providing for a lawyer or community worker to be present at the interrogation. But simply having these procedural safeguards in place is insufficient. There is growing evidence that, due to their vulnerability and lack of knowledge, juveniles have not been able to rely on and assert the rights accorded them.[29] Police training in the proper and effective handling of young people, taking stern disciplinary measures against recalcitrant police officers, and educating young people of their rights are essential remedial measures.

Another area requiring attention is police custody of juvenile suspects. Safeguards protecting the rights of suspects include assigning them to a special police officer (Custody Officer) who is responsible for ensuring that they are fairly and humanely treated, and that detention is lawful and reasonably necessary. Parents, a guardian or an adult nominated by the suspect should be notified of the detention and allowed access to the juvenile. Furthermore, places of detention should have appropriate bedding, adequate toilet facilities, refreshments and recreational provisions.

A third area that needs to be examined concerns complaints by young people of police violence or other misconduct in the course of questioning, custody and other investigative activities. Internal grievance mechanisms for juvenile offenders should be publicised and made accessible to public scrutiny, and officers not directly associated with the station or department should be responsible for receiving and handling complaints. Where not yet available, an Ombudsman's Office should be set up. The Office should have a separate unit to deal with complaints by juveniles, to reduce the period for dealing with complaints, and to publicise its availability to them.

Moving on to cases where the juvenile has been convicted, the special needs and circumstances of juvenile offenders should also be reflected in the sentence. Given the well-documented deleterious effects of institutionalisation on adult prisoners let alone young people, custodial sentences should be avoided whenever possible. Hence, Rule 19 of the Beijing Rules stipulates that:

> The placement of a juvenile in an institution shall always be a disposition of last resort and for the minimum necessary period.[30]

Furthermore, where a custodial sentence is imposed, the Rules require that:

> juveniles in institutions shall be kept separate from adults and shall be detained in a separate institution or part of an institution also holding adults.[31]

The reason for this measure is to prevent juvenile detainees from being brutalised[32] or badly influenced by adult prisoners. With regard to non-custodial sentences, courts should be able to select the most appropriate one from a large range of sanctions. To quote from the *Convention on the Rights of the Child:*

> A variety of dispositions, such as care, guidance and supervision orders; counselling; probation; foster care; education and vocational training programmes and other alternatives to institutional care shall be available to ensure that children are dealt with in a manner appropriate to their well-being and proportionate both to their circumstances and the offence.[33]

The optimal sanction would be one that increases the juvenile's sense of responsibility and remorse for the victim thereby bringing about full-fledged rehabilitation.[34] In respect of sanctions such as probation, community service orders, recognisances and supervision orders, which normally impose conditions on the juvenile offender, there should be safeguards ensuring that these conditions are not unreasonable and onerous. Otherwise, breach of these conditions could result in the imposition of a custodial sentence.

The above discussion has provided examples of areas where the justice and welfare models have both had an input into the handling of juvenile suspects and offenders.[35] Thus, diversionary measures and the provision of basic comforts while in police custody would be matters promoted by the welfare model. On the other hand, procedural safeguards during the investigation stage and concern over any undue impact of punishment on juveniles stem from the justice model. Juveniles are best served in the criminal justice system by adopting this dual approach. While there may be occasional problems in balancing these two models, they are largely surmountable. The following comment on the Australian Law Reform Commission's *Child Welfare Report* is pertinent:

> The Commission concluded that it was not practicable to make a choice between a 'punitive' and a 'therapeutic' approach. Both approaches must be accommodated. Any system designed to achieve social control must take children's needs into account. Similarly, any system which wishes to offer help to the young cannot repudiate the tasks of the criminal law.[36]

Perhaps the best expression of this mixed model is contained in Rule 5 of the Beijing Rules:

> The juvenile justice system shall emphasize the well-being of the juvenile and shall ensure that any reaction to juvenile offenders shall always be in proportion to the circumstances of both the offenders and the offence.

The commentary accompanying this Rule states that in essence, it:

> calls for no less and no more than a fair reaction in any given case of juvenile delinquency and crime.

Fairness in this regard is commensurate with justice and should be the guiding light in all the criminal justice system's dealings with young people.

As a final comment, the emergence of conferencing schemes in various Australian jurisdictions adds the concept of 'restorative justice'[37] to the traditional models of justice and welfare. While both the justice and welfare models place control of the process of reducing juvenile crime in the hands of agents of the state (the police and welfare officials), restorative justice leaves it primarily to the key protagonists, the victim and offender and the community to which they belong. It thereby views crime as an offence against the victim and not the state and that mediation between the offender and victim, in an effort to have the offender agree to make reparation, often leads to reconciliation between the two parties and their respective supporters. Hence, restorative justice differs from the conventional justice and welfare model because it aims to repair the harm caused by the crime, not to punish the crime.[38] The Australian Law Reform Commission and the Human Rights and Equal Opportunity Commission were highly supportive of this victim-centred 'restorative justice' approach:

> The restorative model is often integral to diverting young offenders from the formal court system. It is a contextual model that acknowledges the desirability of balancing juvenile offenders' rights against their responsibilities to the community. The

Inquiry considers that the national standards for juvenile justice should strike a balance between the rehabilitation of offenders and restitution to the victim and the community.[39]

Agreeing with this position, almost every Australian jurisdiction has enacted legislation introducing conferencing schemes. In order to situate the schemes away from the criminal justice system, all but one of them is not run by the police.

# Aboriginal people[40]

Aboriginal Australians constitute less than 2% of the nation's population. Yet they are twenty times more at risk than non-Aboriginal people of coming into contact with the criminal justice system. This staggering figure is strong evidence that Aboriginal people are discriminated against by agents of the criminal justice system and lack equal protection of the law. One possible explanation for this discrimination is the continuing subjugation of Aboriginal people, ever since white settlement began, by powerful groups within the white community.

## Over-policing

The distortion here is unlike the one for juvenile offenders. There, it was a false claim that there was a juvenile crime wave with serious offences on the increase. With regard to Aboriginal people, the distortion lies in their being grossly over-represented as offenders within the criminal justice system. This is borne out by rates of police custody and imprisonment. For instance, one study found that the rate of Aboriginal people held in police custody was 26.9 times that for the rest of the population.[41] The level of Aboriginal people placed in police custody also differed materially between jurisdictions. The highest figure was in Western Australia, where Aboriginal people were 39 times more likely than non-Aboriginal people to be placed in police custody, while Tasmania registered the lowest over-representation of six times. Significant differences in police treatment of Aboriginal people were also evident when certain types of offences were examined.

Imprisonment rates tell the same story of gross over-representation. Diagram 2 shows the percentage of Aboriginal people in the general population and the percentage of Aboriginal adults in prisons throughout Australia.

The 1997 National Correctional Statistics for Prisons draws a similar picture with an overall figure of over 15% of the total prison population comprising Aboriginal people compared with under 2% in the community.[42] There are also studies revealing that proportionally more Aboriginal people than non-Aboriginal people are sentenced to imprisonment for less serious offences. For example, the Royal Commission into Aboriginal Deaths in Custody noted that:

**Diagram 2** Percentage of all people in the community and in prison who are Aboriginal (2003)

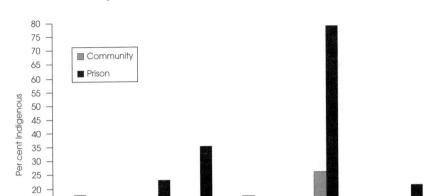

Sources: Australian Bureau of Statistics (ABS) 2004, *Prisoners in Australia*, cat. no. 4517.0, Australian Bureau of Statistics, Canberra; Australian Bureau of Statistics (ABS) 1998, *Experimental projections of the Aboriginal and Torres Strait Islander population*, cat. no. 3231.0, Australian Bureau of Statistics, Canberra; Australian Bureau of Statistics (ABS) 2004, *Population by age and sex*, cat. no. 3201.0, Australian Bureau of Statistics, Canberra.

at the less serious end of the scale, there are proportionately more Aboriginal than non-Aboriginal prisoners held for traffic, good order offences, property offences and for the group of offences known as 'justice procedures', which includes breaches of orders and fine default.[43]

Then there is the disturbing finding that the percentage of Aboriginal prisoners had increased considerably during the four-year period of the Royal Commission into Aboriginal Deaths in Custody as well as the period since the Commission delivered its report.[44] This goes directly against the thrust of the Commission's belief at the very outset of its inquiry that to curb Aboriginal deaths in custody there must be a reduction in the number of Aboriginal people in custody. During the period of the Commission's inquiry, there was nationally a 25% increase of Aboriginal people in prison. New South Wales had the largest increase at 80%, with Victoria a close second at 75%. Western Australia had an increase of 24%, which is particularly alarming given the huge number of Aboriginal prisoners in that jurisdiction.

Taking these figures at face value, the higher rates of Aboriginal people in police custody and in prisons may be simply explained by their proclivity towards criminal behaviour. But an evaluation of the dynamics of police and Aboriginal relations and of judicial perceptions of Aboriginal people offers a quite different and true explanation.

# A more accurate portrayal

In our view, the gross over-representation of Aboriginal people in our criminal justice system is the result of 'over-policing'.[45] The concept of over-policing involves a proactive response by the police to behaviour that they perceive to be disorderly or offensive. This means that, when dealing with Aboriginal people, there is a tendency for police to initiate a confrontation with them. This often leads to an angry verbal or physical response from the Aboriginal people, which results in their being charged for an offence. In contrast, the police normally take a reactive stance in respect of offending by non-Aboriginal people. That is, they tend to take action only after a report has been made by a victim or witness about a criminal incident.

Much of the problem of over-policing is caused by legislatively prescribed public order offences, such as disorderly conduct, offensive behaviour and public drunkenness. These forms of behaviour by Aboriginal people are mostly directed not at a member of the public but at the police officer confronting the Aboriginal person.[46] Politicians implement this type of legislation as a means of social control and the police use it for the same purpose. Taking the cue that good Aboriginal people are ones who are 'reasonably well-behaved' and 'stay in their place', the police use the public order offences to maintain their authority over Aboriginal people who have been defiant or disrespectful towards them. The following observation from an official report on Aboriginal offending in northwestern New South Wales is illuminating:

> It would seem that a popular 'remedy' for the Aboriginal 'problem' has rested on the assumption that law and order would be achieved if Aborigines were made 'invisible' through more policing of the streets and the imposition of curfews etc. There has been an underlying belief that if Aborigines were removed from 'public' places then law and order would be reinstituted.[47]

There is thus a conflict between the police and Aboriginal people over the use of public space. The 'dry area' legislation in New South Wales is a good example of governmental empowerment of police in controlling public space.[48] This legislation makes it an offence to be found drunk or to consume alcohol in certain designated public areas. In many rural townships with sizeable Aboriginal populations, these are precisely the places that Aboriginal people often choose to frequent. Until public drunkenness is decriminalised in all Australian jurisdictions, the pattern will continue of placing Indigenous Australians in police custody for minor public order offenders, and of the disproportionately high rates of deaths of these people while in custody.[49]

Alongside such controlling legislation is the deployment of large police resources to communities with large Aboriginal populations. Studies of police strength in certain rural towns in New South Wales and Western Australia show that the ratio of police to population is noticeably higher in towns with a large

Aboriginal population compared to those with a small population.[50] The National Inquiry into Racist Violence has noted that the high numbers of police in some of these townships was directly due to political lobbying by local councils and chambers of commerce.[51] The lobbying was based on claims of a breakdown in law and order caused by Aboriginal people. The same report also heard evidence of levels of police surveillance and intervention of Aboriginal people that went well beyond those experienced by non-Aboriginal people. The forms of surveillance and intervention included constant police patrols in certain streets and areas; frequent stop and search, and stop and question practices; unlawful arrests and entry into houses; assaults; harassment; and the use of spotlighting and police dogs in particular communities.[52] Of concern also is the use of paramilitary police units against Aboriginal people. For example, in New South Wales, the Tactical Response Group (TRG) was deployed to the rural town of Bourke after a particular disturbance caused by Aboriginal people. The TRG was used again to raid the homes of many Aboriginal people residing in the Sydney suburb of Redfern. A report commissioned by the National Inquiry into Racist Violence described the Redfern raid as follows:

> At an operational level, particular policing practices were legitimised on the basis of 'race' ... the policing operation was, from its inception, designed as an operation in relation to a particular community rather than a series of individuals. It is appropriate therefore to consider these policing practices as constituting institutional racism where the perceived difference of the Aboriginal community was used to legitimise an exceptional use of State force.[53]

The term 'racism' contained in the above comment requires further elucidation. The International Convention on the Elimination of All Forms of Racial Discrimination defines a comparable expression 'racial discrimination' as constituting:

> any distinction, exclusion, restriction or preference based on race, colour, descent, or national or ethnic origin which has the purpose or effect of nullifying or impairing the recognition, enjoyment or exercise, on an equal footing, of human rights and fundamental freedoms in the political, economic, social, cultural or any other field of public life.[54]

Quite clearly, the over-policing of Aboriginal people in the ways described comes within this definition.

This racial discrimination against Aboriginal people might also be found in the judiciary. We have previously noted the findings of studies indicating that Aboriginal offenders are more likely to receive prison sentences for less serious offences than non-Aboriginal offenders committing the same offences. Among some judicial officers, this might be explained by their conscious racist stereotyping of Aboriginal people as essentially different and lesser beings than white people. A South Australian study found that some Supreme Court judges classified Aboriginal people according to colonial perceptions of either the 'noble savage' who was entitled to special consideration, or one who had 'fallen from grace on the way to cultural extinction' and who was associated with criminality.[55] There are also the observations of the Royal Commission into Aboriginal Deaths in Custody on the attitudes of justices of the peace in Western Australia. Many of these justices saw little use in community-based sanctions, preferring custodial sentences instead. They also relied heavily on Clerks of the Court, many of whom were police officers, for advice. The Commission concluded that these justices held paternalistic attitudes that indicated a deep seated ignorance and reflected the 'entrenched racism inherent in the social fibre of the State of Western Australia'.[56] More recently, a study conducted by the Judicial Commission of New South Wales carefully matched juveniles according to factors identifiable prior to sentencing so that any disparity could only be attributed to the sentencing decision.[57] The study found that Aboriginal juvenile offenders received significantly harsher penalties than their Anglo-Australian counterparts, leading the researchers to call upon judges to be aware of conscious and unconscious racial prejudices and any tendency to stereotype such offenders.[58]

However, racism among the judiciary need not be as conscious or direct as these examples. Judicial officers may promote racial discrimination against Aboriginal people by accepting and enforcing the outcomes of over-policing.[59] For example, by making a prior conviction record a factor in sentencing, justices are legitimating the police practices of targeting, arresting and charging Aboriginal people. These practices largely explain why more Aboriginal people appear before the courts in the first place and why they have prior criminal records.

But why, it may be asked, are Aboriginal people over-policed? The answer mainly lies in the history of colonialism in which the police played a significant role in dispossessing the Aboriginal people of their land, removing their children, and giving effect to the policy of assimilation. In some instances, the police were dispensers of summary justice and participants in massacres.[60] This appalling history of police–Aboriginal relations has continued into contemporary times. Thus, in a study of street offences by Aboriginal people, it was revealed that some of the Aboriginal children who were forcibly removed by the police from their families were later the adults who were being arrested by the police for street crimes.[61] The response of Aboriginal people has been aptly described as rebellion. They view the police as instruments of control of the white community bent on perpetuating its policies of subjugation. The resulting disrespect and defiance shown to the police brings demands for more police and greater police powers. Chris Cunneen summarises the explanation and dynamics of over-policing:

> Over-policing must be placed within both an historical and a political context. The historical context of over-policing draws attention to the role of the criminal justice system in the history of colonial relations in Australia. The political context draws attention to the dynamic of Aboriginal resistance and the ongoing processes

of control. Over-policing in this sense should be seen as a process of contestation: the struggle between the imposition of a dominant order and the resistance of a dispossessed cultural minority.[62]

Certainly, not all police have been or are racist towards Aboriginal people. In recent times there have been attempts to improve police–Aboriginal relationships. But the severe damage caused to these relations by past and ongoing instances of over-policing is a long way from being alleviated.

## Remedies

The solution to the current injustice perpetrated against Aboriginal people is obvious. It involves a material change of attitude towards Aboriginal people by politicians, criminal justice administrators including the police and judiciary, and the wider community. For more than two hundred years, Aboriginal people have been dominated to an extraordinary degree by non-Aboriginal people. That domination has produced social, cultural and economic disadvantages, which need to be eliminated for justice to be reinstated. In particular, economic discriminators such as poverty and a lack of stable residence and regular employment experienced by many Aboriginal people are clear reasons for their over-representation in the criminal justice system. These discriminators need to be addressed urgently and effectively. Non-Aboriginal people must be prepared to recognise the need for Aboriginal people to retain their identity as an indigenous and distinct people. Aboriginal people should be provided with resources to enable them to have a degree of control over their lives and futures. Only when concrete measures are effected that place Aboriginal people on an equal basis can a freely negotiated reconciliation between Aboriginal people and non-Aboriginal people occur. This need for attitudinal change is compelled by the *International Convention on the Elimination of All Forms of Racial Discrimination*, Article 1:

(a) Each State Party undertakes to engage in no act or practice of racial discrimination against persons, groups of persons or institutions and to ensure that all public authorities and public institutions, national and local, shall act in conformity with this obligation;

(b) Each State Party undertakes not to sponsor, defend or support racial discrimination by any persons or organisations;

(c) Each State Party shall take effective measures to review governmental, national and local policies, and to amend, rescind or nullify any laws and regulations which have the effect of creating or perpetuating racial discrimination wherever it exists.

Regrettably, this attitudinal change is slow in coming. Pat O'Shane makes the cogent observation that in the aftermath of the Royal Commission's Report into

Aboriginal Deaths in Custody, governments and their institutions were seeking to absolve themselves from responsibility by asserting that the types of safeguards that the Commission had recommended were already in place.[63] If these safeguards had indeed been implemented, why did Aboriginal people in custody continue to die at such an alarming rate? Until governments and their agencies are genuinely committed to change, over-policing of Aboriginal people and the attendant injustices will continue. A decade after the Royal Commission into Aboriginal Deaths in Custody delivered its report, Murray Jones, a prominent Aboriginal activist, gave the following perspective when asked to assess whether anything had been achieved by the Commission:

> The Royal Commission has been a waste of time … [The report was] informative, well-researched and expensive. The government has demonstrated the lengths it will go to gather information. However, while money is spent, thousands of human hours worked and, most importantly, Aboriginal lives continue to fall through the cracks of our society, the equivalent amount of effort not channelled into the recommendations that are the product of reports.[64]

It is hoped that the following sentiments expressed by the then Prime Minister, Paul Keating, when launching the Australian opening of the United Nations Year for the World's Indigenous Peoples, take concrete form:

> And if we have a sense of justice, as well as common sense, we will forge a new partnership [between non-Aboriginal people and Aboriginal people].
>
> As I said, it might help us if we non-Aboriginal Australians imagined ourselves dispossessed of land we had lived on for fifty thousand years—and then imagined ourselves told that it had never been ours.
>
> Imagine if *ours* was the oldest culture in the world and we were told that it was worthless.
>
> Imagine if *we* had resisted this settlement, suffered and died in defence of our land, and then told in history books that we had given up without a fight.
>
> Imagine if non-Aboriginal Australians had served their country in peace and war and were then ignored in history books.
>
> Imagine if *our* feats on sporting fields had inspired admiration and patriotism and yet did nothing to diminish prejudice.
>
> Imagine if *our* spiritual life was denied and ridiculed.
>
> Imagine if *we* had suffered the injustice and then were blamed for it.
>
> It seems to me that if we can imagine the injustice we can imagine the opposite. And we can *have* justice.
>
> I say that for two reasons: I say it because I believe that the great things about Australian social democracy reflect a fundamental belief in justice. And I say it because in so many other areas we have proved our capacity over the years to go on extending the realms of participation, opportunity and care.

Just as Australians living in the relatively narrow and insular Australia of the 1960s imagined a culturally diverse, worldly and open Australia, and in a generation turned the idea into reality, so we can turn the goals of reconciliation into reality. There are good signs that the process has begun.[65]

As part of a sincere reconciliatory attitude towards Aboriginal people, governments should promptly work towards securing several results. These would include either abrogating or drastically reducing the use of public order offences; reducing police numbers and resources in townships with sizeable Aboriginal populations; and tightening the control over paramilitary police units. Above all, there is an urgent need to educate the police about how they are perceived by Aboriginal people and why. Presently, many instances of over-policing are the result of police mismanagement and misinterpretations based on cross-cultural ignorance. The reason why there is so much focus on the police is because society has given them extensive powers. Society needs to ensure that these powers are not misused. As one of the Commissioners into Aboriginal deaths in custody has observed:

> the danger of tolerating [racist] attitudes among police or prison officers is particularly acute, since whilst society entrusts such officers with the wide powers that they exercise, society has a continuing obligation to ensure that abuses and denials of rights by custodians or denial of their duty of care do not occur.[66]

But reconciliation is the result of a two-way process. On their part, Aboriginal people need to appreciate that antagonistic attitudes and responses to police are detrimental to fostering closer relationships between them. There needs to be greater commitment from both Aboriginal people and the police to the development of effective community policing strategies that adopt suitable processes and produce realistic outcomes for members of Aboriginal communities who run afoul with the criminal law.[67] With regard to judicial racism, there is a similar need for education. As previously noted, the Royal Commission into Aboriginal Deaths in Custody found instances of biased sentencing practices against Aboriginal offenders. As an important step in eliminating this injustice, the Commission recommended training of judicial officers in Aboriginal issues, and several jurisdictions have since implemented such cross-cultural training programs.[68] In addition, sentencing judges should regard the entire history of race relations between Aboriginal people and whites as mitigating factors when dealing with certain offences such as offensive behaviour through drunkenness, assaulting the police and resisting arrest.[69]

# Women

In comparison with men, there are few women who are offenders within the criminal justice system. This may be precisely the underlying reason for gender bias in the criminal law and in sentencing practices. To elaborate, since men comprise the vast majority of defendants appearing before the courts, judicially formulated legal principles have inevitably been designed to meet men's rather than women's circumstances and experiences. As for sentencing, the apparent dearth of women offenders could lead the courts to be less concerned with imposing a sentence for deterrence purposes.

First we shall consider the development of certain criminal defences to see how they have been constructed to accommodate the experiences of men but not of women. Women defendants are consequently treated unjustly as they have to mould their own experiences to conform to those of men in order to successfully plead these defences. We shall then consider the opposite effect in relation to sentencing. Instead of discriminating against them, there is some evidence that women offenders are more leniently treated than male offenders by sentencing courts. This raises interesting questions as to why such differential treatment occurs within the criminal justice system.

# Women defendants and criminal defences

## A different experience

It is helpful to place a discussion relating to experience in its factual context. We are here concerned with cases where women defendants have killed their husbands or partners after suffering lengthy periods of violence from them. The general defences of provocation and self-defence available to these women defendants have all been developed on the basis of male experiences and definitions. This is hardly surprising given the overwhelming proportion of men among the judiciary and legal profession. By a process known as legal method, these men determine what facts should be considered as relevant and what facts should be dismissed as irrelevant.[70] Since the experiences of women would normally fall outside those of men, facts based on their experience are likely to be dismissed. Contributing to this male-gendered definition of criminal defences is the fact that a large majority of cases coming before the criminal courts involve male defendants. Accordingly, the courts would feel perfectly comfortable in pronouncing the law to meet the experiences of these defendants. The resulting distortion occurs when women defendants seek to rely on these defences. The women are confronted with the prospect of either failing to plead them successfully, or having to distort their experiences in an effort to fit them into the defences. In the following passage, Stella Tarrant describes this gender inequality:

> the primary structural requirements of the defences work to reproduce the silencing of women in domestic violence because the defences fail to contemplate the power dynamics involved in that violence. A woman's experience of her marital relationship and the killing itself is likely to be systematically skewed. This skewing may preclude access by the woman to the defence; however, even where the

defence is available (and even where it is successful) her experience may be presented and understood in a distorted way.[71]

A presentation of the traditional defences of provocation and self-defence will serve to illustrate this injustice.[72] An examination will then be made of recent efforts by the courts and legislature to rectify gender bias in the law.

Provocation is a defence that, if successfully pleaded, reduces a charge of murder to the lesser offence of manslaughter. The essential requirements of the defence include the defendant having lost her or his power of self-control at the time of the killing due to the provocative conduct of the deceased. These requirements were developed to meet standard cases such as killings immediately following a sudden quarrel or upon the defendant unexpectedly discovering his wife in bed with her lover. Hence, the law has required the provocative conduct of the deceased to have occurred suddenly or unexpectedly, and for the defendant to have killed the provoker very shortly thereafter. This requirement fails to account for women experiencing what has been aptly described as 'constipated rage' resulting in delayed retaliation on the part of women. Additionally, the law confined the provocative conduct to the incident occurring just before the killing. This ignored the social reality of many battered women's experiences of having endured protracted periods of physical and psychological abuse from their batterers. The last seemingly minor episode of violence might well have been the 'last straw, which broke the camel's back'. Yet, the law insisted on regarding this last episode as the primary or relevant provocative incident.

With regard to self-defence, several of its requirements are based on the supposition that the defendant was responding to an isolated and extraordinary assault. The usual situation envisaged by the law is of an isolated contest between two male strangers. This resulted in the requirement that defensive action can be taken only when the assault was in progress or was about to begin. Such a requirement fails to acknowledge the social reality that many battered women live in perpetual danger and fear of being assaulted. For these women, violence is part of their ordinary existence. Another aspect of self-defence that has reflected its bias against women is a requirement of proportionality between the attack and the defensive action taken. This requirement imposes a need to balance with some precision the force threatened by the assailant with that countered by the defender. It would consequently deny the defence to defendants who used a weapon such as an axe or a gun against an unarmed assailant. Many of the cases where women have killed their male batterers fit this description.

Of late, the courts and legislators have become aware of these injustices towards women and sought ways to rectify the position. One method has been to establish procedures that specially take into account the experiences of women. The recent judicial recognition of the so-called 'battered woman syndrome' is a good example of this.[73] The syndrome is not a defence as such but assists in proving certain requirements of defences. A woman manifesting the syndrome is said to be in a depression-like state, becoming immobilised, passive and unable to improve her situation or escape from her batterer. The syndrome is presented in court through clinical expert opinion evidence. The courts have taken this course on the basis that ordinary jurors are not by themselves sufficiently equipped to appreciate the psychological state of battered women. For instance, there was concern that, without expert assistance, jurors would not understand why a frequently battered woman continued to remain with her batterer. The syndrome also helps explain why the defendant might have reasonably believed that her actions were necessary to counteract a life-threatening situation.

However, judicial recognition of 'battered woman syndrome' could well be regarded as perpetuating the bias of the criminal law against women. This development could be construed as yet another instance where a male-dominated judiciary has sought to categorise women from a male perspective. While women's experiences are certainly taken into consideration through the use of the syndrome, women defendants are required to enter into what has been described as 'the gender contract' whereby 'she permits her life to be represented primarily in terms of its domestic, sexual and pathological dimensions'.[74] Hence, a woman relying on the syndrome cannot voice her own experiences; she must have them reconstructed in the form of a medical or scientific discourse. She is labelled irrational, ill and helpless when she may have actually been none of these. Indeed, her act of self-help, which constituted the charge, clearly runs counter to being helpless and is more likely to have been the work of a rational and reasonable mind.

The distortion of women's experiences by the criminal law wreaks injustice. To have a chance of acquittal, women defendants have either to tailor their experiences to fit the perceptions of men, or agree to be construed as irrational and helpless beings.

## A more accurate portrayal

Much has already been said about how women's experiences have been ignored in the application of criminal defences. Thus, for the defence of provocation, the law does not recognise women's experience of 'slow-burning anger', which results in a delayed act of retaliation. The law also fails to give due weight to past provocative incidents, being prepared to regard them only as a backdrop to the latest provocative conduct. The reality may be that women might have lost their self-control and killed because of the cumulative effect of the past provocative incidents and the latest occasion of it. With regard to self-defence, the law ignores the fact that battered women may live in perpetual fear of being assaulted. Furthermore, in requiring that the force applied in self-defence be proportionate to the threatened danger, the defence is denied to women who resort to the use of a weapon to kill their unarmed victims. As for the notion of 'battered woman syndrome', besides categorising normal women as irrational, the law fails to consider other explanations (consistent with women's experiences) as to why a woman did not leave the violent relationship. An obvious explanation could be that she had simply nowhere safe to go and no one she could turn to for protection. The failure of welfare agencies and the police to provide effective support and protection is a very real experience of many battered women.[75]

So long as criminal defences such as provocation and self-defence continue to ignore the experiences of women caught up in violent domestic relationships, the law and the criminal justice system discriminate against them. The resulting injustice could be the difference between a conviction and punishment for murder and a complete acquittal. There is therefore utmost urgency in achieving gender equality in criminal defences. For far too long already, the law has caused women to be subjected to the perceptions of men. Our criminal law must move quickly to set in place the following Article contained in the *Convention on the Elimination of All Forms of Discrimination against Women:*

> State Parties condemn discrimination against women in all its forms, agree to pursue by all appropriate means and without delay a policy of eliminating discrimination against women and, to this end, undertake … to take all appropriate measures … to modify or abolish existing laws, regulations, customs and practices which constitute discrimination against women.[76]

## Remedies

The judiciary and the legislature need to make concerted efforts to ensure that women's experiences are accommodated in criminal defences. To some extent, this has already been done. For instance, as a result of legislation in New South Wales, there is no longer any need for the act of killing to have occurred immediately after the provocative incident. Provided the defendant killed while under loss of self-control, the defence would succeed, even though the retaliation was delayed. This would account for the battered woman's experience of 'constipated rage', which connotes intense anger continuing over a long period of time and exploding when the act of killing eventuated.[77] Some progress has also been made in relation to the law of self-defence. The imminence of the attack is now much more liberally construed, with the law no longer requiring the attack to have started or just about to have commenced when the defendant took defensive action. The attack would be regarded as imminent should the defendant have honestly and reasonably believed that the assailant 'remained in a position of dominance and in a position to carry out the threatened violence at some time not too remote, thus keeping the apprehension ever present in the victim's mind'.[78] This development clearly takes into account the circumstances of a battered woman who lives in perpetual terror of the next attack, which she reasonably believes could occur at any time.

While such recent liberalising of the traditionally male-gendered defences is to be applauded, the bias against women will continue if the modified law is not applied in practice. For this to occur, there needs to be a breakthrough in the legal method used by judges[79] and legal practitioners who argue the cases of women defendants before them. These judges and lawyers, and indeed the wider community, must be educated to displace their male stereotypical perceptions of defence situations and to adopt perceptions that integrate women's circumstances and experiences. Part of this education could stem from expert witnesses who do not 'syndromise' but 'situationise' battered women. As one such expert explained:

> My aim is neither to further reinforce stereotypes of the woman as helpless or passive nor to pathologise her action. By contextualising, the goal is to convey the view that within the particular twisted and horrific reality of the battered woman, her actions were reasonable.[80]

While this process of re-education might be daunting, it must be made for the sake of justice and equality: two cardinal principles of the criminal law and the attendant criminal justice system.

On a much wider plane, law-makers need to pay increasing attention to the views of women on a whole range of criminal justice issues. A failure to do so means that the concerns, experiences and established ways of doing and seeing of half the members of society is ignored. While it is beyond the scope of this book to consider these issues, it would be appropriate to cite a list that has been suggested by various scholars as comprising a premise for developing a feminist criminal justice process. The mere reading of this list should inform the reader that women do have different views and emphases on matters that have thus far been dictated by men.

### Preliminary List of Issues

(1) Violence against children. Should there be any defence ... to assault against children?

(2) Is there too much tolerance in the criminal law for the use of violence? ... A great deal of attention should be paid to the issue of violent sports. At the moment there does not appear to be any limit to the defence of consent to assault. Thus it is possible for boxing to be legal, even though bodily harm, sometimes serious and even fatal, is caused. It is possible that a feminist criminal law would make the prohibition of boxing absolute ... and severely limit the defence of consent to assault.

(3) Are there sufficiently severe limitations on possession and use of firearms? Or do women need access to weapons for defence purposes?

(4) Is there sufficient protection for animals?

(5) Is there sufficient protection for the environment?

(6) Should we change our notions of property, for example, by changing our law

of theft to reflect a willingness to share? Can we learn other values from Aboriginal communities? How much should their perspective be embodied in reform of the criminal law? Are there yet other perspectives which should be taken into account?

(7)  How should the interest in the introduction of new technologies be balanced with respect for reproduction, health and quality of life generally? Is there sufficient protection for workers? Does the criminal law have any appropriate role to play in encouraging the provision of a healthy, safe, non-discriminatory work environment?

(8)  What harm does gambling cause? Empirical data are necessary on who gambles and the effect of gambling on women and children.

(9)  Similarly, with respect to alcohol: the tolerance of alcohol use in our society may have a direct impact on security of the person for women and children. There is a history of women's involvement in this issue.

(10)  Should there ... be a constitutional prohibition on the manufacture or purchase of weapons by the State? Again women have a history of involvement in the peace movement.[81]

The authors conclude with the following comment, which has a direct bearing on the narrower issue of gender bias in criminal defences canvassed above:

> The main theme ... is that the criminal law reform process should not be limited by the range of issues and choices deemed acceptable from a middle-class professional white male perspective. This is particularly important since the ultimate decision-makers, politicians, may be trapped also by the limitations of their own perspective.[82]

## Sentencing women offenders

The assertion has often been made that women are more leniently sentenced than men if convicted, and serve less time than men if a custodial sentence is imposed. A review of various Victorian cases by Richard Fox and Arie Freiberg led them to conclude that '[i]n sentencing, this bias is well entrenched'.[83] Further support for this conclusion comes from empirical studies. For example, in one study by Biles, it was shown that the level of female imprisonment was significantly lower than the percentage of women proceeded against for serious offences.[84] The Victorian judges have been quick to declare that the justification for favouring women in sentencing is not due to male chivalry. Rather, it stemmed from the deterrent aim of punishment. Since few women committed crime when compared to men, deterrent or exemplary sentences were not necessary for women. The judges also thought that public opinion sanctioned a more lenient sentence for women offenders than for male offenders.

However, it is questionable whether women are given more lenient sentences than men outside of Victoria. For example, in a similar study to that of Fox and

Freiberg, Kate Warner could find, in Tasmanian judges, no express sentencing policy that favoured women.[85] To the contrary, she found a Supreme Court judge opining that 'in a society striving for, and largely achieving, sexual equality, no legitimate distinction can or should be drawn between offenders solely upon the basis of gender'.[86] And even with regard to Victoria, judicial attitudes to sentencing of women offenders is more ambivalent than Fox and Freiberg make it out to be. This was the view expressed by the Victorian Sentencing Committee.[87] The committee noted the paucity of information on the sentencing of women in Victoria and called for research in the area. Furthermore, the findings of empirical studies such as the one by Biles can be due to reasons other than judicial leniency towards women. For instance, they could be explained on the basis that women tended to commit the least serious of the range of offences examined when compared with those of men and also tended to have fewer prior convictions than men. Indeed, there are some studies that suggest that women offenders who do not fit into the mould of the conventional woman could be punished more harshly than men.[88] A review of the New South Wales home detention scheme revealed that nearly 27% of persons sentenced to be confined at home instead of in prison were women, although they made up less than 5% of the prison population.[89] However, other explanations may be tendered besides the one of gender bias favouring women offenders. For example, men are likely to commit more violent crimes than women and those found guilty of such crimes cannot serve home detention. Furthermore, sentencing judges may be applying home detention orders to women offenders when previously they would have utilised other more appropriate diversionary options.

Sentencing practice aside, is there any valid justification for favouring women over men in sentencing? Reverting to the reasons given by the Victorian judges, the one about public opinion can be discarded for being question begging as to why more lenient sentences should be given to female offenders. The other reason, based on the low incidence of female criminality and consequently a lesser need for deterrent sentences, carries much more weight. However, although women reoffend less often than men, it has not been clearly established that gender is independently related to reconviction.[90] Thus, any justification for favouring women on account of their gender is unsubstantiated. As against sentencing bias in favour of women is the fact that it runs against the increasing push in society towards doing away with sexual discrimination. Additionally, such a practice might rightly be regarded by male offenders as being unjust. A good example would be of co-offenders convicted of committing exactly the same offence in the same circumstances as a female offender, who were given severer sentences on account of their gender. On balance then, it would seem that any bias favouring women in the sentencing process should be removed. However, when deciding on the appropriate sentence, judges can and should account for the fact that women's criminal conduct may be explained by experiences and circumstances that are quite different to those of men.[91] In so doing, judges should steer clear of the sexist approach of imposing a custodial sentence as a means of 'protecting' women from perceived risks associated with women's choices of lifestyles.[92]

# Intellectually disabled people

Personnel of the criminal justice system and the wider community know very little about intellectually disabled people. Indeed, what little is known tends to be inaccurate, as instanced by their being described as 'mentally handicapped', 'feeble-minded', 'subnormal' or 'mentally retarded'. These are terms that carry pejorative connotations as they suggest some abnormality caused by disease or pathology. There is also a perception held by some that these people are prone to violence. Mindful of this, Commonwealth, Victorian and New South Wales legislation has used the expression 'intellectual disability' because it is not connected with mental or physical illness, has not yet gathered negative connotations, and 'acknowledges that with appropriate services and positive social attitudes, a disability need not become a handicap'.[93] The definition of 'disability' in the United Nations *Declaration on the Rights of Disabled Persons* is also instructive:

> The term 'disabled person' means any person unable to ensure by himself or herself, wholly or partly, the necessities of a normal individual and/or social life, as a result of deficiency, either congenital or not, in his or her physical or mental capabilities.[94]

The Declaration goes on to proclaim that disabled people have the same civil and political rights as other human beings and are entitled to have measures designed to enable them to become as self-reliant as possible.[95]

## Public ignorance

While legislative and international instruments may be accurate in their presentation of intellectually disabled people and their needs, there remains a prevailing community ignorance about them.[96] The ignorance comes in two forms. The first constitutes lack of public awareness of characteristics of intellectual disability. Consequently, they may be treated as people fully capable of looking after and speaking for themselves. This could result in a greater risk of entry into the criminal justice system, since their statements or actions could be misconstrued by police and other criminal justice personnel. The second form of ignorance occurs when the public is made aware of the disability and then perceives it as rendering people incapable of being tried by the courts or as dangerous to the community. The result may be a protracted and unjustified period of custody of these people in an institution.

These projected results have been borne out in empirical studies. For instance, a study has shown that more than one-third of persons appearing before the New South Wales Local Courts on criminal charges may have significant intellectual deficits.[97] Furthermore, while approximately 2–3% of the New South Wales population has a mental disability, they comprise 12–13% of the prison population of that State.[98] It has also been suggested that intellectually disabled people are given longer terms of imprisonment and have a higher rate of recidivism.[99] As one researcher has said:

> [Intellectually disabled persons are] more likely to be arrested, refused bail, convicted, sentenced to imprisonment, receive a longer term of imprisonment and serve a greater percentage of their sentence before being released on parole.[100]

This differential treatment of intellectually disabled people may be explained by the negative stereotyping accorded to them by criminal justice personnel. A Western Australian study examining the attitudes of police and service workers (including lawyers) towards people with an intellectual disability found that some responses of the police and service workers were based on underlying prejudices.[101]

The greater likelihood of intellectually disabled people becoming the subject of and staying within the criminal justice system is justifiable provided they have indeed committed the crimes complained of and are being punished for them. But a great injustice is perpetrated if the reason for their greater representation in the criminal justice system stems from the forms of ignorance previously described.

## A more accurate portrayal

As discussed in chapter 2, most people first become involved with the criminal justice system through police procedures. At this initial phase, many significant admissions and decisions are made that largely determine the eventual outcome of the case. People with intellectual disability may come to the attention of police as a result of their disability.[102] For example, they might be arrested for some minor infringement of public order law. At the police station, the decision may be made to charge them because of the answers they give, the police being ignorant that the disability prevents them from properly comprehending the questions put to them or the information sought by the police. The unfamiliar surroundings of the police station and the inability to understand police detention, interviews and procedures are likely to heighten the anxiety of intellectually disabled people. They might respond either by becoming belligerent or by seeking at all costs to please the police, whom they are likely to regard as people of authority. Either response could have negative effects on police decisions in relation to charging and bail.

A New South Wales inter-departmental committee report on the intellectually disabled and services provided to them listed the following characteristics that place intellectually disabled people at greater risk of entry into the criminal justice system:

1  a desire for recognition and status;
2  a desire to please others;

3   a yearning for acceptance and belonging—an unmet need for meaningful relationships;

4   low self-esteem;

5   poor social skills and inability to deal with problems; and

6   restricted social network and lack of family support.[103]

Hence, a cogent explanation for the greater numbers of intellectually disabled people found in the criminal justice system is the failure by police to identify them. It is only when police are trained to recognise intellectual disability that special procedural safety measures can be brought into play to ensure that police detention and questioning accommodate their needs.

With regard to the community perception that intellectually disabled people are prone to violence, the available evidence is, at best, equivocal. Research suggests that the crimes committed by them are bimodal in distribution.[104] This means that there is a high representation in low-severity and nuisance-type offences, and a high representation in high-severity crimes such as assault and murder. The research also suggests that intellectually disabled people seldom commit sexual offences, such as indecent assault and rape. Suffice it to say that intellectual disability should not be automatically equated with dangerousness or violence. This has an important bearing on the way intellectually disabled people are regarded in the adjudicative, sentencing and correctional stages of the criminal justice system.

When dealing with intellectually disabled people, attention must be given to two competing considerations. On the one hand, there is the principle of normalisation, which asserts that it is in their best interest to be integrated into the community as much as possible. The United Nations *Declaration on the Rights of Disabled Persons* supports this principle by proclaiming that:

> Disabled persons are entitled to the measures designed to enable them to become as self-reliant as possible.[105]
>
> [and]
>
> Disabled persons have the right to live with their families or with foster parents and to participate in all social, creative or recreational activities.[106]

This policy of normalisation requires a recognition of the disadvantages experienced by intellectually disabled people and the provision of appropriate services to meet their special needs. Again, the United Nations *Declaration on the Rights of Disabled Persons* acknowledges this:

> Disabled persons shall be protected against all exploitation, all regulations and all treatment of a discriminatory, abusive or degrading nature.[107]

In a similar vein and more specifically in relation to the criminal justice system, the United Nations *Declaration on the Rights of Mentally Retarded Persons* proclaims that:

if prosecuted for any offence, [a mentally retarded person] shall have right to due process of law with full recognition being given to his degree of mental responsibility.[108]

It would seem that the best course to be taken is to ensure that procedures and services are in place that promote a policy of normalisation but at the same time provide the necessary support and protection to intellectually disabled people as they integrate into the general community.

We shall now consider the problems and remedies of selected aspects of the criminal justice system as they impact on intellectually disabled people. These concern police contact; fitness to be tried and confessional evidence; and sentencing options, including whether it is just to impose lengthy custodial sentences on the basis of societal protection.

# Problems encountered and proposed remedies

## The police and intellectually disabled people

The police, as with many other community services personnel, may not recognise that a person they are questioning has an intellectual disability. This failure may occur because of the person's adaptive skills in masking any deficiency in intellectual functioning, and police lack of training or experience in identification.

Intellectually disabled people may be overly impressed with those in authority and will be likely to respond obligingly to suggestive questioning.[109] Hence, their tendency to answer 'yes' to questions posed by people in authority will place them at a decided disadvantage in police interviews. They may also have difficulties with comprehension, not fully understanding common questions asked by the police nor legal concepts applied during police questioning such as 'the right to remain silent', the standard caution and 'adopting' a record of interview as accurate. Furthermore, intellectually disabled people are likely to experience difficulty in maintaining concentration over the usually long periods of police questioning. All these factors create a real danger that they will be too ready to confess to crimes they did not commit.

To avoid unjustly prosecuting and convicting intellectually disabled people, there should be procedural safeguards firmly in place that account for intellectual disability during the course of police questioning. The New South Wales Law Reform Commission has recommended the development of a statutorily prescribed Code of Practice that is kept at all police stations for consultation by the police, detained persons and other interested persons. The Code would cover matters such as:

* *Identification of intellectual disability.* Guidelines prepared with expert input should list indicators of the possibility of intellectual disability such as difficulty of understanding questions and instructions, short attention span and residence at a group home or institution.

- *Questioning.* Guidelines prepared with expert input should list factors that the police should take into account when questioning a person with an intellectual disability. Factors include the need to pitch the language and concepts used at a level that will be understood, the need to take extra time in interviewing, and the risk of the person's special susceptibility to authority figures.
- *The police caution.* When administering the caution, the police should be aware that persons with an intellectual disability may have difficulty comprehending the concept of the right to silence and the caution, and their need to be reminded periodically of the caution.
- *Adoption of the record of interview.* The standard 'adoption' questions used at the end of the record of interview should be in language appropriate to a person with an intellectual disability.
- *Electronic recording of interview.* As far as practicable, all police interviews with intellectually disabled persons should be electronically recorded.
- *Identification parades.* People with an intellectual disability should not be made to participate in identification parades in circumstances where unfairness to the suspect is likely to result.[110]

The Commission also recommended that questioning of a person with an intellectual disability after arrest should take place only in the presence of a lawyer representing that person. In addition, the police must ask the intellectually disabled person whether he or she wished to have a third person present during police questioning and if this was desired, the police had to take reasonable steps to arrange for this to happen.[111]

Several of these safeguards are already in place in some jurisdictions. For example, the Victorian Office of Intellectual Disability Services runs training programs for police throughout that State 'to help police understand intellectual disability and its effect on charging, interviewing and accessing appropriate crisis resources'. The Victorian courts have also held that the *Anunga* Rules should be extended to cases involving intellectually disabled people.[112] These Rules were introduced in the Northern Territory for the police to follow when interviewing an Aboriginal suspect. The Rules require the presence of a friend of the suspect during police questioning and careful administration of the caution. Similarly, the New South Wales Police Commissioner's Instructions contain certain guidelines in respect of intellectually disabled suspects.[113] They include having present at the police interview a relative, guardian or someone experienced in dealing with intellectually disabled people. The police are also instructed to be aware of their potential difficulties, such as slowness in reacting, short attention span, weak memory or language problems.

## The court process

Our magistrates, judges and lawyers are generally not trained to recognise the characteristics of intellectual disability in people they deal with. This is especially alarming given the sizeable proportion of defendants appearing in court who are intellectually disabled. A court cohort study[114] of New South Wales Local Courts found that possibly as many as one in three defendants will have intellectual difficulties, making it extremely difficult for them to participate adequately in court proceedings.[115] Hence, the most important proposal to achieve justice in this area is to train our judiciary and lawyers to identify the characteristics of intellectual disability.

An important prerequisite to a trial is that an accused person must be 'fit to be tried', that is, be capable of participating fully in the court process. This includes understanding the nature of the charge, giving instructions to lawyers, and following the course of court proceedings in a general sense. Intellectually disabled people may consequently be found unfit to be tried. In some jurisdictions, they may be detained until they are fit to be tried and that might mean indefinitely. The obvious injustice is that these people are detained without the charges against them ever having been proven in court. This injustice is particularly glaring when we note that a sizeable proportion of people who are tried are acquitted. For instance, in Victoria, about 40% of accused people committed for trial are acquitted.[116] Intellectually disabled people who are rendered unfit to plead are therefore denied the opportunity to have their case put before a jury and be acquitted—a chance that is available to other defendants. They will have to cope with charges hanging over their heads until they are found sufficiently fit to be tried, or until the prosecution decides to discontinue with proceedings.[117]

A remedy to this injustice was initially implemented with apparent success in New South Wales and similar schemes have since been introduced in South Australia and Western Australia.[118] Under the New South Wales scheme, should a person be found unfit to be tried and it is determined that this will remain so for the next 12 months, the Attorney-General may order either that the prosecution be discontinued or a special hearing occur. Special hearings are conducted in a similar way to trials, with the jury returning verdicts of 'not guilty', 'guilty on the ground of mental impairment', or 'that, on the limited evidence, the person committed the offence charged'. Where a person is found guilty on the ground of mental impairment he or she will be dealt with in the same way as a legally insane person. Where the qualified finding of guilt is returned, no conviction is recorded, but the court can set a limiting term of detention by reference to any sentence of imprisonment that the person might have received had he or she been convicted of the offence charged. In these cases, the limiting term is the maximum period of detention that the person may undergo. The special hearing terminates criminal proceedings against the defendant. Justice is served by the New South Wales scheme in several respects. The special hearing provides the unfit person with the opportunity to require that the prosecution prove its case as much as possible; the person is discharged where the prosecution cannot prove its case; and the period of detention is not indefinite, being limited by the sentence that the judge would have imposed on any other convicted person.

Besides the issue of fitness to be tried, there are other aspects of the court process that may cause injustices to intellectually disabled people. Mention has already been made of unreliable confessions in the course of police questioning. The same cautionary approach should be taken at the court stage, perhaps in the form of a rule of evidence requiring the confession to be rejected unless circumstances indicated that it is likely to be reliable. An example of such a rule appears in section 85(2) of the *Evidence Act* 1995 (NSW), which states that:

> evidence of the admission is not admissible unless the circumstances in which the admission was made was such as to make it unlikely that the truth of the admission was adversely affected.

This clause requires the court to take into consideration the characteristics of the person making the admission, including intellectual disability.

Another matter needing attention is the special needs of intellectually disabled people who decide to testify in court. The rigours of cross-examination are daunting enough for ordinary witnesses, let alone those with an intellectual disability—they would be more likely to be mentally exhausted by the cross-examination process and to suffer loss of concentration much more quickly. Additionally, they would be more likely to be confused by lengthy questions and those containing double negatives. To ameliorate these problems, the New South Wales Law Reform Commission has proposed that special arrangements for giving evidence should be made for persons with an intellectual disability. These include giving evidence with the assistance of support persons or by way of closed circuit television. The Commission has also recommended providing intellectually disabled persons with the right to make a statement at the trial but not be subject to cross-examination, subject to the court's direction about the length, subject matter and scope of the statement.[119] Measures such as these are in line with the statement contained in the United Nations *Declaration on the Rights of Disabled Persons* that:

> If judicial proceedings are instituted against [disabled people], the legal procedure applied shall take their physical and mental condition fully into account.[120]

## Sentencing

In chapter 8, we noted that the particular characteristics of the offence and offender are relevant to the sentencing decision. Clearly, intellectual disability would be relevant to decisions on the type and length of sentence. More generally, an offender's intellectual disability would have an effect on the types of justifications for punishment relied upon. Hence, the courts have ruled that general deterrence should be given much less weight in a case involving an offender with an intellectual disability 'because such an offender is not an appropriate medium for making an example to others'.[121] Where the offender's intellectual disability gives rise to a propensity for violence, the question becomes whether protracted incarceration is justifiable on the grounds of societal protection and rehabilitation. The High Court in *Veen (No. 2) v The Queen* has frowned upon this and held that societal protection is relevant provided it was considered within the limits imposed by the principle of proportionality.[122] Thus, retribution (or just deserts) is to be regarded as the primary justification in these cases. The New South Wales Law Reform Commission summarised the position on intellectually disabled people and the criminal justice system as follows:

> The use of detention to protect the community is an abandonment of the retribution rationale, being punishment for what a person is expected to do. Detention which is justified as rehabilitation for the detainee is also a rejection of retribution principles. Such forms of detention are contrary to the usual rule that after an individual has undergone the punishment imposed, he or she regains all the privileges accorded to a citizen.[123]

We believe that justice is best served by this approach towards the sentencing of offenders whose intellectual disability is of a kind that makes them dangerous.

Problems remain with the types of sentences to be imposed for intellectually disabled offenders. A major issue is whether these offenders should be diverted from the criminal justice system altogether. This may be supported by the fact that punishment may have little or no effect on many of these offenders, as they have no recollection of the offence nor understand the consequences of their criminal actions. However, the principle of normalisation runs against diversion and argues that if intellectually disabled people are fit to be tried and are found guilty, then the courts should be able to impose the same types of sentences on them as for all other offenders. Currently, the principle of normalisation has won out against diversion. However, this creates other controversies, namely, whether there should be a policy of integration or segregation in respect of custodial sentences, and whether special non-custodial sentences should be devised to meet the needs of intellectually disabled people.

With regard to custodial sentences, the choice is between placing an intellectually disabled offender in the mainstream of the prison community or within a specialised protection unit. The best approach seems to be to promote integration with the mainstream prison community wherever possible, but to provide specialised units for those clearly in need of protection. There is a real danger that other prisoners may abuse and exploit the more vulnerable intellectually disabled prisoners. While specialised units are therefore necessary, every effort should be made to engage people in these units to participate in the general and recreational activities of the mainstream prison. This is the approach taken by Corrective Services Departments in States such as New South Wales, Victoria and Western Australia.[124]

In respect of non-custodial sentencing options, those currently available do not lend themselves well to intellectually disabled offenders. Options such as community service orders, periodic detention, and good behaviour bonds are of limited use because intellectually disabled offenders 'may not understand them and lack the resources and capacity to comply with them'.[125] Likewise, fines are usually inappropriate as most intellectually disabled people belong to the lower socio-economic class. More generally, these people have characteristics that lend themselves to be given custodial rather than non-custodial sentences. These characteristics include being poor, unemployed, lacking in family and community support, and having unstable living conditions. We have already noted the problems of integration and segregation facing intellectually disabled offenders who are imprisoned. Consequently, urgent attention should be given to devise non-custodial sentences that will meet the special characteristics and needs of these offenders. In line with this view, the New South Wales Law Reform Commission has proposed the development of Community Service Order work options that are suitable for persons with an intellectual disability. Under this proposal, a Special Offenders Service would be established to provide specialist supervision and support to people using its services and to liaise with community services agencies to ensure that these people receive appropriate services and accommodation.[126]

Overall, intellectual disability is largely unrecognised by criminal justice personnel such as the police, lawyers and judges. This produces injustice from wrong charges, improper detentions, incorrect convictions and inappropriate sentences. To rectify these injustices, adequate procedural safeguards should be established alongside training of criminal justice personnel to recognise and deal with intellectually disabled people. Where the sentencing of these people is concerned, the principle of normalisation should be adopted, but provision made for special services of various kinds that meet their needs, whether in custody or serving sentences in the community.

# Corporations

Thus far, we have been considering individual people who have committed conventional crimes against other people, such as murder, physical and sexual assault, and property offences such as larceny, housebreaking and robbery. In recent years, however, there has been growing concern about crimes committed by corporations. This concern has been fuelled by empirical evidence revealing that corporations cause more injury to people and loss to property than conventional crimes. Insofar as the criminal justice system continues to punish corporate crime more leniently than conventional crime, or is less rigorous in its enforcement policies, inequality is perpetrated and injustice served. Schrager and Short define corporate crime as:

> illegal acts of omission or commission of an individual or a group of individuals in a legitimate formal organisation in accordance with the operative goals of the organisation which have a serious physical and economic impact on employees, consumers or the general public.[127]

## Disguising the problem

Crimes committed by corporations are hidden in several ways. First there is the use of concepts and accompanying language that disguise the criminality of the conduct, presenting it as a civil wrong warranting a civil remedy rather than punishment. The following comment succinctly describes this portrayal of corporate crime:

> When we enter the arena of business, the talk of crime, of punishment, of just deserts and strong policing vanishes. Instead we are thrown into the world of *self-regulation*. This is the shadowy and closed world where breaches of regulations occur through 'accidents' or 'mistakes' rather than where laws are broken by criminals; the world where licences are revoked or minimum fines are imposed rather than individuals imprisoned.[128]

Second, the media perform a significant role in playing down corporate criminality, emphasising instead the conventional crimes. This is true of both electronic and printed media, which are replete with sensational news of murders, rapes, physical assaults and the purportedly ever increasing rates of housebreaking and robberies. The community is therefore continually exposed to a picture of conventional crime committed by individuals mostly belonging to the lower socio-economic classes of society.

Third, legislation that proscribes corporate crime seldom appears in the mainstream penal statutes. This segregation tends to lessen the severity of the crimes committed by corporations. For example, offences relating to industrial health and safety and pollution frequently cause harm comparable to conventional offences. Yet they are scattered over a miscellany of legislation. This arrangement has even misled the courts. A leading English judge, commenting on the *Trade Descriptions Act* 1968 (UK) said that it 'is not a truly criminal statute. Its purpose is not the enforcement of the criminal law but the maintenance of trading standards'.[129] This disguising of corporate criminal liability is likely to be fuelled by the effective lobbying by corporations to decriminalise the law governing corporations in Australia.[130]

Fourth, there is the concept of corporate criminal liability itself. The current law depends heavily on individualistic conceptions of corporate criminal liability. This is only to be expected from a legal system that has traditionally focused on individual responsibility for criminal behaviour. A good example of the ensuing problems that arise is the difficulty of construing a corporation as capable of committing culpable homicide.[131] This is because the resulting death might have been due to a series of actions performed disparately by a variety of people so that no one individual could be said to have caused the death or possessed the requisite fault for culpable homicide. Another example of the individualisation of current criminal law is its regard of intentional wrongdoing as being more culpable than recklessness or indifference to risk.[132] As corporate crime is predominantly the result of indifference to risk, corporate criminals are likely to be punished less severely than individual criminals.

However, it should be acknowledged that the law has sought to depart from individualisation by devising what may be described as the *Tesco* principle.[133] This principle renders a company criminally liable for an offence where the requisite elements were performed on behalf of the company by the board of directors, the managing director, or a person who has been fully delegated with the board's functions. But, the principle is defective in its failure to include middle-level management, who usually carry out the daily operations of the company.[134] This opens the way for astute directors to evade corporate criminal liability by retaining a formal right to veto or intervene. By exercising this right, directors can distance themselves from the criminal conduct of their middle-level managers.

## A more accurate portrayal

The cost of corporate crime to the community is enormous. With regard to crimes against the person, the National Committee on Violence has observed that 'more Australians perish in industrial accidents than from intentional attacks, and the number of injuries sustained in the workplace dwarfs those occasioned by assault'.[135] With regard to property crimes, the available figures are just as staggering. For instance, the Commonwealth Treasury has estimated that lost revenue from tax fraud amounted to $3 billion a year, and the Australian Medical Association has estimated that $100 million a year is incurred through fraud and over-servicing by medical practitioners.[136] There are also crimes against the environment committed by some corporations, which cause destruction of land and sources of livelihood. Furthermore, corporate crime breeds distrust in the community since the perpetrators are often high ranking and respected people in society.[137]

Despite the damage done by corporate crime, the criminal law and criminal justice system pays little attention to it. We have already noted how legislation proscribing corporate criminality seldom appears in the mainstream penal legislation, and how conceptualisation of this criminality is ill-conceived. Other examples of this reluctance to combat corporate crime include the poor coordination of the efforts of over a hundred regulatory agencies, the scant resources assigned to investigate and prosecute, and the lenient penalties imposed when convictions are secured. This stands in stark contrast to the criminal justice system's approach to conventional crimes. Thus, in New South Wales in the late 1980s, there were about 240 occupational health and safety inspectors compared with 11 000 police. In the same State during the same period, the average fine for a company involved in a workplace fatality was approximately $1800. This may be compared with legislation covering public order offences such as offensive behaviour and swearing, which attract terms of imprisonment for offenders. The low levels of fines imposed on corporate criminals quite clearly lack any significant deterrent effect. More glaring is the fact that corporations are being given the message that they can commit crime provided they are willing to pay a monetary price. Accordingly, corporate executives may decide to regard fines as recurrent business losses that shareholders should bear or else be passed on to consumers.[138]

And what does the public think about all this? Somewhat surprisingly, given media under-reporting of corporate crime, the community has been shown to deeply resent many forms of corporate crime. For instance, in a national survey conducted by the Australian Institute of Criminology, respondents ranked industrial pollution and industrial injury caused by employer negligence only below murder and heroin trafficking in perceived seriousness of 14 crimes.[139] The survey also revealed that public expectations of penalties were much more severe than those currently imposed on corporate offenders. For example, in respect of industrial negligence causing serious injury, a fine of $50 000 was commonly advocated. In reality, the actual case that was used in the survey received a fine of $250 in the South Australian Industrial Court. The significance of these public attitudes is that the system's response to corporate crime is grossly out of sync with public perceptions, and the public then comes to regard the criminal justice system as a tool of the powerful in society.

## Remedies

Beginning with legal conceptualisations of corporate criminal liability, the law should move away from individual blameworthiness to organisational blameworthiness. This would more adequately cover corporate crime, as the criminal conduct of corporations is often the result of employees striving to achieve organisational goals devised by the company's executives. Thus a collective culpability is evident. The *Criminal Code Act* 1995 (Cth) embraces this view of corporate organisational blameworthiness.[140] The provisions of the Code apply both the subjective and objective approaches to fault in corporate criminal liability.[141] Subjective corporate fault may be proven where either the board of directors or a high managerial agent was shown to have intended, known or been reckless of the wrongdoing. It may also be evidenced by the presence of a criminogenic corporate culture, that is, where the corporation's policies and codes of conduct promoted performance of the wrongdoing. Objective corporate fault may comprise the negligence of a corporation as a whole as evidenced by inadequate corporate systems of management, supervision, control and communication. The new legislation is a considerable advancement on the *Tesco* principle discussed earlier, since corporate criminal liability is not confined to the top management level. The legislative approach recognises the diffusion of responsibility within the corporation and that corporate decision-making is often complex and cannot be explained simplistically in terms of the decisions of certain individuals.

In addition to corporate blameworthiness, combating corporate crime could be enhanced by identifying beforehand individuals within the corporation who will be made criminally responsible for any subsequent proscribed harm. This strategy has been successfully implemented in the field of environmental protection where legislation requires corporations to nominate senior company individuals to be personally liable for corporate breaches of the environmental legislation.[142] As a result, company directors have taken their environmental commitments seriously. [143]

Recent debate over corporate homicide cases reveals the tension between imposing standard penalties (including imprisonment) on senior company individuals and treating these cases as little more than health and safety breaches. Doubtless, corporate personnel would take their responsibilities much more seriously if they knew that they would be prosecuted, convicted and punished in the same way as a person convicted of culpable homicide.

Turning to penalties, the legislature should considerably increase the amount of fines and ensure that judges follow suit.[144] The legislature could also explore the use of other penalties especially aimed at corporate offenders. These types of penalties steer clear of traditional fines because they could cripple a company financially if the amount is large, or create unacceptable consequences to innocent shareholders, workers and consumers. One of these alternative penalties is a probation order whereby a court-appointed team of accountants, lawyers, engineers, chemists, and other appropriate experts monitor the standard operating procedures, research programs, communication links or any other structural factors that might be connected with the previous misconduct of the company. The team would then make recommendations, which the company would have to comply with to avoid the probation order being revoked and having to return to the court for resentencing.

Another penalty is the community service order, which would require the offending company to undertake a socially useful project using its expertise and other resources.[145] This would return to the community what the company had previously and illegally reaped. For example, instead of simply imposing a fine for misleading advertising, the errant company could be ordered to use its research facilities to develop safety standards for the product it manufactures, and to undertake other measures that assist in consumer protection. A third penalty could be adverse publicity, which empirical studies have shown to have a marked deterrent effect on corporations.[146] This shame-based strategy has the advantage of being forward-looking, compelling the company towards exemplary behaviour, rather than the usual efforts at achieving retrogressive introspection.[147]

Applying the penalty of imprisonment to corporate criminals will definitely serve as a powerful deterrent. However, the view has been expressed by some that the difficulties in getting a jury to convict of a criminal offence such as manslaughter in the context of corporate homicide are so great that procedural changes are required. For instance, it has recently been suggested in New South Wales that an offence of 'industrial manslaughter' be created, with a lesser maximum penalty than manslaughter under the criminal law, but to be dealt with by the Industrial Relations Commission.[148] Not only would there be no jury, but it also appears to be implicit in this proposal that the onus of proof would be placed on the defendant to prove that he or she exercised all due diligence. We query the proposed abandonment of jury trial and oppose any reversal of the onus of proof. Concerns about 'difficulties in getting convictions' cannot justify abandonment of fundamental principles of criminal justice.

For combat against corporate crime to be truly effective, the numerous regulatory agencies should be better coordinated and streamlined, be provided with sufficient numbers of investigators, and have access to a pool of legal experts equal to those engaged by corporations.[149] There could also be greater use of strict liability offences against corporations to bring about more successful prosecutions.[150]

In the final analysis, gross injustice is perpetrated by having a dual system of criminal justice—one which leaves corporate crime virtually unscathed compared with the rigorous efforts used to combat conventional crime. The following comment suggests the strength of feeling this duality creates:

> If there is no way of implementing justice for the largest and worst offending corporations then it is surely unjust to pursue with such ruthless and cruel tenacity the majority of those eventually condemned to prison. By all means punish those committing violence against us, but when we fail to punish those practising minor acts of [homicide], let us be merciful to those committing comparatively minor acts of violence. If that is too hard to stomach, then the political will should be discovered or constructed so that our government will pursue vigorously and ruthlessly all those, including transnational corporations, who violate laws, particularly those designed to protect our lives and limbs.[151]

# Victims of crime

We have been discussing various distortions within the criminal justice system that have caused injustice to a selection of people as offenders. But injustice may also be incurred on these same groups in their role as *victims* of crime. Much of this injustice is caused by oversight or neglect on the part of the criminal justice system to meet the rights and needs of crime victims. This is contrary to the United Nations *Declaration of Basic Principles of Justice for Victims of Crime and Abuse of Power*, which provides that '[v]ictims should be treated with compassion and respect for their dignity'.[152] For this discussion, the following definition of crime victims in the *Declaration* is adopted:

> 'Victims' means persons who, individually or collectively, have suffered harm, including physical or mental injury, emotional suffering, economic loss or substantial impairment of their fundamental rights, through acts or omissions that are in

violation of criminal laws operative within member states, including those laws proscribing criminal abuse of power.

The oversight or neglect shown to crime victims was largely the result of historical developments in the legal system.[153] Initially, offences were regarded as injury to the interests of individuals. With increased social organisation, crime gradually came to be regarded as injury to the public or the state. While the individual could still initiate a private prosecution, this rarely occurred due to the expense involved. The state took over the prosecution of offenders and left the victim with the roles of reporting incidents of crime to the authorities and serving as a witness for the prosecution.

In recent years, however, crime victims have re-emerged from their effective exclusion. This has been due to several factors. One was criminological interest in the 1960s in studying criminal behaviour in its wider context. This inevitably included the participants, such as the victims, which led to the emergence of the discipline of victimology. Another was the emergence of lobby groups pressing for state-funded compensation for crime victims. A third factor was the increasing community awareness and concern for the plight of victims of domestic violence and sexual assault.

Policy-makers are being made increasingly aware that they can no longer afford to ignore crime victims. Studies have shown that victims may want greater involvement in the prosecution and sentencing processes, want access to more information of the case against the offender, and want to be given compensation, counselling and other support services. Failure to meet these interests of crime victims could lead to their disrespect for the criminal justice system. As a result, victims could withdraw their cooperation in reporting crime incidents, in assisting with the investigation, and as prosecution witnesses at the trial. Their cooperation is crucial in the fight against crime because most crime incidents become known through victim reports, not through police initiative.

The following discussion comments on our selected groups of juveniles, Aboriginal people, women and intellectually disabled people as crime victims. Then, certain rights and needs of crime victims in general will be examined.

## Juveniles as victims

Contrary to popular perceptions of old people being the most likely victims of crime, it is the juvenile who fits this role. Crime victim surveys show that young people aged between 15 and 24 are disproportionately represented as victims in all types of personal crime.[154] A South Australian study has shown that young people between the ages of 15 and 20 were the most likely group to be victims of robbery and that more young people reported being victims of robbery than were apprehended as perpetrators of the offence.[155]

Only in recent years has interest been shown towards crime against children committed in the home. The revelations give rise to much concern. For example, the Queensland Centre for the Prevention of Child Abuse reports that one in four girls and one in eight boys will be victims of sexual assault before they reach their eighteenth birthday.[156] Their chances of being physically assaulted are considerably higher. There is also a national survey for 1995–96 that found that there were nearly 30 000 cases of child abuse and neglect committed by persons with responsibility for caring for the child, such as a parent or guardian.[157]

The greatest attention and concern, however, has been with homeless youth. A vast proportion of these youth are subjected to personal violence. This is consistent with criminological studies showing that victimisation rates are directly related to the degree of exposure to risk in terms of time spent in public places.[158] The immensity of the problem is readily reflected in the huge numbers of homeless youth—conservatively between 20 000 and 25 000 in Australia.[159] Further insight into the victimisation of these youth was gained in a Melbourne study by Christine Alder.[160] The study found that nearly two-thirds of the juveniles interviewed had been physically assaulted and over half sexually assaulted in the previous twelve months. The sources of violence were from strangers, friends or acquaintances as well as the police. Very few of these victims reported the crimes because they distrusted the police or had past experiences that showed the police to be unsympathetic. Perhaps even more alarming was the revelation that many of these injured youth expressed reluctance to seek medical assistance because they distrusted or were uncertain about hospitals. The feelings of powerlessness of these youth and their difficulties in having to struggle alone are a powerful indictment of the police, and health and community services agencies. Alder concluded her study with a call for governmental action:

> The government has to address the economic, educational and welfare policies which deny youth [the] possibility of living safe, independent lives. Young people living away from home should be assisted with access to employment, education and housing opportunities, and the welfare benefits that are available to other adults or to young people living at home. To deny them such access is to structurally determine their vulnerability to exploitation, abuse and violence.[161]

To this could be added that the police, health and community services agencies should become more accessible and acceptable to youth. The present failure of society and the criminal justice system to protect youth from falling victim to crime constitutes a grave social injustice. Recognising this fact, the Australian Law Reform Commission and the Human Rights and Equal Opportunity Commission have called on the Prime Minister to convene a National Summit on Children as a matter of priority. The Summit should be attended by all heads of government, who should find ways to coordinate efforts to assist children from broken homes, and to seek to reduce child abuse, causes of youth offending, youth suicide and youth homelessness.[162] Regrettably, this has still to happen.

# Aboriginal people as victims

The extent of personal violence against Aboriginal people is immense. The National Aboriginal and Torres Strait Islander (NATSI) Survey conducted by the Australian Bureau of Statistics in 1994 estimated assaults to be about five times more prevalent among Aboriginal people than all Australians. A comprehensive Western Australian study using the police computerised offence-information system found that Aboriginal people are 6.5 times more likely to be victims of reported crime than non-Aboriginal people and that Aboriginal women were 10.7 times more likely to be victims of violent crime than non-Aboriginal women.[163] In another study, Aboriginal women in the Northern Territory were found to be grossly over-represented as victims of murder, attempted murder and sexual assaults, and approximately one-third of the Aboriginal female population were gravely assaulted in the year studied.[164] A more recent survey supports these findings by revealing that, although Aboriginal women comprise only 2% of the total female population, they account for 15% of all female homicide victims.[165] In most cases, the violence was associated with alcohol abuse by the perpetrator and occasionally by the victim, which rendered her more vulnerable.[166]

From a law enforcement perspective, an explanation for this alarmingly high rate of personal violence against Aboriginal people is that these occurrences are under-policed. The report of the National Inquiry into Racist Violence contains numerous allegations that police fail to adequately investigate complaints by Aboriginal people in New South Wales, Queensland and Western Australia.[167] This may be contrasted with the strategy of over-policing crimes allegedly committed by Aboriginal people. This is a form of institutionalised racism that should be rigorously countered by the government. It need hardly be stated that Aboriginal people are entitled to exactly the same protection from the police as any other person residing in Australia.

A broader explanation for the gross victimisation of Aboriginal people stems from their displacement in society. The sad story is that much of the source of violence against Aboriginal victims is from other Aboriginal people.[168] With such factors as unemployment, bad housing conditions, poor health, and feelings of worthlessness operating against them, it can only be expected that many Aboriginal people will become violent towards others and themselves. The remedies for this injustice are the same as those canvassed when we dealt with Aboriginal people as offenders. These include effecting a tangible healing between Aboriginal people and non-Aboriginal people; creating among Aboriginal people a sense of well-being and purpose through land rights and identification with their culture; providing resources to improve their levels of employment, health, housing and education; and providing specialist support services to assist Aboriginal crime victims.

## Women as victims

Since the mid-1980s, there has been a dramatic rise in community concern over domestic violence. The usual participants of these domestic conflicts are the male partner as assailant and the female partner as victim. It is difficult to estimate the extent of domestic violence because empirical data is limited. However, broad estimates suggest that physical and sexual assaults on women in the home are rife. This is indicated in a survey finding by the Public Policy Research Centre that 46% of respondents knew someone involved in domestic violence.[169] This and other surveys has led the National Committee on Violence to suggest that 'the behaviour is widespread, almost to the point of being a normal, expected behaviour pattern in many homes'.[170]

A major problem in combating domestic violence is the traditional community perceptions about this behaviour. There is a prevailing attitude that domestic violence is a private matter that should be handled within the family.[171] Consequently, the victims themselves will not contact the police until they believe that the level of violence has reached crisis proportions. Also, neighbours and acquaintances would be disinclined to report instances of domestic violence that they knew about to the police. As for the police, they often prefer to regard violence in the home as a 'social problem' rather than a crime. This leads the police to adopt a conciliatory role, with arrest used as a last resort.[172] The community and police need to be re-educated to regard violence against women in the home in the same way as they regard criminal assaults in the streets. Towards this end, the National Committee on Violence has recommended that where there is sufficient evidence of criminal assault in the home, police should lay charges. Furthermore, such a police policy should be publicised widely, both within the force and to the wider community.[173]

There may be a similar problem in the perceptions about domestic violence held by some of our judges. Lately, the media has brought to public attention several instances of judicial bias against women victims. For example, a Victorian Supreme Court judge in a marital rape case had instructed the jury that there was nothing wrong with a husband using 'rougher than usual treatment' to persuade his wife to have sexual intercourse.[174] Primarily as a result of public outcry over this and other instances of judicial gender bias, training programs have been developed to educate judges about the experiences of women that differ from those of men. The Australian Law Reform Commission has also been given the tasks of examining the extent of judicial gender bias and finding ways to reduce it.[175]

In respect of crime prevention, special needs arise due to the particularly vulnerable position of women who are assaulted in their own homes by their partners. Currently, many States have legislation enabling these women to obtain restraint orders. These are court orders that keep the offending spouse away from the victim by removing him from or limiting his access to the home. Unfortunately, these orders appear to be insufficiently enforced.[176] In line with the views of the National Committee on Violence, the police should be given more powers to enforce these orders.[177] The Committee's recommendations include empowering the police to enter and remain on premises to deal with breaches of restraint orders; authorising the police to take offenders into custody where there is a reasonable belief that this is needed to protect the spouse or children from personal injury; and enabling the police themselves to apply for restraint orders.[178]

Effective support services are also essential for women who leave a violent domestic relationship. Regrettably, women's refuge centres have largely been unable to provide the support and protection needed by these women. The State governments owe it to battered women to supply full financial support to these centres. In this regard, they are reminded of Article 4(g) of the *Declaration on the Elimination of Violence against Women* that:

> States should work to ensure, to the maximum extent feasible in the light of their available resources … that women subjected to violence … have specialized assistance such as rehabilitation, assistance in child care and maintenance, treatment, counseling and health and social services, facilities and programmes, as well as support structures, and should take all other appropriate measures to promote their safety and physical and psychological rehabilitation.

Mention was previously made of women as victims of sexual assault. Under the common law, non-consensual sexual intercourse is prosecuted through the offence of rape. This offence is restrictive in scope, with sexual intercourse narrowly defined as the penetration of the vagina by the penis and with husbands immune from criminal liability for raping their wives. Legislation has widened considerably the scope of sexual assault. The legislative definition of sexual intercourse extends to penetration of the anus (consistent with the move to gender neutrality), the penetration by fingers or objects manipulated by another person, oral sex, and covers not merely the specified sexual connection but also the continuation of sexual intercourse so defined by the legislation. Additionally, marital immunity to rape has been statutorily abolished, and a failure to physically resist a sexual assault does not itself constitute consent. These are welcome changes, which, by deterring potential offenders, afford greater protection to women and other victims of sexual assault.

Despite these improvements in the law, a major problem persists in relation to the issue of consent. In most jurisdictions, the prosecution continues to bear the onerous burden of having to prove beyond reasonable doubt that the victim did not consent and the accused knew this.[179] A new offence of sexual assault has been suggested that dispenses altogether with the need to prove lack of consent or that permits a defence of consent. Instead, the new offence could be defined in terms of sexual conduct in circumstances of coercion or exploitation.[180] Related to the issue of consent is the myth that sexual assaults tend to be committed by strangers, when in fact a majority of cases involve individuals who were acquainted in some way with their victims prior to the commission of the offence.[181] There is also the popular belief, held by many sexual assault victims themselves, that stranger rape is 'real' rape while non-consensual sexual intercourse committed by an acquaintance is not.

In relation to sexual intercourse between acquaintances, there is considerable debate over the possibility of drawing a distinction between voluntary and coerced heterosexual intercourse.[182] Some feminist scholars maintain that it is difficult to know when, if ever, a woman's consent to sexual intercourse with a man is free from constraint in a culture in which the coercion of women by men is positively eroticised. Other feminists argue that a distinction can and should be drawn between the two types of sexual intercourse. Ultimately, the debate turns on interpretative dilemmas in which one individual views a sex act as non-consensual and another regards the same act as consensual. Generally, it may be said that for far too long now, the law relating to sexual assault has paid scant attention to the perceptions and experiences of women engaging in sexual activity with men. Viewed from this perspective, the debate is a positive development.

Another major problem in meting justice in sexual assault cases is getting victims to report the offence. Reasons for not reporting include being ashamed if family and friends were to find out, fear of retaliation from the offender, the perception that the legal process would acquit the attacker or impose a relatively light sentence on him, and worry that the victim would not be believed by the police.[183] In one study, sexual assault victims suggested that the provision of a support person or legal representative right through the legal process would minimise the double victimisation they experienced first at the hands of the assailant and then by the legal system itself.[184] In another study of the experiences of sexual assault victims, it was suggested that provision be made for victims to give their evidence through the production of written statements, closed circuit television and computer technology.[185] In this regard, recent New South Wales legislation requires a legally unrepresented accused to use a court-appointed intermediary to cross-examine a sexual assault victim.[186] Although care should be taken to avoid undermining basic rights of accused persons, these and other concrete measures that assist women to report incidents of sexual assault against them would help to ensure that the offenders are brought to justice.

## Intellectually disabled people as victims

Another group of people who are especially vulnerable to becoming victims of crime are the intellectually disabled. Some of the reasons for this have already been canvassed when we considered them as offenders. These people may lack community survival skills and are the subjects of pervasive ignorance and societal myths.[187] The intellectually disabled may not regard certain behaviour as a crime against them if they lack knowledge about the rights and responsibilities of themselves as citizens. When they do realise that a crime has been committed, they may lack the ability to report the incident or may do so in a way that presents difficulties with investigation and prosecution, or they may lack the emotional energy to follow through the report to court.[188]

There is very little data on the extent of crimes against intellectually disabled people. The National Committee on Violence has noted, however, that such crime must be widespread given that most of these persons are unemployed, unmarried and live in rental accommodation. These are factors that put them at greater risk of victimisation than the general population.[189] A South Australian study has confirmed this suspicion.[190] It showed that intellectually disabled people were more than twice as likely as the non-disabled to be victims of personal violence. They were also more likely to be victims of property offences, such as housebreaking and theft. One rather unexpected finding of the study was that the rate of reporting of crime incidents did not differ significantly between the intellectually disabled and non-disabled populations. However, the researchers did find that reporting was frequently done by a third party, such as a family member or carer, who was known to the intellectually disabled person.

Studies have documented the extent to which intellectually disabled persons have been sexually assaulted by their carers and family members. Many of these victims do not report the crime because they are in a dependent relationship with the perpetrator and fear reprisals should they do so. The problem is compounded by clinical evidence indicating that exposure to violent sexual experiences could lead people with an intellectual disability to inflict the same type of violence on others through sexual role modelling.[191] Appropriate sex education of people with an intellectual disability has been shown to decrease the incidence of sexual abuse of these people. It is therefore imperative that such education be afforded to people with an intellectual disability and, at the same time, for effective measures to be put in place to minimise sexual violence by their carers and family members. On this last matter, the Model Criminal Code Officers Committee has proposed the creation of sexual offences against intellectually disabled people by their carers.[192] These offences provide that the consent of an intellectually disabled person is not a defence unless the giving of that consent was not unduly influenced by the fact that the accused was the carer of the intellectually disabled person.

It is anticipated that victimisation of intellectually disabled people will increase with the current trend towards greater deinstitutionalisation. This is because they will be without a third party or the benefit of a closed environment to assist and protect them against criminal exploitation. One remedy is for psychologists to develop behavioural strategies for these people that would minimise the risks of victimisation.[193] Additionally, the police should implement some routine checking procedure that encourages intellectually disabled people to report crimes against them. There is also a need to establish a governmental body charged with developing safeguards against abuses of people with intellectual disabilities.[194]

These would include the provision of adequate support services for intellectually disabled people who are living in the community. Overall, as the New South Law Reform Commission has recommended, there is a need for high-level coordination among the numerous agencies dealing with people with an intellectual disability, with the aim of safeguarding the rights of these people when they come into contact with the criminal justice system.[195] In this regard, the following observations are specially pertinent:

> [I]t is critical that any response to violence [against intellectually disabled people] recognise the correlation between violence and disadvantage. An understanding of individual needs and difference is important for a respectful and considered response. However, socially constructed difference reinforces negative stereotypes and devalues individuals within the groups so categorised. Challenging the factors that contribute to violence requires an inclusive and collective response spearheaded by members of the most disadvantaged groups and supported by enlightened policy makers and activists for social justice alike.[196]

These observations are equally pertinent when seeking remedies to alleviate the injustices done to other disadvantaged groups such as juveniles, Aboriginal people, and women.

## The rights and needs of crime victims

In this section, some concerns shared by all crime victims will be discussed. These concerns have often been categorised into rights and needs, although the dividing line may be indistinct. By 'rights' is meant that a victim should be given the opportunity to actively participate in the criminal justice system. These rights include 'the provision of relevant information to victims and a pertinent input from them into the criminal justice proceedings [and] [c]oncern for victims' privacy and feelings, decent treatment by the criminal justice system, appropriate reparation and adequate assistance and support'.[197] On the other hand, a victim's 'needs' focus on humanitarian matters, rather than aspects of criminal proceedings. Victims are regarded in the same way as any other disadvantaged group in society such as the aged and unemployed. The concern is with providing services that will assist them in their recovery from the traumas resulting from the criminal incident and to reduce the risk of them being victimised again.

### Information about progress of case

We have previously noted that victims do not like to be undervalued or ignored by the criminal justice system. A clear example of this is their dissatisfaction in not being informed by the police about the progress of the case. Surveys show that victims are interested to know whether the offender was apprehended; the type of charge laid; the decision to grant or refuse bail; the date of hearing; and the eventual outcome of the criminal proceedings.[198] Providing this information to victims meets their right to be consulted and to participate in the criminal justice process. In recognition of this, the United Nations *Declaration of Basic Principles of Justice for Victims of Crime and Abuse of Power* has provided, as part of the victims' access to justice and fair treatment, for information to be supplied to victims about their cases.[199]

In a crime victim survey sponsored by the South Australian Attorney-General's Office, several constructive proposals were made to ensure that victims were adequately informed about the progress of their cases. These included the distribution of pamphlets to victims informing them of their rights; the engagement of a 'victim contact officer' at all major police stations to answer queries from victims; and establishing databases through which information concerning a victim's case could be easily accessed.[200] Many of these proposals have since been implemented.

## Involvement in trial proceedings

Victim participation in the court hearing may be regarded as a right. Traditionally, victims may be called upon to be prosecution witnesses. But with this right comes a need to reduce as much as possible the stress occasioned by cross-examination, difficulties in recalling events, and the fear of retaliation upon encountering the offender again. A somewhat less traditional right is for victims to be consulted about the appropriate charge to be laid or the acceptance of a guilty plea to a lesser offence.[201] Much more controversial is the practice of enabling victims to have their own representation in court, either by themselves or their own lawyer.[202]

A South Australian survey has found that crime victims do not want to represent themselves in court and trusted the prosecution to do so.[203] However, there were many victims who wanted to be actively involved in the decision on charges, or their modification. The reasons for this included 'to put forward their point of view and opinions'; 'to make sure the charge was not lessened'; and 'to know why a particular charge was laid or changed'.[204] This consultation between prosecutors and victims should become normal practice. Another finding of the survey was the plight of victims as witnesses. Recommendations accompanying the survey and relating to this were for prosecutors to explain to victims what was expected of them as witnesses; for victims to be provided with ample opportunity to reread their original statement to refresh their memory well before the court appearance; and for courtroom facilities to be upgraded so as to minimise meetings between victims and alleged offenders.[205]

Some of these recommendations have been given practical effect by the establishment of Victim Assistance Units in several offices of the Director of Public Prosecutions. The creation of Victims of Crime Bureaus and Victims Advisory Boards are other measures that respond to the real needs of crime victims.[206]

## Involvement in sentencing

Crime victims have both a right and a need to be informed about the factors that the sentencing court takes into consideration. This knowledge assists in their understanding of how the sentencing decision was reached, which is crucial to their acceptance that justice was done. The South Australian survey found that very few victims were aware of the sentencing factors and many would have liked to have known about them.[207]

Victims would also like to have the effect of the crime on them taken into consideration when sentencing. Several jurisdictions provide for this through what is described as a victim impact statement.[208] The statement, supplied by the prosecution to the court, contains details of injury and any loss or damage to the victim resulting from the crime. Reservations have been expressed about the use of these statements.[209] One is the possibility of a 'second trial' with the victim being cross-examined on the impact statement. Another is that these statements will create disparity in sentencing. A third reservation is the artificial amplification of victim impact for purely vindictive purposes.

However, these reservations may be countered. With regard to cross-examination of victims, a South Australian study has shown that this has not been a major problem.[210] Furthermore, the risk of revictimisation could be avoided by the court exercising its normal discretion to disallow questions in cross-examination that are improper. As for disparity in sentencing, it can be argued that the problem does not lie with recognising the impact of the crime on victims; rather, it lies with the need for relevant sentencing factors such as this to become known and systematically applied. Only when such a system is in place can consistency in sentencing and the appropriateness of the punishment be achieved.[211] In respect of artificial amplification of victim suffering, this is a real problem that requires close monitoring. Safeguards could include procedures that disentangle:

> those elements of victim impact which are attributable to the offender, from those produced or compounded by the lack of therapeutic services, by insensitivities on the part of the victim's family, or by indiscretions on the part of health and/or criminal justice professionals.[212]

It has been further suggested that victim impact statements should be prepared by professionally trained persons in consultation with the victim.[213] This measure would inject impartiality, objectivity, the use of appropriate language and the restriction of the statement to provable facts, all of which are vital to ensuring fairness in the sentencing process.

The involvement of victims in the decision whether to prosecute, in the trial process, and in sentencing, is strongly supported by the United Nations *Declaration of Basic Principles of Justice for Victims of Crime and Abuse of Power*. Article 6 of the Declaration reads in part:

The responsiveness of judicial and administrative processes to the needs of victims should be facilitated by … (b) [a]llowing the views and concerns of the victims to be presented and considered at appropriate stages of the proceedings where their personal interests are affected, without prejudice to the accused and consistent with the relevant national criminal justice system.

## Restitution and compensation

Restitution refers to the process by which the offender makes good in some way to the victim for the injury or damage caused to the victim. Compensation refers to payment made by the state to recompense the injury suffered by the victim as a result of a crime. The United Nations *Declaration of Basic Principles of Justice for Victims of Crime and Abuse of Power* makes provision for both of these. Article 8 states that restitution from offenders to victims, their families and dependants, should be made available as a sentencing option. And Article 12 urges states to endeavour to provide financial compensation when it is not fully available from the offender or some other source.

As indicated by the Declaration, restitution is preferred to compensation because it supports the notion of accountability on the offender's part with the possibility of some rehabilitative effect. The South Australian survey on crime victims revealed that, while financial payment is preferred by victims, they appear to accept that many offenders can ill afford to provide it.[214] Consequently, victims approve restitution, taking non-monetary alternatives such as community service where offenders work in the community without payment. The study also found that a majority of victims were against the idea of the offender working for them. However, just under half of those interviewed were prepared to meet the offender in a mediation setting with a third party present.[215]

With regard to compensation, several Australian jurisdictions have set up legislative funding schemes for crime victims.[216] The source of funds is from General Revenue,[217] which inevitably means that a statutory limit is imposed on the amount of payment. There are reasons for requiring the amounts of compensation to be increased above their present levels. An inadequate amount may convey the message that the state is little concerned over the victim's suffering. In some circumstances, it is arguable that the state is at least partially responsible for the harm suffered as a result of crime.[218] For example, young people may have engaged in crime partly because the public school system had been deficient in providing them with a basic education and a supportive environment.

## Victim support services

Nearly all victims of crime, irrespective of the type of the offence, experience some trauma. The South Australian survey on crime victims found that 90% of those interviewed had some emotional problems after the offence.[219] These problems were long-lasting, continuing on for many months after the crime had occurred. A similar proportion of victims experienced a financial cost. Besides these immediate emotional and financial effects, there were problems with work, family members becoming upset, and upheavals such as having to move house.

The extent of trauma suffered by crime victims is not matched by assistance in recovery from the effects of crime. The South Australian survey found that many victims were dissatisfied with the dearth of services, including information on support services, advice on crime prevention, financial assistance and counselling.[220] The National Committee on Violence also noted the need to improve services for crime victims. The Committee saw the police as playing a dominant role in providing a network between the victim and other service agencies. It was also aware of the special needs of the select groups of victims discussed in this chapter. In the Committee's words:

> Police must assist in the provision of services that reflect the victim's needs. Integration with other agencies will serve a diversity of requirements—housing, legal assistance, emotional support, security information, and practical assistance. This integration should also increase police and community awareness of the vulnerability of various groups—the physically and mentally disabled, the aged, women, the very young, Aboriginals and other ethnic minorities ensuring services are appropriate for the particular group in need.[221]

Fortunately, several victim support services have been established in recent years. Besides the Victim Assistance Units in offices of the Director of Public Prosecutions, there are a number of non-governmental services such as the Victims of Crime Association of Queensland, the Sydney City Mission Victims of Crime Counselling and Support Service, and the Victims of Crime Assistance League of the Australian Capital Territory. There is also the Restorative Justice Unit established by the New South Wales Department of Corrective Services in 1999.[222] The Unit conducts a victim–offender conferencing program, which operates on a post-sentence basis and has no impact on the punishment of offenders. The program brings together the parties with a view to informing the offender of how the victim has suffered and finding a way of reconciling the victim with the offender.

To conclude our discussion on the rights and needs of crime victims, it is appropriate to note that several jurisdictions such as the Australian Capital Territory, New South Wales, Queensland and Western Australia have legislatively prescribed lists of guidelines to ensure that victims are no longer ignored by the criminal justice system. For example, the Western Australian list, entitled *Guidelines as to how victims should be treated*, provides as follows:[223]

1. A victim should be treated with courtesy and compassion and with respect for the victim's dignity.

2. A victim should be given access to counselling about the availability of welfare, health, medical and legal assistance services and criminal justice compensation.

3. A victim should be informed about the availability of lawful protection against violence and intimidation by the offender.

4. Inconvenience to a victim should be minimized.

5. The privacy of a victim should be protected.

6. A victim who has so requested should be kept informed about—
   (a) the progress of the investigation into the offence (except where to do so may jeopardize the investigation);
   (b) charges laid;
   (c) any bail application made by the offender; and
   (d) variations to the charges and the reasons for variations.

7. A victim who is a witness in the trial of the offender and has so requested should be informed about the trial process and the role of the victim as a witness in the prosecution of the offence.

8. A victim who has so requested should be informed about any sentence imposed on the offender, or any other order made in respect of the offender, as a result of the trial and about any appeal and the result of any appeal.

9. A victim's property held by the Crown or the police for the purposes of investigation or evidence should be returned as soon as possible.

10. Arrangements should be made so that a victim's views and concerns can be considered when a decision is being made about whether or not to release the offender from custody (otherwise than at the completion of a term of imprisonment or detention).

11. A victim who has so requested should be informed about the impending release of the offender from custody and, where appropriate, about the proposed residential address of the offender after release.

12. A victim who has so requested should be informed of any escape from custody by the offender.

Of course, such legislative guidelines are but a first step. Efforts must be made to ensure that these guidelines are discharged in practice and receive the funding required to implement them. Only then will victims of crime believe they are receiving justice in this country.

# Combating terrorism

Thus far, our discussion of criminal justice issues has been of a domestic nature in that the alleged criminal activity and its consequences have occurred wholly within Australia. In recent years, the world has shrunk rapidly due to advances in communications and technology. While this move towards globalisation has brought many benefits, it has an underbelly of crime.[224] Thus, the same techniques of electronic commerce used by legitimate businesses can be used by criminals for fraudulent schemes and money laundering purposes; the various forms of advanced and speedy transportation are available to business people and tourists as well as to people smugglers; and the Internet can be used as much for educational purposes as it can as a tool for illegal Web gambling and paedophile syndicates.

It is beyond the scope of this work to deal with issues of criminal justice spawned by these and other forms of globalised crime. However, we would be remiss not to discuss this phenomenon at all, and have chosen to do so by considering some implications to criminal justice of the so-called 'war on terror' in the aftermath of 11 September 2001. Our choice of this issue is motivated both by the fact that many of the activities of terrorists involve the aforementioned global dimensions of crime and by the major effect the issue has on Australian criminal justice. In particular, we are gravely concerned over the massive expansion of powers and functions by specialist investigative agencies such as ASIO, discussed in chapter 3, and their inevitable targeting of members of specially vulnerable religious and ethnic minority groups in the community. A further concern is that these expansive investigative powers may not only be here to stay, but may be emulated by conventional law enforcement agencies such as the police.

Although terrorism is not a new phenomenon, its globalisation is. It is common for networks of terrorist groups to extend across borders, with the movement of group members, their bombs and weapons greatly facilitated by modern and rapid forms of transportation. Communications between members of these terrorist groups and their sympathisers are aided by the Internet, and the covert funding of these groups is often through the medium of electronic banking.

## The political response to terrorism

In Australia, the dominant view is that 'the maintenance of national security underpins and is the foundation of all our civil liberties rather than the other way around'.[225] This is not at all to downplay the serious dangers that terrorism poses to Australia and its peoples and there is no doubting that strong legally sanctioned counter-measures are warranted. In terms of the competing principles of individual autonomy and community welfare, the latter can be expected to prevail.[226] Societal protection therefore justifies the criminalisation of certain conduct even when the particular individual may have lacked fault in performing such conduct. Furthermore, extra-territorial legislation has been enacted that makes it a crime to injure Australian nationals while they are abroad.[227] This runs counter to the conventional principle of territoriality, which limits nations to enacting laws criminalising activities that have occurred within their national borders.

Along with increased criminalisation, there has been a massive increase in police powers of investigation, search and detention. These powers are largely exercised under a cloak of secrecy at the pre-trial stage, with little or no allowance afforded to judicial intervention. For example, in the Northern Territory, the police may, without warrant, enter premises that are within a designated area of authorisation if they reasonably suspect it to be necessary to do so to enable the surveillance of a person who the police reasonably suspect to have committed or is intending to commit an act of terrorism.[228] The Police Minister's decision in relation to an area of authorisation may not be legally challenged or reviewed.[229] Another example of the extensive powers afforded to crime control agencies is that members of ASIO can detain a person for interrogation for up to 168 hours and, in some cases, even longer.[230] Although detainees will have access to a lawyer, they can be questioned before the lawyer arrives.[231] Detainees who fail to answer questions may be charged with a criminal offence.[232]

The Howard Government has made a connection between terrorism and people smuggling, and regards border protection as an important anti-terrorism measure. Consequently, legislation has been enacted that makes it an offence, punishable with stiff minimum mandatory penalties, to bring into Australia a group of five or more people knowing that they would become illegal immigrants.[233] The Howard Government has indicated that it is committed to extraditing persons from outside of Australia in order to bring them to trial for people smuggling.

Regarding the financing of terrorist activities, there is legislation making it an offence punishable with life imprisonment to provide for or collect funds for this purpose. A person may be guilty of this offence even if he or she had not intended to finance terrorists activities; recklessness will suffice.[234]

## Preserving the rule of law

While the greatly extended scope of criminal responsibility and police powers of investigation, interrogation and detention may be needed to combat terrorism effectively, these measures should be regarded for what they are: extreme and justifiable only so long as there is a real need for them. Emergencies do not last forever, and these special measures should be wound back as soon as the threat of terrorism is overcome.

The guiding light for governments in these troubled times should be the maintenance of 'the rule of law'. As the preamble to the *Universal Declaration of Human Rights* notes:

> it is essential, if man [*sic*] is not to be compelled to have recourse, as a last resort, to rebellion against tyranny and oppression, that human rights should be protected by the rule of law.

A principal feature of the rule of law is that people, including government officials, should be answerable to the law through the courts.[235] Another major feature is that the law should be of such a nature that people will be both able and willing to be ruled by it.[236] For these features to exist, the law must reasonably accord with properly informed public opinion and general social values. This can happen only when there is public trust and confidence that the government is not manufacturing or manipulating information concerning terrorist activities.

Alongside a vigilant public is the need for a strong judiciary to ensure that the rule of law is maintained even in times of high public danger. The following comment by an English judge is pertinent:

> In this country, amid the clash of arms, the laws are not silent. They may be changed, but they speak the same language in war as in peace. It has always been one of the pillars of freedom, one of the principles of liberty ... that the judges are no respecters of persons and stand between the subject and any attempted encroachments on his [or her] liberty by the [government], alert to see that any coercive action is justified in law.[237]

On this view, the Northern Territory and ASIO laws mentioned previously are untenable for shielding from judicial scrutiny governmental encroachments upon civil liberties. Ultimately, we contend that, when enacting legislation to counter the threat of terrorism, the government should endeavour to strike an appropriate balance between security concerns and civil rights. It could do so by adopting the premise that such legislation should adhere as closely as possible to the ordinary criminal law and criminal procedure; and that the legislation should comply with human rights principles contained in international law.[238]

# Conclusion

Injustice is no respecter of people. It may affect offenders as well as victims of crime, and it cuts across age, race, gender and class. Injustice is also not confined to a particular part of the criminal law or criminal justice system. It may be present in the definition of the crime itself, operate through the exercise of police and prosecutorial discretions, appear in the rules of evidence and procedure, and arise in various other ways in the course of the trial, sentencing and appeal hearings.

However, there are some people who are more prone than others to receiving unjust treatment at the hands of the criminal law and criminal justice system. What these people have in common is their distance from the centres of power in our society that inspire, direct and administer criminal justice. Consequently, their interests are not properly protected and their values, experiences and perceptions ignored. It is only through active political lobbying by these discriminated groups or others supportive of their cause that the injustices against them may be acknowledged by those in power and remedial measures put in place. Yet this is a sorry state of affairs for a system of criminal justice that claims to be centred on principles of fairness, equality and moral rightness.

Rather than waiting to hear reports of injustices before taking action, legislators, judges, lawyers and criminal justice administrators should actively seek out those areas in need of reform and implement appropriate remedies. This imperative to take a proactive approach stems not only from an inherent sense of rightness. It also comes from international legal covenants, ratified by Australia, that recognise basic rights and standards to which every human being is entitled.[239] It is only when those people wielding the power behind the criminal justice system regard these basic tenets as inviolable, that we can begin to hope that justice for all is an attainable goal.

## Notes

1   Article 26 and ratified by Australia in 1980.

2   W. Chambliss and R. Seidman, *Law, Order and Power*, John Wiley & Sons, Reading, MA, 1971, p. 4. Authors' emphasis.

3   A. Freiberg, R. Fox and M. Hogan, *Sentencing Young Offenders*, Sentencing Research Paper No. 11, Law Reform Commission and Commonwealth Youth Bureau, Canberra, 1988.

4   For further details see P. Grabosky and P. Wilson, *Journalism and Justice: How Crime is Reported*, Pluto Press, Sydney, 1989.

5   H. Sercombe, 'Easy Pickings: The Children's Court and the Economy of News Production', paper presented to Youth 93: The Regeneration Conference, Hobart, November 1993; S. Hall, C. Critcher, T. Jefferson, J. Clark and B. Roberts, *Policing the Crisis*, Macmillan, London, 1978, p. 57.

6   See M. Wilkie, 'Crime (Serious and Repeat Offenders) Sentencing Act 1992: A Human Rights Perspective', *University of Western Australia Law Review*, 22, 1992, p. 187; R. White, 'Tough Laws for Hard-Core Politicians', *Alternative Law Journal*, 17, 1992, p. 58. The controversial legislation has since been replaced by the *Young Offenders Act* 1994 (WA), Div. 9. However, another type of mandatory minimum sentencing scheme is still in place in Western Australia: see chapter 8, p. 286.

7   Compare the 'just deserts' model of sentencing discussed in chapter 8, p. 276.

8   Australian Law Reform Commission and Human Rights and Equal Opportunity Commission, Report No. 84, *Seen and Heard: Priority for Children in the Legal Process*, AGPS, Canberra, 1997, para. 18.3.

9   New South Wales Youth Justice Coalition, *Kids in Justice: A Blueprint for the '90s*, Sydney, 1990, pp. 21–2. The studies relied on for these findings were the Australian Institute of Criminology report The Costs of Juvenile Crime and Crime Prevention, 1990; S. Mukherjee, *Age and Crime*, Australian Institute of Criminology, Canberra, 1983; A. Freiberg, R. Fox and M. Hogan, *Sentencing Young Offenders*, Sentencing Research Paper No. 11, Australian Law Reform Commission, Sydney, and Commonwealth Youth Bureau, Canberra, 1988; and R. White, 'Making Ends Meet: Young People, Work and the Criminal Economy', *Australia and New Zealand Journal of Criminology*, 22, 1989, p. 136. See further J. Wundersitz, 'Some Statistics on Youth Offending: An Inter-jurisdictional Comparison' in F. Gale, N. Naffine and J. Wundersitz (eds), *Juvenile Justice: Debating the Issues*, Allen & Unwin, Sydney, 1993, p. 18; and C. Cunneen and R. White, *Juvenile Justice: An Australian Perspective*, Oxford University Press, Melbourne, 1995, pp. 97–101.

10   For studies, see Queensland Criminal Justice Commission, *Youth, Crime and Justice in Queensland*, Brisbane, 1992, pp. 43–6; M. Cain, *Recidivism of Juvenile Offenders in New South Wales*, NSW Department of Juvenile Justice, Sydney, 1996, p. 1.

11   F. Morgan, 'Contact with the Justice System over the Juvenile Years' in L. Atkinson and S.A. Gerull (eds), National Conference on Juvenile Detention, Canberra, 1993, p. 180; C. Coumarelos, *Juvenile Offending: Predicting Persistence and Determining Cost-effectiveness of Interventions*, NSW Bureau of Crime Statistics, Sydney, 1994, p. 7.

12   Australian Institute of Criminology, 'Youth Justice: Criminal Trajectories', *Trends and Issues in Criminal Justice*, No. 265, Canberra, 2003, pp. 3–4.

13   New South Wales Youth Justice Coalition, 1990, p. 36.

14   R. White and C. Alder (eds), *The Police and Young People in Australia*, Cambridge University Press, Melbourne, 1994, p. 205; H. Blagg and M. Wilkie, 'Young People and Policing in Australia: The Relevance of the United Nations Convention on the Rights of the Child', *Australian Journal of Human Rights*, 3, 1997, p. 134.

15   Australian Institute of Criminology, *Public Attitudes on Dealing with Juvenile Offenders*, Canberra, 1989.

16   Australian Institute of Criminology, *Trends and Issues in Criminal Justice*, No. 265, as above, p. 5.

17   For an overview of pre-court diversion, see J. Wundersitz, 'Pre-court Diversion: The Australian Experience' in A. Borowski and I. O'Connor (eds), *Juvenile Crime, Justice and Corrections*, Longman, Melbourne, 1997, p. 281.

18   Adopted by the General Assembly in November 1985.

19   See J. Seymour, *Dealing with Young Offenders*, Law Book Co., North Ryde, NSW, 1988, pp. 224–77; Australian Law Reform Commission and Human Rights and Equal Opportunity Commission, 1997, paras 18.38–18.44.

20   Queensland Criminal Justice Commission, 1992, p. 22.

21   *Children (Protection and Parental Responsibility) Act* 1997 (NSW).

22   W. Fisher, S. Garkawe and D. Heilpern, 'Summary Sanitation: The Extension of Police Powers Over Children in New South Wales', *Southern Cross University Law Review*, 1, 1997, p. 120.

23   Australian Law Reform Commission and Human Rights and Equal Opportunity Commission, 1997, para. 18.78.

24   See A. Morris and G. Maxwell, 'Juvenile Justice in New Zealand: A New Paradigm', *Australian and New Zealand Journal of Criminology*, 26, 1993, p. 72.

25   The scheme was established by the *Young Offenders Act* 1993 (SA). See J. Wundersitz, 'Family Conferencing and Juvenile Justice Reform in South Australia' in C. Alder and J. Wundersitz (eds), *Family Conferencing and Juvenile Justice: The Way Forward or Misplaced Optimism?*, Australian Institute of Criminology, Canberra, 1994, p. 87. A note of warning has been expressed over the propriety of using family group conferencing to Indigenous young people: see C. Cunneen, 'Community Conferencing and the Fiction of Indigenous Control', *Australian and New Zealand Journal of Criminology*, 30, 1997, p. 292.

26   The Convention was ratified by Australia in December 1990.

27   New South Wales Youth Justice Coalition, 1990, p. 37.

28   For a detailed discussion of the ensuing areas and others requiring protection of a juvenile's rights, see New South Wales Youth Justice Coalition 1990, chapters on 'Police' and 'Detention Centres'.

29  N. Naffine and J. Wundersitz, 'Trends in Juvenile Justice' in D. Chappell and P. Wilson, *The Australian Criminal Justice System in the Mid 1990s*, Butterworths, North Ryde, 1994, p. 235.

30  See also the *Convention on the Rights of the Child*, Article 37(b).

31  Rule 26.3.

32  See D. Heilpern, *Fear or Favour*, Federation Press, Annandale, 1998, for a horrific account of sexual assault of young prisoners in NSW prisons.

33  Article 40(4).

34  In line with this, s. 4(f) of the *Juvenile Justice Act* 1992 (Qld) states that a child who commits an offence should be 'held accountable and encouraged to accept responsibility for the offending behaviour'.

35  See D. Palmer and R. Walters, 'Crime Prevention Camps for Youth "At Risk": Blurring the Boundaries of Care and Control' in C. Simpson and R. Hil (eds), *Ways of Resistance: Social Control and Young People in Australia*, Hale and Iremonger, Sydney, 1995, p. 161.

36  Seymour, 1988, p. 245.

37  This concept is based on the notions of restoration and reintegrative shaming propounded by J. Braithwaite in his seminal work, *Crime, Shame and Reintegration*, Cambridge University Press, Cambridge, 1989.

38  K. Daly and H. Hayes, 'Restorative Justice and Conferencing in Australia', *Trends and Issues in Crime and Justice*, No. 186, Australian Institute of Criminology, Canberra, 2001, p. 2.

39  Australian Law Reform Commission and Human Rights and Equal Opportunity Commission, AGPS, 1997, para. 18.34.

40  This term is used to designate peoples of Aboriginal and Torres Strait Islander descent.

41  C. Cunneen and D. McDonald, *Keeping Aboriginal and Torres Strait Islander People Out of Custody*, ATSIC, Canberra, 1997, pp. 20–1.

42  *Correctional Statistics: Prisons*, Canberra, 1997, p. 14.

43  Royal Commission into Aboriginal Deaths in Custody, Final Report, Vol. 1, Canberra, 1991, p. 208. See also Cunneen and McDonald, 1997, pp. 23–4.

44  See C. Cunneen, 'Aboriginal Imprisonment During and Since the Royal Commission into Aboriginal Deaths in Custody', *Current Issues in Criminal Justice*, 3, 1992, p. 351. See also Australian Institute of Criminology, *Trends in Crime and Criminal Justice*, No. 153, 'Australian Deaths in Custody and Custody-related Police Operations 1999', Australian Institute of Criminology, Canberra, 2000.

45  See generally G. Gardiner, *Indigenous People and Criminal Justice in Victoria*, Centre for Australian Indigenous Studies, Monash University, Clayton 2001.

46  See R. Jochelson, 'Aborigines and Public Order Legislation in New South Wales', *Contemporary Issues in Criminal Justice*, 34, 1997, pp. 14–15.

47  C. Cunneen and T. Robb, *Criminal Justice in North-west New South Wales*, New South Wales Bureau of Crime Statistics and Research, Sydney, 1987, pp. 192–3. See further C. Cunneen, *Conflict, Politics and Crime. Aboriginal Communities and the Police*, Allen & Unwin, Crows Nest, 2001, ch. 8.

48  *Local Government (Street Drinking) Amendment Act* 1990 (NSW). See K. Kitchener, 'Street Offences and the Summary Offences Act (1988): Social Control in the 1990s' in C. Cunneen (ed.), *Aboriginal Perspectives on Criminal Justice*, Sydney University Institute of Criminology, Sydney, 1992, p. 22; J. White, 'Power/Knowledge and Public Space: Policing the Aboriginal Towns', *Australian and New Zealand Journal of Criminology*, 30, 1997, p. 275.

49    L. Collins and J. Mouzos, 'Deaths in Custody: A Gender-specific analysis', *Trends and Issues in Crime and Justice*, No. 238, Canberra, 2002, pp. 5–6. Specifically, the study found that a higher proportion of Aboriginal women were in police custody at the time of their deaths for public order offences than non-Aboriginal women.

50    For a summary of the findings of these studies, see C. Cunneen, 'Policing and Aboriginal Communities: Is the Concept of Over-policing Useful?' in Cunneen, 1992, pp. 82–3 and 86–7.

51    Human Rights and Equal Opportunity Commission's report, *Racist Violence*, AGPS, Canberra, 1990, p. 93.

52    As above, pp. 82–8.

53    C. Cunneen, *Aboriginal-Police Relations in Redfern: With Special Reference to the 'Police Raid' of 8 February 1990*, Report commissioned by the National Inquiry into Racist Violence, Sydney, 1990, pp. 35–6.

54    Article 1(l). Australia ratified the Convention in 1975.

55    C. Charles, 'Sentencing Aboriginal People in South Australia', *Adelaide Law Review*, 13, 1991, p. 90.

56    Final Report, Vol. 1, 1991, pp. 116–17.

57    P. Gallagher and P. Poletti, *Sentencing Disparity and the Ethnicity of Juvenile Offenders*, Sydney, 1998.

58    Gallagher and Poletti, 1998, p. 25.

59    C. Cunneen, 'Judicial Racism' in S. McKillop (ed.), *Aboriginal Justice Issues*. Proceedings of the Australian Institute of Criminology Conference, 23–5 June 1992, Australian Institute of Criminology, Canberra, 1993, p. 117.

60    See further Cunneen and Robb, 1987.

61    NSW Anti-Discrimination Board. *A Study of Street Offences by Aborigines*, Sydney, 1982.

62    C. Cunneen, 'Policing and Aboriginal Communities: Is the Concept of Over-policing Useful?' in C. Cunneen (ed.), 1992, p. 90.

63    P. O'Shane, 'Aborigines and the Criminal Justice System' in C. Cunneen (ed.), 1992, pp. 5–6.

64    M. Hoey and M. Flynn, '*Deaths in Custody. The Royal Commission: 10 years on*' (2001) 26 *Alternative Law Journal* 196.

65    Speech delivered in Redfern, NSW, 10 December 1992.

66    Royal Commission into Aboriginal Deaths in Custody, *Interim Report*, 1988, p. 45.

67    Cunneen and McDonald, 1997, pp. 119–21.

68    Recommendation 96 of the Final Report. See J. Stubbs, C. Cunneen, J. Chan, J. Travaglia and L. Inge, *Cross Cultural Awareness for the Judiciary*, Final Report, Australian Institute of Judicial Administration, Melbourne, 1996.

69    This was advocated by Murphy J in the High Court case of *R v Neal* (1982) 42 ALR 609. See further, chapter 8, pp. 265–6.

70    M. J. Mossman, 'Feminism and Legal Method: The Difference it Makes', *Australian Journal of Law and Society*, 3, 1986, pp. 44–5; M. Davies, *Asking the Law Question*, Law Book Co, Sydney, 1994, p. 191.

71    S. Tarrant, 'Something is Punishing Them to the Side of Their Own Lives: A Feminist Critique of Law and Laws', *University of Western Australia Law Review*, 20, 1990, p. 585.

72    For a more detailed discussion, see S. Yeo, 'Resolving Gender Bias in Criminal Defences', *Monash University Law Review*, 19, 1993, p. 104.

73    For a debate on whether the recognition of the syndrome is advantageous to women, see J. Stubbs, 'Battered Woman Syndrome: An Advance for Women or Further Evidence of the

Legal System's Inability to Comprehend Women's Experiences?', *Current Issues in Criminal Justice*, 3, 1991, p. 267; P. Easteal, 'Battered Woman Syndrome: Misunderstood?', *Current Issues in Criminal Justice*, 3, 1992, p. 356; J. Stubbs, 'The (Un)reasonable Battered Woman? A Response to Easteal', *Current Issues in Criminal Justice*, 3, 1992, p. 359; S. Yeo, 'Battered Woman Syndrome: In Between Syndrome and Conviction', *Current Issues in Criminal Justice*, 4, 1992, p. 75.

74    A. Worral, *Offending Women: Female Lawbreakers and the Criminal Justice System*, Routledge, London, 1990, p. 31.

75    E. Sheehy, J. Stubbs and J. Tolmie, 'Defending Battered Women on Trial: The Battered Woman Syndrome and its Limitations', *Criminal Law Journal*, 16, 1992, p. 369.

76    Article 2(f). The Convention was ratified by Australia in 1983.

77    Rather than modifying the defence of provocation, the Tasmanian legislature has recently abolished the defence on the ground that it is too male-gendered: see R. Bradfield, 'The demise of provocation in Tasmania', *Criminal Law Journal*, 27, 2003, p. 318.

78    Borrowing the words of *Zanker v Vartsokas* [1988] 34 A Crim R 11 at 16, a case on the requirement of imminent threat in the crime of assault.

79    Training programs that educate judges about gender bias have been developed at both Commonwealth and State levels. Further recommendations for judicial training can be expected from the Australian Law Reform Commission's current reference on *Equality and the Law*, Discussion Paper 54, Sydney, 1993.

80    P. Easteal, *Less than Equal: Women and the Australian Legal System*, Butterworths, Sydney, 2001, p. 56.

81    C. Boyle, M. Bertrand, C. Lacerte-Lamontagne and R. Shamai, 'Feminist Visions in Criminal Law' in J. Russell (ed.), *A Feminist Review of Criminal Law*, Minister of Supply and Services, Ottawa, 1985, para. 6.2.

82    As above, para. 6.3.

83    Fox and Freiberg, 1985, p. 465. The authors refer to two unreported cases of the Victorian Full Court, namely, *Sumner* (4 October 1972) and *Stokes* (29 May 1981).

84    D. Biles, 'Prisons and Prisoners in Australia' in D. Chappell and P. Wilson (eds), *The Australian Criminal Justice System*, 2nd edn, Butterworths, Sydney, 1977, p. 352. Biles' study found the level of female imprisonment to be only 2.6% compared to over 12% of the number of people charged with serious crimes who were females.

85    K. Warner, *Sentencing in Tasmania*, Sydney, 1991, p. 271. There is well-documented research overseas which indicates that the sentencing equation for women is much more complicated than one of 'biology equals leniency': see N. Morris, 'Sex and Sentencing', *Criminal Law Review*, 1988, p. 168.

86    *Tracey* (unreported serial no. 38/1987) per Wright J.

87    Victorian Sentencing Committee, Report, Vol. 1, 1988, p. 372. See also R. Douglas, 'Is Chivalry Dead? Gender and Sentence in the Victorian Magistrates' Courts', *Australian and New Zealand Journal of Sociology*, 23, 1987, p. 343.

88    E. Hiller, 'Women, Crime and Criminal Justice: The State of Current Theory and Research in Australia and New Zealand', *Australian and New Zealand Journal of Criminology*, 15, 1982, pp. 74–5; NSW Youth Justice Coalition, 1990, p. 26.

89    Reported in the *Sydney Morning Herald*, 28 February 1998. For a commentary of the scheme, see M. Liverani, 'Slow Take-up for Home Detention', *Law Society Journal*, 36, 1998, p. 42.

90    D. Farrington and A. Morris, 'Sex, Sentencing and Reconviction', *British Journal of Criminology*, 23, 1983, p. 243.

91    P. Carlen, 'Future Trends in Women's Crimes and Women's Imprisonment', paper presented at the Australian Institute of Criminology Seminar in Hobart, 21 October 1987, pp. 12–13; T. Henning, 'Psychological Explanations in Sentencing Women in Tasmania', *Australian and New Zealand Journal of Criminology*, 28, 1995, p. 298.

92    E. Moore, 'Alternatives to Secure Detention for Girls' in Atkinson and Gerull, 1994; J. Bargen, 'In Need of Care: Delinquent Young Women in a Delinquent System' in Atkinson and Gerull, 1994.

93    E. Cocks, *An Introduction to Intellectual Disability in Australia*, Australian Institute on Intellectual Disability, Canberra, 1989, p. 39.

94    Article 1. The Declaration was adopted by the General Assembly in 1975 and constitutes a schedule to the *Human Rights and Equal Opportunity Commission Act* 1986 (Cth).

95    Articles 4 and 5.

96    Human Rights and Equal Opportunity Commission, *Human Rights and Mental Illness*, Canberra, 1993, p. 4.

97    New South Wales Law Reform Commission, Research Report 4, 'People with an Intellectual Disability and the Criminal Justice System: Appearances Before Local Courts', Sydney, 1993; and New South Wales Law Reform Commission, Research Report 5, 'People with an Intellectual Disability and the Criminal Justice System: Two Rural Courts', Sydney, 1996.

98    S. Hayes and D. McIlwain, *The Prevalence of Intellectual Disability in the New South Wales Prison Population: An Empirical Study*, Report to the Criminology Research Council, Canberra, 1988, p. 47.

99    M. Ierace, 'Acting for the Intellectually Disabled Offender', *Law Society Journal*, 25, 1987, p. 43.

100   S. Bright, 'Intellectual Disability and the Criminal Justice System: New Developments', *Law Institute Journal*, 63, 1989, p. 933.

101   J. Cockram, R. Jackson and R. Underward, 'People with an Intellectual Disability and the Criminal Justice System: The Family Perspective', paper presented at the Sixth Joint National Conference of the National Council of Intellectual Disability and the Australian Society for the Study of Intellectual Disability, Perth, 1994, p. 16.

102   R. Hearn, 'Policing or Serving? The Role of Police in the Criminalisation of Young People with Mental Health Problems', *Youth Studies Australia*, 12, 1993, p. 40.

103   Inter-departmental Committee on Intellectually Handicapped Adult Offenders in New South Wales, *The Missing Services*, Sydney, 1985, p. 24.

104   Hayes and McIlwain, 1988, p. 11.

105   Article 5.

106   Article 9. See also Article 4 of the United Nations *Declaration on the Rights of Mentally Retarded Persons* (1971).

107   Article 10.

108   Article 6.

109   For a study confirming this and other perceptions and experiences of intellectually disabled people towards the police, see New South Wales Law Reform Commission, Research Report 3, *People with an Intellectual Disability and the Criminal Justice System: Consultations*, Sydney, 1993, paras 4.10–4.12.

110 New South Wales Law Reform Commission, Report 80, *People with an Intellectual Disability and the Criminal Justice System*, Sydney, 1996, recommendations 5 and 6.

111 New South Wales Law Reform Commission, Report 80, recommendations 7 and 8.

112 *Narula* (1986) 22 ACR 409. See J. Goldhar, 'People with Intellectual Disabilities and the Criminal Justice System', *Law Institute Journal*, 63, 1989, p. 856.

113 Instruction 155, paras 1.22–1.23.

114 This is a study of people appearing before a court within a given time frame.

115 New South Wales Law Reform Commission, Research Report 4, *People with an Intellectual Disability and the Criminal Justice System: Appearances Before Local Courts*, Sydney, 1993, and Research Report 5, *People with an Intellectual Disability and the Criminal Justice System: Two Rural Courts*, Sydney, 1996.

116 Law Reform Commission of Victoria, Report No. 34, *Mental Malfunction and Criminal Responsibility*, Melbourne, 1990, para. 118.

117 Real case examples are described in the Victorian Law Reform Commission's Report, paras 116–17.

118 The New South Wales scheme was introduced under the *Mental Health (Criminal Procedure) Act* 1990 (NSW) and has received the general approval of the New South Wales Law Reform Commission, Report 80. For a more detailed description of the scheme, see the New South Wales Law Reform Commission, Report 80, paras 5.9–5.18. The South Australian scheme was introduced in 1995 and the Western Australian scheme in 1996.

119 New South Wales Law Reform Commission, Report 80, recommendations 29 and 30.

120 Article 11.

121 *Letteri* (unreported, NSW CCA, 18 March 1992) referring to various Victorian case authorities.

122 (1978) 164 CLR 465.

123 New South Wales Law Reform Commission, *People with an Intellectual Disability and the Criminal Justice System*, Issues Paper, Sydney, 1992, para. 6.20.

124 See New South Wales Law Reform Commission, Report 80, paras 11.4–11.22.

125 Submission of the New South Wales Intellectual Disability Rights Service to the New South Wales Law Reform Commission, in Issues paper, para. 6.14.

126 New South Wales Law Reform Commission, Report 80, recommendations 58 and 59.

127 L. Schrager and J. Short, 'Toward a Sociology of Organizational Crime', *Social Problems*, 25, 1977, p. 409.

128 C. Cunneen, 'Law, Order and Inequality' in J. O'Leary and R. Sharp (eds), *Inequality in Australia: Slicing the Cake*, Heinemann, Melbourne, 1991, pp. 327–8.

129 *Wings Ltd v Ellis* [1985] 1 AC 272 at 293 per Lord Scarman.

130 R. Tomasic, 'Sanctioning Corporate Crime and Misconduct: Beyond Draconian and Decriminalisation Solutions', *Australian Journal of Corporate Law*, 2, 1992, p. 84.

131 S. Perrone, 'Workplace Fatalities and the Adequacy of Protection', *Law in Context*, 13, 1995, p. 81.

132 See chapter 8, p. 262.

133 After the name of the House of Lords case which developed the principle: *Tesco Supermarkets Ltd v Nattrass* [1972] AC 153. For examples of Australian cases adopting the principle, see *Collins v State Rail Authority of New South Wales* (1986) 5 NSWLR 209;

*S & Y Investments (No. 2) Pty Ltd v Commercial Union Assurance Co. of Australia Ltd* (1986) 85 FLR 285; *Hamilton v Whitehead* (1988) 63 ALJR 80.

134   For a detailed discussion of this and other problems of the *Tesco* principle, see B. Fisse and J. Braithwaite, *Corporations, Crime and Accountability*, Cambridge University Press, Cambridge, 1993.

135   National Committee on Violence, *Violence: Future Directions for Australia*, Canberra, 1990, p. 52. For the view that the tobacco industry should be criminalised for harming smokers, see J. Liberman and J. Clough, 'Corporations that Kill: The Criminal Liability of Tobacco Manufacturers', *Criminal Law Journal*, 26, 2002, p. 223.

136   C. Cunneen, in J. O'Leary and R. Sharp (eds), *Inequality in Australia: Slicing the Cake*, Heinemann, Melbourne, 1991, p. 329. For the prospect of fraudulent activity in the superannuation industry in future years, see Australian Institute of Criminology, *Trends and Issues in Crime and Criminal Justice*, No. 56, 'Superannuation Crime', Canberra, 1996.

137   G. Acquaah-Gaisie, 'Corporate Crimes: Criminal Intent and Just Restitution', *Australian Journal of Corporate Law*, 13, 2001, p. 220.

138   See B. Fisse, 'Sanctions against Corporations: Economic Efficiency or Legal Efficiency?', Transnational Corporations Research Project, University of Sydney, Sydney, 1986, pp. 9–10.

139   Australian Institute of Criminology, *Trends and Issues in Crime and Criminal Justice*, No. 4, 'How the Public Sees Sentencing: An Australian Survey', Australian Institute of Criminology, Canberra, 1987.

140   In particular, see Part 2.5 of the Act. For a critique of the legislation, see T. Woolf, 'The Criminal Code Act 1995 (Cth): Towards a Realist Vision of Corporate Criminal Liability', *Criminal Law Journal*, 21, 1997, p. 257.

141   These two approaches were presented in chapter 1, p. 15. For further discussion, see Fisse, 1986, pp. 19–25.

142   For example, *Environment Protection Act* 1993 (SA), s. 129.

143   A. Hopkins, *Making Safety Work: Getting Management Commitment to Occupational Health and Safety*, Allen & Unwin, Sydney, 1995, pp. 105–7.

144   For a recent proposal of this nature, see the Australian Competition and Consumer Commission, 'Criminal Sanctions and increased pecuniary penalties', submission to the Trade Practices Act Review, 2002. The ACCC's submission is analysed in J. Clarke and M. Bagaric, 'The desirability of criminal penalties for breaches of Part IV of the Trade Practices Act', *Australian Business Law Review*, 31, 2003, p. 192.

145   As above, pp. 30–5.

146   T. Makkai and J. Braithwaite, 'Praise, Pride and Corporate Compliance', *International Journal of the Sociology of Law* , 21, 1993, p. 73; Fisse, 1986, pp. 25–30.

147   That is, making erring corporations identify and rectify those of its procedures and processes which caused the harm. See J. Braithwaite, *Crime, Shame and Reintegration*, Cambridge University Press, Cambridge, 1989, ch. 9.

148   'NSW will introduce industrial manslaughter regime, says Minister', *OHS alert*, 21 July 2004. Incidentally, in August 2004, the Commission convicted two mine managers and a surveyor for the deaths of several coal miners, and ordered them to pay stiff fines. These were the first convictions in the 200-year history of the NSW coal mining industry despite more than 3000 miners killed in the State's coal mines: see *Sydney Morning Herald*, 10 August 2004.

149 Measures implemented by the Australian Securities and Investments Commission (formerly the Australian Securities Commission) have been in the right direction: see K. Fairall, 'The Corporations Law: Likely Directions for 1993', *Journal of Corporate Management*, 45, 1993, p. 5. See chapter 3 of this book for a discussion of the ASC's efforts at crime investigation.

150 See chapter 1, p. 20.

151 Box, 1983, p. 79. We have replaced 'genocide' with 'homicide' in the quotation because we feel that the former is too strong a term.

152 Article 4. The Declaration was adopted by the United Nations General Assembly in 1985.

153 See R. Davis, F. Kunreuther and E. Connick, 'Expanding the Victim's Role in the Criminal Court Dispositional Process: The Results of an Experiment', *Journal of Criminal Law and Criminology*, 75, 1984, p. 491.

154 Australian Bureau of Statistics, *Recorded Crime-Victims, Australia, 2003*, Canberra, 2004, p. 14.

155 D. Tait, 'Cautions and Appearances: Statistics About Youth and Police' in White and Alder, 1994, p. 70.

156 Queensland Criminal Justice Commission, 1992, p. 9.

157 A. Broadbent and R. Bentley, *Child Abuse and Neglect, Australia, 1995–96*, Child Welfare Series 17, Canberra, 1997, p. 25.

158 M. Stafford and O. Galle, 'Victimisation Rates, Exposure to Risk and Fear of Crime', *Criminology*, 22, 1984, p. 173.

159 Human Rights and Equal Opportunity Commission, *Our Homeless Children*, Canberra, 1989, p. 69. The Commission acknowledged that the figure could be as high as 70 000.

160 C. Alder, 'Victims of Violence: The Case of Homeless Youth', *Australian and New Zealand Journal of Criminology*, 24, 1991, p. 1.

161 Alder, 1991, p. 13.

162 Australian Law Reform Commission and Human Rights and Equal Opportunity Commission, 1997, paras. 5.43–5.45.

163 R. Harding, R. Broadhurst, A. Ferrante and N. Loh, *Aboriginal Contact with the Criminal Justice System and the Impact of the Royal Commission into Aboriginal Deaths in Custody*, Hawkins Press, Perth, 1995, pp. 20–3.

164 A. Bolger, Aboriginal Women and Violence: A Report for the Criminology Research Council and the Northern Territory Commissioner of Police, Darwin, 1991.

165 J. Mouzous, 'New Statistics Highlight High Homicide rate for Indigenous Women', *Indigenous Law Bulletin*, 4, 1999, pp. 16–17.

166 G. Gardiner and T. Takagi, 'Indigenous Women and the Police in Victoria: Patterns of Offending and Victimisation in the 1990s', *Current Issues in Criminal Justice*, 13, 2002, pp. 313–16.

167 Human Rights and Equal Opportunity Commission, Racist Violence, Canberra, 1990, pp. 107–8; See also, Cunneen above, 2001, pp. 160–5.

168 While Aboriginal women suffer from extremely high rates of domestic violence, reporting a violent partner to the police is unlikely because family breakups are contrary to Aboriginal culture: see P. Greer, 'Aboriginal Women and Domestic Violence in New South Wales' in J. Stubbs (ed.), *Women, Male Violence and the Law*, Institute of Criminology, Sydney, 1994. See further, Australian Institute of Criminology, 'Indigenous and Non-indigenous Homicides in Australia. A Comparative Analysis', *Trends and Issues in Crime and Criminal Justice*, No. 210, Australian Institute of Criminology, Canberra, 2001.

169  *Community Attitudes Towards Domestic Violence in Australia: Social Survey Report*, Sydney, 1988. See also Young People and Domestic Violence: Partnerships against Domestic Violence, 2000: <http://www.ncp.gov.au/ncp/publications/no10.htm>.

170  *Violence: Directions for Australia*, 1990, pp. 33–4.

171  Public Policy Research Centre, *Community Attitudes Towards Domestic Violence in Australia: Social Survey Report*, Sydney, 1988.

172  H. McGregor and A. Hopkins, *Working for Change: The Movement against Domestic Violence*, Allen & Unwin, Sydney, 1991, ch. 7.

173  *Violence: Directions for Australia*, 1990, pp. 188–9.

174  See 'Editorial: Educating the Judiciary on Gender Bias', *Criminal Law Journal*, 17, 1993, p. 155; K. Gosman, 'Judges on Trial. Are They Asking For It?', *Sydney Morning Herald*, 14 May 1993, p. 9; B. Hocking, 'The Presumption Not in Keeping with *Any* Times: Judicial Re-Appraisal of Justice Bollen's Comments Concerning Marital Rape', *Australian Feminist Law Journal*, 1, 1993, p. 152.

175  Australian Law Reform Commission, Discussion Paper 54, *Equality Before the Law*, Sydney, 1993.

176  H. Katzen, *'How Do I Prove I Saw His Shadow?' Responses to Breaches of Apprehended Violence Orders: A Consultation with Women and Police in the Richmond Local Area Command of New South Wales*, 2000.

177  *Violence: Directions for Australia*, 1990, pp. 183–4.

178  Cf. J. Scutt, *Women and the Law: Commentary and Materials*, Law Book Co., Sydney, 1990, pp. 451–9, who argues that the concept of restraint orders is problematic because it treats as a civil matter what is really a criminal assault.

179  B. McSherry, 'Constructing Consent' in P. Easteal (ed.), *Balancing the Scales: Rape, Law Reform and Australian Culture*, Federation Press, Sydney, 1998, p. 30.

180  S. Bronitt and B. McSherry, *Principles of Criminal Law*, Law Book Co., Sydney, 2001, p. 597.

181  L. Trimboli, 'Women as Victims and Offenders', *Contemporary Issues in Crime and Justice*, 22, 1995, p. 6.

182  See N. Naffine, 'A Struggle Over Meaning: A Feminist Commentary on Rape Law Reform', *Australian and New Zealand Journal of Criminology*, 27, 1994, p. 100.

183  See J. Silverii, 'The Trials of Sex', *Law Institute Journal*, 77, 2003, p. 18, for a good account of why women who make up the vast majority of sexual assault victims are fearful of the legal system.

184  Real Rape Law Coalition, *No Real Justice: The Interim Report of a Confidential Phone-In on Sexual Assault*, Melbourne, 1991, p. 47.

185  New South Wales Department for Women, *Heroines of Fortitude: The Experiences of Women in Court as Victims of Sexual Assault*, Sydney, 1996.

186  *Criminal Procedure Act* 1986 (NSW), s. 294A, introduced by the *Criminal Procedure Amendment (Sexual Offence Evidence) Act* 2003 (NSW).

187  See generally K. Johnson, R. Andrew and V. Topp, *Silent Victims: A Study of People with Intellectual Disabilities as Victims of Crime*, Office of the Public Advocate, Carlton, 1988.

188  See generally K. Howe, 'Violence against women with disabilities—an overview of the literature', 2000: at <http://www.wwda.org.au/keran.htm>.

189  *Violence: Directions for Australia*, 1990, p. 43.

190 C. Wilson and N. Brewer, 'The Incidence of Criminal Victimisation of Individuals with an Intellectual Disability', *Australian Psychologist*, 27, 1992, p. 114. See also H. Cattalini, *Access to Services for Women with Disabilities who are Subject to Violence: Report for the National Committee on Violence against Women*, Canberra, 1993, p. 12.

191 S. Hayes, 'Sexual Violence Against Intellectually Disabled Victims' in P. Easteal (ed.), *Without Consent: Confronting Adult Sexual Violence*, Australian Institute of Criminology, Canberra, 1993, p. 201.

192 *Chapter 5, Sexual Offences Against the Person*, 1999, Model Criminal Code, ss. 5.2.29–5.2.31. Similarly, the Victorian Law Reform Commission is strongly in favour of protecting intellectually impaired people from sexual exploitation by their carers: see VLRC, 'Protecting the vulnerable', *Law Institute Journal*, Vol. 77, 2003, p. 85.

193 As above, p. 116.

194 The Office of the Public Advocate in Victoria is an example.

195 New South Wales Law Reform Commission, Report 80, recommendations 48–54.

196 Howe, as above, in the conclusion.

197 United Nations Secretariat, *Victims of Crime*, Document A/CONF. 121/6, 1985, p. 46.

198 Office of Criminal Statistics, South Australian Attorney-General's Department, *Victims and Criminal Justice*, Adelaide, 1990; New South Wales Task Force, *Services to Victims of Crime*, Sydney, 1987. See further, T. Booth, 'Voices after the killing: Hearing the stories of family victims in New South Wales', *Griffith Law Review*, 10, 2001, p. 25.

199 Article 6(a). The Declaration was adopted by the General Assembly in 1985.

200 Office of Criminal Statistics, *Victims and Criminal Justice*, 1990, p. 59.

201 See G. Flatman and M. Bagaric, 'The Victim and the Prosecutor: The Relevance of Victims in Prosecution Decision-making', *Deakin Law Review*, 6, 2001, p. 238.

202 This is known as the *partie civile* model and is found in some European jurisdictions.

203 Office of Crime Statistics, *Victims and Criminal Justice*, 1990, p. 42.

204 As above, p. 49.

205 As above, p. 59.

206 For example, see *Victims Rights Act 1996* (NSW), Parts 3 and 4.

207 As above, p. 48.

208 For example, see *Criminal Law (Sentencing) Act 1989* (SA), s. 7; *Sentencing Act 1991* (Vic), Part 6 Div. 1A; *Sentencing Act 1995* (WA), ss. 13, 24–6. See also New South Wales Law Reform Commission, Report 79, *Sentencing*, 1996: Sydney, recommendations 3–10.

209 See M. Hinton, 'Expectations Dashed: Victim Impact Statements and the Common Law Approach to Sentencing in South Australia', *University of Tasmania Law Review*, 14, 1995, p. 81; T. McCarthy, 'Victim Impact Statements: A Problematic Remedy', *Australian Feminist Law Journal*, 3, 1994, p. 175; C. Sumner, 'Victim Participation in the Criminal Justice System', *Australian and New Zealand Journal of Criminology*, 20, 1987, pp. 207–9.

210 E. Erez, L. Roeger and F. Morgan, *Victim Impact Statements in South Australia: An Evaluation*, Office of Crime Statistics, SA Attorney-General's Department, Series c, No. 6, Adelaide, 1994.

211 Chapter 8 was devoted to this subject.

212 *Violence: Directions for Australia*, 1990, p. 181.

213 M. Hinton, 'Guarding Against Victim-authored Victim Impact Statements', *Criminal Law Journal*, 20, 1996, p. 310.

214   Office of Criminal Statistics, *Victims and Criminal Justice*, 1990, pp. 44–5.

215   As above, p. 46.

216   For example, see *Victims Rights Act* 1996 (NSW); *Victims of Crime Assistance Act* 1996 (Vic); *Criminal Offences Victims Act* 1995 (Qld).

217   In Tasmania, there is legislation making compensation orders compulsory for property damage, with the offender having to pay compensation from their own pockets. This arrangement has not worked well in practice: see K. Warner and J. Gawlik, 'Mandatory compensation orders for crime victims and the rhetoric of restorative justice', *Australian and New Zealand Journal of Criminology*, 36, 2003, p. 60.

218   Warner and Gawlik, as above, p. 73.

219   As above, p. 58.

220   As above, p. 59.

221   *Violence: Directions for Australia*, 1990, p. 191.

222   J. Bargen, 'The *Young Offenders Act* 1997 (NSW): The Beginning of Restorative Organisational Reforms in Juvenile Justice in New South Wales?', conference paper, Restorative Justice Conference, Brisbane, 22–3 July, 1999; T. Booth, 'Delivering Justice to Victims of Crime', *Law Society Journal*, 40, 2002, p. 64.

223   *Victims of Crime Act* 1994 (WA), Schedule 1.

224   See generally, M. Findlay, *The Globalisation of Crime*, Cambridge University Press, Cambridge, 1999.

225   J. Hocking, 'National Security and Democratic Rights: Australian Terror Laws', *Sydney Papers*, 16, 2004, p. 92.

226   See chapter 1.

227   *Criminal Code* (Cth), s. 104.

228   *Terrorism (Emergency Powers) Act* 2003 (NT), s. 20.

229   As above, s. 12.

230   *Australian Security Intelligence Organisation Amendment (Terrorism) Act* 2003, s. 34HC. See further chapter 3, p. 101.

231   As above, s. 34TB.

232   As above, s. 34G.

233   See chapter 8, p. 286.

234   *Criminal Code* (Cth), s. 103.1.

235   S. Bronitt, 'Constitutional Rhetoric *v* Criminal Justice Realities: Unbalanced Responses to Terrorism?', *Public Law Review*, 14, 2003, p. 76.

236   See generally G. Walker, *The Rule of Law*, Melbourne University Press, Melbourne, 1988.

237   *Liversidge v Anderson* [1942] AC 206 at 244 per Atkin LJ.

238   M. Robinson, UN High Commissioner for Human Rights, UN Doc E/C/N.4/2002/18 (27 February 2002), para. 2; J. Dempsey, 'Civil Liberties in a Time of Crisis', *Human Rights*, 29, 2002, pp. 8–10.

239   A laudable example of legislative recognition of these conventions is s. 562AC of the *Crimes Act* 1900 (NSW), which concerns apprehended violence orders. The provision expressly refers to the principles of the *Declaration on the Elimination of Violence Against Women*.

# Bibliography

Acquaah-Gaisie, G., 2001, 'Corporate Crimes: Criminal Intent and Just Restitution', *Australian Journal of Corporate Law*, 13, p. 220.

Alder, C., 1991, 'Victims of Violence: The Case of Homeless Youth', *Australian and New Zealand Journal of Criminology*, 24, p. 1.

Arenson, K., 1996, 'Causation in the Criminal Law: A Search for Doctrinal Consistency', *Criminal Law Journal*, 20, p. 189.

Aronson, M., 1992, *Managing Complex Criminal Trials: Reforms of the Rules of Evidence and Procedure*, Institute of Judicial Administration, Melbourne.

Aronson, M. I., Hunter, J. B. and Weinberg, M. S., 1988, *Litigation: Evidence and Procedure*, Butterworths, Sydney.

Asche, A., 1991, 'The Trial Judge, the Appeal Court and the Unsafe Verdict', *Criminal Law Journal*, 15, p. 416.

Ashworth, A., 1983, *Sentencing and Penal Policy*, Butterworths, London.

Ashworth, A., 1986, 'Criminal Justice, Rights and Sentencing: A Review of Sentencing Policy and Problems' in Potas, I. (ed.), *Sentencing in Australia: Issues, Policy and Reform. Proceedings of a seminar on Sentencing: Problems and Prospects*, Australian Institute of Criminology, Canberra.

Ashworth, A., 1998, 'Four Techniques for Reducing Sentences' in von Hirsch, A. and Ashworth, A. (eds), *Principled Sentencing: Readings on Theory and Practice*, Oxford University Press, Oxford, p. 229.

Ashworth, A., 2003, *Principles of Criminal Law*, 4th edn, Oxford University Press, Oxford.

Ashworth, A. and Steiner, E., 1990, 'Criminal Omissions and Public Duties: The French Experience', *Legal Studies*, 10, p. 153.

Australian Bureau of Statistics, 2004, *Recorded Crime-Victims, Australia, 2003*, AGPS, Canberra.

Australian Bureau of Statistics, 1998, 'Law and Justice Issues', *Indigenous Australians*, AGPS, Canberra.

Australian Institute of Criminology, 1986, 'How the Public Sees Crime: An Australian Survey', *Trends and Issues*, 2, Canberra.

Australian Institute of Criminology, 1987, 'How the Public Sees Sentencing: An Australian Survey', *Trends and Issues*, 4, Canberra.

Australian Institute of Criminology, 1989, *Public Attitudes on Dealing with Juvenile Offenders*, Canberra.

Australian Institute of Criminology, 1990, Report on *The Cost of Juvenile Crime and Crime Prevention*, Canberra.

Australian Institute of Criminology, 1995, 'Infringement Notices: Time for Reform?', *Trends and Issues*, 50, Canberra.

Australian Law Reform Commission, 1975, Report No. 2, *Criminal Investigation*, Sydney.

Australian Law Reform Commission, 1980, *Sentencing Federal Offenders*, Interim Report No. 15, Sydney.

Australian Law Reform Commission, 1983, *Privacy*, Report No. 22, Sydney.

Australian Law Reform Commission, 1985, *Evidence*, Interim Report No. 26, Sydney.

Australian Law Reform Commission, 1987, *Contempt*, Report No. 35, Sydney.

Australian Law Reform Commission, 1987, *Sentencing: Procedure*, Discussion Paper No. 29, Sydney.

Australian Law Reform Commission, 1988, *Sentencing*, Report No. 44, Sydney.

Australian Law Reform Commission, 1992, *Multiculturalism and the Law*, Report No. 57, Sydney.

Australian Law Reform Commission, 1993, *Equality before the Law*, Discussion Paper No. 54, Sydney.

Ayling, C. J., 1984, 'Comment—Corroborating Confession', *Wisconsin Law Review*, pp. 1121–90.

Baldwin, J. and McConville, M., 1979, *Jury Trials*, Oxford University Press, Oxford.

Baldwin, K. and Bottomley, A. K., 1978, *Criminal Justice: Selected Readings*, Part II, Martin Robertson, Oxford.

Bargen, J., 1992, 'Going to Court CAP in Hand', *Current Issues in Criminal Justice*, 4(2), pp. 118–40.

Bargen, J., 1994, 'In Need of Care: Delinquent Young Women in a Delinquent System' in Atkinson, L. and Gerull, S. A. (eds), *National Conference on Juvenile Detention: Conference Proceedings*, Australian Institute of Criminology, Canberra.

Bargen, J., 1999, 'The *Young Offenders Act* 1997 (NSW): The Beginning of Restorative Organisational Reforms in Juvenile Justice in New South Wales?', Restorative Justice Conference, Brisbane, 22–23 July.

Basten, J., Richardson, M., Ronalds, C. and Zdenkowski, G. (eds), 1982, *The Criminal Injustice System*, Legal Services Bulletin, Sydney.

Bean, P., 1976, *Rehabilitation and Deviance*, Routledge and Keagan Paul, London.

Bean, P., 1981, *Punishment*, Martin Robertson, Oxford.

Bentham, J., 1962, 'Principles of Penal Law', Bowring, J. (ed.), *Works*, Edinburgh.

Bersten, M., 1990, 'Making ICAC Work: Effectiveness, Efficiency and Accountability', *Current Issues in Criminal Justice*, 1(2), p. 67.

Biles, D., 1977, 'Prisons and Prisoners in Australia' in Chappell, D. and Wilson, P. (eds), *The Australian Criminal Justice System*, 2nd edn, Butterworths, Sydney.

Blagg, H. and Wilkie, M., 1997, 'Young People and Policing in Australia: The Relevance of the United Nations Convention on the Rights of the Child', *Australian Journal of Human Rights*, 3, p. 134.

Blanch, R., 1991, *Prosecution Policy and Guidelines of the Director of Public Prosecutions*, Office of the DPP, Sydney.

Blom-Cooper, L. and Morris, T., 1996, 'The Penalty for Murder: A Myth Exploded', *Criminal Law Review*, p. 707.

Blumstein, A., Cohen, J, Martin, S. and Tonry, M. (eds), 1983, *Research on Sentencing: The Search for Reform*, Vols 1 and 2, National Academy Press, Washington.

Bolger, A., 1991, *Aboriginal Women and Violence: Report for the Criminology Research Council and the Northern Territory Commission of Police*, Darwin.

Booth, T., 2001, 'Voices after the Killing: Hearing the Stories of Family Victims in New South Wales', *Griffith Law Review*, 10, p. 25.

Bottom, B., 1984, *Without Fear or Favour*, Sun Books, Melbourne.

Bottomley, K. and Coleman, C., 1984, 'Law and Order: Crime Problem, Moral Panic, or Penal Crisis?' in Norton, P. (ed.), *Law and Order in British Politics*, Gower, Aldershot.

Bourke, J., 1993, 'Misapplied Science: Unreliability in Scientific Test Evidence', *Australian Bar Review*, 10, p. 123.

Bowen, J. K., 1986, 'Suspect's Rights and Police Duties', *Law Institute Journal*, p. 1344.

Box, S., 1983, *Power, Crime and Mystification*, Tavistock, London.

Boyle, C., Bertrand, M., Lacerte-Lamontagne, C. and Shamai, R., 1985, 'Feminist Visions in Criminal Law' in Russell, J. (ed.), *A Feminist Review of Criminal Law*, Minister of Supply and Services, Ottawa.

Bradfield, R., 2003, 'The Demise of Provocation in Tasmania', *Criminal Law Journal*, 27, p. 318.

Braithwaite, J., 1989, *Crime, Shame and Reintegration*, Cambridge University Press, Cambridge.

Bright, J., 1989, 'Intellectual Disability and the Criminal Justice System: New Developments', *Law Institute Journal*, 63, p. 933.

Bronitt, S., 2003, 'Constitutional Rhetoric v Criminal Justice Realities: Unbalanced Responses to Terrorism?', *Public Law Review*, 14, p. 76.

Brown, D., 1977, 'Criminal Justice Reform: A Critique' in Chappell, D. and Wilson, P. (eds), *The Australian Criminal Justice System*, Butterworths, Sydney, p. 471.

Brown, D., 1997, *PACE Ten Years On: A Review of the Research*, Research Study No. 155, Home Office, London, p. 171.

Brown, D., 2002, 'The Politics of Law and Order', *Law Society Journal*, 40, p. 64.

Brown, D. and Neal, D., 1988, 'Show Trials: The Media and the Gang of Twelve' in Findlay, M. and Duff, P. (eds), *The Jury Under Attack*, Butterworths, Sydney, p. 135.

Brown, D. and Willke, M. (eds), 2002, *Prisoners as Citizens: Human Rights in Australian Prisons*, Federation Press, Sydney.

Cain, M., 1996, *Recidivism of Juvenile Offenders in New South Wales*, NSW Department of Juvenile Justice, Sydney, p. 1.

Carlen, P., 1987, 'Future Trends in Women's Crimes and Women's Imprisonment', paper presented at the Australian Institute of Criminology Seminar, Hobart.

Carlen, P. and Worral, A., 1987, *Gender, Crime and Justice*, Oxford University Press, Milton Keynes.

Carrington, K., Dever, M., Hogg, R., Bargen, J. and Lohrey, A., 1992, *Travesty! Miscarriages of Justice*, Pluto Press, Sydney.

Carroll, V., 1992, 'The Trials and Tribulations of the Jury', *Sydney Morning Herald*, 20 August, p. 13.

Cashman, P., 1982, 'Representation in Criminal Cases' in Basten, J., Richardson, M., Ronalds, C. and Zdenkowski, G. (eds), *The Criminal Injustice System*, Legal Services Bulletin, Sydney.

Cashman, P., 1987, 'Legal Representation in Lower Courts' in Zdenkowski, G., Ronalds, C. and Richardson, M. (eds), *The Criminal Injustice System*, Vol. 2, Pluto Press, Sydney.

Challinger, D. (ed.), 1988, *Bail or Remand?* Australian Institute of Criminology, Canberra.

Chambliss, W. and Seidman, R., 1971, *Law, Order and Power*, John Wiley & Sons, Reading, MA.

Chan, J., 1987, 'The Limits of Sentencing Reform' in Zdenkowski, G., Ronalds, C. and Richardson, M. (eds), *The Criminal Injustice System*, Vol. 2, Pluto Press, Sydney.

Chan, J., 1992, *Doing Less Time*, Sydney Institute of Criminology, Sydney.

Chappell, D. and Wilson, P., 1989, *Australian Policing: Contemporary Issues*, Butterworths, Sydney.

Chappell, D. and Wilson, P. (eds), 1993, *The Australian Criminal Justice Systems—the Mid 90s*, Butterworths, Sydney.

Charles, C., 1991, 'Sentencing Aboriginal People in South Australia', *Adelaide Law Review*, 13, pp. 90–6.

Choo, A. L-T., 1989, 'Abuse of Process and Pre-trial Delay: A Structured Approach', *Criminal Law Journal*, 13, pp. 178–87.

Christie, N., 1993, *Crime Control as Industry*, Routledge, London.

Clarke, J. and Bagaric, M., 2003, 'The Desirability of Criminal Penalties for Breaches of Part IV of the Trade Practices Act', *Australian Business Law Review*, 31, p. 192.

Cocks, E., 1989, *An Introduction to Intellectual Disability in Australia*, Australian Institute on Intellectual Disability, Canberra.

Cohen, S., 1985, *Visions of Social Control*, Polity Press, Oxford.

Colvin, E., 1989, 'Causation in Criminal Law', *Bond Law Review*, 1, p. 253.

Committee of Inquiry into the Enforcement of Criminal Law in Queensland, 1977, *Report* (the Lucas Report), Brisbane.

Commonwealth Attorney-General's Department, 1995, *The Justice Statement*, p. 102.

Commonwealth Director of Public Prosecutions, 1990, *Prosecution Policy of the Commonwealth*, 2nd edn, AGPS, Canberra.

Constitutional Commission, 1988, *Final Report*, AGPS, Canberra.

Corns, C., 1991, 'Evaluating the National Crime Authority', *Law Institute Journal*, pp. 829–30.

Corns, C., 1992, 'Inter-agency Relations: Some Hidden Obstacles to Combating Organised Crime', *Australian and New Zealand Journal of Criminology*, 25, p. 169.

Corns, C., 2004, 'Videotaped Evidence in Victoria: Some Evidentiary Issues and Appellate Court Perspectives', *Criminal Law Journal*, 43.

Costigan, F., 1984, *Royal Commission on the Activities of the Federated Ship Painters and Dockers Union, Final Report*, Canberra.

Costigan, F., 1986, 'Control of Organised Crime with Reflections on Sydney', *Proceedings of the Institute of Criminology*, p. 10.

Coumarelos, C., 1994, *Juvenile Offending: Predicting Persistence and Determining Cost-effectiveness of Interventions*, NSW Bureau of Crime Statistics, Sydney, p. 7.

Criminal Justice Commission, 1992, *Youth, Crime and Justice in Queensland*, Brisbane.

Criminal Justice Commission, 1993, *Report on A Review of Police Powers in Queensland*, Brisbane.

Criminal Law Officers Committee of the Standing Committee of Attorneys-General, 1992, *Final Report: Model Criminal Code: General Principles of Criminal Responsibility*, Canberra.

Cunneen, C., 1988, 'An Evaluation of the Juvenile Cautioning System in NSW', *Proceedings of the Institute of Criminology*, 75, pp. 21–38.

Cunneen, C., 1990, *Aboriginal–Police Relations in Redfern: With Special Reference to the 'Police Raid' of 8 February 1990*, Report commissioned by the National Inquiry into Racist Violence, Sydney.

Cunneen, C., 1991, 'Law, Order and Inequality' in O'Leary, J. and Sharp, R. (eds), *Inequality in Australia: Slicing the Cake*, Heinemann, Melbourne.

Cunneen, C., 1992, 'Judicial Racism' in McKillop, S. (ed.), *Aboriginal Justice Issues, Proceedings of the Australian Institute of Criminology Conference*, 23–25 June 1992, Canberra.

Cunneen, C., 2001, *Conflict, Politics and Crime: Aboriginal Communities and the Police*, Allen & Unwin, Crows Nest.

Cunneen, C. and McDonald, D., 1997, *Keeping Aboriginal and Torres Strait Islander People in Custody*, ATSIC, Canberra, p. 27.

Cunneen, C. and Robb, T., 1987, *Criminal Justice in North-west New South Wales*, New South Wales Bureau of Crime Statistics and Research, Sydney.

Cunneen, C. and White, R., 1995, *Juvenile Justice: An Australian Perspective*, Oxford University Press, Melbourne, p. 97.

D'Amato, A., 1989, 'The Ultimate Injustice: When a Court Misstates the Facts', *Cardozo Law Review*, 11, p. 1313.

Damaska, M. R., 1986, *The Faces of Justice and State Authority*, Yale University Press, New Haven, CT.

Davies, M., 1994, *Asking the Law Question*, Law Book Co, Sydney.

Davis, K. C., 1975, *Police Discretion*, West Publishing, Saint Paul.

Davis, R., Kunreuther, F. and Connick, E., 1984, 'Expanding the Victim's Role in the Criminal Court Dispositional Process: The Results of an Experiment', *Journal of Criminal Law and Criminology*, 75, p. 491.

Dempsey, J., 2002, 'Civil Liberties in a Time of Crisis', *Human Rights*, 29, p. 8.

Dempster, Q., 1992, *Honest Cops*, pp. 116–20, ABC Books, Sydney.

Devlin, P., 1965, *The Enforcement of Morals*, Oxford University Press, London.

Disney, J., Redmond, P., Basten, J. and Ross, S., 1986, *Lawyers*, 2nd edn, Law Book Co., Sydney.

Dixon, D., 1991, 'Common Sense, Legal Advice and the Right of Silence', *Public Law*, p. 240.

Dixon, D., 1991, 'Politics, Research and Symbolism in Criminal Justice: The Right of Silence and the Police and Criminal Evidence Act', *Anglo-American Law Review*, p. 43.

Dixon, D., 1997, *Law in Policing: Legal Regulation of Police Practices*, Clarendon Press, Oxford.

Dixon, D. (ed.), 1999, *A Culture of Corruption: Changing an Australian Police Service*, Hawkins Press, Sydney.

Dixon, D., Bottomley, K., Coleman, C., Gill, M. and Wall, D., 1990, 'Safeguarding the Rights of Suspects in Police Custody', *Policing and Society*, 1, p. 124.

Dobinson, I. and Ward, P., 1985, *Drugs and Crime*, NSW BCS&R, Sydney.

Douglas, R., 1987, 'Is Chivalry Dead? Gender and Sentence in the Victorian Magistrates' Courts', *Australia and New Zealand Journal of Sociology*, 23, p. 343.

Dowd, J., 1990, 'Committal Reform: Radical or Evolutionary Change', *Current Issues in Criminal Justice*, 2(2), p. 10.

Easteal, P., 1992, 'Battered Woman Syndrome: Misunderstood?', *Current Issues in Criminal Justice*, 3(3), p. 356.

Easteal, P., 2001, *Less than Equal: Women and the Australian Legal System*, Butterworths, Sydney, p. 56.

Edney, R., 2001, 'Use of the Prisoners' Dock under Australian Criminal Law: Desirable Practice or Impediment to a Fair Trial?', *Criminal Law Journal*, 25, p. 194.

Edney, R., 2003, 'Sentencing of Indigenous Offenders in Victoria', *Law Institute Journal*, 32, p. 32.

Emmins, C., 1986, *A Practical Approach to Sentencing*, Blackstone Press, London, p. 47.

Evatt, H., 1938, *Rum Rebellion*, Angus and Robertson, Sydney.

Evland, S., 1993, 'Truth in Sentencing: A Koori Perspective', unpublished research paper.

Fairall, K., 1993, 'The Corporations Law: Likely Directions for 1993', *Journal of Corporate Management*, 45, p. 5.

Fairall, P. and Yeo, S., 2005, *Criminal Defences*, 4th edn, Butterworths, Sydney.

Farrington, D. and Morris, A., 1983, 'Sex, Sentencing and Reconviction', *British Journal of Criminology*, 23, p. 229.

Feinberg, J., 1984, *Harm to Others*, Oxford University Press, New York.

Findlay, M., 1982, *The State of the Prison: A Critique of Reform*, Mitchellsearch, Bathurst.

Findlay, M., 1983, 'The Politics of Prison Reform' in Findlay, M., Egger, S. and Sutton, J. (eds), *Issues in Criminal Justice Administration*, George Allen & Unwin, Sydney, p. 139.

Findlay, M., 1984, 'The Possibility of a Criminal Justice Corrections Model', *Proceedings of the Institute of Criminology*, 60, p. 11.

Findlay, M., 1986, 'Acting on Information Received: Myth Making and Police Corruption', *Journal of Studies in Justice*, 2.

Findlay, M., 1988, 'The Demise of Corrections' in Cullen, B., Dowding, M. and Griffin, J. (eds), *Corrective Services in NSW*, Law Book Co., Sydney, p. 326.

Findlay, M., 1992, 'Impact of Criminal Justice Administration on the Penal Sanction', *Current Issues in Criminal Justice*, 3(3), p. 339.

Findlay, M., 1993, 'Prosecutorial Discretion and the Conditional Waiver: Lessons from the Japanese Experience', *Current Issues in Criminal Justice*, 4(2), p. 175.

Findlay, M., 1995, 'International Rights and Australian Adaptions: Recent Developments in Criminal Investigation', *Sydney Law Review*, 17, p. 278.

Findlay, M., 1999, *The Globalisation of Crime*, Cambridge University Press, Cambridge.

Findlay, M., 2001, 'Jury Comprehension and Complexity: Strategies to Enhance Understanding', *British Journal of Criminology*, 41, p. 56.

Findlay, M., 2003, *Introducing Australian Policing*, Oxford University Press, Melbourne.

Findlay, M., 2004, 'The "Demise of Corrections" Fifteen Years On: Any Hope for Progressive Punishment', *Current Issues in Criminal Justice*, 2, p. 57.

Findlay, M. and Duff, P. (eds), 1988, *The Jury Under Attack*, Butterworths, Sydney.

Findlay, M. and Grix, J., 2003, 'Challenging Forensic Evidence? Observations on the Use of DNA in Certain Criminal Trials', *Current Issues in Criminal Justice*, 14(3), p. 269.

Findlay, M. and Henham, R., 2005, *Transforming International Criminal Justice*, Willan, Devon (forthcoming).

Findlay, M. and Hogg, R., 1988, *Understanding Crime and Criminal Justice*, Law Book Co., Sydney.

Finnane, M., 1997, *Punishment in Australian Society*, Oxford University Press, Melbourne.

Fisse, B., 1986, 'Sanctions against Corporations: Economic Efficiency or Legal Efficiency?', Transnational Corporations Research Project, University of Sydney, Sydney.

Fisse, B., 1990, *Howard's Criminal Law*, 5th edn, Law Book Co., Sydney.

Fisse, B., 1992, 'Towards a Framework for the Design of Sanctions Against Corporations: Differential Implementation of the Criminal law, Elements of Sanction Design, and the Punitive Length of the Chancellor's Foot', unpublished conference paper.

Fitzgerald, M. and Simm, J., 1982, *British Prisons*, Basil Blackwell, London.

Flatman, G. and Bagaric, M., 2001, 'The Victim and the Prosecutor: The Relevance of Victims in Prosecution Decision-making', *Deakin Law Review*, 6, p. 238.

Flynn, M., 'One Strike and You're Out!', *Alternative Law Journal*, 22, p. 72.

Foucault, M., 1977, *Discipline and Punishment*, Penguin, Harmondsworth, UK.

Fox, R., 1987, 'Controlling Sentencers', *Australian and New Zealand Journal of Criminology*, 20, p. 218.

Fox, R., 1988, 'The Killings of Bobby Veen: The High Court on Proportion in Sentencing', *Criminal Law Journal*, 12, p. 339.

Fox, R., 1991, 'Order Out of Chaos: Victoria's New Maximum Penalty Structure', *Monash University Law Review*, 17, p. 106.

Fox, R., 1992, *Victorian Criminal Procedure*, Oxford University Press, Melbourne.

Fox, R., 1994, 'The Meaning of Proportionality in Sentencing', *Melbourne University Law Review*, 19, p. 489.

Fox, R., 1995, 'Infringement Notices: Time for Reform', *Trends and Issues*, Australian Institute of Criminology, 50.

Fox, R. and Freiberg, A., 1985, *Sentencing: State and Federal Law in Victoria*, Oxford University Press, Melbourne.

Fox, R. and Freiberg, A., 1985, 'The Laws of Australia', *Criminal Sentencing*, 12, Law Book Co., Sydney.

Frank, J., 1949, *Law and the Modern Mind*, Coward-McCann Inc., New York.

Freckelton, I. and Selby, H. (eds), 1988, *Police in Our Society*, Butterworths, Sydney.

Freiberg, A., 1988, 'Jury Selection in Trials of Commonwealth Offences' in Findlay, M. and Duff, P. (eds), *The Jury Under Attack*, Butterworths, Sydney, p. 117.

Freiberg, A., 2000, 'Australian Drug Courts', *Criminal Law Journal*, 24, p. 213.

Freiberg, A. and Morgan, N., 2004, 'Between Bail and Sentence: The Conflation of Disposition Options', *Current Issues in Criminal Justice*, 15, p. 220.

Freiberg, A., Fox, R. and Hogan, M., 1988, *Sentencing Young Offenders*, Sentencing Research Paper No. 11, Australian Law Reform Commission, Sydney, and Commonwealth Youth Bureau, Canberra.

Galbally, R. J., 1991, 'Corporate and Commercial Crime: The New Emphasis', *Law Institute Journal*, p. 826.

Gans, J., 2001, 'Something to Hide: DNA, Surveillance and Self Incrimination', *Current Issues in Criminal Justice*, 13(2), p. 168.

Gardiner, G., 2001, *Indigenous People and Criminal Justice in Victoria*, Centre for Australian Indigenous Studies, Monash University, Clayton.

Gardiner, G. and Takagi, T., 2002, 'Indigenous Women and the Police in Victoria: Patterns of Offending and Victimisation in the 1990s', *Current Issues in Criminal Justice*, 13(3), p. 313.

Garland, D., 1985, *Punishment and Welfare*, Gower, Aldershot.

Garland, D., 1990, *Punishment and Modern Society*, Clarendon Press, Oxford.

Gillies, P., 1990, *The Law of Criminal Conspiracy*, Federation Press, Annandale.

Goldhar, J., 1989, 'People with Intellectual Disabilities and the Criminal Justice System', *Law Institute Journal*, 63, p. 856.

Goode, M., 1992, 'Codification of the Australian Criminal Law', *Criminal Law Journal*, 16, p. 5.

Goode, M., 2004, 'Codification of the Criminal Law', *Criminal Law Journal*, 26, p. 226.

Gorta, A., 1991, 'Impact of the Sentencing Act 1989 on the NSW Prison Population', *Current Issues in Criminal Justice*, 3, p. 308.

Grabosky, P. and Wilson, P., 1989, *Journalism and Justice: How Crime is Reported*, Pluto Press, Sydney.

Greenawalt, L., 1987, 'Punishment' in Kadish, S. (ed.), *Encyclopaedia of Crime and Justice*, Free Press, New York.

Greenberg, D. and Humphries, D., 1980, 'The Co-optation of Fixing Sentencing Reform', *Crime and Delinquency*, 26.

Griffiths, T. and Ayres, A., 1967, 'A Postscript to the Miranda Project: Interrogation of Draft Protesters', *Yale Law Journal*, 77, p. 300.

Hall, S., Critcher, C., Jefferson, T., Clark, J. and Roberts, B., 1978, *Policing the Crisis*, Macmillan, London.

Harding, R., 1988, 'Jury Performance in Complex Commercial Cases' in Findlay, M. and Duff, P. (eds), *The Jury Under Attack*, Butterworths, Sydney.

Harding, R., 1992, 'Prison Privatisation in Australia: A Glimpse of the Future', *Current Issues in Criminal Justice*, 4(1), p. 9.

Harding, R., Broadhurst, R., Ferrante, A. and Loh, N., 1995, *Aboriginal Contact with the Criminal Justice System and the Impact of the Royal Commission into Aboriginal Deaths in Custody*, Hawkins Press, Sydney, p. 20.

Hart, H. L. A., 1963, *Law, Liberty and Morality*, Oxford University Press, London.

Hart, H. L. A., 1968, *Punishment and Responsibility: Essays in the Philosophy of Law*, Oxford University Press, Oxford.

Hartnell, A. G., 1993, 'Regulatory Enforcement by the ASC: An Interrelationship of Strategies' in Grabosky, P. and Braithwaite, J. (eds), *Business Regulation and Australia's Future*, Australian Institute of Criminology, Canberra.

Hay, D., Linebaugh, P. and Thompson, E. P., 1975, *Albion's Fatal Tree*, Allen Lane, London.

Hayes, S. and McIlwain, D., 1988, *The Prevalence of Intellectual Disability in the New South Wales Prison Population: An Empirical Study*, Report to the Criminology Research Council, Canberra.

Hearn, R., 1993, 'Policing or Serving? The Role of Police in the Criminalisation of Young People with Mental Health Problems', *Youth Studies Australia*, 12, p. 40.

Heilpern, D., 1998, *Fear or Favour*, Federation Press, Annandale.

Hickie, D., 1985, *The Prince and the Premier*, Angus & Robertson, Sydney.

Hiller, E., 1982, 'Women, Crime and Criminal Justice: The State of Current Theory and Research in Australia and New Zealand', *Australian and New Zealand Journal of Criminology*, 15, p. 152.

Hinton, M., 1995, 'Expectations Dashed: Victim Impact Statements and the Common Law Approach to Sentencing in South Australia', *University of Tasmania Law Review*, 14, p. 81.

Hocking, J., 2004, *Terror Laws: ASIO, Counter-terrorism and the Threat to Democracy*, University of New South Wales Press, Sydney.

Hocking, J., 2004, 'National Security and Democratic Rights: Australian Terror Laws', *Sydney Papers*, 16, p. 92.

Hoey, M. and Flynn, M., 2001, 'Deaths in Custody. The Royal Commission: 10 Years On', *Alternative Law Journal*, 26, p. 196.

Hogg, R., 1987, 'The Politics of Criminal Investigation' in Wickham, G., *Social Theory and Legal Politics*, Local Consumption Publications, Sydney, p. 120.

Hogg, R., 1988, 'Criminal Justice and Social Control: Contemporary Developments in Australia', *Journal of Studies in Justice*, 2, p. 89.

Hogg, R. and Brown, D., 1998, *Rethinking Law and Order*, Pluto Press, Sydney.

Howard, M. N., 1991, 'The Neutral Expert: A Plausible Threat to Justice', *Criminal Law Review*, p. 98.

Hudson, J., Morris, A., Maxwell, G. and Galaway, B., 1996, *Family Group Conferences: Perspectives on Policy and Practice*, Federation Press, Sydney.

Hughes, R., 1988, *The Fatal Shore: A History of the Transportation of Convicts to Australia*, Pan, London.

Human Rights and Equal Opportunity Commission, 1989, *Our Homeless Children*, Canberra.

Human Rights and Equal Opportunity Commission, 1990, *Racist Violence*, Canberra.

Human Rights and Equal Opportunity Commission, 1993, *Human Rights and Mental Illness*, Canberra.

Human Rights and Equal Opportunity Commission, 1997, *Seen and Heard: Priority for Children in the Legal Process*, Canberra.

Ierace, M., 1987, 'Acting for the Intellectually Disabled Offender', *Law Society Journal*, 25, p. 42.

Ierace, M., 1989, *Intellectual Disability: A Manual for Criminal Lawyers*, Redfern Legal Centre Publishing, Sydney.

Independent Commission Against Corruption, 1990a, *Annual Report to 30 June 1990*, Sydney.

Independent Commission Against Corruption, 1990b, *Report on Investigation into North Coast Land Development*, Sydney.

Independent Commission Against Corruption, 1991, *Annual Report to 30 June 1991*, Sydney.

Independent Commission Against Corruption, 1992, *Report on the Metherell Resignation and Appointment*, Sydney.

Independent Commission Against Corruption, 1993a, *Report on Investigation into the Use of Informers*, Vol. 1, Sydney.

Independent Commission Against Corruption, 1993b, *Report on Investigation into the Use of Informers*, Vol. 2, Sydney.

Indermaur, D., 'Public Perception of Sentencing in Perth, Western Australia', *Australian and New Zealand Journal of Criminology*, 20, p. 163.

Inquiry into the Death of David John Gundy (Commissioner J. H. Wootten), 1991, *Report*, Canberra.

Institute of Criminology, 2002, *Crisis in Bail and Remand: Seminar Papers*, Sydney.

Interdepartmental Committee on Intellectually Handicapped Adult Offenders in New South Wales, 1985, *The Missing Services*, Sydney.

Jackson, H., 2003, 'Child Witnesses in the Western Australian Criminal Courts', *Criminal Law Journal*, 27, p. 199.

James, G., 1990, 'The Future of Committals', *Criminal Law Journal*, 14, p. 145.

Johnson, K., Andrew, R. and Topp, V., 1988, *Silent Victims: A Study of People with Intellectual Disabilities as Victims of Crime*, Office of the Public Advocate, Carlton.

Kadish, S., 1987, *Blame and Punishment: Essays in the Criminal Law*, Macmillan, New York.

Kalven, H. and Zeisel, H., 1966, *The American Jury*, Little Brown, Boston.

Katzen, H., 2000, *'How Do I Prove I Saw His Shadow?' Responses to Breaches of Apprehended Violence Orders: A Consultation with Women and Police in the Richmond Local Area Command of New South Wales*.

Kemp, D., 1992, 'Legal Aid in the Early 1900s: A Broad View of a Bleak Picture', *Alternative Law Journal*, 17, p. 124.

Kenny, R., 2004 *An Introduction to the Criminal Law of Queensland and Western Australia*, Butterworths, Sydney.

Kirby, M. D., 1979, 'Controls over Investigation of Offences and Pre-trial Treatment of Suspects', *Australian Law Journal*, 53, p. 632.

Kitchener, K., 1992, 'Street Offences and the Summary Offences Act (1988): Social Control in the 1990s' in Cunneen, C. (ed.), *Aboriginal Perspectives on Criminal Justice*, Sydney University Institute of Criminology, Sydney.

Lacey, N., 1988, *State Punishment: Political Principles and Community Values*, Routledge, London.

Law Reform Commission of Victoria, 1990, Report No. 34, *Mental Malfunction and Criminal Responsibility*, Melbourne.

Legal Aid Commission of NSW, 1997, *Annual Report 1997*, Sydney.

Legal and Constitutional Committee of the Legislative Council of the Victorian Parliament, 1985, *Report on the Burden of Proof in Criminal Cases*, Melbourne.

Leaver, A., 1997, *Criminal Investigation*, Law Book Co., Sydney.

Leaver, A., 1997, *Investigating Crime: A Guide to the Powers of Agencies Involved in the Investigation of Crime*, LBC Information Services, Sydney.

Lovegrove, A., 1998, 'Judicial Sentencing Policy, Criminological Expertise and Public Opinion', *Australian and New Zealand Journal of Criminology*, 31, p. 287.

Makkai, T. and Braithwaite, J., 1993, 'Praise, Pride and Corporate Compliance', *International Journal of the Sociology of Law*, 21, p. 73.

Mason, S., 1992, 'Background Paper: Evidence and Procedure Reforms', unpublished conference paper, Melbourne.

Mathiesen, T., 1974, *The Politics of Abolition*, Martin Robertson, London.

Mathiesen, T., 1990, *Prison on Trial: A Critical Assessment*, Sage, London.

McBarnet, D., 1981, *Conviction—Law, the State and the Construction of Justice*, Macmillan, London.

McCarthy, T., 1994, 'Victim Impact Statements: A Problematic Remedy', *Australian Feminist Law Journal*, 3, p. 175.

McDonald, D., 1990, *Royal Commission into Aboriginal Deaths in Custody: National Police Custody Survey*, Research Paper No. 13, Canberra.

McGregor, H. and Hopkins, A., 1991, *Working for Change: The Movement against Domestic Violence*, Allen & Unwin, Sydney.

Meagher, D., 2002, 'Black and White is Always Grey: The Power of the Police to Conduct a Strip Search in Victoria', *Criminal Law Journal*, 26, p. 43.

Mitchell, R., 1973, *South Australian Criminal Law and Penal Methods Reform: Report No. 1: Sentencing and Corrections*, Adelaide.

Moffitt, A. R., 1985, *Quarter to Midnight: The Crisis for Australia*, Sydney.

Moir, P. and Eijkman, H. (eds), 1992, *Policing Australia: Old Issues, New Perspectives*, Macmillan, Melbourne.

Moore, M., 1993, *Act and Crime: The Theory of Action and its Implications for Criminal Law*, Oxford University Press, Oxford.

Moore, E., 1994, 'Alternatives to Secure Detention for Girls' in Atkinson, L. and Gerull, S. A. (eds), *National Conference on Juvenile Justice: Conference Proceedings*, Australian Institute of Criminology, Canberra.

Morgan, F., 1993, 'Contact with the Justice System over the Juvenile Years' in Atkinson, L. and Gerull, S. A. (eds), *National Conference on Juvenile Detention*, Canberra, p. 180.

Morgan, N., 2002, 'Why we should not have Mandatory Penalties: Theoretical Structures and Political Realities', *Adelaide Law Review*, 23, p. 141.

Morris, A., 1988, 'Sex and Sentencing', *Criminal Law Review*, p. 163.

Morris, N., 1974, *The Future of Imprisonment*, University of Chicago Press, Chicago.

Morris, N., 1979, 'The Sentencing Disease', *Judges Journal*, 18(3), p. 9.

Mossman, M. J., 1986, 'Feminism and Legal Method: The Difference it Makes', *Australian Journal of Law and Society*, 3, p. 30.

Mukherjee, S., 1983, *Age and Crime*, Australian Institute of Criminology, Canberra.

Naffine, N., 1994, 'A Struggle Over Meaning: A Feminist Commentary on Rape Law Reform', *Australian and New Zealand Journal of Criminology*, 27, p. 100.

Naffine, N. and Wundersitz, J., 1994, 'Trends in Juvenile Justice' in Chappell, D. and Wilson, P. (eds), *The Australian Criminal Justice System in the Mid 1990s*, Butterworths, North Ryde, p. 235.

Nagle, J., 1978, *Report of the Royal Commission into NSW Prisons*, NSW Government Printer, Sydney.

National Committee on Violence, 1990, *Violence: Directions for Australia*, Canberra.

National Legal Aid Advisory Committee, 1991, *Legal Aid for the Australian Community*, Canberra.

Neal, D., 1992, *The Rule of Law in a Penal Colony: Law and Power in Early NSW*, Cambridge University Press, Melbourne.

New South Wales Anti-Discrimination Board, 1982, *A Study of Street Offences by Aborigines*, Sydney.

New South Wales Bureau of Crime Statistics and Research, 1987, 'Bail in NSW', *Crime and Justice Bulletin*, 2, p. 1.

New South Wales Bureau of Crime Statistics and Research, 1989, 'Court Delay and Prison Overcrowding', *Crime and Justice Bulletin*, 6.

New South Wales Bureau of Crime Statistics and Research, 1992, 'Understanding Committal Hearings', *Crime and Justice Bulletin*, 18, p. 1.

New South Wales Bureau of Crime Statistics and Research, 1993, 'Grappling with Court Delay', *Crime and Justice Bulletin*, 19, p. 1.

New South Wales Bureau of Crime Statistics and Research, 1997, 'Hung Juries and Majority Verdicts', *Crime and Justice Bulletin*, 36.

New South Wales Bureau of Crime Statistics and Research, 2002, 'Absconding on Bail', *Crime and Justice Bulletin*, 68.

New South Wales Bureau of Crime Statistics and Research, 2004, 'Evaluation of the *Bail Amendment (Repeat Offenders) Act* 2002', *Crime and Justice Bulletin*, 83, p. 1.

New South Wales Department for Women, 1996, *Heroines of Fortitude: The Experiences of Women in Court as Victims of Sexual Assault*, Sydney.

New South Wales Law Reform Commission, 1986, *The Jury in a Criminal Trial*, Report No. 48, Sydney.

New South Wales Law Reform Commission, 1987, *Procedures from Charge to Trial: Specific Problems and Proposals*, Vol. 1, Sydney.

New South Wales Law Reform Commission, 1990, *Police Powers of Detention and Investigation after Arrest*, Report No. 66, Sydney.

New South Wales Law Reform Commission, 1992, *People with an Intellectual Disability and the Criminal Justice System*, Issues Paper, Sydney.

New South Wales Law Reform Commission, 1993, *People with an Intellectual Disability and the Criminal Justice System: Appearances Before Local Courts*, Research Report 4, Sydney.

New South Wales Task Force, 1987, *Services to Victims of Crime*, Sydney.

New South Wales Youth Justice Coalition, 1990, *Kids in Justice—A Blueprint for the 90s*, Sydney.

Nicholson, J., 1992, 'Resentencing Serious Offenders: A Commentary on the New South Wales Model', *Criminal Law Journal*, 16, p. 216.

Norrie, A., 2001, *Crime, Reason and History: A Critical Introduction to Criminal Law*, 2nd edn, Butterworths, London,.

Norton, P. (ed.), 1984, *Law and Order in British Politics*, Gower, Aldershot.

O'Connell, T. and Moore, D., 1992, 'A New Juvenile Cautioning Program', *Rural Society*, 2.

O'Regan, R., 1979, *Essays on the Australian Criminal Code*, Law Book Co., Sydney.

Odgers, S., 1985, 'Police Interrogation and the Right to Silence', *Australian Law Journal*, 59, p. 78.

Odgers, S., 1986, 'Evidence of Sexual History in Sexual Offence Trials', *Sydney Law Review*, 11, p. 73.

Odgers, S., 1988, 'Regulating Police Interrogation—Back to First Principles' in Freckelton, I. and Selby, H., *Police and Society*, Butterworths, Sydney.

Odgers, S., 2004, *Uniform Evidence Law*, 6th edn, Law Book Company, Sydney.

Office of Criminal Statistics, South Australian Attorney-General's Department, 1990, *Victims and Criminal Justice*, Adelaide.

Parliamentary Joint Committee on the National Crime Authority, 1988, *The National Crime Authority—An Initial Evaluation*, Report, Canberra.

Parliamentary Joint Committee on the National Crime Authority, 1989, *Third Report*, Canberra.

Parliament of New South Wales, Committee on the ICAC, 1993, *Review of the ICAC Act*, Sydney.

Parliament of the Commonwealth of Australia, Joint Statutory Committee on Corporations Securities, 1991, *Use Immunity Provisions in the Corporations Law and Australian Securities Commission Law*, Canberra.

Petre, C., 1984, 'View from the Jury Room', *National Times*, 4–10 May.

Potas, I. (ed.), 1987, *Sentencing*, Australian Institute of Criminology, Canberra.

Potas, I., 1991, 'The Sentencing Act 1989: Impact and Review', *Current Issues in Criminal Justice*, 3(3), p. 318.

Public Policy Research Centre, 1988, *Community Attitudes Towards Domestic Violence in Australia: Social Survey Report*, Sydney.

Queensland Criminal Justice Commission, 1992, *Youth, Crime and Justice in Queensland*, Brisbane, p. 43.

Re, L., 1984, 'Eyewitness Identification: Why So Many Mistakes?', *Australian Law Journal*, 58, p. 509.

Reiman, J., 1979, *The Rich Get Richer and the Poor Get Prison*, John Wiley, New York.

Review of Commonwealth Criminal Law, 1991, *General Principles of Criminal Responsibility*, Fifth Interim Report, Canberra.

Richardson, M., 1997, 'A Background to the Current Legal Aid Funding Issues', *Current Issues in Criminal Justice*, 9(2).

Rinaldi, F., 1983, 'Dismissal of Crown Appeals Despite Inadequacy of Sentence', *Criminal Law Journal*, 7, p. 306.

Robberds, L., 1990, 'The National Crime Authority: A National Perspective on the Investigation of Organised Crime', *Current Issues in Criminal Justice*, 1(2), p. 25.

Robinson, P. and Darley, J., 1994, *Justice, Liability and Blame*, Westview Press, Boulder.

Roden, A., 1992, 'Submission to the Parliament of New South Wales Committee on the ICAC on its Discussion Paper of September 1992', Submission, Sydney.

Rowan-Robinson, J. and Watchman, P., 1990, *Crime and Regulation*, T. and T. Clark, Edinburgh.

Royal Commission into Aboriginal Deaths in Custody (Commissioner Muirhead) 1988, *Interim Report*, Canberra.

Royal Commission into Aboriginal Deaths in Custody, 1991, *Final Report*, Vol. 1, Canberra.

Royal Commission of Inquiry into the Chamberlain Convictions (Commissioner, Justice T. R. Morling), *Commonwealth Parliamentary Paper*, No. 192/1987.

Royal Commission on Criminal Procedure (chaired by Sir Cyril Phillips), 1981, *Report* (HMSO Cmnd 8092), London.

Rozenes, M., 1993, 'Prosecuting Regulatory Offences', conference paper, Sydney.

Sallmann, P., 1983, 'The Criminal Trial on Trial: A Response to Some Recent Criticisms', *Australian and New Zealand Journal of Criminology*, 16, p. 31.

Sallmann, P., 1992, 'A Note on Judicial Education in Australia: An Australian Institute of Judicial Administration Perspective', *Journal of Judicial Administration*, 2, p. 28.

Sallmann, P. and Willis, J., 1984, *Criminal Justice in Australia*, Oxford University Press, Melbourne.

Sanders, A., 1997, 'From Suspect to Trial' in Maquire, M., Morgan, R. and Reiner, R. (eds), *The Oxford Handbook of Criminology*, Oxford University Press, Oxford, p. 1051.

Schrager, L. and Short, J., 1977, 'Toward a Sociology of Organizational Crime', *Social Problems*, 25, p. 407.

Scott, G., 'A Model Criminal Code', 1992, *Criminal Law Journal*, 16, p. 350.

Scull, A., 1984, *Decarceration: Community Treatment and the Deviant: A Radical View*, Polity Press, Oxford.

Scutt, J., 1990, *Women and the Law: Commentary and Materials*, Law Book Co., Sydney, p. 451.

Senate Standing Committee on Constitutional and Legal Affairs, 1982, *Report on the Burden of Proof in Criminal Proceedings*, Canberra.

Senate Standing Committee on Constitutional and Legal Affairs, 1983, *Report on National Crime Authority Bill*, Canberra.

Seymour, J., 1988, *Dealing with Young Offenders*, Law Book Company, North Ryde.

Sheehy, E. A., 1991, 'Feminist Argumentation before the Supreme Court of Canada in *Seaboyer; Gayme*: The Sound of One Hand Clapping', *Melbourne University Law Review*, 18, p. 450.

Sheehy, E., Stubbs, J. and Tolmie, J., 1992, 'Defending Battered Women on Trial: The Battered Woman Syndrome and its Limitations', *Criminal Law Journal*, 16, p. 369.

Shroff, D., 2003, 'The Future of Guideline Judgments', *Current Issues in Criminal Justice*, 14(3), p. 316.

Shute, S., 1998, 'The Place of Public Opinion in Sentencing Law', *Criminal Law Review*, p. 465.

Silverii, J., 2003, 'The Trials of Sex', *Law Institute Journal*, 77, p. 18.

Skolnick, J., 1966, *Justice Without Trial: Law Enforcement in Democratic Society*, John Wiley & Sons, New York.

Spears, D., 1999, 'Sentencing Discretion: Sentencing in the Jurisic Age', *University of New South Wales Law Journal*, 22, p. 300.

Stafford, M. and Galle, O., 1984, 'Victimisation Rates: Exposure to Risk and Fear of Crime', *Criminology*, 22, p. 173.

Stevenson, N. N., 1982, 'Criminal Cases in the NSW District Court: A Pilot Study' in Basten, J., Richardson, M., Ronalds, C. and Zdenkowski, G. (eds), *The Criminal Injustice System*, Australian Legal Workers Group (NSW) and Legal Services Bulletin, Sydney, p. 106.

Stewart, Justice D., 1983, *Royal Commission into Drug Trafficking*, p. 9.

Stubbs, J., 1991, 'Battered Woman Syndrome: An Advance for Women or Further Evidence of the Legal System's Inability to Comprehend Women's Experiences?', *Current Issues in Criminal Justice*, 3(2), p. 267.

Stubbs, J., 1992, 'The (Un)reasonable Battered Woman? A Response to Easteal', *Current Issues in Criminal Justice*, 3, p. 359.

Sumner, C., 1987, 'Victim Participation in the Criminal Justice System', *Australian and New Zealand Journal of Criminology*, 20, p. 195.

Tait, D., 1994, 'Cautions and Appearances: Statistics About Youth and Police' in White, R. and Alder, C. (eds), 1994, *The Police and Young People in Australia*, Cambridge University Press, Melbourne, p. 70.

Tarrant, S., 1990, 'Something is Pushing Them to the Side of Their Own Lives: A Feminist Critique of Law and Laws', *University of Western Australia Law Review*, 20, p. 573.

Temby, I., 1991, 'ICAC: Working in the Public Interest', *Current Issues in Criminal Justice*, 2, p. 11.

Thomas, D., 1979, *Principles of Sentencing*, 2nd edn, Heinemann, London.

Tomasic, R., 1992, 'Sanctioning Corporate Crime and Misconduct: Beyond Draconian and Decriminalisation Solutions', *Australian Journal of Corporate Law*, 2, p. 84.

Tomasic, R. and Dobinson, I., 1979, *The Failure of Imprisonment: An Australian Perspective*, George Allen & Unwin, Sydney.

Travis, G., 1983, 'Police Discretion in Law Enforcement: A Study of Section 5 of the NSW Offences in Public Places Act 1979' in Findlay, M., Egger, S. and Sutton, J. (eds), *Issues in Criminal Justice Administration*, George Allen & Unwin, Sydney.

United Kingdom Criminal Law Revision Committee, 1972, Eleventh Report, *Evidence (General)*, London.

United Nations Secretariat, 1985, *Victims of Crime*, Document A/CONF. 121/6, 1985.

Victorian Law Reform Commission, 2003, 'Protecting the Vulnerable', *Law Institute Journal*, 77, p. 85.

Victorian Premier's Drug Advisory Council, *Drugs and Our Community*, Melbourne, 1996.

Victorian Sentencing Committee, 1987, *Sentencing*, Discussion Paper, Melbourne.

Victorian Sentencing Committee, 1988, *Sentencing*, Vols 1 and 3, Melbourne.

Vinson, T. and Homel, R., 1973, 'Legal Representation and Outcome: A Progress Report on the Relation Between Legal Representation and the Findings of Courts of Petty Sessions throughout New South Wales', *Australian Law Journal*, 47, p. 133.

Von Hirsch, A., 1987, 'Guidance by Numbers or Words? Numerical versus Narrative Guidelines for Sentencing' in Wasik, M. and Pease, K. (eds), *Sentencing Reform: Guidance or Guide Lines?*, Manchester University Press, Manchester.

Von Hirsch, A. and Jareborg, N., 1991, 'Gauging Criminal Harm: A Living Standard Analysis', *Oxford Journal of Legal Studies*, 11, p. 1.

Von Hirsch, A. and Ashworth, A., 1992, 'Not Not Just Deserts: A Response to Braithwaite and Pettit', *Oxford Journal of Legal Studies*, 12, p. 83.

Wald, S., Ayres, R., Hess, R., Schantz, M. and Whitebread, C., 1967, 'Project, Interrogations in New Haven: The Impact of Miranda', *Yale Law Journal*, 76, p. 1573.

Walker, N., 1991, *Why Punish?*, Oxford University Press, Oxford.

Warner, K., 1991, *Sentencing in Tasmania*, Federation Press, Sydney.

Warner, K., 2003, 'The Role of Guideline Judgments in the Law and Order Debate in Australia', *Criminal Law Journal*, 27, p. 8.

Warner, K. and Gawlik, J., 2003, 'Mandatory Compensation Orders for Crime Victims and the Rhetoric of Restorative Justice', *Australian and New Zealand Journal of Criminology*, 36, p. 60.

Watson, R., Blackmore, A. and Hosking, G. , 1997, *Criminal Law*, Law Book Co., Sydney.

Weatherburn, D., 1983, 'Sentencing for What?' in Findlay, M., Egger, S. and Sutton, J. (eds), *Issues in Criminal Justice Administration*, George Allen & Unwin, Sydney.

Weatherburn, D., 1988, 'Sentencing Principles and Sentence Choice' in Findlay, M. and Hogg, R. (eds), *Understanding Crime and Criminal Justice*, Law Book Co., North Ryde, p. 269.

Weinberg, M., 1978, 'The Consequences of Failure to Object to Inadmissible Evidence in Criminal Cases', *Melbourne University Law Review*, 11, p. 408.

Westling, W. T. and Waye, V., 1996, 'Promoting Fairness and Efficiency in Jury Trials', *Criminal Law Journal*, 20.

White, R., 1989, 'Making Ends Meet: Young People, Work and the Criminal Economy', *Australian and New Zealand Journal of Criminology*, 22, p. 136.

White, R., 1992, 'Tough Laws for Hard-core Politicians', *Alternative Law Journal*, 17, p. 58.

White, R. and Alder, C. (eds), 1994, *The Police and Young People in Australia*, Cambridge University Press, Melbourne, p. 205.

Whitrod, R., 1986, 'The Victim's Role in the Sentencing Process' in Potas, I. (ed.), *Sentencing in Australia: Issues, Policy and Reform, Proceedings of a Seminar on Sentencing: Problems and Prospects*, Australian Institute of Criminology, Canberra.

Wilkie, M., 1992, 'Crime (Serious and Repeat Offenders) Sentencing Act 1992: A Human Rights Perspective', *University of Western Australia Law Review*, 22, pp. 187–96.

Williams, G., 1979, 'The Authentication of Statements to the Police', *Criminal Law Review*, p. 14.

Williams, G., 1963, *The Proof of Guilt*, 3rd edn, Stevens and Sons, Oxford.

Williams, Justice E., 1980, *Australian Royal Commission of Inquiry into Drugs*, Report, Canberra.

Wilson, C. and Brewer, N., 1992, 'The Incidence of Criminal Victimisation of Individuals with an Intellectual Disability', *Australian Psychologist*, 27, pp. 114–17.

Wilson, P., 1982, *Black Death White Hands*, George Allen & Unwin, Sydney.

Wilson, P., Walker, J. and Mukherjee, S., 1986, 'How the Public Sees Crime: An Australian Survey' in Wilson, P. (ed.), *Trends and Issues in Crime and Criminal Justice*, No. 2, Canberra.

Wood, J., 1996, *Royal Commission into the NSW Police Service: Final Report*, Sydney.

Woodward, Justice P., 1979, *New South Wales Royal Commission into Drug Trafficking*, Report, Sydney.

Worral, A., 1990, *Offending Women: Female Lawbreakers and the Criminal Justice System*, Routledge, London.

Wundersitz, J., 1993, 'Some Statistics on Youth Offending: An Interjurisdictional Comparison' in Gale, F., Naffine, N. and Wundersitz, J. (eds), *Juvenile Justice: Debating the Issues*, Allen & Unwin, Sydney, p. 18.

Wundersitz, J., 1994, 'Family Conferencing and Juvenile Justice Reform in South Australia' in Alder, C. and Wundersitz, J. (eds), *Family Conferencing and Juvenile Justice: The Way Forward or Misplaced Optimism?*, Australian Institute of Criminology, Canberra, p. 87.

Wundersitz, J., 1997, 'Precourt Diversion: The Australian Experience' in Borowski, A. and O'Connor, I. (eds), *Juvenile Crime, Justice and Corrections*, Longman, Melbourne, p. 281.

Yabsley, M., 1990, *Prisons: Firm but Fair*, Department of Corrective Services, Sydney.

Yeo, S., 1988a, 'Self-defence: From Viro to Zecevic', *Australian Bar Review*, 4, p. 251.

Yeo, S., 1988b, 'The Demise of Excessive Self-defence in Australia', *International and Comparative Law Quarterly*, 37, p. 348.

Yeo, S., 1990, *Compulsion in the Criminal Law*, Law Book Co., North Ryde.

Yeo, S., 1991, 'Necessity under the Griffith Code and the Common Law', *Criminal Law Journal*, 15, p. 17.

Yeo, S., 1992, 'Battered Woman Syndrome: In Between Syndrome and Conviction', *Current Issues in Criminal Justice*, 4(1), p. 75.

Yeo, S., 1993, 'Resolving Gender Bias in Criminal Defences', *Monash University Law Review*, 19, p. 104.

Young, W., Tinsley, Y. and Cameron, N., 2000, 'The Effectiveness and Efficiency of Jury Decision-making', *Criminal Law Journal*, 24, p. 89.

Zdenkowski, G., 1986, 'Sentencing: Problems and Responsibility' in Chappell, D. and Wilson, P. (eds), *The Australian Criminal Justice System—The Mid–80s*, Butterworths, Sydney.

Zdenkowski, G., Ronalds, C. and Richardson, M. (eds), 1987, *The Criminal Injustice System*, Vol. 2, Pluto Press, Sydney.

Zimring, F. and Hawkins, G., 1973, *Deterrence: The Legal Threat in Crime Control*, University of Chicago Press, Chicago.

# Index